T0396658

Domain-Specific Bodies of Knowledge in
Project Management – **Volume 4**

Developing a Body of Knowledge for Green Construction Project Management

Domain-Specific Bodies of Knowledge in Project Management

Print ISSN: 2811-0889
Online ISSN: 2811-0897

Series Editor: Mohan M Kumaraswamy
*(The University of Hong Kong, Hong Kong and
The University of Moratuwa, Sri Lanka)*

Published:

Vol. 4   *Developing a Body of Knowledge for Green Construction
Project Management*
edited by Amos Darko (University of Washington, Seattle, USA) and
Albert P C Chan (The Hong Kong Polytechnic University, Hong Kong)

Vol. 3   *Building a Body of Knowledge in Project Management in
Developing Countries*
edited by George Ofori (London South Bank University, UK)

Vol. 2   *Managing Information Technology Projects:
Building a Body of Knowledge in IT Project Management*
edited by Srinath Perera (Western Sydney University, Australia) and
Robert Eadie (Ulster University, UK)

Vol. 1   *Building a Body of Knowledge in Construction Project Delivery,
Procurement and Contracting*
edited by Giovanni C Migliaccio (University of Washington, USA)
and Pramen P Shrestha (University of Nevada Las Vegas, USA)

Domain-Specific Bodies of Knowledge in
Project Management – **Volume 4**

Editor-in-Chief: Mohan M Kumaraswamy
The University of Hong Kong, Hong Kong
The University of Moratuwa, Sri Lanka

Developing a Body of Knowledge for Green Construction Project Management

Editors

Amos Darko
University of Washington, Seattle, WA, USA

Albert P C Chan
The Hong Kong Polytechnic University, Hong Kong

Sponsored by

Published by

World Scientific Publishing Co. Pte. Ltd.

5 Toh Tuck Link, Singapore 596224

USA office: 27 Warren Street, Suite 401-402, Hackensack, NJ 07601

UK office: 57 Shelton Street, Covent Garden, London WC2H 9HE

Library of Congress Cataloging-in-Publication Data

Names: Darko, Amos, editor. | Chan, Albert P. C., editor.

Title: Developing a body of knowledge for green construction project management /
    editors: Amos Darko, University of Washington, Seattle, USA,
    Albert P C Chan, The Hong Kong Polytechnic University, Hong Kong.

Description: New Jersey : World Scientific, [2025] | Series: Domain-specific bodies of knowledge
    in project management, 2811-0889 ; volume 4 | Includes bibliographical references.

Identifiers: LCCN 2024002488 | ISBN 9789811251412 (hardcover) |
    ISBN 9789811251429 (ebook) | ISBN 9789811251436 (ebook other)

Subjects: LCSH: Construction industry--Materials management. |
    Sustainable buildings--Design and construction. | Project management.

Classification: LCC HD9715.A2 D428 2025 | DDC 624.068/7--dc23/eng/20240202

LC record available at https://lccn.loc.gov/2024002488

British Library Cataloguing-in-Publication Data

A catalogue record for this book is available from the British Library.

For any available supplementary material, please visit
https://www.worldscientific.com/worldscibooks/10.1142/12700#t=suppl

Desk Editors: Nambirajan Karuppiah/Nicole Ong

Typeset by Stallion Press
Email: enquiries@stallionpress.com

https://doi.org/10.1142/9789811251429_fmatter

Foreword

For good reason, "sustainability" is a word on the lips of everyone today. Our burning of fossil fuels has released huge amounts of greenhouse gases into the atmosphere that are now significantly altering the composition of the atmosphere, engendering long-lasting changes in weather patterns and temperatures. This in the long run will totally change the ecosystems that support our lives and existence on this planet.

The impacts of these changes in the climate are already being felt very strongly across the globe. Here in Hong Kong, for example, we have been incessantly threatened by the impacts of climate change, such as very hot weather, over the years, but this threat is becoming even more and more severe recently. Just last month (September 2023), we were fiercely hit by Super Typhoon Saola, the strongest typhoon that we have seen in five years. Exactly a week after that, we were again fiercely hit by a record-breaking rainstorm, the highest record since records began in 1884.[a] The storm brought a heavy rainfall that flooded metro stations and turned roads into rivers. According to the government, at least two people were killed and more than 140 were injured during the rainstorm, not to mention the numerous trees that were destroyed and the landslides that were caused by the typhoon. This year (2023) has also seen some of the hottest weather in history in Hong Kong, with record-breaking consecutive sunny

---

[a]See https://www.info.gov.hk/gia/general/202310/04/P2023100300488.htm, accessed 12 October 2023.

and very hot days for September, which remained hotter than normal. As the climate continues to warm, the intensity, severity, and frequency of extreme weather events are anticipated to increase.

While almost everything we do emits the greenhouse gas emissions that are causing these problems, construction is among the activities that emit most of the greenhouse gases into the atmosphere. The negative sustainability impact of the sector does not end here. Construction is also a major source of air pollution, waste generation, and raw materials, energy, water, and other natural resources consumption.

To tackle these challenges and keep the Sustainable Development and Paris Agreement Goals within reach, we need to embrace sustainable and green construction. Many construction companies are nowadays doing a very good job in this direction, but the question remains whether they have an adequate supply of the knowledgeable and skilled managers needed to manage and deliver such green construction projects effectively and efficiently. In my experience, many project managers in the industry are not knowledgeable, specialized, and skilled at green construction. They are just and still experimenting with their traditional project management processes and practices, which in most cases fail to successfully deliver the desired sustainable and green outcomes for the project client (owner).

We need to educate, train, and address the pressing shortage of project managers who are knowledgeable, specialized, and skilled at green construction. This is why I am so excited about this book. The objective of this book is to equip industry practitioners, researchers, and students with the core project management knowledge and skills needed to successfully deliver green construction projects. The authors have well achieved this objective by bringing together key topics that address the unique aspects of green construction project management. The book is an important resource and publication for anyone who wants to learn about the process of successfully managing green construction projects. Not only project managers will benefit from this book but also other professions associated with the construction sector, such as project owners and developers, designers, facility managers, construction managers, surveyors, and contractors, will benefit. The book will play a key role in addressing our sustainability challenges through the development of green construction projects. I hope you will find this book to be extremely timely and useful for addressing the critical and unique aspects of green construction project management.

Sr Wong Kwok Leung, Paul
The Hong Kong Institute of Surveyors

Preface

The world is in a period of sustainability breakdown: the triple planetary crisis of climate change, nature and biodiversity loss, and pollution and waste; a global health and well-being crisis; the overexploitation of natural resources; and extinction. With the construction industry being a foremost contributor to these challenges, we need rapid systemic changes in this industry if we are to avoid catastrophic sustainability crises in the years ahead.

When we were approached by Professor Mohan M. Kumaraswamy, Editor-in-Chief of the World Scientific book series *Domain-Specific Bodies of Knowledge in Project Management*, to put together a book on a body of knowledge for green construction project management, we asked ourselves one important question: Can this book contribute to achieving the above goal of making positive changes in the construction industry toward sustainability? Our answer to that question was a resonant "yes," thus we did not hesitate to take up the initiative to produce this book.

Green or sustainable construction is one of the biggest opportunities the construction industry has to make the deep systemic changes required to improve its sustainability performance and impact. But the challenge that we see having worked in this field over the past 10 years is that project managers cannot deliver successful green construction projects through conventional project management processes and practices, which were used when we created the sustainability challenges that we currently face. As the wise saying of Albert Einstein goes, "we cannot solve our problems with the same thinking we used when we created them." We must change the way we manage and deliver our construction projects if we are going to have a chance to reduce consumption, emissions, pollution, and waste while maximizing human health, safety, well-being, happiness, and quality of life, as well as profitability as envisioned in the Paris Agreement and United Nations Sustainable Development Goals.

This is what this book is about. Project management bodies of knowledge are quite common, but the 18 chapters in this book together provide a comprehensive project management body of knowledge that addresses the unique aspects of green construction projects specifically. We have worked to understand and report on all that we could about the development of the project management and green construction professions over the years. We have also examined several project management standards, frameworks, and methodologies. What we discovered is that lean and agile project management methodologies are the best for optimizing the delivery of successful green construction projects. In addition to suggesting solutions to the pressing challenges facing green construction project managers at a time of climate and sustainability emergency, we have also provided strategies and instruments for integrating sustainability into the project management of our construction projects. A number of changes to project management that are needed to ensure success in green construction projects are proposed. We show you how cutting-edge digital technologies can be used and applied to improve the delivery of green construction projects.

We hope that *Developing a Body of Knowledge for Green Construction Project Management* will be your extremely valuable resource, companion, and guide to managing and delivering your next green construction project. This book further shows you how you can play a vital role in achieving the decarbonization, carbon neutrality, or Net Zero carbon goals set out in the Paris Agreement through the way you manage and deliver your green construction project. We present real-world case studies from various sources to tell success stories of green construction project management and to serve as a reference point for successful green construction project management and delivery.

So, grab a cup of coffee or tea, kick back, and let's help you find out how to manage and deliver successful green construction projects by making relevant changes to your project management processes and practices from scope, risk, procurement, stakeholder, health and safety, energy, postconstruction, and life cycle management through to design decision-making and digital delivery.

Amos Darko
University of Washington

Albert P.C. Chan
The Hong Kong Polytechnic University

About the Editors

Amos Darko is an Assistant Professor in the Department of Construction Management at the University of Washington (UW), Seattle, USA. Prior to joining UW in 2023, Dr. Darko was a Research Assistant Professor at The Hong Kong Polytechnic University (PolyU), Hong Kong, from 2020 to 2023. Dr. Darko earned his Ph.D. degree from PolyU in 2019 and worked there as a Postdoctoral Fellow from 2019 to 2020. Dr. Darko also earned his BSc degree (first-class honors) from Kwame Nkrumah University of Science and Technology (KNUST), Ghana, in 2014 and worked there as a Research and Teaching Assistant from 2014 to 2015. Dr. Darko's research interests include sustainability, sustainable built environment, green or sustainable construction, green building, modular construction, project management, and digital technologies including building information modeling and artificial intelligence. Dr. Darko has published numerous papers in leading international peer-reviewed journals, conferences, books, and industry guides and reports. His papers have been rated as highly cited and hot papers by the Web of Science. His paper is the most cited paper of all time in the *International Journal of Construction Management*. He has also been ranked among the world's top 2% most cited scientists by Elsevier BV and Stanford University. Dr. Darko's work has been applied in the construction industry in the forecasting, monitoring, management, and enhancement of the performance of construction projects. Dr. Darko has received several awards for his outstanding work, including the Green Talents Award from the German Federal Ministry of Education and Research in 2020, the Global Top Peer Reviewer Award from the Web of Science Group in 2019, the Outstanding Overseas Young Scholars Award from Central South University in 2019, the Best Construction Technology and Management Student Award from KNUST in 2014, and Best and Highly Commended Paper Awards in 2020, 2023, and 2024. Dr. Darko has received and managed competitive research grants worth a significant amount of money from various sources, including the Research Grants Council of Hong Kong and Chief Secretary for Administration's Office of Hong Kong. Dr. Darko is an Associate Editor of *Green Building and Construction Economics*, an Associate Editor of *Humanities and Social Sciences Communications*, and an Academic Editor of *Advances in Civil Engineering*. He can be reached at amos.darko@connect.polyu.hk; adarko@uw.edu.

Albert P.C. Chan is a Chartered Construction Manager, Engineer, Project Manager, and Surveyor by profession. Professor Chan has worked in a few tertiary institutions both in Hong Kong and overseas. He was a Senior Lecturer and Deputy Head of the School of Building and Planning at the University of South Australia, Australia. Professor Chan joined the Department of Building and Real Estate of The Hong Kong Polytechnic University (PolyU), Hong Kong, in 1996 and was the Associate Head (Teaching) from 2005 to 2011, Associate Dean and Interim Dean of the Faculty of Construction and Environment from 2011 to 2013 and from 2013 to 2014, respectively. He was Head of the Department of Building and Real Estate from 2015 to 2021 and is currently the Dean of Students, Associate Director of Research Institute for Sustainable Urban Development, Able Endowed Professor in Construction Health and Safety, Chair Professor of Construction Engineering and Management, and Chief Warden of PolyU Students Halls of Residence. Professor Chan's research interests include project management and project success, construction procurement and relational contracting, public–private partnerships, and construction health and safety. Professor Chan's research has had a real and significant impact on the construction industry resulting in changes in policy decisions. His recommendations have been incorporated in the Construction Industry Council Guidelines on "Site Safety Measures for Working in Hot Weather" since April 2013. He has produced over 1,000 research outputs in refereed journal papers, international refereed conference papers, consultancy reports, and other articles. He has won numerous prestigious research paper and innovation awards since 1995. Professor Chan served as an expert member in the Built Environment Panel of FORMAS, Swedish Research Grants Council. He was also an expert member to assess the research performance of the Faculty of Architectural and the Built Environment, TU Delft, the Netherlands in 2016. Professor Chan has served as an expert member of the Engineering Panel of the Research Grants Council, HKSAR since 2015. Professor Chan holds an MSc in Construction Management and Economics from the University of Aston in Birmingham, UK, and a Ph.D. in Project Management from the University of South Australia. He has been an Adjunct Professor in a number of universities. Professor Chan was also a Founding Director of Construction Industry Institute, Hong Kong, which was a joint research institution developed by industry and the academia. He can be reached at albert.chan@polyu.edu.hk.

About the Contributors

Nazirah Zainul Abidin, PhD, is an Associate Professor in the School of Housing, Building and Planning at Universiti Sains Malaysia, Malaysia. An avid researcher in the field of quantity surveying, sustainable construction, green building management, environmental performance, and value management with many completed and active research grants. She has published in various indexed journals and presented in international conferences. She is currently a member of Board of Quantity Surveyors Malaysia, Royal Institution of Surveyors Malaysia, and Institute of Value Management Malaysia. She can be reached at nazirah_za@usm.my.

Adeleye Ayoade Adeniran is an accomplished professional with a strong background in the field of surveying and valuation. His professional qualifications as a Registered Surveyor & Valuer (Estate Surveyors and Valuers Registration Board of Nigeria) and a Chartered Valuer (Royal Institution of Chartered Surveyors) demonstrate his expertise in the industry. Ayo's academic achievements are equally impressive, holding a BSc in Estate Management, an MSc in Housing Development and Management, and a PhD in Construction Management. His educational background indicates a comprehensive understanding of various aspects related to real estate, housing development, and construction management. Ayo has extensive years of lecturing experience in real estate. As a Research Associate at Nelson Mandela University, South Africa, Ayo's research focus is on post-construction management and the circular economy. His work aligns with the United Nations Sustainable Development Goal 11, which aims to make cities and human settlements inclusive, safe, resilient, and sustainable. Ayo's contributions to the academic world are evident through his numerous research publications, book chapters, conference proceedings, and the authorship of a book on a relevant subject. His expertise and academic achievements have also positioned him as a supervisor for honors, master's, and doctoral students, enabling him to share his knowledge and mentor future professionals in the field. Overall, Ayo's qualifications, research focus, and commitment to sustainability make him a valuable asset to the academic community and the sustainable development agenda. He can be reached at ayoadeniran111@gmail.com.

Emmanuel Adinyira, PhD, is a Professor of Construction Project Management in the Department of Construction Technology and Management at the Kwame Nkrumah University of Science and Technology, Ghana. His areas of specialization include construction project management, construction safety, health and environment, and construction education and training. He has served as a guest editor, editor, sectional editor, editorial board member, and reviewer for several national and international journals and conferences. His global experience in construction education and training includes working as a Visiting Scholar at Loughborough University, UK, among others. He can be reached at eadinyira.cap@knust.edu.gh.

Kofi Agyekum, PhD, is a Senior Lecturer of Building Science, Engineering, and Materials in the Department of Construction Technology and Management at the Kwame Nkrumah University of Science and Technology, Ghana. His specialization areas include construction health and safety, building biology, circular economy in construction, building pathology, and sustainable and lean construction. He serves as an Associate Editor, an Editorial Board Member, and a reviewer for several national and international journals. Currently, he is the Team Leader of the Building Science, Engineering, and Materials Research Team in the Department of Construction Technology and Management at the Kwame Nkrumah University of Science and Technology. He can be reached at agyekum.kofi1@gmail.com.

Tayyab Ahmad is an Assistant Professor in the Department of Civil and Architectural Engineering at Qatar University, Qatar. He received his PhD from the University of Melbourne, Australia, in May 2020. He has degrees in Architectural Engineering and Construction Management. He has expertise in building energy efficiency, sustainable design optimization, project success frameworks, decision-making frameworks, Building Information Modelling (BIM), and life cycle assessment. His PhD research is about investigating project success in green buildings. During his brief academic career, he has worked in different academic positions in Australia, Hong Kong, and most recently Qatar. His research has investigated best practices of green building project planning, design, construction, and delivery. His research is aimed at improving the practice in Architecture, Engineering, and Construction (AEC) industry to meet the needs of the present without compromising the ability of future generations to meet their own needs. He can be reached at tayyab@qu.edu.qa.

Ali Alashwal is currently a Senior Lecturer in project management at Western Sydney University, Australia. He completed his PhD in Building and Construction Economics in 2012. He has vast experience in academia and practice in the areas of construction management, project management, and architecture. He holds two credentials as a Project Management Professional (PMP) from the Project Management Institute, the USA, and a Certified Practicing Project Practitioner (CPPP) from the Australian Institute of Project Management. His involvement in over 10 research projects enriched his experience in research management and research methodologies and enabled him to publish over 80 papers. He is well versed in different univariate and multivariate data analyses, particularly partial least squares structural equation modeling (PLS-SEM). Dr. Alashwal has completed different research projects focusing on enhancing construction project performance and sustainability. Currently, he is conducting research on construction waste minimization and construction workers' mental health. He can be reached at a.al-ashwal@western sydney.edu.au.

Laura Melo de Almeida is a Lecturer in building design and construction management at Western Sydney University, Australia. She completed her

PhD in Environmental Engineering in 2020. In addition to her recent academic experience, she has significant professional experience in sustainability, building design, and engineering, including managing her own company for 5 years. Dr. Laura is a Professional Engineer recognized by Engineers Australia and the Portuguese Order of Engineers. She has obtained the qualifications of Green Associate for LEED (USGBC, US) and Green Star (GBCA, AUS) rating tools and Energy Saving Professional (ADENE, PT). She was involved in rating more than 100 buildings according to the European Energy Performance of Buildings Directive, including green buildings assessments using LEED and Green Star tools, among others. Additionally, her assistance in the delivery of the Sustainable Energy Action Plan aligned with the European Covenant of Mayors for Climate and Energy gave her a holistic understanding of a Sustainable Process. Her research focused on sustainable areas such as occupant behavior, energy building simulation, and climate change led her to publish around 20 papers. Furthermore, she was the editor of the recent book *Understanding Australian Construction Contractors* published by Routledge in 2023. She has successfully targeted the areas of energy efficiency and indoor environmental quality. Currently, she is conducting research on climate change's impact on energy performance, circular economy, occupant behavior, and biomimicry. She can be reached at l.almeida@westernsydney.edu.au.

Judith Amudjie holds a BSc (Hons) degree in Quantity Surveying and Construction Economics and an MPhil in Construction Management from the Department of Construction Technology and Management at the Kwame Nkrumah University of Science and Technology, Ghana. Her research interests include circular economy in construction, ethics in construction, sustainable construction, construction health and safety, and construction project management. She would soon commence her PhD studies in Construction and Real Estate Management at the Department of Building and Real Estate at The Hong Kong Polytechnic University, Hong Kong. She has obtained several publications by co-authoring in very reputable peer-reviewed journals and book chapters in construction-related issues in Ghana and has also participated in some international conferences. She is a Peer Reviewer and holds a recognized peer review certificate from the Web of Science Academy in the UK. Additionally, she has carried out several reviews for Scopus-indexed journals. She is a team member of the building science, engineering, and materials research team in the Department of Construction Technology and Management. She can be reached at juamudjie@gmail.com.

Emma Ayesu-Koranteng is a highly qualified and dedicated construction professional with a passion for various aspects of the construction industry. As a Chartered Construction Manager (CIOB), she possesses a recognized and prestigious qualification that showcases her expertise and commitment to the field. Her role at Nelson Mandela University, South Africa, as a Senior Lecturer and Head of Department for the Department of Building & Human Settlement Development indicates her extensive experience and leadership capabilities in academia. Emma's specific areas of interest and expertise include Mass Timber Construction, Construction Health & Safety, Sustainable Construction, and Construction Contractor Development. These areas reflect her commitment to promoting environmentally friendly and safe construction practices, as well as fostering the growth and development of construction contractors. As a co-leader of the CLT (Cross-Laminated Timber) Engagement unit and a Project Manager for Mass Timber research projects at the university, Emma actively contributes to the advancement of knowledge and innovation in the construction industry, particularly regarding sustainable and modern construction materials and techniques. Her dedication to student engagement and learning is evident in her teaching approach. Emma consistently provides stimulating and relevant materials to her students, keeping their learning objectives in mind. She is attentive to their needs, focusing on test preparedness and adapting her teaching methods based on student feedback. Overall, Emma is a results-oriented construction expert who is committed to the success of her students and promoting a comprehensive understanding of construction practices. Her passion for sustainable construction and contractor development further highlights her commitment to making a positive impact on the construction industry and the environment. She can be reached at emma.ayesu-koranteng@mandela.ac.za.

Zahirah Mokhtar Azizi, PhD, is an Assistant Professor in the Department of Architecture and Built Environment at Northumbria University, UK. Her research interests are in the areas of decarbonization, sustainable and smart cities, digital built environment, social value, and circular economy. She is a member of the Construction, Process and Management research group at Northumbria. She has worked together on research and consultancy projects with industry, such as one with North East England Climate Coalition (NEECCo) on a study aimed at better understanding how to decarbonize social housing in the region. She has contributed to several key publications in peer-reviewed journals and delivered presentations at various conferences. She can be reached at zahirah.azizi@northumbria.ac.uk.

Victoria Burrows has dedicated her career to radically improving the sustainability of the built environment, by transforming the way that it is designed, constructed, operated, and repurposed. As Director of Advancing Net Zero at the World Green Building Council (WorldGBC), Victoria is responsible for a pioneering global program to accelerate total decarbonization of the sector by 2050, working with a network of Green Building Councils and industry stakeholders to identify solutions to barriers and challenges to accelerating uptake. Victoria is the driving force behind the Net Zero Carbon Buildings Commitment, an industry leadership initiative demonstrating that action to decarbonize building portfolios by 2030 or sooner can unlock the solutions needed for the entire sector to reach its goals. The Whole Life Carbon vision for total sector decarbonization that was developed under this program is now reflected in the UNFCCC Human Settlements Climate Action Pathway, and through the UN's Climate Change Conference of Parties (COP), in collaboration with the High-Level Climate Champions (HLCCs), used to call for bolder and more ambitious regulation from national governments. Victoria has served on the Expert Advisory Group for the Science Based Targets Initiative, the World Economic Forum's Green Building Principles, and as a judge for prestigious industry awards. With a technical background in the sustainable development industry across the world, ranging from client-side advisory services, green building rating tool consultancy, and an onsite Head of Sustainability for a major international contractor, Victoria brings a combination of technical and strategic expertise to the mission, to identify the approaches, solutions, and technologies needed to transform the sector. Victoria has a degree in Architecture and Environmental Design from the University of Nottingham, UK, and co-authored the book *A Whole System Approach to High-Performance Green Buildings*. She can be reached at vkburrows@gmail.com.

Linyan Chen is a Postdoctoral Fellow in the Department of Building Real Estate at The Hong Kong Polytechnic University, Hong Kong. She obtained the PhD degree jointly offered by The Hong Kong Polytechnic University, Hong Kong, and Tongji University, China, in 2023. Prior to her doctoral studies, she obtained her ME and BS degrees in Management Science and Engineering and Construction Cost from Zhengzhou University of Aeronautics, China, in 2017 and 2013, respectively. Her research interests span various areas, including green buildings, sustainable construction, building energy retrofitting, urban risk management, and construction and demolition waste management. She has authored 14 papers, which have been published in renowned journals and international conferences, such as *Building and Environment, Journal of Cleaner Production*, and *Environmental Science and Pollution Research*. Furthermore, she has contributed chapters to two books. She also serves as a reviewer of renowned academic journals, such as *Sustainable Development*. Driven by a desire for interdisciplinary research, she actively engages with researchers in other fields, such as artificial intelligence and digital twins. By forging these interdisciplinary collaborations, she seeks to leverage cutting-edge technologies and methodologies to improve energy efficiency in existing building stock. She can be reached at linyan.chen@connect.polyu.hk.

Caleb Debrah is currently a PhD student in the Department of Building and Real Estate at The Hong Kong Polytechnic University, Hong Kong, and a Visiting Scholar in the Powell Center for Construction and Environment of M. E. Rinker Sr. School of Construction Management at the University of Florida, USA. His PhD research focuses on 'green finance in green building'. He obtained both MSc and BSc degrees in Construction Management from the Kwame Nkrumah University of

Science and Technology. His publications have been rated as highly cited by the Web of Science. He is a member of the Project Management Institute (PMI), Ghana Institute of Construction, Ghana Institute of Surveyors (probationary member), and the Hong Kong Green Building Council (student member). His research interests cover green financing, project bonds financing, green building, green and sustainable cities, construction innovation and management, sustainability, and sustainable development. He can be reached at caleb.debrah@connect.polyu.hk.

Sevilay Demirkesen received her BSc degree in civil engineering from Istanbul Technical University, Turkey, in 2010, MSc degree in construction engineering and management program from the Illinois Institute of Technology, USA, in 2011, and PhD degree in construction management from Bogazici University, Turkey, in 2016. She also has industry experience and worked as a design engineer at IHI Infrastructure Systems from 2012 to 2013. Following her graduation from Bogazici University, she was a Postdoctoral Research Associate with Project Production Systems Lab (P2SL) at the University of California, Berkeley, from 2016 to 2018. She is currently an Associate Professor in the Department of Civil Engineering at Gebze Technical University, Turkey. Her research interests are lean construction, sustainability, construction health and safety, performance management, and risk management. She can be reached at demirkesen@gtu.edu.tr.

Cheng Siew Goh is a Professional Surveyor and Academic. Her subject knowledge lies in sustainability, green buildings, life cycle management, risk management, construction project management, and construction innovations. She has undertaken several individual and joint research projects to produce high-quality research outputs and her works have been published in peer-reviewed journals, conference proceedings, and books. Her expertise is highly recognized where she has been invited to serve as reviewer for several peer-reviewed journals and international conferences. She can be reached at gohkeanu@yahoo.com.

Chathuri Gunarathna is a Research Assistant in the School of Property Construction and Project Management at RMIT University, Australia.

She completed her PhD in Built Environment at RMIT University in 2023. Her research investigated the opportunities for blockchain application in distributed solar energy projects. She received a BSc (Hons) in Quantity Surveying degree with first-class honors from the University of Moratuwa, Sri Lanka, in 2013. Her research interests include distributed solar energy applications, blockchain technology in energy sector, Building Integrated Photovoltaics (BIPV) application, energy communities, blockchain-enabled information management, and supply chain integration and management. Chathuri is also a member of the Solar Energy Application Laboratory (SEAL) at RMIT University. She can be reached at chathuri.gunarathna@rmit.edu.au.

Bon-Gang Hwang is a Professor and Deputy Head (Research) in the Department of the Built Environment at the National University of Singapore, Singapore. He was also the former Director of Center for Project Management and Construction Law and the former Director of BSc, Project and Facilities Management program offered by the department. He received his BSc in Architectural Engineering from Han Yang University, South Korea, and master's and doctorate in Civil, Architectural, and Environmental Engineering from the University of Texas at Austin, USA, with a specialty in Construction Engineering and Project Management. With over 25 years of experience in the built environment industry of USA, Singapore, and South Korea, he has served on the advisory board and consulted in various areas for both public and private organizations. His current research interests are in the areas of project and technology management, green building and infrastructure project management, project/enterprise performance analytics and innovations, and project/enterprise risk management and decision support system. He has delivered over 150 invited speeches at various international conferences, seminars, and workshops and published over 240 journal papers, conference papers, books, book chapters, research reports, and short articles to top-tier international refereed journals, conference proceedings, and publishers. He can be reached at bdghbg@nus.edu.sg.

Sajani Jayasuriya is a Lecturer in the construction management discipline at the School of Property Construction and Project Management at

RMIT University, Australia. She completed her doctoral degree at RMIT University in the area of stakeholder management and Public-Private Partnerships. Her bachelor's degree was in Quantity Surveying with a first class from the University of Moratuwa, Sri Lanka. She is a member of the Australian Institute of Quantity Surveyors (AIQS) and she is the school accreditation manager. She has collaborated on research projects locally and internationally. She is an active member of the Solar Energy Application Laboratory (SEAL) at RMIT. She has also worked in the industry and is passionate about finding solutions to industry-based issues. Her research areas include stakeholder management, public–private partnerships, renewable energy transition, affordable housing, and women in construction. She can be reached at sajani.jayasuriya@rmit.edu.au.

Victoria Maame Afriyie Kumah is currently a Postgraduate Student reading a Master of Science (MSc) in Construction Management. She is also a research assistant in the Department of Construction Technology and Management at the Kwame Nkrumah University of Science and Technology, Ghana. Her research interests lie in Green and Sustainable Construction, Circular Economy, and Digital Technologies. She has authored and co-authored publications in her current field. She is a team member of the building science, engineering, and materials research team in the Department of Construction Technology and Management. She can be reached at victoria1kum@gmail.com.

Sijekula Mbanga is a Full Professor and Chair for Human Settlement Development and Management at Nelson Mandela University, South Africa. He holds a Doctor of Philosophy in Administration, with a focus on intergovernmental development planning and management. Sijekula is an active member of several professional organizations related to human settlements and development. Sijekula is a registered member of SAAPAM, SAMEA, GISSA, IHSP-SA, ISOCARP, and SAPI. Before joining the university, Sijekula held senior and executive management positions in various departments in the Eastern Cape provincial government. He is involved in various advisory committees, research collaborations, and editorial boards in the field of human settlements and development.

Sijekula's research interests cover integrated approaches to development management, sustainable livelihoods, spatial transformation, green construction, human settlement policies, local government capacity, and indigenous knowledge systems in infrastructure development. He is passionate about community development and social justice activism, aiming to address issues of poverty, malnutrition, homelessness, and inequality. Sijekula believes in transdisciplinary and multisector approaches to achieve sustainable development outcomes. Sijekula is actively engaged in international research collaborations, including projects with partners in Germany and the USA. He is dedicated to promoting positive change and development both in academia and within the communities he works closely with. He can be reached at sijekula.Mbanga@mandela.ac.za.

Stephen Au Ling Ming has been the Managing Director and Founder of MTECH Engineering Co. LTD since 1995. He received the award of China 2007 Top 100 Innovative Enterprise Leader in 2008. MTECH is a leading information technology company that provides building information modeling, lean construction, and product life cycle management solutions and consulting services to the building construction and manufacturing industry in Hong Kong and China. MTECH received the Award of Hong Kong Most Valuable Companies 2017. Stephen AU has more than 30 years of experience in international business for information technology in the building construction and manufacturing industry. He got the Outstanding PolyU (The Hong Kong Polytechnic University) Alumni Award 2017 in recognition of his distinguished professional accomplishments and significant contributions to the industries and his alma mater in technology research and development and deployment. He is a Professional Member of The Hong Kong Institute of Building Information Modelling (HKIBIM), Director of Business and Technology Development of FJ005 (Indoor Positioning with BIM), and External Examiner of VTC (Vocational Training Council) for the Part Time course of Certificate in Revit Level 1 from 2021 to 2023 and holds many other external appointments. Stephen AU holds a Higher Diploma of Applied Science from PolyU, Hong Kong (1982), an MBA of Strategic Marketing from the University of HULL, UK (1999), and a Master of Advanced Business Practice (knowledge management for continuous product innovation) from the University of

South Australia, Australia (2007) and is currently a Student of the Doctor of International Real Estate and Construction program at PolyU (2022–2025). He can be reached at stephenau@mtech.com.hk.

Eric Obiaw Mireku is a Forestor and a Pastor originally from Kwahu, Eastern region. He has a bachelor's degree in Natural Resource Management from the Kwame Nkrumah University of Science and Technology, Ghana, and an MPhil in Project Management from the same university. He is an ISO-accredited inspector of timber, who has been with the Forestry Commission for almost 10 years, where he serves as a northern sector assistant operations manager. He is currently on three projects at the commission. He is a trainer, mentor, and coach to several young people. He can be reached at ericmirekuobiaw@gmail.com.

Lukuman Musibau is a highly qualified individual with an extensive academic background in the field of real estate. His PhD in Real Estate from Universiti Teknologi Malaysia, Malaysia, and MSc in Housing from the University of Ibadan, Nigeria, demonstrate his expertise and dedication to advancing knowledge in the domain of real estate and housing. As a Registered Estate Surveyor and Valuer (RSV), Lukuman is recognized as a certified professional in the field, equipped with the necessary skills to carry out property surveys, valuations, and related services. Currently serving as the Head of the Department of Estate Management and Valuation at Federal Polytechnic Ede, Nigeria, Lukuman is actively involved in academic administration and contributes to the development of future professionals in the field of estate management and valuation. Beyond his academic engagements, Lukuman has substantial public service experience. He has worked as a Senior Special Assistant/Sub-National Consultant in the Office of the Deputy Chief of Staff (DCoS) to the Executive Governor of Osun State, Nigeria. This role likely involved providing advisory support and contributing to policy initiatives in the area of real estate and related sectors. Additionally, Lukuman has served as a Technical Assistant on MDGs (Millennium Development Goals) and SDGs (Sustainable Development Goals) to both the Presidency and the Osun State Government in Nigeria. In these positions, he might have played a crucial role in aligning government initiatives with the sustainable development agenda, with a focus on real estate development and housing. Overall, Lukuman's academic qualifications, professional certifications, and public service experience make him a highly competent and valuable professional in the real estate and housing sectors, contributing to both academia and the development of sustainable policies and projects in Nigeria. He can be reached at lukuman.musibau@federalpolyede. edu.ng.

Goodenough D. Oppong is currently taking a Postdoctoral Fellow position at The Hong Kong Polytechnic University, Hong Kong, upon completing his doctoral study in Construction Management Field from the same university. He is a certified construction management professional and has substantial research and practical experience in the construction industry over the past decade. His research interests include the management of numerous stakeholders who enter the project space, the performance evaluation and benchmarking systems for construction projects, the utilization of blockchain-enabled smart contracts in construction projects, and the management of large construction projects. He is also engaged with industry organizations in developing and implementing practical solutions including project performance monitoring systems, project planning, and contingency estimation tools, and project cost and time prediction tools based on artificial intelligence. His present research project focuses on developing a computerized system for monitoring and benchmarking hospital project performance. He can be reached at dennis. oppong@polyu.edu.hk.

Emmanuel Kingsford Owusu is a Research Assistant Professor in Construction and Real Estate Economics in the Department of Building and Real Estate at The Hong Kong Polytechnic University, Hong Kong. Prior to assuming this role, he was a Postdoctoral Fellow in the same Department. Dr. Owusu was a recipient of the Hong Kong PhD Fellowship Scheme Award and holds first-class honors in Quantity Surveying and Construction Economics from Kwame Nkrumah University of Science and Technology, Ghana. His research focuses on Construction and Real Estate Finance, Infrastructure Procurement Automation, Engineering Ethics, Quantity Surveying Digitization, and Urban Infrastructure

Economics, Policy, and Governance. He can be reached at emmanuel.kingsford.owusu@polyu.edu.hk.

Sivakumar Palaniappan completed his B.E. (Civil Engineering) from the Madurai Kamaraj University, Master of Science (by Research) from the Building Technology and Construction Management Group at the Department of Civil Engineering, Indian Institute of Technology Madras, Chennai, and Doctoral Degree from the Department of Civil and Environmental Engineering at Arizona State University, USA. Before pursuing his doctoral degree, Dr. Sivakumar Palaniappan worked in the industry for two years in the area of application of information technology tools. Dr. Sivakumar Palaniappan has been a faculty member at IIT Madras since 2010 and teaches courses such as Construction Planning and Control, Quality Management, and Sustainable Construction for graduate students. His research interests are in the areas of embodied energy assessment of materials and construction processes, life cycle assessment, life cycle energy analysis, green buildings, and low carbon buildings. He can be reached at sp@iitm.ac.in.

L. Pinky Devi completed her B.E. (Civil Engineering) from the Viswesvaraya Technological University, M.Tech. (Construction Engineering and Management) from the Manipal University, and Doctoral Degree (Civil Engineering with specialization in the areas of Sustainable Construction) from the Indian Institute of Technology Madras, Chennai. Before pursuing her doctoral degree, Dr. Pinky Devi worked at the Brigade Group (one of the largest real estate development organizations) in Bangalore for two years. Her research interests are in the areas of embodied energy assessment of materials and construction processes and life cycle energy analysis of buildings. Dr. Pinky Devi has been working as an Associate Professor at the Nagarjuna College of Engineering and Technology in Bangalore since 2017. Dr. Pinky Devi teaches courses in the areas of construction engineering and management and conducts training programs for professionals from the Government and Industry organizations at regular intervals. She can be reached at pinkydevi@gmail.com.

Hayford Pittri is a Research Assistant in the Department of Construction Technology and Management at the Kwame Nkrumah University of Science and Technology, Ghana. He holds a bachelor's degree in Quantity Surveying and Construction Economics and a master's degree in Construction Management from Kwame Nkrumah University of Science and Technology. Hayford is a corporate member of the Ghana Institute of Construction and a student member of the American Concrete Institute (Kwame Nkrumah University of Science and Technology Chapter). He is a proficient reviewer for the *Journal of Engineering, Design and Technology*. His research interests are in the areas of Health and Safety, Immersive Technologies, BIM, and Sustainable construction. Hayford has published several peer-reviewed journal papers in top journals, such as *Engineering, Construction and Architectural Management* (Emerald publishing) and *International Journal of Construction Management* (Taylor and Francis). He is a team member of the building science, engineering, and materials research team in the Department of Construction Technology and Management. He can be reached at hayfordp09e@gmail.com.

Emel Sadikoglu received her BSc degree in civil engineering and MSc degree in construction management from Bogazici University, Turkey, in 2018 and 2021, respectively. She is currently working toward her PhD degree in construction management at Gebze Technical University, Turkey. She has been working as a Research and Teaching Assistant at the Department of Civil Engineering of Gebze Technical University. Her research interests include but are not limited to lean construction, agility, sustainability, occupational health and safety, and digital technologies in the construction industry. She has already published in several peer-reviewed journals in the context of construction management studies. She can be reached at esadikoglu@gtu.edu.tr.

Mohammad Sakikhales is a Senior Lecturer in Construction Management and Property Development at the University of Greenwich. Motivated by his background in both Architecture and Project Management, he is teaching and researching multidisciplinary areas related to digital transformation from multiple perspectives including technology, process, and sustainability perspectives. Across these areas, he researches (1) technical topics, such as building information modeling, digital twins, virtual and augmented reality, and Internet of Things, (2) management topics including engineering and construction project management and the development of innovative management approaches specifically nonlinear methods, such as agile management, and (3) the impact of digitalization of built environment on sustainability including BIM-based building performance simulation and Net Zero design and refurbishment. He can be reached at m.sakikhales@greenwich.ac.uk.

Ron Schipper, MSc (1971), is the Sustainability Program Manager at the Municipality of Waddinxveen (Netherlands) and an independent researcher. "Different projects for a better life" captures his drive, finding possibilities for sustainability transitions in every project and portfolio is his daily business. Today he is one of the well-known recognized experts in the field of sustainability in project management with over a dozen papers and several books published and various practical contributions toward organizations adopting this topic. Ron is also an External Examiner in the MSc Project, Programme and Portfolio Management at HU University of Applied Science in the Netherlands. He can be reached at rpj.schipper@gmail.com.

Winston Shakantu is a Full Professor of Construction Management at Nelson Mandela University, South Africa. He has been inducted into the South African Council for the Project and Construction Management Professions as a Professional Construction Manager (Pr.CM), and the Chartered Institute of Building as a Corporate Member and a Chartered Construction Manager. Winston's teaching interests are in Construction Management in general with specific interests in Innovative Technologies in Construction and how these are applied and affect Materials and Methods in Construction. Professor Shakantu's research interests stretch across the broad area of Construction Management. Specific areas of interest have been eclectic, ranging from Construction Cost Control through Risk Management to Supply Chain Logistics Management at bachelor's, master's, and PhD levels. Completed research includes Construction Sustainability, Indigenous Construction Technology, Small, Micro, and

Medium Enterprise Contractors, Construction Logistics, Risk Management, and Health and Safety. His current research interest and work is on new developments in construction management, such as information and communication technology, innovative technology, and building information modeling. Much of the recent research has been in Construction Automation and Digitalization. Professor Shakantu has supervised research projects for honors, master's, and PhD students. He has supervised 22 PhD candidates to successful completion. Professor Shakantu has published more than 200 papers in book chapters and journals and presented papers at conferences in Africa, Europe, North America, Asia, and Oceania. He has been invited to review papers and join the peer-review panels for numerous international journals and conferences. He can be reached at winston.shakantu@mandela.ac.za.

Ming Shan is currently a Professor and Deputy Head of the Department of Engineering Management, School of Civil Engineering, Central South University, China. Prior to his employment at Central South University, Dr. Shan worked in the Department of Building, National University of Singapore, as a Research Fellow. Dr. Shan received his dual PhDs in Construction Management from The Hong Kong Polytechnic University in 2015 and Tongji University in 2016, respectively. He was also a Visiting Fellow at the Department of Civil and Environmental Engineering, The University of Auckland, from September 2015 to February 2016. Dr. Shan's research is mainly concentrated on professional ethics in construction, organizational issues in megaprojects, construction productivity, and sustainable construction management. Dr. Shan has participated in several research projects funded by the National Natural Science Foundation of China and Singapore Economic Development Board. Dr. Shan has produced nearly 80 research outputs in refereed journal papers, international refereed conference papers, and consultancy reports. He can be reached at ming.shan@csu.edu.cn.

Gilbert Silvius (1963) is a Professor of Applied Sciences at Wittenborg University of Applied Sciences in the Netherlands, an Associate Professor at HU University of Applied Sciences Utrecht in the Netherlands, and a Visiting Professor at the University of Johannesburg in South Africa. He has authored several books and over 50 academic journal articles and is a recognized expert in the field of sustainability in project management. For his work on this topic, Gilbert received the GPM 2013 sustainability award and a 2020 Outstanding Contribution IPMA research award. As a practitioner, Gilbert has over 30 years of experience in organizational change and IT projects and is a member of the international enable2change network of project management experts. Gilbert holds a PhD degree in information sciences from Utrecht University, the Netherlands, and masters' degrees in economics and business administration. He is also a certified project manager, scrum master, and product owner. He can be reached at mail@gilbertsilvius.nl.

Nilmini Weerasinghe is a Lecturer (ECDF) in Civil and Infrastructure Engineering Discipline at RMIT University, Australia. She completed her PhD in built environment at RMIT University in 2021. She received a BSc (honors) in Facilities Management degree with a first-class from the University of Moratuwa, Sri Lanka, in 2013. She is an active member of the Solar Energy Application Laboratory (SEAL) at RMIT. She previously served as a Lecturer (sessional) at Victoria University, Australia, and the University of Moratuwa. She conducts various research projects with the collaboration of international and local research partners. As a scholar in the building and construction sector, she is savvy in data mining techniques such as modeling and machine learning and MATLAB programming. Her main research interests are sustainable construction technologies, solar building envelop, asset management, modeling, and machine learning techniques. She can be reached at nilmini.weerasinghe@rmit.edu.au.

Rebecca Yang is an Associate Professor in the School of Property Construction and Project Management at RMIT University, Australia. She is a scholar of building, construction, and distributed renewable energy who undertakes pure and applied research that can provide innovative solutions to the industry by integrating theories with cutting-edge technologies. She has established the Solar Energy Application Lab at RMIT and led many academics, research students, and research assistants from multiple projects to support energy transformation through greater solar adoption in the building sector and the urban environment. She is also a board member of the Australian PV Institute. She can be reached at rebecca.yang@rmit.edu.au.

Sitsofe Kwame Yevu is a Lecturer in Construction Management in the School of Architecture, Building and Civil Engineering at Loughborough University, UK. He has a PhD degree in Construction Engineering and Management from The Hong Kong Polytechnic University, Hong Kong, and worked there as a Postdoctoral Fellow after completing his doctoral degree. Having a bachelor's and master's in building technology and procurement management, Sitsofe's research focuses on exploring digital technologies for sustainable solutions in construction circular economy, sustainable or green supply chain, low-carbon and Net Zero buildings, and modular construction. He has published several articles in leading journals and presented at international conferences. He is a reviewer for several journals in the domain and has been an invited speaker at seminars. With a collaboration network spanning from Australia through Asia, Europe, and Africa to the United States, Sitsofe always seeks to leave a research footprint that is solution-oriented and relevant to the built environment and future society. He can be reached at s.k.yevu@lboro.ac.uk.

Tarek Zayed, PhD, PE, PEng, FASCE, FCSCE, FHKIE, is a Professor and Associate Head of Research in the Department of Building and Real Estate at The Hong Kong Polytechnic University, Hong Kong. Dr. Zayed has a PhD, MSc, and BSc in Construction Engineering and Management. He received his Ph.D. from Purdue University, West Lafayette, Indiana, USA, in May 2001. He conducted research on modular construction; infrastructure/asset management; simulation, fuzzy, optimization, risk assessment, data mining, and artificial intelligence applications in construction; and performance, budget allocation, and life cycle cost analysis for municipal underground systems. He has more than 30 years of professional experience working in the construction industry training and in academic posts in the USA, Canada, Egypt, and Hong Kong. Dr. Zayed has published more than 550 journal and conference articles and performed research with a significant amount of funding from government and private funding agencies. He is serving as an Associate Editor of the *ASCE's Journal of Pipeline Systems Engineering and Practice, the*

Canadian Journal of Civil Engineering, and Buildings, MDPI. Dr. Zayed is also a fellow of the Hong Kong Institution of Engineers (HKIE), the American Society of Civil Engineers (FASCE), and the Canadian Society for Civil Engineering (FCSCE). He is ranked among the top 1.0% of scholars in civil engineering worldwide, based on a study by Stanford University. He can be reached at tarek.zayed@polyu.edu.hk.

Xianbo Zhao is an Associate Professor in the School of Engineering and Technology at Central Queensland University, Australia. Dr. Zhao joined Central Queensland University in 2014. He holds bachelor's and master's qualifications in Construction Management from Southeast University (China) and a PhD degree in Building awarded by the National University of Singapore (NUS), Singapore. Dr. Zhao has been conducting research into the issues surrounding the management of civil and building construction and built environment. Dr. Zhao has over 140 peer-reviewed publications in the field of building and construction management. His research output has gained national and international recognition as evidenced by publications in leading journals, high citations, and international awards. Dr. Zhao was selected as Australia's Top Researcher in Architecture and one of the Rising Stars of Research in Sustainable Development in *The Australian's Research Magazine* in 2021. He was among the World's Top 2% Researchers in Building and Construction compiled by Stanford University in 2020–2022. He can be reached at b.zhao@cau.edu.au.

Acknowledgments

This book would not have been possible without the support and contributions of many people. Many thanks to the Series Editor-in-Chief, Professor Mohan M. Kumaraswamy, for his support throughout this project. Thanks also to Mr. John Stuart, Senior Commissioning Editor of World Scientific, for his patience and encouragement. Further thanks to Professor Mohan M. Kumaraswamy and Mr. John Stuart for championing this book. Thanks go to The Hong Kong Institute of Surveyors (HKIS) for sponsoring this book. Thanks to Sr Wong Kwok Leung, Paul, HKIS President, for generously writing the foreword. A special note of thanks goes to all the contributors for the high-quality chapters in this book. Thanks also to the many experts and academics who reviewed each of the individual chapters and offered helpful suggestions and corrections. Thanks to Professor Bon-Gang Hwang for his support in the initiation of this project. Like any knowledge creation project, producing a book such as this demands a significant amount of time commitment. Thanks to our families for their understanding and support, for indulging the time spent on this book, and for sharing our enthusiasm for green construction.

Contents

List of Figures

List of Tables

Chapter 1

Introduction: Background, Need, and Rationale for Developing a Body of Knowledge for Green Construction Project Management

Amos Darko[*] and Albert P. C. Chan[†]

[*]*University of Washington, Seattle, WA, USA*

[†]*The Hong Kong Polytechnic University, Hung Hom, Hong Kong*

1.1. Background

Green construction isn't going anywhere, so it's time for construction firms in all sectors of the industry to embrace it.

— Autodesk

The *process* of constructing buildings is a major contributor to energy use and emissions that drive climate change worldwide, accounting for over 30% of global final energy use and energy- and process-related carbon emissions. The process is also a massive consumer of natural resources, water, and raw materials, and it generates significant amounts of waste. In the US, for example, 600 million tons of construction and demolition waste were generated in 2018 (US Environmental Protection Agency, 2022). Water, noise, and air pollution associated with the process that negatively impacts people's health, well-being, happiness, and quality of life in myriad ways are also worth mentioning. In addition, the process is full of complexity, risk, and uncertainty and requires great technical and technological interventions for efficient and effective delivery of the project. We wanted to stop here but nature and biodiversity loss, land degradation, and deforestation due to construction developments are other critical concerns.

These facts show that the construction process can be held accountable for significantly contributing to the sustainability challenges that humanity currently faces — from the triple planetary crisis of climate change, nature and biodiversity loss, and pollution and waste to the general sustainability breakdown! Climate change, for instance, "is the most pressing issue facing humanity today" (United Nations, 2022). To solve it, we need to cut the carbon emissions from the construction process now — highlighting the urgency of immediate action and "step change" in the construction process.

These decisive issues represent not only challenges for the construction industry but also tremendous opportunities for the industry to build back better — reducing negative impacts while creating positive impacts on the environment, society, and economy.

Green construction unlocks these opportunities for the utilization of the industry. Many in the industry have already realized this and are shifting from conventional to green construction nowadays (Autodesk, 2022). But what is green construction? It refers to the process of constructing buildings in a "green" or "sustainable" manner. What does this actually mean? It's about building with green or "sustainability" in mind. It's also about the actual construction of the building itself, not the operation of the finished building (Forestell, 2019). However, the operation and even the eventual maintenance, renovation, and demolition of the building can also become green if the process of construction itself was green. Green construction focuses on maximizing human health, well-being, happiness, and quality of life, using fewer resources, as well as reducing waste, pollution, and negative impacts of the construction process on the environment, such as carbon emissions. It addresses environmental, social, and economic sustainability issues, impact, and performance in the construction process. This is what distinguishes green construction projects from their conventional counterparts that are built with no green in mind. While many have used the terms "green" and "sustainable" interchangeably, others have attempted to differentiate between them by claiming that "green" is concerned only with the environmental dimension of sustainability, while "sustainable" takes a broad environmental, social, and economic approach. This book shares the first school of thought and uses the terms interchangeably. That is to say that the terms "green" and "sustainable" are used to mean the same thing — environmental, social, and economic sustainability.

Green construction is special! Going green requires several changes to the [conventional] construction process, such as using green or sustainable materials; using innovative methods such as modular construction to help reduce waste as much as possible in the context of circular economy; using less energy and water, and reducing carbon emissions; proper, integrated planning, design, and delivery process to make the process truly green; sourcing non-toxic chemicals for use on site; and using innovative and creative solutions and advanced technologies to increase the efficiency, effectiveness, and productivity of the process. Project managers must have the ability to identify and overcome challenges that come with this new method of construction. They must have the specialized knowledge and skills required to help them overcome these challenges and successfully deliver green construction projects. This is the core rationale for developing this specialized body of knowledge for green construction project management (PM), which is further explored in the rest of this chapter.

Despite the global and special importance of green construction projects, there is a lack of a *comprehensive* body of knowledge for their management. There exist bodies of knowledge in PM in general and books on selected areas of green construction PM specifically. But this is the first attempt at consolidating and developing a more comprehensive body of knowledge for green construction PM specifically. Green construction projects are increasingly becoming more and more important and prominent, and the global market for green construction projects is expanding exponentially. For instance, the "2022 Global Status Report for Buildings and Construction" indicated that in 2021, the number of green certifications increased by 19% across the world compared with 2020 (United Nations Environment Programme, 2022). In addition, a 2022 research report by Verified Market Research indicated that the global green construction materials market size was worth USD 271.90 billion in 2021 and is forecasted to reach USD 635.47 billion by 2030 (Verified Market Research, 2022). It is therefore important and timely to help project managers develop the specialized knowledge and skills needed to successfully complete green construction projects. This book provides a PM body of knowledge that addresses the unique aspects of this field and thereby is directly applicable to green construction projects. It provides both conceptual principles as well as practical case studies on PM processes and practices in green construction projects. This book should be useful to practitioners, researchers, and students of green construction PM and anyone seeking to develop green construction PM knowledge and skills.

1.2. Need and rationale for this book

Increasing global imperatives to address sustainability issues and concerns have boosted the importance and prominence of green construction projects worldwide. However, project managers may lack the specialist knowledge and/or technical skills to overcome the unique challenges to successfully deliver suitably sustainable green projects (ManagePlaces, 2020). This book aims to address this shortfall by unearthing, refining, and synergizing the hitherto scattered gems of experiential and theoretical knowledge, into a unified body of knowledge for green construction PM.

Green construction projects are special because they are fundamentally different from their conventional counterparts from several perspectives. Most importantly, they have sustainability as a primary project goal, which engenders most of the differences between them and conventional projects. To achieve this sustainability goal, green construction projects use more special technologies, materials, processes, practices, strategies, measures, features, infrastructures, and facilities that possess less environmental and health impact (Hwang *et al.*, 2017). While this is good, it can make green construction projects more complicated and expensive.

In addition, green construction projects come with higher staffing requirements, with additional staff including, and especially, green professionals, such as green design consultants, air quality consultants, life cycle assessment experts, energy and carbon experts, green building assessors, sustainability consultants, waste managers, and environmental consultants. This may increase the possibility of more conflicts, claims, and litigations, and therefore the need for greater team coordination, communication, and collaboration between the multidisciplinary and interdisciplinary experts, to avoid such conflicts, claims, and litigations. Careful planning and design are required to integrate green measures. This can make the design process more complicated and time-consuming when compared with conventional projects. There is also the need for more advanced project sustainability performance studies, analyses, calculations, modeling, simulations, representations, and visualizations. The necessity to undergo and achieve formal green assessment and certification further increases the uniqueness, complexity, and uncertainty of green construction projects. When such certification is a project goal, extensive sustainability documentation, reporting, submission, verification, and processing are required (Robichaud & Anantatmula, 2011). At times, even appeal procedures come in if the applicant is not happy with the green assessment and certification results, further complicating and delaying the project. There are many other factors that make green construction projects really special and very different from other types of construction projects, such as waste management, reduction, reuse, and recycling requirements.

These crucial issues make green construction projects riskier, and more complex and uncertain, with green construction projects facing numerous challenges caused by poor PM (Bon-Gang, 2018). Not only are they usually completed with a "cost premium," but they also face more cost and schedule overruns than conventional projects (Hwang *et al.*, 2017; Hwang & Leong, 2013). It has been reported in the literature that many green construction projects experience rework and greater health and safety risks to workers (Hwang *et al.*, 2016; Dewlaney *et al.*, 2012; Bon-Gang, 2018). Good PM is critical to solving these problems and has never been more important, highlighting the critical need for this book.

Moreover, the world is now in a state of climate emergency (United Nations Environment Programme, 2023), with many cities and people already feeling and suffering the impacts of the climate emergency first-hand. We are not going to waste your time talking about the impacts of the climate emergency, as we all know and feel them. But, recently, in May 2023, we saw record-breaking rainfalls and floods that left many people dead or homeless in Italy, where Mount Etna volcano further discharged heavy smoke and ash into the atmosphere which seriously impaired visibility. We saw similar rainfalls causing severe flash floods, landslides, and disruptions in Saudi Arabia. In Canada, from only January to May 2023, over 600 intense wildfires have been seen in Alberta and British Columbia alone, burning nearly 1 million acres of forests and land and forcing over 29,000 people to evacuate their homes and communities (Department of Commerce, 2023). Smoke from the wildfires traveled into the US, and several states including Wisconsin, Montana, Washington, and Nebraska issued air quality warnings (Rao, 2023). Breathing in smoke from wildfires is linked to many respiratory and health problems. The Department of Commerce (2023) stated the following:

> According to local experts, this type of "ferocious" wildfire activity isn't typical this early in the year, and firefighters don't normally see such a large area burned at once. Additionally, a news release issued by the government of Alberta stated the region is experiencing unusually hot, dry conditions this spring, which makes it an ideal environment for fires to spread. A provincial state of emergency in Alberta was declared on May 6, 2023.

The question is as follows: Why are all these extreme weather events happening and affecting all corners of the world? One may argue that they are natural disasters; yes those are natural. However, there must be a reason why these natural disasters are becoming more common and are no longer as normal as they once were. Who is responsible? One of the best answers is rising global temperatures. But what causes the global temperatures to rise? One answer is human activities. We are the cause of our own problems. Our activities, such as the use of energy in the building construction process, that require the burning of fossil fuels that releases carbon emissions into the earth's atmosphere are the main cause of the rising global temperatures. According to the World

Meteorological Organization (2023), climate impacts become increasingly severe with rising temperatures, as higher temperatures mean more extreme weather, sea level rise, melting ice and glaciers, and ocean heat and acidification. In addition, rising temperatures have extensive implications for human health, well-being, happiness, quality of life, and safety, the environment, water availability, access, and management, and food security.

To solve these challenges and save people and the planet, there is an urgent need to take aggressive and concrete actions to rapidly cut carbon emissions that fuel the continuous rise in global temperatures. With the construction process of buildings being a big contributor to these carbon emissions, there's no doubt that green construction will continue to be prioritized in the global toolkits and solutions to deliver the transformative change required to decarbonize the global economy in line with the Paris Agreement. This is one of the reasons why green construction is the future. It is a movement that would never go away — it is here to stay! As Autodesk (2022) indicated, "construction firms that ignore this are at risk of getting left behind." PM has a significant role to play in successfully delivering green construction projects to save the world.

1.3. Green construction project management

As indicated in Chapter 2, this book adopts the Chartered Institute of Building's (2014) definition of PM: "the overall planning, coordination, and control of a project from inception to completion aimed at meeting a client's requirements in order to produce a functionally viable and sustainable project that will be completed safely, on time, within authorized cost, and to the required quality standards."

What we like about this definition compared with many other PM definitions in existence is the focus on producing a "sustainable project." But this refers to the sustainability of the completed project — the project output. It is not clear whether the client's requirements and responsibilities of PM in this definition involve making the actual construction process sustainable as well. It seems that for this definition, safety, time, cost, and quality are the main success criteria or key performance indicators (KPIs) in the construction stage.

Producing a sustainable project does not necessarily mean that the process of producing the project itself is also sustainable. Kevin Forestell is the Co-Founder and CEO of DOZR, a construction equipment firm. In his article "Green Construction vs. Green Buildings: Understanding the Important Difference," it is mentioned:

> ... a building or area can become green certified even if the process of construction itself was not completed with sustainability in mind. To get green certified you need the applicable infrastructure, technologies, appliances, and design to make it green. Yet the process of building it isn't even taken into consideration. A sustainable project is one thing, but green or sustainable construction is a whole game of its own. Since it is not required, very few contractors consider or think about it in their site building plan. That doesn't mean that green construction doesn't benefit contractors or that more contractors shouldn't take it into consideration more often.

In fact, the practice of producing "green certified" projects through unsustainable construction processes has never been a good practice in the world of sustainability. Considering the climate emergency crisis that we currently face and the triple planetary crisis of climate change, nature and biodiversity loss, and pollution and waste that we highlighted earlier, for example, this practice needs to be stopped immediately. Overlooking the sustainability of the construction process itself (i.e., green construction) means missed opportunities to deal with all those significant embodied carbon emissions, waste generation, and pollution associated with the construction process stage and materials. In such a situation, the climate and sustainability challenges that the world faces can never be addressed. For example, addressing operational carbon impact from the operation of the completed sustainable project alone is not enough to address the global climate crisis. This is because as energy efficiency, renewable energy, and cleaner production improve and reduce the carbon emissions from operational energy, embodied carbon from the construction process and materials will become the leading source of carbon emissions from the buildings and construction sector in the future. Moreover, the impacts of embodied carbon associated with the construction process stage and materials are irreversible postconstruction. After the project is constructed, any negative impacts that resulted from the processes and materials that have already been used to construct it cannot be undone (Bouchard, 2023). In addition, how can we address sustainability challenges if the massive waste and pollution from the construction process are not dealt with? It is impossible. Hence, delivering a sustainable project while the process of delivering it itself isn't sustainable too must not be entertained and encouraged.

Contractors who care about the survival and prosperity of themselves and their families, their companies, and the common good do not ignore green construction in the face of the climate crisis and other sustainability challenges. Those who ignore it may be out of business soon, as green construction becomes a vital business strategy for many contractors as the world, the industry, and clients prioritize the increasing urgency for solutions to the triple planetary crisis and other sustainability challenges.

The PM definition needs to consider this. We, therefore, based on the Chartered Institute of Building's (2014) definition of PM, define green construction PM as follows:

> the 'sustainable' overall planning, coordination, and control of a project from inception to completion aimed at meeting a client's requirements in order to produce a functionally viable and sustainable project that will be completed safely, on time, within authorized cost, and to the required quality and 'sustainability' standards.

This definition emphasizes that, first, the overall project planning, coordination, and control work of the project manager need to be sustainable. This means that sustainability of the PM process is a critical client requirement and must be carefully considered right from the start of the project. Second, with this definition, the project manager is tasked not only with delivering a functionally viable and sustainable project but also with making sure that the process of constructing or delivering the project itself is completed with sustainability (environmental, social, and economic), safety, time, cost, quality, and other client's project requirements in mind, carefully considered and addressed. In short, green construction PM transforms the conventional PM KPI model by adding to the model sustainability of the (1) PM process, (2) construction or project delivery process, and (3) output of the project as a critical client requirement. (See Chapter 6 for more on "Considering Sustainability in Construction PM".)

The consideration of sustainability makes green construction PM a specialized and skilled profession (Kubba, 2010). The green construction project manager is under great pressure to meet all the sustainability requirements of the client in addition to meeting all the prevailing conventional requirements (e.g., cost, time, quality, and safety) as well. One new challenge this brings is ensuring that the project is delivered within acceptable time and cost constraints despite the consideration of sustainability requirements. For the project to be considered a successful project, it is required to avoid any cost premium, 'time premium', as well as cost overruns and schedule delays — a challenging task for the green construction project manager, knowing that green measures and green certification, if not well managed, usually add extra costs and time. But when well-managed, green projects are successfully delivered with no added costs and time and no cost and time overruns. There are many successful cases where no extra costs were incurred to successfully deliver green projects. Lisa Fay Matthiessen and her colleagues have documented many of them (Matthiessen & Morris, 2004). However, such successes require competent, effective, and efficient green construction project managers.

With this in mind, just as taxi (small vehicle) drivers are not allowed to operate large/heavy vehicles (e.g., trucks) unless they have the required commercial driver's license, conventional construction project managers must not be allowed to manage green construction projects unless they have the required green construction PM "license." But what is the green construction PM license? It is what qualifies a project manager as a green construction project manager. This includes working experience managing green construction projects successfully. According to Yudelson (2009), experience with green construction projects is a key qualification for two reasons. First, project managers with little or no experience will naturally allot to their fees a "risk premium," with the hope of getting paid for their "learning curve" by the first client. Second, project managers with experience, in contrast, will bring written standard specifications, research and knowledge of alternative materials, ability to pick team members right, and simpler moves and shortcuts to get to sustainability. Instead of allotting a risk premium to their fees, they would rather save the project efforts, time, and money because their simpler moves and shortcuts usually translate to less effort, time, and money from utilizing simpler or fewer systems. Besides, they are more likely to treat sustainability requirements as "business as usual," not as an additional burden to their conventional PM and delivery processes.

Other attributes that qualify the green construction project manager are knowledge of sustainability science, building science, biodiversity or climate change science, green construction technologies and practices, energy, carbon, water and waste management, and efficiency enhancement strategies; green accreditations in relevant green construction project rating tools (see Chapter 3 for more on green construction project rating tools); knowledge of building codes and heating, ventilation, and air conditioning (HVAC) systems; excellent people skills needed to communicate clearly both in writing and orally; familiarity with innovative, smarter, and greener ways of working; superior analytical skills needed for interpreting data, energy, water, and carbon models; and financial calculations (Northeast Sustainable Energy Association, 2023), just to mention a few. Chapter 5 covers more on the PM knowledge areas and skills that green construction project managers must possess. It is important that the green construction project managers continue training, educating, and developing themselves and staying with well-developed needed skills and informed (ManagePlaces, 2020). This book is a valuable resource and companion in this journey.

Lauren Bradley Robichaud and Vittal Anantatmula are among those who have conducted interesting PM studies of green construction projects. The essential message from their studies is that "the unique characteristics of green construction require adjustments to conventional PM processes and practices to minimize risks and improve the chances of delivering the project successfully." In other words, "in order for project managers to deliver green construction projects successfully, modifications must be made to conventional PM processes and practices" (Robichaud & Anantatmula, 2011). While this message further stresses the importance of this book, examples of suggested specific adjustments to conventional PM processes and practices to optimize the delivery of green construction projects include the following:

- Including in project needs assessment/definition, sustainability goal, green certification level, and budget allocated to green initiatives.

- Involving a "cross-discipline team" from the very beginning of and throughout the project. The team must be selected based on their knowledge and experience with all phases of green construction, as well as their familiarity with the market and product type. Green-accredited professionals are optimal and strongly recommended.
- Prioritizing "charrettes" as a required PM practice. According to Robichaud and Anantatmula (2011), communication and coordination across a multidisciplinary and interdisciplinary team is the most significant challenge to delivering a successful green construction project. Charrettes have the potential to solve this challenge through effective communication, collaboration, and coordination. They bring together all the project stakeholders to work collaboratively to create solutions that are desired by "all" — an integrated team and process in effect. The National Charrette Institute (n.d.) and Roggema (2014) offer lots of resources on understanding charrettes and how to conduct successful charrettes.
- Involving all stakeholders, including the community, in project site selection. This is addressed if a good charrette process has been completed as suggested above.
- Involving an experienced green construction project manager, an integrated team and process, and specialized technology to facilitate the processes of documentation and submission for the green certification in a way that does not harm the cost and schedule of the project.
- Introducing a "construction with kickoff meeting" that incorporates a green construction education and training module for onsite construction workers. It is also essential that after construction begins, regular onsite meetings are held with the whole site workforce. Such regular meetings should also include education and training sessions on green construction. Continual education and training throughout the project are essential to ensure achievement of green construction project goals in an effective and efficient manner.

It is hoped that the important information and penetrating insights from the various chapters of this book will be useful to the reader in successfully understanding and implementing various green construction PM processes and practices.

1.4. Structure of this book

This book is organized as follows. It has 18 chapters. This introductory chapter presents the background, need, and rationale for developing a body of knowledge for green construction PM. The remaining 17 chapters are organized in two parts.

Part 1 has three chapters that provide an introduction to PM, as well as to green construction projects and their PM methodologies and frameworks.

Specifically, Chapter 2 provides an introduction to key concepts and fundamental knowledge of projects and PM and discusses the rich history of PM across different industries; the importance and challenges of PM; the main generic PM standards, frameworks, and methodologies, with case studies of their application; and the current, emerging, and future trends of the knowledge and practice of PM.

Chapters 3 and 4 describe green construction projects and their PM methodologies and frameworks, respectively. Topics covered include but are not limited to green construction projects, rating tools, policies, success stories, benefits, PM issues and challenges, case studies, and green construction projects and the UN Sustainable Development Goals.

Part 2 has 14 chapters that tackle processes and practices involved in managing green construction projects through to successful completion, for which practical case studies are introduced.

Specifically, Chapter 5 offers a systematic examination of issues regarding the green construction project manager and their activities in a green construction project.

Chapter 6 tackles the integration of sustainability into PM. The areas of impact of sustainability on PM with a focus on the management of construction projects are identified and analyzed.

Chapter 7 provides a "special chapter" on how PM can impact Net Zero construction as a part of green construction.

Chapter 8 discusses current approaches and processes of project scope management and illustrates how they can be applied in green construction projects.

Chapter 9 explores how green construction project design leaders (architects and engineers) determine building solutions and examines the motivations for their decision behavior.

Chapter 10 identifies the risks that are closely associated with green construction and presents methods to analyze these risks. A series of risk response measures are proposed to deal with the critical risks.

Chapter 11 presents a thorough discussion on the use of green criteria in procurement management to promote green construction for projects.

Chapter 12 deliberates on effective stakeholder management processes and practices in green construction projects.

Chapter 13 compares health and safety (risks and performance) in green and conventional construction projects, inspects green rating tools regarding their effect on health and safety, and reviews safety management elements in green and conventional construction projects.

Chapter 14 entails the concepts as well as a detailed understanding of "success" for green construction projects.

Chapter 15 presents a framework and models for assessing the energy use of onsite construction processes along with the identification of several technological and operational parameters.

Chapter 16 surveys the need for postconstruction management of green projects through adopting management techniques to ensure sustainability. Postconstruction management strategies for green projects are discussed.

Chapter 17 examines how life cycle management contributes to green construction by offering a more systematic and holistic view in examining the costs and benefits of green construction projects throughout their entire life cycle.

Chapter 18 concludes this book by tackling digital green construction PM as an emerging and future trend in green construction PM.

Across these chapters, practical case studies are offered to demonstrate and support the practical application of discussed concepts, processes, and practices in green construction PM.

References

Autodesk. (2022). Green construction: A growing global trend — How to build green today and what to expect tomorrow. PDF. Available at: https://construction.autodesk.com/resources/guides/green-construction-a-growing-global-trend/ (accessed on 16 December 2022).

Bon-Gang, H. (2018). *Performance and Improvement of Green Construction Projects: Management Strategies and Innovations.* Kidlington, UK: Butterworth-Heinemann.

Bouchard, M. (2023). Make sustainable construction material choices with the winning combination of the embodied carbon in construction calculator (EC3) and autodesk construction cloud. Available at: https://construction-blog.autodesk.com/embodied-carbon-in-construction-calculator-ec3-and-autodesk-construction-cloud/ (accessed on 28 July 2023).

Chartered Institute of Building. (2014). *Code of Practice for Project Management for Construction and Development* (5th edn.). West Sussex, UK: John Wiley & Sons, Ltd.

Department of Commerce. (2023). Wildfires rage in Western Canada. Available at: https://www.nesdis.noaa.gov/news/wildfires-rage-western-canada (accessed on 30 May 2023).

Dewlaney, K. S., Hallowell, M. R., & Fortunato III, B. R. (2012). Safety risk quantification for high performance sustainable building construction. *Journal of Construction Engineering and Management, 138*(8), 964–971.

Forestell, K. (2019). Green construction vs green buildings: Understanding the important difference. Available at: https://dozr.com/blog/green-construction (accessed on 30 June 2021).

Hwang, B. G. & Leong, L. P. (2013). Comparison of schedule delay and causal factors between traditional and green construction projects. *Technological and Economic Development of Economy, 19*(2), 310–330.

Hwang, B. G., Shan, M., & Tan, E. K. (2016). Investigating reworks in green building construction projects: Magnitude, influential factors, and solutions. *International Journal of Environmental Research, 10*(4), 499–510.

Hwang, B. G., Zhu, L., Wang, Y., & Cheong, X. (2017). Green building construction projects in Singapore: Cost premiums and cost performance. *Project Management Journal, 48*(4), 67–79.

Kubba, S. (2010). *Green Construction Project Management and Cost Oversight.* Burlington, USA: Architectural Press.

ManagePlaces. (2020). Project management for green construction. Available at: https://www.manageplaces.com/construction/project-management-for-green-construction/ (accessed on 20 June 2021).

Matthiessen, L. F. & Morris, P. (2004). *Costing Green: A Comprehensive Cost Database and Budgeting Methodology.* Davis Langdon.

National Charrette Institute. (n.d.). NCI Charrette System™. Available at: https://www.canr.msu.edu/nci/nci-charrette-system/ (accessed on 16 March 2022).

Northeast Sustainable Energy Association. (2023). Green building project manager. Available at: https://nesea.org/content/green-building-project-manager (accessed on 27 July 2023).

Rao, D. (2023). Extreme weather events of 2023. Available at: https://theweek.com/in-depth/1021278/2023-extreme-weather (accessed on 30 July 2023).

Robichaud, L. B. & Anantatmula, V. S. (2011). Greening project management practices for sustainable construction. *Journal of Management in Engineering*, 27(1), 48–57.

Roggema, R. (2014). *The Design Charrette: Ways to Envision Sustainable Futures*. Dordrecht: Springer Netherlands.

United Nations (2022). What is the triple planetary crisis? Available at: https://unfccc.int/blog/what-is-the-triple-planetary-crisis (accessed on 12 May 2022).

United Nations Environment Programme. (2022). *2022 Global Status Report for Buildings and Construction: Towards a Zero-emission, Efficient and Resilient Buildings and Construction Sector*. Nairobi, Kenya: United Nations Environment Programme.

United Nations Environment Programme. (2023). The climate emergency. Available at: https://www.unep.org/climate-emergency (accessed on 2 February 2023).

US Environmental Protection Agency. (2022). Construction and demolition debris: Material-specific data. Available at: https://www.epa.gov/facts-and-figures-about-materials-waste-and-recycling/construction-and-demolition-debris-material (accessed on 16 December 2022).

Verified Market Research. (2022). Green building materials market size and forecast. Available at: https://www.verifiedmarketresearch.com/product/green-building-materials-market/ (accessed on 14 June 2022).

World Meteorological Organization. (2023). Global temperatures set to reach new records in next five years. Available at: https://public.wmo.int/en/media/press-release/global-temperatures-set-reach-new-records-next-five-years (accessed on 20 May 2023).

Yudelson, J. (2009). *Green Building Through Integrated Design*. New York, USA: The McGraw-Hill Companies, Inc.

Part 1

Project Management and Green Construction Projects

Chapter 2

Introduction to Project Management

Amos Darko[*], Goodenough D. Oppong[†], and Albert P. C. Chan[†]

[*]*University of Washington, Seattle, WA, USA*

[†]*The Hong Kong Polytechnic University, Hung Hom, Hong Kong*

This chapter introduces the concepts and fundamental knowledge of projects and project management (PM). The rich history of PM across different industries is reviewed to reveal the essential progress made. The importance of PM and the challenges that PM faces in contemporary times are discussed. The main generic standards, frameworks, and methodologies that are available in the PM world are reviewed, with case studies explored for exemplification of their application in real life. In the end, the current, emerging, and future trends of the knowledge and practice of PM are discussed as a reference point for the PM community.

2.1. What is a project?

Over the past years, when the knowledge and practice of project management (PM) thrived, many people and organizations have attempted to provide an appropriate definition for a "project." Among the numerous definitions, one of the authoritative general definitions is found in "BS 6079-2:2000 Project Management Vocabulary," which refers to a project as follows:

> A unique process, consisting of a set of coordinated and controlled activities with start and finish dates, undertaken to achieve an objective conforming to specific requirements, including constraints of time, cost, and resources.

The Project Management Institute (PMI) (2013) provided another authoritative definition of a project: "a temporary endeavor undertaken to create a unique product, service, or result." According to PMI (2013), a project can generate the following:

- a product that can be either a component of another item, an enhancement of an item, or an end item in itself,
- a service or a capability to perform a service,
- an improvement in an existing product or service lines, or
- a result, such as an outcome or document.

These definitions indicate that projects could range from anything simple and minor to anything complex and large. Examples of projects include developing an algorithm for a new computer program, undertaking an agricultural program, developing a medical facility, developing a new phone model, solving a mathematical problem, undertaking a research study, developing a new animal breed, constructing transport infrastructure, undertaking a movie production, undertaking a political campaign, lunching spaceships and satellites, carrying out military operations, developing medical solutions for health problems, and so on. A very famous project was NASA's Apollo program which enabled American astronauts to make 11 spaceflights and walk on the moon from 1968 to 1972. As can be observed, the list of projects could be unending and cuts across all sectors of the economy and spheres of life.

2.2. Origination of projects

According to the European Commission (2021), projects may be initiated for several reasons, including new products or services requested by clients/customers, market demands or opportunities for new products or services, changes in legal frameworks or organizational needs, improvements required upon conducting audits, counter products or services introduced by competitors, adoption of advanced technologies and methodologies, merging departments and integrating related processes, updating existing organizational processes, relocating businesses or organizations to new premises, raising awareness on specific topics, improving existing services and businesses, establishing proof of concepts, and migrating data to new information management systems. Other reasons may include environmental emergencies, recovery from disasters, social needs, and political opportunism. For instance, the Year 2000 (Y2K) project was carried out simultaneously by different organizations across the globe. The project was initiated to transform the dating format of the entire computing world to allow for better storage and management of historical computing data and information across millenniums.

2.3. Characteristics of projects

While projects are characterized by high levels of complexity, uncertainty, and uniqueness, reviewing several PM scholarly works and the definitions above reveals that there are some features that a project generally has, which include the following:

- Individual projects are unique in nature. A new project should be easily differentiable from other projects even if they are all similar. The uniqueness of a project is defined by the scale, scope, composition, type, client constraints, site conditions, external effects, project participants and organization, technology adopted, etc.
- Every project has specific goals and objectives. The goals and objectives are the targets that all effort investments must seek to achieve.

- Each project is a temporary activity and is defined with time boundaries. Thus, the expected beginning and ending dates are specified to translate a project from "imagination/ghost" status to "realistic" status. However, the time boundaries may experience modifications during the actual execution of the project.
- Every project requires the use of multiple resources. The resources serve as the inputs and could be in the form of materials and products, finance, staff, etc.
- Each project requires the application of certain knowledge and expertise from different fields.
- Individual projects are naturally executed within risky and uncertain environments and contexts. The real world is yet to attain an ideal and perfect status, and many contextual factors are unpredictable or inaccurately predictable. This creates a great headache for project managers to maneuver through the uncertainties and risks and still be able to deliver expected results.
- Each project is executed by assembling teams from diverse backgrounds and following an interdisciplinary approach to achieve common goals.
- Every project follows a typical life cycle and maturity curve. The project life cycle may include phases, such as conception, planning, designing, procurement, construction, commissioning, operation, and close out.
- Each project is flexible and dynamic and allows for necessary changes to initial plans and arrangements.
- Every project should be measurable in terms of success or failure.
- All these features make projects highly complicated enterprises.

2.4. Types of projects

There are several categorizations of projects in extant PM literature. The categorizations are done based on some similarities among the projects. Agreeing on how projects should be categorized is an important step underlying the development of new PM tools and techniques that are applicable to and effectual on different project types (Crawford *et al.*, 2005). The classification of projects into types could be based on several parameters, including the size or scale, complexity, organizational condition, geographical location, industrial sector characteristics, stage within life cycle, nature of work, procurement approach, mode of operation, financing source, and output or product. The categorization used in this chapter follows the work of Lock (2013).

2.4.1. *Type 1 projects*

Type 1 projects are always physical in nature and result in tangible outputs. These projects cover civil engineering, construction, petrochemical, mining, and quarrying works. Civil engineering projects include roads, railways, waterways, waste management, land reclamation, coastal works, environmental projects, and highways, among others. Construction projects are mainly buildings for commercial, residential, industrial, and institutional use. An important characteristic is that the projects must be executed in a specific location during the implementation phase. The scope and composition are often significantly detailed prior to the start of a project in location, and the flexibility allows for accommodating changes in initial plans. The extent of risk component is based on the complexity and complication of the project. For instance, a complex mega infrastructure project may be exposed to more risk items than a small building project. The projects often make use of a lot of technological, material, financial, and human resources. The workforce mostly comprises a high percentage of blue-collar workers and a low percentage of white-collar workers. Accordingly, shortage of skilled and unskilled workers is a common problem of these projects due to their labor-intensive nature. The project teams assemble different managerial specialists to perform specific roles such as cost, quality, time, safety, design, and environmental management in the projects. Sometimes, several consortiums come together to provide funding and resources for the implementation of huge projects where this is not possible with a single organization. Given that these projects are geographically expansive in nature and impact the social, environmental, and economic experiences of several stakeholders, project managers must be skilled in not only delivering technical responsibilities but also building social and communicative relationships with affected people. Examples of Type 1 projects include the following:

- The Great Wall of China (400 BC–AD 1600).
- Burj Khalifa Skyscraper of Dubai (2004–2009).

2.4.2. *Type 2 projects*

Type 2 projects are generally manufacturing projects, which create products or outputs that are physical and tangible in nature. Type 2 projects include, for example, the manufacture of aircraft, sea vessels, machines, automobiles, space vehicles, missiles, and rockets. The products or outputs of manufacturing projects sometimes serve as inputs for the implementation of Type 1 projects. For instance, concrete components are manufactured in factories and transported to the site for assembling into a building or bridge structure. Manufacturing projects are executed in a factory, workshop, or laboratory under a properly controlled environment, and the products or outputs are transported to users or for installation in different locations. Often, the complexity and detailing of manufacturing projects necessitate that different organizations develop specialized parts in separate locations and then assemble them elsewhere into the product. For demonstration, the engine, wings, and body of an airplane could be manufactured in different locations or countries and then assembled elsewhere for delivery to clients. The challenging management functions in such international Type 2 projects entail coordinating the project activities in different locations, managing organizational complexity, ensuring effective communication, and resolving conflicting technical standards (Lock, 2013). The scope and composition of the project are usually very detailed, with little flexibility and allowance for changes due to the high inherent risks. Similarly, these projects engage a lot of technological, financial, material, and human resources. Relatively, more blue-collar workers are employed on the projects than white-collar workers. The project teams are most often not co-located but distributed with respect to the number of parts production factories or laboratories. Examples of Type 2 projects include the following:

- The USS Gerald R. Ford (CVN-78) Aircraft Carrier project of the US Navy,
- Project Apollo of the US National Aeronautics and Space Administration (NASA).

2.4.3. *Type 3 projects*

Type 3 projects cover information technology (IT) projects and management or business change projects. Change projects are new initiatives or solutions required to modify how an organization is run, change how business is carried out, or answer critical business questions facing organization. The typical case for these projects could be company relocation, implementation of new technology, organizational restructuring (e.g., mergers and acquisitions), organizational cultural change, conducting feasibility study, or undertaking marketing campaign. These projects do not produce tangible and physical outputs as found with the earlier project types. Failure to undertake some of these necessary projects could create dysfunctional organizations or downward business growth. For instance, where newer software programs are not installed on hospital computer systems for managing healthcare operations, there could potentially be problems with the effective delivery of service in terms of increased waiting times, increased ambulance response time, higher mortality rates, and so on. Apart from businesses, several non-profit organizations (e.g., government departments, professional organizations, charitable foundations, social institutions, and disaster relief organizations) carry out management projects under Type 3 projects. The scope and composition may not be very detailed at the beginning but instead improve in the process. Intellectual, technological, and financial resources are required to execute these projects. Usually, these projects are self-financed by individual companies or through contributions from donors. Examples of Type 3 projects include the following:

- Netflix, Inc. transforming DVD services to online streaming from 2007,
- British Airways business restructuring from 1981.

2.4.4. *Type 4 projects*

Type 4 projects are pure scientific research projects that sometimes produce innovative and profitable outcomes. Research projects are scientific endeavors undertaken to answer theoretical or practical questions in the real world and potentially add to the current human knowledge and understanding. Since the outputs or products are often intangible and disseminated through journal articles, conferences, forums, reports, and books, research projects could sometimes be carried out from unrestricted locations. However, the data collection component (e.g., experiment) is carried out in a specific location (e.g., scientific laboratory). Research projects are highly risky, utilize a lot of financial resources and research personnel, solicit the inputs of several participants, involve a significant level of cross-discipline and/or cross-jurisdiction collaboration, and generate unpredictable outcomes. The goals and objectives of research projects are often challenging to frame from the start as researchers may be partially or totally unaware of the likely outcomes. This realistic experience calls for proper control measures in the form of capping budgets in correspondence with available funding, conducting regular stage-gate reviews, and re-evaluating the possible value of the projects. Whereas positive feedback alerts the continuation of the projects, negative feedback should help researchers to decide on terminating or continuing the projects. Project directors and leaders must possess significant management and social skills to optimize the intellectual strengths of researchers and promote good relationships among them (Lock, 2013).

2.5. Roles and impact of projects in business

Projects are an essential part of all organizations that participate in the economic or business environment. Organizations make decisions to invest in projects at specific times based on strategic business reasons. Through the implementation of projects, organizations can transform their endeavors, processes, activities, or functions to attain their strategic business objectives. Such strategic projects may be triggered by deliberate, emergent, or imposed reasons in organizations to create some expected outcomes and benefits toward the fulfillment of business objectives. Projects are aligned with the characteristics of the respective investments such that the needed resources are procured by the funding organizations and assigned to the implementation of projects today in hopes of realizing the expected outcomes and benefits tomorrow. It is important for organizations to accurately interpret the investments made in projects and the results that should follow in the future, even if the results are non-financial in nature. The funding organizations are viewed in the economic or business context of projects as the investors who have expectations of making positive returns over a defined period. Just as positive returns are the motivation for financial investments in business, even so are expected outcomes and benefits the inspiration for investments in projects. Although there are many factors influencing the decision of funding organizations to support project implementation and investment plans, the most important factor, according to Zwikael and Smyrk, is the convincing potential of projects to create target outcomes and benefits at specified times (Zwikael & Smyrk, 2019).

When project outcomes and benefits are properly managed (see Section 2.7), organizations can realize the maximum potential returns on their investments over time. However, only a few organizations carry out effective processes for the management of outcomes and benefits realization. Many organizations do not have any processes in place at all. These organizations are failing to take advantage of the opportunity to guarantee that their projects create the target strategic value and impact necessary for driving business success. Even several high-performing organizations hardly pay sufficient attention to the management of project outcomes and benefits. These organizations might be effective at executing projects to meet the defined success criteria but utterly fail at linking back the project outputs to business objectives and realizing the outcomes and benefits, largely due to the absence of effectual processes for identifying the target outcomes and benefits from the initiation phase of the projects. Noticeably, organizations that embrace PM principles as the critical driver of change ensure good alignment of project to business strategy, significantly better business results, and valuable impact on products and services. A disciplined PM approach includes paying meticulous attention to the management of project outcomes and benefits realization as early as possible.

In fact, organizations that adopt a disciplined approach to PM waste 67% fewer financial resources on projects than their counterparts (PMI, 2016).

It is important to mention that the global economic environment is under the constant threat of change and evolution. The approaches and methods with which organizations participate in the economic environment require corresponding revision and updating always. The unavoidable competition in the economic environment has driven out and keeps driving many once-successful organizations out of business. Projects and PM approaches are implemented by organizations as the strategic capability for driving change to improve their participation in business. Therefore, the perpetual survival and success of organizations in the economic environment hinge on the strategic implementation of projects to transform internal processes and methodologies to deliver competitively potent products and services.

2.6. Project success and failure

An essential phenomenon in PM is the determination of what constitutes "success" or "failure" of a project. (See Chapter 14 for "Green Construction Project Success.") People will always share different opinions about the definition of project success or failure based on their personal experiences with and understanding of the project venture. While a client assesses a project to be successful based upon meeting cost, time, and quality/performance requirements, end-users could regard the same project as a failure upon realizing that the promised benefits are in shortfall over time. Other stakeholders, such as the public, contractors, consultants, local communities, politicians, and government departments, may prefer other parameters for judging the success or failure of the project. Therefore, the ultimate success of a project is attainable where all stakeholder groups are largely satisfied (Lock, 2013). In understanding the success or failure of a project, two parameters are useful for consideration, i.e., critical success factors (CSFs) and success criteria. CSFs are the important management functions, processes, or factors that must be fulfilled in a project to achieve successful outcomes. Sometimes, the presence of CSFs may not be easily seen but their absence may create a significant success gap in the project. From extant literature, generic CSFs of projects include the following (Cooke-Davies, 2004; Horine, 2013; Lock, 2013; Lester, 2014):

- Sound project business case
- Clear project purpose, goals, and objectives
- Clear project scope, approach, and deliverables
- Capable and competent project team
- Project alignment with organizational goals
- Suitable organizational structure and culture
- Strong sense of relationship, collaboration, and teamwork
- Clearly defined roles and responsibilities
- Adequate funds and project resources
- Clarifying technical performance requirements
- Effective project planning, monitoring, and control systems
- Effective management of project risks
- Stakeholder support and commitment
- Effective benefits management and realization
- Suitable project strategy
- Effective project leadership and top management support
- Effective and consistent project communications
- Realistic project targets in terms of, for example, time and cost
- Rigorous change and conflict management
- Good surrounding political atmosphere
- Good contractual documentation
- Well-designed reporting systems

Success criteria, on the other hand, refer to the performance areas by which the success of a project is evaluated. Success criteria are also presented in the literature as key performance indicators (KPIs) and include the following (Cooke-Davies, 2004; Horine, 2013; Lester, 2014):

- Time
- Cost
- Quality
- Technical performance
- Scope
- Safety
- Reliability
- Sustainability

- Benefits realized
- Stakeholder satisfaction
- Long-term business relationships

Apart from CSFs and success criteria, it is also important to understand that there are also failure factors underlying and fueling challenges in projects. The presence of these factors must be noticed early and corrected where possible, otherwise the project is doomed to fail. Corrections are less expensive at the early stages of the project than at later stages. Some failure factors of projects identified by researchers include the following (Horine, 2013; Lock, 2013):

- Non-alignment of project with organization
- Vague project definition
- Insufficient support of top management
- Poor management of stakeholders
- Unclear and conflicting roles and responsibilities
- Communication problems
- Inadequate project resources
- Underperforming project team
- Misjudging the impact of project changes
- Planning inefficiencies
- Funding and cashflow difficulties
- Flawed risk assessment and management
- Difficulties with change control management
- Unspecified completion criteria
- Incompatible project strategy
- Ineffective progress tracking and monitoring
- Too optimistic project cost, schedule, and benefits estimates
- Unforeseen project execution problems

2.7. Realizing project benefits and outcomes

Projects are generally initiated with the intention of solving realistic problems while giving due consideration to growing or new market demand, business opportunities, or statutory requirements. The implementation of projects typically results in outputs, outcomes, and benefits to society and several stakeholders. The outputs are the direct products delivered at the end of the execution phase of the project. PM efforts are usually applied to successfully accomplish the outputs, and the project teams are disbanded afterward. The outcomes are the direct results obtained from utilizing the project outputs. The benefits are the qualitatively and quantitatively measurable results or improvements at the extreme end of project utilization that offer value to the sponsor and other relevant project stakeholders. They are the transformation of the needs and expectations of stakeholders into quantifiable results, and they sum up to the ultimate value of the project. Figure 2.1 and Table 2.1 illustrate and exemplify the outputs, outcomes, and benefits of projects. The outcomes and benefits should advisably be captured in the business case of the project and clearly communicated to the relevant stakeholders for better monitoring of the realization process and timing. The business case provides justification for carrying out the project as against other options, by presenting the convincing possibility of successful delivery and the significant net benefits arising from a typical cost–benefit analysis. It is used to secure the

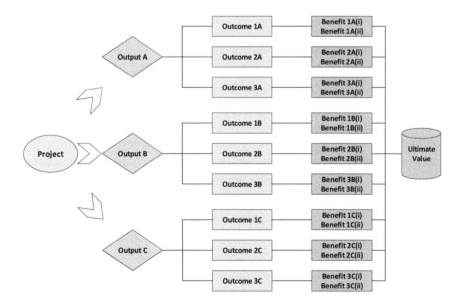

Figure 2.1.   Process of creating outcomes and benefits.

Table 2.1.   Examples of outputs, outcomes, and benefits.

Project outputs	• New road and bridge network • Hospital • Shipyard • Software • New management methodology • Implementation of employee benefits
Project outcomes	• More efficient traveling time • Production and service improvement • Cybersecurity improvement • Noticeable business change • Minimization of production cost • Higher level of control of project activities • Improvement of staff retention
Project benefits	• 15% improvement in productivity • 10% increase in revenues • 23% improvement in product sales • 45% reduction in traveling time • 25% reduction in the project cost • 65% reduction in annual cyber attack • 55% reduction in staff attrition

buy-in of sponsors and stakeholders from the start and further align project progress to the realization of business goals. The inability of project teams to specify project scope, take in stakeholder expectations, and build a strong business case that highlights the outcomes and benefits could expose projects to high failure rates. There are many instances where the planned outcomes and benefits of projects are not realized at all or only realized partially. Arguably, the more time and energy expended on defining, refining, and communicating the business case, the better the chances of project success in terms of outcomes and benefits realization.

Benefits management encompasses efforts in identifying, analyzing, quantifying, prioritizing, and delivering the expected project benefits to target stakeholders. The project benefits management plan is a special document that holds the detailed definition of target benefits and answers how and when the benefits are to be realized and sustained in the project, and what systems would be used to measure the benefits at the end. It is developed from the data and information captured in the project business case and needs assessment. Its development commences very early at the project initiation stage and spells out key features, such as the expected tangible and intangible benefits, the strategic alignment of the target benefits to the business objectives of the organization, the project stakeholders to receive the benefits, the timeline for delivering the benefits to the stakeholders, the metrics required to accurately estimate the realized benefits and success by extension, the persons or organizations in charge of monitoring and reporting the realization of the benefits over time, the potential risks that accompany the realization of the benefits in the short- and long-term, and the account of how the resulting business value of the project will fit into the ongoing core operations of the organization. Naturally, it takes a great deal of effort and an iterative process for a project team to develop and sustain a proper benefits management plan that will be useful over the project life cycle. The onus is on the project team and the sponsor working collaboratively to guarantee that the project benefits management plan together with the business case, PM plan, and project charter are in continuous alignment with organizational business objectives across the project life cycle. To ensure stronger benefits realization, organizations must implement the most critical and strategic initiatives that exert greater positive impact on the project, introduce prudent and simple processes to underlie the implementation of benefits-oriented project activities, enhance the talents and capabilities of project teams in delivering project objectives, and create an "enabling environment" to encourage the culture of change (PMI, 2017a, 2021).

2.8. Project management definition and history

2.8.1. *What is project management?*

There are many different definitions in existence for what is meant by "PM." While we do not intend to review such definitions, the fifth edition of the *Code of Practice for Project Management for Construction and Development* provides a summary of several definitions of PM. This book adopts the Chartered Institute of Building's (2014) definition of PM: "the overall planning, coordination, and control of a project from inception to completion aimed at meeting a client's requirements in order to produce a functionally viable and sustainable project that will be completed safely, on time, within authorized cost, and to the required quality standards."

2.8.2. *History of project management*

PM is not new. It has a very long history with the entire existence of humanity on the face of the earth. There is great history about how the Great Pyramids of Egypt and other engineering masterpieces (the Great Wall of China, the Coliseum, the Hanging Gardens of Babylon, and Stonehenge) were put together by engaging a lot of workforces over long durations. Oftentimes, the engineers and architects played the PM role by planning, scheduling, implementing, and monitoring several processes and activities until the expected outputs and outcomes are attained (Seymour & Hussein, 2014). The unfortunate reality is that the PM perspectives were not put into proper documentation though the principles were applied in achieving such great engineering feats. From the mid-20th century, PM started the journey of formalization into a contemporary study field. In providing an analytical description of the historical progress of contemporary PM, scholars have attempted classifying the historical years into periods. To simplify the presentation, much broader periods are adopted for classifying the historical years.

2.8.2.1. *First period of project management history*

Though contemporary PM is taken from the 1950s, there are some significant precursors that must be looked at. Hence, the first period of contemporary PM is taken from the 1900s to 1940s. The growth of industrialization and demand for ammunition production during World War I led to the advent of industrial engineers and management scientists, and typical examples given by Kanigel (1997) are Elton Mayo and Frederick W. Taylor. Taylor promoted labor productivity by adopting the principle of "efficiency over working longer and harder." Henry Ford introduced the Model T automobile to the world in 1908 and afterward popularized production line manufacture to project managers. In 1903, a Polish economist called Karol Adamiecki published his work on an invention, the harmonogram, to visualize interdependent processes. Though the harmonogram was not broadly received or adopted then in the Western world due to the publication language barrier, it is believed to have formed the basis for the development of the Gantt charts (Marsh, 1975; Seymour & Hussein, 2014). Henry Gantt, working under Taylor, developed the renowned Gantt Charts somewhere between 1910 and 1915, which are still very profitable to modern PM. Gantt charts emphasize the value of fragmenting projects into relatively smaller tasks that are manageable and largely interrelated and interdependent. Gantt charts were reportedly adopted in huge projects during World War I and the Hoover Dam project and Interstate Highway project construction (Seymour & Hussein, 2014). The Gantt charts were preferred to the then underdeveloped critical path method (CPM) because the charts enabled easy activity rescheduling, work allocation to machines and people, worker days-off schedule, etc. from a simple setup on office walls (Lock, 2013). Professionally, project coordinators were appointed in the US Army Air Corps in the 1920s (Morris, 1994), and project officers and engineers became popular in companies in the 1930s (Morris, 2011).

2.8.2.2. *Second period of project management history*

The second period of contemporary PM ranged from the 1950s to 1970s, and it witnessed the application of management science. After the time of World War II, industrialization, construction, and engineering boomed because there was a need to redevelop human civilization from the rubble. In 1953, the US military established special project offices that allowed contractors to work on whole systems of weapons on a project basis under the responsibility and control of a "project manager" (Johnson, 2002). The earliest recognition of an established matrix "PM organization" is attributed to the Martin (Marietta) Company in 1953 (Johnson, 1997). Project managers started to adopt two planning and control tools for managing projects. The US defense establishment developed the Program Evaluation and Review Technique (PERT) in 1957 to compute the fastest time for constructing nuclear submarine Polaris, whereas E.I. du Pont de Nemours Company developed a similar technique called CPM to accurately estimate the time and cost for constructing a large chemical plant project (Verma, 1996). The PERT tool emerged to solve the problem of complexity and uncertainty surrounding project scheduling, especially where several scenarios are involved and need to be properly visualized. The PERT and CPM techniques became highly recognized among construction and manufacturing industries because the advent of large computer systems improved their processing and updating speed. Another significant history was mandating the adoption of the Work Breakdown Structure (WBS) method for new projects sharing similar context with Polaris (Seymour & Hussein, 2014). WBS is a coherent and hierarchical fragmentation of project into smaller portions named work packages or deliverables to assist project managers in paying detailed attention to their successful execution in complex environments. Later, the human relational perspective of PM was infused mainly into European project organizations. The contributions of management practices such as negotiation, conflict resolution, communication, stress management, and leadership to project success started to be considered within organizations (Verma, 1996). A lot of companies started showing genuine commitment toward the welfare, health, and safety of the employees, and there was a general law-based fight to discourage all manner of discrimination in the workplace.

In terms of professional organizations and bodies, the International Project Management Association (IPMA), PMI, and other European PM associations commenced contemporaneously. IPMA was formally established in 1965 initially as a forum for cross-learning the experience and knowledge of network planning practitioners in Europe. IPMA, as a supervising federation, has witnessed tremendous growth and currently houses several national PM associations across the globe to provide necessary PM training and enhancement to the members. Likewise, PMI was initiated by five volunteers in 1969 for sharing member experiences, discussing issues, and promoting best practices and tools in PM. PMI is the mother organization overseeing several affiliate chapters in most world nations, with close to 700,000 registered members in its PM community. Generally, these professional organizations and bodies offer services including standards development, education, research, publication, networking prospects, and professional accreditations in PM.

The perspective of the professional organizations and bodies was mainly that of middle management; while it focused on the challenges of achieving project goals and the relevant methods and tools to apply accordingly, it was scarcely about the successful execution of projects. Then, the common experience of projects performing poorly started deteriorating into a worse case (Morris, 2011). The application of the recommended "best practices" was rather in the wrong paradigm, and this resulted in unmet expectations in some projects. For instance, Concorde's rival in the US did not have effective PM practices to handle the opposition of stakeholders, and consequently, the project failed to receive funding approval from Congress and was canceled in 1970 (Horwitch, 1982). Later, the causes of success and failure of projects were given increasing attention. Many scientific studies and investigations on project performance were commissioned by several government departments and organizations, such as the US Department of Defense, the World Bank, the US General Accounting Office, the UK National Audit Office, academic institutions, and research bodies. Morris and Hough (1987) reviewed 34 studies on project success and failure and reported on 1,544 programs and projects of the 1960s and 1970s. As identified, the factors that led to project failure include vague project definition, ill-defined success criteria, quality assurance problems, unsuitable contracting approach, deficient support of top management, technological problems, negative political environment, ineffective cost and time control, limited workforce, exchange rate and inflation, and marketing problems. The scope of these factors extends far beyond the typical PM criterion of cost emphasized in textbooks and publications (Morris, 2011).

2.8.2.3. *Third period of project management history*

The third period of contemporary PM spanned the 1980s and early 1990s, and this was when the dependency on IT became apparent. In the preceding period, it took the responsibility of IT experts to operate the PM systems as the few mainframe computers were generally unfriendly and difficult to use. The rise in the development of multitasking personal computers and IT capable of processing and organizing complex data amounted to better communication and connectivity within the PM space. PM systems for personal computers were popularized and made commercially available by several companies, making access to PM techniques much easier. A lot of the PM systems in this period were based upon the

Projects Resource Organization Management Planning Technique II (PROMPT II) model, which got modified later into the PRojects In Controlled Environments (PRINCE) model of PM (Bizness Académie, 2012). Project managers were able to run several PM tasks (e.g., scheduling and resource allocation) with installed software by themselves and there was less dependency on special IT experts who were behind the mainframe computers. The computer graphics and interfaces were significantly advanced and there were printers present in project managers' local offices that produced intricate and colorful charts. Project managers were able to easily manage and control complex project schedules from the computer screens and printout charts (Kwak, 2002). However, at the same time, productivity could not correspond with the level of technological growth in PM because the project managers developed an interest in the technology itself more than the tasks it was intended to manage. Notably, team members would often gather around computer screens and raise questions that were geared toward developing their computer literacy skills and becoming far less dependent on IT experts rather than focusing on solving project problems with the PM systems. While activity-on-arrow network software was getting outmoded, planners had resorted to using activity-on-node networks on their personal computers for scheduling purposes. Naturally, data processing times were reduced drastically such that project managers could immediately receive up-to-date scheduling information at an arm's stretch for incorporating into progress reports and project changes (Lock, 2013).

While the 1970s witnessed the multiplication and refinement of different PM applications, tools, and techniques, the subsequent years saw attempts to integrate the same into generic principles and practices that are commonly applicable to majority of projects. This means that PM would become a systematic discipline and approach instead of just a pool of individual tools and techniques. Professional organizations and bodies took the great responsibility of publishing books that summarize PM developments and applications. The Association for Project Management (APM), which is the UK member association of IPMA, published the initial edition of their Body of Knowledge (APM-BoK) book in 1992, and it has been revised to the 7th edition as of 2019. The APM-BoK captures several knowledge areas of PM, comprising implementation strategy, life cycle options and choices, establishing governance and oversight, shaping the early life cycle, assurance, learning and maturity, transition into use, engaging stakeholders, leading teams, working professionally, defining outputs, integrated planning, and controlling deployment. Prior to 1989, IPMA started some advanced courses with the aim of improving the competencies of professionals in project, program, and portfolio management. Similarly, a significant contribution of PMI is the publication of the Project Management Body of Knowledge (PMBOK) Guide in 1987, with the latest (i.e., seventh) edition released in 2021. The PMBOK Guide was largely based on a 1983 white paper named the "Ethics, Standards, and Accreditation Committee Final Report." The PMBOK Guide represented efforts to properly record and standardize commendable PM principles and practices, and it has grown into the standard for the global industry (Seymour & Hussein, 2014). The first edition presented eight knowledge areas of PM, comprising the management of project time, cost, quality, resources, scope, communications, procurement, and risk, with the addition of integration and stakeholders later. In the current edition, the knowledge areas have been somewhat transformed into performance domains, namely stakeholders, team, development approach and life cycle, planning, project work, delivery, measurement, and uncertainty. Though the Project Management Professional (PMP) certification offered by PMI was started earlier in 1984 to acknowledge skills and experience in PM, the PMBOK Guide later became a core underlying factor. Both the APM-BoK and the PMBOK Guide present an up-to-date understanding on the several developments in PM relevant for improving success in global industries. Besides, many conferences, symposiums, forums, and seminars have been organized by IPMA and PMI to offer professional development and networking opportunities to project managers all over the world.

In the 1980s, the emphasis on PM techniques and tools started expanding from the implementation phases, as experienced in previous periods, to equally include the front-end phase of projects. Barnes and Wearne (1993) stated that "the evolution of techniques of PM has moved progressively from concentration upon the problems apparent at the tail end towards the front end — from downstream to upstream. The emphasis for PM now is [to] start with attention to a project's needs and risks as a whole so as to anticipate the potential problems and shrink the risks."

Accordingly, emphasis was put on determining needs and demands, conducting feasibility studies, analysis of values and benefits, management of risks, and starting up projects generally. The front-end analysis was made possible by the availability of powerful personal computers and the latest control information to people at the workplace. Again, many externalities including stakeholders (e.g., communities, government agencies, and political groups) and physical environmental constraints became relevant in the PM sphere. The stakeholders exert high levels of pressure on projects such that project managers are forced to create holistic project solutions to fulfill the numerous "legitimate" needs and demands of stakeholders. The needs and demands of stakeholders in projects are usually social, environmental, and economic in nature. Moreover, the PM discipline gained recognition as a suitable methodology for analyzing and responding to changes, as well as initiating and accomplishing desired changes in projects (Stretton, 2007).

The management ideology called the theory of constraints, introduced by Eliyahu M. Goldratt in "The Goal" novel, was a significant contribution to PM. The ideology is about aiding organizations to continuously realize their goals based on the principle that the goal accomplishment rate of a goal-tailored system is limited by a minimum of one constraint (Cox & Goldratt, 1986). In 1986, a PM framework referred to as the scrum model was introduced in the field of software development and later extended to research, marketing, sales, and advanced technologies fields, which made use of several small teams in the process. The approach of the scrum model is holistic and flexible, whereby products are strategically developed by a team acting as a unit to attain set goals, and it contrasts with the traditional, sequential approach (Takeuchi & Nonaka, 1986). The 1994 CHAOS report issued by the Standish Group presented success and failure profiles of real projects in the IT sector. The aim of the Standish Group is to regularly present the true picture of projects and their environments so that relevant recommendations based on collective wisdom are provided to improve industrial success (Seymour & Hussein, 2014).

There were several projects executed in the period that portray the application of high technology and PM techniques and tools. The English-France Channel project (1989–1991) was contextually international and involved several stakeholders from both countries. A lot of adjustments were made to the objectives, cost, and schedule of the project, while the language and communication differences were coordinated, and the success metrics were standardized for common application. The Space Shuttle Challenger project (1983–1986) that ended in a fatal disaster drew attention to core PM dimensions, including risk management, quality management, and group dynamics. In addition, the XV Calgary Olympic Winter Games (1988) successfully adopted PM principles for its event management program (Kwak, 2002).

2.8.2.4. *Fourth period of project management history*

The fourth period of contemporary PM ranges from the mid-1990s to the 21st century (i.e., 1996–2022). IT excelled to become the driver of change and a platform to help project managers do their best work. The upgraded PRINCE2 model was released in 1996. In the following year (1997), the alternative tool named Critical Chain Project Management (CCPM) was developed for planning and managing projects. Distinct from CPM and PERT, the CCPM tool was based on the theory of constraints, and it puts emphasis on the resources needed to carry out a project instead of using specific project tasks (Goldratt, 1997). The underlying ideas involve regarding the availability of resources when determining the true critical path, eliminating contingencies from the activity level and instead handling them at the project level as buffers, and only handling a single activity at a time in the fastest possible way. To implement these suggested ideas successfully, project managers must adapt to needful behavioral changes easily, e.g., when it becomes necessary to sometimes deal with unavoidable multitasking (Morris, 2011). As the status of the PMBOK Guide was speedily advancing in keeping the concepts and principles of PM well defined and reliable, the globally renowned Institute of Electrical and Electronics Engineers (IEEE) formally embraced it as their benchmark for PM. PMI received accreditation in 1999 as an American National Standards Institute (ANSI) standards developer and was acknowledged as the first organization to attain the ISO 9001 recognition for its certification program (Barron & Barron, 2009). IPMA also commenced the certification of individual PM professionals in 1998 and the assessment and certification of organizations in 2012. Over time, industries witnessed significant advancement in the professionalism of the PM community, leading to the firming of the PM discipline, effective PM functions, and project value creation and benefits realization (Section 2.7). Despite the relevance of the bodies of knowledge, they are driven highly by the practical application of PM tools and techniques, and the theoretical premises and interdependencies underlying the practices are still left unaddressed (Sanz *et al.*, 2018). In 2001, the Agile manifesto comprising 12 key operational principles to enhance the performance of teams in software development projects was issued. The manifesto revealed four core values as favoring individuals and interactions over processes and tools, working software over comprehensive documentation, customer collaboration over contract negotiation, and responding to change over following a plan. Since agile projects are highly risky and much more flexible to adapt to changes, agile PM focuses on delivering outputs and creating business value instead of necessarily adhering to a defined process as commonly observed in conventional PM (Fernandez & Fernandez, 2008).

In the early 2000s, the main suppliers of PM software started to offer enterprise-level computer platforms that allow usage on multiple projects by multiple account holders. This strategic supplier decision opened discussions that PM approaches and results could vary for different project types (e.g., manufacturing, building, and research projects), project size (e.g., small, large, and mega projects), project contexts (e.g., industry, environment, and technology), and organizational level (e.g., low-level management, middle-level management, and top-level management). Meanwhile, enterprise resource planning suppliers, such as Hewlett-Packard Company, Oracle Corporation, and SAP, added PM components and interfaces to professional PM packages (such as Microsoft and Primavera). Latterly, the more IT (e.g., mobile telecommunications, broadband, internet, and satellite) grew and revolutionized traditional business practices, the more complex computing algorithms and web-based applications were developed for project planning and control, helping project managers to increase project communication capabilities and accomplish numerous tasks in lesser time and with higher accuracy. Modeling power too has been improving with the use of Microsoft Excel, computer-aided design and engineering software, 4D simulation, and artificial intelligence products (Morris, 2011). The advantages of web-based applications for PM encompass easy access on mobile devices, personal computers, and large enterprise resource planning systems without requiring the installation of software packages. Developments in IT that allow PM applications to function extensively over extranets and minimize time and distance significantly are assisting project teams to communicate and coordinate better in projects. In several industries, it has become mandatory to sustain effective communication and coordination among project teams, following the shrinkage of project schedules, geographical dispersion of project team members, and the involvement of external partners and suppliers (Roe & Elton, 1998).

In the 21st century, program management has grown to become a discipline that is more commercially driven than PM. PMI (2021) states that a program is "related projects ... managed in a coordinated manner to obtain benefits not available from managing them individually." As noted by the UK Office of Government and Commerce (2003), "while programs deal with outcomes, projects deal with outputs." Apart from program management being extensively promoted by APM, PMI, and other establishments, there is significant attention given to it in scholarly research publications. Moreover, the principle of project governance has gained high recognition in the PM space, partially deriving from the conspicuous malfeasance in big corporations such as the accounting scandals that hit Enron Corporation and WorldCom in 2001 and 2002, respectively, and the subsequent enforcement of laws and refining of corporate actions (Morris, 2011). Lessons were learned from these prior incidences and APM accordingly formulated some guiding principles for PM to include configuring the business strategy and the project plan correctly, openly reporting the true status and risk of the project, and conducting regular third-party "assurance" reviews (APM, 2004). In practice, stage gate review, peer review, and peer assist are used as mechanisms for governing projects. Besides, the concepts of organizational learning, PM offices, and PM maturity became prominent experiences. Projects were perceived as purpose vehicles for creating new knowledge opportunities to help organizational learning. The temporal and unique nature of projects, however, presents obstacles against effectual organizational learning (Morris, 2011). PM offices perform functions, such as holding best practices, organizing skills development activities, reporting the status of projects, and initiating project reviews (Hobbs & Aubry, 2008). Many inconclusive PM maturity models have been introduced, including the OPM3® product of PMI and the PMMM and P3M3 frameworks of the UK Office of Government and Commerce, for benchmarking the competency and capability levels of project managers and organizations (Morris, 2011). It must be emphasized that professional qualifications awarded by management schools, universities, and professional organizations were attained by people who underwent significant training and proved their capabilities (Lock, 2013).

Two main projects are used to represent PM in this period, i.e., the Year 2000 (Y2K) project and the Iridium project. The Y2K project was an effort to resolve a global computing crisis of converting the prior dating style of two-digit format to full representation. In the 1950s, dates were acceptably represented with the last two digits of the year of reference. Later, this phenomenon managed to penetrate the computing world, and programmers used it to design storages of mainframe and personal computers to minimize the already expensive cost of storing data files and databases. This approach naturally created a problem because new centuries will represent dates similarly. For instance, the date "00" could equally represent the years 1700, 1800, 1900, and 2000, and the date "78" could likewise mean 1778, 1878, 1978, and 2078, with no better distinguishing features. This dating approach would be unusable after the millennium year 2000; therefore, there was a sharp deadline to fix this problem and get the computers functioning correctly by January 1st, 2000, at 12 am. The PM features of the Y2K project include the following: the setting of a specific goal, objectives, and a deadline for the project; the independent involvement of several organizations around the globe to equally resolve the problem; the application of different practices, techniques, and tools by several organizations to resolve the same problem; and the common availability of detailed reports from several organizations on their independent progresses made. Numerous organizations established physical or virtual project offices to manage several stakeholders, ensure seamless transition into the new century, provide coordination of efforts, monitor progress, and implement risk management plans. This prompted the PM community on the relevance of project offices and risk management practices (Kwak, 2002). The Iridium project was initiated by

Motorola, Inc. in November 1998, 11 years after the development of the engineering concept, to provide worldwide communication services to people via a network of low-earth-orbiting satellites. The project seemed convincing because of a generally positive perception obtained from screening a target segment of more than 200,000 people, interviewing 23,000 people across 42 countries, and surveying about 3,000 corporations. Analysts referred to the very qualified top management team of the company as an excellent reason for the success of the project. In a short while, after defaulting on USD 1.5 billion in loans, Iridium filed for one of the largest bankruptcies in the history of the US, and the services were subsequently terminated (Finkelstein & Sanford, 2000). The program office was created to house project control managers, software engineers, and analysts for managing the project. Sophisticated PM software including Primavera Project Planner was engaged to manage complex and interdependent project scheduling (Fabris, 1996).

2.8.2.5. *Immediate future of project management*

Having explored the history of PM, it is essential to forecast the near future experiences in the PM field. In 2009, the US News & World Report ranked PM in third place, after leadership/negotiation skills and business analysis, as the most valued skills required by employers (O'Brochta, 2014). According to PMI (2017b), there will be a huge growth in the demand for project managers compared to other occupations across organizations in many countries in the coming years. By 2027, PM job opportunities will grow by 33% to nearly 88 million in total, as project managers have become significant contributors to productivity. PM is a key role in achieving great project results in many industries, such as information services and technology, engineering and construction, business, healthcare implementation, finance and economic services, education, manufacturing, advertising and marketing, mining, tourism and hospitality, and agriculture. However, the foreseeable consequence is that related talent scarcity could result in risks amounting to about USD 208 billion in GDP (PMI, 2017b). The COVID-19 pandemic affected many workplaces globally, with employers implementing an alternative approach by allowing employees to work from home. Global Workplace Analytics (2022) predicts that

25–30% of the workforce in the US alone will still work from home after the pandemic. This phenomenon may expand and become the reality in several industries given the availability of technological support to circumvent natural challenges. Virtual PM is growing into a mainstream role in industries to eliminate or minimize the challenges of resource, time, and distance in projects. For instance, project managers could continue monitoring and tracking tasks and activities in remote offices far away from the actual workplaces. Future project managers will face critical challenges, such as adapting to the dynamic project environment and organizational structure, coordinating multidisciplinary knowledge and skills, acclimatizing to newer technologies and tools, collecting the appropriate information from huge databases, communicating effectively with diverse people, and addressing climate change, health, well-being, value, sustainability, safety, quality, equality, diversity and inclusion, and productivity crises. Some of the changes in the industry brought about by these challenges have been reflected in the latest sixth edition of the *"Code of Practice for Project Management for the Built Environment,"* but it is anticipated that even greater changes may occur in the industry in the future, prompting greater challenges the PM profession may have to face up to. The need to address sustainability in particular highlights the importance and timeliness of this book. The PM history is summarized in Table 2.2.

Table 2.2.   Summary of PM history.

Periods	Contexts
1900s to 1940s	• Advent of industrial engineers and management scientists • Labour productivity by principle of efficiency over working harder • Popularization of production line manufacture • Introduction of harmonogram and Gantt charts • Project coordinators, officers, and engineers played the 'project manager' role
1950s to 1970s	• Application of management science • Establishment of special project offices that allowed contractors to work under the responsibility and control of a 'project manager' • Establishment of the matrix PM organization • Popularization of planning and control tools, e.g., PERT, CPM, and WBS

Table 2.2. (*Continued*)

Periods	Contexts
	• Infusion of the human relational aspect of PM into project organizations • Increasing attention was paid to the causes of project success and failure • IPMA, PMI, and other European professional associations initiated
1980s to mid-1990s	• Less dependence on IT specialists running PM systems on mainframe computers • Rise of IT and personal computer applications running PM systems • More efficient and quicker connectivity and information exchange in projects • Systematizing PM into a formal discipline and approach • Initial versions of APM-BoK and PMBOK books were published to summarize PM developments and applications • Attention increased on project, program, and portfolio management • Start of PM competence benchmarking, i.e., PMP certification • PM emphasis expanded from the execution phase to the frontend phase of projects • The theory of constraints, scrum model, and initial CHAOS report were noticeable
Mid-1990s to 21st century	• IT became the driver of change and the performance of project managers • The upgraded PRINCE2 and CCPM were launched to aid PM • PMBOK Guide was formally embraced by IEEE as their benchmark for PM • PMI received accreditation from ANSI and attained ISO 9001 recognition • IPMA commenced the certification of PM professionals and organizations • Industries witnessed significant advancement in the professionalism of PM • Agile manifesto was issued to enhance the performance of project teams • Advanced computer and web-based applications revolutionized professional PM • Professional bodies widely promoted project, program, and portfolio management as well as project governance • Organizational learning, PM offices, and PM maturity concepts became prominent
Immediate future	• Huge growth in the demand for project managers than other professions • Virtual PM will become common in several industries

2.9. Importance of project management

Projects are the central means through which organizations create outcomes, benefits, and value for sponsors and several stakeholders. In the contemporary economic world, organizations are burdened with the daunting task of managing projects successfully amidst tightened budgets, compressed schedules, scarcer resources, and rapidly advancing technology. The entire economic environment is dynamically changing, and organizations are compelled to consistently embrace PM approaches for optimizing project benefits and value delivery to remain competitive in the market. The formalization and advancement of PM approaches have proven to be relevant for project implementation. As identified by PMI (2017a) and Wallace (2016), the following are important benefits of carrying out PM:

- PM presents tools and techniques to help projects attain established success criteria and contribute to organizational evolution over time.
- PM tools and techniques make organizations extra effective and efficient at producing broader sets of outputs given the same input resources.
- PM promotes communication and a singular sense of purpose among project team members and thus, helps overcome natural or artificial boundaries separating different functional groups within organizations.
- PM optimizes opportunities for innovation, research, and development, which enables faster and timely development of new products via the efforts of multidisciplinary teams.
- Where the whole life cycle of a project is considered in the PM process, project teams can provide useful advice and recommendations for ensuring success at all project stages.
- Friendly competition among project team members and within functional groups is useful for uplifting their morale and motivation for better performance on projects.
- PM provides a proper system for effectively managing changes and dynamics that accompany complex, risky, and costly projects, which would otherwise be doomed to fail.

- PM principles equip project managers with great flexibility to direct project progress toward the best outcomes and benefits while balancing the influence of constraints on the project at the same time. For instance, scope changes or rework will likely affect project cost and time.
- The standardized techniques and methodologies for managing projects, as captured in several bodies of knowledge, provide sound and logical bases for regulating PM practice across all industries around the globe. This commonly spoken "management language" helps unify industries from different countries and makes the PM profession more mobile and versatile.
- PM approaches help project organizations to offer task orientation to project team members and personnel.
- PM approaches enhance the predictability of project outcomes and the effective design of solutions to solve project problems. Thus, reasonable decisions could be made on identifying, recovering, or terminating failing projects as early as possible with the guidance of PM approaches.
- PM generally helps increase the chances of project success, meet business objectives, and satisfy the expectations of stakeholders.
- PM approaches empower organizations to optimally utilize limited resources to deliver the right products or outputs at the right time.
- PM approaches help organizations to sustain competitive market performance and adjust PM plans where necessary in response to the impact of changing business environment.

2.10. Challenges facing project management today

The advantages of embracing PM approaches generally outweigh the disadvantages; hence reality has dawned on innumerable global organizations to adopt PM as a launching pad for achieving success. The consideration of several objectives on the way to attain project outcomes and benefits is very useful in PM practice, and yet it is challenging because of the numerous years required for professionals to gather relevant skills and experiences to be able to do it on real projects. Wallace (2016) identified the typical challenges of PM to include the following:

- To get PM systems working effectively, experienced personnel are drawn from different functional groups to participate in project teams for a part of their time. Failure to put this practice under proper control could undermine the performance of functional groups as the key personnel would literally have to divide their time and focus on attending to both roles.
- Naturally, there is significant competition over resource (e.g., finance, personnel, materials, support systems, and time) distribution across ongoing projects and functional groups under the control of organizations. Relatively, projects with higher profiles are assigned more resources whereas projects with lower profiles are assigned fewer resources, based on the linear assumption that the higher the profile, the more the resource requirements. This assumption is too simple, fails sometimes, and creates internal challenges for effective and efficient PM.
- Oftentimes, the managers of functional groups may disagree with the diversion of scarce organizational resources from undertaking some key functional activities to executing projects.
- Sometimes, the personnel themselves resent being assigned to project teams as they think that the outputs of their original functional groups are more relevant than the projects. This mindset could dominate the personnel and negatively affect their performance on projects.
- Modern-day PM requires the forming of diverse and multidisciplinary project teams, which are already difficult to form and manage given the possibility of conflicts among members. The lack of high-level communication within project teams keeps personnel in disagreement and misalignment with project objectives.
- The PM discipline is complex and multifaceted in nature, and it requires years of training and practical experience for professionals to develop the necessary skillsets for performing roles commendably on projects. Some project teams are intentionally set up as a mix of more experienced and less experienced professionals to allow for learning and improvement. However, this may create mismatched skill sets and significantly affect the overall effectiveness and efficiency of such project teams.

- Contemporary high-level computerized tools are developed as support systems to help project teams carry out PM functions. However, it could take a lot of effort and time for project teams to pass the training and become adequately competent to use the computerized tools for managing projects.
- As compared to pure function systems, personnel are expected to be more flexible while working in PM systems of organizations. PM personnel must exercise a commendable degree of flexibility and adaptability to be prepared for and responsive to changes.
- Project teams have the herculean task of impressing stakeholders to obtain their approval and support for project implementation. This is indeed difficult given the increasing list of stakeholder expectations and demands in projects that could easily outweigh all practical PM efforts.
- The true proof of PM success is observable across the life cycle of projects. However, as project teams are usually disbanded after the execution phase of projects, it is a great challenge to coordinate all PM factors that should translate into success across the life cycle of projects.

Today, these challenges are compounded with the need for PM to drive a significant change in performance in terms of sustainability, value, quality, productivity, collaboration, health, safety, well-being, leadership, risk, and knowledge and information.

2.11. Current generic project management standards, frameworks, and methodologies

2.11.1. *Project management standards and guides*

A standard refers to an acceptable benchmark by which actions or endeavors are executed and evaluated. PM standards are the common benchmarks designed for guiding, monitoring, and evaluating project execution process. Efficient and effective project delivery as well as better outcomes and benefits are anchored in a calculated PM process and not just a random undertaking. Successful PM is often inseparably connected with program and portfolio management as well as their governance. Several standards have been developed by organizations and institutions for enhancing the capabilities and competencies of professionalism in the PM world. Major PM standards discussed in this book include the ISO series, PMBOK, IPMA ICB4, APM-BoK, P2M, and PRINCE2.

2.11.1.1. *The ISO series*

The ISO series offers guidance on various aspects of project, program, and portfolio management practice, including planning, control, governance, benefits realization, and business change. ISO 21500 covers the organizational context and underlying principles for carrying out and improving project, program, and portfolio management. ISO 21502 specifies top practices that are highly esteemed for producing good results in PM contexts. It addresses concepts of PM, requirements for formalizing PM, integrated PM practices, and practices for managing a project. ISO/TR 21506 attempts to provide definitions for common terms used in project, program, and portfolio management environments. ISO 21508 presents information on the purpose and benefits of earned value management, incorporation of earned value management into project and program management, basic requirements for and use of earned value management system, and overview of earned value management processes. ISO 21511 tackles the principles, features, benefits, applications, integration, and relationships associated with WBS within the context of project and program management. ISO 21503 emphasizes the principles, requirements, and practices of program management, such as the description of specific roles and responsibilities of professionals that constitute good and acceptable practices. ISO 21505 communicates the correct contexts and guidance for conducting project, program, and portfolio governance and is useful for the assessment, assurance, and verification of such governance functions. ISO 21504 documents guidance on the principles, concepts, and practices of program and portfolio management. ISO 10006 delineates some principles and practices of quality management that are enforced in projects to impact the realization of quality objectives. All listed ISO standards are useful for any size and type of public or private organizations and can be adapted to suit specific project, program, or

Table 2.3.   ISO series on project, program, and portfolio management.

ISO code	Description	Publication year
ISO 21504	Guidance on portfolio management	2022
ISO 21503	Guidance on program management	2022
ISO 21500	Context and concepts	2021
ISO 21502	Guidance on PM	2020
ISO/TR 21506	Vocabulary	2018
ISO 21508	Earned value management	2018
ISO 21511	Work breakdown structures	2018
ISO 21505	Guidance on governance	2017
ISO 10006	Guidance on quality management in projects	2017

portfolio environments. Table 2.3 captures the series of published ISO standards for project, program, and portfolio management.

2.11.1.2. *PMBOK standard guide*

In the previous editions, the PMBOK guidance standards carefully align the discipline and functions of PM around several business processes that enable the implementation of reliable and formalized practices. This allows for the documentation of the best practices by which performance against the business processes can be evaluated and business processes can be enhanced to undercut threats and optimize efficiency. PM is evolving rapidly and so the intrinsically prescriptive process-based standards are giving way to principle-based standards to underlie the complete value delivery sphere instead of just focusing on deliverables. Hence, from the sixth edition to the seventh edition of the globally prominent PMBOK, there is a substantive transformation of the PM guidance standards to a set of applicable principles statements (Figure 2.2). The latest PMBOK comes with two parts, namely the standard for PM and a guide to the PMBOK. The principles statements encapsulate commonly accepted objectives for core PM practices and functions, and they offer general constraints within which project teams could flexibly execute duties and provide several options to retain alignment with the purpose of the principles. Upon

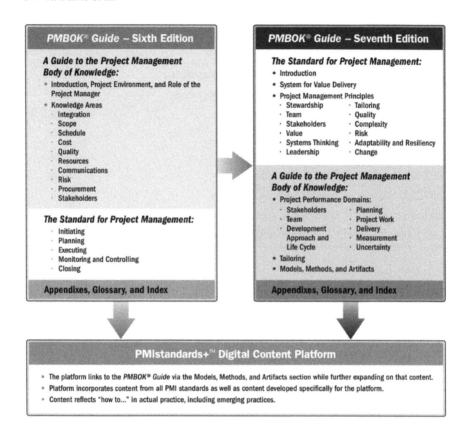

Figure 2.2.   Transformation of the global PMBOK standards.
Source: PMI (2021).

defining the principles statements, project teams can guide their PM capabilities, align relevant PM methodologies, and evaluate the effectiveness of
their PM capabilities across the complete value delivery scope from predictive perspective to adaptive perspective. The systems approach to value
delivery has pragmatically shifted the emphasis from mere project, program, and portfolio management and governance to the actual value chain
connecting them and other business capabilities to perfecting business
strategies, values, and objectives of organizations. The eight performance
domains constitute a PM system of interactive, interconnected, and interdependent management capabilities that are applied by organizations

collectively to attain expected project outcomes and benefits. Following the system for value delivery, project teams assess the effectiveness of the performance domains by using outcome-oriented measures instead of process- or output-based measures, such as keeping to defined project procedures. As contended by PMI, the developed PMIstandards+™ presents an up-to-date comprehensive knowledge body on evolving PM standards via an interactive digital platform (PMI, 2021).

2.11.1.3. *APM-BoK standard book*

The latest edition of the APM-BoK comprises a collection of principles and processes of the PM professional field. PM has advanced to the state of recognizing the influence of project-based work (i.e., project, program, and portfolio) in attaining business objectives for beneficial change realization at the strategic and operational levels. The APM-BoK recognizes the flexible ability of organizational leaders and professionals to select different forms of life cycle from one fashioned to manage premeditated change in a linear manner to one fashioned to manage emergent change in an additive, repetitive, or dynamic manner. Many organizations adopt hybrids of linear and repetitive life cycle approaches. The first aspect of this book looks at the available alternatives regarding the best project-based work structures and the relevant strategic decisions to support and facilitate the achievement of specific objectives for beneficial organizational change. The management of change initiatives using a structured approach guarantees that beneficial changes are entrenched within and aligned with the organization's operational approach to realize long-term success and impact. The second aspect focuses on preparation for change in terms of emphasizing the practices crucial for the shaping of early life cycle; the assurance, learning, and maturity of mid-life cycle; and the transition of late life cycle into use for project-based works. The third aspect covers people and behaviors, and it specifically discusses the common project professional skills and responsibilities, the engagement and influencing of stakeholders, and the building and management of teams, with the motive of revealing that project-based work is grounded in people's ability to work collaboratively and cooperatively. The final aspect is about planning and managing deployment and

Table 2.4.   Main knowledge areas of APM-BoK.

Knowledge areas	
Setting up for success	**People and behaviors**
Implementing strategy	Engaging stakeholders
Life cycle option and choices	Leading teams
Establishing governance and oversight	Working professionally
Preparing for change	**Planning and managing deployment**
Shaping the early life cycle	Defining outputs
Assurance, learning, and maturity	Integrated planning
Transition into use	Controlling deployment

considers on one side the detailing of objectives, requirements, success criteria, quantifiable benefits, best-value alternatives, and scope definition and on the other side the commitment to monitoring and reporting of deployment and managing risks, problems, and variations in a systematic manner (APM, 2019). When broken down, the 4 aspects are constituted by 12 main knowledge areas and 80 subtopics applicable to managing project-based work (Table 2.4).

2.11.1.4. *IPMA ICB4 standard*

Version 4.0 of the IPMA Individual Competence Baseline (ICB4) is a global standard for assessing individual competence in project, program, and portfolio management. It presents an all-inclusive checklist of required components of competence, representing full mastery of related management areas, and further underlines the development of competence of individual professionals for the management of projects, programs, and portfolios. As projects commence and close with the involvement of diverse people, the successful execution of projects has the competence of individuals at its heart. Individual competence is defined in plain English as the "application of knowledge, skills, and abilities in order to achieve the desired results." The ICB4 framework comprises perspective, people, and practice competence areas in project,

Table 2.5.   Overview of the components of individual competence.

Components of competence		
Perspective	**People**	**Practice**
Strategy	Self-reflection and self-management	Design
Governance, structures, and processes	Personal integrity and reliability	Requirements, objectives, and benefits
Compliance, standards, and regulations	Personal communication	Scope
Power and interest	Relationships and engagement	Time
Culture and values	Leadership	Organization and information
	Teamwork	Quality
	Conflict and crisis	Finance
	Resourcefulness	Resources
	Negotiation	Procurement and partnership
	Results orientation	Plan and control
		Risk and opportunities
		Stakeholders
		Change and transformation
		Select and balance

program, and portfolio management (IPMA, 2015). Altogether, 29 components of the perspective, people, and practice competencies in the project environment are shown in Table 2.5.

2.11.1.5. *P2M standard guide*

Issued by the Project Management Association of Japan, the third edition of the P2M is a standard guidebook of project and program management for enterprise innovation. The features of P2M are to create a singular

knowledge body by connecting and optimizing the previously individual-
ized knowledge areas of program management and PM, as well as to sub-
sume Japan's industrial strengths into the knowledge body. The P2M
guidebook is mission-focused, thus, it enhances business value by considering external environmental changes and breaking ground for solutions to
complex problems and challenges in projects. It is fundamentally set up
with a value-creation methodology to focus on and achieve the program's
mission as directed by the broader strategy or mission of the organization.
The P2M guidebook is structured into major knowledge bodies covering
program management, PM, business management foundation, knowledge
foundation, and human capability foundation (PMAJ, 2017). The knowledge areas covered under these knowledge bodies are captured in Table 2.6.

2.11.1.6. *PRINCE2 standard*

PRINCE2 is a *de facto* standard adopted by the government of the UK,
and it is prominent in the UK private sector and the general global community as well. It is a standard written description of a typically structured
PM system whereby projects are ordered into specific steps to allow for
logical and organized implementation to achieve established objectives. It
is a process-oriented methodology that offers an easily customizable and
scalable template for managing different types and sizes of projects.
Individual processes come with carefully defined key inputs and outputs
in addition to the activities to be executed to achieve specified objectives.
The framework presented by PRINCE2 necessitates projects to have organized and controlled commencement (i.e., organizing and planning prior
to jumping into action), organized and controlled middle (i.e., keeping
projects properly organized and controlled in process), and organized and
controlled finish (i.e., concluding projects well after accomplishing what
is necessary). PRINCE2 encompasses seven principles, seven themes, and
seven processes for managing projects. The seven principles are continued
business justification, learning from experience, defining roles and
responsibilities, managing by stages, managing by exception, focusing on
products, and tailoring to suit the project. The seven themes comprise
business case, organization, quality, plans, risk, change, and progress. The
seven processes include starting up a project, directing a project, initiating

Table 2.6. Overview of the P2P knowledge coverage.

Structure of the P2P knowledge body

PM	Program management	Business management foundation
Project and PM	Program and program management	Strategy formulation
Integration management	Program integration management	Business enterprises and programs
Stakeholder management	Program strategy and risk management	Program strategy method
Scope management	Value assessment management	Project organization management
Resource management		Project finance management
Time management	**Human capability foundation**	Information management and infrastructure
Cost management	What is human capability foundation?	
Risk management	Capability of manager for practicing P2M	**Knowledge foundation**
Quality management	Human capability foundation on program/project	Systems approach
Procurement management	Leadership	Knowledge and information assets
Communication management	Communication skills and creation of community	Value and value assessment
	Multicultural correspondence	

a project, controlling a stage, managing product delivery, managing a stage boundary, and closing a project (Figure 2.3). PRINCE2 is beneficial because it encloses tested best PM practices, applies generally to all project types, offers common vocabularies for all project people, explicates the roles and responsibilities of participants, helps participants to focus on project success and business case, and represents diverse stakeholders properly in project decisions (PRINCE2, 2017).

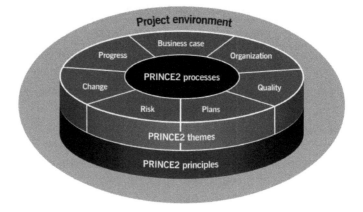

Figure 2.3.   The structure of PRINCE2.

Source: PRINCE2 (2017).

2.11.2. *Project management methodologies and frameworks*

A methodology is a system or collection of methods that are employed for investigating a study area or implementing a standard practice. Specifically, a PM methodology is defined by Firend (2019) as "the combination of logically related practices, methods, and processes that determine how best to plan, develop, control, and deliver a project throughout the continuous implementation processes until successful completion and termination." A framework, on the other hand, offers a structure and direction for carrying out an endeavor. A PM framework refers to a collection of standard processes, models, and techniques that are utilized for initiating, planning, executing, controlling, and closing a project. While PM framework provides an overview of the implementation of guidelines, PM methodology provides strict rules and practices for executing a project. Although there are inherent differences between the two, some methodologies are equally referred to as frameworks in the PM community, e.g., agile. Hence, the use of methodology herein is largely interchangeable with framework. PM methodologies assist project managers to direct, monitor, and improve project delivery and further enable organizations to accomplish results in line with strategic objectives. The choice of PM methodology dictates how work packages are prioritized and executed to achieve project objectives. Several PM methodologies are reviewed in the following sections.

2.11.2.1. *Waterfall*

This is a traditional PM methodology whereby work packages or tasks are carried out in a linear, finish-to-start fashion. It is only after one task is completed that a subsequent one can follow in the project process. Thus, the project process flows absolutely in a single direction, and this technically precludes any sort of complex and networked project task execution. The negative side of this methodology is that once the stage is completed, it is almost impossible to return to the same stage even for the purpose of correcting errors. The methodology is applicable where project goals are clear and unchangeable, and project is highly predictable but may be unsuitable where project requirement picture is bleak and changeable.

2.11.2.2. *Agile*

Agile methodology emerged to somewhat address gaps and frustrations in using too simplistic traditional PM methodologies, such as waterfall. The agile methodology enables different project tasks/steps to be implemented side-by-side in a complex setting and incorporates any new knowledge and discovery in the process of accomplishing objectives. With great emphasis on project team cooperation and collaboration, it provides an approach for projects to rapidly adapt to change, creativity, innovation, and invention in the business environment by encouraging the use of iterative models. Project teams can make relevant changes as and when necessary, without the need to wait until the end. It offers faster data-based and change-driven execution of tasks and is appropriate for projects with high tendency of change, unclear expected goals and outcomes, and limited time to start.

2.11.2.3. *Scrum*

Scrum methodology is a type of agile PM framework that splits work into a series of short-lasting cycles called "sprints." Usually, the team organizes a backlog of project tasks around sprint durations, and during a scrum sprint, stand-up team meetings are conducted daily to report on the accomplishments of the previous day, the task objectives of the new day, and the roadblocks hindering successful completion of tasks. Upon the completion of a sprint, the achievements and effectiveness of the team are reviewed through a retrospective meeting. The scrum methodology is about getting the best effectiveness and efficiency out of a team of people to deliver project tasks faster. It does not prescribe any tools, techniques, or procedures for its usage. Instead, it emphasizes how the entire team ought to cooperate, collaborate, communicate, self-organize, work together, and monitor and overcome obstacles to execute project tasks optimally and successfully. With the background knowledge that projects are unpredictable and complex, it is applicable for teams that are absolutely dedicated and without strong constraints of time and resources.

2.11.2.4. *Critical path method*

CPM helps develop a PM model based on a collection of tasks, allocated durations, interdependencies between the tasks, and deliverable goals. It explores the most critical project tasks through logical and practical sequencing of activities and estimation of the longest possible duration of each sequence. The model comprises four basic components, namely analysis of the critical paths, computation of floats, computation of the early start and early finish times, and computation of late start and late finish times. The critical path in the model is determined by resolving the longest sequence of activities that should be completed without prolongation for the whole project to be successfully completed. With this model at hand, the team can manipulate and set priorities among project activities as well as efficiently allocate resources based on scheduling flexibility. It underlies rescheduling to ensure the optimization of team effectiveness toward completing project assignments on time.

2.11.2.5. *Critical chain project management*

CCPM is a form of conventional, sequential PM methodology. It utilizes the theory of constraints and the principle of "buffers" to determine enhanced durations of activities and manage tasks and resource-dependent activities of projects. It highlights the resources that must be invested as inputs into the project system to achieve predicted performance. Upon identifying the most critical project tasks, the available resources are critically allocated by prioritization to the several tasks for better achieving set deadlines. It helps minimize the completion durations of individual project stages and control the common experience of budget overruns to generate more accurate deliverables.

2.11.2.6. *Event chain methodology (ECM)*

ECM puts emphasis on events (i.e., all sorts of external risk factors) that exert influence on project tasks and schedules. The external risk factors are assessed and considered in project decisions, and the team becomes cognizant of and prepared for such potential risks. The objective of ECM is to effectively manage these events so that plans are revised in accordance and projects remain on course. As quantitative and qualitative analyses and risk monitoring are key features of ECM, it is advantageous for risk planning and response strategizing.

2.11.2.7. *Extreme project management (XPM)*

XPM methodology enables the team to make allowance for changes during the execution phase to keep project on the right course. As changes occur during a project, the expected outputs and outcomes, quality, budgets, and resources of the project may change in the same way. XPM's premise in PM is to explore, identify, and eliminate any redundant parts and delay issues. The fundamental purpose is to minimize labor, expenditure, and time requirements and maximize value-added activities to attain maximum outputs and outcomes of the project.

2.11.2.8. *Six Sigma*

Six Sigma is a methodology that has to do with process improvement and quality development by analyzing the requirements of customers in a better way, eliminating, or minimizing potential defects across all delivery phases, and ensuring consistency in the outputs and outcomes of a project.

It has implication for financial returns and holds that the greatest success of a project is hinged on the whole organization's buy-in and support, minimizing process variations, enhancing the accuracy and speed of process implementation, and defining, controlling, measuring, and improving process characteristics. It can be adopted for improving or optimizing existing business processes with the DMAIC framework (i.e., Define, Measure, Analyze, Improve, and Control) and creating new business processes and products with the DMADV framework (i.e., Define, Measure, Analyze, Design, and Verify). It is compatible with other PM methodologies (e.g., agile and lean) and can be employed in almost all organizations and projects.

2.11.2.9. *Lean*

Lean methodology is aimed at maximizing the value offered to customers and at the same time minimizing resource wastage borne by the organization at all phases by continuously enhancing task and product delivery processes. Thus, organizations can create optimized value for their customers with the use of minimum resources by cutting down on wastes (i.e., muda, muri, and mura). Lean principles comprise defining value, mapping value stream, creating flow, establishing pull, and pursuing perfection. The methodology reaches perfect application when the satisfaction of customers is sustained and increasing value is created through the implementation of optimized processes. It is generally useful for cutting out fat to optimize process flow, multiply value for customers, and eventually reduce time and cost of production.

2.11.2.10. *Kanban*

Kanban methodology is focused on optimized flow of work processes, with the visualizing help of the Kanban board to set restrictions for the volume of work that should be in progress and analyze the entire flow to effect constant improvements rather than on cyclical processes. Kanban supports cross-functionality and enhances the productivity of teams, and it concerns how project tasks are continuously executed while avoiding an overload of the team at any point in time. It begins with visualizing all needful tasks of the team, prioritizing tasks, and limiting workloads of the team, implementing the most important task efficiently and effectively, and then focusing on the next most important task to create the best flow of work. The benefits include ease of visual presentation of current bottlenecks and progress status of work, ease of making changes when needed, ease of aligning and carrying along the whole team, and saving of time for the team and management.

2.11.2.11. *Hybrid*

There is no single PM methodology that is a one-size-fits-all approach for managing diverse projects successfully. Hybrid methodologies optimize the strengths and minimize the weaknesses of the separate methodologies for much better PM. A typical example of a hybrid methodology is scrumban, which combines scrum and Kanban.

2.12. Limitations of current generic project management standards, frameworks, and methodologies

The PM standards, frameworks, and methodologies have proven to be relevant for managing projects in industries. However, these tools have inherent challenges and limitations that need to be addressed, as outlined in the following. These challenges and limitations represent the superficial generic case and do not focus on a specific PM standard, framework, or methodology:

- The PM standards, frameworks, and methodologies are undergoing constant modifications and improvements, with the main objective of enhancing success rates in the changing project environments. Reviewing these tools revealed that there are significant variances in terms of vocabulary, approaches, and concepts. This creates realistic divisions on the broad "PM pie" that are currently difficult to reconcile across numerous industries. The source organizations and institutions have yet to collaborate and resolve these variances to make knowledge exchange and adaptation easier and more beneficial across different PM communities.

- It must be acknowledged that the "project manager" role is not fully professionalized yet. This situation, for instance, encourages original architects, engineers, and surveyors to often take the PM responsibilities in projects. This professionalization gap could be partly attributed to the lack of adequate and compatible knowledge bodies on PM practice. PM professionals must have sufficient materials for guidance to execute their responsibilities to standard levels.

- The 21st century is acclaimed for the notable rise in technological developments, automation, and digitization of various sectors of the economy. Developments such as artificial intelligence and machine learning are joining forces with the natural human thought process to make better decisions around real-world phenomena. The PM field is lagging because the developed standards, frameworks, and methodologies have not been digitized to a large extent. Many of these tools are just written instructions and cannot serve the project environment to the fullest without being digitized.

- A great limitation has to do with the mismatch between project environments and the available PM standards, frameworks, and methodologies. Undoubtedly, environmental factors could greatly influence the operational success of specific PM standards, frameworks, and methodologies and the overall success of projects. Some elements captured in these tools could be referenced to specific industries of origination and application. This situation necessitates extra efforts to be invested in some scenarios in terms of customizing these tools to become suitable for "external" project types and environments.

2.13. Case studies on applications, success, and failure of current generic project management standards, frameworks, and methodologies

The PRINCE2 standard was employed by Vocalink to deliver excellent and quality payment services to their clients. The reason is to plan for the worst scenarios to readily address problems and issues as and when they arise in the course of service delivery within the context of an open culture. Vocalink processes both local and international automated payments, offers ATM switching solutions, and runs the Bacs services. By capacity, Vocalink processed 91 million payments in a single day and a staggering 9 billion payments in 1 year. About 94% of UK's payroll goes through the payment system provided by Vocalink, and risks and errors that are not properly mitigated or managed could be detrimental to both Vocalink and clients. As every single payment is important, the system must work to perfection. Applying PRINCE2 principles consistently enhanced the robustness of the processes and practices of Vocalink (*SUCCESS*).

The waterfall methodology was applied for managing a drought situation in San Joaquin Valley, California, US. A state of emergency was issued upon the drastic shortage of rainfall that eventually affected agricultural production, residential life, businesses, and general living conditions in the region. A USD 500 million project was started to solve the problem and diversify the water supply system in the region. The methodology helped the project managers to make the needful decisions to solve the specific problem successfully in 2013 and further became useful in other similar large-scale projects (*SUCCESS*).

IBM is globally renowned for developing computer software and hardware technologies. IBM adopted agile scrum to redevelop and improve business operations to the extent that it now offers a unique management tool called Rational Team Concert, which integrates agile development domain. IBM carried out changes in three main aspects of process, people, and tools. Eventually, the implementation of agile scrum brought a lot of improvements to IBM such as faster delivery time, reduced defects, better maintenance, and higher innovation (*SUCCESS*).

The former Minnesota Mining and Manufacturing Company, which is currently referred to as 3M, is a constant name on the Fortune 500 list that operates in the fields of industry, worker safety, health care, and consumer goods. Today, more than 60,000 3M products ranging from medical products to electronic circuits are used in homes, businesses, schools, hospitals, and other industries. At a certain point, the company decided to start offering turn-key systems and software components that will be utilized in the radio frequency identification track and trace industry. 3M originally followed the traditional waterfall methodology but faced some roadblocks.

The methodology could not support the dynamic nature of software development, particularly in reducing the overall development cost and speeding up the development process (*FAILURE*). Subsequently, 3M adopted agile with scrum methodology for software development, requiring several changes and resulting in rewarding outcomes. The inherent potential of scrum teams to be readily self-organized in responding swiftly to customer requirements and pushing priorities was worth the invested efforts (*SUCCESS*).

Microsoft Corporation is a leading technology firm that manufactures computer devices and develops several software products. Microsoft adopted the Six Sigma methodology upon observing a drop in their win/loss review process. Originally, there was no effective approach for analyzing the win/loss process of sales groups because the field leaders were disengaged from the centralized Microsoft process and utilized their own different practices. Six Sigma was adopted to understand their true competitive position by evaluating whom their sales groups were winning or losing against regarding marketplace opportunities. It was relevant because increasing marketplace opportunities were impacting Microsoft's revenues and stakeholder values. Eventually, Microsoft was able to minimize the drop in their win/loss review process and identified that sales efforts were mainly driven by front-line sellers who have better knowledge of sales (*SUCCESS*).

A Malaysian automotive components manufacturing company implemented the lean methodology in its manufacturing process and the observed success led to an award by Malaysia Japan Automotive Industries Cooperation (MAJAICO) in 2007. MAJAICO is a 5-year project implemented to develop the Malaysian automotive industry and enhance its competitive position as a worldwide automotive powerhouse, by introducing continuous improvement processes in companies through the implementation of lean manufacturing. By implementing lean manufacturing, the company's goal was to reduce inventory levels to minimize or eliminate other wastes, such as overproduction, excessive motion, waiting times, excessive processing, excessive transportation, and defective products. The results showed a significant reduction in the inventory levels and by this means controlled other wastes (*SUCCESS*).

The Kanban methodology was applied at the International Committee of the Red Cross for their humanitarian micro-economic initiatives focusing on enhancing the economic condition of low-income households and families whose sources of income have suffered from conflicts in Iraq. Donations were made to households and families to support them in establishing income-generating businesses in line with their expertise and skills. Given that this project was spread across multiple phases with several overlapping steps and activities, Kanban visualization board and cards pushed Red Cross to rapidly achieve their organizational strategies in Iraq for 2019. The project leaders could monitor the "work-in-progress" areas or unfinished activities easily and thereby multiply efforts to get such activities and milestones completed successfully (*SUCCESS*).

2.14. Current, emerging, and future trends in project management

In the years ahead, PM may undergo massive transformation to match up with the continuous changes (e.g., new needs, contexts, complexities, and globalization of relationships) apparent in the project environment and improve success stories. Understanding the trends of the PM field may inform the revision of PM standards, frameworks, and methodologies to produce the needed results. The Chartered Institute of Building (2022) has recognized the evolution and its latest sixth edition of the *"Code of Practice for Project Management for the Built Environment"* reflects relevant changes and challenges. According to Germán *et al.* (2021), the current, emerging, and future trends in the PM field include the following:

- The project concept is gradually departing from just being an instant transitional hand-off between strategy and ongoing operational process. As such, PM must focus more on formulating strategies to guide the best decisions and actions to deliver long-term benefits and value to the project organization and stakeholders.
- Virtualization and digital transformation of the project process by using modern technological opportunities. The details encompass making

use of artificial intelligence, machine learning, automation, cloud computing, big data, speedy communication, decision support systems, and process visualization in managing projects. Possibly, virtual project teams will manage entire projects effectively from distant places through global connectivity without the need for face-to-face meetings.

- Professionalization of PM in the industry. As of now, PM is not fully seen as a unique profession despite the efforts invested by way of professional institutions and knowledge bodies. There is a need to understand the benefits of PM, promote the profession, and build its impact by constructing the appropriate professional pipeline from "starter to charter."

- Globalization of PM in the "Industry 4.0" and "Industry 5.0" eras. This will create an industry-wide workforce comprising organizations with changing corporate cultures and project teams that are diversified in terms of distance and culture in the new cosmopolitan "Gig Economy."

- PM has gradually progressed from fixing technical problems to enabling transformation and change in high-performing organizations. The new thinking of PM is about highly swift, empowered, and focused implementation of strategies, beyond just functional coupling of systems with processes. Project teams need to develop and implement more agile, responsive, and flexible PM approaches for the successful execution of projects.

- PM will engage more and more with multicultural and multi-institutional contexts. The daunting responsibility will be how the stakeholders emerging from these contexts are effectively integrated into projects.

- Proper definition of the roles of the PM offices in alignment with the adaptation and customization of PM methodologies for specific projects. PM offices will support project managers to accomplish daily tasks and overall enterprise goals.

- The working conditions are changing rapidly and unendingly, so the future project environment framework must be built around volatility, flexibility, uncertainty, complexity, opportunity, and ambiguity. PM must tackle all these dimensions effectively to be successful.

- Change management is a regular PM trend now and into the future. Change management encompasses embracing, mitigating, reducing, or increasing changes in a project. Effective change management is a key area that project managers must focus on to overcome the challenges in the project environment and increase success rates.
- The open innovation culture will become normal and promote more collaborative networks and practices in industries. More organizations will be willing and ready to combine efforts in delivering project outputs and outcomes.
- Although the concept of sustainability has been explored in PM, it is still the greatest challenge facing the globe, particularly in the built environment. The future of PM is to fully embed sustainability practices into all project life cycle discourses by following a holistic approach. This trend is the key premise of this book, particularly Chapter 6.
- One new concept in PM is the "project economy," which is supposed to be a fundamental paradigm shift for organizations. Project economy requires that project managers are empowered with the right skills, capabilities, and competencies needed to transform ideas and imaginations into reality through projects. It also requires that organizations deliver benefits and value to diverse recipients by executing projects successfully, providing expected products, and aligning to value streams. It diverts PM attention from processes and controls to benefits and value and helps project managers concern themselves with rapidly delivering the elements with the greatest value.

2.15. Summary

This chapter has introduced the topic of PM, its core concepts, history, and developments. A project is a process, activity, or endeavor that is unique, complex, temporary, goal-oriented, measurable, flexible, dynamic, risky, uncertain, and executed by diverse teams and with multiple resources. Projects are initiated for various reasons, such as new product or service requests, organizational needs, adopting advanced technologies and methodologies, updating existing organizational processes, and establishing proof of concepts. They can be categorized into four main types: (1) civil engineering, construction, petrochemical, and mining projects, (2) manufacturing projects, (3) IT projects and management or business change projects, and (4) pure scientific research projects. Projects serve as how organizations implement business strategies, create and manage outcomes and benefits, realize returns on investments, and maintain success and survival in the highly competitive economic environment.

The contemporary PM era is divided into four consecutive periods of 1900s to 1940s, 1950s to 1970s, 1980s to early 1990s, and mid-1990s to the 21st century. During the first period, the growth of industrialization and demand for ammunition production during World War I led to the advent of industrial engineering and management science, witnessed typically by harmonogram and Gantt charts. The second period saw the booming of management science, industrialization, construction, and engineering to help redevelop human civilization after World War II, with the prominence of PERT, CPM, and WBS methods. IPMA, PMI, and other European PM associations commenced contemporaneously. The third period recorded the rise of IT and computer applications running PM systems. The initial APM-BoK and PMBOK books were published to improve the competencies of practitioners. The fourth period presented excelling IT driving change and aiding project managers to do their best work in projects. Competency certification, PM maturity models, knowledge body updates, and program and portfolio management became popular.

The most prominent generic PM standards issued by well-renowned institutions and organizations are the ISO series, PMBOK, IPMA ICB4, APM-BoK, P2M, and PRINCE2. Besides, the common PM frameworks and methodologies comprise waterfall, agile, scrum, CPM, CCPM, ECM, XPM, Six Sigma, lean, Kanban, and scrumban. These PM tools are useful for monitoring, improving, and evaluating project execution, accomplishing results in line with strategic objectives, as well as enhancing the capabilities and competencies of practitioners. Case studies revealed the success and failure stories regarding the application of these PM tools. Meanwhile, these PM tools are limited in terms of differences in terminologies and approaches, lack of adequate and compatible knowledge bodies, lack of digitization, and mismatch with changing project environments.

PM is undergoing massive transformation to catch up with the continuous changes happening in the project environment and enhance success rates. The trends include focusing on long-term project benefits and value delivery; virtualization and digital transformation of the PM process; advancing PM to a fully recognized professional status; globalization of PM; engagement of multicultural and multi-institutional environments; redefining the roles of PM offices; redefining project environment as volatile, flexible, uncertain, complex, and ambiguous; open culture of organizational collaboration; fully embedding sustainability into PM; and applying the project economy concept.

Having introduced the topic of PM in this chapter, the following chapter introduces the topic of green construction projects, knowing that this book is about green construction PM.

References

Association for Project Management. (2004). *Directing Change: A Guide to Governance of Project Management*. High Wycombe, UK: Association for Project Management.

Association for Project Management. (2019). *APM Body of Knowledge* (7th edn.). Buckinghamshire, UK: Association for Project Management.

Barnes, N. M. L. & Wearne, S. H. (1993). The future for major project management. *International Journal of Project Management*, *11*(3), 135–142.

Barron, M. & Barron, A. R. (2009). History of project management. Available at: https://scholar.google.com/scholar?hl=en&as_sdt=0%2C5&q=History+of+Project+Management+Merrie+Barron%2C+PMP%2C+CSM+Andrew+R.+Barron&btnG=#aHR0cHM6Ly9jcm9uZmEuc3dhbi5hYy51ay9SZWNvcmQvY3JvbmZhMzQxNjkvRG93bmxvYWQvMDAzNDE2OS0wNjA2MjA2MjAxNzE5MDQxMC5wZGGZAQEAw (accessed on 22 September 2022).

Bizness Académie. (2012). A short history of PRINCE2®. Available at: http://biznessacademie.com/en/2012/08/a-short-history-of-prince2/ (accessed on 23 September 2022).

Chartered Institute of Building. (2014). *Code of Practice for Project Management for Construction and Development* (5th edn.). West Sussex, UK: John Wiley & Sons, Ltd.

Chartered Institute of Building. (2022). *Code of Practice for Project Management for the Built Environment* (6th edn.). Hoboken, NJ, USA: John Wiley & Sons, Ltd.

Cooke-Davies, T. (2004). Project success. In J. K. Pinto & P. W. Morris (Eds.), *The Wiley Guide to Managing Projects*. New Jersey, USA: John Wiley & Sons, Inc.

Cox, J. & Goldratt, E. M. (1986). *The Goal: A Process of Ongoing Improvement.* Great Barrington, USA: North River Press.

Crawford, L., Hobbs, B., & Turner, R. (2005). *Project Categorization Systems: Aligning Capability with Strategy for Better Results*. Newton Square, PA: Project Management Institute.

European Commission. (2021). *The PM² Project Management Methodology Guide 3.0.1.* Luxembourg: Centre of Excellence in Project Management (CoEPM²), The European Commission, DIGIT.

Fabris, P. (1996). Ground control. *CIO Magazine*, April 1.

Fernandez, D. J. & Fernandez, J. D. (2008). Agile project management — Agilism versus traditional approaches. *Journal of Computer Information Systems, 49*(2), 10–17.

Finkelstein, S. & Sanford, S. H. (2000). Learning from corporate mistakes: The rise and fall of Iridium. *Organizational Dynamics, 29*(2), 138–148.

Firend, A. R. (2019). Methodologies in project management. https://doi.org/10.32893/IJBMR.2019/AMII.19/11.11.

Germán, M. M., Javier, A. B., Eulalia, J. G., & Begoña, M. E. (2021). Project management methodologies: Challenges and trends. The PM2 case. In *Proceedings of the 25th International Congress on Project Management and Engineering*, 6th–9th July, (pp. 92–108). Alcoi, Spain.

Global Workplace Analytics. (2022). Work-at-home after Covid-19 — Our forecast. Available at: https://globalworkplaceanalytics.com/work-at-home-after-covid-19-our-forecast (accessed on 8 October 2022).

Goldratt, E. (1997). *Critical Chain*. Great Barrington, USA: North River Press.

Hobbs, B. & Aubry, M. (2008). An empirically grounded search for a typology of project management offices. *Project Management Journal, 39*(1_suppl), S69–S82.

Horine, G. M. (2013). *Project Management: Absolute Beginner's Guide* (3rd edn.). Indiana, USA: Que Publishing.

Horwitch, M. (1982). *Clipped Wings: The American SST Conflict*. Cambridge, MA: MIT Press.

International Project Management Association. (2015). *Individual Competence Baseline for Project, Programme and Portfolio Management (Version 4.0)*. Nijkerk, The Netherlands: International Project Management Association.

Johnson, S. B. (1997). Three approaches to big technology: Operations research, systems engineering, and project management. *Technology and Culture*, *38*(4): 891–919.

Johnson, S. B. (2002). *The Secret of Apollo: Systems Management in American and European Space Programs*. Baltimore, USA: The Johns Hopkins University Press.

Kanigel, R. (1997). *The One Best Way: Frederick Winslow Taylor and the Enigma of Efficiency*. London, UK: Little, Brown and Company.

Kwak, J. H. (2002). Brief history of project management. In E. G. Carayannis, Y. H. Kwak, & F. T. Anbari (Eds.), *The Story of Managing Projects: A Global, Cross-disciplinary Collection of Perspectives*. New York, NY: Quorum Books.

Lester, A. (2014). *Project Management, Planning and Control: Managing Engineering, Construction and Manufacturing Projects to PMI, APM and BSI standards* (6th edn.). Oxford, UK: Elsevier Ltd.

Lock, D. (2013). *Project Management* (5th edn.). Surrey, UK: Gower Publishing Limited.

Marsh, E. R. (1975). The harmonogram of Karol Adamiecki. *Academy of Management Journal*, *18*(2): 358–64.

Morris, P. W. G. (1994). *The Management of Projects*. London, UK: Thomas Telford.

Morris, P. W. G. (2011). A Brief History of Project Management. In P. W. G. Morris, J. Söderlund, & J. Pinto (Eds.), *The Oxford Handbook of Project Management* (pp. 47–48). Oxford, UK: Oxford University Press.

Morris, P. W. G. & Hough, G. H. (1987). *The Anatomy of Major Projects*. Chichester, UK: Wiley and Sons.

O'Brochta, M. (2014). Project management essentials — Beyond the basics: You know you are a project manager when... In *Proceedings of PMI® Global Congress*, 25th to 28th October, Phoenix Convention Center, Phoenix, Arizona, US. Newtown Square, PA: Project Management Institute.

Project Management Association of Japan. (2017). *P2M: A Guidebook of Program and Project Management for Enterprise Innovation* (3rd edn.). Tokyo, Japan: Project Management Association of Japan.

Project Management Institute. (2013). *A Guide to the Project Management Body of Knowledge (PMBOK® Guide)* (5th edn.). Newtown Square, Pennsylvania: Project Management Institute, Inc.

Project Management Institute. (2016). *The Strategic Impact of Projects: Identify Benefits to Derive Business Results*. Newtown Square, Pennsylvania, USA: Project Management Institute.

Project Management Institute. (2017a). *A Guide to the Project Management Body of Knowledge (PMBOK® Guide)* (6th edn.). Newtown Square, Pennsylvania, USA: Project Management Institute.

Project Management Institute. (2017b). Project management job growth and talent gap 2017–2027. Available at: https://www.pmi.org/learning/careers/job-growth (accessed on 7 October 2022).

Project Management Institute. (2021). *A Guide to the Project Management Body of Knowledge: PMBOK® Guide* (7th edn.). Pennsylvania, USA: Project Management Institute, Inc.

PRINCE2 (2017). *Managing Successful Projects with PRINCE2®* (6th edn.). UK: The Stationery Office.

Roe, J. & Elton, J. (1998). Bringing discipline to project management. *Harvard Business Review*, 76(2), 153–160.

Sanz, G. C., Nadal, J. O., & Robert, J. V. (2018). Project management. In C. Machado, and J. P. Davim (Eds.), *Micro MBA: Theory and Practice*. Berlin, Germany: Walter de Gruyter GmbH.

Seymour, T. & Hussein, S. (2014). The history of project management. *International Journal of Management & Information Systems (IJMIS)*, 18(4), 233–240.

Stretton, A. (2007). A short history of modern project management. *PM World Today*, 9(10), 1–18.

Takeuchi, H. & Nonaka, I. (1986). The new new product development game. *Harvard Business Review*, 64(1), 137–146.

UK Office of Government and Commerce. (2003). *Managing Successful Programmes*. Norwich, UK: The Stationery Office.

Verma, V. (1996). *The Human Aspects of Project Management: Human Resource Skills for the Project Manager, Volume 2*. Project Management Institute.

Wallace, W. (2016). *Project Management*. UK: Edinburgh Business School, Heriot-Watt University.

Zwikael, O. & Smyrk, J. R. (2019). *Project Management: A Benefit Realisation Approach*. Switzerland: Springer Nature Switzerland AG.

Chapter 3

Introduction to Green Construction Projects

Amos Darko[*], **Caleb Debrah**[†,‡], **and Albert P. C. Chan**[†]

[*]*University of Washington, Seattle, WA, USA*
[†]*The Hong Kong Polytechnic University, Hung Hom, Hong Kong*
[‡]*University of Florida, Gainesville, FL, USA*

This chapter overviews the concepts and development of green construction projects, policies, and success stories. The tangible and intangible benefits of green construction projects are discussed. A summary and evolution of the existing green construction project rating tools are provided. We explain how green construction projects align with 11 of the 17 UN Sustainable Development Goals (SDGs). Green construction project planning and design are described. In addition, the increasing importance of green construction projects globally is clarified. We then present examples of green construction projects and policies in the US, UK, Hong Kong, and other countries. The role of the World Green Building Council and its 70 plus members in promoting green construction projects is described. We present the history, the status, and the future of green construction projects to inform stakeholders of available opportunities for research and development. Moreover, some green construction project management (PM) issues and challenges are discussed. Finally, we present real-world case studies of three PM success stories of green construction projects in the US, China, and Ireland.

3.1. Understanding green construction projects

3.1.1. *What is a green construction project?*

As defined in Chapter 1, green construction is the process of constructing buildings in a "sustainable" manner. A green construction project has sustainability in mind as a primary project goal. In a green construction project, environmental, social, and economic impact and performance are critical client considerations that must be addressed right from the project inception through to the completion stage. A green construction project focuses on maximizing human health, well-being, happiness, and quality of life, using fewer resources, as well as reducing waste, pollution, and negative impacts of the construction process on the environment, such as carbon emissions (United States Environmental Protection Agency, 2016). In a nutshell, a green construction project addresses environmental, social, and economic sustainability issues, impact, and performance in its construction process. By so doing, it reduces negative impacts and creates positive impacts on the environment, society, and economy, preserving precious natural resources. A green construction project may have a sustainability mandate that supports the management framework for the planning, coordination, and control of the project to meet the sustainability requirements of the client and other project stakeholders. It must be noted that a green construction project must meet not only sustainability requirements but also conventional requirements, such as cost, time, quality, and safety. This can make green construction projects very challenging. Efficient and effective project management (PM) is thus a necessary recipe for success in green construction projects.

3.1.2. *Green versus conventional construction projects*

Conventional construction projects primarily focus on cost, time, and quality as the main indicators of performance (Kibert, 1994; McKim *et al.*, 2000). Usually, the success criteria for such projects do not include sustainability. Consequently, conventional construction projects are commonly known and criticized to be energy, carbon, resources, water, materials, waste, and pollution (noise, air, and water pollution)-intensive.

Efforts to reduce negative and create positive environmental, social, and economic impacts during the construction process are not a priority. Project delivery methods such as design-build, construction management-at-risk, and design-bid-build are typically implemented for conventional construction projects (Kibert, 2016). Contractors are often selected based on the "lowest bid" criterion, which often results in a poor-quality project with no sustainability performance consideration.

Green construction projects, on the other hand, are sustainable in their approach. Their key sustainable features have been discussed in Section 3.1.1. In terms of project delivery, while some argue that the design-build method is best for maximizing the sustainability parameter of green construction projects (Kibert, 2016; Xia & Olanipekun, 2023), others argue that a more innovative method such as integrated project delivery (IPD) is best (Dixon, 2010). IPD is strongly recommended for its ability to *integrate people, systems, business structures, and practices into a process that collaboratively harnesses the talents and insights of all participants to optimize project results, increase value to the owner, reduce waste, and maximize efficiency through all phases of design, fabrication, and construction* (The American Institute of Architects, 2007). IPD integrates all project participants ranging beyond the basic trinity of owner, architect, and contractor. It ensures highly effective early coordination, communication, and collaboration among all participants throughout the project, which is a key ingredient for success in green construction projects, as highlighted in Chapter 1.

In green construction procurement, special attention is given to green requirements and specifications in the contract document, usually found in green construction rating tools (Glavinich, 2008) (see Section 3.1.4. See also Chapter 11 for more on "Green Construction Project Procurement Management"). Contracts are usually awarded based on experience in past green projects rather than just the lowest bid. Likewise, qualified green professionals with accreditations such as Leadership in Energy and Environmental Design (LEED) Accredited Professionals (LEED APs) who are specialized and skilled in green construction principles are preferred during green construction projects (Hwang & Tan, 2012; Kibert, 2016). As such, *Green Request for Proposals* is used to recruit green professionals such as construction managers, project managers, architects, engineers, and consultants who possess a comprehensive knowledge and understanding of green construction projects (Hwang & Tan, 2012).

3.1.3. *Tangible and intangible benefits of green construction projects*

There are several tangible and intangible benefits associated with green construction projects. The tangible benefits are readily identified, quantified in unit terms, and converted to dollars (Kee, 2004; Thurimella & Padmaja, 2014). For instance, the adoption of environmentally sustainable construction practices contributes to reduced operational expenses by virtue of energy conservation, while concurrently enhancing the creditworthiness of both green construction initiatives and environmentally conscious borrowers. According to the International Finance Corporation (IFC) (2019), green construction augments property worth by 7% owing to a higher resale value compared to conventionally constructed residences in the US. Nevertheless, it is worth noting that intangible benefits, which constitute significant advantages but are often difficult to precisely quantify, are frequently overlooked in cost analyses (Kubba, 2012). Such benefits as improved air quality, occupant satisfaction, and health, well-being, happiness, and quality of life are not easy to quantify (Green Building Council of Australia, 2006) and thus are regarded as intangible benefits of green construction projects. Most of the intangible benefits belong to the social sustainability dimension and the difficulty in their quantification may explain why they are mostly neglected, making social sustainability the most neglected aspect of sustainability in green construction projects. Approaches should be developed for the easy and accurate quantification of the intangible benefits of green construction projects because "what can't be measured can't be improved." Figure 3.1 presents some tangible and intangible benefits of green construction projects.

3.1.4. *Green construction project rating tools*

As defined by the World Green Building Council (WorldGBC) (2022a), green construction project rating tools — also known as certification — are tools used to assess, rate, certify, and recognize project sustainability

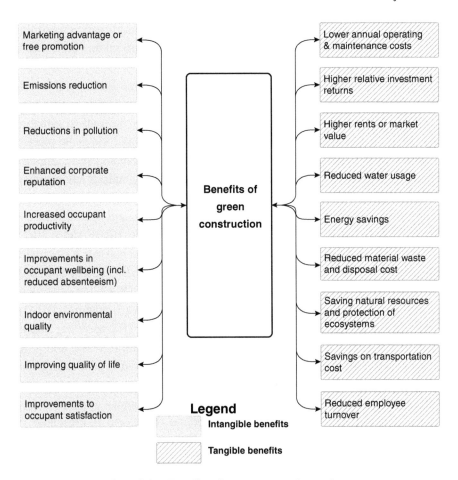

Figure 3.1.   Benefits of green construction projects.

performance. The development of such tools commenced in 1990, when the world's first, the UK Building Research Establishment Environmental Assessment Method (BREEAM), was established. Shortly after that, the France High Quality Environmental standard (HQE) and the US LEED were introduced in 2000 (Reed *et al.*, 2009). Over the past years, many countries have also introduced their own rating tools. This is because green construction is highly context-specific and therefore such context-specific rating tools are needed to address the sustainability needs and priorities of specific locations. The rating tools of one location are not directly applicable to another location. Factors such as climatic conditions and the availability of materials define the approach to green construction in each context.

Most of the rating tools are developed by the Green Building Councils in each region or country. They are usually voluntary rather than mandatory. The structure of these rating tools is similar and covers several sustainability performance categories for different project types and life cycle phases. Categories in various rating tools mainly include sustainable sites, land use and ecology, energy and atmosphere, water efficiency, indoor environmental quality, materials, waste and resources, location and transportation, innovation, regional priority, education and awareness, and health and well-being. The most widely applied rating tools include BREEAM, LEED, Green Globes, ENERGY STAR (US), Japan's Comprehensive Assessment System for Building Environmental Efficiency (CASBEE), Green Building Tool, Excellence in Design for Greater Efficiencies (EDGE), the Australian Green Star, NABERS Energy (Australia), Green Mark (Singapore), BEAM Plus (Hong Kong), and China Green Building Label (Harris *et al.*, 2020). EDGE, for instance, has been widely used to assist design teams and project owners in assessing the most cost-effective ways to integrate energy and water savings and reduce embodied energy in materials used in new construction and existing buildings (IFC, 2016). A summary of some major green construction project rating tools around the world is presented in Table 3.1.

3.1.5. *Green construction projects and the sustainable development goals*

In 1987, "*Our Common Future*," also known as the Brundtland Report, of the World Commission on Environment and Development presented the modern definition of sustainable development: "*development that meets the needs of the present without compromising the ability of future generations to meet their own needs*" (Brundtland, 1987).

As indicated earlier, green construction promotes efficient use of resources and reduces negative impacts on the environment, preserving it for us and for future generations. The ultimate goal of green construction is to ensure that the process of constructing buildings has little to no

Table 3.1.   Some major green construction project rating tools.

Europe	Americas	Asia	Africa and rest of the world
BREEAM (UK)	LEED (US & Canada)	BEAM Plus (Hong Kong)	Green Star (Australia, also used in New Zealand)
DGNB system (Germany)	US DOE (Department of Energy) Design Guide	Green Building Label (China)	Green Star SA (South Africa also used in Ghana)
GBC Home (Italy)	WBDG (Whole Building Design Guide (US)	Green Mark (Singapore)	Green Star SA Kenya
GRESB (Netherlands)	BREEAM (Canada)	LEED (China and India)	Green Building Tool (South Africa)
HQE (France)	HOK Sustainable Design Guide (US)	CASBEE (Japan)	NABERS Energy (Australia)
Strategic Environmental Assessment (SEA)	Green Globes (US and Canada)		IFC EDGE (Global)
ENVEST	ENERGY STAR (US)		
Office Scorer	Green Key Global (Canada)		
The Green Guide to Specification	International Green Construction Code (IgCC) (US)		
Sustainability Checklists (e.g., SEEDA; BRE)			
Environmental Impact Assessment (EIA)			

negative impact on the environment, society, and economy. Green construction is therefore critical to shaping a sustainable built environment and planet. It addresses the environmental, social, and economic issues of habitat and community context of construction in the spirit of sustainable development (Kibert, 2004). The objective of green construction appears to be underpinned by the UN Sustainable Development Goals (SDGs).

Arguably, green construction projects generally promote 11 out of the 17 SDGs: Goals 3, 6, 7, 8, 9, 10, 11, 12, 13, 15, and 17.

Green construction projects align with SDG 3 through reduction in emissions and air pollutants, and improvements in human health, well-being, happiness, satisfaction, productivity, and quality of life (WorldGBC, 2018). By using renewable energy technologies, green construction projects support SDG 7 to achieve affordable and clean energy. In addition, green construction projects promote decent work and economic growth (SDG 8) through the creation of decent green jobs and green skills development toward low-carbon transition (WorldGBC, 2021). For instance, developing greener construction projects in the UK could deliver about 50,000 jobs by 2030 (HM Government, 2020). Green construction projects promote SDG 9 (industry, innovation, and infrastructure) by providing equitable, high-quality urban and regional infrastructure. They also address SDG 10 (reduced inequalities) by safeguarding human health, ensuring decent living standards, and eliminating energy poverty while offering employment opportunities and upholding human rights for workers. Green construction projects are an integral part of any sustainable cities and communities (SDG 11) development plan (Debrah & Owusu-Manu, 2021; Debrah *et al.*, 2022a). The benefits of green construction projects such as reduction in energy and water consumption promote responsible consumption and production (SDG 12). Green construction projects contribute to the achievement of SDG 13 (climate action) by prioritizing clean and efficient energy usage and implementing adaptation and mitigation measures to decarbonize the buildings and construction sector. Furthermore, these projects promote SDG 15 (life on land) by ensuring access to nature for all and implementing nature-based solutions that enhance resilience, support biodiversity, and protect ecosystem services (WorldGBC, 2021). Besides, green construction projects are critical to achieving the Paris Agreement goals. Chapter 7 talks more about the Paris Agreement.

3.1.6. *Green construction project planning and design*

Project planning is vital for project success. It involves team selection, establishing documentation systems, initiating material procurement, creating schedules and milestones, and other activities necessary for project execution (Menches *et al.*, 2008). It is the primary step in helping project teams set up a concept, procedure, and project scope definition for controlling and executing construction projects (Menches *et al.*, 2008). Green construction projects prioritize a comprehensive and integrated planning and design process right from the project's inception. This is to ensure that unique green design features are integrated into the project in an innovative and collaborative manner (Kibert, 2016). Yudelson (2010) identifies three cardinal aspects of green construction design: indoor lighting, building materials, and layout. Lighting design incorporates energy-efficient fixtures, strategic window placement for natural lighting, and the use of efficient fluorescent lighting. It is extremely important to ensure that energy-efficient lighting systems are adequately incorporated into the design. Building layout is critical to enhancing the energy efficiency of the project through techniques, such as good orientation to promote natural ventilation. Green construction emphasizes the use of sustainable materials to promote environmental sustainability. This includes incorporating recyclable bamboo flooring and utilizing non-toxic materials, such as formaldehyde-free cabinets and paint, which are free from harmful toxins.

3.2. Green construction projects as a global agenda

The global demand for buildings and floor area is steadily rising. According to the UN Environment Programme (UNEP), the floor area of building stock is expected to double by 2060. To avoid increasing negative impacts, buildings must be constructed "right" from the outset — a green construction approach. Green construction is accepted globally as a means to deliver sustainability in the construction sector. This is evident in the role of governments around the world through various green construction ambitions and policies. For instance, the "*2021 Global Status Report for Buildings and Construction*" of the UNEP revealed that 136 countries mention building emissions and reduction ambitions in 2020 as part of their Nationally Determined Contributions (NDCs) under the Paris Agreement (UNEP, 2021). The above statistics highlight the importance attached to green construction projects globally. IFC (2022) notes that governments adopt a variety of fiscal and non-fiscal incentives to motivate green construction. Non-fiscal incentives encompass a range of measures to promote green construction, including public advocacy, capacity building, incentives from national, local, and city governments, alternative compliance options with green construction codes, regulatory flexibility, benefits such as extra floor allowance, expedited permits, technical assistance, national recognition programs, net metering, and the use of green taxonomy. In addition to non-fiscal measures, fiscal policies and incentives play a crucial role in encouraging developers to adopt green construction practices. These can include capital adequacy requirements, prudential norms such as loan-to-value or loan-to-income ratios, tax breaks, property tax incentives, grant and subsidy programs, loan programs, and discounts on permit fees. The following sections overview the development of green construction projects and policies around the globe.

3.2.1. *Green construction projects and policies in the US*

The US is a leader in green construction. LEED is the prominent and widely accepted green construction project rating tool in the US. More than 100,000 construction projects have participated in the LEED certification (USGBC, 2022b). Other major green construction project rating tools used in the US include Green Globes and ENERGY STAR (Kubba, 2012). Local governments employ various innovative policy designs and incentives to promote green construction beyond rating tools. These include property tax reassessment moratoriums, parking incentives, green funds, green roof mandates, electricity bill discounts, recertification requirements, and mandatory investments with positive returns. Matisoff *et al.* (2016) found that 70 cities offer development density bonuses, while over 90 cities provide rebates, fee reductions, or expedited permitting. Additionally, 25 cities offer tax reliefs and grants as financial incentives. Some states and cities adjust incentives based on the scale of the proposed project, offering greater incentives for green activities in development projects that are larger in scale. Furthermore, nine municipalities incentivize certification without explicitly mentioning LEED.

The US federal government commits to making its buildings and construction more sustainable. The Energy Policy Act (2009) allocated USD 31 billion to green construction and conservation. As such, the government has been offering tax breaks and incentives for efficiency upgrades of buildings. Likewise, the Energy Independence and Security Act (2007) includes requirements for high-performance green federal buildings and construction (The Office of the Federal Environmental Executive, 2010). The US Environmental Protection Agency's construction activities are guided by the Green Building Strategy (2008). The Department of Environmental Services has established the Green Building Incentive Program, which enables developers to request an increased building area if their project obtains LEED certification. Additionally, many funding sources for green construction projects have been provided by the agency to encourage government organizations, industries, homeowners, and NGOs to access grants, tax credits, and loans. States such as Maryland, New York, and Oregon offer tax credits for expenditures on projects that meet specific energy efficiency criteria. The US Department of Agriculture requires LEED Silver certification, while the US Department of Energy mandates LEED Gold for new construction projects. Other departments, including the US Department of Defense and the US Department of State, encourage adherence to LEED but do not impose strict certification tier requirements.

3.2.2. *Green construction projects and policies in the UK*

BREEAM is the leading green construction project rating tool in the UK (Parker, 2012). Numerous local authorities in the UK incorporate BREEAM into their local development frameworks for new construction projects. BREEAM serves as a planning condition for many of these projects, although the specific rating requirements may differ among different authorities. Subject to certain project thresholds, projects occupied by health authorities and government estates require BREEAM "Excellent" for new projects and "Very Good" for retrofit projects. Green construction plays a significant role in the *"The Ten Point Plan for a Green Industrial Revolution"* in the UK. For green construction projects, an investment of around GBP 1 billion in public finance and GBP 11 billion in private investment is expected to realize 16% emissions reduction (of 2018 levels) in buildings and construction in the UK. The investment will also support about 50,000 jobs in the sector by 2030. Within the green construction project framework, the UK established a heat and buildings strategy in 2021. In line with the aforementioned developments, a comprehensive energy-related product policy framework was introduced. This policy aims to promote the use of energy-efficient products that consume fewer resources and materials, resulting in carbon savings and assisting households and businesses in reducing their energy expenses with minimal effort. To achieve this objective, the UK has set a target of installing 600,000 heat pumps per year by 2028. Additionally, homes constructed in accordance with the Future Homes Standard are expected to be "zero carbon ready" and reduce emissions by 75–80% compared to conventionally built homes. Initiatives of green home finance are also expected to enhance the energy efficiency of approximately 2.8 million homes and upgrade about 1.5 million homes to meet energy performance certificate/standard requirements by 2030. Furthermore, the public sector aims to achieve a 50% reduction in direct emissions by 2032 compared to a baseline set in 2017. Other green construction project schemes and incentives in the UK include the Green Homes Grant, Public Sector Decarbonization Scheme, Homes Upgrade Grant, Social Housing Decarbonization Fund, and the extension of the Energy Company Obligation to 2026. These policies and incentives are intended to strengthen energy efficiency requirements in the UK, especially toward making the buildings and construction sector greener, as envisioned in the *"The Ten Point Plan for a Green Industrial Revolution"* (HM Government, 2020).

3.2.3. *Green construction projects and policies in Hong Kong*

BEAM Plus, launched in 2010, is Hong Kong's leading green construction project rating tool. BEAM Plus is a voluntary scheme designed specifically for high-rise and high-density cities in subtropical climates. It provides a comprehensive set of performance criteria addressing various sustainability aspects throughout the life cycle of buildings, including planning, design, construction, commissioning, management, operation, and maintenance. The BEAM Plus Project Directory and Statistics shows that as of 5 July 2023, there are a total of 2,225 finally assessed, provisionally assessed, and registered BEAM Plus projects in Hong Kong. By 2020, 41 new government construction projects in the city achieved gold rating or higher under BEAM Plus (HKGBC, 2022). These projects have saved around 370 million kWh of electricity (an equivalent annual consumption for 110,000 households) (HKSAR, 2021). The total Gross Floor Area (GFA) of projects registered under BEAM Plus has exceeded 74,500,000 square meters (HKGBC, 2023). Hong Kong also incorporates other green construction project rating tools, such as LEED, Green Building Design Label, and Green Mark. The Holiday Inn Express Hong Kong SOHO is the first high-rise hotel building project to achieve platinum or equivalent ratings in all these rating tools (Chan & Leung, 2018).

Incentive schemes, such as the GFA concession scheme, are available to promote green construction projects in Hong Kong. Since the introduction of the GFA concession scheme in 2011, more than 60% of new construction projects have applied for BEAM Plus assessment, and approximately 95% of these projects have received GFA concessions, as estimated by the BEAM Society Limited. BEAM Plus certification is a prerequisite for granting up to 10% GFA concessions for green construction projects (Harris *et al.*, 2020). Furthermore, in Hong Kong, capital expenditure invested in the installation or construction of energy-efficient building systems registered under the Energy Efficiency Registration Scheme for Buildings by the Electrical and Mechanical Services Department qualifies for accelerated tax deduction. Eligible organizations that achieve ratings of "Excellent" or "Very Good" under the Energy Use Aspect of BEAM Plus Existing Buildings V2.0 Selective Scheme can also receive subsidies for assessment fees. There is also funding assistance for Energy Efficiency Improvement Works. Generally, these policies, as part of *"Hong Kong's Climate Action Plan 2050,"* are intended to increase energy savings in commercial projects (15–20%) and residential projects (10–15%) by 2035 (HKSAR, 2021). As such, there are more stringent energy efficiency standards for both new and existing building projects.

To reduce energy intensity by 40% by 2025, the government established the *"Energy Saving Plan for Hong Kong's Built Environment 2015–2025+."* A progress of 30% reduction in energy intensity in Hong Kong was estimated in 2021. Additional incentives in Hong Kong include offering subsidies of up to HKD 0.5 million on a matching basis for implementing energy-saving improvements in different types of projects. Other policies such as the Buildings Energy Efficiency Ordinance, Mandatory Energy Efficiency Labelling Scheme, Government's Energy Saving targets, and the District Cooling System are measures toward electricity conservation and energy savings in Hong Kong.

3.2.4. *Green construction projects and policies in other countries*

Several other countries have also developed policies to promote the development of green construction projects. This section focuses on some of the policies and developments in other countries, including countries in Europe, Africa, Asia, Australia, and South America.

The European Union (EU) takes the lead in developing policies and promoting green construction projects. The EU's Renovation Wave strategy adopts the principle of "life cycle thinking and circularity" to reduce the carbon intensity of buildings throughout their entire life cycle (European Commission, 2020). Member states are required to come up with strategies for achieving an energy-efficient and decarbonized building stock by 2050 (European Parliament, 2021). Examples of specific policies and incentives in some European countries include the following:

- **Bulgaria:** 100% real estate tax exemption for 10 years for project owners who install renewable energy technologies (IFC, 2019).
- **Germany (Darmstadt):** Compensation of up to €5,000 for users of green roofs to cover implementation costs (Shafique *et al.*, 2018).
- **Peru (San Borja, Arequipa, Cusco, Miraflores, and Surco):** Height bonus incentives for green construction of commercial, educational, and residential projects certified under EDGE, BREEAM, or LEED

(IFC, 2022). Specific requirements include features, such as green roofs, setbacks from the curb, visible green gardens, bicycle racks, and waste segregation, as well as compliance with the "National Technical Code for Sustainable Construction."

In Africa, while green construction projects and policies are relatively novel, South Africa is regarded as a leader in the subregion. The Green Star South Africa rating tool launched in 2007 has been employed to certify over 700 green construction projects. This rise in green certifications could be attributed to the "award" incentive implemented by the Green Building Council of South Africa (GBCSA) to accelerate adoption. A municipality in South Africa, eThekwini, offers refunds or reductions in property rates on projects that have an "as built" rating certificate granted by the GBSCA. In addition, the government has introduced tax incentives to promote energy savings. In Sekondi-Takoradi (Ghana), there is a 30% reduction in building permit fees for commercial and residential projects that are green-certified. In Kenya's national green fiscal incentives policy framework, there are tax incentives for using 50% recycled content in the manufacturing of local building materials, importation/manufacturing of water-saving devices, construction material reuse, and solar passive structures. The Kenya National Treasury offers total tax exemption on interest income for securities and bonds that are utilized for raising funds specifically for green construction projects that adhere to the Green Bond Standards. African leaders, policymakers, and practitioners should look at developing more green construction projects and policies to address climate and sustainability challenges.

In Asia, Singapore provides financial incentives for Green Mark retrofitting. China launched the Green Building Label in 2006, which is widely accepted and applied nationwide. Some local governments in China mandate a minimum of 1-star certification for new construction projects (Harris *et al.*, 2020). China's 14th Five-Year Plan (2021–2025) includes plans for low-carbon cities and green construction mandates (Vaughan, 2021). The government has established subsidies, environmental taxes, technical standards for production, a carbon trading mechanism, and a total emissions standard to deal with economic activities that have negative impacts (Zhang *et al.*, 2019). Other relevant Chinese policies include Assessment Standard for Green Building (GB/T50378-2019), Environmental Protection Law (2014 Revision), Resolution of the Standing Committee of the National People's Congress on Making Active Responses to Climate Change (2009), and the Prevention and Control of Solid Waste Pollution (2004 Revision) (Yang *et al.*, 2021).

Mandaluyong, a city in the Philippines, collaborated with IFC to establish "Green Buildings Ordinance." Property owners who comply with the regulations are rewarded with various incentives, including a 50% discount on real property tax for installed machinery that meets the requirements of the ordinance. In Japan, 13 local governments mandate large-scale construction projects to submit a "CASBEE Assessment Result Sheet." Similarly, projects over 5,000 square meters in total floor area are required to conduct their own assessment in compliance with the "Tokyo Green Building Guidelines" and prepare and submit a Green Building Plan to the government (ISEP, 2009; Bureau of Environment Tokyo Metropolitan Government, 2018). Since 2010, it has been mandatory to consider the introduction of equipment to use renewable energies in large-scale new construction projects in Japan (Bureau of Environment Tokyo Metropolitan Government, 2018). Green projects that achieve the CASBEE B+ class will be eligible for an increase in the maximum allowable floor area as a reward.

Presently, 24 Japanese local governments employ the "Sustainable Building Reporting System" regulation that targets the housing and commercial sectors (CASBEE, 2022). In Japan, tax deductions are provided for the installation of equipment that is energy efficient, including LEDs, highly insulated windows, and high-efficient air conditioning systems in residential projects (IFC, 2019). The Bank of Bangladesh requires commercial banks to offer discounted financing rates of 9% for the additional costs incurred in implementing green measures for light industry projects (IFC, 2022). The Bank of Indonesia has announced a 5% increase in the maximum loan-to-value ratio for green properties (IFC, 2019). The Pune Municipal Corporation (India) grants extra floor area ratios of 3–7% for improvement in energy, water, and materials up to 50% (IFC, 2022). Lebanon has launched a National Energy Efficiency and Renewable

Energy Action, under which the private sector receives affordable credits from commercial banks for energy efficiency, renewable energy, and green construction project developments (IFC, 2022).

Australia and other countries in the rest of the world have also made significant progress in green construction project development. NABERS Energy rating is mandatory for office projects beyond 1,000 square meters in Australia (Harris *et al.*, 2020). In Argentina, residential projects incorporating LED lighting up to 140,000, solar hot water collectors, and insulation Class B are eligible for a 10% VAT exclusion. In Colombia, technical solutions and project design services such as energy-efficient air conditioning systems and insulation can receive up to 25% income tax deduction as well as 19% VAT exclusion (IFC, 2022). These play a key role in driving the development of green construction projects.

3.2.5. *World Green Building Council and its members*

WorldGBC is a global action network of over 70 Green Building Councils around the world that promotes sustainability — climate action, health and well-being, and resources and circularity — in the buildings and construction sector (WorldGBC, 2022b). It influences over 81% of the global built environment (WorldGBC, 2021). The first Green Building Council, which is the USGBC, was founded in 1993 by Rick Fedirizzi, David Gottfried, and Mike Italiano to promote sustainability-focused practices in buildings and construction. The success story of the USGBC served as a model for other countries to begin their own Green Building Councils. To coordinate the activities of these Green Building Councils, the WorldGBC was then established in 1999. Since then, the WorldGBC global membership has grown from 9 to over 70 members and affiliates at different membership stages: established, emerging, and prospective. At present, there are Green Building Councils in all parts of the world: Europe (over 20 members), the Americas (over 15), Asia-Pacific (over 15), Africa (over 5), and the Middle East and North Africa (MENA, over 5) (see Figure 3.2) (WorldGBC, 2022c, 2022d).

WorldGBC members collectively support governments and businesses to promote environmental, social, and economic impacts and

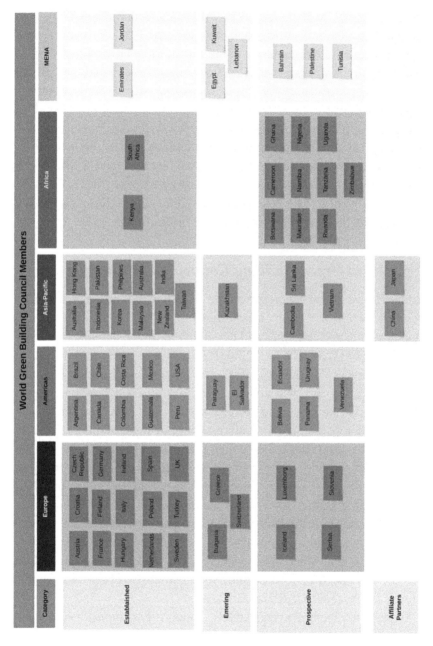

Figure 3.2.   WorldGBC members list.

performances in the built environment on global, national, regional, and local levels — making green construction projects a truly global agenda (WorldGBC, 2022c, 2022d).

3.3. The history, present, and future of green construction projects

The urgent need to address global sustainability challenges gave rise to the need for green construction projects. The green construction movement is rooted in the 1970 energy crisis which required energy-saving approaches. The use of active and passive solar design and tighter building envelopes became necessary (Kibert, 1994; The Office of the Federal Environmental Executive, 2010). Green construction has now become very popular due to increased demand, favorable government policies and initiatives, and available green construction materials and technologies (Darko, 2019; Darko *et al.*, 2019). There is growing evidence for the ability to improve the quality of life of people and a robust business case for the further development of the green construction market (WorldGBC, 2023). Hence, green construction continues to impact and transform the construction industry, while revolutionizing perceptions of design, habitation, and operation of buildings. Today, green construction is seen as one of the best approaches to make buildings and construction sustainable. It is accepted as a global solution for sustainable cities, communities, and neighborhoods (USGBC, 2022a). The role of government in promoting green construction projects is critical. Many governments reported ambitious targets for the buildings and construction sector in their NDCs. According to the UN Framework Convention on Climate Change (UNFCCC) (2021), cross-cutting measures applicable to residential, commercial, and industrial construction projects were the second most prioritized subarea communicated in submitted NDCs for domestic mitigation as of July 2021. Similarly, energy-efficiency improvements in buildings and construction were the second most frequently indicated mitigation priority area related to supply and end-use of energy. The integration of ambitious targets, goals, and policies into national legislative, regulatory, and planning processes by various countries is an indication of governments' commitment toward achieving the goals of the Paris Agreement. Yang *et al.* (2021) suggested that a combination of environmental taxes, green subsidies, and carbon trading would serve as more effective policy instruments for promoting the development of green construction projects. However, IFC (2019) has noted that developing countries face challenges in implementing efficient strategies for mandating and incentivizing the scaling up of green construction projects. Continuous research and development in developing countries, especially those in Africa and Asia, are necessary to overcome this challenge. This is because developing countries possess enormous untapped investment prospects for green construction projects, especially in green finance (IFC, 2019; Debrah *et al.*, 2022b).

Green finance offers opportunities to increase green construction project development across the world (Debrah *et al.*, 2022b). It represents the biggest investment opportunity of US\$24.7 trillion by 2030 (IFC, 2019). Insights from the Country Climate and Development Reports of the World Bank Group have indicated that sustainability challenges can be addressed but only if policies are well designed and financing is available (The World Bank Group, 2022). Stakeholders such as governments, private investors, developers, owners, and financial institutions should collaborate to stimulate investment in green construction projects, especially in developing countries. Besides, future green construction projects should prioritize Net Zero over net-to-gross floor area to meet global emissions reduction targets. The world should move from voluntary to mandatory green construction rating tools. Implementing mandatory tools can effectively ensure the incorporation of green measures from the beginning, offsetting the need for costly retrofits in the future (UNFCCC, 2021). Additionally, policies that simplify processes and procedures for green construction, such as expediting construction permits, can serve as a cost-effective approach to encourage the adoption of green construction projects (IFC, 2019). Moreover, the increasing interest in artificial intelligence and machine learning and other digital technologies in green construction opens up opportunities to incorporate emerging technologies into green construction practices (Debrah *et al.*, 2022c). Emerging technologies such as blockchain technology, digital twins, artificial intelligence of things, robotics, and 3D/4D printing offer opportunities to revolutionize green construction project development. Similarly, building information modeling provides a means to transform conventional construction practices to assess the impact of the design process on the life cycle of a construction project (Raouf and Al-Ghamdi, 2009; Ansah *et al.*, 2019).

3.4. Project management issues and challenges in green construction projects

Green construction projects face several PM issues and challenges (Chan *et al.*, 2018; Darko and Chan, 2017). Similar to conventional projects, green construction projects face challenges related to planning, schedule, costs, execution, resources, and project stakeholders. In addition, green construction project managers encounter unique challenges to meet sustainability objectives.

Both Shi *et al.* (2013) and Hwang and Ng (2013) highlighted that most of the challenges faced by green construction project managers are planning-related. Challenges such as extended planning and approval procedures for new green technologies and recycled materials, as well as difficulties in understanding and implementing green specifications within contract details, can impact project schedules and costs. Furthermore, the productivity of design and construction in green projects is currently lower compared to conventional projects due to practitioners still being on a learning curve in implementing green practices. Besides, green designs can be more complicated than conventional designs. The complexities associated with integrating green and integrated design process requirements into designs demand more time and this may affect the schedule of procurement, construction, and project closure. Green certification requirements and stakeholders' unfamiliarity often lead to cost increases, project delays, and productivity losses. Hence, the unfamiliarity with green technologies and technical difficulties during the construction process may lead to time and cost overruns. With more green construction projects, green professionals will gather more experience and become proficient in using green technologies.

On the other hand, the myth that sustainability costs more inhibits green development. The perception of higher costs is the most common barrier associated with green construction. Since the higher cost of green construction technologies and materials could result in cost over-runs, project managers are critical of managing and delivering green projects within allocated budgets. Innovative strategies such as optimal value engineering, reducing waste, right-sizing and structure, low-e windows, energy-saving appliances, and solar PVs are now available to reduce the additional construction cost of going green. Besides, green construction should be viewed as a holistic approach to promoting healthy communities and sustaining quality lives. From a life cycle perspective, green construction is known to be inexpensive (Gabay *et al.*, 2014; Hwang *et al.*, 2017), but this may not be attractive to the developer or investor who has no long-term interest in the operation or leasing of the project. Hence, it is crucial for the project manager to devise strategies to contain costs during the project implementation.

Other constraints in green construction PM include misaligned incentives, short hold periods versus long building lifespans, uncertainties in climate change and regulations, limited green suppliers, uncertain performance of materials and equipment, restrictions on emerging technologies, imperfect specifications, regional variations in understanding the green concept, lack of knowledge, limited evaluation tools, and added maintenance responsibilities. In Section 4.1, we see a further elaboration of some of the green construction PM challenges.

3.5. Project management success stories in green construction projects

Green construction projects provide opportunities "to do right by planet and people." There is global evidence of increasing acceptance and willingness to pay for green construction projects due to the tangible and intangible benefits (WorldGBC, 2018). Some green construction PM success stories are offered in the following to serve as a useful reference point for future green construction PM.

Akron Children's Hospital project is a LEED Gold-certified 100-bed neonatal intensive care unit in the US (Ohio). To maximize innovation, beauty, and performance, the project utilized an IPD approach to ensure positive impacts for all stakeholders. Evidence-based design and Lean Six Sigma PM methodologies informed decisions throughout the design and construction stages. This led to completing the project under budget by USD 44 million and ahead of schedule by 54 days with zero change orders. In comparison with the national average for healthcare facilities in the US, this green hospital project has resulted in 50% energy cost savings, 54% energy consumption savings, 49% greenhouse gas emissions reduction, 67% improvement in patient/family satisfaction, and 76% improvement in staff satisfaction (WorldGBC, 2018). So far, the project has received three awards: The Silver Recognition Evidence-Based Design Touchstone Award; The Center for Health Design in 2017 and the Honor Award; and New Construction, AIA Akron Chapter in 2015 (HKS, 2022).

The Hub project in Shanghai (China) offers another green construction PM success story. This project has attained a 3-star rating in the China Green Building standard. It stands as the city's inaugural low-carbon business district, encompassing office towers, hotels, and malls. The project incorporates multiple energy-saving strategies, including a solar hot water system, stormwater and greywater recycling systems, as well as co-generation from a central district plant for the supply of chilled water and hot water. Moreover, it benefits from convenient transportation options, such as high-speed rails, metros, and domestic flights (Arup, 2022).

The Central Bank of Ireland (*Dublin*) is the first office building project to achieve BREEAM Outstanding. It utilizes a mixed-mode ventilation strategy to reduce energy consumption and features a building management system that controls volume control dampers for fresh air supply. Local override switches are also provided for end users. The project uses a combined heat and power plant to reduce project emissions and operational energy costs. This has led to the reduction of the project's energy use by 70% in comparison to Irish Building Regulations. To promote sustainable transportation and reduce private vehicle use, the project has implemented 300 cycle racks, 30 showers, and e-charge car parking spaces for staff. Additionally, the project specified Forestry Stewardship Council-certified timber to achieve two credits for responsibly sourcing the materials (BRE Group, 2022).

3.6. Summary

Green construction projects are here to stay. They do not only support climate change mitigation and adaptation actions, but they also present a viable business case for investors. Intangible benefits of green construction projects such as improved indoor environmental quality leading to improved occupant satisfaction and well-being fuel the increasing development and adoption. The role of government and the private sector in promoting green construction projects through voluntary green construction rating tools have shaped the market. However, mandatory rating tools are necessary to achieve higher sustainability goals in buildings and construction.

References

Arup. (2022). The Hub — The city's first low carbon business district. Available at: https://www.arup.com/projects/the-hub-shanghai (accessed on 20 September 2022).

BRE Group. (2022). Central Bank of Ireland is the first office building in Ireland to achieve BREEAM Outstanding — BRE Group. Available at: https://bregroup.com/case-studies/breeam-case-studies-real-estate/central-bank-of-ireland-is-the-first-office-building-in-ireland-to-achieve-breeam-outstanding/ (accessed on 22 September 2022).

Brundtland, G. H. (1987). What is sustainable development. *Our Common Future*, *8*(9), 1–40.

Bureau of Environment Tokyo Metropolitan Government. (2018). Green building program (Tokyo Metropolitan Government). ESCAP Policy Documents Management. Available at: https://policy.asiapacificenergy.org/node/2611 (accessed on 2 September 2022).

CASBEE. (2022). Welcome to CASBEE website!! Available at: https://www.ibec.or.jp/CASBEE/english/ (accessed on 20 September 2022).

Chan, A. P. C., Darko, A., Olanipekun, A. O., & Ameyaw, E. E. (2018). Critical barriers to green building technologies adoption in developing countries: The case of Ghana. *Journal of Cleaner Production*, *172*, 1067–1079.

Chan, I. & Leung, M.-Y. (2018). *Sustainable Development Worldwide: Costs of Green Buildings*. Hong Kong, China: Hong Kong Institute of Surveyors.

Darko, A. (2019). Adoption of green building technologies in Ghana: Development of a model of green building technologies and issues influencing their adoption. Available at: https://theses.lib.polyu.edu.hk/handle/200/9924 (accessed on 20 September 2022).

Darko, A. & Chan, A. P. C. (2017). Review of barriers to green building adoption. *Sustainable Development, 25*(3), 167–179.

Darko, A., Chan, A. P. C., Huo, X., & Owusu-Manu, D.-G. (2019). A scientometric analysis and visualization of global green building research. *Building and Environment, 149*, 501–511.

Debrah, C. & Owusu-Manu, D.-G. (2021). An apposite framework for green cities development in developing countries: The case of Ghana. *Construction Innovation, 22*(4), 789–808. https://doi.org/10.1108/CI-08-2020-0132.

Debrah, C., Chan, A. P. C., & Darko, A. (2022c). Artificial intelligence in green building. *Automation in Construction, 137*, 104192. https://doi.org/10.1016/j.autcon.2022.104192.

Debrah, C., Chan, A. P. C., & Darko, A. (2022b). Green finance gap in green buildings: A scoping review and future research needs. *Building and Environment, 207*, 108443. https://doi.org/10.1016/j.buildenv.2021.108443.

Debrah, C., Darko, A., Chan, A. P. C., Owusu-Manu, D. G., & Edwards, D. J. (2022). Green finance in green building needs under the Paris Agreement. *IOP Conference Series: Earth and Environmental Science, 1085*(1), 012033.

Debrah, C., Owusu-Manu, D.-G., Amonoo-Parker, Lord, Baiden, B. K., Oduro-Ofori, E., & Edwards, D. J. (2022a). A factor analysis of the key sustainability content underpinning green cities development in Ghana. *International Journal of Construction Management*, 1–10. https://doi.org/10.1080/15623599.2022.2068786.

Dixon, C. (2010). Straight green: Project delivery methods and their impact on green building. Available at: https://www.wconline.com/articles/86791-straight-green-project-delivery-methods-and-their-impact-on-green-building (accessed on 18 March 2022).

European Commission. (2020). *A Renovation Wave for Europe: Greening Our Buildings, Creating Jobs, Improving Lives*. Brussels: European Commission. Available at: https://ec.europa.eu/energy/sites/ener/files/eu_renovation_wave_strategy.pdf (accessed on 22 September 2022).

European Parliament. (2021). Energy efficiency | Fact Sheets on the European Union | European Parliament. Available at: https://www.europarl.europa.eu/factsheets/en/sheet/69/energy-efficiency (accessed on 2 September 2022).

Gabay, H., Meir, I. A., Schwartz, M., & Werzberger, E. (2014). Cost-benefit analysis of green buildings: An Israeli office buildings case study. *Energy and Buildings*, *76*, 558–564. https://doi.org/10.1016/j.enbuild.2014.02.027.

Glavinich, T. E. (2008). *Contractor's Guide to Green Building Construction.* New Jersey, USA: John Wiley & Sons.

Green Building Council of Australia (2006). *Dollars and Sense of Green Buildings: Building the Business Case for Green Commercial Buildings in Australia.* Green Building Council of Australia, Barangaroo, NSW, Australia.

Harris, T. W., Song, J., Yu, F., & Wong, A. (2020). Green building rating systems: Energy benchmarking study. *Civic Exchange*. Available at: https://civic-exchange.org/report/green-building-rating-systems-energy-benchmarking-study/ (accessed on 20 September 2022).

HKGBC. (2022). BEAM plus project directory. Available at: https://www.hkgbc.org.hk/eng/beam-plus/beam-plus-dir-stat/BEAMPlusDirectory/beamplus-directory.jsp (accessed on 22 September 2022).

HKGBC. (2023). BEAM plus. Available at: https://greenbuilding.hkgbc.org.hk/posts/view/BEAMPlus_Intro (accessed on 12 March 2023).

HKS. (2022). Akron children's hospital Kay Jewelers Pavilion — Case Study. HKS architects. Available at: https://www.hksinc.com/what-we-do/case-studies/akron-childrens-hospital-kay-jewelers-pavilion/ (accessed on 2 September 2022).

HKSAR. (2021). *Hong Kong's Climate Action Plan 2050.* 66. Available at: https://cnsd.gov.hk/wp-content/uploads/pdf/CAP2050_booklet_en.pdf (accessed on 11 March 2024).

HM Government (2020). The ten point plan for a green industrial revolution. GOV.UK. Available at: https://www.gov.uk/government/publications/the-ten-point-plan-for-a-green-industrial-revolution (accessed on 12 September 2022).

Hwang, B. G. & Tan, J. S. (2012). Green building project management: Obstacles and solutions for sustainable development. *Sustainable Development*, *20*(5), 335–349.

Hwang, B.-G. & Ng, W. J. (2013). Project management knowledge and skills for green construction: Overcoming challenges. *International Journal of Project Management*, *31*(2), 272–284.

Hwang, B.-G., Zhu, L., Wang, Y., & Cheong, X. (2017). Green building construction projects in Singapore: Cost premiums and cost performance. *Project Management Journal*, *48*(4), 67–79. https://doi.org/10.1177/875697281704800406.

IFC. (2016). About EDGE. GBCI. Available at: https://gbci.org/press-kit-edge (accessed on 23 September 2022).

IFC. (2019). *Green Buildings: A Finance and Policy Blueprint for Emerging Markets*. The World Bank, Washington, D.C., USA.

IFC. (2022). Fiscal vs non-fiscal government incentives. *EDGE Buildings*. Available at: http://edgebuildings.com/marketplace/governments/ (accessed on 25 September 2022).

ISEP. (2009). CASBEE for Japanese local government programs. Green Local Government Portal. Available at: http://www.climate-lg.jp/en/programs/id_003.html (accessed on 24 September 2022).

Kats, G. (2003). *Green Building Costs and Financial Benefits*. Boston, MA: Massachusetts Technology Collaborative.

Kee, J. E. (2004). Cost-effectiveness and cost-benefit analysis. In Wholey *et al.* (Eds.) *Handbook of Practical Program Evaluation* (pp. 506–541), Wiley, San Francisco, USA.

Kibert, C. J. (1994, November). Establishing principles and a model for sustainable construction. In *Proceedings of the First International Conference on Sustainable Construction*, pp. 6–9, Tampa, Florida, USA.

Kibert, C. J. (2004). Green buildings: An overview of progress. *Journal of Land Use & Environmental Law*, *19*(2), 491–502.

Kibert, C. J. (2016). *Sustainable Construction: Green Building Design and Delivery* (4th edn.), New Jersey, USA: John Wiley & Sons, Hoboken, New Jersey, USA.

Kubba, S. (2012). *Handbook of Green Building Design and Construction: LEED, BREEAM, and Green Globes*. Butterworth-Heinemann, Oxford, UK.

Matisoff, D. C., Noonan, D. S., & Flowers, M. E. (2016). Policy monitor — Green buildings: Economics and policies. *Review of Environmental Economics and Policy*, *10*(2), 329–346. https://doi.org/10.1093/reep/rew009.

McKim, R., Hegazy, T., & Attalla, M. (2000). Project performance control in reconstruction projects. *Journal of Construction Engineering and Management*, *126*(2), 137–141.

Menches, C. L., Hanna, A. S., Nordheim, E. V., & Russell, J. S. (2008). Impact of pre-construction planning and project characteristics on performance in the US electrical construction industry. *Construction Management and Economics*, *26*(8), 855–869. https://doi.org/10.1080/01446190802213511.

Parker, J. (2012). *The Value of BREEAM: A Bsria Report*. BSRIA, Bracknell, Berkshire, UK.

Raouf, A. M. & Al-Ghamdi, S. G. (2019). Effectiveness of project delivery systems in executing green buildings. *Journal of Construction Engineering and Management, 145*(10), 03119005.

Reed, R., Bilos, A., Wilkinson, S., & Schulte, K.-W. (2009). International comparison of sustainable rating tools. *Journal of Sustainable Real Estate, 1*(1), 1–22. https://doi.org/10.1080/10835547.2009.12091787.

Shafique, M., Kim, R., & Rafiq, M. (2018). Green roof benefits, opportunities and challenges — A review. *Renewable and Sustainable Energy Reviews, 90*, 757–773.

The American Institute of Architects. (2007). Integrated project delivery: A guide. Available at: https://zdassets.aiacontracts.org/ctrzdweb02/zdpdfs/ipd_guide.pdf (accessed on 22 September 2022).

The World Bank Group. (2022). Climate and development: An agenda for action — Emerging insights from World Bank Group 2021–2022 country climate and development reports. Available at: http://hdl.handle.net/10986/38220 (accessed on 1 February 2023).

The Office of the Federal Environmental Executive. (2010). The federal commitment to green building: Experiences and expectations. Available at: https://archive.epa.gov/greenbuilding/web/pdf/2010_fed_gb_report.pdf (accessed on 22 September 2022).

Thurimella, A. K. & Padmaja, T. M. (2014). Economic models and value-based approaches for product line architectures. In *Economics-Driven Software Architecture* (pp. 11–36). Morgan Kaufmann, Amsterdam, Netherlands.

UN Environment and International Energy Agency. (2017). Towards a zero-emission, efficient, and resilient buildings and construction sector, Global status report 2017, 48. Available at: https://worldgbc.org/article/global-status-report-2017/ (accessed on 11 March 2024).

UNEP. (2021). 2021 global status report for buildings and construction. UNEP. Available at: http://www.unep.org/resources/report/2021-global-status-report-buildings-and-construction (accessed on 22 September 2022).

UNFCCC. (2021). Nationally determined contributions under the Paris Agreement. Synthesis report by the secretariat. UNFCCC. Available at: https://unfccc.int/documents/306848 (accessed on 22 September 2022).

United States Environmental Protection Agency (2016). Green building | US EPA. Available at: https://archive.epa.gov/greenbuilding/web/html/about.html#1 (accessed on 22 September 2022).

USGBC. (2022a). Mission and vision. USGBC. Available at: https://www.usgbc.org/about/mission-vision (accessed on 20 September 2022).

USGBC (2022b). Press: Benefits of green building. USGBC. Available at: https://www.usgbc.org/press/benefits-of-green-building (accessed on 22 September 2022).

Vaughan, S. (2021). Guest article: A new plan ahead | *SDG Knowledge Hub* | IISD. Available at: https://sdg.iisd.org:443/commentary/guest-articles/a-new-plan-ahead/ (accessed on 21 September 2022).

WorldGBC. (2018). Doing right by planet and people: The business case for health and wellbeing in Green Building. *WorldGBC*.

WorldGBC. (2021). WorldGBC annual report — 2021. World Green Building Council. Available at: https://worldgbc.org/sites/default/files/WorldGBC%202021%20Annual%20Report.pdf (accessed on 11 September 2022).

WorldGBC. (2022a). About green buildings. Available at: https://www.worldgbc.org/about-green-building (accessed on 22 September 2022).

WorldGBC. (2022b). Rating tools. Available at: https://www.worldgbc.org/rating-tools (accessed on 21 May 2022).

WorldGBC. (2022c). Our mission. Available at: https://www.worldgbc.org/our-mission (accessed on 18 January 2022).

WorldGBC. (2022d). Our green building councils. Available at: https://www.worldgbc.org/our-green-building-councils (accessed on 13 January 2022).

WorldGBC. (2023). The business case for green building: A review of the costs and benefits for developers, investors and occupants. Available at: https://worldgbc.org/article/the-business-case-for-green-building-a-review-of-the-costs-and-benefits-for-developers-investors-and-occupants/ (accessed on 16 January 2023).

Xia, B. & Olanipekun, A. O. (2023). Project delivery methods and green building projects: The owner's perspective. In Giovanni and Shrestha (Eds.), *Building a Body of Knowledge in Construction Project Delivery, Procurement and Contracting* (pp. 88–106). World Scientific Publishing, Singapore.

Yang, Z., Chen, H., Mi, L., Li, P., & Qi, K. (2021). Green building technologies adoption process in China: How environmental policies are reshaping the decision-making among alliance-based construction enterprises? *Sustainable Cities and Society*, *73*, 103122.

Yudelson, J. (2010). *The Green Building Revolution*. Island Press, Washington, D.C., USA.

Yudelson, J. & Meyer, U. (2013). *The World's Greenest Buildings: Promise Versus Performance in Sustainable Design*. Routledge, London, UK.

Zhang, L., Xue, L., & Zhou, Y. (2019). How do low-carbon policies promote green diffusion among alliance-based firms in China? An evolutionary-game model of complex networks. *Journal of Cleaner Production*, *210*, 518–529.

© 2025 World Scientific Publishing Company
https://doi.org/10.1142/9789811251429_0004

Chapter 4

Green Construction Project Management Methodologies and Frameworks

Linyan Chen[*], **Amos Darko**[†], **and Albert P. C. Chan**[*]

[*]*The Hong Kong Polytechnic University, Hung Hom, Hong Kong, China*
[†]*University of Washington, Seattle, WA, USA*

Green construction brings new challenges and requirements to project management (PM), making the exploration of PM methodologies and frameworks that are suitable for green construction essential. This chapter provides an overview of green construction PM methodologies and frameworks. First, new challenges faced in green construction projects are described. Second, common PM methodologies and frameworks are introduced. In the end, the PM methodologies and frameworks that are suitable for green construction projects are highlighted. This chapter concludes that lean and agile facilitate better performance of green construction and significantly improve project quality. PM teams are prone to implement hybrid approaches of multiple PM methodologies, which show more advantages than single methodologies. This chapter broadens practitioners', researchers', and students' knowledge of the PM methodologies and frameworks in green construction and enhances their PM capability, leading to delivering more successful projects and achieving a sustainable future in the construction industry.

4.1. Challenges faced in green construction projects

There are several differences between green and conventional construction projects. Sustainable attempts and technologies of green construction projects might affect the cost, schedule, and other aspects of project performance, bringing new challenges to PM. This section summarizes the challenges of green construction PM.

4.1.1. *Cost premiums*

It is well known that the sustainable materials, technologies, systems, and techniques applied in green construction projects can lead to higher initial construction costs than conventional projects. The cost of the sustainable material compressed wheat boards can be as much as 10 times higher than that of conventional plywood (Hwang & Tan, 2012). Highly efficient equipment and systems (e.g., heat pumps and radiant flooring), green construction methods (e.g., modular construction), and green certification also contribute to the higher costs of green construction projects. This issue of higher costs has been a long-lasting barrier to adopting and promoting green construction projects.

Our brief review of a few selected previous independent studies showed that the green construction cost premium can be in the range from 2% to more than 20% (Bond, 2011; Meron & Meir, 2017; Uğur & Leblebici, 2018; Vyas & Jha, 2018; Doan *et al.*, 2021). Although green construction projects have various positive impacts on the environment, society, and economy, it must be noted that not every client is willing to pay the premium. However, a study by Ade and Rehm (2020) showed that clients who have sustainability knowledge and awareness are increasingly willing to pay the cost premium because of the benefits green construction projects provide in better living environment and improved human health. Despite such a positive sign, as Yudelson (2009a) clearly pointed out in his book "*Sustainable Retail Development: New Success Strategies,*" the cost premium is still the single most important, principal issue in green construction projects because benefits are apparent. He states the following:

> It is a truism that costs are real and present-tense, but benefits are speculative and future-tense. This means that a client makes an investment in

green construction features and certification by paying more in initial costs, but with the hope of getting some significant return over time. This is not an unreasonable thing to do, but right now it is an exercise in leadership in the industry to commit to a strong green construction program.

To address this challenge, the project manager should have the ability to identify and select sustainable options that lead to delivering the green construction project within acceptable cost constraints for the client.

4.1.2. *Cost overruns*

Many global construction projects are facing the dilemma of cost overruns and green construction projects are no exception. A 2015 McKinsey & Company report shows that only 31% of construction projects came within 10% of their cost estimates, and most megaprojects were over budget (McKinsey & Company, 2015). The challenge of cost overruns is more alarming in green construction projects, with research indicating that green construction projects experience more cost overruns than conventional construction projects (Hwang *et al.*, 2017).

Factors such as incomplete design documents, adverse weather, project complexity, inaccurate cost estimation, changes within scope, poor PM, insufficient knowledge of green construction, unfamiliarity with green construction methods and equipment, project size, project type, and inflation have been identified to be leading to the cost overruns (Jamaludin *et al.*, 2014; Subramani *et al.*, 2014). Among these factors, inaccurate cost estimation is considered to be the root cause of the cost overruns in green construction projects. This is because although it is true that the other factors pose risks to the project, if such risks are properly identified and factored into the cost estimation, then they could be avoided. If the cost estimation is inaccurate, then cost overruns seem a predetermined result putting the project already on the way to failure from the start. To improve the accuracy of cost estimation in green construction projects, project managers should look at more accurate cost estimation methods, such as reference class forecasting (Flyvbjerg, 2006), building information modeling (Autodesk, 2023), and artificial intelligence and machine learning.[1] The adoption of digital technologies for the cost estimation stands out as particularly significant to improving accuracy. Digital technologies hold the potential to revolutionize the cost estimation process and accuracy. To facilitate their use, it is vital for the industry to share data and information on green construction project costs, and data transparency and authenticity should also be ensured. (See Chapter 18 for more on "Digital Green Construction PM.")

Lisa Fay Matthiessen and her colleagues propose the following "budgeting methodology" for green construction projects (Matthiessen & Morris, 2004):

> The only effective way to budget for sustainable features within buildings is to identify the goals and build an appropriate cost model for them. If they are seen as upgrades or additions, the cost of the elements will also be seen as an addition. It is possible to establish goals and budgets from the very beginning of the project. Other methods are ineffective and unnecessary.

The "appropriate cost model" that is called for in this budgeting methodology is something that digital technologies such as artificial intelligence and machine learning can offer, as highlighted above.

In fact, cost is the most significant issue in green construction projects. The combined risk of cost premiums and cost overruns alone can make the work of the project manager as daunting as possible. This means that the green construction project manager is under greater pressure to avoid both additional costs for going green as well as cost overruns. This combined risk has also been playing a key part in discouraging the adoption of green construction projects. It makes sense for people to avoid any project that comes with a higher initial cost and at the same time overruns the already high costs at completion. It is difficult to justify such an investment from the economic point of view. Therefore, the importance of the role of the project manager in ensuring tight cost controls to avoid cost premiums and overruns has never been so vital.

---

[1] An application of machine learning in green building project cost estimation can be found in Darko *et al.* (2023).

4.1.3. *Schedule delays*

Schedule performance is another crucial aspect of a construction project. Green construction projects can take more time and have a higher risk of delay. This schedule challenge is similar to the cost challenge highlighted in Sections 4.1.1 and 4.1.2, and these two challenges are interrelated because schedule delays can increase costs. When the project is delayed, extra resource inputs in labor, materials, and plant and equipment might need to be deployed, increasing the chances of exceeding the initial cost estimate. Integrated approaches to managing cost and schedule simultaneously in green construction projects are thus strongly recommended.

Studies have shown that the schedule of green construction projects is usually longer than that of conventional construction projects (Hwang *et al.*, 2013; Shrestha & Pushpala, 2012). They have also tried to document green construction project schedule delays and the common causes of such overruns (Hwang *et al.*, 2015). The reasons come from different angles, but again, just as in the case of cost overruns discussed in Section 4.1.2, the root cause of schedule delays is considered to be the inaccurate estimation of the duration required for a green construction project. The recommendations provided in Section 4.1.2 for improving the accuracy of cost estimation apply to schedule estimation as well. In addition, schedule estimation is also covered in the machine learning application case given.

Green design is an integrated process, considering more elements than conventional design. In theory, the construction time of green projects is shorter than conventional projects. However, the reality is the opposite. If stakeholders are not familiar with green construction projects and have no clear list of additional works for the green requirements, they may hold blind optimism on the schedule. Moreover, the integrated design process needs more time to address the green requirements in the design stage, and successful execution cannot live without a good PM capability. More time may be needed for further studies and analyses, charrettes, and meetings during the design stage.

The materials, techniques, technologies, and systems might be more complicated because of their green attributes, which may cause difficulties in management and schedule delays. Therefore, the PM team needs to be familiar with the green characteristics and practice in the execution.

In addition, the time needed to pursue and obtain green certifications should be well considered in the project estimates. It is recommended to spend time on a solid planning and design stage to get the project estimates right before the actual construction starts. The project is headed straight for failure if the cost and schedule estimates to begin with are faulty. But spending time to successfully identify and fix potential cost and time issues preconstruction can go a long way in saving the project significant amounts of money and time later, for example, during the construction stage. So, it is about spending more money and time on planning and design to save money and time later in the project, as good planning and design in place usually means fewer change orders, for instance, later (Yudelson, 2009b). Flyvbjerg and Gardner (2023) stated that "planning is relatively cheap and safe; delivering is expensive and dangerous. Good planning boosts the odds of a quick, effective delivery, keeping the window on risk small and closing it as soon as possible."

4.1.4. *Technical difficulties*

Green construction requires alternative construction materials, techniques, technologies, and systems (Lam *et al.*, 2011). Renewable energy (e.g., solar) and innovative energy models and automatic system controls are encouraged (Singh, 2018). Sustainable wood, bamboo, low-carbon concrete, and recycled and non-toxic materials are some of the alternative construction materials to be considered in green construction. It is best when these materials are locally sourced to avoid or reduce carbon emissions associated with transportation. Alternative construction techniques may include rammed earth, sandbag, cob, timber-framed, compressed earth blocks, sun-dried bricks, thatched roof, and wattle and daub construction. But can they be made modular to unlock and drive further sustainability benefits?

Green technologies can be more complex than conventional ones, and the complexities should be fully addressed in the construction. Otherwise, the overall project performance may be affected by such complexities. For example, installing solar panels on the façade or roof of the building needs sufficient time to consider the material integration (Shi *et al.*, 2013). Difficulties brought by green technologies incorporate several aspects.

Applying green materials and equipment has some uncertainty, which, if not well addressed, can lead to low efficiency in green construction (Shi *et al.*, 2013). Project team members may not be familiar with green technologies, and experienced managers and workers are lacking. Besides, green specifications are essential for green construction (Lam *et al.*, 2010). They provide clear goals and targets and specify energy-efficient equipment for the project. The lack of such specifications hinders green construction technology adoption. In addition, while integrating green technologies into the project, there is a critical need to consider and address the interactions between different components (Hoffman & Henn, 2008). All these issues entail technical challenges that the green construction PM team must face up to.

4.1.5. *More communication between stakeholders*

Good communication between stakeholders is important in green projects (Kim *et al.*, 2017). If all stakeholders have a common goal and stay on the same page through effective and efficient communication, it is likely to achieve a successful project. However, in a construction project, conflicts among stakeholders are commonplace, and green initiatives might exacerbate such conflicts. Small firms with simple and direct communication channels might not be affected by communication issues (Shan *et al.*, 2020). But green construction projects usually comprise a large number of stakeholders ranging from green professionals, such as green design consultants, air quality consultants, life cycle assessment experts, energy and carbon experts, green building assessors, sustainability consultants, waste managers, and environmental consultants, to government departments. Managing communications between such a large number of stakeholders is a critical challenge in green construction projects. Project managers need to maintain good communication and collaboration with both internal and external stakeholders. Communications management among stakeholders ensures that the information flow is smooth and that information sharing is correct and timely (Woo *et al.*, 2016). It helps clarify the responsibilities of stakeholders. Besides, communications management provides the right work procedures for the workers in the frontier, ensuring the smooth progress of the projects and benefiting troubleshooting and effective feedback. Digital technologies such as building information modeling can allow the project manager to optimize communication and collaboration in the green construction project.

4.2. Project management methodologies and frameworks

Section 2.11.2 reviewed several current "generic" PM methodologies and frameworks. Prior to discussing the PM methodologies and frameworks that are specifically suitable for green construction projects in this section, it is imperative to revisit the generic ones. Common standardized PM methodologies and a brief introduction of each are provided in Table 4.1. Customized PM methodologies need to be applied in specific contexts, such as green construction, which is the focus of the following section.

Selecting a suitable PM methodology is a challenge for the project team and the whole company. The PM methodology selected has a significant effect on the business and procurement processes, organizational structure, and most importantly the success of the project (Joslin & Müller, 2015). Project managers are prone to choose the methodology they are familiar with, so the number of options is usually limited. But rather various factors, such as the requirements of the project, reporting system, project team expertise, and risk probability, should be considered in the selection decision-making (Kononenko & Kharazii, 2014). Researchers have proposed three criteria to optimize the selection of PM methodologies when the project team has sufficient knowledge, including the work content of the project, management cost, and the risks associated with adopting the methodology (Kononenko & Kharazii, 2014). This means that correct risk identification and analysis of the PM methodology is essential for the selection process. Both qualitative and quantitative approaches should be well applied.

4.3. Green construction project management methodologies and frameworks

Not all PM methodologies are suitable for green construction projects. For example, extreme programming PM methodology is commonly applied in

Table 4.1. Common PM methodologies.

Code	PM methodologies	Characteristics	Advantages	Disadvantages
1	Waterfall	Linear and sequential; Static	Simple; Organized view; Easy to control each phase	Not flexible; No room for errors
2	Critical path method (CPM)	The most critical tasks are found and lined up to formulate a critical path	Clear project priorities	Time-consuming for deciding a path
3	Critical chain PM (CCPM)	Similar to CPM and focusing on resource availability; Inserting buffers in project scheduling	Easy-to-view workload	Buffers may slow progress
4	Agile	Iterative; People-centric; Breaking down the project cycle into smaller segments	Highly flexible; Faster turnaround time	Difficult to predict resources and measure progress
5	Kanban	Prioritizing and visualizing the project tasks on customizable boards	Clear; Simple; Bird's-eye view of progress	Not suitable for complex projects
6	Scrum	Decomposing work to actionable tasks; Following Agile methodology; Focusing on scrum sprint meetings	Visible individual efforts of team members; Easy to change based on feedback	Lack of a definite deadline; Not suitable for large teams
7	Extreme programming	Agile software; Focusing on the customers' requirements; Iterative processes	Change quickly; Error avoidance	Hard to track updates; Additional work; Customers participant
8	Lean	Eliminating wastes and leaving only the essentials; Tighter budgets and shorter deadlines	Saving money; Higher quality	Low inventory levels could be risky

(Continued)

Table 4.1.   (*Continued*)

Code	PM methodologies	Characteristics	Advantages	Disadvantages
9	Adaptive project framework (APF)	Adapting to changing situations; Breakdown structure to determine goals and evaluate results	Flexible; Suitable for the situation that the team has no idea of the project's purpose	Unsuitable for large-scale projects; Limited control over the projects
10	PRiSM (Projects integrating Sustainable Methods)	Known as green PM; Principles-based; Sustainable; Eco-friendly; Using in large-scale construction projects	Positive social impact; Low energy consumption; Reducing waste	Difficulty in sourcing suppliers; Involvement of all stakeholders in every phase
11	Six sigma	Driven by data; Statistics-based quality improvement process; Aiming to eliminate bugs and defects	Improving the quality of products; Extremely thorough process	Constant upgrades can be costly; Requiring statistical analysis
12	Lean six sigma	Combining the zero-waste approach of Lean with the bug-fixing abilities of Six Sigma	Benefits of two methodologies; Improving overall productivity	Needing many resources; Requiring a cross-functional team

software development projects. It can quickly respond to the frequently changing requirements of customers, delivering software projects successfully. For green construction projects, in order to deliver the project successfully on budget and on time, the frequent change orders associated with the extreme programming PM methodology are not recommended. As suggested in Section 4.1.3, freezing project design and requirements early before the actual construction begins is much better for a green construction project to avoid additional future costs associated with change orders. Therefore, extreme programming PM methodology may not be a good choice for green construction projects. This section discusses PM methodologies and frameworks that are suitable for green construction projects.

4.3.1. *Lean*

Lean thinking is about using fewer resources in the production system for the delivery of the same products to customers (Krafcik, 1988). This is directly related to the idea of using fewer resources in green construction projects to preserve the world's limited resources for future generations. Lean originated from Toyota Production System (TPS) in the 1950s, aiming to produce more and better vehicles with fewer resource inputs (e.g., time, costs, and labor hours) (Womack *et al.*, 2007). The efficient production system is based on just-in-time deliveries, Jidoka technical pillars, flexible workforces, and total quality control (Monden, 2011).

Lean projects differ from conventional projects in many aspects, such as the PM goal, phase structure, and relationship (Ballard & Howell, 2003). Conventional lean thinking cuts waste and improves efficiency and productivity (Womack & Jones, 1997), all of which are critical facets of green construction projects, as highlighted in Chapters 1 and 3. In production systems, waste means activities that do not add value to projects and customers. Therefore, the goal of lean thinking has become finding approaches to adding values to projects and customers. Cruz *et al.* (2020) proposed five core principles of lean PM to achieve this goal, as shown in Figure 4.1.

The first principle is to identify the activities that create values. The activities in PM include the activities that create value and those that do

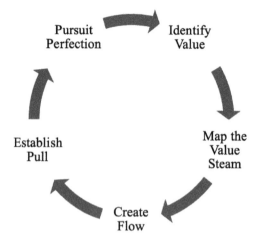

Figure 4.1.   Five principles of lean PM.

not create value. Some of the no-value activities are still necessary because they are critical parts of PM, while some are unnecessary. These are called waste. The primary goal of lean methodology is to eliminate this waste. The second principle is to map the value stream. The value stream shows the value generation process, including all the actions and people involved. It provides an overview of value generation and identifies the waste. The third principle is to create flow. It aims to ensure the smooth workflow of the PM team. Sometimes, projects need cross-functional teamwork, so it is better to break up work and visualize the workflow to check whether bottlenecks and interruptions exist. The fourth principle is to establish a pull system. The pull system optimizes resources and guarantees that the team can pull the work if there is a demand. The last principle is to pursue perfection. PM is dynamic and changes, so the work needs to be improved continuously based on the lean methodology (Cruz *et al.*, 2020).

Not every approach in lean could be applied to construction because construction and manufacturing processes differ (Howell, 1999). Unlike manufacturing products, construction projects are unique and complex. Additionally, the external environment of construction projects is full of uncertainty. Koskela (1992) first discussed the approach to applying the lean methodology in construction activities and conducted a conceptual analysis and synthesis. Combining construction with the lean methodology led to what is known today as "lean construction" (Ballard & Howell, 2003).

The Lean Construction Institute (2022) defines lean construction as a construction project delivery process that applies lean methods or lean thinking to maximize the value of projects and eliminate waste. The Last Planner® System, first proposed by Ballard, is a critical part of lean construction, providing a pull system for the project design (Koskela *et al.*, 2002; Li *et al.*, 2020). Besides, lean construction techniques incorporate Concurrent Engineering, Value Steam Mapping, and Daily Huddle Meetings (Paez *et al.*, 2005). Three essential elements in lean construction are teamwork, creative thinking, and focusing on problems. Lean construction also needs proactive approaches from stakeholders as well as a capable workforce (Ogunbiyi *et al.*, 2014; Paez *et al.*, 2005).

Lean construction and green construction have different ideologies, but they could make joint efforts and contribute to successful, sustainable, and high-performance projects (Maris & Parrish, 2016). Due to the advantages of waste reduction and resource conservation, lean practice is associated with green solutions (Marhani *et al.*, 2013). When lean and sustainability work together in green construction projects, benefits in waste reduction, environment improvement, project values, and people's health and safety are amplified. Besides, lean construction affects green construction from all the three dimensions of environmental, social, and economic (Ogunbiyi *et al.*, 2014). For example, the high-cost premiums of green construction projects could be reduced through the lean methodology. Moreover, lean construction offers more value to the client, increasing the environmental and social values of green construction projects (Pandithawatta *et al.*, 2020). In addition, lean principles help optimize green construction project design, certification, and construction processes (Riley *et al.*, 2005; Sadikoglu *et al.*, 2022). Given these benefits, the concept of a lean-green approach has been proposed to achieve sustainability and deal with waste (Birgün & Kulaklı, 2022).

Pandithawatta *et al.* (2020) proposed an integrated lean-green construction framework. The simplified framework, shown in Figure 4.2, includes six aspects: continuous improvements, cycle time, flexibility, simplicity, variability, and transparency. Many others have also proposed

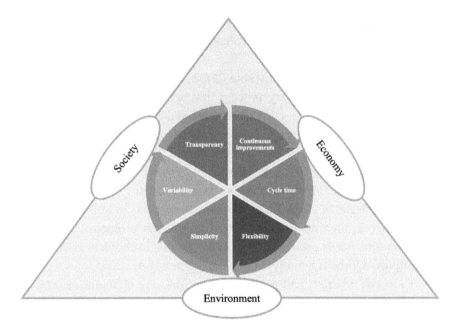

Figure 4.2.   Integrated lean-green construction framework.

similar frameworks to facilitate green construction PM and delivery (Banawi & Bilec, 2014; Moradi & Sormunen, 2022). Combining the lean and green concepts promotes the whole life cycle benefits of green construction projects.

4.3.2. *Agile*

Agile has become popular since 2001 (Schmitt & Hörner, 2021). It accepts and responds to changes quickly rather than following a plan constantly. It is commonly applied in self-organizing, cross-functional teams and similar to extreme programming, it is typically used for software development projects (Abrahamsson *et al.*, 2017; Cohen *et al.*, 2004). Ribeiro and Fernandes (2010) indicated that the agile manifesto declares four values:

- individuals and interactions over processes and tools,
- working software over comprehensive documentation,

- customer collaboration over contract negotiation,
- responding to change over following a plan.

Agile is an umbrella concept that includes many agile methods, such as extreme programming, scrum, Kanban, and adaptive project framework (Cohen *et al.*, 2004). Different agile methods could be combined in one application. For example, scrumban is a combination of scrum and Kanban methods. It divides a project into small sections as scrum and displays a workflow vividly as Kanban (Alavi *et al.*, 2022). In response to fast-changing markets, enterprises utilize agile to adapt business processes to a dynamic environment and unstable external circumstances (Schmitt & Hörner, 2021).

Lean and agile are not synonymous, although some studies mentioned the term "lean" when they introduced agile methodology, and sometimes agile is confused with lean in practice (Owen *et al.*, 2006). Lean tends to use operational techniques to optimize resources, while agile aims to complete projects and deliver products in an unpredictable environment (Sanchez & Nagi, 2001). It is believed that lean requires efficiency in a stable circumstance, and agile requires rapid and effective feedback (Naim & Barlow, 2003). Based on the work of Owen *et al.* (2006), the differences between lean methodology and agile methodology are shown in Table 4.2. Overall, agile methodology seeks the possibility to enhance values and rebuilds orders in chaos, so the status was called "chaordic" (Hock, 1999).

Due to the quick response to changes and flexibility in an agile organization, small and medium enterprises seek the agile methodology to improve their management and enhance their resilience when facing unforeseen shifts in construction activities (Ribeiro & Fernandes, 2010).

Table 4.2. Differences between lean and agile methodologies.

Aspect	Lean	Agile
Origination	• Toyota Production methods • Systems thinking	• Software development • Complexity theory
Characteristics	• Value adding • Waste reduction • Performance management • Pull system	• Emergent value • Rapid feedback • Embedded customer • Multi-disciplinary teams

Research shows that significant uncertainty exists in construction projects even at the beginning of construction (Howell *et al.*, 1993). PM members can capture project requirements and apply agile, taking scope control as an ongoing task (Owen *et al.*, 2006).

The literature has summarized three basic principles of agile PM as flexible and constant planning, iterative development, and self-directed teams (Albuquerque *et al.*, 2020). Agile PM could be utilized in many stages of construction projects, including the predesign, design, and construction stages (Owen *et al.*, 2006). It is easier to implement agile in the design stage because it helps significantly improve construction project values to customers. Agile PM encounters greater resistance in the construction stage, mainly from the subcontractors and employees. Besides, the management mode has path dependency, hindering the application of agile principles. It takes time to constitute multiskilled and self-managing teams and workforces that adapt to agile.

Research shows that agile PM contributes to social sustainability, including realizing diversity, self-organization, learning capacity, and trust (Obradović *et al.*, 2019). The concepts of sustainability and agility are complementary, helping PM teams improve project performance. Meanwhile, an agile green workforce is the prerequisite of an agile organization (Alavi & Mirmohammadsadeghi, 2021).

The agile methods suitable for construction projects have been discussed, and the agile methodology benefits green construction PM from many aspects. Agile could be combined with green construction project rating tools. In a green construction project, the agile principle could be applied in the energy management system to combine the central power generation grids and local community energy generation (Clark II & Eisenberg, 2008). Furthermore, combining agile PM and building information modeling is a wise choice. This combination facilitates an integrated product delivery, improves the construction process, and delivers economic sustainability benefits (Tomek & Kalinichuk, 2015).

4.3.3. *Hybrid*

Construction has significant negative effects on the environment, society, and economy, urgently appealing to sustainable initiatives. Construction activities are highly project-oriented. The increasing market demand and fast-changing external environment require integrated PM methodologies. Many studies combine multiple PM methodologies and investigate the application in practice.

Many previous studies investigated the combination of lean and agile, which solves most of the issues in market competition (Towill & Christopher, 2002). Integrating lean and agile PM enhances successful project delivery and gains the capability to adapt to a dynamic and robust PM environment (Albuquerque *et al.*, 2020). However, case studies show that organizations seldom adopt lean and agile PM together, as social factors (e.g., organizational culture and structures) are highlighted as the main barriers. Moreover, interviews show that the workforce lacks the basic knowledge of lean project development and agile PM, which hinders the combination to some extent.

In addition, researchers hold various opinions on how to combine lean and agile PM. The preference is slightly different. Some opinions support implementing agile in the design stage and switching to lean in the construction stage, namely "leagile" (Naim and Barlow, 2003), while some opinions demonstrate that lean is the foundation and agile brings flexibility to projects, namely "agilean" (Demir *et al.*, 2012).

Similar to manufacturing, construction is a production process, creating values with materials, labor, technologies, and information (Koskela, 1992). Although construction products have unique characteristics compared with manufacturing products, high similarities exist when projects implement offsite construction. Offsite construction means some components are produced in offsite factories and assembled onsite (Russell *et al.*, 2012). Offsite construction alleviates the side effects of construction activities on the environment, reducing the noise, dust, and waste at the construction site. Due to the environmental-friendly feature, offsite construction is considered a part of green construction (Wuni *et al.*, 2020).

Since building components are easy to produce repeatedly in the factory, offsite construction is more common in the building sector. Mostafa *et al.* (2016) proposed a framework to combine lean and agile in offsite construction, showing privileges in waste reduction and quick response to clients' requirements. In the supply chain, lean principles are applied in upstream industries, optimizing production processes of building components in the offsite factory, while agile principles are implemented in downstream industries, contributing to flexible changes in dynamic construction (Mostafa *et al.*, 2016; Purvis *et al.*, 2014).

Some studies explored combination frameworks of other multiple PM methodologies. Lean construction and critical chain PM are integrated to minimize the waste in the schedule (e.g., defects, overproduction, waiting, unnecessary, and motion), eliminating the additional construction time (Ariyanti *et al.*, 2021). Banawi and Bilec (2014) developed a framework that integrated lean, green, and Six Sigma to improve the quality of projects. The specific methods include value stream mapping, life cycle assessment, cause–effect diagram, and Pareto chart, and the process is as follows:

- **Step 1:** Value stream mapping and life cycle assessment are applied to identify the waste and quantify its environmental impacts.
- **Step 2:** If waste exists in the construction process, the Six Sigma tools, such as the cause–effect diagram and Pareto chart, could be applied to eliminate waste.
- **Step 3:** The waste reduction and its environmental impacts are quantitatively analyzed by value stream mapping and life cycle assessment to re-evaluate the effects.

Combining multiple PM methodologies magnifies the advantages of different methodologies, improving the efficiency of green construction PM. The application of integrated methodologies to green construction projects can be summarized as follows. First, integrated methodologies are applied to new construction methods, such as modular and offsite construction. Integrated methodologies could optimize the production process of prefabrication components and integrated modules, and the connections with onsite construction can be strengthened. Since green construction faces new challenges, the second approach is to utilize integrated methodologies to solve complex issues and try to add more value to the construction, achieving the environmental, social, and economic sustainability of green construction projects.

4.4. Summary

This chapter has provided an overview of green construction PM methodologies and frameworks. The chapter had two main objectives highlighting new challenges brought to the PM world by green construction projects and highlighting PM methodologies and frameworks that are suitable for green construction projects. Green construction projects face various challenges, such as cost premiums, schedule delays, cost overruns, technical difficulties, and more communication among stakeholders. The most suitable PM methodologies for green construction projects are lean and agile. While lean reduces waste in green construction projects, agile brings flexibility to the projects. Besides, multiple PM methodologies can be combined for application in green construction projects to achieve joint efforts on project performance improvement. This chapter broadens practitioners', researchers', and students' knowledge of the PM methodologies and frameworks for green construction projects and enhances their PM capability, leading to delivering successful projects and a sustainable future in the construction industry.

References

Abrahamsson, P., Salo, O., Ronkainen, J., & Warsta, J. (2017). Agile software development methods: Review and analysis. *arXiv preprint arXiv*:1709.08439.

Ade, R. & Rehm, M. (2020). The unwritten history of green building rating tools: A personal view from some of the 'founding fathers.' *Building Research and Information, 48*(1), 1–17.

Alavi, S. & Mirmohammadsadeghi, S. (2021). Introducing a green agile workforce. *Journal of Soft Computing and Decision Support Systems, 8*(1), 18–24.

Alavi, S., Zeinalnezhad, M., & Mousavi, E. (2022). Prioritisation of GPM activities from lean-agile-resilience perspective using fuzzy analytic hierarchy process. *Journal of Fuzzy Extension and Applications, 3*(3), 263–278.

Albuquerque, F., Torres, A. S., & Berssaneti, F. T. (2020). Lean product development and agile project management in the construction industry. *Revista de Gestão, 27*(2), 135–151.

Ariyanti, F. D., Putri, A. C., & Ningtyas, D. A. (2021). Implementation of lean construction and critical chain project management (CCPM) for waste management and work estimation on the Ciawi dam construction project. *IOP Conference Series: Earth and Environmental Science* (Vol. 794, No. 1, p. 012074). IOP Publishing.

Autodesk. (2023). Building Information Modeling. Available at: https://www.autodesk.com/solutions/aec/bim (accessed on 17 January 2023).

Ballard, G. & Howell, G. (2003). Lean project management. *Building Research & Information, 31*(2), 119–133.

Banawi, A. & Bilec, M. M. (2014). A framework to improve construction processes: Integrating lean, green and six sigma. *International Journal of Construction Management, 14*(1), 45–55.

Birgün, S. & Kulaklı, A. (2022). Eliminating the barriers of green lean practices with thinking processes. In *Digitizing Production Systems: Selected Papers from ISPR2021, October 07-09, 2021 Online, Turkey* (pp. 372–383). Cham: Springer International Publishing.

Bond, S. (2011). Barriers and drivers to green buildings in Australia and New Zealand. *Journal of Property Investment & Finance, 29*, 494–509.

Charvat, J. (2003). *Project Management Methodologies: Selecting, Implementing, and Supporting Methodologies and Processes for Projects.* Hoboken, NJ: John Wiley & Sons, Inc.

Clark II, W. W. & Eisenberg, L. (2008). Agile sustainable communities: On-site renewable energy generation. *Utilities Policy, 16*(4), 262–274.

Cohen, D., Lindvall, M., & Costa, P. (2004). An introduction to agile methods. *Advances in Computational, 62*(3), 1–66.

Cruz, A., Tereso, A., & Alves, A. C. (2020). Traditional, agile and lean project management — A systematic literature review. *The Journal of Modern Project Management, 8*(2), 86–95.

Darko, A., Glushakova, I., Boateng, E. B., & Chan, A. P. C. (2023). Using machine learning to improve cost and duration prediction accuracy in green building projects. *Journal of Construction Engineering and Management, 149*(8), 04023061.

Demir, S. T., Bryde, D. J., Fearon, D. J., & Ochieng, E. G. (2012). Re-conceptualizing lean in construction environments-'the case for "AgiLean" project management.' In *48th ASC Annual International Conference Proceedings* (pp. 1–9). Birmingham, UK.

Doan, D. T., Wall, H., Hoseini, A. G., Ghaffarianhoseini, A., & Naismith, N. (2021). Green building practice in the New Zealand construction industry: Drivers and limitations. *Green Building, 12*(5), 946–955.

Flyvbjerg, B. (2006). From Nobel prize to project management: Getting risks right. *Project Management Journal, 37*(3), 5–15.

Flyvbjerg, B. & Gardner, D. (2023). *How Big Things Get Done: The Surprising Factors that Determine the Fate of Every Project, from Home Renovations to Space Exploration and Everything in Between.* USA: Penguin Random House.

Hock, D. (1999). *Birth of the Chaordic Age.* San Francisco, CA: Berrett-Koehler Publishers.

Hoffman, A. J. & Henn, R. (2008). Overcoming the social and psychological barriers to green building. *Organization & Environment, 21*(4), 390–419.

Howell, G. A. (1999). What is lean construction-1999. In *Proceedings IGLC* (Vol. 7, p. 1). Berkeley, CA: Citeseer.

Howell, G., Laufer, A., & Ballard, G. (1993). Uncertainty and project objectives. *Project Appraisal, 8*(1), 37–43.

Hu, M. & Skibniewski, M. J. (2021). A review of building construction cost research: Current status, gaps and green buildings. *Green Building & Construction Economics, 2*(1), 1–17.

Hwang, B. G. & Tan, J. S. (2012). Green building project management: Obstacles and solutions for sustainable development. *Sustainable Development, 20*(5), 335–349.

Hwang, B. G., Leong, L. P., & Huh, Y. K. (2013). Sustainable green construction management: Schedule performance and improvement. *Technological and Economic Development of Economy, 19*(sup1), S43–S57.

Hwang, B. G., Zhao, X., & Tan, L. L. G. (2015). Green building projects: Schedule performance, influential factors and solutions. *Engineering Construction and Architectural Management, 22*(3), 327–346.

Hwang, B. G., Zhu, L., Wang, Y., & Cheong, X. (2017). Green building construction projects in Singapore: Cost premiums and cost performance. *Project Management Journal, 48*(4), 67–79.

Jamaludin, S. Z. H. S., Mohammad, M. F., & Ahmad, K. (2014). Enhancing the quality of construction environment by minimizing the cost variance. *Procedia-Social and Behavioral Sciences, 153*, 70–78.

Joslin, R. & Müller, R. (2015). Relationships between a project management methodology and project success in different project governance contexts. *International Journal of Project Management, 33*(6), 1377–1392.

Kim, J. J., Goodwin, C. W., & Kim, S. (2017). Communication turns green construction planning into reality. *Journal of Green Building, 12*(1), 168–186.

Kononenko, I. & Kharazii, A. (2014). The methods of selection of the project management methodology. *International Journal of Computing, 13*(4), 240–247.

Koskela, L. (1992). *Application of the New Production Philosophy to Construction* (Vol. 72). Stanford: Stanford University.

Koskela, L., Howell, G., Ballard, G., & Tommelein, I. (2002). The foundations of lean construction. In R. Best & G. de Valence, G. (Eds.), *Design and Construction* (pp. 211–226). London, UK.

Krafcik, J. F. (1988). Triumph of the lean production system. *Sloan Management Review, 30*(1), 41–52.

Kumara, P. (2017). Applicability of agile project management for construction projects (Doctoral dissertation).

Lam, P. T., Chan, E. H., Chau, C. K., Poon, C. S., & Chun, K. (2011). Environmental management system vs green specifications: How do they complement each other in the construction industry? *Journal of Environmental Management, 92*(3), 788–795.

Lam, P. T. I., Chan, E. H. W., Poon, C. S., Chau, C. K., & Chun, K. P. (2010). Factors affecting the implementation of green specifications in construction. *Journal of Environmental Management, 91*(3), 654–661.

Lean Construction Institute. (2022). What is lean construction? Available at https://leanconstruction.org/lean-topics/lean-construction/ (accessed on 20 September 2022).

Marhani, M. A., Jaapar, A., Bari, N. A. A., & Zawawi, M. (2013). Sustainability through lean construction approach: A literature review. *Procedia-Social and Behavioral Sciences, 101*, 90–99.

Maris, K. & Parrish, K. (2016). The confluence of lean and green construction practices in the commercial buildings market. In *Annual Conference of the International Group for Lean Construction* (Vol. 24), Boston, MA.

Matthiessen, L. F. & Morris, P. (2004). *Costing Green: A Comprehensive Cost Database and Budgeting Methodology*. Davis Langdon.

McKinsey and Company. (2015). Infrastructure productivity: How to save $1 trillion a year. Available at https://www.mckinsey.com/business-functions/operations/our-insights/infrastructure-productivity (accessed on 20 December 2022).

Meron, N. & Meir, I. A. (2017). Building green schools in Israel. Costs, economic benefits and teacher satisfaction. *Energy and Buildings, 154*, 12–18.

Monden, Y. (2011). *Toyota Production System: An Integrated Approach to Just-in-time*. Boca Raton, FL: CRC Press.

Moradi, S. & Sormunen, P. (2022). Lean and sustainable project delivery in building construction: Development of a conceptual framework. *Buildings, 12*(10), 1757.

Mostafa, S., Chileshe, N., & Abdelhamid, T. (2016). Lean and agile integration within offsite construction using discrete event simulation: A systematic literature review. *Construction Innovation*, *16*(4), 483–525.

Naim, M. & Barlow, J. (2003). An innovative supply chain strategy for customized housing. *Construction Management and Economics*, *21*(6), 593–602.

Obradović, V., Todorović, M., & Bushuyev, S. (2019). Sustainability and agility in project management: Contradictory or complementary? In *Advances in Intelligent Systems and Computing III: Selected Papers from the International Conference on Computer Science and Information Technologies, CSIT 2018, September 11–14, Lviv, Ukraine* (pp. 522–532). Lviv, Ukraine: Springer International Publishing.

Ogunbiyi, O., Goulding, J. S., & Oladapo, A. (2014). An empirical study of the impact of lean construction techniques on sustainable construction in the UK. *Construction Innovation*, *14*(1), 88–107.

Owen, R., Koskela, L., Henrich, G., & Codinhoto, R. (2006). Is agile project management applicable to construction? In *Proceedings IGLC-14*, Chile.

Paez, O., Salem, S., Solomon, J., & Genaidy, A. (2005). Moving from lean manufacturing to lean construction: Toward a common sociotechnological framework. *Human Factors and Ergonomics in Manufacturing & Service Industries*, *15*(2), 233–245.

Pandithawatta, T., Zainudeen, N., & Perera, C. (2020). An integrated approach of lean-green construction: Sri Lankan perspective. *Built Environment Project and Asset Management*, *10*(2), 200–214.

Purvis, L., Gosling, J., & Naim, M. M. (2014). The development of a lean, agile and leagile supply network taxonomy based on differing types of flexibility. *International Journal of Production Economics*, *151*, 100–111.

Ribeiro, F. L. & Fernandes, M. T. (2010). Exploring agile methods in construction small and medium enterprises: A case study. *Journal of Enterprise Information Management*, *23*(2), 161–180.

Riley, D., Sanvido, V., Horman, M., McLaughlin, M., & Kerr, D. (2005). Lean and green: The role of design-build mechanical competencies in the design and construction of green buildings. In *Construction Research Congress 2005: Broadening Perspectives* (pp. 1–10). San Diego, CA.

Russell, K., Sittimont, K., Chun, O., & Moe, W. (2012). Procuring OSM: Baseline models of off-site manufacture business processes in Australia. In *Proceedings of the 16th Pacific Association of Quantity Surveyors Congress*. Pacific Association of Quantity Surveyors (PAQS)/Pertubuhan Ukur, Jurutera dan Arkltek, Surveying, Brunei (pp. 1–10), The Empire Hotel, Brunei Darussalam.

Sadikoglu, E., Demirkesen, S., & Zhang, C. (2022). Identifying the commonalities between lean construction and LEED requirements. In *Construction Research Congress 2022* (pp. 269–277). Arlington, VA.

Sanchez, L. M. & Nagi, R. (2001). A review of agile manufacturing systems. *International Journal of Production Research, 39*(16), 3561–3600.

Schmitt, A. & Hörner, S. (2021). Systematic literature review — Improving business processes by implementing agile. *Business Process Management Journal, 27*(3), 868–882.

Shan, M., Liu, W.-Q., Hwang, B.-G., & Lye, J.-M. (2020). Critical success factors for small contractors to conduct green building construction projects in Singapore: Identification and comparison with large contractors. *Environmental Science and Pollution Research International, 27*, 8310–8322.

Shi, Q., Zuo, J., Huang, R., Huang, J., & Pullen, S. (2013). Identifying the critical factors for green construction — An empirical study in China. *Habitat International, 40*, 1–8.

Shrestha, P. P. & Pushpala, N. (2012). Green and non-green school buildings: An empirical comparison of construction cost and schedule. In *Construction Research Congress 2012: Construction Challenges in a Flat World* (pp. 1820–1829), West Lafayette, IN.

Singh, C. S. (2018). Green construction: Analysis on green and sustainable building techniques. *Civil Engineering Research Journal, 4*(3), 555638.

Subramani, T., Sruthi, P., & Kavitha, M. (2014). Causes of cost overrun in construction. *IOSR Journal of Engineering, 4*(6), 1–7.

Tomek, R. & Kalinichuk, S. (2015). Agile PM and BIM: A hybrid scheduling approach for a technological construction project. *Procedia Engineering, 123*, 557–564.

Towill, D. & Christopher, M. (2002). The supply chain strategy conundrum: To be lean or agile or to be lean and agile? *International Journal of Logistics, 5*(3), 299–309.

Uğur, L. O. & Leblebici, N. (2018). An examination of the LEED green building certification system in terms of construction costs. *Renewable and Sustainable Energy Reviews, 81*, 1476–1483.

Vyas, G. S. & Jha, K. N. (2018). What does it cost to convert a non-rated building into a green building? *Sustainable Cities and Society, 36*, 107–115.

Womack, J. P. & Jones, D. T. (1997). Lean thinking — Banish waste and create wealth in your corporation. *Journal of the Operational Research Society, 48*(11), 1148.

Womack, J. P., Jones, D. T., & Roos, D. (2007). *The Machine that Changed the World: The Story of Lean Production-Toyota's Secret Weapon in the Global Car Wars that is Now Revolutionizing World Industry*. Simon and Schuster, New York.

Woo, C., Kim, M. G., Chung, Y., & Rho, J. J. (2016). Suppliers' communication capability and external green integration for green and financial performance in Korean construction industry. *Journal of Cleaner Production, 112,* 483–493.

Wuni, I. Y., Shen, G. Q., & Osei-Kyei, R. (2020). Sustainability of off-site construction: A bibliometric review and visualized analysis of trending topics and themes. *Journal of Green Building, 15*(4), 131–154.

Yudelson, J. (2009a). *Sustainable Retail Development: New Success Strategies*. Springer Science & Business Media.

Yudelson, J. (2009b). *Green Building Through Integrated Design*. New York: The McGraw-Hill Companies, Inc.

Part 2

Managing Green Construction Projects

https://doi.org/10.1142/9789811251429_0005

Chapter 5

The Green Construction Project Manager

**Kofi Agyekum, Eric Obiaw Mireku,
Emmanuel Adinyira, Judith Amudjie,
Victoria Maame Afriyie Kumah,
and Hayford Pittri**

*Kwame Nkrumah University of Science and
Technology, Kumasi, Ghana*

There have been concerns over the state of climate change and the construction industry's impact on the measures put in place to implement climate change initiatives. One of the significant contributions of the construction industry toward improving the environment is the introduction of green construction. Unfortunately, the implementation of green construction projects is plagued with several challenges, including the project management (PM) techniques required to carry out specific tasks. This chapter offers a systematic examination of the issues regarding the green construction project manager and their activities in a green construction project. The chapter begins with a critical examination of the definition of a green construction project manager. It then discusses the key attributes required of an effective green construction project manager. The competencies required of a green construction project manager are also discussed. Following these, the roles and duties of the green construction project manager are elaborated. In addition, the

135

challenges faced by green construction project managers are discussed. These discussions lead the chapter to identify the best practices for developing an effective green construction project manager. This chapter contributes significantly to the emerging green construction PM field by critically examining the green construction project manager. The issues covered can open the debate on the possibility of creating a route or a framework to certify professionals as green construction project managers.

5.1. Introduction

The construction industry is fast changing with challenges, such as shortage in skills, advancement of information and communication technologies, and increase in global prioritization of sustainable development, climate change, and environmental protection, hence the need for adaptation in project managers' role concerning construction project management (PM) (Hwang & Tan, 2012). The sustainability concept has captured global attention and gained significant recognition in the last 10–15 years. As such, many industry players are shifting toward sustainable development and implementing green measures. The construction industry is no exception (Silvius *et al.*, 2012; Hwang & Tan, 2012). Construction players, either researchers or practitioners, have made a significant effort toward achieving sustainable construction and development (Silvius *et al.*, 2012). The drive toward implementing green measures in the construction project life cycle became necessary and critical due to the negative impact of construction activities on the environment. It is said that the construction industry consumes a high amount of energy and other natural resources. This impact significantly affects the environment, society, and the economy (Agyekum *et al.*, 2021). In an attempt by construction players to mitigate the negative environmental impact of construction activities and ensure efficient use of resources, the concept of green building emerged (Retzlaff, 2010).

A "green" building is a building that, in its design, construction, or operation, reduces or eliminates negative impacts and can positively impact our climate and natural environment. Various studies have shown that the construction of green buildings features the critical element of sustainability: the environment, economy, society, and other important factors, such as technology and management (Love *et al.*, 2013). Shen *et al.* (2017) argued strongly that green buildings need a high degree of green technological capability. The introduction of advanced green technology will improve the efficiency of buildings in terms of sustainability. However, different green technologies do not inherently mean that project stakeholders have the required capacity to master and apply them efficiently to realistic projects to achieve better results. To undertake green construction projects to achieve client satisfaction and stakeholder expectations, there is a need for a competent and effective project manager. The project manager's competency has been an important critical success factor for effective and efficient green building delivery and adoption (Shen *et al.*, 2017). A green construction project is a project which seeks to eliminate adverse effects of the construction process on the environment, society, and economy. Such projects not only eliminate the damage but also create buildings that have a positive impact on the environment, society, and economy.

Conventionally, the construction project manager pays significant attention to planning, implementation, management, and control of construction activities surrounding the three primary construction objectives, i.e., time, cost, and quality (Sang *et al.*, 2018). They ensure timely and accurate dissemination of information, develop project team members, and coordinate project participants. The conventional project manager may not rely on these roles alone when managing green projects. This is because delivering green project objectives will require new technologies, ecofriendly materials, reliable simulation analysis, and complex architectural designs, presenting new challenges to the construction PM profession (Sang *et al.*, 2018; Li *et al.*, 2019). Furthermore, project managers may have to deal with a broader spectrum of stakeholders and participants. The scope of communication between project managers, stakeholders, and project participants has to be expanded accordingly. Due to this problem, there is a need to modify conventional PM practices to equip project managers with the necessary knowledge and skills for successful green construction project delivery.

Therefore, this chapter seeks to equip PM practitioners, researchers, and students with a systematic examination of green construction project manager issues and their activities in a green construction project. The chapter comprises six sections (Sections 5.2–5.7) and the introduction. Section 5.2 critically examines the definitions of a green construction project manager. Section 5.3 critically analyzes the key attributes and competencies required of an effective green construction project manager. Section 5.4 discusses the roles and duties of the green construction project manager. Also, the challenges faced by green construction project managers are identified and discussed in Section 5.5. Section 5.6 discusses the best practices for developing an effective green construction project manager. Section 5.7 concludes the chapter.

5.2. Definition of a green construction project manager

Project managers play critical roles in the success of construction projects. Research has shown that they can influence over 40% of project success (Sang *et al.*, 2018). Given that the construction industry remains a human-intensive industry in the face of advancement and development in science and technology, the role of project managers in achieving green construction goals and objectives cannot be overemphasized (Sang *et al.*, 2018). According to the *Project Management Body of Knowledge Guide* (PMBOK Guide, 6th Edition), a project manager is the person assigned by the performing organization to lead the team responsible for achieving the project objectives. While Meredith *et al.* (2017), as cited by Lokman *et al.* (2017), define a project manager as an individual with the duty to ensure the flow of a project from planning, constructing, and getting the approval for each construction project, Sang *et al.* (2018) describe a project manager as an individual responsible for communication and coordination with stakeholders, such as the owner and supervisory agencies. The project manager needs to lead the project team and promote sincere cooperation among members to achieve project objectives. In terms of project objectives, green construction must achieve added goals in contrast to conventional construction, namely energy, land, water, material savings, and environmental friendliness (Hwang *et al.*, 2017). Against this background, a green construction project manager could be defined as "an individual with additional competencies in green construction appointed by the performing organization to lead the team responsible for delivering the sustainable project to meet its conventional and sustainability objectives."

5.3. An effective green construction project manager: Attributes and competencies

PM competencies have been extensively researched in various fields, including human resource management and organizational management. Competency is defined as knowledge, skills, and characteristics that influence individual performance (Parry, 1996). It is also a set of skills and attributes that workers require to do their jobs effectively (Lokman *et al.*, 2017). In the view of Rothwell *et al.* (1999), it is a body of knowledge or skills needed to produce a specific output.

Since a project manager is in charge of overseeing the flow of a project from planning to construction and receiving approval for each development project, they should acquire various skills and knowledge to manage projects effectively. Studies have identified managerial skills such as social skills, decision-making skills, problem-solving skills, and recognizing opportunities and managing changes as key personal attributes influencing project success (Lokman *et al.*, 2017). The project manager competency development (PMCD) framework identifies three domains: knowledge, performance, and personal competencies. The Project Management Institute (PMI) (2008), through the application of the PMCD, identified three thematic areas (technical PM, leadership, and strategic and business management) as critical to PM competence. To achieve the full benefits of PM, project managers should be able to effectively apply PM knowledge areas (technical PM) in achieving desired project outcomes, guide, motivate, direct a team (leadership), as well as enhance organizational performance and business outcome (PMI, 2008).

Dainty *et al.* (2010) created a competency-based performance framework in projects, including information gathering, team leadership, and impact and influence. PMI (2008) has also identified scope management, schedule management, cost management, quality management, integration management, resource management, risk management, stakeholder management, procurement management, and communication management as the 10 essential knowledge areas for effective PM.

Green construction projects are known to contribute to the conventional success criteria of construction projects. In addition to delivering construction projects on time and budget as well as ensuring that quality objectives are achieved, green construction projects must also achieve energy efficiency, favorable environmental quality, sustainable site planning and management, materials and resources efficiency, water efficiency, and innovation (Sang *et al.*, 2018). These objectives present additional challenges and responsibilities to project managers. Since project managers may be confused and unfamiliar with complex construction methods, new designs, and the use and shortage of green materials (Sang *et al.*, 2018), there is a need for their competencies to be developed to handle such projects. The project managers' competency has frequently been identified as an important critical success factor for effective and efficient green construction project delivery and adoption (Shen *et al.*, 2017). This means comprehending the essential attributes and competencies that a project manager should possess to manage green construction projects (Hwang & Ng, 2013). These attributes and competencies are presented in the form of the knowledge areas and skills required by the project managers to manage green construction projects.

5.3.1. *Project management knowledge areas essential for green construction project delivery*

PM applies processes, methods, skills, knowledge, and experience to achieve specific project objectives according to the project acceptance criteria within agreed parameters (Association for Project Management, 2019). To effectively manage projects, project managers must tailor relevant knowledge and skills to achieve project objectives within agreed parameters or expectance criteria (Lokman *et al.*, 2017). According to Hwang and Ng (2013), PM competency is acquired through knowledge acquisition, skill development, and the application of relevant skills and knowledge in achieving project objectives. Researchers and institutions have carried out many studies to determine the relevant and applicable knowledge needed to ensure that project objectives are achieved within an acceptable criterion. As indicated earlier, PMI (2017) has highlighted 10 essential knowledge areas that project managers should possess and apply throughout the PM processes. The 10 knowledge areas include integration management, scope management, schedule management, quality management, risk management, procurement management, cost management, stakeholder management, communication management, and resource management.

Project integration management consists of "processes and activities to identify, define, combine, unify, and coordinate the various processes and PM activities within the PM Process Groups." Within this knowledge area, one can choose resource allocation, balance competing demands, examine any alternative approaches, and manage the interdependencies among the PM knowledge areas. Project scope management involves the "processes required to ensure that the project includes all the work required, and only the work required to complete the project successfully." In this knowledge group, the project manager must be able to define and control what is and is not included in the project. Project schedule management consists of the "processes required to manage the project's timely completion." Within this knowledge area, the project manager must be able to plan schedule management, define the various activities, sequence the actions, estimate activity durations, develop a schedule, and control the developed schedule. The project cost management knowledge area includes the "processes involved in planning, estimating, budgeting, financing, funding, managing, and controlling costs to complete the project within the approved budget." In this knowledge group, the project manager must be able to plan cost management, estimate costs, determine the budget, and control costs.

Project quality management considers the "processes for incorporating the organization's quality policy regarding planning, managing, and controlling project and product quality requirements to meet stakeholders' objectives." In this process group, the project manager seeks to plan quality management, manage quality, and control quality. Project resource management considers the "processes to identify, acquire, and manage the resources needed to complete the project." The project manager must plan resource management, estimate activity resources, acquire resources, develop a team, manage the team, and control the resources. In project communication, the processes necessary to "ensure that the information needs of the project and its stakeholders are met through the development of artefacts and implementation of activities designed to achieve effective information exchange" are considered. The project manager must be able to plan communications management, manage communications, and monitor communications in this knowledge area. The project risk management knowledge area considers "processes of conducting risk management planning, identification, analysis, response planning, response implementation, and monitoring risk on a project." The project manager plays a vital role in this knowledge area by ensuring the proper planning of risk, identifying risks, performing qualitative and quantitative risk analyses, planning risk responses, implementing risk responses, and monitoring risk. Project procurement management looks at the "processes necessary to purchase or acquire products, services, or results needed from outside the project team." The project manager must be able to plan procurement management, conduct procurements, and control procurements. The processes required to "identify the people, groups, or organizations that could impact or be impacted by the project, to analyze stakeholder expectations, and their impacts on the project, and to develop appropriate management strategies for effectively engaging stakeholders in project decisions and execution" fall in project stakeholder management.

To achieve an effective PM program, each of the 10 knowledge areas contains processes that must be completed within its discipline. Project cost management, for example, includes processes such as resource planning, cost estimating, cost budgeting, and cost control that are required to ensure that the project is completed within the approved budget. On the other hand, project risk management is concerned with the process of identifying, analyzing, and responding to project risk. Among the activities are risk identification, risk quantification, and response development.

The construction industry remains a human-intensive industry in the face of advancement and development in science and technology. As the number of green construction projects rises, so the demand for skilled professionals to design, build, manage, and maintain specialized green facilities and services increases. Organization and management of staff are the critical focus of project managers (Sang *et al.*, 2018). In an attempt to develop PM competency for green construction project delivery, many studies have been conducted to determine the essential project knowledge areas critical to green construction project delivery. Hwang and Ng (2013) identified 10 knowledge areas and concluded cost management, communication management, and schedule management as the three most essential knowledge areas for green construction project delivery. The other knowledge areas are health and safety management, risk management, conflict and dispute management, stakeholder management, materials, and resources management, claims management, and human resource management.

The knowledge areas identified by Hwang and Ng (2013) were limited to the PMBOK. To complement the efforts of Hwang and Ng (2013), backed by recommendations of Hwang and Ng (2013), Marcelino-Sadaba *et al.* (2015), Hamid *et al.* (2012), and Lokman *et al.* (2017), through a comprehensive literature review, identified 18 knowledge areas that are relatively new and peculiar to green construction project delivery. Table 5.1 summarizes and provides explanations of these knowledge areas.

Table 5.1. New knowledge areas which green construction project managers must possess.

Knowledge	Description
Green construction materials management	The selection of green construction materials should be aligned with green construction goals and objectives and must improve environmental performance
Sustainable standards	Project managers should know the sustainable/green standards to set sustainable goals/objectives in designing green construction projects
Sustainable goals/ objectives	Project managers should set sustainable goals/objectives as early as the design phase to meet environmental building performance criteria and should be explicit and measurable as well as meeting green construction rating criteria
Sustainable/green designs	Knowledge on designing green construction projects to fulfill environmental criteria such as energy efficiency, water efficiency, and selection of green construction materials

(Continued)

Table 5.1.   (*Continued*)

Knowledge	Description
Green strategies	Knowledge on better building sustainability performance, lower operational cost, protection of the health of building residents, and energy saving for achieving sustainability goals
Green requirement	Knowledge of the requirement to build green is typically found in the specifications of contract documents
Sustainable practices	Project managers should perform sustainable practices during green construction
Familiarity with green products and their market	Project managers should be familiar with green products and their markets to align with sustainability goals
Sustainable procurement	Knowledge on meeting organization needs for goods, achieving value for money for organization, society, and economy while minimizing damage to the environment
Sustainable construction	Project managers should select a proper construction method that will result in quite different outcomes in terms of sustainability
Air quality management	Knowledge of managing air quality in the green construction project
Water efficiency	Knowledge of how to use water efficiently during green construction
Life cycle assessment	Knowledge of life cycle assessment when designing green construction project
Environmental knowledge	Project managers should be able to obtain environmental knowledge and adopt them as early as the design phase of the green construction project
Civil engineering and construction	Knowledge of civil engineering and construction in a sustainable manner to prevent impacts of construction on the environment
Green construction project delivery system	Knowledge of how to deliver green construction projects for sustainability
Site management	Knowledge of impacts of green construction on soil and landfill
Team management	Project managers should select new members by identifying and classifying their abilities and needs and coordinating and delegating tasks based on their competency

Source: Adapted from Lokman *et al.* (2017).

5.3.2. *Project management skills essential for green construction project delivery*

To ensure effective PM, PM professionals must possess a balanced mix of skills, general management expertise, and other competencies (PMI, 2017). Hard PM skills aid in PM efficiency. However, the combined economic and industry volatility effects mean that PM professionals must manage more complex projects and deal with people-related issues and emerging concepts and technology (Zuo *et al.*, 2016). The roles of PM professionals have been expanded beyond technical expertise to include other competencies that will ensure effective alignment of internal and external stakeholders' expectations and management. To achieve shared understanding, PM practitioners must know the significance of resolving people-related issues among various stakeholders (Ruuska & Vartiainen, 2003). PMI (2017) identifies the need for project managers to understand interpersonal skills such as leadership, team building, motivation, communication, influencing, decision-making, political and cultural awareness, negotiation, trust building, and conflict management in their PMBOK Guide. PMI's findings agree with the International Project Management Association (IPMA) (Caupin, 2006), which defines the skills competency to consist of technical, behavioral, contextual competencies, and people factors.

According to Edum-Fotwe and McCaffer (2000), PM professionals must possess specific and general skills. Specific skills refer to knowledge and are directly related to projects. In contrast, general skills, such as leading, communicating, negotiating, and problem-solving, provide a solid foundation for developing PM skills. They further asserted that general skills form a large part of developing PM abilities. They are frequently required for the project manager to work effectively with knowledgeable specialists. Zuo *et al.* (2016) concluded that there is a statistically significant causal relationship between a project manager's soft skills and critical success factors of construction projects, which contributes to the overall success of projects. In their work, conflict management, teamwork, motivational, cognitive, and leadership skills were identified as the top soft skills relevant for construction PM.

To complement the efforts of practitioners, researchers, and industry players, many studies have been carried out to determine essential soft skills that will enhance the application of PM knowledge in achieving successful green construction project delivery. PM professionals will have to tailor the right mix of knowledge and skills to manage the challenges that confront green construction project delivery in a particular region or context.

Teamwork, leadership, communication, decision-making, analytical skills, problem-solving, etc., are the most essential skills for green construction project delivery. In a study conducted by Hwang and Ng (2013), analytical skill was necessary to address planning-related challenges associated with green construction project delivery. In addition, decision-making skills were critical to managing project-related challenges associated with green construction project delivery. In a similar study, Lokman *et al.* (2017) concluded that 21 skills are believed to be essential to green construction project delivery. According to Hwang and Ng (2013) and Senaratne and Hewamanage (2015), the genuine desire to work cooperatively with others rather than separately or competitively is required for persuading the team to perform well; hence teamwork cannot be undermined in achieving green construction project objectives. Senaratne and Hewamanage (2015) opined that the leadership qualities of green construction project managers could not be undermined; project managers should have the ability and skill to inspire and influence team members in achieving green objectives. Table 5.2 provides a summary explanation of skills for green construction project managers.

5.4. The role and duties of the green construction project manager

As a result of the increasing complexity of green projects' criteria, the project manager's role, tasked with the overall management of a building's different development phases, is becoming increasingly crucial for attaining pre-established sustainability goals (Borg *et al.*, 2020). During the implementation of green construction projects, a significant aspect considered is the sustainable design which rests with the architects and

Table 5.2.   Skills required by green construction project managers.

Skill	Description
Teamwork	The genuine intention to work cooperatively with others instead of separately or competitively is a prerequisite for influencing the team to perform desirably
Leadership	Refers to the intention to serve as a leader of a team or other groups. Although it implies a desire to lead others and can be manifested in formal authority and responsibility, effective team leadership also requires the leader to know when *not* to act authoritatively if they are to extract the best out of the team
Communication	Project managers should be able to efficiently communicate with all parties involved in the green construction project to fulfill the sustainability goals
Decision making	Ability to take appropriate actions under limited time, information, and resources or use good judgment to resolve problems
Analytical and holistic thinking	Refers to the need to develop an understanding of a situation or problem by breaking it into components or tracing the causes and implications of a situation systematically
Problem-solving	During the design and construction stages, some unexpected operational and technical problems that can cause pollution may arise. Project managers should generate fast solutions that can significantly improve the environmental performance of building projects
Chairing meeting	This skill is under general skills. The general abilities provide much of the foundation for developing PM skills. They are often essential for the project manager to function effectively with their specialist knowledge
Document and knowledge sharing	Skill in sharing documents and knowledge with all green construction project participants
Continuous learning	This is important since constructing green construction projects introduces many new concepts such as life cycle management and building information modeling that will penetrate the minds of construction practitioners. Therefore, project managers should be able to keep learning new knowledge and update their knowledge structure constantly

(*Continued*)

Table 5.2.   (*Continued*)

Skill	Description
Delegation	Ability to effectively distribute tasks to other members of an organization or assign actual decision-making authority to qualified subordinates
Negotiation	Negotiation skills of the PM are called for (i) scope, cost, and schedule objectives, (ii) changes to scope, cost, or schedule, (iii) contract terms and conditions, (iv) resource availability and utilization
Human behavior	The project manager has to see the general functions associated with the project. These include managing human systems, logistics, information flows, and organizational relationships
Presentation	Project manager should be able to present all information (and related to green construction) understandably to all project participants
Proactive planning and visualization	Project manager should be able to predict and visualize one step ahead in managing the green construction project
Collective implementation	Skill in interdependency, good communication, and client facilitation
Evaluation	Project manager should be able to evaluate all circumstances in green construction project construction
Innovation	Project manager should be innovative since green construction projects require new technologies and use different materials
Onsite practical skill	Information and technology skills, learning skills, and application skills
Personnel quality	It consists of teamwork potential, creativity, ownership, management, delivery of solutions to clients, interpersonal communication skills, and organization skills
Ethics	Ability to analyze both the project results and processes under classic ethic perspectives (virtue, ethics/utilitarianism, deontology/social contract)

Source: Adapted from Lokman *et al.* (2017).

engineers (Borg *et al.*, 2020). However, the various complexities found in such green projects require the input of other professional figures, such as the sustainable or green construction project manager. Hope and Moehhler

(2014) posit that the green construction project manager could be suited to deliver on the promised sustainability of proposed building projects. This means that the green construction project manager must be responsible for the overall management of the different phases of sustainable building.

As a project manager, one must focus on getting from an idea to an implemented project to a steady state (Tharp, 2012). A project manager may not be focused on longer-term issues such as what happens to the product as it is being manufactured, used, and disposed of. On the contrary, a project manager must take a broad view of their role and evolve from "doing things right" to "doing the right things," as advised by Tharp (2012). This means taking responsibility for the project's results, including the sustainability aspects of that result. The developed product or service does not go away once it is handed over (Tharp, 2012). It impacts the world, a reasonable period of operation, and ultimate disposal. Hence, the role of the green construction project manager is critical.

The green construction project manager is expected to be trained in sustainability and sustainable project processes to manage green construction projects. This training is necessary to enable the green construction project manager to deliver sustainable development projects (Marcelino-Sadaba *et al.*, 2015). Once this training is attained, the green construction project manager must adequately perform his/her roles. Borg *et al.* (2020) indicated that the role of the project manager in green construction spans the entire life of a project, i.e., from preconstruction to project decommissioning. In bringing this to the conventional PM, researchers, including Silvius *et al.* (2012), have suggested the possibility of integrating sustainability principles in groups of processes in conventional PM (see Chapter 6). Although possible, the researchers indicated that each process group could have unique sustainability issues that must be considered. According to PMI (2017), the PM process groups are initiating, planning, executing, monitoring, and closing.

For instance, in the initiating and planning groups, sustainability could be considered in the scope and objectives of the project. The executing and monitoring process groups enable the integration of sustainability into creating project results. In the closing process group, the project results are handed over. In this process group, a significant aspect of sustainability is represented. For projects that have their results rejected, they cannot be considered sustainable. This is because, for such projects, there is a tendency to waste resources, materials, and energy; hence, the required performance is not achieved. The researchers also concluded that all sustainability principles could influence the initiating, planning, and execution process groups, not the monitoring and closing process groups. The construction process is typically divided into four essential phases: i.e., preconstruction, construction, operation, and decommissioning (Borg *et al.*, 2020). Some PM outlines separate these phases into five, i.e., project initiation (planning), project planning (preconstruction), project execution (construction), project monitoring and control (performed concurrently within construction), and project closure (close-out). For this chapter which is in line with that discussed in the broader literature, the role of the green construction project manager is discussed under four phases of the construction life cycle as follows: preconstruction (made up of the initiation and planning process groups), construction (made up of the execution and monitoring and control process groups), operation (made up of the monitoring and control process group), and decommissioning (made up of the close-out process group).

5.4.1. *The roles of the green construction project manager in the preconstruction phase of projects*

The green construction project manager has a critical role to play during the preconstruction phase of green construction projects. Within this phase, the need for a project manager is crucial because this phase is the most critical step toward delivering the green project (Zulkiffli & Latiffi, 2019). The green construction project manager must strive hard to integrate the concept of sustainability into their practices at this phase. This means that specific sustainability attributes must be attained.

According to Morgese (2014), the green construction project manager must *set defined and agreed sustainable project objectives with the client.* This is crucial since a misunderstood or poorly defined project scope could result in project inefficiencies (Borg *et al.*, 2020). The green construction project manager must provide the necessary advice to comply with regulations and agreed standards (Maltzman & Shirley, 2010). There are several standards and certification systems in place with specific criteria. The green construction project manager must be able to advise on the particular standard needed for a specific project and must be able to understand and interpret it. Another role that the green construction project manager could perform at this phase is to have and engage with a sustainability-conscious project team and stakeholders (Armenia *et al.*, 2019; Crawford, 2013). There is a need for both the project team and the stakeholders to understand the sustainability issues associated with the project. The green construction project manager must convince the stakeholders about the concept of sustainability and the value of the green project. These engagements tend to curb most of the misunderstandings encountered in the project.

Another important role that the green construction project manager plays is *developing a sustainable business case/investment analysis with life cycle costing* (Agyekum *et al.*, 2020; Kibert, 2013). In the view of Borg (2020), this is necessary to understand the construction and operational costs and the actual economic benefits associated with the project. The green construction project manager must establish and convince investors of the overall trends and benefits of investing in green projects, such as their tenants' attractiveness, cost-effectiveness, increased productivity and worker satisfaction, increased rental rates, and lower operating costs.

Sustainable building design is the practice of creating structures and using environmentally responsible processes and resource efficiency throughout the life cycle of a building. Such designs can reduce operating costs and carbon footprints and increase building resiliency. In ensuring that this is achieved, the green construction project manager could *ensure that the designs are produced to meet the six fundamental principles of sustainable building designs as outlined by the National Institute of Building Sciences*. The design must optimize site potential, maximize energy use, protect and conserve water, optimize building space and materials use, enhance indoor environmental quality, and optimize operational and maintenance practices (Whole Building Design Guide, WBDG, 2021). The green construction project manager must ensure a sustainable project design and briefing/content (Borg, 2020).

The green construction project manager must also *ensure green project sequencing and scheduling* (Morgese, 2014). Scheduling involves listing the activities, deliverables, and milestones within a project. Project sequencing involves evaluating capital projects where the finance manager decides whether or not to invest in a future project based on the outcome of one or more current projects. Similar to any project, sequencing and scheduling are essential in green construction projects. Hence, the need for the green construction project manager to carry out this task.

The green construction project manager must play a key role in *sustainable procurement*. Sustainable procurement involves using procurement strategies and decision-making tools that support broader social, economic, and environmental factors. It involves organizations meeting their needs for goods, services, works, and utilities in a way that achieves value for money on a whole life basis in terms of generating benefits not only for the organization but also for society and the economy while minimizing damage to the environment (Sustainable Procurement Taskforce, 2006). Though procurement officers oversee procurement activities, procurement is the sole responsibility of the entire project team. As a result, the green construction project manager has a role to play in the purchasing process of an organization. In line with that stipulated by PMI, when planning procurement activities, the green construction project manager must be able to evaluate marketplace conditions; products, services, and results that are available in the marketplace; suppliers, including past performance and reputation; typical terms and conditions for products, services, and results for the organizations; and unique local requirements. The green construction project manager must examine the products to be procured on specific dimensions of sustainability, such as resource use, non-renewables inclusion, impact on climate change, impact on ecosystems throughout the product supply chain, and impact on human health. The green construction project manager could work with other professionals to ensure whether supplier evaluations include specific sustainability criteria, whether obligations and requirements regarding sustainability are encoded in contracts, and whether the entire supply chain is transparent in terms of sustainability priorities.

Another critical role played by the green construction project manager at this phase is *ensuring risk management toward sustainability*. Similar to conventional construction projects, various risks are associated with green construction projects, as seen in Chapter 10. However, these risks may not be the same because of the incorporation of new concepts involved in the projects' social, environmental, and economic aspects and the use of new equipment and materials in the construction practices of such projects. Furthermore, managing the conservative behavior of stakeholders involved in such projects and the involvement of certification bodies may all come with their risks. There is a need for the green construction project manager to foresee these potential risks during the project's preconstruction phase and find appropriate ways to manage them before the project commences.

The green construction project manager must also *ensure that the project documents are cross-checked for compliance with agreed standards before the project commences.* This will help to deal with any unforeseen circumstances that may affect the entire project.

5.4.2. *The roles of the green construction project manager in the construction phase of projects*

The project manager is responsible for the success of the entire construction project. This means that in addition to the other phases of the construction project, the roles of the project manager during the construction phase are critical. Similar to the conventional project manager, the green construction project manager also has specific roles to play during the construction phase of a green project to ensure its success. Among the roles are the following:

Organizing a kickoff meeting with stakeholders to transmit sustainable plans (Maltzman & Shirley, 2010; Taylor, 2010; Robichaud & Anantatmula, 2011). The kickoff meeting is the first meeting between the stakeholders (i.e., the project manager, the client, and the team). The green construction project manager uses this meeting to orient the team about sustainable plans to ensure the successful completion of the project. At this meeting, the green project's objectives and the client's requirements are thoroughly discussed to ensure that all the stakeholders are on common ground. Though the green construction project manager may not delve deeper into specific task deadlines at this stage, the high-level green project schedule must be communicated to the stakeholders.

Furthermore, the green construction project manager must ensure that everyone understands what is in and out of the scope of the project. The deliverables expected of the project team must also be well discussed. It is also important that the green construction project manager identifies each subgroup working on specific aspects of the project at this meeting. A brief description of their roles must be spelt out at each construction phase.

Another role of the green construction project manager at this phase is to *provide details on the communication channels, meeting schedules, and the PM technologies he will be using to manage the sustainable project.* According to Robichaud and Anantatmula (2011), a green construction kickoff meeting must include a sustainable education component for onsite construction personnel; monthly onsite meetings are required by the entire site workforce and include periodic education and training sessions on green construction. Sustainability requirements must be reviewed with each subcontractor before commencing work.

Again, at this phase, the green construction project manager *is responsible for project sequencing and scheduling for sustainability* (Taylor, 2010; Morgese, 2014). The green construction project manager must highlight the importance of logistics plans for materials, human resources, procurement, and the schedule of project activities (Borg *et al.*, 2020) and ensure that these are handled in the most sustainable and efficient way possible.

Since the green project will be constructed in line with green standards and certification systems, such as Building Research Establishment Environmental Assessment Method (BREEAM), Leadership in Energy and Environmental Design (LEED), and Excellence in Design and Greater Efficiencies (EDGE), there is a need for the green construction project manager to ensure that all control mechanisms are put in place to ensure full compliance with the requirements. Another vital role is *monitoring and ensuring compliance with regulations agreed standards, or requirements* (Maltzman & Shirley, 2010; Marcelino-Sadaba *et al.*, 2015). Violations of any of the requirements could be associated with legal battles later. A compliance management system could be developed and instituted to prevent these problems from arising during the construction phase. The green construction project manager could double as the project compliance manager and ensure that the company observes legal standards and in-house policies concerning the sustainable project they are undertaking.

The green construction project manager is also *responsible for the risk identification and implementation of sustainability management practices* at this phase (Crawford, 2013; Morgese, 2014; Silvius *et al.*, 2017). Risk management and knowledge management applications are essential critical success factors for green construction projects (Borg *et al.*, 2020). Managing risks in green construction projects is important to achieving the project objectives regarding time, cost, quality, safety, and sustainability. Javed *et al.* (2020) revealed that high initial costs, inexperienced contractors and subcontractors, consideration of life cycle inflation, and experience in green construction PM are significant risks associated with green construction projects. To manage these risks, the green construction project manager must be conversant with specific strategies (e.g., the Project Risk Management framework) to effectively manage risks in green construction projects and keep their organizations competitive within the business environment.

5.4.3. *The roles of the green construction project manager in the operation phase of projects*

The role of the project manager also spans the operation phase of projects. The operation phase of a building includes all impacts during the use of that building, including maintenance, repair, replacement, refurbishment, operational energy use, and operational water use, among others. The green construction project manager has specific roles to perform during the operation phase of a green construction project. The green construction project manager *must coordinate testing and commissioning, project closure, certifications, and compliances* (Robichaud & Anantatmula, 2011). The importance of testing and commissioning, while ensuring building compliance with initial stipulated criteria, is an essential final step in green project processes (Borg *et al.*, 2020). Green construction commissioning is essential in ensuring that the building systems function as intended and outlined in the project criteria (Robichaud & Anantatmula, 2011). The commissioning authority could be hired by the green construction project manager from the onset and must understand the owner's goals and investments. Other equally important roles that the green construction project manager could perform at this phase include *coordinating handover of operations manual and training operators*; *coordinating handover of management, operation, and maintenance plans*; and *obtaining post-occupancy evaluation surveys to learn for future prospects* (Taylor, 2010; Robichaud & Anantatmula, 2011; Silvius & Schipper, 2014; Borg *et al.*, 2020).

5.4.4. *The roles of the green construction project manager in the decommissioning phase of projects*

Decommissioning is shutting down a building and/or removing it from operation or use. Decommissioning will protect a building and its systems, reduce ongoing costs, and reduce hazards and other risks until the future of the building has been determined. The roles of the green construction project manager are numerous in the decommissioning phase of green construction projects. The roles include *coordinating feasibility studies for adaptive reuse rather than demolition* (Elefante, 2012) and *extending the service life of the sustainable building stock* (Borg *et al.*, 2020). Before an existing stock is demolished, it must be thoroughly examined. This examination could potentially lead to ascertaining the building's sustainable value, which can possibly be optimized through adaptive reuse (Borg *et al.*, 2020). The green construction project manager must be able to *coordinate sustainable decommissioning plans*. During the decommissioning phase, the green construction project manager *monitors the building for compliance with regulations, agreed standards, or requirements* (Maltzman & Shirley, 2010; Marcelino-Sadaba *et al.*, 2015). Another important role of the green construction project manager at this phase is to *coordinate and implement a site waste management policy plan per context* (Elefante, 2012). *Risks identification and management toward sustainability* could also be carried out by the green construction project manager (Borg *et al.*, 2020).

5.5. Challenges faced by green construction project managers

Green construction project managers face several challenges. These challenges may include but are not limited to planning-related issues, client-related issues, external issues, project-related issues, material and equipment-related issues, project team-related issues, and labor-related issues. The critical challenges as reported in the literature are expounded in the following sections.

5.5.1. *Planning-related challenges*

As indicated by Hwang and Ng (2013), most of the challenges that project managers face when executing green construction projects are related to planning. The planning stage is expected to ensure that team members introduce sustainability principles to improve the result by ensuring that all building systems work cooperatively in the most sustainable manner (Glavinich, 2008). Unfortunately, this is not the case as serious problems are encountered during this stage. The most commonly observed planning challenges that green construction project managers encounter are the longer time required for the preconstruction process, difficulty comprehending green specifications, and a lengthy approval process for new technologies, according to Hwang and Ng (2013). Other planning-related challenges reported in the literature include the adoption of different contract forms of project delivery, design, structure, and orientation of the building, planning of different construction sequences and techniques, the lengthy approval process for new green technologies within the organization, and difficulty in comprehending the green specifications in the contract details (Ozumba *et al.*, 2020). It is worthy to note that the effort put in during the project's detailed design, construction, and rest phase is critical to success. The green construction project manager must be well equipped with green construction skills and techniques to control these planning-related issues.

5.5.2. *Project-related challenges*

The project-related challenges are those challenges associated with carrying out the project. These challenges are prevalent during the actual execution of the project. These challenges have been identified to include difficulty in approving payment disbursement to suppliers and subcontractors, difficulty in assessing the progress of completion in green construction projects, difficulty in the selection of subcontractors in providing green construction services, greater amount of time needed to implement green construction practices on site, and extensive alteration and variation with the design during the construction process (Ozumba *et al.*, 2020).

5.5.3. *Client-related challenges*

Having a clear and detailed understanding of the client's green objective is key to the success of any green construction project. In their study, Hwang and Ng (2013) emphasized the need for project managers to understand clients' green objectives, most importantly, when focusing on achieving green certification. Key among the client-related challenges faced by green construction project managers are specific budget specifications of the green project, the objective of the building project, the required date of completion, the level of risks borne by the client on the application of green technologies, the extensive time needed by the client to make specific decisions, and special requests from clients regarding specified green technologies to be used (Ozumba *et al.*, 2020). These challenges pose a serious threat to completing the project on schedule.

5.5.4. *Project team-related challenges*

The busy schedule of the green construction project manager's daily activities means that problems are often ignored with the hope of disappearing. Unfortunately, this is not the case because when the problems compound, they eventually expound and normally have dire consequences on the project's success. The green construction project manager normally faces project team-related challenges in the form of conflict with the architect over the type of material to use, lack of communication among project team members, frequent meetings with green specialists, green consultant delay in providing information, conflict of interest between consultant and project manager, specific performance required for green construction projects, material and equipment-related challenge, and high cost of green material and equipment, among others (Ozumba *et al.*, 2020). As a green construction project manager, one must balance the elements of a complex project time, money, scope, and people. There is a need for them to be able to balance their busy schedules with attending to issues that can potentially affect the project. Green construction project managers can only achieve this by effectively developing their PM skills. One can evaluate their skills and work to improve the areas lacking. Through training programs and continuous professional education, green construction project managers can learn best practices that can help them overcome such project team-related challenges.

5.6. Developing effective green construction project managers

To be a great project manager, one must be fully vested in organizational success as a strategic business partner. That person must be able to roll with inevitable setbacks. With various uncertainties such as the COVID-19 pandemic, managing projects has become more complex. There is a need for project managers to fully develop themselves to become highly effective in managing projects in such uncertain circumstances.

An effective project manager has the required competencies and skills to lead and manage projects and teams. The green construction project manager is the one who has the necessary knowledge and ability reserve (competence and skill) to allow them to deliver the project as efficiently as possible. Faced with challenges associated with a complicated construction process involved in green construction, the professional competencies of the green construction project manager must be developed to enable them to effectively deliver projects. Despite the advent of science and technology, construction is still human-intensive. This makes most project managers focus their attention on the organization and management of their staff (Sang *et al.*, 2018). With their different working backgrounds and cultural knowledge, there is a need to standardize the competencies of project managers. There could be standardized ways of selecting project managers for particular projects. Some of these standardizations could be introduced as part of the move to develop effective green construction project managers for the construction industry.

Selecting an effective project manager has always been a hot issue in the engineering sector (Sang *et al.*, 2018). Notwithstanding, if one can define who an effective project manager is, most of the challenges associated with their selection could be dealt with. For this chapter, an effective green construction project manager is defined as "one whose ability and knowledge reserve (competence and skill) can enable them to deliver the project as efficiently as possible." This definition implies that an effective green construction project manager is one whose competencies have been fully developed. Several PM competency areas have been proposed. Green construction project managers must establish four competency areas to manage green construction projects: leadership and organization, basic literacy, target management, and emotional intelligence.

5.6.1. *Effectively developing their leadership and organizational abilities*

Effective leaders develop new leadership skills to complement those that made them successful as managers (Kumar, 2009). Leadership skills are not the same as management skills. This is because solid management skills can be gained through experience and practice; however, leadership skills can be learned, and leadership skills can be developed (Kumar, 2009). This implies that green construction project managers can learn to improve their leadership abilities to become effective leaders in their field. Hwang and Ng (2013) reported leadership to be one of the essential skills of green construction project managers. Other researchers, including Sang *et al.* (2018), identified the attributes associated with leadership and organizational competency to include cooperation, engaging in communication, teamwork, and conflict management. As a green construction project manager, one must make a conscious effort to improve their leadership skills. In enhancing their leadership skills, they must learn new ways of cooperating with others, communicating, improving teamwork on the project, and conflict management. Developing these attributes could enable green construction project managers to develop different ways of understanding the team members because of their diversified nature, learn different ways of giving contexts to project goals, learn and improve on ways to obtain feedback from team members, and learn how to trust team members and learn to lead by example. In addition to these, Kumar (2009) suggests that any project manager's most essential leadership skills must start with motivating and inspiring teams and individuals. This is important in the case of green construction project managers, especially considering the unique and complex nature of green construction projects.

5.6.2. *Effectively developing their basic literacy*

Sang *et al.* (2018) summarize the attributes of this competency to include professional knowledge, information seeking and management, and learning. This implies that the green construction project manager must have professional expertise in the PM skills and techniques needed to deliver the green construction project. Where necessary, the green construction project manager must be able to seek and manage the required information needed to deliver the project. Again, the green construction project manager must learn new and emerging trends required in such an area. The essential knowledge areas in which green construction project managers are required to be able to manage green construction projects include green construction material management, sustainable standards, goals and objectives, sustainable/green design, green strategies, green requirements and practices, and green procurement, among others (Lokman *et al.*, 2017). These knowledge areas must be fully developed to enable the green construction project manager to carry out the project to meet its objectives. The green construction project manager must constantly seek information on new ways to plan, monitor, and control project delivery and support processes while considering the project's life cycle's environmental, economic, and social aspects. The green construction project manager could learn appropriate ways to better manage the project to benefit the stakeholders from the knowledge gained.

5.6.3. *Effectively developing ways to improve target management skills*

The PMBOK Guide divides the target management into three, i.e., project time, cost, and quality. Dulewicz and Higgs (2005) indicated that resource management is a crucial PM competency. According to Sang *et al.* (2018), critical attributes in the target management criteria are resource management, financial management, risk management, and health and safety management. This implies that the green construction project manager must be conversant with these attributes and develop ways to improve them effectively. In green construction projects, resource management involves using all resources (i.e., humans, plants, and materials) to manage the project efficiently. Efficient resource management in green projects will reduce overall operating costs, improve productivity and profitability, and enhance the competitiveness of the project (Aghili *et al.*, 2016). Green construction project managers must develop effective resource management plans to manage the resources wisely. A new trend in managing resources is the introduction of digital tools (i.e., acquiring and making use of the right resource management software), a subject tackled in Chapter 18. Conflicts, risks, and health and safety issues highly impact the cost of green construction projects. The green construction project manager must develop ways (this could be context-specific) to deal with conflicts and risks that may arise in the project's life cycle. The green construction project manager could seek training on some conflict resolution strategies. In addition to this, being abreast with some current tips for handling health and safety issues in green construction projects could help save lives and money. Chapter 13 deals with health and safety management in green construction projects.

5.6.4. *Effectively developing their emotional intelligence skills*

Emotional intelligence is a key competency that every project manager must possess. Boyatzis (2009) believes that competencies are behavioral manifestations of emotional intelligence. In the construction project network, emotional intelligence could trigger events that affect the mood of employees (Tang *et al.*, 2020). Green construction project managers must develop their emotional intelligence skills to ensure that the project is completed without hitches. The critical attributes of emotional intelligence include interpersonal skills, emotional control ability, and understanding and adapting to local culture (Sang *et al.*, 2018). The green construction project manager must develop their interpersonal skills, improve their emotional control ability, and understand and adapt to local cultures. To develop their interpersonal skills, the green construction project manager must develop new and alternative ways to enable them to pay attention to the management of team members. Finding ways to develop a strong relationship with key members of the project irrespective of their demographic backgrounds could help improve their interpersonal skills. Among the ways is that the green construction project manager must be able to perceive the feelings and thoughts of their employees, making room to listen to the thoughts and ideas of employees, among others. As a core factor that influences how leaders manage daily work (Jordan & Lindebaum, 2015), green construction project managers must be able to develop their emotional control abilities. It is a crucial function to analyze emotions if they occur (Gareis, 2004). This will enable the project manager to plan and carry out strategies and activities to deal with them. Emotions can be managed throughout the project's life, i.e., from start to finish. The green construction project manager must be able to develop mechanisms that can manage emotions in the project start process, controlling process, during the resolution of crises, and in the project close-down process. Table 5.3 summarizes competencies which green construction project managers must develop and how they can develop them effectively.

Table 5.3.   Summary of competencies which green construction project managers must develop.

Competency	How to effectively develop it
Leadership and organization	As a green construction project manager, one must make a conscious effort to improve their leadership skills. In enhancing their leadership skills, they must learn new ways of co-operating with others, communicating, improving teamwork on the project, and conflict management. Developing these attributes could enable green construction project managers to develop different ways of understanding the team members because of their diversified nature; learn different ways of giving contexts to project goals; learn and improve on ways to obtain feedback from team members; learn how to trust team members, and learn to lead by example

(Continued)

Table 5.3.   (*Continued*)

Competency	How to effectively develop it
Basic literacy	The green construction project manager must develop their knowledge in green construction material management, sustainable standards, goals and objectives, sustainable/green design, green strategies, green requirements and practices, green procurement, etc. The green construction project manager must constantly seek information on new ways to plan, monitor, and control project delivery and support processes whiles considering the environmental, economic, and social aspects of the life cycle of the project
Target management	Critical attributes of target management are resource management, financial management, risk management, and health and safety management. Green construction project managers must develop effective resource management plans to manage the resources wisely A new trend in managing the resources is the introduction of digital tools (i.e., acquiring and making use of the right resource management software) The green construction project manager must develop ways (this could be context-specific) to deal with conflicts and risks that may arise in the project's life. The green construction project manager could seek training on some conflict resolution strategies In addition to this, being abreast with some current tips for handling health and safety issues in green construction projects could help save lives and money
Emotional intelligence	Critical attributes of emotional intelligence include interpersonal skills, emotional control ability, and understanding and adapting to local culture To develop their interpersonal skills, the green construction project manager must develop new and alternative ways (e.g., perceive the feelings and thoughts of their employees, making room to listen to the thoughts and ideas of employees) that can enable them to pay attention to the management of the team members Emotions can be managed throughout the project's life, i.e., from start to finish. It is a crucial function to analyze emotions if they occur. This will enable the project manager to plan and carry out strategies and activities to deal with them. The green construction project manager must be able to develop mechanisms that can manage emotions in the project start process, controlling process, during the resolution of crises, and in the project close-down process

5.7. Summary

The need to achieve sustainability in all facets of life is well acknowledged. Sustainability has become widespread in policy-oriented research as a target that public policies must achieve. Therefore, sustainability must be included as part of a strategy that balances social development, economic growth, and environmental development. Similar to other industries, the construction industry is gradually shifting from conventional practices toward more sustainable practices. This is seen in the many related sustainability research and activities currently receiving massive attention. Of late, the demand for green or sustainable projects has increased. Technically, green construction can be complex because it involves using multidisciplinary designers and engineers with green expertise and multicultural project teams at several levels. In addition to their conventional roles (i.e., time, cost, and quality), project managers must seek to drive the green agenda. The increasing demand for green construction, coupled with heightened perceptions of the risks associated with going green, means that project managers will be responsible for managing tighter budgets with tighter profit margins on green projects. The possible complicated nature of green construction projects may make it difficult for conventional project managers to manage.

The rising demand for green projects puts pressure on project managers to seek knowledge in this field to play a leading role in green construction projects. Notwithstanding, if the project manager is well equipped with knowledge regarding green construction projects, this challenge could be overcome. This chapter explores and discusses the green construction project manager who must be well equipped to lead and manage such projects. The chapter offers PM practitioners, researchers, and students a systematic examination of the issues regarding the green construction project manager and their activities in a green construction project. It critically examined the definition of a green construction project manager and its roles in green construction projects. It further identified and critically analyzed the competencies and attributes required of a green construction project manager to lead and manage green construction projects. The challenges faced by green construction project managers were also identified and discussed. The chapter discussed some best practices for developing an effective green construction project manager to manage and lead such projects effectively.

References

Aghili, N., Mohammed, A. H. B., & Sheau-Ting, L. (2016). Key practice for green building management in Malaysia. *MATEC Web of Conferences, 66,* 00040. The Fourth International Building Control Conference, 2016, Kuala Lumpur, Malaysia, 7–8 March 2016.

Agyekum, K., Botchway, S. Y., Adinyira, E., & Opoku, A. (2021). Environmental performance sustainability indicators for assessing sustainability of projects in the Ghanaian construction industry, *Smart and Sustainable Built Environment.* DOI: 10.1108/sasbe-11-2020-0161.

Agyekum, K., Opoku, A., Oppon, J. A., & Opoku, D.-G. J. (2010). Obstacles to green building project financing: An empirical study in Ghana. *International Journal of Construction Management.* DOI: 10.1080/15623599.2020. 1832182.

Armenia, S., Dangelico, R. M., Nonino, F., & Pompei, A. (2019). Sustainable project management: A conceptualization-oriented review and a framework proposal for future studies. *Sustainability, 11,* 2664.

Association for Project Management. (2019). What is project management? Available at: https://www.apm.org.uk/resources/what-is-project-management/#:~:text=Definition,a%20finite%20timescale%20and%20budget (accessed on 15 April 2022).

Borg, R., Gonzi, R. D., & Borg, S. P. (2020). Building sustainably: A pilot study on the Project Manager's contribution in delivering sustainable construction projects — A Maltese and international perspective. *Sustainability, 12*(20200), 10162.

Caupin, G.-M. (2006). ICB: IPMA competence baseline, Version 3.0. International Project Management Association, Zurich, Switzerland, pp. 1–199.

Crawford, L. (2013). Leading sustainability through projects. In A. J. G. Silvius & J. Tharp (Eds.), *Sustainability Integration for Effective Project Management* (pp. 235–244). Hershey, PA, USA: IGI Global Publishing.

Dainty, A. R. J., Cheng, M. I., & Moore, D. R. (2010). A competency-based performance model for construction project managers. *Construction Management and Economics, 22,* 877–886.

Dulewicz, V. & Higgs, M. (2005). Assessing leadership styles and organizational context. *Journal of Management in Psychology, 20,* 105–123.

Edum-Fotwe, F. T. & McCaffer, R. (2000). Developing project management competency: Perspectives from the construction industry. *International Journal of Project Management, 18*(2), 111–124.

Elefante, C. (2012). The greenest building is one that is already built. *Forum Journal, 27*, 62–72.

Gareis, R. (2004). Emotional project management. In *Paper Presented at PMI® Research Conference: Innovations, London, England.* Newtown Square, PA: Project Management Institute.

Glavinich, T. E. (2008). Contractor's guide to green building construction. In *Management, Project Delivery, Documentation, and Risk Reduction.* John Wiley & Sons, Inc., Hoboken, New Jersey, USA, p. 1–255.

Hamid, Z. A., Ali, M. C., Kamar, K. A. M., Zain, M. Z. M., Ghani, M. K., Rahim, A. H. A., & Kilau, N. M. (2012). Towards a sustainable and green construction in Malaysia, *Malaysian Construction Research Journal, 11*(2), 55–64.

Hope, A. J. & Moehler, R. (2014). Balancing projects with society and environment: A project, programme and portfolio approach. *Procedia Social and Behavioural Science, 119*, 358–367.

Hwang, B. G. & Tan, J. S. (2012). Green building project management: Obstacles and solutions for sustainable development. *Sustainable Development, 20*(5), 335–349.

Hwang, B. G., Shan, M., & Supa'at, N. N. B. (2017). Green commercial building projects in Singapore: Critical risk factors and mitigation measures. *Sustainable Cities and Society, 30*, 237–247.

Hwang, B.-G. & Ng, W. J. (2013). Project management knowledge and skills for green construction: Overcoming challenges. *International Journal of Project Management, 31*(2), 272–284.

Javed, N., Thaheem, M. J., Bakhtawar, B., Nasir, A. R., Khan, K. I. A., & Gabriel, H. F. (2020). Managing risk in green building projects: Toward a dedicated framework. *Smart and Sustainable Built Environment, 9*(2), 156–173

Jordan, P. J. & Lindebaum, D. (2015). A model of within person variation in leadership: Emotional regulation and scripts as predictors of situationally appropriate leadership. *Leadership Quarterly, 26*, 594–605.

Kibert, C. J. (2013). *Sustainable Construction: Green Building Design and Delivery.* Hoboken, NJ, USA: Wiley.

Kumar, V. S. (2009). Essential leadership skills for project managers. In *Paper presented at PMI® Global Congress 2009 — North America, Orlando, FL.* Newtown Square, PA: Project Management Institute.

Li, Y., Song, H., Sang, P., Chen, P. H., & Liu, X. (2019). Review of critical success factors (CSFs) for green building projects. *Building and Environment, 158*, 182–191.

Lokman, M. A. A., Abdullah, M. N., Asmoni, M., & Shaari, N. (2017). Exploring competencies for green building project manager. *Internal Journal of Real Estate Studies*, *11*(3), 13–30.

Love, P., Niedzweicki, M., Bullen, P., & Edwards, D. (2013). Achieving the green building council of Australia's world leadership rating in an office building in Perth. *Journal of Construction Engineering and Management*, *138*, 651–660.

Maltzman, R. & Shirley, D. (2010). *Green Project Management* (1st edn.). Boca Rat on, FL, USA: CRC Press.

Marcelino, Sadaba, S., Gonzalez-Jaen, L. F., & Perez-Ezcurdia, A. (2015). Using project management as a way to sustainability. From a comprehensive review to a framework definition, *Journal of Cleaner Production*, *99*, 1–16.

Meredith, J. R., Shafer, S. M., & Mantel, S. J. (2017). *Project Management: A Strategic Managerial Approach* (10 edn.) (pp. 1–544). John Wiley & Sons, Hoboken, New Jersey, USA.

Morgese, P. (2014). *Handbook for sustainable projects. Global Sustainability and Project Management.* Lexington, MA, USA: CreateSpace Independent Publishing Platform.

Ozumba, A., Chothia, T., Booi, Z., & Madonsela, N. (2020). Sustainability in project management practice. *MATEC WEB of Conferences*, *312*, 02015.

Parry, S. B. (1996). The quest for competencies. *Training*, *33*(7), 48–54, 56.

PMI. (2008). *A Guide to the Project Management Body of Knowledge.* PMBOK® Guide, Newtown Square, Pennsylvania, USA.

Project Management Institute. (2017). A guide to the project management body of knowledge. Available at: https://www.pmi.org/pmbok-guide-standards/foundational/PMBOK (accessed on 20 March 2022).

Retzlaff, R. (2010). Developing policies for green buildings: What can the United States learn from the Netherlands? *Sustainability: Science, Practice and Policy*, *6*(1), 28–38.

Robichaud, L. B. & Anantatmula, V. S. (2011). Greening project management practices for sustainable construction. *Journal of Management in Engineering*, *27*, 48–57.

Rothwell, W. J., Sanders, E. S., & Soper, J. G. (1999). *ASTD Models for Workplace Learning and Performance: Roles, Competencies, and Outputs.* American Society for Training and Development.

Ruuska, I. & Vartiainen, I. (2003). Critical project competences — A case study. *Journal of Workplace Learning*, *15*(7/8), 307–312.

Sang, P., Liu, J., Zhang, L., Zheng, L., Yao, H., & Wang, Y. (2018). Effects of project manger competency on green construction performance: The Chinese context, *Sustainability*, *10*(10), 3406.

Senaratne, S. & Hewamanage, P. R. (2015). The role of team leadership in achieving LEED certification in a green building project. *Built Environment Project and Asset Management*, *5*(2), 170–183.

Shen, L., Zhang, Z., & Long, Z. (2017). Significant barriers to green procurement in real estate development. *Resources, Conservation and Recycling*, *116*, 160–168.

Silvius, A. J. G. & Schipper, R. (2014). Sustainability in project management: A literature review and impact analysis. *Social Business*, *4*, 63–96.

Silvius, A. J. G., Kampinga, M., Paniagua, S., & Mooi, H. (2017). Considering sustainability in project management decision making. An investigation using Q-methodology, *International Journal of Project Management*, *35*, 1133–1150.

Silvius, M. G., van den Brink, M. J., Schipper, M. R., Planko, M. J., & Köhler, M. A. (2012). *Sustainability in Project Management*. Taylor and Francis, London, UK.

Sustainable Procurement Taskforce. (2006). Procuring for the future. Available at: https://assets.publishing.service.gov.uk/government/uploads/system/uploads/attachment_data/file/69417/pb11710-procuring-the-future-060607.pdf (accessed on 22 January 2022).

Tang, H., Wang, G., Zheng, J., Luo, L., & Wu, G. (2020). *How Does the Emotional Intelligence of Project Managers Affect Employees' Innovative Behaviour and Job Performance? The Moderating Role of Social Network Structure Hole*. Sage Open, New York, USA.

Taylor, T. (2010). *Sustainability Interventions for Managers of Projects and Programmes*. London, UK: Dashdot Enterprises Ltd.

Tharp, J. (2012). Project management and global sustainability. In *Paper Presented at PMI® Global Congress 2012 — EMEA, Marsailles, France*. Newtown Square, PA: Project Management Institute.

Whole Building Design Guide, WBDG, (2021). Sustainable. Available at: https://www.wbdg.org/design-objectives/sustainable (accessed on 18 January 2022).

Zulkiffli, N. A. & Latiffi, A. A. (2019). Review on project manager's leadership skills in the pre-construction phase of sustainable construction projects. *MATEC Web of Conferences*, *266*, 01011.

Zuo, J., Zhao, X., Nguyen, Q. B. M., Ma, T., & Gao, S. (2018). Soft skills of construction project management professionals and project success factors: A structural equation model. *Engineering, Construction and Architectural Management*, *25*(3), 425–442.

https://doi.org/10.1142/9789811251429_0006

Chapter 6

Considering Sustainability in Construction Project Management

Gilbert Silvius[*,†] and Ron Schipper[‡]

*[*]HU University of Applied Sciences Utrecht,
Utrecht, The Netherlands*

*[†]University of Johannesburg,
Johannesburg, South Africa*

*[‡]Municipality of Waddinxveen,
The Netherlands*

Sustainability is one of the most important challenges of our time. How can prosperity be developed without compromising the lives of future generations? These sustainability concerns are also critical in the construction industry, as buildings and construction projects are significant resource sinks and consumers of energy. The industry therefore needs to take meaningful action in order to reduce its negative impact on climate and society. Given the central role of projects in the construction industry, the concepts of sustainability have more recently also been linked to project management (PM). From the emerging sustainability school of PM, two types of relationships between sustainability and PM appeared: the sustainability of the deliverable that the project realizes and the sustainability of the process of delivering and managing the project. Based on the available literature, this chapter identifies the areas of impact of sustainability on PM with a focus on the management of construction projects, such as recognition of context, stakeholders, project objectives and specifications, risk management, dimensions of project success, and project team. The chapter also includes examples and instruments for the integration of sustainability into PM. The chapter concludes that the project manager has a pivotal role in the sustainability of her project and that sustainable PM involves managing a project's social, environmental, and economic impacts by an approach that considers uncertainty, flexibility, complexity, and opportunity.

6.1. Introduction

Concerns about the balance between economic growth, social well-being, and the use of natural resources emerged as early as the 18th century (for example, Von Carlowitz, 1713; Malthus, 1798). However, it took until the second half of the 20th century before the concerns about sustainability and sustainable development became broadly recognized as a political, societal, and managerial challenge (Dyllick & Hockerts, 2002). The 1972 report *The Limits to Growth* (Meadows *et al.*, 1972) predicts that the exponential growth of world population and world economy will result in depleting Earth's natural resources and in damaging Earth's atmosphere.

Buildings are seen as significant resource sinks (Borg *et al.*, 2020). Energy consumption in buildings accounts for around 40% of the total energy consumption in Europe (Vella *et al.*, 2020), and the building industry also uses significant resources, from construction to eventual demolition of buildings. "Green" or "sustainable" construction is therefore one of the most prominent developments in the construction industry. A significant responsibility for the realization of sustainable buildings rests on architects and engineers who design these buildings. However, project managers also play a role in sustainable construction, as project managers are typically tasked with overseeing the detailed design and construction of specific aspects of buildings (Borg *et al.*, 2020).

This relationship between sustainability and project management (PM) is being addressed in a growing number of studies and publications

(Silvius & Schipper, 2014; Aarseth *et al.*, 2017; Sabini *et al.*, 2019). From the emerging literature on the integration of sustainability and PM, two types of relationships between sustainability and PM appeared (Silvius & Schipper, 2015; Kivilä *et al.*, 2017): the sustainability of the project's "product," the deliverable that the project realizes, and the sustainability of the "process" of delivering and managing the project. The first relationship, which we labeled a "sustainable project," is well studied and addressed, for example, in relationship to ecodesign and for the construction of "green" buildings. The second relationship, "sustainable PM," is less established, and one of the most important global PM trends today (Alvarez-Dionisi *et al.*, 2016; Gemünden, 2016). Silvius (2017) concludes that sustainability should be considered a new "school of thought" in PM.

It is this integration of the concepts of sustainability into construction PM that this chapter addresses. The remainder of the chapter is organized as follows. In the following paragraph, the concepts of sustainability are discussed, after which in the following paragraph these concepts are related to projects and the impact of sustainability on PM is analyzed. In the final paragraphs of the chapter, the available instruments and tools for the integration of sustainability into construction PM and their application are discussed.

6.2. Sustainability and responsibility

In order to be able to consider sustainability in PM, this paragraph discusses the main concepts of sustainability and societal responsibility.

The earlier mentioned *Limits to Growth* report fueled a public debate, leading to the installation of the UN "World Commission on Development and Environment," named the Brundtland Commission after its chair. In their report, the Brundtland Commission defines sustainable development as "development that meets the needs of the present without compromising the ability of future generations to meet their own needs" (World Commission on Environment and Development, 1987). By stating that "in its broadest sense, sustainable development strategy aims at promoting harmony among human beings and between humanity and nature," the report implies that sustainability requires also a social and an environmental perspective, next to the economic perspective, on development and performance. The vision that societal goals, such as economic growth, social well-being, and a wise use of natural resources, are interrelated and either one of these goals cannot be realized without considering and affecting the other two got widely accepted (Keating, 1993). In his book *Cannibals with Forks: the Triple Bottom Line of 21st Century Business*, John Elkington identifies this as the "Triple Bottom Line" (TBL) or "Triple-P (People, Planet, Profit)" concept: sustainability is about the balance or harmony between economic sustainability, social sustainability, and environmental sustainability (Elkington, 1997).

6.2.1. *Triple bottom line*

The TBL evolved into a set of perspectives for assessing, reporting, or communicating the impact of human actions on nature and society, forming the foundation of many sets or frameworks of sustainable development indicators that aim to measure, communicate, or evaluate an organization's societal impact or performance (Bell & Morse, 2003). However, this operationalization also introduces the risk that the interrelations between the three perspectives are overlooked and that the social, environmental, and economic perspectives are each considered in isolation. A holistic understanding of the integration of economic, environmental, and social perspectives is therefore considered one of the key concepts of sustainability (Linnenluecke *et al.*, 2009).

6.2.2. *Life cycle orientation*

Dyllick and Hockerts (2002) conclude that sustainability is about consuming the income and not the capital. In other words, organizations should not "consume" their capacity to produce and create value in the future. From an economic perspective, this concept is a generally accepted accounting principle that states that in the calculation of profit, the capital in the organization should be preserved. And where in accounting this principle created the nominalism versus substantialism debate, considering the principle from a social or environmental perspective supports the substantialism view. Sustainability implies that "the natural capital remains intact. This means that the source and sink functions of the environment should not be degraded. Therefore, the extraction of renewable resources should not exceed the rate at which they are renewed, and the absorptive capacity of the environment to assimilate waste, should not be exceeded" (Gilbert *et al.*, 1996).

However, the fact that the impacts of human actions and behavior may not be visible in the short term provides a challenge. In order not to compromise "the ability of future generations to meet their needs," as stated in the Brundtland definition, sustainability requires a balance between both short and long terms. This balance leads to the concept of life cycle orientation.

One strategy to realize an equilibrium between resource extraction and resource renewal is logically decreasing the levels of production and consumption until the extraction rate reaches the equilibrium level. However, with the projected increase in world population and our "linear economy" value chains, this strategy severely limits the quality of life and is not considered a viable option (Sukhdev, 2013). Another strategy to prevent the depletion of natural resources is that of the "circular economy": a concept that aims to realize resource minimization and the adoption of cleaner technologies by promoting the benefits of recycling residual waste materials and byproducts. In the circular economy, raw materials and resources are processed from used products, thereby minimizing waste and the need for extraction of "virgin" resources. McDonough and Braungart (2002) elaborate on the concept of the circular economy in their "cradle2cradle" concept with the principle that "waste equals food," suggesting continuous cycles of production and consumption, without waste.

The concept of circularity highlights the "systems change" that development toward sustainability (sustainable development) needs. In this systems change, sustainable development is a shared responsibility between authorities, companies, and consumers, which can only be realized in cooperation. In the 1990s, the concept of sustainable development therefore also got applied to businesses and organizations, thereby creating a link between sustainable development and (Corporate) Social Responsibility (CSR) (Ebner & Baumgartner, 2006).

6.2.3. *Stakeholder orientation*

(C)SR is defined by the International Organization for Standardization (ISO) 26000 as the "responsibility of an organization for the impacts of its decisions and activities on society and the environment, through transparent and ethical behavior that: contributes to sustainable development, including health and the welfare of society; takes into account the expectations of stakeholders; is in compliance with applicable law and consistent with international norms of behavior; is integrated throughout the organization and practiced in its relationships" (International Organization for Standardization, 2010). In this definition, the earlier discussed concepts of TBL and life cycle orientation can be recognized. Next to these concepts, the definition also mentions the expectations of stakeholders. In the so-called "stakeholder theory," Freeman (2007) developed the notion that all stakeholders of a company or an organization, and not just the shareholders/financiers, have the right and legitimacy to receive adequate management attention that considers their interests (Julian *et al.*, 2008). The interests of all stakeholders should be embraced by the organization and win-win situations should be sought (Eskerod & Huemann, 2013). An orientation on stakeholder's interests is therefore an inevitable concept of an organization's role in, and responsibility for, sustainable development.

6.2.4. *Responsibility, accountability, and transparency*

The ISO 26000 definition of (C)SR also highlights the responsibility and accountability that an organization has for the societal impact of its decisions and actions, and the transparency and ethicality of its behavior. This ethical dimension is an inseparable aspect of CSR (Dahlsrud, 2008; Carroll, 1991) and introduces a normative, values-based, element. Sustainability is a value-based concept, reflecting values and ethical considerations of society (Robinson, 2004; Martens, 2006). And its integration into business decisions and actions should go beyond being compliant with legal obligations. Carroll (1991) illustrated this in his seminal "Pyramid of CSR" model (Figure 6.1), by positioning the ethical responsibility of an organization separately from its legal responsibility. Dahlsrud (2008) therefore points out the voluntariness dimension of CSR.

Figure 6.1.   The pyramid of CSR.

Carroll's pyramid model includes a philanthropic dimension. However, its position in the model expresses that philanthropy by organizations is seen as being less important than the other three components of CSR (Kakabadse *et al.*, 2005).

The concepts and sources discussed in this paragraph elaborated on the meaning and contents of sustainability, as we apply this in this chapter.

6.3. Projects and sustainability

6.3.1. *Projects as instruments of change*

The Project Management Institute, the most influential professional organization of project managers, defines a project as "a temporary endeavor undertaken to create a unique product, service, or result" (Project Management Institute, 2021). This definition emphasizes the temporary aspects of a project and its output-oriented nature. In the so-called task perspective on projects, projects are seen as temporary efforts to carry out given tasks (Andersen, 2008). The project is ideally performed detached from its organizational environment so that the project team can fully concentrate on carrying out the task. The environment should therefore not interfere with the execution of the project, and PM is focused on the planning and control processes within the project.

However, there is more to projects than just the intended output. In what is recognized as the organizational perspective, projects are considered from a more contextual perspective. In this perspective, a project is "a temporary organization, established by its base organization to carry out an assignment on its behalf" (Andersen, 2008). In an organizational perspective, the main purpose of a project is value creation in or for the base organization. And as value creation comes with changes in that organization, close cooperation between the base organization and the project is essential to the success of the project. PM is therefore focused on the relationships between the project and the base organization.

Andersen (2008) did not imply a hierarchy between the two perspectives. No single perspective is best, and the way people perceive reality depends on their position, experience, knowledge, context, etc. Anderson went on to state that "it should not be very surprising that project managers with a technical background, working on building or construction projects with a strictly defined set of requirements, see the world differently from managers with a social science background, working on organizational change projects where the purpose is to improve working relations between employees." However, from a sustainability perspective, the two perspectives are not equally preferable. Sustainable development in essence is "a process of change," according to the World Commission on Development and Environment (1987). Combining the change perspective on projects and the requirement of change that sustainability entails, Marcelino-Sádaba *et al.* (2015) observe that "projects are the ideal instrument for change." This view refers more to the change orientation that can be found in the organizational perspective on projects than to the task perspective.

The sustainability "school of thought" in PM adopts a societal perspective on projects and considers projects as instruments to realize societal change (Silvius, 2017). A recent study into the "projectification" of three Western European countries showed that projects account for roughly one-third of economic activity (Schoper *et al.*, 2018), which justifies this societal perspective. However, the role of projects in society is not limited to economic value. The sustainability school elaborates on this societal role by considering also the social and environmental impact of projects. Silvius and Schipper (2014) point to the recognition of this societal context of projects as the starting point for considering sustainability in PM.

6.3.2. *Sustainable project management*

As projects are defined by their temporary nature, the relationship between sustainability and PM bears some challenges. Marcelino-Sádaba *et al.* (2015) observe a "lack of integration of sustainability and PM," where "organizations, nowadays are increasingly keen to include sustainability in their business. PM can help make this process a success, but little guidance is available on how to apply sustainability to specific projects" (Marcelino-Sádaba *et al.*, 2015).

As was mentioned already, the relationship between sustainability and PM can be interpreted in two ways (Huemann & Silvius, 2017): "sustainability of the project and sustainability by the project." In one of the first publications on sustainability and PM, Labuschagne and Brent (2005) link these two interpretations by elaborating on the earlier discussed concept of life cycle orientation. In the context of projects, a life cycle orientation logically implies that the full life cycle of a project, from its conception to its disposal, should be considered. However, Labuschagne and Brent argue that when considering sustainability in PM, not just the total life cycle of the project (for example, initiation–development–execution–testing–launch) should be taken into account but also that of the "output" the project produces, being a change in products, assets, systems, processes, or behavior. This result, in their words: the "asset," should also be considered over its full life cycle, being something like design–develop–manufacture–operate–decommission–disposal. As Labuschagne and Brent were applying life cycle orientation in the manufacturing industry, this asset has a productive phase ("operate"), in which it generates value by producing products or services. Elaborating on the life cycle view even further, Labuschagne and Brent conclude that the life cycles of these products or services that the asset produces should also be considered.

Following this reasoning, Silvius and Schipper (2024) define sustainable PM as "the planning, monitoring, and controlling of project delivery and support processes, with consideration of the environmental, economic, and social aspects of the life cycle of the project's resources, processes, deliverables, and effects, aimed at realizing benefits for stakeholders, and performed in a transparent, fair, and ethical way that includes proactive stakeholder participation." Next to the interaction between life cycles that Labuschagne and Brent pointed out, this definition includes the four concepts of sustainability and responsibility that were discussed earlier in this chapter.

Sustainable PM implies a scope shift in PM (Silvius *et al.*, 2012): from managing time, budget, and quality, to managing social, environmental, and economic impact (Haugan, 2012).

6.4. Considering sustainability in project management

The concepts of sustainability identified earlier have an impact on the way projects are executed and managed. Sabini *et al.* (2019) conclude that the impact of "sustainability" on PM tools, techniques, and methodologies is one of the main topics in sustainable PM literature. For example, Maltzman and Shirley (2010), Silvius *et al.* (2012), and Tharp (2013) specify the impact of sustainability on PM in "impact areas," such as the identification of relevant stakeholders, the recognition of benefits in the business case, the assessment of risks, etc. And in our structured analysis of 164 selected publications on sustainability in PM,[1] we describe 14 "areas of impact" of sustainability. This paragraph discusses the consideration of sustainability in PM, and the impact on PM practices that results from this. As a framework to analyze and describe this impact, we have chosen the "Management practices for a project" (International Organization for Standardization, 2020) as defined in the ISO21502 standard. These practices describe "the individual PM practices that should be considered throughout a project" (International Organization for Standardization, 2020).

A starting point for our analysis is the understanding that the consideration of sustainability starts with the recognition of the context of the project. Integrating the dimensions of sustainability in PM inevitably implies a broader consideration of this context (Silvius *et al.*, 2012;

---

[1] Silvius and Schipper (2014).

Tharp, 2013). Both the time and the spatial boundaries of the context are stretched when considering sustainability.

6.4.1. *Planning*

According to ISO, "the purpose of planning is to define the requirements, deliverables, outputs, outcomes, and constraints, and to determine how the project's objectives should be achieved." Integrating sustainability into PM suggests that the content, intended output/outcome, and quality criteria of the project are based on a holistic view (Gareis *et al.*, 2013), including the TBL perspectives economic, environmental, and social, and developed together with a broad group of stakeholders (Eskerod & Huemann, 2013). Considering sustainability will therefore influence the specifications and requirements of the project's deliverables or output, and the criteria for the quality of the project (Eid, 2009; Maltzman & Shirley, 2010; Taylor, 2010), for example, the inclusion of environmental or social aspects in the project's objective and intended output and outcome (Silvius *et al.*, 2012).

Next to these content-related aspects of the project, the consideration of the earlier discussed concepts of sustainability and responsibility may also influence the approach to planning. Sabini and Silvius (2022) argue that the integration of sustainability increases the complexity of the project and that therefore a more dynamic approach to PM, one that also embeds a non-deterministic perspective on PM, is required. In other words, PM should address the variability in project phenomena and employ appropriate theoretical and methodological approaches (Padalkar & Gopinath, 2016). For project planning, this implies an increased focus on the goal and the value of the project, instead of the deliverables and objectives (Sabini & Silvius, 2022), and so a more outcome than output-oriented approach to project planning. It is expected that an adaptive approach to project planning, based on agile principles, is more suitable for this, than a predictive approach.

6.4.2. *Cost and benefit management*

ISO states that "the purpose of cost management is to establish the financial controls to be used throughout the project life cycle to facilitate delivery of the project within the approved budget," while "the purpose of benefit management is to assist the sponsoring organization and the customer in realizing the desired benefits of a project from the project's outcomes, as described in the project's business case or other similar documentation." In line with the reference to Sabini and Silvius (2022) above, the planned or aspired benefits, which represent the goal and thereby the justification of the project, should get adequate attention. These benefits will also need to reflect the concepts of sustainability discussed earlier (Silvius *et al.*, 2012). The identification of benefits, and also costs, will need to be expanded to include also non-financial factors that refer to, for example, social or environmental aspects (Weninger & Huemann, 2013).

Next to the content of identified benefits and costs, the consideration of sustainability also influences the process of valuing these in a business case that provides a justification for the project. Silvius (2015) suggests that a financial Return on Investment calculation by definition does not comply with the concepts of sustainability, especially the TBL concept of economic, social, and environmental benefits. He therefore concludes that considering sustainability in the business case of a project needs a multi-criteria approach to investment evaluation, with consideration of both financial and non-financial criteria (Silvius, 2015).

6.4.3. *Scope management*

ISO states that "the purpose of scope management is to facilitate the creation of the deliverables, outputs, and outcomes to achieve the stated objectives of the sponsoring organization or customer. Scope management enables only formally approved work to be incorporated into the project. The scope should be an integrated part of the project's plan." Scope management may apply to a project's goals, benefits, objectives, deliverables, and/or activities (Doloi, 2014). The earlier mentioned broader contextual consideration resulting from the concepts of sustainability stretches the scope of consideration in PM (Silvius *et al.*, 2012; Tharp, 2013). Silvius *et al.* (2017) illustrate the recognition of the broader context of "Sustainable PM," compared to "Traditional PM" or "Modern PM/Management of Projects," as in Figure 6.2.

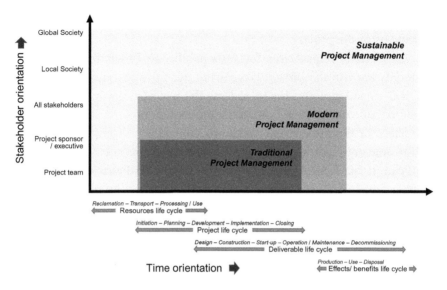

Figure 6.2.   The broadened scope of sustainable PM.

The broadened contextual orientation builds upon the interacting life cycles as proposed by Labuschagne and Brent (2005) and combines this concept with a wider stakeholder orientation, which includes a reference to the (local and global) society. This broadened scope of consideration that sustainable PM implies still requires scope management, as "scope creep" may still lead to an unmanageable project. However, scope management should include a collective sensemaking about the goal and intended outcome of the project (Sabini & Silvius, 2022) and be limited to "guarding" the scope of work as laid down in the project plan.

6.4.4. *Resources management*

According to ISO, "the purpose of resources management is to determine the resources needed to deliver the scope of the project in terms of quality, quantity, and optimum usage. Resources should be an integrated part of the project's plan. Resources can include people, facilities, equipment, materials, infrastructure, and tools. Resources management should involve planning, managing, and controlling resources to determine the resource quality, quantity, and necessary optimization needed for achieving the objectives of the project."

An obvious impact area for sustainability in PM is the selection of materials used in the project (Akadiri *et al.*, 2013; Silvius *et al.*, 2012). Logical considerations should address the use of hazardous substances, pollution, and energy use, both in the production process as well as in the use phase of the project and remaining life cycle. An important sustainability concept regarding the materials used in the project is therefore the application of a life cycle perspective (Brent & Petrick, 2007). This implies considering not only the materials' price/quality relationship and sustainability impact for use in the project's deliverable but also the impact of their production supply chain and aspects such as reusability and recyclability at the decommission stage of the project's deliverable.

Another area of impact of sustainability is the project organization and management of the project team. Social considerations, such as equal opportunity, non-discrimination, and personal development, can be put to practice in the management of the project team (Silvius & Schipper, 2014). Also, aspects such as commuting distance, digital/hybrid working opportunities, and work–life balance may be considered in the organization and management of the team.

6.4.5. *Schedule management*

Schedule management includes "sequencing activities, estimating activity durations, and developing and controlling the schedule, as committed to by the team undertaking or impacted by the work. Activities should be logically sequenced to support the development of a realistic, achievable, and controllable schedule. Activities within the project should be described with dependencies in order to determine the critical path or to identify alternative approaches," according to ISO. Taylor (2010) recognizes the opportunities for considering sustainability in project planning, scheduling, and sequencing. He challenges project managers to think beyond "how things are normally done" and provides several examples. One of the examples is offsite fabrication rather than onsite. Modular versus stick-built construction. This provides possible sustainability advantages of less waste, reduced delivery costs, better use of resources, opportunities to increase labor skills, opportunities for job creation in poorer locations, economies of mass production, etc. A study by Dallasega and Rauch (2017) confirmed positive economic, environmental, and social benefits from an optimized onsite/offsite project work design.

Sustainable PM also implies performing the project as efficiently as possible, with minimal idle resources or waiting times (Maltzman & Shirley, 2010). Schedule management should therefore balance optimizing the schedule with a more detailed planning with building in buffers and flexibility in order to be able to absorb the inevitable deviations from the plan.

6.4.6. *Risk management*

ISO states that "the purpose of risk management is to increase the likelihood of achieving the project's objectives. Identified risks and options for addressing each risk should be an integrated part of the project's plan." A risk is defined as an uncertain event or a set of events that, should it occur, will have an effect on the achievement of objectives (Office of the Government Commerce, 2010). However, when looking at this definition from a sustainability perspective, some questions may come up (Silvius, 2016). For example, "Are we, next to the economic risks, considering also environmental risks, impacts, and effects? Are we considering also social risks, impacts, and effects? Are we considering long-term risks, impacts, and effects? Are we considering risks related with the disposal phase? Are we considering risks also in our "sphere of influence"? Are we considering risks, impacts, and effects also for other/all stakeholders? Are the/all stakeholders also involved in the risk management process? Is the risk management process transparent and performed in an ethical way?" (Silvius, 2016).

With the inclusion of the concepts of sustainability in PM, the assessment of potential risks will need to evolve (Winnall, 2013). The questions above logically lead to a broader identification of risks related to the project's resources, processes, deliverables, and effects (Silvius *et al.*, 2012). The UN Global Compact principles prescribe that organizations should take a precautionary approach to environmental and social challenges (Silvius, 2016). This precautionary principle is based on the understanding that in environment-society system interactions, the complexity, indeterminacy, irreversibility, and nonlinearity have reached a level at which it is more efficient to prevent damage rather than ameliorate it (De Bakker *et al.*, 2010). The Deepwater Horizon oil spill disaster of 2010 may be an illustration that the economically oriented project risk management methods and techniques are less suitable for the management of societal and environmental risks.

6.4.7. *Issues management*

In the view of ISO, "the purpose of issue management is to resolve issues such that there is no negative impact on the achievement of the project's objectives." The broader consideration of a project's context and content, that the concepts of sustainability suggest, also leads to an elaborated recognition of issues in the project. First of all, the TBL concept suggests that social and environmental issues are also recognized, but second, the concept of life cycle orientation suggests that issues are identified based not only on their impact on the project's objectives/outputs but also on their impact on the project's goals/outcomes. So, both on the width of the content, as on the depth of the orientation, the issues management process in PM is affected and needs to evolve.

6.4.8. *Change control*

According to ISO, "the purpose of change control is to control changes to the project and deliverables and to formalize acceptance or rejection of these changes." From a sustainability perspective, changes in the project bear the risk of creating waste: waste in the form of work that has been performed, but through the change turns out to be unnecessary, or in the form of additional planning and management efforts that the change requires. Preventing waste, however, does not imply that changes to the project should never be accepted. Changes during the project are often required in order to adapt the project's output to changes in the environment or new insights. Reluctance to change may therefore also lead to waste in the form of necessary rework in later stages, or loss of value from the use of the project's deliverable.

Changes are a reality in dynamic project environments and should therefore be "absorbed" by the project organization, instead of "handled." As was already indicated at the PM practice planning, the integration of sustainability requires a more dynamic approach to PM, in which the variability of project phenomena is standard, and appropriate methods and approaches are deployed (Padalkar & Gopinath, 2016). An adaptive approach to project planning, in which changes in requirements and priorities are considered the norm and are therefore not leading to alterations of the project's plan or schedule, is suggested to be more fitting the increased dynamics and complexity of sustainable PM (Silvius *et al.*, 2012).

6.4.9. *Quality management*

ISO indicates that "the purpose of quality management is to increase the likelihood that outputs are fit for purpose or use." The life cycle orientation of sustainability implies that the usability of a project's deliverables and outputs is an important criterion for assessing the success of the project (Pade *et al.*, 2008; Craddock, 2013). Usability and the expected benefits of this use should therefore also be considered in the quality management of the project, which means that quality and acceptance criteria for the project's outputs should be goal-oriented and not necessarily deliverable-oriented. These criteria should also reflect the life cycle approach and the TBL concept and include economic, environmental, and social aspects of the outputs and outcomes of the project.

6.4.10. *Stakeholder management*

ISO indicates that "the purpose of stakeholder engagement is to enable the needs, interests, and concerns of stakeholders to be identified, understood, and addressed sufficiently to enable the objectives to be met. Project stakeholders should be identified, analyzed, documented, and engaged throughout the project." In the publications about sustainability in PM, the topic of stakeholder management is frequently addressed (for example, by Eskerod and Huemann (2013), Bal *et al.* (2013), and Labelle and Leyrie (2013)). Integrating a sustainability perspective in PM implies a more holistic view of project stakeholder management (Huemann *et al.*, 2016) and suggests a more open and proactive engagement of stakeholders (Silvius & Schipper, 2014). "Specifically, it calls for different values. Values like transparency and fairness constitute a management for stakeholder approach" (Huemann *et al.*, 2016). Labelle and Leyrie (2013) suggest a change in terminology from stakeholder management to "stakepartner" management to express this change in PM philosophy and practice.

The concepts of sustainability increase the number of stakeholders to be identified in the project (Tharp, 2013; Eskerod & Huemann, 2013) and bring new perspectives to the project (AlWaer *et al.*, 2008). Typical "sustainability stakeholders" may be environmental protection pressure groups, human rights groups, non-governmental organizations, etc. (Silvius *et al.*, 2012). Several authors (for example, Pade *et al.*, 2008; Perrini & Tencati, 2006) emphasize the importance of stakeholder participation in projects. This principle logically impacts stakeholder management and the communication processes in PM (Silvius & Schipper, 2014). However, the intention behind "participation" goes beyond the process of stakeholder management and communication. Stakeholder participation isn't so much a specific process, as it is an attitude with which all PM processes are performed (Silvius & Schipper, 2014). According to the ISO 26000 guideline, proactive stakeholder engagement is one of the basic principles of sustainability (International Organization for Standardization, 2010). Stakeholder participation requires "a process of dialogue and ultimately consensus-building of all stakeholders as partners who together define the problems, design possible solutions, collaborate to implement them, and monitor and evaluate the outcome" (Goedknegt & Silvius, 2012). Also, Eskerod and Huemann (2013) link sustainable development, projects, and the role of stakeholders and conclude that there is a need "to incorporating stakeholders and their interests in more PM activities."

6.4.11. *Communication management*

ISO indicates that "the purpose of communication management is to enable stakeholder interactions that are effective and likely to contribute to the successful delivery of the project's outcomes and the successful realization of benefits." Following the concept of responsibility, account-ability, and transparency, considering sustainability in PM would imply proactive and open communication about the project (Silvius & Schipper, 2014), which would also cover social and environmental effects, both short and long terms (Khalfan, 2006; Taylor, 2010; Silvius *et al.*, 2012).

Barendsen *et al.* (2021) explored the ways (internal) sustainability communication is organized and perceived in the context of sustainable PM. In the case they studied, there was no uniform understanding of sus-tainability among project team members and the different modes of sus-tainability communication did not meet project team members' needs. These findings illustrate the importance of effective communication of sustainability-related aspects of the project, as a basis for improving the (sustainability) impact of the project.

6.4.12. *Managing organizational and societal changes*

In the view of ISO, "the purpose of managing organizational and societal change is to enable the project's desired outcomes to be delivered." Earlier in this chapter we discussed the organizational perspective on projects, in which projects are seen as temporary organizations to do work to bring about beneficial change (Turner, 2014). Elaborating this change perspec-tive to the societal level is one of the defining characteristics of the sus-tainability "school of thought" in PM (Silvius, 2017).

When considered from an organizational change perspective, the handover of the project's output or deliverable to the stakeholders that are expected to start using this deliverable in order to create benefits for them, their organization or society, is a critical phase. This handover, logically planned for the final stages of the project, does not always get adequate attention from the project organization, as "the job has been done." For example, Eid (2009) suggests that the closing phase of a project offers the least opportunities for integrating sustainability. However, Pade *et al.* (2008) and Silvius *et al.* (2012) point out the importance of the closing processes for a more sustainable project result. The success of the hand-over of the project's deliverables and the acceptance of the project result are important aspects of a project's sustainability. The importance of the project's handover should be reflected in the management attention this aspect gets, for example, in the engagement with the stakeholders of the handover during the project's life cycle. Early and open engagement with these stakeholders is often an enabler of a successful handover. Failed or non-accepted projects can hardly be considered sustainable, given the waste of resources, materials, and energy they represent.

6.4.13. *Reporting*

According to ISO, "the purpose of reporting is to provide the current status, forecast, and analysis of the project. Reporting should be aligned with the current, and possibly updated, project documentation and determined from an analysis of PM information." The impact of the concepts of sustainability on project reporting elaborates on what was already argued in the communication management of the project. Sustainability implies proactive and open communication about the project, which also applies to the status and progress of the project. And as the project progress reports logically result from the agreed project objectives, scope of work, milestones, business case, etc. also the content of the project's status and progress reports will be influenced by the inclusion of sustainability aspects in the objectives and processes of the project (Perrini & Tencati, 2006).

6.4.14. *Information and documentation management*

ISO states that "the purpose of information and documentation management is to enable relevant and reliable information (physical and digital) to be available to those undertaking work and making decisions." At first glance, little impact of the concepts of sustainability on the information and documentation management of the project might be expected. However, the information within and about the project is an enabler for communication, controlling, reporting, and eventually also learning improving and learning. The consideration of sustainability in these PM practices therefore also impacts the information and document management of the project, both its content and its processes.

6.4.15. *Procurement*

According to ISO, "the purpose of procurement is to source products and services bought as part of resourcing the work that are of appropriate quality, represent value for money and can be delivered when needed within an acceptable level of risk." Not just in the materials used but also in the processes concerned with procurement and selection of suppliers, sustainability needs to be considered (Silvius & Schipper, 2014). For example, valuing the sustainability performance of potential suppliers in supplier selection (Taylor, 2010). Next to this, the UN Global Compact principles point out that preventing bribery and non-ethical behavior in a project's procurement processes (Tharp, 2013), both by members of the project organization and by potential suppliers and authorities, also is part of sustainable PM.

6.4.16. *Lessons learned*

ISO indicates that "the purpose of learning lessons is to benefit from experience, avoid repeating mistakes and disseminate improved practices to benefit current and future projects teams." As sustainability in projects and PM is still a developing topic, extracting learnings from practice is extremely important. Both on the process of considering sustainability in the execution and management of the project, as well as on the solutions for making the project's deliverable more sustainable, new knowledge needs to develop. Logically, the project's objectives and quality requirements build upon the available knowledge, but as sustainability is considered a "wicked" problem, solutions to sustainability challenges will also develop bottom up from practice (Neugebauer, 2016). It is therefore crucial that the knowledge of these solutions is effectively captured during the project and made available for future use. We already identified organizational learning as one of the impact areas of sustainability in PM, in our earlier cited structured analysis of 164 selected publications on sustainability in PM. Organizations should learn from their projects in order to not "waste" energy, resources, and materials on their mistakes in projects (Eid, 2009; Silvius *et al.*, 2012).

Reflecting on the impact of the concepts of sustainability on PM, analyzed above, it may be concluded that considering sustainability impacts all aspects of PM. The growing body of literature on sustainable PM, however, still includes some gaps. Some of the management practices discussed above are quite well covered in literature, whereas others have received little attention. For example, the integration of sustainability in the management practices of stakeholder engagement, benefit management, and procurement has been analyzed in several articles. However, other PM practices, such as risk management, scheduling, and resources management, that also are expected to be impacted by sustainability considerations, lack deeper discussion in academic literature.

6.5. Practical implementation

The impact of sustainability on the practices of PM, as described in the preceding paragraph, has been identified by numerous studies. However, its practical application in organizations is not easily carried out (Chofreh *et al.*, 2019). Sustainability is understood intuitively but remains difficult to express in concrete, operational terms (Briassoulis, 2001). Martens and Carvalho (2016) observe that organizations need a methodology for the effective implementation of sustainable PM in all processes and phases of PM. And as methodologies for PM are often based on or derived from standards for PM, the following section discusses how some of these standards address sustainability.

6.5.1. *Sustainability in the standards of project management*

Sustainability is increasingly being integrated into the industry standards of PM. For example, the International Project Management Association Individual Competence Baseline version 4 (ICB4) (International Project Management Association, 2015) explicitly refers to sustainability in its "Perspective" competence element "Compliance, regulations, and standards," which includes the indicator "Identify, and ensure that the project complies with relevant sustainability principles and objectives." The description of this key competence indicator states that the project manager should be able to "assess the impact of the project on the environment and society" and that he/she "researches, recommends, and applies measures to limit or compensate negative consequences." With the explicit reference to the effects of the project's processes and products on the environment and society, the ICB4 acknowledges the relation between projects and sustainability and establishes a role for the project manager in this relationship. Also, the ISO 21505 standard on the governance of project, program, and portfolio management (International Organization for Standardization, 2017) refers explicitly to sustainability and states that "the governance of projects, programs, and portfolios should reflect the organization's commitment to ethical values and sustainability."

Likewise, the latest edition of the Project Management Institute's Guide to the PM Body of Knowledge (Project Management Institute, 2021) explicitly refers to sustainability under the principle of stewardship. The guide states that stewardship encompasses responsibilities both within and external to the organization and includes in the external responsibilities "environmental sustainability," "use of materials and natural resources," as well as the impact on social communities (Project Management Institute, 2021).

A specific sustainability-oriented standard is Projects Integrating Sustainability Methods, PRiSM (Carboni *et al.*, 2018). PRiSM integrates the consideration of sustainability into PM processes, by performing a sustainability impact analysis in the project initiating or planning phases. The results of this sustainability impact analysis are documented in a "Sustainability Management Plan" (SMP) for the project. Throughout the project life cycle, the SMP is managed and at the closure of the project, the sustainability aspects of the project are reviewed in a meeting that also includes the sustainability or CSR officer of the organization. A specific and new sustainable PM methodology such as PRiSM may not be adopted by the market quickly. However, it provides a model and a number of methods or practices that can inspire organizations to integrate sustainability considerations into their existing PM methodologies.

6.5.2. *Instruments for assessing sustainability impact*

With sustainability now being integrated into standards and practice, the following question remains: What practical instruments and tooling are available to enable the project manager to assess a project's environmental, economic, and social impact? Good intentions do not automatically lead to behavior. For example, in our research,[2] we found that a distinct group of project managers, the "pragmatics," need practical knowledge, tools, and results in order to consider the sustainability aspects of their projects. In order to assess sustainability in the project, the project manager can logically choose to use an unstructured method to assess the sustainability impact of the project, for example, brainstorming together with members of the project team, or a structured method. In the last years, a number of structured "project sustainability impact analysis" instruments have been published, of which 16 were reviewed and discussed by us.[3] Based on this review, we make a number of observations.

The perspectives of the TBL are a recurring element in most instruments, however, the operationalization of the different perspectives in criteria or indicators differs. Consensus on how to measure and assess sustainability has therefore not emerged yet and many specialists actually question whether or not a universal list is even possible, given the wide variety of conditions and the differences in values in different contexts (Silvius, 2015). We therefore suggest that the criteria for assessing sustainability should be configured to the context and specifics of the project. As criteria for the materiality or relevance of a criterion, the industry and strategy of the organizations involved in the project are indicated, as well as the type of project.

A second observation is that most project sustainability impact analysis instruments recognize the different levels of impact of a project: impacts related to the project's process ("sustainability of the project") and impacts related to the project's product ("sustainability by the project"). In their nature, most instruments are assessment models, with some earlier ones being simple checklists, and two others being developed as

---

[2] Silvius and Schipper (2020a).
[3] Silvius and Schipper (2020b).

maturity models, that also include an assessment instrument. In their applicability, the instruments are mixed. Some are developed with a focus on a specific industry, whereas others have a more generic orientation (Silvius & Schipper, 2020b).

Based on their nature and their assessed impact, we categorized the project sustainability impact assessments (SIA) into three groups.

6.5.2.1. *Rudimentary checklists*

Early attempts to provide practical guidance for the consideration of sustainability in PM included the checklists developed by Shen *et al.* (2007) and Silvius (2010). Both these checklists were developed in expert studies. Both checklists develop indicators for the assessment of the sustainability impact of projects, based on the TBL perspectives of social impact, environmental impact, and economic impact. The checklist of Shen *et al.* (2007) applies this SIA to the phases of the project and its deliverable, from inception to demolition.

6.5.2.2. *Incidental study-based project SIA instruments*

The largest group of instruments consists of academically published project SIA instruments or methodologies. These project SIA instruments are mostly developed in empirical case studies (single or multiple), although some, for example, PSIA (Tam, 2017) and PSEM (Szabo, 2016), are more conceptually developed. Notwithstanding the potential quality of these instruments, no further applications of or experiences with these instruments have been documented, beyond their initial or incidental study.

6.5.2.3. *Further developed project SIA instruments*

Of three project sustainability impact assessment instruments, multiple applications and studies were published. They were therefore classified as more impactful. These three instruments are Wa-Pa-Su Project Sustainability rating system (Poveda & Lipsett, 2012), Sustainable PM Maturity Model (SPM3) (Silvius & Schipper, 2010; 2015), and the P5 Standard for Sustainability in PM (GPM Global, 2013, 2016).

Two of these three, SPM3 and P5 instruments of Green Project, were also published in multiple versions, indicating that these instruments are not one-off developments but that they are applied, studied, and updated.

A sustainability impact assessment method that is specifically aimed at assessing, rating, and certifying the sustainability of buildings is Building Research Establishment Environmental Assessment Method (BREEAM). BREEAM has expanded from its original focus on individual new buildings at the construction stage to encompass the whole life cycle of buildings from planning to in-use and refurbishment. BREEAM includes several sustainability categories for the assessment, generally management, energy, health and well-being, transport, water, materials, waste, land use and ecology, and pollution.

Leadership in Energy and Environmental Design (LEED) is another popular green building certification program used worldwide. It includes a set of rating systems for the design, construction, operation, and maintenance of green buildings, homes, and neighborhoods that aims to help building owners and operators to be environmentally responsible and use resources efficiently.

As BREEAM and LEED are mainly focused on buildings and their usage, their coverage of the PM process is limited.

6.6. Conclusion: Sustainable project management as a mind shift

This chapter analyzed and described the scope shift that considering sustainability in the content and the process of planning, organizing, managing, and governing a project implies, from managing time, budget, and quality to managing social, environmental, and economic impact (Silvius *et al.*, 2012).

However, the impact of sustainability on PM is more than adding a new perspective or aspect to processes and formats of the current PM standards. Adding new perspectives to the way projects are considered also adds complexity (Sabini & Silvius, 2022; Silvius *et al.*, 2012). PM therefore needs to adopt a holistic, adaptive, and less predictive approach (Gareis *et al.*, 2013). The traditional PM paradigm of controlling the "iron triangle" performance criteria of time, budget, and quality suggests a level of predictability and control that does not fit the "wicked" character of sustainability challenges and solutions. The integration of sustainability therefore also requires a paradigm shift (Silvius *et al.*, 2012), from a "predict & control" paradigm to a "prepare & commit" paradigm that is characterized by uncertainty, flexibility, complexity, and opportunity.

The basis for the scope shift and the paradigm shift described above is the way the PM professional sees her/his role (Crawford, 2013). Project managers are well positioned to play a significant role in the implementation of the concepts of sustainability in organizations and businesses (Tharp, 2013; Silvius & Schipper, 2020a). However, project managers are observed to be reluctant in using the influence they have on the sustainability of the project, as they are uncertain about how this would influence their relationship with the project owner (Silvius & De Graaf, 2019). Integrating sustainability requires that project managers take up responsibility for the sustainability of their projects and act as partners of and peers to stakeholders (Crawford, 2013; Tam, 2010). This requires a mind shift in the project manager (Silvius & Schipper, 2014). In this mind shift, the change a project realizes is no longer the exclusive responsibility of the project sponsor, but also the responsibility of the project manager, with ethics and transparency as a basic touchstone. Sustainable PM requires that the role of the project manager evolves from that of a planning and control-oriented manager to a co-creating and shaping leader. Figure 6.3 summarizes the three shifts that sustainable PM implies (Silvius & Schipper, 2014).

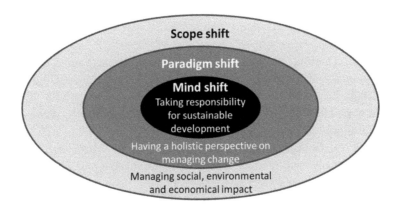

Figure 6.3.   The three shifts of sustainable PM.

References

Aarseth, W., Ahola, T., Aaltonen, K., Økland, A., & Andersen, B. (2017). Project sustainability strategies: A systematic literature review. *International Journal of Project Management, 35*(6), 1071–1083.

Akadiri, P. O., Olomolaiye, P. O., & Chinyio, E. A. (2013). Multi-criteria evaluation model for the selection of sustainable materials for building projects. *Automation in Construction, 30*, 113–125.

Alvarez-Dionisi, L. E., Turner, R., & Mittra, M. (2016). Global project management trends. *International Journal of Information Technology Project Management, 7*(3), 54–73.

AlWaer, H., Sibley, M., & Lewis, J. (2008). Different stakeholder perceptions of sustainability assessment. *Architectural Science Review, 51*(1), 48–59.

Andersen, E. S. (2008). *Rethinking Project Management: An Organisational Perspective*. Harlow: Prentice Hall.

Bal, M., Bryde, D., Fearon, D., & Ochieng, E. (2013). Stakeholder engagement: Achieving sustainability in the construction sector. *Sustainability, 6*, 695–710.

Barendsen, W., Muß, A., & Silvius, A. J. G. (2021). Exploring team members' perceptions of internal sustainability communication in sustainable project management. *Project Leadership & Society, 2*, 100015. 1–13.

Bell, S. & Morse, S. (2003). *Measuring Sustainability Learning from Doing*. London: Earthscan.

Brent, A. C. & Petrick, W. (2007). Environmental Impact Assessment (EIA) during project execution phases: Towards a stage-gate project management model for the raw materials processing industry of the energy sector. *Impact Assessment and Project Appraisal, 25*(2), 111–122.

Briassoulis, H. (2001). Sustainable development and it's indicators: Through a (Planner's) Glass Darkly. *Journal of Environmental Planning and Management, 44*(3), 409–427.

Carboni, J., Duncan, W., González, M., Milson, P., & Young, M. (2018). *Sustainable Project Management*. The GPM Reference Guide, GPM Global.

Carroll, A. B. (1991 July–August). The pyramid of corporate social responsibility. *Business Horizon*, pp. 39–48.

Chofreh, A. G., Goni, F. A., Malik, M. N., Khan, H. H., & Klemeš, J. J. (2019). The imperative and research directions of sustainable project management. *Journal of Cleaner Production, 238*, 1–14.

Craddock, W. T. (2013). How business excellence models contribute to project sustainability and project success. In A. J. G. Silvius & J. Tharp (Eds.),

Sustainability Integration for Effective Project Management. Hershey, PA: IGI Global Publishing.

Crawford, L. (2013). Leading sustainability through projects. In A. J. G. Silvius & J. Tharp, (Eds.), *Sustainability Integration for Effective Project Management* (pp. 235–244). Hershey, PA: IGI Global Publishing.

Dahlsrud, A. (2008). How corporate social responsibility is defined: An analysis of 37 definitions. *Corporate Social Responsibility and Environmental Management, 15*(1), 1–13.

Dallasega, P. & Rauch, E. (2017). Sustainable production supply chains through synchronized production planning and control in engineer-to-order enterprises. *Sustainability, 9*(10), 1888.

De Bakker, K. (2011). *Dialogue on Risk; Effects of Project Risk Management on Project Success.* Groningen: University of Groningen.

Doloi, H. (2014). Managing scope and configuration. In R. Turner (Ed.), *Gower Handbook of Project Management* (5th edn.) pp. 161–178. Farnham, UK: Routledge.

Dyllick, T. & Hockerts, K. (2002). Beyond the business case for corporate sustainability. *Business Strategy and the Environment, 11*, 130–141.

Ebner, D. & Baumgartner, R. J. (2006). The relationship between sustainable development and corporate social responsibility. Available at: www.crrconference.org (accessed on 12 April 2013).

Eid, M. (2009). *Sustainable Development & Project Management.* Cologne: Lambert Academic Publishing.

Elkington, J. (1997). *Cannibals with Forks: The Triple Bottom Line of 21st Century Business.* Oxford: Capstone Publishing Ltd.

Eskerod, P. & Huemann, M. (2013). Sustainable development and project stakeholder management: What standards say. *International Journal of Managing Projects in Business, 6*(1), 36–50.

Freeman, R. E., Harrison, J. S., & Wicks, A. C. (2007). *Managing for Stakeholders: Survival, Reputation, and Success.* Yale: Yale University Press.

Gareis, R., Huemann, M., Martinuzzi, R.-A., Weninger, C., & Sedlacko, M. (2013). *Project Management & Sustainable Development Principles.* Newton Square, PA: Project Management Institute.

Gemünden, H. G. (2016). From the editor: Project governance and sustainability — Two major themes in project management research and practice. *Project Management Journal, 47*, 3–6.

Gilbert, R., Stevenson, D., Girardet, H., & Stern, R. (Eds.). (1996). *Making Cities Work: The Role of Local Authorities in the Urban Environment.* Clerkenwell: Earthscan Publications Ltd.

Goedknegt, D. & Silvius, A. J. G. (2012). The implementation of sustainability principles in project management. In *Proceedings of the 26th IPMA World Congress*, Crete, pp. 875–882. 29–31 October.

GPM Global. (2013). *P5 Standard for Sustainability in Project Management Version 1*. GPM Global.

GPM Global. (2016). *P5 Standard for Sustainability in Project Management Version 1.5.1*. GPM Global.

Haugan, G. (2012). *The New Triple Constraints for Sustainable Projects, Programs, and Portfolios*. Boca Raton, FL USA: CRC Press.

Huemann, M. & Silvius, A. J. G. (2017). Editorial: Projects to create the future: Managing projects meets sustainable development. *International Journal of Project Management*, 35(6), 1066–1070.

Huemann, M., Eskerod, P., & Ringhofer, C. (2016). *Rethinking Project Stakeholder Management*. Newtown Square: Project Management Institute.

International Organization for Standardization. (2010). *ISO 26000, Guidance on Social Responsibility*. Geneva.

International Organization for Standardization. (2012). *ISO 21502:2020, Guidance on Project Management*. Geneva.

International Organization for Standardization. (2017). *ISO 21505:2017, Guidance on Governance of Project, Programme and Portfolio Management*. Geneva.

International Project Management Association. (2015). *Individual Competence Baseline Version 4*. Nijkerk, The Netherlands: International Project Management Association.

Julian, S. D., Ofori-Dankwa, J. C., & Justis, R. T. (2008). Understanding strategic responses to interest group pressures. *Strategic Management Journal*, 29, 963–984.

Kakabadse, N. K., Rozuel, C., & Lee-Davies, L. (2005). Corporate social responsibility and stakeholder approach: A conceptual review. *International Journal of Business Governance and Ethics*, 1, 277–302.

Keating, M. (1993). *The Earth Summit's Agenda for Change*. Geneva: Centre for our Common Future.

Khalfan, M. M. A. (2006). Managing sustainability within construction projects. *Journal of Environmental Assessment Policy and Management*, 8(1), 41–60.

Labelle, F. & Leyrie, C. (2013). Stakepartner management in projects. *The Journal of Modern Project Management*, 1, 32–43.

Labuschagne, C. & Brent, A. C. (2005). Sustainable project life cycle management: The need to integrate life cycles in the manufacturing sector. *International Journal of Project Management, 23*(2), 159–168.

Linnenluecke, M. K., Russell, S. V., & Griffiths, A. (2009). Subcultures and sustainability practices: The impact on understanding corporate sustainability. *Business Strategy and the Environment, 18*(7), 432–452.

Malthus, T. R. (1798). *An Essay on the Principle of Population.* J. London: Johnson.

Maltzman, R. & Shirley, D. (2010). *Green Project Management.* Boca Raton, FL USA: CRC Press.

Marcelino-Sádaba, S., Pérez-Ezcurdia, A., & González-Jaen, L. F. (2015). Using project Management as a way to sustainability. From a comprehensive review to a framework definition. *Journal of Cleaner Production, 99,* 1–16.

Martens, M. L. & Carvalho, M. M. (2016). Sustainability and success variables in the project management context: An expert panel. *Project Management Journal, 47*(6), 24–43.

Martens, P. (2006). Sustainability: Science or fiction? *Sustainability: Science, Practice, & Policy, 2*(1), 1–5.

McDonough, W. & Braungart, M. (2002). *Cradle to Cradle: Remaking the Way We Make Things.* Berkeley, US: North Point Press.

Meadows, D. H., Meadows, D. L., Randers, J., & Behrens, W. W. (1972). *The Limits to Growth.* Washington D.C., US: Universe Books.

Neugebauer, F., Figge, F. & Hahn, T. (2016). Planned or emergent strategy making? Exploring the formation of corporate sustainability strategies. *Business Strategy and the Environment, 25*(5), 323–336.

Office of the Government Commerce. (2010). *Management of Risk: Guidance for Practitioners.* Norwich.

Padalkar, M. & Gopinath, S. (2016). Six decades of project management research: Thematic trends and future opportunities. *International Journal of Project Management, 34*(7), 1305–1321.

Pade, C., Mallinson, B., & Sewry, D. (2008). An elaboration of critical success factors for rural ICT project sustainability in developing countries: Exploring the Dwesa case. *The Journal of Information Technology Case and Application, 10*(4), 32–55.

Perrini, F. & Tencati, A. (2006). Sustainability and stakeholder management: The need for new corporate performance evaluation and reporting systems. *Business Strategy and the Environment, 15*(5), 286–308.

Poveda, C. & Lipsett M. (2012). Wa-Pa-Su project sustainability rating system: Assessing sustainability in oil sands and heavy oil projects. In C. A. Brebbia & T.-S. Chon (Eds.), *Environmental Impact* (pp. 115–128). Southampton: WIT Press.

Project Management Institute. (2021). *A Guide to Project Management Body of Knowledge (PMBOK Guide)* (7th edn.). Newtown Square, PA: Project Management Institute.

Robinson, J. (2004). Squaring the circle: On the very idea of sustainable development. *Ecological Economics, 48*(4), 369–384.

Sabini, L. & Silvius, A. J. G. (2022). Embracing complexity in sustainable project management. In G. Winch (Ed.), *Research Handbook on Complex Project Organizing*. Cheltenham, U.K.: Edward Elgar Publishing.

Sabini, L., Muzio, D., & Alderman, N. (2019). 25 years of 'sustainable projects'. What we know and what the literature says. *International Journal of Project Management, 37*, 820–838.

Schoper, Y.-G., Wald, A., & Ingason, H. T. (2018). Projectification in Western economies: A comparative study of Germany, Norway and Iceland. *International Journal of Project Management, 36*(1), 71–82.

Shen, L. Y., Hao, J. L., Wing-Yan Tam, V., & Yao, H. (2007). A checklist for assessing sustainability performance of construction projects. *Journal of Civil Engineering and Management, 13*(4), 273–281.

Silvius, A. J. G. (2010). Report workshop 2. In H. Knoepfel (Ed.), *Survival and Sustainability as Challenges for Projects*. Zurich: International Project Management Association.

Silvius, A. J. G. (2015). Sustainability evaluation of IT/IS projects. *International Journal of Green Computing, 6*(2), 1–15.

Silvius, A. J. G. (2016). Integrating sustainability into project risk management. In S. Bodea, A. Purnus, M. Huemann, & M. Hajdu (Eds.), *Managing Project Risks for Competitive Advantage in Changing Business Environments*. Hershey, U.S.: IGI Global.

Silvius, A. J. G. (2017). Sustainability as a new school of thought in project management. *Journal of Cleaner Production, 166*, 1479–1493.

Silvius, A. J. G. & De Graaf, M. (2019). Exploring the project manager's intention to address sustainability in the project board. *Journal of Cleaner Production, 208*, 1226–1240.

Silvius, A. J. G. & Schipper, R. (2010). A maturity model for integrating sustainability in projects and project management. In *24th IPMA World Congress*, Istanbul. 1–3 November.

Silvius, A. J. G. & Schipper, R. (2014). Sustainability in project management: A literature review and impact analysis. *Social Business*, *4*(1), 63–96.

Silvius, A. J. G. & Schipper, R. (2015). Developing a maturity model for assessing sustainable project management. *Journal of Modern Project Management*, *3*(1), 16–27.

Silvius, A. J. G. & Schipper, R. (2020a). Exploring variety in factors that stimulate project managers to address sustainability issues. *International Journal of Project Management*, *38*, 353–367.

Silvius, A. J. G. & Schipper, R. (2020b). Sustainability impact assessment on the project level; A review of available instruments. *The Journal of Modern Project Management*, *8*(1), 240–277.

Silvius, A. J. G., Kampinga, M., Paniagua, S., & Mooi, H. (2017). Considering Sustainability in Project Management Decision Making; An investigation using Q-methodology. *International Journal of Project Management*, *35*(6), 1133–1150.

Silvius, A. J. G., Schipper, R., Planko, J., van der Brink, J., & Köhler, A. (2012). *Sustainability in Project Management*. Farnham: Gower Publishing.

Sukhdev, P. (2013). Transforming the corporation into a driver of sustainability. In L. Starke (Ed.), *Worldwatch Institute, State of the World 2013: Is Sustainability Still Possible?* (pp. 143–153). Washington, U.S.: Island Press.

Szabo, L. (2016). Sustainability, creativity and innovation in project management. *Vezetéstudomány/Budapest Management Review*, *47*(10), 3–18.

Tam, G. (2010). The program management process with sustainability considerations. *Journal of Project, Program & Portfolio Management*, *1*(1), 17–27.

Tam, G. (2017). *Managerial Strategies and Green Solutions for Project Sustainability*. Hershey, US: IGI Global Publishing.

Taylor, T. (2010). *Sustainability Interventions — For Managers of Projects and Programmes*. Sanford: The Higher Education Academy — Centre for Education in the Built Environment.

Tharp, J. (2013). Sustainability in project management: Practical applications. In A. J. G. Silvius & J. Tharp (Eds.), *Sustainability Integration for Effective Project Management*. (pp. 182–193). Hershey, PA: IGI Global Publishing.

Turner, R. (2014). Projects and their management. In R. Turner (Ed.), *Gower Handbook of Project Management* (5th edn.). (pp. 19–34). Farnham, UK: Routledge.

Von Carlowitz, H. C. (1713). *Sylvicultura Oeconomica: Oder Haußwirthliche Nachricht und Naturmäßige Anweisung zur Wilden Baum-Zucht*. Leipzig: Braun.

Weninger, C. & Huemann, M. (2013). Project initiation: Investment analysis for sustainable development. In A. J. G. Silvius & J. Tharp (Eds.), *Sustainability Integration for Effective Project Management*. (pp. 144–159). Hershey, U.S.: IGI Global Publishing.

Winnall, J.-L. (2013). Social sustainability to social benefit: Creating positive outcomes through a social risk. In A. J. G. Silvius & J. Tharp (Eds.), *Sustainability Integration for Effective Project Management*. (pp. 95–105). Hershey, PA: IGI Global Publishing.

World Commission on Environment and Development. (1987). *Our Common Future*. Great Britain: Oxford University Press.

Chapter 7

Project Management in Pursuit of Net Zero Construction

Victoria Burrows

World Green Building Council, London, UK

Net Zero construction is a subset of green construction, and this is a special chapter because of most urgency to the world at the moment is achieving Net Zero by 2050, in order to significantly reduce the risks and impacts of climate change, such as the ferocious wildfires that destroy many lives, properties, and forests, as we saw in Chapter 1. As Oxford University Professor Bent Flyvbjerg and *The New York Times* bestselling author Dan Gardner stated in their recent award-winning book *How Big Things Get Done*, "no task is more urgent today than mitigating the climate crisis — not only for the common good but for your organization, yourself, and your family." This chapter is critical to achieving the Net-Zero-by-2050 goal from the perspective of project management (PM) for the built environment. It is arguably the first of its kind. The uniqueness of the chapter is further boosted by being authored by the authority leading the global action toward "Advancing Net Zero" for the built environment. Collaboration and commitment are required from global construction bodies in order to achieve the decarbonization goals set out in the Paris Agreement. As such, the World Green Building Council has identified PM as a key facilitator in the pursuit of Net Zero and the broad adoption of sustainable building. This chapter explores the Net Zero initiative and its core components, how PM can impact Net Zero construction as a part of green construction, and strategies for aligning and enhancing the aforementioned efforts.

7.1. A Net Zero overview

7.1.1. *An introduction to the Net Zero initiative*

The World Green Building Council (WorldGBC) catalyzes the uptake of sustainable built environments for everyone, everywhere. As a global action network of over 70 Green Building Councils around the world, we are transforming the building and construction sector across three strategic areas: climate action, health and well-being, and resources and circularity.

As members of the UN Global Compact, we work with businesses, organizations, and governments to drive the ambitions of the Paris Agreement and UN Global Goals for Sustainable Development (SDGs). Through a systems-change approach, our network is leading the industry toward a Net Zero carbon, healthy, equitable, and resilient built environment.

Net Zero represents a critical milestone toward achieving sustainable development goals and creating a more circular economy. It is achievable but requires commitment and investment from both private and public sectors on a global scale. Furthermore, it must be combined with other approaches, such as the development of renewable energy sources and green financing for maximum effectiveness.

With the right combination of policies and investments in sustainability initiatives, Net Zero can be achieved in a cost-effective way that supports economic growth while reducing emissions rapidly enough to avoid catastrophic climate change. By reducing global emissions, we can achieve greater balance in the amount of carbon dioxide released into our atmosphere and subsequently offset the effects of rising temperatures. It is essential that we continue to work toward this goal if we are to secure a prosperous future for generations to come.

A multidisciplined, cross-border effort is required to bring about the necessary change: a global movement that includes investing in renewable energy sources, promoting energy efficiency via reduced demand, and adopting new technologies that are capable of offsetting harmful greenhouse gas emissions. In doing so, it is possible to reduce the global temperature rise significantly over time, eventually leading to a Net Zero, low-carbon economy.

The benefits of such an economy include decreased air and water pollution, better public health, economic growth, and a safer climate for future generations. High-performance buildings contribute toward the Net Zero economy by optimizing resource usage, utilizing low-carbon materials, using energy efficiently, and either generating all the energy they need onsite or procuring externally generated renewable energy.

With Net Zero efforts gaining increased attention from both businesses and governments around the world, it is clear that this approach will be a key part of any comprehensive effort to combat climate change and achieve global sustainability. If we are to achieve the target of Net Zero emissions by 2050, a holistic approach across all aspects of the built environment along with strong political will is needed to reach this goal.

7.1.2. *Advancing Net Zero*

Advancing Net Zero is WorldGBC's global program working toward total sector decarbonization by 2050. The initiative sees Green Building Councils working across the network to develop tools, programs, and resources to promote the urgency and achievability of Net Zero carbon buildings and build industry capacity to deliver them.

By advocating for a sustainable, efficient, healthy, and resilient built environment, we can create tangible improvements in our communities, which bring us closer to achieving our decarbonization goals. Improved buildings mean better air quality, reduced global warming potential, increased comfort levels in indoor spaces, and enhanced savings in energy costs. Ultimately, these factors lead to lower greenhouse gas emissions over time while improving the quality of life for people around the world.

In order for these initiatives to be successful, built environments must be designed with sustainability, efficiency, health, and resilience in mind. These goals can be achieved through the use of energy-efficient technologies, such as renewable energy systems, smart building materials, and green or sustainable construction practices.

It is critical that governments support Net Zero initiatives by providing incentives and subsidies to businesses that choose to adopt them. Ideally, cities should advocate for policies that promote green infrastructure development, such as green roofs and urban gardens. Broad educational campaigns should be launched to raise awareness about climate change issues among citizens, so they become more engaged in Net Zero initiatives. By taking these steps, we can accelerate the adoption of a Net Zero mindset, on macro and micro scales.

Advancing Net Zero is a journey and an integral part of a wider systemic shift toward a more sustainable built environment. As part of the transition toward total sector decarbonization, the WorldGBC advocates for a holistic approach to sustainability that also enables tangible environmental and social co-benefits in support of the SDGs.

7.1.2.1. *Meeting Net Zero targets*

The building industry is one of the largest contributors to greenhouse gas emissions due to its reliance on fossil fuels and, mainly, a lack of performance standards that leads to inefficiencies, poor design, and the over consumption of energy. In order to meet Net Zero targets, the industry must make significant changes in terms of both technology and policy. Technologies such as renewable energy sources, green building materials, advanced insulation systems, and smart automation systems need to be adopted by the industry at large.

Additionally, local governments should establish policies that encourage sustainable architecture practices, such as rainwater harvesting, greywater reuse, efficient heating and cooling systems, and increased use of natural light. Educational initiatives must be implemented to raise awareness among project managers, architects, and building managers about the importance of reducing their environmental impact in order to achieve Net Zero targets. By taking these steps, the building industry can become a vital partner in mitigating climate change.

The building industry must also take into account the social and economic consequences of their policies and technological changes. For example, renewable energy sources may be more expensive than traditional forms of energy, making them inaccessible to some lower-income organizations. Green building materials may also not be available or feasible for many smaller construction projects. To address these issues, governments should offer incentives for builders who adopt renewable energy sources and other sustainable practices, as well as provide access to more affordable green materials for small-scale projects. By looking at both the environmental and economic implications of their actions, the building industry can create a future that is both prosperous and environmentally responsible.

When designing and constructing building projects to meet Net Zero goals, it is important to consider the following key elements:

Energy efficiency: Energy efficiency focuses on reducing the amount of energy used in a building by actively regulating the temperature and ventilation systems within a space. This can be done through installing high-performance insulation materials, controlled ventilation, and efficient lighting systems. Energy Star-rated appliances should be selected for use in the building where possible.

Renewable energy sources: Renewable energy sources such as solar power or wind turbines can also be used to generate electricity for the building. It is important to identify the best source for each location based on climate and conditions to ensure optimum performance of these systems over time.

Water conservation: Water conservation should also be taken into consideration for a Net Zero building. This can involve selecting water-efficient appliances and fixtures, installing rainwater collection systems, and harvesting greywater for reuse.

Material selection: Material selection is an important factor to consider when constructing a Net Zero building. It is critical to select construction materials that are sustainable and ecofriendly and that enhance the whole life performance of the building. Ideally, decision-makers — project managers — should select locally sourced materials that reduce the carbon footprint of transportation while ensuring quality craftsmanship.

By carefully considering each of these key elements when planning, designing, and constructing a building project to meet Net Zero goals, it is possible to create energy-efficient buildings that are environmentally friendly. Shifts in construction site practices are enabling positive progress, but their broader adoption must increase.

Fossil fuel-free construction has the potential to significantly reduce emissions associated with the industry, and it can play an important role in helping us reach our sustainability goals.

Lean construction has become increasingly popular among industry professionals. The approach seeks to reduce waste and inefficiency during construction by streamlining processes, improving workflows, and introducing value-adding activities.

Modular construction has introduced the exciting prospect of buildings, or parts of buildings, being made in prefabricated units in a factory setting before they are transported to the site for installation. This allows for increased efficiency, faster build times, better quality control, and reduced waste. Perhaps better still is that it provides greater flexibility in design as the parts can be easily reconfigured to meet changing requirements.

It's essential that infrastructure be designed to support a circular economy. The industry can accomplish this by ensuring that buildings can be adapted and deconstructed and materials reused to create material banks for future projects.

7.1.3. *Innovation in pursuit of Net Zero*

As businesses continue to strive for greater sustainability, innovation in products and services is seen as a major driver of decarbonization. Companies have the potential to create new technologies, practices, and business models that can reduce or even eliminate their carbon footprints. This ranges from cleaner energy sources, such as wind and solar power, to developing sustainable materials for construction.

Organizations may need to consider changing how they deliver goods and services by utilizing digital technology instead of physical transportation. By embracing innovative solutions, companies can significantly improve their impact on climate change while also creating long-term economic growth. This could lead to major progress toward meeting global decarbonization goals.

Innovation does not just mean investing in green technologies and sustainable practices. It also means adapting to a changing market, responding to customer needs, and integrating new technologies into organizational structures. For instance, businesses can make use of big data analytics and AI-powered automation tools to reduce energy consumption or find ways to reallocate resources more efficiently. Companies can use blockchain technology to better track emissions or create incentives for reducing carbon outputs.

By embracing such innovations, organizations can reduce their impact on the environment while still being competitive in the market. Innovation is essential for businesses that want to contribute to decarbonization efforts in a meaningful way. Companies must be willing to take risks and invest in creative solutions that will lead them toward cleaner, greener operations.

7.1.4. *Barriers to achieving Net Zero*

It is vital that we work to close the gaps that are preventing wider implementation of Net Zero initiatives. Despite the availability of proven approaches and technologies that make Net Zero buildings achievable today, they're not being deployed sufficiently or at scale because current designs are not being challenged. We must confront the perceived barriers to the spread of systemic solutions; complacency can't be justified when there is so much to gain through their adoption.

Knowledge gaps can be bridged by asking the right questions and understanding the decisions and actions that need to be taken in order to achieve Net Zero. Project managers need a clear view of all aspects of design, building materials and systems, energy use, and resource management in order to make decisions that deliver impact.

We must embrace technology and tools that can provide insight into performance over time. For example, life cycle assessment software allows users to understand the environmental impact of their choices throughout a building's entire life cycle, from raw material extraction through to construction and operation. Similarly, utilizing data analytics can enable researchers, designers, and engineers to assess the effectiveness of specific technologies or strategies before committing to their use.

Gaps in implementation are solvable by bringing existing solutions and technologies to scale. This would increase the accessibility and affordability of energy-efficient buildings, reduced carbon emissions, and a higher level of infrastructure performance without putting undue pressure on budgets.

The construction value chain must develop the capability to implement improved building design through the use of high-performance materials, renewable energy sources, and advances in automation and digitization. It is important to create awareness among project managers, architects, engineers, and contractors about the possibilities of Net Zero construction. This can be achieved through training, open dialog, and collaboration opportunities, as well as by involving stakeholders in the design process. Furthermore, public–private partnerships and government incentives have the potential to facilitate large-scale adoption of Net Zero construction strategies and technologies.

Policy frameworks present a major opportunity for governments to reduce their emissions. However, there are numerous concerns that must be addressed. There are currently only 80 countries with building energy codes and standards in place and a startling 66% with none at all. Most countries are not tracking the in-use performance of buildings, which comes at the cost of valuable insights and creates further knowledge gaps.

Political instability can also be a major hindrance. Political shifts can cause drastic changes in policy, making it hard to maintain a consistent long-term plan to reach Net Zero targets. In some cases, this has led to abrupt changes in direction, which have made it difficult for countries and companies to keep up with new regulations or technological advancements.

Financial gaps create an array of challenges too. To put this into perspective, for every dollar spent on energy efficiency, USD 37 is spent on conventional construction. The upside is that this presents a USD 24.7 trillion investment opportunity as we work toward 2030. It's critical that the industry utilizes verification systems to mobilize finances that support this goal. The verification process provides assurance that all processes are taken in accordance with a given set of criteria, encouraging transparency and accountability, as well as long-term performance monitoring. These systems can be tailored to suit the specific needs of each construction project in order to ensure better outcomes for all stakeholders.

This lattice of obstacles must be addressed if we are going to make progress on global Net Zero goals. We need greater investment in research and development of technologies; increased financing from public, private, and international sources; public support for new regulations and technologies; and stable policies that can be implemented in the long term. Only then will we be able to make tangible progress toward a low-carbon future.

7.2. Defining Net Zero buildings

Net Zero buildings are increasingly seen as essential for achieving sustainability goals in the built environment and have been adopted by many governments, organizations, and individuals around the world. The application of the principles of Net Zero will depend on the project type, scale, location, and climate. Most Net Zero buildings incorporate many of the same elements, which include low-carbon materials, energy efficiency, renewable energy sources, and responsible waste disposal. The balance of each of these components determines which definition to apply to a project (as per Figure 7.1) (WorldGBC, 2022b).

In addition to reducing carbon emissions associated with traditional construction methods, these structures offer numerous economic benefits, including reduced operating expenses, increased property values, and improved occupant health and comfort. Net Zero buildings represent an effective way to meet both the energy demands of today's society and the environmental challenges of our future.

First and foremost, Net Zero structures must be well insulated and airtight, which helps prevent heat loss and ensures that no extra energy is expended for heating or cooling the space. Furthermore, they should make use of passive design principles, such as natural ventilation and daylighting, to reduce the need for artificial lighting and mechanical systems. Additionally, Net Zero buildings should employ renewable sources of

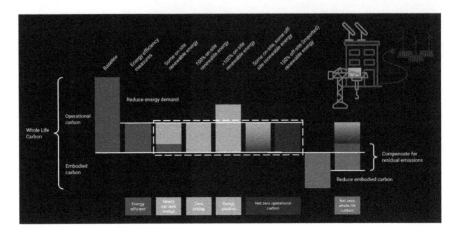

Figure 7.1.   Definitions of Net Zero buildings.

Source: https://worldgbc.org/advancing-net-zero/what-is-a-net-zero-carbon-building/.

energy, such as solar photovoltaics or wind turbines, in order to generate electricity from renewable sources. Finally, these buildings usually feature advanced energy storage systems designed to store any excess energy generated so that it can be used when needed. By combining all of these components, Net Zero buildings are able to dramatically reduce their reliance on traditional fossil fuels and become truly sustainable. In this way, they can help reduce greenhouse gas emissions and contribute to a more sustainable future.

En route to total decarbonization of the built environment, we call upon the industry to adopt the whole life carbon approach that addresses emissions from operational energy use in buildings and the embodied carbon which comes from the building materials and construction process.

Net Zero buildings are energy-efficient by design, and they achieve their status by utilizing a combination of sustainable and renewable technology that includes the following:

- Onsite solar photovoltaic systems
- Geothermal systems

- Wind turbines
- Heat pumps
- Energy-efficient windows and insulation
- Natural lighting techniques
- Rainwater recycling systems
- Smart appliances and building automation technologies
- Effective monitoring

In addition to these measures being taken to reduce energy consumption, design strategies must also be implemented in order to maximize natural ventilation, daylighting, and passive cooling. These aspects should be considered during the early stages of design so that the building's heating, cooling, and lighting needs can be addressed in a comprehensive manner.

Net Zero buildings also aim to reduce water consumption through low-flow fixtures, water harvesting, and recycling systems. Rainwater harvesting is one way of collecting and storing water for use in non-drinking applications, such as flushing toilets or watering plants. Greywater systems can also be used to treat wastewater onsite for reuse within the building. By leveraging these technologies, it's possible to dramatically reduce the amount of fresh water needed from municipal sources.

Net Zero buildings are designed with the intention of producing no waste over the course of their lifetime. Strategies for diverting waste from landfills include composting and recycling, as well as implementing waste management systems such as zero-waste policies. By taking the necessary steps to become a Net Zero building, it's possible to make a positive contribution toward reducing our carbon footprint.

Taking embodied carbon and materials into account is integral to the total carbon footprint of a building. Throughout a building's life cycle, embodied carbon accounts for around 11% of total energy use and about one-third of its total emissions. The type and amount of materials used can also significantly affect how much energy is consumed over time. For example, using renewable or recycled materials can reduce a building's embodied carbon footprint, while low-carbon insulation and efficient windows can lower its energy consumption.

Net Zero buildings present an exciting opportunity for project managers, architects, engineers, and builders to create innovative designs that are both energy-efficient and environmentally friendly. The challenge is in finding ways to incorporate these strategies into existing designs without sacrificing comfort or aesthetics. With careful planning and collaboration between all stakeholders, Net Zero buildings can be achieved that are not only sustainable but also highly functional and aesthetically pleasing. The onus is on government bodies, through both regulations and procurement practices, and the construction value chain to implement these strategies and contribute to a more sustainable future.

7.3. The Net Zero Carbon Buildings Commitment

The Net Zero Carbon Buildings Commitment from the WorldGBC recognizes leadership action by businesses, organizations, cities, and subnational governments in tackling operational and embodied carbon emissions from the building and construction sector (WorldGBC, 2022a).

Achieving total sector decarbonization requires deep collaboration across the entire value chain, and radical transformation in the way buildings are designed, built, occupied, and deconstructed.

The commitment seeks to accelerate this transition by setting high-performance targets that promote circularity, reuse of buildings and materials, whole life cycle thinking, high-performance operations, and ultimately a shift away from fossil fuels.

Its tenets consider the whole life cycle impact of buildings, and it builds on the WorldGBC's Whole Life Carbon Vision and best practice principles for implementation.

The commitment sets the goal of 2030 for existing buildings to reduce their energy consumption and eliminate emissions from energy and refrigerants, and subsequently, that new developments and major renovations are built to be highly efficient, powered by renewables, with a maximum reduction in embodied carbon and compensation of all residual upfront emissions.

Based on submissions from the current signatories, the status of the commitment is as follows:

- 171 total signatories
- 20,000 assets
- 7.3 million tons of CO_2 emissions accounted for
- >\$427 billion annual turnover

The commitment promotes a reduction-first, outcomes-based approach to decarbonization, which gives signatories the flexibility to develop bespoke action plans for their specific portfolio profile based on best practice principles that reduce both consumption and emissions.

Annual reporting of verified progress toward decarbonization goals enables the collection of data to inform low-carbon choices, relevant benchmarks and targets, best practice methods to incorporate, and associated costs reduced. A greater uptake helps accelerate market transformation and leads to significant sector emission reductions.

Finally, WorldGBC advocates for halving emissions of the building and construction sector by 2030, and the total decarbonization of the sector by 2050. Therefore, as we transition, we also recognize the value of offsets as a means to compensate for and neutralize the residual impacts of the sector, and to facilitate positive social and environmental impact in pursuit of overall Net Zero emissions, such as nature-based solutions or building retrofit credits.

As this is a global challenge requiring collective local solutions, the commitment is outcomes focused and action based. Thus, in order to prevent and mitigate embodied emissions, increase resource efficiency, and stimulate the development and market supply of low-carbon products, the sector must reduce and account for its impact on the environment and natural resources through design and construction. Furthermore, it must generate a strong and urgent demand to activate the necessary finance to decarbonize materials, construction, and heavy industry processes.

7.4. Net Zero operational and whole life carbon

Operational and whole life carbon are two different methods of measuring the carbon footprint of a building. Operational carbon is calculated to measure emissions generated through its operations, helping identify direct emission sources associated with the building and making it useful for setting targets and monitoring progress toward reducing those emissions.

Whole life carbon takes into account all the emissions associated with the building throughout its life cycle — from raw material extraction to disposal at the end of life. This method allows us to look beyond our own operations and understand how we can influence upstream activities that could have an even greater impact on overall emissions.

By looking at the full life cycle of a product, in this case a building, it gives us a better understanding of the emissions associated with our activities and can help us identify opportunities to reduce them. These two approaches provide more detailed information that allows organizations to develop strategies for reducing their carbon footprint in a more effective way. They also enable comparisons to be made between different products or activities based on their relative contribution to overall emissions reductions, enabling firms to make informed decisions about how best to achieve their sustainability goals. Both methods are essential tools for helping businesses meet their climate commitments and transition toward Net Zero operations.

By deploying these strategies, companies can better understand where they currently stand in terms of emissions, as well as identify where opportunities exist to reduce them and set meaningful targets for the future. These data can then be used to inform decision-making, support investments in new technologies, and ensure that progress is being made toward Net Zero goals. With these powerful tools at their disposal, organizations can take action and make the necessary changes needed to create a sustainable future.

7.4.1. *Operational carbon*

Achieving Net Zero operational carbon is an increasingly prominent goal for organizations around the world. Eliminating all of an organization's emissions from operations and activities is a noble and necessary pursuit. This goal can be achieved through a variety of strategies, such as energy efficiency upgrades, renewable energy investments, green building standards, and finally, offsetting any residual emissions.

To reach Net Zero operational carbon, organizations must identify their sources of emissions and develop plans for eliminating or offsetting them. Organizations that are able to achieve Net Zero operational carbon set an example for others in the industry and inspire positive environmental impact on a global scale.

Transitioning to a low-carbon economy should also involve stakeholders throughout the process. Employees and customers may be able to provide valuable insight into ways to achieve greater efficiency or alternative solutions. Net Zero operational carbon is a critical step in reaching our global climate change objectives, but it cannot be achieved without strong leadership from business leaders around the world.

7.4.2. *Whole life carbon*

Net Zero whole life carbon refers to buildings that are designed, constructed, and operated in a way that minimizes energy consumption, optimizes renewable energy sources, and also reduces embodied carbon emissions. This approach requires an integrated design process that takes into account the entire life cycle of a building, from its inception to demolition.

It involves using materials with low or no embodied carbon, such as timber or recycled materials, along with energy efficiency measures, such as insulation and window glazing. By reducing the total amount of embodied carbon in a building's construction and operation over its lifetime, Net Zero whole life carbon offers significant potential for meeting sustainability goals.

A recent WorldGBC report by Adams *et al.* (2019) on the topic had the following to say:

> While minimizing upfront carbon is vitally important, we must not risk creating adverse or negative outcomes for both operational carbon and whole life carbon. We therefore need to be conscious of the impacts that our upfront carbon decisions will have on whole life carbon. This is especially true for material selection where each material represents impacts and reduction opportunities throughout the whole life cycle, and we must design with these in mind. A low embodied carbon building

that performs poorly in operation creates adverse financial, environmental, and social implications. To achieve our vision, we cannot address one without the other and so must take urgent action to tackle upfront carbon while designing with whole life carbon in mind.

As the concept gains popularity among the construction and design industries, a number of initiatives and tools are being developed to facilitate this approach. Some Green Building Councils have developed a zero-carbon certification that recognizes projects which have achieved Net Zero whole life carbon. Additionally, numerous software packages are available to help architects and engineers assess embodied carbon in building materials in order to independently verify performance.

7.5. Adopting a whole system approach

The whole system approach to sustainable green building utilizes an integrated, holistic strategy to manage a building's life cycle. It encompasses the entire development process from the initial design stage through to the end of life. The aim of this approach is to ensure that every decision made during the construction and management of a building takes into account its environmental impact and sustainability potential in order to create buildings with reduced operational costs, improved occupant quality of life, and long-term benefits for the environment.

This approach considers numerous interrelated factors, such as energy efficiency, water conservation, material selection, and waste management, while also incorporating social considerations, such as accessibility requirements and health and safety regulations. All these elements are taken into consideration when developing a comprehensive plan to meet the needs of the building and its occupants.

The whole system approach seeks to create buildings that are as resource-efficient, low-impact, and cost-effective as possible. It also takes into account local environmental conditions and the life cycle of a building's materials, components, and systems in order to develop solutions that are tailored to each project's unique needs. Furthermore, it aims to promote the use of renewable energy sources wherever possible in order to reduce reliance on fossil fuels.

By taking a holistic view of sustainability when planning and constructing buildings, developers can ensure they are creating structures that will not only be beneficial for today but for generations to come. This is an essential part of developing an environmentally responsible and economically viable future that aligns with the Paris Agreement.

The challenge lies in making sure that all stakeholders involved in the building process — from project managers and architects to contractors and suppliers — are aware of their role in implementing this approach as part of an overall plan. Through education, training, and collaboration, all parties must fully understand the implications of undertaking a project that employs this future-minded approach.

7.6. Net Zero project management

7.6.1. *Net Zero project management*

Net Zero project management (PM) is a comprehensive approach to managing projects with a focus on reducing or eliminating carbon emissions. It requires a thorough understanding of environmental, economic, and social sustainability principles. Every Net Zero-oriented project should include an integrated plan that outlines goals, objectives, strategies, and tactics for achieving the desired result, and every decision should be evaluated against this framework (Bakshi, 2022).

Establishing clear communication between stakeholders and making sure everyone understands their role within the project are key to success. Proper monitoring techniques must be employed to measure progress and re-evaluate the design as needed to stay on track. With careful planning and consideration, Net Zero projects can be successfully managed to create a more sustainable future.

Project managers are uniquely positioned to create and implement strategies that can make a real difference in advancing Net Zero initiatives. By utilizing an integrated approach to PM, they can develop comprehensive plans that promote sustainability while still meeting the needs of stakeholders.

Project managers must possess both technical and soft skills in order to effectively manage Net Zero projects. Technical know-how is required so that the decision-makers understand how their choices impact the end goal, ensuring buy-in from all stakeholders and agreement on project outcomes. Ultimately, successful PM requires having a strategic plan in place before starting and constantly monitoring progress throughout each stage until completion.

Stakeholders must be consulted throughout the process, so their interests are taken into consideration and their ideas incorporated into future plans. This involves taking time to understand each stakeholder's individual goals and motivations in order to create buy-in and support for the initiative.

Internally, project managers should focus on creating a culture of collaboration within teams by fostering open communication, working together toward common objectives, and holding each other accountable for results. This will lead to more effective project execution and enable teams to develop creative solutions that maximize sustainability.

It's imperative that project managers come to grips with the complexities of Net Zero initiatives and the potential implications of their decisions. They should be aware that their actions can have long-term consequences both on the environment and on their reputation as leaders in sustainability. By doing research and staying up to date with best practices, they can make sure that their projects are successful over time.

7.6.2. *Principles of Net Zero project management*

Net Zero PM is a framework that can be used to help teams identify, prioritize, and manage projects with the goal of achieving Net Zero carbon emissions. By setting expectations upfront and building sustainability into decision-making, it helps ensure that projects are designed and executed with long-term goals in mind.

The principles of Net Zero PM include the following:

- setting clear targets,
- making sure all stakeholders understand their roles and responsibilities,

- designing for flexibility,
- monitoring progress on a regular basis,
- creating systems for tracking results, and
- establishing feedback loops to inform future decisions.

By employing these principles, teams can maximize the chances of success while minimizing environmental impact. Following this approach encourages an innovative mindset that can lead to a ripple effect of sustainable decisions. It is an effective way for organizations to take meaningful action toward mitigating climate change and leading the way with sustainably minded PM.

In order to ensure Net Zero PM efforts are successful, teams must have a good understanding of the goals and objectives of their project. This means that individual team members need to be aware of the big picture, as well as their own roles and responsibilities within it. They should also be prepared to adjust their strategies in response to changing circumstances or new information.

Additionally, it is important that everyone involved understands how the concepts of sustainability and Net Zero emissions apply to the project at hand so they can make informed decisions with these values in mind. It is essential that teams track progress and results on a regular basis. This will enable them to make necessary changes or course-correct if goals are not being met.

Net Zero PM is becoming increasingly important as we strive for greener solutions to reduce our carbon footprints. As such, it is necessary for every business or organization to understand its responsibilities when it comes to implementing these programs. Net Zero PM is an effective way for organizations to ensure that sustainability is at the forefront of their decision-making process. Crucially, it serves as a launch point for organizations to take meaningful action toward mitigating climate change. By setting clear targets and establishing systems for tracking progress, teams can maximize the implementation and effectiveness of sustainable choices. Ultimately, this approach ensures that projects will be designed and executed with long-term decarbonization goals remaining a priority.

7.6.3. *Things to consider for Net Zero project management*

When it comes to formulating plans for Net Zero building projects, there are some key factors that organizations need to consider. While a universal, one-size-fits-all solution would be ideal, it would be impractical to apply. Prudence suggests that a balanced approach is preferable to meet the specific needs of each project.

Organizations should ask the following:

- How does the building affect our staff and their productivity?
- Does it have a negative environmental impact?
- Does it achieve a balance between sustainability and value for money?
- Have we accounted for all the aspects we have influence over?
- Is the building working optimally?
- How does it compare to similar structures?
- Where can we create improvements?
- Is the building delivering on its purpose?
- Does it provide business benefits?

The answers will often be determined by each organization's approach and ethos. Design and construction are key stages in the implementation of Net Zero initiatives, but the true measure of a building's effectiveness can be found when looking at its in-use performance.

Schäfer and Zuberer (2022) of EY Global summed this up when discussing Net Zero:

> Construction companies that move quickly to develop strategies and business models that help their clients and themselves get them one step closer to achieving Net Zero by 2050 will have a significant competitive advantage. By adopting a life cycle perspective of both individual products and entire sustainable buildings, construction-related companies can understand their CO_2 contribution in the larger context and make adjustments that benefit everyone.

7.6.4. *Key stakeholders and their roles in Net Zero project management*

The key stakeholders in a Net Zero construction project may vary depending on the specific project, but in general, they would include the following:

Owner/Client: The owner or client is the individual or organization that is responsible for initiating and funding the project. They may have specific goals and objectives for the project, such as achieving Net Zero energy use, reducing carbon emissions, or minimizing environmental impact.

The owner or client should provide clear guidance on project goals and expectations, allocate sufficient resources for the project, and collaborate closely with the PM team to ensure that the project is delivered on time, within budget, and to the required standards.

Architects: Architects are responsible for designing the building or structure, taking into account the owner's goals, local building codes, and sustainable design principles. They may work closely with other stakeholders, such as engineers, contractors, and sustainability consultants.

The role requires architects to have a deep understanding of sustainable design principles, be able to develop and communicate a clear design vision, and collaborate effectively with other stakeholders to ensure that the design meets the project goals and requirements.

Contractors: Contractors are responsible for overseeing the construction of the building or structure. They should work closely with architects, engineers, and other stakeholders to ensure that the project is built according to the plans and specifications.

Contractors should have a strong track record in sustainable construction practices, be able to manage the construction process effectively, and collaborate closely with other stakeholders to ensure that timing and budget expectations are met.

Engineers: Engineers are responsible for designing and implementing systems such as HVAC, lighting, and renewable energy systems.

They should work closely with architects, contractors, and sustainability consultants to ensure that the buildings maximize energy efficiency and minimize environmental impact.

Their role requires a deep understanding of sustainable building systems, the design and implementation of complex systems, and the ability to integrate these systems seamlessly into building designs.

Sustainability consultants: Sustainability consultants are responsible for providing expert advice on sustainable design and construction practices. They work alongside owners, architects, contractors, and engineers to develop sustainability strategies and to ensure that projects meet their goals.

They should possess a deep understanding of sustainable design and construction practices, be able to provide expert advice on sustainability strategies, and collaborate effectively with other stakeholders to ensure that the project meets the required Net Zero standards.

7.7. Creating organizational change through effective project management

In order to establish a culture of sustainability and achieve Net Zero emissions in construction, professionals need to re-evaluate their PM principles. Net Zero ambitions cannot be reached overnight, but the speed of progress will quicken if the construction sector strives for greener practices.

With world economies under pressure, it's asking a lot of the construction sector to increase productivity, meet targets, and stay within budgets while also prioritizing sustainability. Advocating for better materials, wider use of technology, and effective waste management are all necessary steps, but PM also has a significant role to play in any organization's progress toward sustainability.

Project managers must be agile enough to adapt as challenges arise in their organizations. Cultivating this style of response creates teams that are equipped to put Net Zero principles into action. It's a transition that takes time, effort, and the will of all stakeholders. Organizations have to position themselves to deliver the necessary response to the climate crisis.

Industry bodies must prioritize education initiatives that equip the global workforce with the necessary skills to implement Net Zero methodologies. Modernizing the capabilities of workers will enable sustainable construction efforts to filter into wider use. Furthermore, shifting the industry's thinking will promote the adoption of a sustainably minded approach to construction for generations to come.

Building teams with cross-functional capability is essential in order to realize the full scope and sustainable potential of each project. By placing the focus on results, processes can be adapted as needed to reach them. That's where the agility of project managers is able to affect noticeable change. It may seem counterintuitive in a sector that's dominated by deadlines and rigid structure, but PM strategies have to embrace flexibility in order to meet changing conditions.

Embedding sustainability principles within the ethos of an organization can be fast-tracked by way of PM procedures that are derived from those same principles. It creates room for structural changes in the company and new roles that support sustainability. Support from decision-makers should eventually lead to renewed organizational strategies that recognize and prioritize Net Zero goals across the board.

Sustainability should always be considered during any process or decision. To make this happen, organizations need to understand how different business areas can help achieve sustainability goals. A unified and collaborative approach is essential if organizations are to entrench sustainable practices and principles. Ultimately, Net Zero presents an opportunity for project managers to improve their organizations' long-term success and secure a greener future.

7.7.1. *Organizational-level requirements for Net Zero project management*

Net Zero construction projects require a holistic approach to PM, which considers all aspects of the project's design, construction, operation, and maintenance. At an organizational level, the following aspects should be addressed to achieve meaningful results:

Leadership and commitment: Commitment from leadership is critical to the success of any Net Zero project. The organization must be committed to the goal of achieving Net Zero carbon emissions and have a clear understanding of the benefits and challenges that will arise.

Collaboration and communication: All stakeholders, including architects, engineers, contractors, suppliers, and facility managers, must collaborate and communicate effectively to ensure that everyone is aligned with Net Zero objectives and requirements.

Knowledge and expertise: Net Zero construction projects require specialized knowledge and expertise in areas, such as energy efficiency, renewable energy, building science, and sustainable design. Organizations must ensure that they have the necessary skills and knowledge to manage projects effectively.

Planning and design: Planning and design processes must take into account each site's location, climate, and available resources. Comprehensive project plans should be developed that include clear goals, timelines, and milestones.

Technology and innovation: Net Zero construction projects require the use of advanced technologies and innovative solutions to achieve the desired results. Organizations must stay up to date with the latest technology trends and ensure that projects incorporate the most appropriate and effective solutions.

Measurement and verification: To ensure that carbon emission goals are achieved, organizations must establish robust measurement and verification plans that include regular monitoring, data analysis, and reporting to stakeholders.

Continuous improvement: Net Zero PM is an ongoing process that requires continuous improvement. Organizations must continually evaluate project performance, identify areas for improvement, and implement changes to achieve better results.

7.7.2. *Project-level requirements for Net Zero project management*

To achieve Net Zero targets, PM teams need to take several requirements into consideration for each project:

Energy efficiency: Projects must prioritize energy efficiency in their design and construction, including the use of materials and techniques that reduce energy consumption and improve insulation. This requires careful planning and coordination among the design and construction teams.

Renewable energy sources: Onsite renewable energy sources must be able to generate enough power to meet the building's energy needs. PM teams must carefully assess the location and orientation of the building to optimize the use of these sources.

Water efficiency: Every project must prioritize water efficiency through the use of improved fixtures, rainwater harvesting, and deliberate conservation measures. PM, design, and construction teams must collaborate to integrate water efficiency into the project's overall plan.

Waste management: Minimizing waste during construction and operation is imperative to staying on track toward Net Zero targets. This includes the use of recycled and sustainable materials and the implementation of recycling programs for materials that can't be reused.

Monitoring and reporting: PM teams must develop a system for monitoring a building's energy use and renewable energy generation, as well as water use and waste management. This information should be regularly reported to stakeholders to ensure transparency and accountability.

Commissioning: Projects must undergo a commissioning process to ensure that all systems and equipment are installed and operate correctly. This is an important milestone to ensure buildings are meeting their Net Zero energy goals.

Maintenance: Projects must include a maintenance plan to ensure that all systems and equipment are regularly inspected and maintained for optimal performance and energy efficiency.

7.7.3. The challenges of Net Zero project management

Achieving Net Zero targets and reducing greenhouse gas emissions present some significant challenges for construction PM. These challenges include the following:

Complex design: Careful design and planning are required to integrate energy-efficient features, such as insulation, solar panels, and efficient heating and cooling systems. This can make the design process more complex and time-consuming when compared with traditional buildings.

Higher costs: Net Zero construction can be more expensive than traditional construction due to the use of specialized materials and technology. This can create challenges for project managers who need to balance costs with the desire for energy efficiency.

Tight schedules: Net Zero construction projects often have tight schedules due to the need to meet specific energy goals. The challenge for project managers is to ensure that every aspect of the construction process is carefully planned and executed to avoid delays.

Skilled labor shortage: Building Net Zero structures requires skilled labor with specialized training and expertise. The shortage of skilled workers in the construction industry can make it difficult to find qualified personnel to work on Net Zero projects.

Limited availability of materials: Some materials used in Net Zero construction are not as widely available as traditional materials. This can create challenges for project managers who need to source materials from a limited pool of suppliers.

Regulatory challenges: Building codes and regulations can vary widely depending on the location of the project. Project managers must stay up to date on local codes and regulations to ensure that their projects meet all necessary requirements.

7.8. Enhancing Net Zero project management

7.8.1. *Strategies to enhance Net Zero project management*

As organizations strive toward achieving Net Zero targets, PM plays a crucial role in ensuring the successful implementation of sustainable building practices. Project managers can employ several strategies to improve and enhance Net Zero construction in their own capacity, as well as from an organizational standpoint.

From the outset, project managers should establish clear sustainability goals at the beginning of the project and make sure all team members understand them. By defining what Net Zero means for each project, it outlines measurable targets and a clear path to achieving them. Developing a comprehensive project plan that accommodates the many components of Net Zero construction ensures a concerted effort from all parties involved in the process.

Conducting an energy audit gives project managers a clear view of the energy consumption patterns of the site. This helps them identify areas that can be improved and enhanced to achieve Net Zero energy consumption. It also enables them to prioritize the incorporation of renewable energy sources that reduce greenhouse emissions and generate energy for the building. The aim is to reduce reliance on non-renewable energy sources as much as possible.

Project managers must monitor and optimize a building's energy use to ensure that it is not using more energy than necessary, during and after construction. This can be achieved by implementing a sustainability management system that ensures sustainability goals are being met throughout each project's life cycle. These systems include regular sustainability audits, performance tracking, and reporting, which enable project managers to monitor and evaluate outcomes and identify areas for improvement.

Technology is a vital asset that streamlines and improves PM efforts. Its varied implementation enables project managers to pursue Net Zero targets from multiple angles. Modern developments such as building information modeling (BIM) can help identify potential sustainability issues early in the design process, and passive design strategies can help reduce energy consumption and improve overall energy efficiency. Taking advantage of automated systems simplifies the tasks of controlling a building's heating, ventilation, and air conditioning systems, as well as its lighting and other energy-consuming systems.

The effectiveness of PM is ultimately determined by communication and collaboration. By engaging with owners, architects, engineers, contractors, suppliers, and regulatory bodies, project managers can align everyone's efforts to the same sustainability goals. A joint commitment is key to achieving sustainable project outcomes throughout a building's life cycle.

7.9. Improving the construction value chain

Improving the construction value chain requires increased collaboration between parties involved in building projects, such as developers, architects, engineers, and contractors. Open channels of communication can lead to better understanding of project requirements, better coordination of workflows, and more efficient use of resources. Greater transparency can be achieved through shared information on budgets, schedules, and materials which can further enhance efficiency gains.

An increased adoption rate for new technology will provide significant growth for the industry. Recent innovations in artificial intelligence (AI), virtual reality, robotics, and 3D printing are allowing for faster design processes and more accurate estimates of construction costs, resulting in faster project completion and lower overall costs. The use of mobile devices on construction sites can help increase the accuracy of data collected on site and streamline operations by providing real-time updates to all parties involved.

Improved safety measures are essential for enhancing the value chain. By introducing more stringent safety protocols and training workers on safe practices, construction sites can be made safer while also minimizing delays due to accidents or incorrect usage of materials. This could lead to fewer disruptions and ultimately result in a better-finished product as well as cost savings from reduced downtime.

With improved supply chain management, businesses can ensure that the materials and resources used are of the highest quality and delivered on time. It's essential that technology such as BIM and prefabrication techniques be incorporated into projects to increase their efficiency. Measures that improve the way the industry operates can be leveraged into sustainability gains that deliver positive impact on a broad scale.

These tools are increasingly being used for design planning, material selection, delivery, as well as during construction on site.

Smart systems provide a wealth of benefits to both contractors and owners alike, due to their ability to collect large amounts of data quickly, accurately track progress throughout development stages, monitor performance metrics, generate reports, predict potential problems before they arise, and provide detailed insights into the project. Automation helps to reduce manual labor, improve efficiency and accuracy in construction processes, and cut costs by eliminating errors or delays. Automated systems have also been proven to increase safety on job sites by reducing the risk of human error or injury due to dangerous conditions.

As technology continues to evolve, so do the opportunities available for the use of smart systems and automation in building construction. Smart systems will continue to become more intuitive and user-friendly, with better capabilities for collecting and analyzing data that can be used to make positive changes in how buildings are designed and constructed. This shift toward smarter technologies is likely to result in a future where projects are completed faster, cheaper, and safer than ever before.

7.9.3. *Reducing emissions in the value chain*

Construction companies can reduce their CO_2 emissions in the value chain by opting to use ecofriendly materials. This includes sustainably sourced wood, stone, and other natural building materials, and products produced with 100% renewable energy. Manufacturers of building components, such as bricks and doors, should look to use sustainable production processes that are energy-efficient and have minimal environmental impact.

Organizations can also look to invest in more efficient machinery and equipment. Investing in machines with higher fuel efficiency or electric-powered tools will help reduce GHG emission from fuel consumption during construction activities. Further consideration should be given to investment in renewable energy sources, such as solar panels and wind turbines, which generate electricity without emitting any GHG emissions.

The industry is actively working to reduce the amount of waste it generates, but more can be done. Strides can be made by aiming for zero-waste construction sites and implementing strategies such as reusing materials or donating surplus supplies to local communities. Ensuring that waste is disposed of responsibly and recycled where possible will help further reduce carbon dioxide emissions in the value chain.

By investing in ecofriendly materials, more efficient machinery and equipment, and reducing their waste output, construction companies can significantly reduce their CO_2 emissions throughout the entire value chain. Doing so will not only benefit the environment but also have positive impacts on company profits through reduced energy costs and improved public perception. As such, these strategies are an important consideration for any construction businesses seeking to reduce their environmental impact.

7.9.4. *Improving process efficiency in the value chain*

Process efficiency is a key factor in the productivity and profitability of any construction project. By streamlining processes, teams can achieve greater consistency in output and reduce operational costs. One way to do this is by implementing process automation tools that can automate mundane tasks, freeing up time for workers to focus on more value-adding activities.

Automated systems also help ensure accuracy in data collection and reporting, which is essential for decision-making and overall success. Additionally, process optimization techniques provide an effective way to identify areas of opportunity within existing processes and eliminate waste. By looking at how materials are used throughout the entire value chain — from suppliers to final consumers — teams can efficiently identify areas where they can improve their operations. Ongoing training of personnel and investments in technologies with the potential to improve process efficiency are essential for success. By taking a proactive approach to improving process efficiency, construction teams can ensure their operations remain efficient, productive, and profitable.

Companies that develop strategies to continually optimize their processes will be best positioned to stay ahead of the competition while achieving greater operational efficiency and customer satisfaction. Investing in process automation tools, adopting lean construction principles, providing training opportunities, and investing in innovative technologies can all help ensure that key processes within the construction value chain are streamlined and optimized for maximum results. This is increasingly critical as competition intensifies and companies strive to make better use of existing resources while ensuring customer satisfaction and sustainability efforts both remain at a high level.

7.9.5. *Closing material loops in the value chain*

Circular economy strategies are being implemented in the construction industry, with a particular focus on closing material loops within the value chain. Closing material loops involves reusing or repurposing materials instead of disposing of them, which has multiple benefits such as reducing waste and emissions associated with production processes. It also contributes to increased resource efficiency and cost savings for businesses. For example, reuse of construction materials can help reduce costs related to raw material purchases. This directly contributes to the UN's Sustainable Development Goals set by reducing carbon dioxide emissions from production processes, conserving natural resources, and creating jobs in green industries.

An effective way to implement circular economy strategies is through life cycle assessment analysis. This process can be used to identify the environmental impacts of materials at different stages of their life and helps to develop strategies for mitigating those impacts. It is also a useful tool for assessing the sustainability potential of building materials, which is important when selecting materials during construction projects.

Another valuable strategy for closing material loops in the construction value chain is to use recycled or reused materials that include high-quality salvaged materials from previously demolished buildings, as well as scrap materials from production processes. Recycled and reused material can also offer cost savings compared to purchasing new products since it has already been produced without additional energy or resources being expended. Many businesses now offer upcycling services to convert scrap material into usable components for construction projects, and this further contributes to waste reduction in the industry.

Circular economy strategies are becoming increasingly popular within the construction industry as they offer multiple benefits to businesses, including cost savings and increased sustainability. It is important for businesses in the construction sector to ensure they are taking responsibility by creating systems that are able to capture and store information on the approaches they are taking. This can help track progress and ensure compliance with sustainability regulations in a transparent manner, thus driving continuous innovation in the industry. These measures are key factors in closing material loops within the construction value chain.

7.10. Energy efficiency and sustainable construction

Energy-efficient buildings incorporate the principles of energy efficiency in their design and construction. These buildings are designed to reduce energy consumption by using materials, technologies, and practices that optimize the use of natural resources while minimizing the impact on the environment.

These principles can be applied to residential homes, commercial buildings, or public facilities. Common features of energy-efficient buildings include passive solar heating and cooling systems, reduced lighting demands through proper window placement, improved insulation material and techniques, high-efficiency HVAC systems, increased air sealing measures to reduce infiltration losses, and green roofs with native vegetation to absorb heat in summer months and reduce air conditioning costs.

By implementing these strategies during the design and construction phases, it can create the dual effect of reducing the structure's carbon footprint and decreasing its operating costs. Furthermore, investing in energy-efficient buildings can yield attractive returns over time through possible tax credits, utility bill savings, and increased property value.

Employing professional contractors that specialize in green building practices will help ensure that all aspects of the project are carried out with sound knowledge and experience to achieve optimal performance. Designers now have access to sophisticated design modeling software that helps predict energy performance based on design, and ways to further improve. With proper planning and execution, energy-efficient buildings are viable investments that provide long-term economic advantages without sacrificing comfort or aesthetic value.

7.10.1. *Essential components of energy-efficient buildings*

Energy-efficient buildings require properly insulated floors, walls, and windows to maintain comfortable temperatures and reduce the amount of energy needed for heating and cooling. Building materials with low thermal conductivity are ideal for reducing energy consumption. For example, using double- or triple-glazed windows, which contain two or three layers of air between panes of glass that act as an insulator, can significantly reduce heat transfer.

Utilizing natural ventilation prevents excess energy use due to mechanical systems such as fans or other energy-efficient measures including demand responsive HVAC systems. Stakeholders must be mindful of best practices for energy efficiency in buildings in order to take full advantage of strides made in sustainable construction.

The development of sustainable construction methodologies is an integral part of global efforts to reduce environmental impact, improve occupant comfort, and increase operational savings. Cost-effective technologies with proven track records are readily available, and once incorporated they can provide long- and short-term benefits that directly support sustainability goals. And emerging technologies such as hydrogen boilers present further opportunities for integrating solutions.

Organizations can create immediate impact by incorporating these components into new buildings or retrofitting existing buildings to further enhance their sustainability. This includes utilizing solar PV arrays for electricity generation or installing solar collectors for hot water heating; geothermal systems for space conditioning; wind turbines for power generation; and green roofs to promote rainwater harvesting. These strategies ensure that energy-efficient designs are achieved, while reducing the amount of energy consumed over the life cycle of the building.

Electrifying existing buildings is an important step to reduce reliance on gas and fossil fuels, which are becoming increasingly scarce resources. By replacing existing systems with electricity-powered alternatives, building owners can take advantage of more efficient, cost-effective solutions that will help them meet sustainable development goals.

A common method of electrifying an existing building is through the installation of a microgrid. These small, local electrical grids can provide power to a single building or multiple buildings, and they allow for the integration of renewable energy sources, such as solar and wind, into the existing electricity infrastructure. A resulting benefit of this is that fully electrified buildings incorporating renewable energy are financially attractive for investment.

Progress may be incremental, but widespread integration of sustainability into construction projects will deliver multiple user benefits, combat climate change, and improve resource efficiency. As technology continues to evolve, so will the possibilities for energy-efficient construction. It's essential for the global construction community to embrace these new technologies and continue to promote sustainable construction to ensure a more energy-efficient future.

7.11. Final considerations

7.11.1. *Climate change and the built environment*

The relationship between climate change and the built environment is a complicated one. Volumes of empirical evidence have confirmed that the global rise in temperatures can be directly attributed to climate change. Its impact is being felt by populations in various climates across a range of geographical regions, and the severity of the crisis is increasing.

We spend a significant majority of our lives within buildings, with the internal environment having a profound impact on our health, happiness, productivity, and well-being. However, the reality is that buildings are a major contributor to greenhouse gas emissions. The energy we use to heat, light, ventilate, cool, and operate our buildings accounts for up to half of the total national emissions in most developed countries. Urbanization trends are set to further increase the urgency of the situation.

Climate change will shape our world for generations to come, and the only way we will be able to navigate it while preserving our way of life is by taking urgent action to address its root causes. This must include extensive change from the construction industry that considers how buildings are designed, how we interact with them, the materials we use to build them, and their associated energy consumption.

By taking into account factors such as climate, building materials, and architecture when designing and constructing buildings, we can significantly reduce their greenhouse gas emissions. The global built environment has a major effect on climate change and by making sustainable decisions in our design practices, we have the potential to make a great contribution in the fight against it.

In order to reduce emissions from buildings and improve their sustainability performance, it is important to understand how the design and construction processes affect energy usage and emissions in different climates. For example, in tropical regions where temperatures are generally warmer than other areas, building materials that are highly reflective can be used to reduce solar gain, thereby reducing the need for air conditioning and decreasing emissions.

Likewise, the use of passive design elements such as natural ventilation, low-emissivity windows, and daylighting technologies can help to control temperatures inside buildings and reduce the amount of energy needed for heating or cooling. Additionally, renewable energy sources such as solar photovoltaic systems can be used to provide a clean source of electricity for buildings with minimal emissions. Green roofs are also becoming increasingly popular in urban planning as they provide insulation from extreme temperatures while helping to purify the air in cities.

Incorporating sustainable design practices into our construction processes can reduce energy consumption and emissions while creating healthier and more comfortable spaces. These include the use of renewable building materials and efficient energy consumption, as well as measures that limit deforestation and disruption of ecosystems caused by construction activities. By recognizing the importance of this issue and taking action to address it, we can make great strides in fighting climate change.

As climate change becomes an ever-increasing concern in the building industry, sustainable methods and materials have become integral parts of best practices. Factoring climate change into building design helps to reduce the impact of global warming and allows for buildings to be constructed with materials that can withstand varying weather conditions. Building designs should take into account the local climate, including temperature ranges, humidity levels, and precipitation amounts.

These considerations will help architects create efficient structures that are able to maintain comfortable indoor temperatures while reducing the need for supplemental heating and cooling systems.

To achieve maximum efficiency in a structure, factors such as thermal control, insulation, proper glazing techniques, air-flow management systems, and energy-efficient lighting should be considered during the planning stages of construction projects. Additionally, by using certifications, such as LEED or BREEAM, project managers, architects, and builders are able to ensure that their designs meet certain standards for ecoefficiency. By incorporating energy efficiency measures from the beginning stages of construction projects, it presents the opportunity to create buildings that are not only energy-efficient but also resilient in the face of changing climatic conditions.

In addition to reducing energy consumption, factoring climate change into building design can also reduce the amount of construction waste produced, helping to protect the environment. By instituting environmentally conscious practices, the industry can help mitigate the effects of climate change while providing safe and comfortable living spaces for occupants. Deep consideration of climate change in relation to flexible building design promotes a more sustainable future for us all.

7.11.2. *Achieving the Paris Agreement*

The Paris Agreement, adopted in December 2015, is a landmark international agreement aimed at significantly reducing global greenhouse gas emissions. Specifically, the goal of the Paris Agreement is to limit the global temperature rise to well below 2°C above pre-industrial levels.

In order to achieve its goals, nations must commit to ambitious climate action. This includes setting nationally determined contributions (NDCs) that outline the actions each country will take to reduce emissions and help adapt to climate change. These contributions are designed to be tailored toward a particular country's circumstances, including its level of economic growth, development, and resources available. NDC commitments may include efforts such as improving energy efficiency standards or accelerating renewable energy deployment among other measures.

Countries should work together on international cooperation initiatives in areas such as capacity building and technology transfer. By increasing access to clean energy sources and modernizing infrastructure across borders, it is possible to improve global resilience against climate change while developing low-emission economies. Coordinated efforts to reduce emissions from deforestation and land degradation, as well as ocean protection measures, are also important for achieving the Paris Agreement's goals.

The commitment of all nations is required if we are to have a realistic chance at limiting global warming to 1.5°C or lower by the end of this century. It is only through collective action that we can maximize our chances of success in combating climate change and protecting our planet's future.

Unfortunately, there are various barriers which prevent countries from joining and implementing the Paris Agreement in a timely manner. One such barrier is lack of political will or commitment. Many nations are facing domestic issues which take precedence over environmental concerns, which limits their ability to commit resources toward climate action initiatives over other areas such as healthcare or education. Additionally, some countries may be unwilling to make significant changes that might disrupt economic growth.

Another barrier to consider is the difficulty of reaching agreements between nations with differing views on climate change. In some cases, countries may have divergent goals for reducing emissions; this could lead to disagreements about implementing a global solution which works for everyone. Further difficulty may be encountered when attempting to coordinate policies across multiple borders and jurisdictions.

Some countries simply lack the capacity and resources required to implement the Paris Agreement in practical terms. This includes financial resources as well as technical knowledge and expertise needed to develop effective strategies and action plans for climate change mitigation and adaptation. Without access to technology or infrastructure that could help them reduce their emissions, it becomes even more difficult for them to contribute to the global effort.

In spite of these barriers, the global community must continue to develop and implement solutions that enable nations to work together toward a more sustainable future. If we are to achieve the goals outlined in the Paris Agreement, a collective and concerted effort is imperative.

7.12. Conclusion

The construction industry has a crucial role to play in helping the world achieve its climate change targets set out in the Paris Agreement. Buildings and infrastructure account for nearly half of global energy-related CO_2 emissions and are responsible for a significant share of air pollution. Reducing their environmental impact is vital for people and the planet, especially as demand continues to grow.

The industry must support the development of green infrastructure, and globally, government bodies have the responsibility of incentivizing them to do so. By embracing more sustainable materials and technologies, prioritizing green infrastructure initiatives, and encouraging energy efficiency measures in buildings across the globe, this essential sector can be part of an effort to drastically reduce global CO_2 emissions. No other industry is better positioned to make an immediate and significant contribution to climate change.

The Paris Agreement provides a global framework for nations to take action on climate change, aiming to keep global warming well below 2°C above pre-industrial levels. To meet this goal, countries must take concrete steps to reduce emissions, increase renewable energy sources, and invest in adaptation measures that reduce the impacts of climate change. Effective PM is a crucial conduit to implement these actions.

PM is well-suited to helping mitigate the effects of climate change due to its focus on organization, goal setting, and problem solving. By leveraging PM techniques, organizations can take action that helps reduce carbon emissions as well as create a framework for adaptation in the face of changing environmental conditions.

PM enables organizations to adopt a structured approach to planning, resourcing, and executing their Net Zero ambitions. It provides the platform for collaborative efforts from multiple stakeholders in order to achieve total sector decarbonization together. Global partnerships such as the BuildingToCOP coalition advocate for frontrunner action from non-state actors, and support countries that recognize the potential of the built environment to reduce emissions and adapt to climate change. This is slowly translating into increased policy and investor requirements, requiring the sector to adapt and mobilize toward high-performance outcomes.

A clear focus on continuous improvement, flexibility, and collaboration will allow teams to quickly respond to new challenges or opportunities while still working toward overall Net Zero goals. This allows for greater agility and responsiveness when addressing the urgency of climate change and promotes improved coordination of resources and teams across borders.

PM tools can assist in monitoring and evaluating potential climate change impacts. This includes forecasting future trends in temperature, precipitation, and other variables, as well as assessing risk mitigation strategies. Best practices will ensure that the necessary data is collected and analyzed in order to provide reliable results which can be used to inform decision-making or set goals for reducing emissions.

In order to build resilience in communities around the world, PM principles must champion energy efficiency and develop plans with realistic milestones and the necessary resources to be completed timeously. These strategies may also be useful when creating policies that are intended to regulate carbon emissions from business activities or processes. With a clear understanding of both organizational objectives and external requirements, project managers can rely on effective policies that meet the needs of both stakeholders and the environment.

In pursuit of Net Zero, PM is a powerful tool for taking action against climate change that helps organizations and individuals plan, monitor, and evaluate their efforts toward mitigating its effects. By leveraging these techniques, we can create better outcomes for businesses and for our planet.

References

Adams, M., Burrows, V., Richardson, S., & World Green Building Council. (2019). Bringing embodied carbon upfront. Available at: https://worldgbc. s3.eu-west-2.amazonaws.com/wp-content/uploads/2022/09/22123951/ WorldGBC_Bringing_Embodied_Carbon_Upfront.pdf (accessed on 14 December 2022).

Bakshi, A. (2022). Re-thinking project management can facilitate Net Zero in construction. Available at: https://www.pbctoday.co.uk/news/energy-news/re-thinking-project-management-facilitate-transition-net-zero-in-construction/111285/ (accessed on 5 November 2022).

Flyvbjerg, B. & Gardner, D. (2023). *How Big Things Get Done: The Surprising Factors that Determine the Fate of Every Project, from Home Renovations to Space Exploration and Everything in Between.* USA: Penguin Random House.

Schäfer, A. & Zuberer, J. (2022). How construction companies can combine profitable growth with Net Zero. Available at: https://www.ey.com/en_gl/strategy/how-construction-companies-can-combine-profitable-growth-with-net-zero (accessed on 2 November 2022).

World Green Building Council. (2022a). The commitment. Available at: https://worldgbc.org/thecommitment/ (accessed on 10 November 2022).

World Green Building Council. (2022b). What is a net zero carbon building? Available at: https://worldgbc.org/advancing-net-zero/what-is-a-net-zero-carbon-building/ (accessed on 28 October 2022).

Chapter 8

Green Construction Project Scope Management

Ali Alashwal and Laura Melo de Almeida

Western Sydney University, Penrith, Australia

Project scope includes a detailed description of the outcomes or mission of the project. Project scope development is the basis for defining other project components, such as schedule, cost, quality, regulatory compliance requirements, and risk. The purpose of this chapter is to discuss the current approaches and processes of project scope management and show how they can be applied in green construction projects. The predictive and iterative approaches of project scope development are discussed in this chapter. This chapter provides a detailed description of project scope management processes from project initiation to closure, and the requirements to ensure that the green asset is kept as "green" throughout its life cycle. Project scope management processes comprise different models, tools, and artifacts, coordinated by stakeholders as part of developing the green construction project. Besides, this chapter highlights some issues of scope management of green construction projects. This chapter concludes that stakeholders' integrative approach, the agility of design, and the utilization of relevant tools such as Green Assessor are crucial processes for effective scope management.

8.1. Introduction

Developing project scope is one of the initial steps conducted early in the project life cycle and serves as the basis for developing other project elements such as schedule, cost, and quality baselines. Providing a clear scope definition is important so the project team's expectations meet other stakeholders' expectations, specifically the owner and end users. Proper scope development and management can be the turning point to achieve project success. Project scope shows the boundary of the project to determine the deliverables and components that should be included and excluded from the project.

Project scope is defined by the Project Management Institute (PMI) (2017) as the detailed description of the outcome (e.g., building) of the project in specific, tangible, and measurable terms. The outcome description includes details of the functions, features, components, and characteristics of the building. The scope also includes the work or activities performed to execute and deliver the building. Therefore, scope management includes product scope management and project scope management.

This chapter provides a detailed explanation of project scope management processes and their application in green construction projects. This chapter consists of the following sections: project scope approaches including predictive and adaptive, scope management processes based on ISO and the Project Management Body of Knowledge (PMBOK) Guide, green construction scope management, and issues of green construction scope management. This chapter concludes with highlights on how the scope of a green construction project can be managed effectively by introducing new processes and tools relevant to this type of project.

8.2. Scope development approaches

The purpose of project scope management is to facilitate the realization of project deliverables and outcomes. Developing a clear project scope description and outcomes is the first step to developing and managing other project elements including time, cost, quality, and risk. An important step toward developing a clear scope definition and ensuring project success is to establish an agreement among key project stakeholders about project deliverables. However, it is not possible to develop a full description of the outcome of the project, especially at the initiation or planning stages. In fact, project scope development is an iterative process. This means that the scope cannot be fully developed at the early stage of the project but requires refinement during the planning and executing stages until the outcome (i.e., building) is achieved. The iterative process of scope development requires the active involvement of the owner, project management (PM) team, and end users in the development process.

Two common approaches are used to develop project scope and deliver outcomes, which are predictive life cycle and adaptive life cycle. PMI (2021) defines the project development approach as the method to create and evolve the outcome during the project life cycle. Choosing the appropriate development approach for a project depends mainly on project characteristics, scope stability, requirements certainty, and the level of flexibility to adopt change (PMI, 2021). Besides scope, other factors that affect choosing between these two approaches are organizational context, characteristics of the project team, time requirements, and budget requirements (Thesing *et al.*, 2021). The project life cycle consists of several phases and provides a basic framework to manage project work. Project phases, which are logically connected activities to complete one or more deliverables such as design and construction, can be arranged as sequential, iterative, or overlapping. Project phases have the following features. Each phase is unique and has attributes such as a unique name, specified duration, and specified cost and resources. Mostly, construction activities consist of sequential phases but can also have overlapping or iterative activities. For example, the construction phase follows the design phase. However, some construction activities can begin before the design can be fully completed (overlapping). On the other hand, as construction work commences, the original design can be amended to reflect the actual situation on site (iterative). Table 8.1 shows a summary of the differences between the predictive and adaptive approaches. The following sections provide more details about the predictive and adaptive scope development.

Table 8.1.   Differences between predictive and adaptive project development approaches.

	Predictive development	Adaptive development
1. Deliverables	Defined at the beginning of the project	Developed over multiple iterations (scope defined or approved when iteration begins)
2. Change level	Low	High
3. Scope development	Full baseline at the beginning of the project	Product backlog (list of highest-priority items/requirements for each iteration)
4. Stakeholders engagement	At the beginning of the project or to validate deliverables	Ongoing for each iteration
5. Scope management processes	Collect requirements, define scope, and create WBS performed at the beginning of the project and updated using integrated change control	Collect requirements, define scope, and create WBS are repeated at the beginning of the iteration
6. Scope baseline	Scope baseline (scope statement, WBS, and WBS dictionary)	Backlogs (product requirements and user stories)

Source: Adapted from PMI (2017).

8.2.1. *Predictive scope development*

The predictive approach is also known as waterfall (Thesing *et al.*, 2021). In this approach, project scope can be, to a great extent, developed earlier in the project life cycle. Project requirements and deliverables are almost fixed. Mostly, construction activities are performed once to produce the building. Changes to project scope during the execution phase are controlled and managed carefully. The main purpose of controlling the scope is to manage cost and reduce changes to design and project components. Figure 8.1 provides an example of a predictive development approach for a construction project. In this example, the scope is developed during the early phase of the project (e.g., design stage). The execution of the project is based on predetermined requirements and plans. The phases are completed sequentially. The project starts in the first phase (e.g., feasibility study) and completes in

Figure 8.1.   Example of predictive project life cycle and sequential phases.

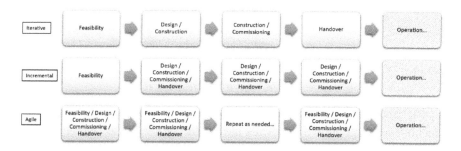

Figure 8.2.   Examples of adaptive project life cycles.

the last phase (i.e., commissioning or hand-over). The project boundary is defined by these phases. The outcome of the project (e.g., building) is transitioned to the operation stage after handing over the project.

8.2.2. *Adaptive scope development*

In the adaptive approach, the project scope can be determined early in the project life cycle, but time and cost estimates are modified as more information becomes available and the team develops a better understanding of project requirements. Components of construction projects may be delivered using some forms of the adaptive approach but usually not the whole project. The adaptive approach is most often used in projects that require a great level of flexibility in defining project requirements or when the project is delivered as multiple components. This approach involves iterative processes of planning, testing, and executing, which are repeated as needed until the outcome is achieved. The different forms of adaptive development approaches are iterative, incremental, and agile life cycles, as shown in Figure 8.2.

Table 8.2.   Project life cycles and project scope.

Life cycle	Requirements	Project activities	Delivery	Goal
Predictive	Fixed	Performed once for the entire project	Single delivery	Manage cost
Iterative	Flexible	Repeated until correct	Single delivery	Correctness of solution
Incremental	Flexible	Performed once for a given increment	Frequent small deliveries	Speed
Agile	Flexible	Repeated until correct	Frequent small deliveries	Customer value

Source: Adapted from PMI (2017).

Usually, the iterative approach has a single delivery (e.g., a building). Incremental and agile approaches have small deliveries as outcomes. The purpose of the iterative approach is to ensure the correctness of the outcome while the purpose of the incremental approach is the speed of delivery of the product. The purpose of the agile approach is to provide value to customers via frequent deliveries and feedback (PMI, 2017). Table 8.2 summarizes the differences between the four life cycles. It is uncommon that the whole construction project is delivered using the adaptive approach, specifically the incremental or agile life cycles. Therefore, this chapter focuses on the predictive approach to describe the processes of scope management, as shown in the following section.

8.3. Project scope management processes

The International Organization for Standardization (ISO) identified three processes of project scope management, which are Defining the Scope, Controlling the Scope, and Confirming the Scope Delivery (ISO, 2020). The purpose of the first process, Defining the Scope, is to confirm how the project is contributing to the objectives of the sponsoring organization. Defining the scope includes also identifying project requirements and how these requirements can be delivered and accepted by the sponsor or owner. This process establishes the scope baseline, which is the basis that will be used to accept the deliverables during the execution stage to complete the project.

The purpose of the second process, Controlling the Scope, is to compare the approved scope baseline to the actual deliverables and determine variances. The purpose of this process is also to maximize the positive and minimize the negative impacts of scope changes. Changes should be incorporated into the scope baseline and other project baselines including schedule and cost baselines. Lastly, Confirming the Scope Delivery focuses on accepting deliverables based on predefined criteria. This process ensures that the sponsoring organization, users, and other stakeholders are ready to receive the deliverables. The stakeholders should confirm that the deliverables and other ancillary results are completed according to the quality standards and other requirements.

The sixth edition of the PMBOK Guide covers other processes in more detail (PMI, 2017). The project scope management processes are Plan Scope Management, Collect Requirements, Define Scope, Create Work Breakdown Structure (WBS), Validate Scope, and Control Scope. These processes follow the predictive approach of project development (waterfall). The processes are covered during the planning, execution, monitoring and control, and closure stages. As shown in Figure 8.3, these processes are organized so each process has inputs, tools and techniques, and outputs. The outputs of a process can be the inputs of the subsequent process. The following sections explain these processes in detail.

8.3.1. *Plan Scope Management*

The purpose of Plan Scope Management is to document how the scope of the project will be defined, validated, and controlled. This process, which is performed at the planning stage of the project, can be formal (i.e., requires some authority to approve it) or informal (i.e., conducted as part of the routine practices). Plan Scope Management explains how the scope will be managed throughout the whole project life cycle. Expert judgment (e.g., project manager with prior experience in developing similar plans) is one of the main tools to develop this plan. One output of this process is the Scope Management Plan, which is a subsidiary component of the overall plan of the project (called the PM Plan). Scope Management Plan is sometimes generic and can be used for several similar projects to save time.

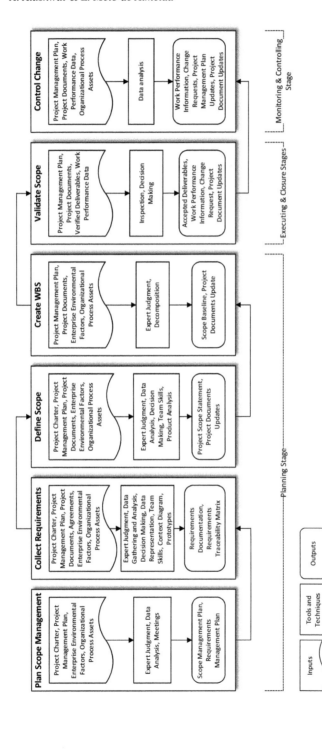

Figure 8.3.   Project scope management processes.

Source: Adapted from PMI (2017).

This document provides important details such as how the scope statement will be prepared, how the WBS will be created and maintained, how the scope will be changed and who authorizes the change, and how project deliverables will be formally accepted. Another output of this process is the Requirements Management Plan, which describes how project requirements can be collected, analyzed, and managed. This document may include details of configuration management activities (e.g., how the change will be initiated and managed across the project organization boundaries), requirements prioritization process, and requirements capturing tools (PMI, 2017).

8.3.2. *Collect Requirements*

Collect Requirements is the process of eliciting and analyzing the needs of project stakeholders and subsequently, transferring the needs into deliverables. Active involvement of project stakeholders is essential to performing this process. Often, many issues happen in the project due to the misunderstanding of stakeholders' needs and how the needs are communicated effectively to the managerial and execution teams. Thus, the seamless understanding of project requirements between all stakeholders is important for scope development. The identification of project requirements is useful for developing other components of the project, such as the WBS. Different tools and techniques can be used to collect project requirements, such as interviews, questionnaire surveys, focus groups, the Delphi technique, and benchmarking. Other tools used in construction include Quality Function Deployment (QFD) (Abdul-Rahman *et al.*, 1999) and mock-ups or three-dimensional (3D) modeling. QFD can be used to translate the client's requirements into technical characteristics and prioritize requirements to be considered in scope development during the design stage (Delgado-Hernandez *et al.*, 2007). The most common form of 3D modeling in construction is building information modeling (BIM). The collected project requirements can be categorized into business, stakeholder, and technical solutions. The requirements can be recorded in the Requirements Traceability Matrix (RTM) document, which connects requirements and deliverables (PMI, 2017). The RTM provides a description of how the requirements contribute to business value and project objectives, which is used to track the requirements and manage changes in project scope during project execution.

8.3.3. *Define Scope*

Define Scope is the process of selecting the final project requirements from the requirements documentation. Scope definition can be an iterative process, where requirements are selected and refined during different stages of the project. The requirements can be identified using different tools, such as data analysis, decision-making, and product analysis (PMI, 2017). The selected requirements can subsequently be developed into a detailed description of the final deliverables. The output of this process is the scope statement, which provides a detailed description of the major deliverables, related work, and final components of the product (i.e., building). The scope statement may contain project acceptance criteria and scope exclusions. Acceptance criteria include, for example, the time required to complete the project, specifications, safety requirements, and environmental regulatory requirements. Scope exclusions are activities, services, or deliverables that are excluded from the project to ensure a clearer scope definition. For instance, the delivery of a project may exclude the following services and activities: onsite hazardous waste man-agement service, additional drawing revisions based on value manage-ment study, and as-built drawings. Scope exclusions are usually included in the contract or agreement under exclusion clauses. Developing the project scope statement is important to complete other planning work (e.g., Create WBS), guide the work during execution, evaluate whether changes during the construction are within project scope, and provide a basis to measure project success.

8.3.4. *Create WBS*

WBS is defined by Larson and Gray (2021) as "a hierarchical method that successively subdivides the work of the project into smaller detail." The project can be divided into three to five levels of deliverables, subdeliver-ables, and work packages, as shown in Figure 8.4. Dividing the project into smaller components is useful to facilitate estimating and managing

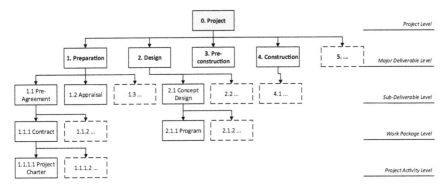

Figure 8.4.   Example of WBS.

the work. Creating WBS is the first step to developing a project schedule and budget. The work packages of WBS can be further decomposed into smaller activities to facilitate estimating and managing the work. Therefore, WBS helps the managerial team to determine the duration and cost of activities, identify the resources required to complete the work, and identify milestones to monitor the progress of work. The WBS can be created using top-down or bottom-up methods. The top-down method can be used when there is not much information available about the components of the project (e.g., during the early stage of the project). In this case, the major deliverables of the project can be developed based on project stages such as initiation, design, construction, and so on. If more details become available about project activities and components, the bottom-up method can be used by rolling 100% of all the work activities and packages up to the higher levels of deliverables and eventually the full project level. In the bottom-up method, the main deliverables of the WBS may include the project components arranged based on the work sequence, such as detailed drawings, earthwork, superstructure, and so on. WBS can also be created using a standardized template available in the sponsoring organization or the PM office.

The outputs of this process include the Scope Baseline, which is the approved version of the scope statement, WBS and work packages, and WBS-associated documents, such as the WBS Dictionary and planning packages (PMI, 2017). WBS Dictionary provides additional details such as the description of work to be completed, responsible organization and resources required to execute the work, cost center number associated with each work package or activities, milestone list, cost estimation, quality requirements, and other details as needed. The WBS can be linked to the Organizational Breakdown Structure (OBS) to determine organizational hierarchy and organizational units, or individuals required to complete the work. The integration between WBS and OBS is useful to identify responsibilities and communication channels and coordinate different work.

8.3.5. *Validate Scope*

Validate Scope is defined as the formal acceptance of project deliverables. This process is similar to Confirming the Scope Delivery process of ISO. Validate Scope can be performed periodically to accept project deliverables as they are completed during the construction stage. This process is different from the Control Quality process in that the latter is about ensuring the correctness of deliverables. Acceptance criteria should be established early during project planning through the Plan Scope Management process to facilitate accepting the deliverables. The onsite inspection is one of the common tools used to verify deliverables. Validate Scope outcomes include accepted deliverables, work performance information (WPI), and change requests. The project can be completed when all deliverables are accepted. The WPI includes details of the status of deliverables, which can be used to provide an indicator of the performance of the project. Change requests can be created if inspected deliverables are not according to the pre-defined criteria and/or there is a need to correct or modify the deliverables. The main methods to respond to changes in projects are corrective action, preventive action, or defect repair (PMI, 2017).

8.3.6. *Control scope*

Scope creep is one of the main issues facing construction projects. Scope creep occurs when the changes to project scope extend beyond the ability of the managerial team to control the expansions in time, cost, and resources available to complete the work. Many examples of how scope creep has affected projects are available in practice, such as the Big Dig freeway project and the Denver Airport baggage handling system (Larson & Gray, 2021). The purpose of the Control Scope process is to manage changes when they occur and analyze the impact of change on project schedule, cost, quality, and risk. The change can also be managed by considering new elements or project components in project baselines, such as cost baseline. The integrated change control process can be used to manage changes (PMI, 2017). As shown in Figure 8.5, the integrated change control process is commenced with a request to modify, add, or eliminate a deliverable. The request is analyzed to determine its influence on project schedule, cost, quality, and risk. For example, a Green Assessor (who is responsible for the assessment process and must be a recognized and certified professional by the selected rating tool) may initiate a

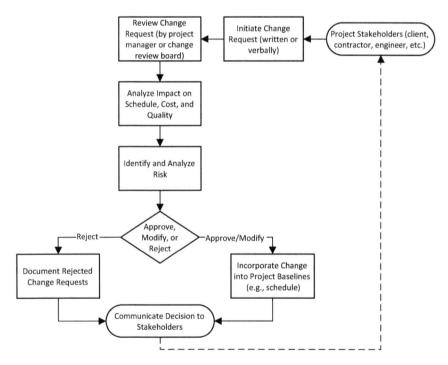

Figure 8.5.   Integrated change control process.
Source: Adapted from PMI (2017).

request during the design stage to replace some building materials with recycled materials to enhance the score of the building when applying for a Green Star rating. While this change would increase the project's Green Star rating, it may influence project cost, time, and/or quality. The overall cost of the project may be reduced if the owner receives a tax rebate as a result of using green materials. However, the quality of recycled materials may not be based on the client's requirements. In addition, the recycled materials may require more time to be delivered to the project and therefore additional time should be added to the project schedule. Based on this analysis and the identification of new risks, the change request can be approved, modified, or rejected. If the request is approved, the change will be incorporated into project baselines such as the project schedule baseline to include additional time if needed. The outcome of the analysis, whether the request is approved or rejected, should be documented and communicated to the main stakeholders.

8.4. Green construction and scope management processes

Green construction is an actual representation of the concepts expressed under the United Nations sustainable development goals (SDGs) aligned with commitments from the Paris Agreement (Ikudayisi *et al.*, 2022; Schmidt-Traub *et al.*, 2017). Green construction has a holistic approach to the built environment and aims to reduce the scarce use of resources by minimizing the external impacts on the natural environment due to the misuse or excessive use of natural resources, such as water, energy, and raw materials. Additionally, green construction contributes to sustainable developments and promotes quality of life in modern societies, enhancing the health and well-being of humans, as well as economic prosperity. Therefore, the main goal of green construction is to mitigate the impact of buildings and other construction outcomes on global warming, reduce the environmental impact related to pollution externalities and resource depletion, and protect the natural environment during construction work. To ensure the previous goals are met, green construction projects are assessed against a series of impact categories to ensure all the required sustainable and efficiency attributes are met (GBCA, 2021). Green construction projects have to comply with several environmental and energy requirements, such as improved thermal comfort, indoor air quality, water and energy efficiency, promotion of accessibility, implementation of renewable energies, daylighting considerations, and using non-polluting materials (Ching & Shapiro, 2021; Ikudayisi *et al.*, 2022). Aside from the environmental considerations, green construction takes the Triple Bottom Line (TBL) approach considering the project's environmental, social, and economic impacts from a local and regional perspective, accounting for its effects on the community and neighborhood connectivity (Retzlaff, 2009). Green construction projects not only promote the creation of green jobs and improve productivity but also enhance morale, meet societal goals of equity and equality, increase competitiveness, and robustly emphasize nature protection (Ching & Shapiro, 2021). Throughout a green construction certification process, it stresses a life cycle approach. Several stages are taken into consideration, which are planning/preparation, design, pre-construction, construction, operations/use, and end-of-life stages. Figure 8.6 represents the main stages and assessment methodologies included within each stage.

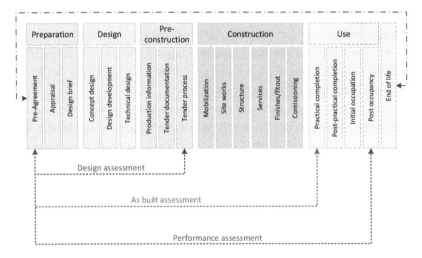

Figure 8.6. Stages and processes of green project assessment.

Source: Adopted from GBCA (2021).

The operation and end-of-life stages are not part of the project life cycle, but they influence how the scope is developed and elaborated.

One of the first steps in a green construction management process is selecting the rating tool for which the building will be certified. There are several tools available worldwide, as we saw in Chapter 3. The most common tools available are the Building Research Establishment Environmental Assessment Method (BREEAM) and Leadership in Energy and Environmental Design (LEED). BREEAM was the first tool launched in 1990, in the United Kingdom, by the Building Research Establishment (BRE). Then, in 1993, the United States Green Building Council (USGBC) started the development of LEED, which was launched in 1998. The Green Building Council of Australia (GBCA) launched in 2003 the Green Star rating system[1] (He *et al.*, 2018). All these tools are similar, not only in the criteria used to perform the assessment but also in the different types of construction projects that are possible to be rated. The main differences are the type of scoring systems, terminologies, and the weight of each credit and database. For example, BREEAM assesses new construction, refurbishment and fit out, in-use, communities, home quality mark, and infrastructure, former CEEQUAL (Civil Engineering Environmental Quality Assessment and Awards Scheme), this last one is more directed to public infrastructures and civil engineering works. Similarly, LEED rates building design and construction, interior design and construction, residential, cities and communities, and building operations and maintenance. All these tools are based on a holistic approach to assessing the building or project through performance criteria.

The green construction rating is not compulsory but is encouraged. The incentives for green construction are qualified as (1) external, which are forced by imposed conditions or requirements from the government to receive a specific benefit; (2) financial, referred to as taxes, rebates, or grants; (3) internal, based on people's free will and interest in green construction. The internal incentives may be related to human

---

[1] Examples of other green rating tools are as follows: Comprehensive Assessment System for Building Environmental Efficiency (CASBEE) in Japan since 2001, Green Mark Scheme in Singapore since 2005, Assessment Standard for Green Building (ASGB) in China since 2006, Pearl Rating System for Estidama in Abu Dhabi Urban Planning Council since 2008, and Green Star South Africa rating system since 2008.

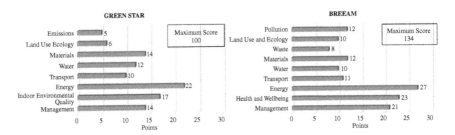

Figure 8.7.   Examples of differences between rating tools.

Source: Adopted from Mattoni *et al.* (2018).

well-being, market demand, and recognition for owning a green construction, based on personal values and norms or due to persuasion and inspiration of positive examples (Olubunmi *et al.*, 2016). The owner or developer may opt for green construction or not and select the performance criteria for which the project will be certified. If the aim is toward a higher classification/score, depending on the tool, the project must comply with almost all the requirements from different criteria (Glavinich, 2008). The most common generic criteria under a green construction process are management, indoor environmental quality, energy, transport, water, materials, land use and ecology, emissions, and pollution. Depending on the tool, each criterion has a specific weight (Mattoni *et al.*, 2018), as shown in Figure 8.7.

Similar to the traditional PM process, the documentation on how the scope of the green construction project will be defined, validated, and controlled is defined at the early stages of the project. During the planning stage, all requirements for the project are clearly defined and put into perspective throughout the whole project life cycle of the building. However, in this case, expert judgment is not provided by just one party, such as the project manager, but with the integration of all stakeholders involved in the process (Ikudayisi *et al.*, 2022). Green construction processes have a multicriteria approach that analyzes the environmental impacts of buildings using Life Cycle Assessment or analysis (LCA). This analysis is based on the requirements defined under ISO 14040:2006 (Environmental Management — Life Cycle Assessment — Principles and Framework) on a regional and global scale (Mattoni *et al.*, 2018; Retzlaff, 2009).

As addressed previously, green construction projects are process-oriented and focus on outcome achievement. The final aim is to build a high-performance building that significantly surpasses the minimum standards of base legislation or requirements. To ensure this high performance and meet all the designed requirements, the Green Assessor must engage in several visits (depending on the selected rating system) to evaluate the project. The Green Assessor is also considered an expert judgment tool (PMI, 2017) and is used to undertake the site visit process. The site visits intend to confirm adherence to the prescribed construction process and project documentation (Glavinich, 2008). During a performance or operations assessment, the Green Assessor must perform audits every 2 or 5 years (depending on the tool) to check if the building is operating efficiently and can maintain the performance rated previously (Ade & Rehm, 2019; Glavinich, 2008). One year after commencing building operations, an audit is performed, or 3 years after, to analyze if the building is operating in accordance with the rating.

8.5. Issues of green construction scope management

Cost is a major factor that influences project scope definition. Green construction projects may represent additional costs compared to traditional construction. The extra costs associated with green construction projects may represent a barrier to green construction and the actual perception of its benefits (Hu & Skibniewski, 2021; Richardson & Lynes, 2007). The Life Cycle Costs (LCC) of a green construction include costs of the initial investment, repair and replacement, refurbishment, and operation costs. The initial investment includes the costs of planning, design, and construction (materials, machinery, labor, and utilities). These costs are commonly designated as capital costs, or the costs incurred before the operation stage (Hu & Skibniewski, 2021). According to Hu and Skibniewski (2021), initial costs are divided into soft costs related to the rating process and hard costs, which are the ones included during the construction stage, such as labor, materials, equipment, and overhead costs. The rating process represents an initial extra cost, increasing the total construction cost between 4% and 11%. Implementing green strategies, such as materials, technical systems, and other green solutions, will increase expenses during the initial stages of a building (Hwang & Tan, 2012; Uğur & Leblebici, 2018). Hu and Skibniewski (2021) argue that, depending on the type of construction, location, and rating level, a maximum of 3–7% is expected but can go up to 46% for the developer. The developer pays most of these extra costs, leading to a sense of uneven distribution of benefits compared to the advantages that tenants will experience throughout the life cycle. These advantages are related to savings in water or energy uses. Other issues include lack of awareness of green products by contractors and developers, the complexity of a green construction code, and its time-consuming process (He *et al.*, 2018; Hwang & Tan, 2012), which all can make project scope development a difficult process.

Another critical aspect associated with green construction is the operations and maintenance stage. Maintaining a green building operation throughout its lifetime is a complex management and maintenance task. Green maintenance practices represent higher costs, constant communication, and regular onsite visits and audits of the building. There is also the need for extra expertise and commissioning practices, which in the long run will lead to a tendency to return to old traditional practices (Wu *et al.*, 2019). Nevertheless, adopting green construction practices cannot be viewed from a limited perspective of the initial investment. The impact of green construction must be translated throughout its whole life cycle within the TBL approach. Green construction will also carry several benefits. For example, one benefit is the risk mitigation of sustainability factors as the reduction of environmental and occupational risks. These can be related to the reuse of materials, translating into less waste disposal and lawsuits due to environmental legislation non-compliance or lack of efficiency (Hwang & Tan, 2012; WorldGBC, 2013). Green buildings have higher profits related to leasing and sales rates. Tenant demand tends to increase by about 26% in green buildings, which would lead to an increase in the net building income by 13% (GBCA, 2020; Hwang & Tan, 2012). The GBCA (2020) highlights that green buildings reduce, on average, greenhouse gas emissions by 55% when compared to regular buildings. New and retrofitted green buildings have an expectable increase in asset value of more than 30%, with paybacks between 6 and 7 years and anticipated cost reduction of 8–9% over 5 years period. Some researchers argue that retrofitting has less impact on the environment when compared to new construction. By decreasing energy use, it prolongs the life cycle of a building, increasing its value and promoting safer and healthier environments for occupants (Jagarajan *et al.*, 2017; Retzlaff, 2009). For example, retrofitting mechanical systems reduces 20% of the mechanical system's costs and improves energy efficiency by 20% (Horman *et al.*, 2006). It is supported that green construction will increase by 10 times the financial benefits, but others highlight that there is no difference between a green construction project and a conventional one (Uğur & Leblebici, 2018). Moreover, on the social side, green construction improves occupants' health and well-being with fewer sick days reported, which can increase performance by 10% and promote cognitive benefits such as an increase in strategic thinking, crisis response, and information use, over 130% (GBCA, 2020). Investors and tenants are now more actively searching for sustainable products, increasing the demand for green construction (GBCA, 2020).

Another issue associated with green construction projects is the different stakeholders involved in the project with various and, sometimes, contradicting requirements. As shown in Figure 8.8, the main stakeholders of a green construction project include the developer, owner, and tenant or end users. The main requirements include higher sales price for developers, lower exit yield for the owner, and health and well-being for tenants. There are common requirements among those stakeholders such as lower refurbishment costs and higher value of the building. The different requirements of stakeholders may make scope definition and management difficult.

On the other hand, green construction will require a significant change in a company. In a green construction project, it is very common to work with a network of partners. According to Mokhlesian and Holmén (2012), companies may need to restructure their business model, in terms of value, workforce, and structure of costs. It is crucial to increase the level of information and expertise, as well as the level of cooperation among all parties involved in the project. Another problem pointed out by the researchers is in the selection of materials and their impact on the environment (Mokhlesian & Holmén, 2012). Moreover, the reuse of waste products and their handling is costly, and sometimes complex process.

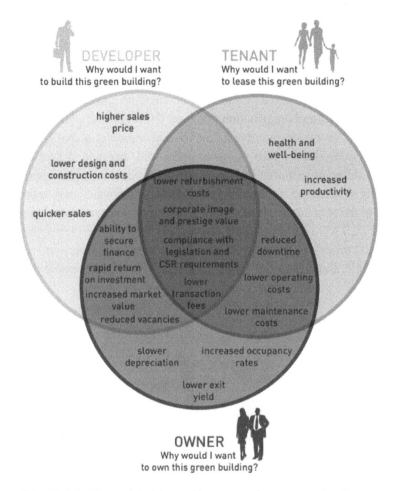

Figure 8.8.   Stakeholders and decision-making process for green construction.
Source: Adopted from WorldGBC (2013).

8.6.   Effective green construction project scope management

One of the main characteristics of green construction is the integration of a "job-sharing" approach and large multidisciplinary teams (Lützkendorf & Lorenz, 2006; Retzlaff, 2009). At the early stage of the project, all key stakeholders should be involved in scope developing processes including engineers, architects, developers, owners, construction contractors, and clients. The key stakeholders are required to collaborate intensively during the definition of the project, design, and documentation. To produce a high-performance green construction project, intensive interdisciplinary collaboration is crucial to share an in-depth understanding and decision-making of green strategies and construction practices (Horman *et al.*, 2006; Hwang & Tan, 2012). However, interdisciplinary teams represent a challenge. Issues such as unfamiliarity with the assessment tool, frequent design changes, limited skills, miscommunication, lack of organization, and limited understanding of complex tools, such as simulation software, may represent a delay in the process. To address this problem, an integrated design process model (IDPM) was created by researchers, which "describes the major tasks and processes required for effective delivery of the design" (Horman *et al.*, 2006; Ikudayisi *et al.*, 2022). Figure 8.9 shows an example of an IDP.

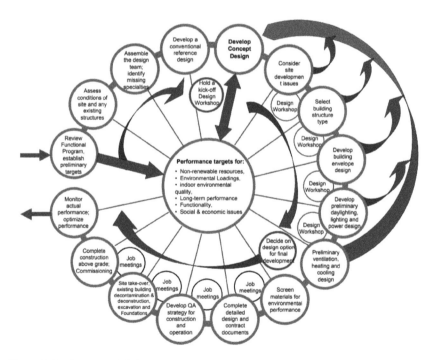

Figure 8.9.   Integrated design process.

Note: Sequence of steps is approximate and may vary according to project needs.

Source: Adopted from Larsson (2009).

The model includes all the development stages from design and clearly defines the workflow and hierarchical flowchart, identifying critical steps and interactions of processes and components. BIM can be used as a key tool to enhance the green construction process and facilitate system thinking, decision-making, construction and design processes, documentation management, and life cycle analysis (Glavinich, 2008; Ikudayisi *et al.*, 2022).

The main decision-makers in a green construction process are the developers, owners or clients, Green Assessor, managerial team, and contractors. These parties are responsible for green construction development and delivery. Finally, the last party involved is represented by a technical coordinator administering the selected rating tool.

The complexity of the process varies according to the type of the project, size, cost, and desirable rating (Ikudayisi *et al.*, 2022). The attributes and scope depend on the main goals of the client. Other aspects such as information sharing, location, climate, activities, and local regulations may add to a project's complexity. A common software platform for exchanging information will significantly improve communication, quality of design, and efficiency of the process, reducing costs and time (Glavinich, 2008). The cost of green construction can be reduced through appropriate management, environmental strategies, transparency among all parties, and a mature supply chain. The evolution of green construction processes is only possible with the collaboration between the industry and governments aiming to define new strategies to move toward more sustainable practices (GBCA, 2020). The integration of these strategies and stakeholders since the beginning is, therefore, crucial (WorldGBC, 2013).

8.7. Summary

This chapter has covered development approaches and processes of project scope management based on common standards of PM including ISO and the PMBOK Guide. The main processes explained in detail in this chapter are Plan Scope Management, Collect Requirements, Define Scope, Create WBS, Validate Scope, and Control Scope. Similar to other construction projects, green construction projects often use the predictive (waterfall) development approach. However, the scope definition of this type of project is difficult. This is because green construction projects involve different stakeholders who have different requirements and needs. Green construction projects face different challenges highlighted in this chapter such as the need for specialized expertise and cost increases due to special project requirements (e.g., green certification process or using sustainable materials).

The processes of project scope management as explained in this chapter can be applied in green construction projects. However, this type of project requires the focus on some additional processes and tools and techniques to ensure appropriate scope definition and control. At the early stage of the green construction project and to define the project components, a suitable green construction rating tool should be selected. The requirements of the rating tool will determine project components. Several specific tools and techniques of green construction projects are required to define project scope, such as the Green Assessor, who also acts as a key project stakeholder. Auditing the project during the operation stage is an important process to help reflect on and develop the design and scope of other projects in the future. The involvement of other project stakeholders such as end users is crucial to collecting project requirements. Collaboration among project stakeholders as highlighted in this chapter is a key process to ensure an appropriate definition of project scope and mutual understanding among the stakeholders on the project's outcome. Therefore, the integrated design process can be applied for more effective design and planning of the green construction project. BIM is an enabling tool for this process. Although this chapter adopts the predictive approach of project development, the scope of green construction projects should be developed with a great level of flexibility during the planning stage. Therefore, a great level of agility during the design stage is required to ensure the most optimized and effective design solution is produced. This flexibility allows the scope to be developed by adopting new technologies and innovative design ideas to produce a valuable outcome that responds to the requirements of different project stakeholders.

References

Abdul-Rahman, H., Kwan, C., & Woods, P. C. (1999). Quality function deployment in construction design: Application in low-cost housing design. *International Journal of Quality & Reliability Management, 16*(6), 591–605. https://doi.org/10.1108/02656719910268198.

Ade, R. & Rehm, M. (2019). The unwritten history of green building rating tools: A personal view from some of the 'founding fathers.' *Building Research & Information, 48*(1), 1–17. DOI: 10.1080/09613218.2019.1627179.

Ching, F. D. K. & Shapiro, I. M. (2021). *Green Building Illustrated.* Hoboken, New Jersey, USA: John Wiley & Sons.

Delgado-Hernandez, D. J., Bampton, K. E., & Aspinwall, E. (2007). Quality function deployment in construction. *Construction Management and Economics, 25*(6), 597–609. https://doi.org/10.1080/01446190601139917.

GBCA. (2020). Green Star in focus: The business case. Available at: https://new. gbca.org.au/news/gbca-media-releases/gbca-builds-powerful-and-positive-case-green-star/.

GBCA. (2021). General purpose financial report | For the year ended 30 June 2021. Sydney, Australia.

Glavinich, T. E. (2008). *Contractor's Guide to Green Building Construction. Management, Project Delivery, Documentation, and Risk Reduction.* Hoboken, New Jersey, USA: John Wiley & Sons, p. 262.

He, Y., Kvan, T., Liu, M., & Li, B. (2018). How green building rating systems affect designing green. *Building and Environment, 133*, 19–31. DOI: 10.1016/j.buildenv.2018.02.007.

Horman, Michael J., David R. Riley, Anthony R. Lapinski, Sinem Korkmaz, Michael H. Pulaski, Christopher S. Magent, Yupeng Luo, Nevienne Harding, and Peter K. Dahl. (2006). Delivering green buildings: Process improvements for sustainable construction. *Journal of Green Building, 1*(1), 123–140.

Hu, M. & Skibniewski, M. (2021). Green building construction cost surcharge: An overview. *Journal of Architectural Engineering, 27*(4). DOI: 10.1061/(asce)ae.1943-5568.0000506.

Hwang, B.-G. & Tan, J. S. (2012). Green building project management: Obstacles and solutions for sustainable development. *Sustainable Development, 20*(5), 335–349. DOI: 10.1002/sd.492.

Ikudayisi, A. E., Chan, A. P. C., Darko, A., & Adegun, O. B. (2022). Integrated design process of green building projects: A review towards assessment metrics and conceptual framework. *Journal of Building Engineering, 50.* DOI:10.1016/j.jobe.2022.104180.

ISO. (2020). *ISO 21502: Project, Programme and Portfolio Management — Guidance on Project Management.* Switzerland: International Standard.

Jagarajan, R., Abdullah Mohd Asmoni, M. N., Mohammed, A. H., Jaafar, M. N., Lee Yim Mei, J., & Baba, M. (2017). Green retrofitting — A review of current status, implementations and challenges. *Renewable and Sustainable Energy Reviews, 67*, 1360–1368. DOI: 10.1016/j.rser.2016.09.091.

Larson, E. W. & Gray, C. F. (2021). *Project Management: The Managerial Process* (8 edn.). Irwin: McGraw-Hill.

Larsson, N. (2009). The integrated design process; history and analysis. International initiative for a sustainable built environment. Available at: https://www.iisbe.org/system/files/private/IDP%20development%20-%20 Larsson.pdf.

Lützkendorf, T. & Lorenz, D. P. (2006). Using an integrated performance approach in building assessment tools. *Building Research & Information*, *34*(4), 334–356. DOI: 10.1080/09613210600672914.

Mattoni, B., Guattari, C., Evangelisti, L., Bisegna, F., Gori, P., & Asdrubali, F. (2018). Critical review and methodological approach to evaluate the differences among international green building rating tools. *Renewable and Sustainable Energy Reviews*, *82*, 950–960. DOI: 10.1016/j.rser.2017.09.105.

Mokhlesian, S. & Holmén, M. (2012). Business model changes and green construction processes. *Construction Management and Economics*, *30*(9), 761–775. DOI: 10.1080/01446193.2012.694457.

Olubunmi, O. A., Xia, P. B., & Skitmore, M. (2016). Green building incentives: A review. *Renewable and Sustainable Energy Reviews*, *59*, 1611–1621. DOI: 10.1016/j.rser.2016.01.028.

PMI. (2017). *A Guide to the Project Management Body of Knowledge: PMBOK® Guide* (6th edn.). Newtown Square, PA: Project Management Institute.

PMI (2021). *A Guide to the Project Management Body of Knowledge: PMBOK® Guide* (7th edn.). Newtown Square, PA: Project Management Institute.

Retzlaff, R. C. (2009). Green buildings and building assessment systems — A new area of interest for planners. *Journal of Planning Literature*, *24*(1), 3–21. DOI: 10.1177/0885412209349589.

Richardson, G. R. A. & Lynes, J. K. (2007). Institutional motivations and barriers to the construction of green buildings on campus. *International Journal of Sustainability in Higher Education*, *8*(3), 339–354. DOI: 10.1108/146763707 10817183.

Schmidt-Traub, G., Kroll, C., Teksoz, K., Durand-Delacre, D., & Sachs, J. D. (2017). National baselines for the sustainable development goals assessed in the SDG index and dashboards. *Nature Geoscience*, *10*(8), 547–555. DOI: 10.1038/ngeo2985.

Thesing, T., Feldmann, C., & Burchardt, M. (2021). Agile versus waterfall project management: Decision model for selecting the appropriate approach to a project. *Procedia Computer Science*, *181*, 746–756.

Uğur, L. O. & Leblebici, N. (2018). An examination of the LEED green building certification system in terms of construction costs. *Renewable and Sustainable Energy Reviews, 81*, 1476–1483. DOI: 10.1016/j.rser.2017.05.210.

WorldGBC. (2013). Business case for green building. A review of costs and benefits for developers, investors and occupants. Available at: https://www.worldgbc.org/sites/default/files/Business_Case_For_Green_Building_Report_WEB_2013-04-11-2.pdf.

Wu, X., Zhao, W., & Ma, T. (2019). Improving the impact of green construction management on the quality of highway engineering projects. *Sustainability, 11*(7). DOI: 10.3390/su11071895.

Chapter 9

Green Construction Project Design Decision-making: The Role of Design Leaders

Zahirah Mokhtar Azizi[*] and **Nazirah Zainul Abidin**[†]

[*]*Northumbria University, Newcastle upon Tyne, UK*

[†]*Universiti Sains Malaysia, Penang, Malaysia*

Green construction is viewed as instrumental to achieving a low-carbon future through reducing the carbon impacts of the built environment. To achieve this, it is imperative to ensure that buildings are designed with sustainable outcomes. Sustainable outcomes of a project are mostly determined by decisions made during the early design process, which place design leaders (architects and engineers) at the forefront of influencing green construction. Based on the theories of resource mobilization and rational choice, this chapter explores how design leaders determine building solutions and examine the motivations for their decision behavior. The chapter concludes that the design leader's decision behavior is conditioned by extrinsic and intrinsic motivations which affect rational choice. These motivations are represented by the design leader's intuition, personal values, contextual background factors, and cost perception. Although design leaders have the capability to influence the construction climate through internal project dynamics, this is determined by the integration of extrinsic and intrinsic motivations that guide rational choice. The chapter contributes to a comprehensive understanding of design leaders' roles as cognitive instruments capable of influencing practical changes for green construction implementation.

9.1. Introduction

As people's awareness of sustainability improves, a rising number of organizations are exploring pathways to sustainable development goals to ensure future business survival (Cillo *et al.*, 2019). Green construction has received much attention around the world over recent years in response to the adverse effects of global warming. However, it is unrealistic to expect change to occur overnight. To ensure an effective transformation, Abidin *et al.* (2013) stressed the importance of internal action enablers to strengthen the platform for action to pursue green construction. Internal action enablers refer to interest and commitment, policies and management, and resources and capabilities within organizations. While various regulatory strategies exist to support green initiatives, it is important for construction practitioners to participate in sustainable actions for regulatory strategies to work (Zhang *et al.*, 2011). Genuine interest and commitment of construction practitioners in sustainability are key driving factors to realizing change as it influences decisions and actions in construction practice. This would promote organizational policies and management strategies to align with sustainability principles and the development of resources and capabilities to deliver sustainable solutions. Despite the related environmental, economic, and social benefits, developments in green construction have frequently faced managerial obstacles arising from key project stakeholders (Mok *et al.*, 2018).

The focus of this chapter is on construction practitioners involved in the design of a project, namely architects and engineers, henceforth referred to as design leaders. Design leaders play fundamental roles in determining building solutions, placing them in a position to influence a project's design outcome (Darko *et al.*, 2017). Typically, design decisions for a construction project often prioritize economic considerations (Penadés-Plà *et al.*, 2016). However, it is now imperative to design buildings that fully consider the balance of economic, environmental, and social factors (Ferreira *et al.*, 2013). This is important as the sustainable outcomes of a project are mostly determined by decisions made during the early design process. Design leaders have a great deal of influence as key decision-makers in the design process in motivating the introduction of green construction in the built environment (Mooi, 2014). The task of implementing green construction, however, is a complex one because it calls into question the values that are prioritized in a development (Goh & Rowlinson, 2015). As a result, this will have varying and even conflicting perspectives on its implementation. Thus, the choice for green construction and how it manifests in practice may be considered differently from one design leader to another. The main question this chapter seeks to address is as follows: What drives design leaders to adopt green construction?

The majority of studies examining the drivers for green construction have focused on government regulations and policies, but more work is needed to understand how construction stakeholders behave in response to these regulations on a practical level. It is viewed that the effectiveness of regulations can only improve through this understanding (Darko & Chan, 2016). Murtagh *et al.* (2016) emphasized that individual behavior is driven by intrinsic and extrinsic motivations that either support or frustrate the action for green construction. Research has shown that intrinsic motivations are more likely to induce an individual's perception and guide behavior (Harpine, 2015). Thus, it is important to understand what drives individuals, specifically design leaders, to engage in green construction. There are surprisingly few studies that have investigated these factors despite the pivotal role of design leaders in project decision-making (Murtagh *et al.*, 2016). It is therefore not known how extrinsic and intrinsic motivations of individual design leaders impinge on project decisions related to green construction. In the research conducted for this chapter, the decision behavior of design leaders is considered from a sociological lens, focusing on the link between design leaders and pro green construction action frames in a construction project. This perspective views the behavior of design leaders as shaped by the social landscape in which the project is situated (macro) and by the social interaction within the project organization (micro). Adapting several interrelated social theories to the domain of green construction, we can examine how project decisions are affected by macro level and micro level conditions. This chapter aims to build an understanding of how design leaders make reasonable assessments of building solutions in a project and explore how that affects the future of the built environment. The chapter defines the process of decision-making for design leaders and examines the impact of extrinsic and intrinsic motivations on the design leader's decision behavior.

9.2. Review of design leaders' role in green construction

9.2.1. *Designing for green construction implementation*

Design is irrefutably an integral stage of a construction project as it establishes the boundaries for expanding project resources and defines the desired outcome. In light of this, it is important to view design leaders as being the key agents driving project realization (Darko *et al.*, 2017). Design leaders form the middle management within a construction society and respond to variations in the industry climate by adapting and/or maintaining habits, roles, and routines. Decisions made by design leaders reflect practical business priorities as well as deeper intrinsic qualities. It is not uncommon for design leaders to be at odds with two good values, and to have to make an acceptable trade-off when the safest option, for example, may not be the most sustainable (Gorp & Poel, 2008). In producing a design, it is often a question of design ethics, which appeared to have a wide knowledge gap that was largely underdeveloped (Fry, 2009). Recognizing this knowledge gap, Purdy (2015) asserted the importance of upholding design ethics on the basis that it would define the world we live in. However, the discussion of design ethics has been sporadic over the last three decades and has yet to achieve steady traction in practice or in academia (Chan *et al.*, 2018).

Isa *et al.* (2013) stated that decisions in construction are governed by strategic and tactical interests that meet the project objectives and are weighed against the anticipated returns and benefits. Thus, design leaders need to consider what is feasible for the project, such as choosing economical design solutions over more sustainable ones that can be more expensive. It is widely accepted that green construction brings various sustainability benefits to the built environment, such as better energy and water efficiency, as well as improved health and work productivity (Sev, 2009; Son *et al.*, 2011). For example, using timber material as opposed to concrete in buildings can lead to reduced embodied carbon emissions as well as transportation emissions during the construction stage (Sandanayake *et al.*, 2018). However, these benefits can only be realized over a long period of time and need to be communicated at a strategic level. Choi (2009) pointed out that long-term benefits are only appealing when there is strong demand for them from end users. If end users created a market demand for green construction, then decisions at project implementation level would support design solutions that respond to this demand. However, a reality check would reveal that this market, despite showing a growing trend, has not dominated the industry at large. This makes it difficult for design leaders to rationalize design choices for green construction from a practical point of view.

To catalyze the creation of a green market and support green initiatives, governments around the world have introduced policies and legislations to encourage green construction. The UK construction industry, for example, has increased environmental requirements and social demand for greener products in order to seed opportunities for green growth in the construction supply chain (HM Government, 2013). The Malaysian government is committed to advancing sustainability as one of the key themes in the Twelfth Malaysia Plan, 2021–2025, which aims to achieve a prosperous, inclusive, sustainable Malaysia (Unit, 2021). Despite this, green construction has yet to become mainstream and problems related to unsustainable development continue to persist (EPU, 2018). These unsustainable practices can be attributed to the high costs of green construction, which are driven by increased material input costs (Mansur *et al.*, 2016). For example, expensive green technologies remain the leading barrier in green construction implementation (Chan *et al.*, 2017). The problem is especially prevalent in developing countries such as Ghana where cost barriers are a major concern (Chan *et al.*, 2018). In view of this, design leaders need to consider solutions against tight project constraints and simultaneously balance economic, environmental, and societal interests. Developing countries such as China are also facing challenges of rapid urbanization and unsustainable planning practices (Choguill, 2008;

Wang *et al.*, 2014; Yu and Cai, 2012). The problems are exacerbated by policies that inhibit the inclusion of community members in planning decisions (Chen *et al.*, 2015). China's unsustainable practices can be attributed to poor revenue-sharing mechanisms for developers and long payback periods with low-profit gains (Shi *et al.*, 2017). Even in the absence of such challenges, innovative construction solutions are often constrained by perceptions of cost and economic benefits (Coimbra & Almeida, 2013).

Research has found that green construction is effectively achieved when design leaders invest in thoughtful decision-making for sustainability as opposed to relying on external third-party nudges (Brandt & Svendson, 2013). An inclusive setting of intense and broad discussions and information exchange is critical to reach competent outcomes and greater efficiency in working methods (Rosenström & Kyllönen, 2007). Good quality decisions are more likely achieved through group discussions and consensus between project stakeholders (Korkmaz *et al.*, 2011). Group discussions could also influence an individual's position to change through persuasion, group pressure, and willingness to compromise (Brandt & Svendson, 2013). While this supports the idea that management and technological innovation can improve organizational sustainability performance (Zhang *et al.*, 2019), design leaders have a more fundamental impact on the decision to choose a desirable green construction design alternative (Pan *et al.*, 2011). Following this, it can be reasoned that the ability to achieve green construction is dependent on whether design leaders are motivated and engaged in green construction discourse. The more design leaders participate in green construction discourse, the more positive influence they may exert. However, it is not yet clear what factors affect this into demonstrable action frames.

9.2.2. *Factors affecting green construction*

Applying sustainability strategies within the building design may come as part of the design leader's role or assumed alongside other responsibilities. Nevertheless, it is recognized that while some efforts to pursue green construction will work, others will not as many variables dictate this accomplishment ranging from market demand to stakeholder partnerships. For design leaders to pursue green construction effectively, they would need to have access to the necessary support and resources, such as financial provisions, policies and regulations, and the participation of other industry stakeholders (Knight & Paterson, 2018). Without these, any effort to put green construction into action would not likely succeed. This effect aligns with the doctrine of social movement, which is characterized by individuals who aim to achieve a common goal in a loosely coordinated effort (Grey, 2004). Efforts to encourage green construction from a bottom-up approach can thus, be viewed as a form of social movement in the building sector. Klandermans and Oegema (1987) described social movements in four processes: forming mobilization potentials, forming and motivating recruitment networks, arousing motivation to participate, and removing barriers to participation. In short, there needs to be a capacity of people who are motivated toward a shared vision and coalesce to build movement power. The Resource Mobilization Theory (RMT) prescribes that the success of any social movement depends on its engaging group organization and access to substantial resources such as money, materials, political influence, and the media to be used toward the movement's cause (Jenkins, 1983; Oberschall, 1973; Beuchler, 2000; Buechler, 2016). Design leaders can be viewed as the primary agents positioned to manage and mobilize resources to accomplish project goals. Given the central role of design leaders in guiding the project outcomes, it is crucial to analyze their behavioral intentions as an indicator of their readiness to mobilize resources toward green construction.

9.2.3. *Rational choice of design leaders*

While the literature has shed light on the various challenges accompanying green construction (Bond & Perrett, 2012; Hwang *et al.*, 2017a; Chan *et al.*, 2018), limited studies have sought to explain what drives some individuals to be more involved in green construction than others. Brandt and Svendson (2013) stated that green construction could only be forwarded if the benefits gained are non-negative, which means that no drawback or inconvenience was felt in comparison to its alternative.

However, even if many of these challenges are removed, there is no promise that green construction would then become the intended solution as a result. The design leaders' discretionary action in this regard is difficult to predict, especially in terms of how sustainable design solutions are considered in all environmental, economic, and social spheres. The Rational Choice Theory (RCT) informs that observing the behavior of individual actors can help us to understand the wider social and economic behavior and assumes that individuals make intelligible decisions based on which alternative provides the best outcomes for them personally (Hackett & Dissanayake, 2014). The theory corroborates the human tendency to choose a course of action that is most in line with their personal preferences and predicts that decisions are usually purposeful and self-interested (Durant *et al.*, 2017). According to Elster (2009), RCT starts from desires, which is grounded by beliefs and rationalized against information before transforming into action (see Figure 9.1). In simpler terms, the decision-maker will assess the information available beside its own beliefs to decide on how best to realize their desire. What this suggests is that people who undertake action for green construction are moved by a personal conviction or self-serving benefit for doing so, and this action is enabled by the knowledge and support to be had. This shows that, depending on personal beliefs, one may or may not be inclined to lead action for green construction.

RCT is widely used in the fields of economics and sociology to explain the determinants of individual choices (Scott, 2000). On this premise, this chapter adopts a sociological lens to explore the associated

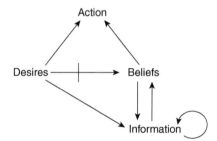

Figure 9.1.   Rational choice theory.

Source: Adopted from Elster (2009).

factors influencing design leaders' rationality of choice which leads to tangible actions. Past studies in green construction decision-making have largely focused on investment decisions at a strategic level (Zhao *et al.*, 2019; Qian *et al.*, 2015; Joachim *et al.*, 2015). The motivations of implementing green construction at an operational level from the design leader's standpoint have not been fully explored or well understood. Applying RMT and RCT to the construction field, this chapter critically analyzes the motivations that stimulate design leaders to opt for green construction action frames, providing a theoretical explanation to the whys of conventional decision behavior. It is hoped that this will provide a fresh perspective and a better understanding of the practical challenges of engaging in green construction, which can be used to predict the proclivities for green construction and improve future actions.

9.3. Conceptual framework

The interpretation of behavior can be conveyed in the rational choice explanation of action (Elster, 2009). This chapter focuses on the rationality of design leaders as key agents selecting design options with regard to the available resources and project goal. Zhang *et al.* (2019) emphasized that behavior toward green construction is induced by the extrinsic and intrinsic motivations of project stakeholders. This affects rational choice in the decision to pursue green construction based on explicit or tacit knowledge and beliefs of the decision-maker (Brockmann & Anthony, 2002). Thus, this chapter believes that the design leaders' decisions are influenced by extrinsic and intrinsic motivations that render tangible action frames. Extrinsic motivations are external rewards or outcomes that drive actions, such as policies, legislation, incentives, and market trends. They are governed by the prospect of instrumental loss and gain. Intrinsic motivations, on the other hand, are internal drivers of action, such as inner satisfaction and sense of purpose (Deci, 1972). Verdugo (2012) stated that extrinsic and intrinsic motivations are fundamental enablers to drive sustainability into clear action frames. Extrinsic motivations can be viewed as elements providing the platform for action through means of support to mobilize people for a purpose. Examples of this include project funds allowing for green construction, skills and

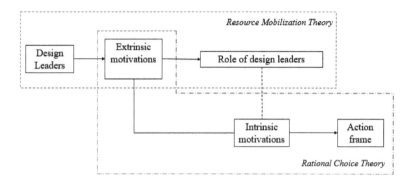

Figure 9.2.   Conceptual framework of RMT and RCT in green construction.

knowledge in green construction, policies driving green construction, and unanimity of other stakeholders. These are analogous to resources described in RMT. While these exist, the other compelling driver is intrinsic motivations of the design leader which are desires moved by personal beliefs as specified by RCT. Based on the doctrine of RMT and RCT explained above, this chapter proposes the conceptual framework shown in Figure 9.2 to describe the design leader's rational choice in relation to the extrinsic and intrinsic motivations activating action frames for green construction. It demonstrates that the availability of resources as RMT suggests is only half the work of a social movement's development and success. As explained in RMT, resources are tangible elements that can be worked toward a social movement's goal. In the context of green construction, having resources alone, while valuable, would be ineffective unless it is optimized and driven by the role of design leaders. That said, the design leader's behavior may be explained by the rationality of choice. Deduction by rational choice is generally influenced by their intrinsic motivations. Thus, extrinsic motivations to undertake green construction action (ranging from various things affecting the project environment) are only survived by the existence of intrinsic motivations (linked to personal beliefs) of the design leader. It is therefore reasoned that the rationality of decisions for green construction can be represented by the combined process of Resource Mobilization and Rational Choice that translate into certain actions.

Based on the discussion above, this chapter offers the following postulations:

(1) Design leaders are key agents of green construction as they are positioned to affect resource mobilization at project delivery.
(2) Extrinsic motivations may influence the role of design leaders in mobilizing resources to achieve a desired outcome.
(3) Intrinsic motivations (linked to personal beliefs) induce the rationality of choice of design leaders in concluding action frames for the project.
(4) Extrinsic motivations for green construction can only be effective with the reciprocal readiness of intrinsic motivations of design leaders.
(5) The development of action frames for green construction is embedded in the combined process of resource mobilization and rational choice of design leaders.

This conceptual framework establishes a sociological perspective for refining our understanding of the conditions under which action frames for green construction will or will not be realized. It provides deeper insight into the interrelationship between extrinsic and intrinsic motivations and underlines the importance of dynamic participation of design leaders in pro green construction action. Appreciating the "why" behind design leaders' action frames helps enable better prediction of the project outcomes. Thus, by conceptualizing relationships, we can better understand and manage the factors affecting design leaders' participation so that the desired outcomes can be achieved (Zaltman *et al.*, 1985).

9.4. Research methodology

The goal of this chapter is to reimagine the role of design leaders by applying and synthesizing existing social theories in the context of green construction. This chapter critically analyzed the principles of Resource Mobilization and Rational Choice theories to explain, predict, and develop an understanding of green construction through the design leaders' role.

The analysis was based on deductive reasoning of the related theories, which explored the conceptual underpinnings of the issue under study to construe meaning. Deductive reasoning starts out with a general statement, or hypothesis, and examines the possibilities to reach a specific, logical conclusion (Hyde, 2000). This approach uses "pattern matching" to test theories by finding a logical coherence within a system of statements. If the case data matches the predicted pattern of outcomes of the theory, then the theory is supported (Campbell, 1975). Table 9.1 shows the pattern matching of RMT and RCT with green construction as the case data.

Table 9.1.   Pattern matching of RMT and RCT with green construction.

Related theory	Hypothesis	Case data
Resource Mobilization Theory (RMT)	For a social movement to be successful, it has to accumulate and mobilize key resources toward its cause	Green construction is a social movement. Therefore, for green construction to be successful, it has to accumulate and mobilize key resources toward its cause Consequently, the availability of key resources may act as extrinsic motivations that affect the effectiveness of the design leader's role in undertaking green construction
Resource Mobilization Theory (RMT)	Resources include money, people's time and skill, materials, political influence and the media	Resources include project budget, design leader's time and skill in undertaking green construction in the design process, alliances with other stakeholders, and attention from the wider polity
Resource Mobilization Theory (RMT)	Resource mobilization potential is determined by the degree of group organization and collective action	The ability to mobilize project resources is determined by the weight of the design leaders' role and their collective action Therefore, design leaders must be unanimous in their actions to mobilize resources for green construction

Table 9.1.   (*Continued*)

Related theory	Hypothesis	Case data
Rational Choice Theory (RCT)	People are rational; People only participate in a movement if the benefits surpass the costs	Design leaders will only participate in green construction if they believe that the benefits surpass the costs
Rational Choice Theory (RCT)	When deciding on something, people perform their own personal cost and benefit analysis based on their beliefs and the information available to them to pursue the best possible outcome	Design leaders balance the costs and benefits of design solutions and choose the one that provides the best possible outcome in proportion to their beliefs and the project information Their personal beliefs represent intrinsic motivations inducing the rationality of choice of the design leader The project information represents extrinsic motivations inducing the rationality of choice of the design leader

An original conceptual framework (shown in Figure 9.2) is developed from the synthesis of RMT and RCT that connects the subject of design leaders and green construction to broader areas of knowledge (Abend, 2013). This framework forms the primary step in the theory-then-research strategy for theory building (Reynolds, 1971). The strategy comprises of a continuous, reiterative interaction process between theory development and empirical inquiry until the theory is made explicit (Kaplan, 2017; Reynolds, 1971).

The framework offers a renewed perspective on green construction implementation by describing what leads to design leaders' action frames using RMT and RCT constructs. This was used to investigate the elements that contribute to an enabling environment for design leaders to adopt green construction practices, defining the process knowledge of how design leaders influence green construction action. Process knowledge is the understanding of how something works and what it means (Dubin, 1976). Its purpose is to generate a theory that extends existing knowledge by bridging interrelated concepts that describe the underlying thought and reasoning in performing design tasks (Marsick, 1990). Kaplan (2017) describes good theories as having rigor and relevance that follow a logical cognitive style in their development with clear and coherent construction. Nevertheless, theory building involves two kinds of expertise, i.e., knowledge and experience (Lynham, 2002). This chapter forms the pioneering step of theory building (knowledge) which help build better grounding on the factors that drive design leaders' action for green construction.

9.5. Results and discussion

The conceptual framework introduces the theory that the design leaders' action frames are conditioned by extrinsic and intrinsic motivations. These motivations reflect the societal–environment interactions of design leaders within and outwith the project. McLaughlin (2011) claimed that social evolution occurred parallel to climate change in which changes can be seen in society's adaptation and vulnerability to climate change. However, it is not known what social evolution must transpire for green construction. For a long time, the construction industry has struggled to develop a clear understanding of the sustainability challenges to support green construction delivery and often focus on apparent matters without delving into the conceptual matters. This is important to ensure that organizational environments can be adapted to harmonize with green construction. The right kind of organizational leadership would provide collective vision, strategy, and direction toward the common goal of a sustainable future (Opoku *et al.*, 2015). This chapter attempts to explain the conditions in which these can be met to enable pro green construction action frames in a construction project.

9.5.1. *Extrinsic and intrinsic motivations on the design leader's decision behavior*

RMT emphasizes the importance of availability of resources to accomplish organizational goals. Design leaders continually access and regulate financial, political policies, and talent resources to support action frames.

Their role as resource mobilizers provides the opportunity to consider green construction when engaged in decision-making tasks. Design leaders can leverage on this platform using proper organizational tactics to influence decisions for sustainability implementation.

However, this ability is determined by extrinsic and intrinsic motivations. Extrinsic motivations can exist in the form of project requirements, awards, policies, incentives, and regulations driving green construction. There have been many discussions around these as the main determining factor to the success of green construction, but there is surprisingly little evidence to support this. Accomplishing green construction in order to fulfill external goals becomes difficult when designers are not prepared to manage the tensions in green construction design or lack the ability to do so effectively. Intrinsic motivations driven by genuine interest and personal values provide a strong sense of conviction for green construction far beyond the impetus of extrinsic motivations. Nevertheless, it is difficult for design leaders to act based on intrinsic motivations alone if they do not align with project goals. This points toward the need for both extrinsic and intrinsic motivations as essential conditions to create a conducive environment for green construction to thrive. The design leader's decision behavior can be interpreted through RCT which assumes decisions are purposeful and driven by maximum utility function. As long as decisions for green construction benefit both extrinsic and intrinsic motivations and do not detract from project goals, design leaders would be able to apply action frames toward green construction.

9.5.1.1. *Intuition*

Sauter (1999) reported that managers increasingly used intuition in decision-making, which exercises unstructured and spontaneous techniques of consideration based on earlier experience to recognize patterns of conditions and draw conclusions even when information is incomplete. Intuitive thoughts are often helpful for familiar situations but tend to reach conclusions too quickly and ignore relevant facts. As constant decision-makers, design leaders are susceptible to using the same technique and oversimplifying analyses using prevailing data to facilitate decision-making. The assumption induces a tendency to respond in obvious patterns as opposed to employing slow analytical methods in order to ensure efficiency. Thus, "rational choice" is often based on incomplete information and preconceived beliefs that form the intuition of the design leader. This makes the design leader a vital part of green construction development as it is crucial for design leaders to be able to quickly assess the benefits of green construction and intuitively consider elements of green construction within their decisions (Kibert, 2012). Consequently, design leaders with an intuition prone toward green construction (based on their past experience and knowledge) will routinely administer decisions with sustainability in mind.

9.5.1.2. *Personal values*

Decision-making is in many ways a conflict resolution process between inner goals, others' goals, and competing goals (Svenson, 1996). In construction, most critical decision problems are related to design. Design is irrefutably an integral process of a building project and has a significant impact on the building outcome. Decisions made by the design leaders such as which problems to solve and why, and who should benefit from the design, are not just a reflection of rational cognitive judgments but reveal deeper intrinsic qualities, such as one's values and moral intensity (Jones, 1991). It is not uncommon for design consultants to be faced with value conflicts where they need to choose between two good values and make an acceptable trade-off (Gorp & Poel, 2008). Stern *et al.* (1999) clarified that people's behavior is characterized by their values, which then shapes their beliefs. What this means is that action for green construction is moved by some altruistic or moral justification for pursuing green construction or is motivated by self-serving interests (Aliagha *et al.*, 2013). This shows that design leaders with personal values that align with sustainability interests may be more likely to follow decisions in support of green construction.

9.5.1.3. *Contextual background*

The first key step in a decision-making process is recognizing the objective and criteria for which the following diagnosis shall relate to, and a solution is formulated (Ferreira, *et al.*, 2013). However, an individual's decision behavior is normally filtered through culture, experience, and personal values (Adanali, 2016; Li, 2017; Cherry, 2022). Thus, how one perceives sustainability will vary from person to person based on the contextual background from which they operate. Reaction or inaction to participate in green construction practices is contingent upon intrinsic and extrinsic motivations of the decision-maker (McLaughlin, 2011, Seidel, *et al.*, 2010). What this suggests is that the ability to deliver green construction is dependent on various factors affecting the individual design leader. For example, design leaders who have better experience, access to technology, skills, and project culture would achieve a more productive delivery of green construction (Hwang *et al.*, 2017b). These can be viewed as extrinsic motivations as they enable the means to undertake green construction effectively. An inhibited contextual background caused by the lack of experience and skills, a supportive project and industry culture, access to technology, and regulatory framework endorsing green construction would frustrate actions for green construction and construct a negative perception.

9.5.1.4. *Cost perception*

Typically, decision problems in construction are focused on their relevance to cost-effectiveness (Penadés-Plà *et al.*, 2016). However, cost has been a continuous debate both theoretically and practically on the choice for sustainable construction (Abidin, 2010). This chapter believes that cost could predominantly influence the rationale of decision-makers' alternate choices by modifying habits, routines, and roles. Theoretical evidence indicates that decisions for green construction could only be supported when its benefits promoted economic interests (Newton & Newman, 2015). There has been a plethora of literature on green construction costs that have confused, broadened, and deepened our knowledge. Nevertheless, the gap in the literature suggests that green construction is often misjudged, and considerations of cost have not included all aspects affecting the cost of green construction projects. The fragmented information in the literature may promote a perception that rears decisions and undermines the full potential of sustainability implementation. With cost being such an uncertain variable, it acts as an extrinsic (de)motivation for green construction. Depending on the experience and knowledge of the design leader, perception of cost can influence the design leader's beliefs about green construction and consequently inspire or deter action for green construction.

9.6. Conclusion and implications

9.6.1. *Subheadings*

This chapter takes a nuanced approach to understanding the internal process of implementing green construction practices from the perspective of design leaders. The conceptual framework presented here shows the conditions which foster an enabling environment for design leaders to adopt green construction practices. Using interrelated concepts from the social sciences, we analyzed how RMT's conception of resources and RCT's premise of logical deduction can reveal the enabling and constraining aspects of green construction.

Based on this hypothesis, the chapter concludes that design leaders are a major determinant of green construction as they have the capability to affect the construction climate through internal project dynamics, i.e., directing decisions toward green construction action. The perspective of design leaders as cognitive instruments in applying action frames within the project environment can be used to address sustainability implementation using internal organizational strategies. This chapter emphasizes the importance of design leaders as agents of change in promoting pro-green solutions in construction projects. Where design leaders have agencies over the building solution, they are able to affect change through strategic decision-making. The first objective of this chapter is to define the process of decision-making for design leaders. This is illustrated by the conceptual framework proposed herein, which constitutes their ability to mobilize resources to achieve a specific aim and to make rational choices in line with their desires. Thus, framing green construction actions requires the design leader to be able to have leverage on key resources, such as funds, skills and knowledge, policies and regulatory frameworks, and stakeholder partnerships.

However, opportunities to undertake green construction actions are also affected by extrinsic and intrinsic motivations. The second objective of this chapter is to examine the impact of extrinsic and intrinsic motivations on the design leader's decision behavior. The design leader's decision behavior is conditioned by extrinsic and intrinsic motivations which affect rational choice. These motivations are represented by the design leader's intuition, personal values, contextual background factors, and cost perception. Consistency of these motivations with green construction determines the decision behavior of design leaders. It is therefore concluded that green construction can only be realized where the design leaders have strong personal values, an intuition oriented to green construction, supportive conditions of the contextual background from which they operate, and a positive cost perception. This indicates that the development of action frames for green construction is not only reliant on the ability of the design leader to mobilize key resources toward green construction but also the motivations underpinning rational choice in their decision behavior.

9.6.2. *Implications of the findings*

The theoretical framework can be used to define the means of motivating green construction and demonstrate the importance of design leaders' participation in this endeavor. The RMT depicts how the *status quo* of built environment may be transformed by proper internal organizational tactics, whereas the RCT affirms the need for design leaders to actively respond to green construction practice through deliberate choices. Design leaders interact with extrinsic and intrinsic motivations to generate a response to building solutions. The existence of extrinsic motivations can appeal mobilization of resources to a specific goal, confirming to RMT. Thus, performance of the design leader's role may be driven by extrinsic motivations. However, extrinsic motivations do not produce permanent changes and can lose impact in the long term. This chapter considers the other influence of intrinsic motivations that affect rational choice of the design leader. It can be reasoned that action frames are more holistically explained by observing the collective stimulations of extrinsic and intrinsic motivations in the context of RMT and RCT. This chapter reports the findings of a critical literature synthesis based on two social theories that informs the theoretical foundations of design leaders' participation in green construction.

Acknowledgments

Acknowledgment to "Ministry of Higher Education Malaysia for Fundamental Research Grant Scheme with Project Code: FRGS/2/2014/SS05/USM/02/3."

References

Abend, G. (2013). *The Meaning of Theory: Sociological Theory*. San Francisco, CA: Berrett-Koehler Publishers.

Abidin, N. Z. (2010). Investigating the awareness and application of sustainable construction concept by Malaysian developers. *Habitat International*, *34*(4), 421–426.

Abidin, N. Z., Yusof, N. A., & Othman, A. A. (2013). Enablers and challenges of a sustainable housing industry in Malaysia. *Construction Innovation*, *13*(1), 10–25. https://doi.org/10.1108/14714171311296039.

Adanali, Y. K. (2016). Rational choice theory as a model to apply to cultural behavior. *Nişantaşı Üniversitesi Sosyal Bilimler Dergisi*, *4*(1), 61–83.

Bond, S. & Perrett, G. (2012). The key drivers and barriers to sustainable development of commercial property in New Zealand. *Journal of Sustainable Real Estate*, *4*(1), 48–77.

Brandt, U. S. & Svendsen, G. T. (2013). Is local participation always optimal for sustainable action? The costs of consensus-building in Local Agenda 21. *Journal of Environmental Management*, *129*, 266–273.

Brockmann, E. N. & Anthony, W. P. (2002). Tacit knowledge and strategic decision making. *Group & Organization Management*, *27*(4), 436–455.

Campbell, D. T. (1975). Degrees of freedom and the case study. *Comparative Political Studies*, *8*(2), 178–193.

Chan, A. P. C., Darko, A., & Ameyaw, E. E. (2017). Strategies for promoting green building technologies adoption in the construction industry — An international study. *Sustainability*, *9*(6), 969.

Chan, A. P. C., Darko, A., Olanipekun, A. O., & Ameyaw, E. E. (2018). Critical barriers to green building technologies adoption in developing countries: The case of Ghana. *Journal of Cleaner Production, 172*, 1067–1079.

Cherry, K. (2022). How heuristics help you make quick decisions. Verywell Mind. Available at: http://psychology.about.com/od/hindex/g/heuristic.htm (accessed on 10 October 2018).

Choguill, C. L. (2008). Developing sustainable neighbourhoods. *Habitat International, 32*(1), 41–48.

Cillo, V., Petruzzelli, A. M., Ardito, L., & Del Giudice, M. (2019). Understanding sustainable innovation: A systematic literature review. *Corporate Social Responsibility and Environmental Management, 26*(5), 1012–1025. https://doi.org/10.1002/csr.1783.

Coimbra, J. & Almeida, M. (2013). Challenges and benefits of building sustainable cooperative housing. *Building and Environment, 62*, 9–17.

Darko, A. & Chan, A. P. C. (2016). Critical analysis of green building research trend in construction journals. *Habitat International, 57*, 53–63. https://doi.org/10.1016/j.habitatint.2016.07.001.

Darko, A., Zhang, C., & Chan, A. P. (2017). Drivers for green building: A review of empirical studies. *Habitat International, 60*, 34–49.

Deci, E. L. (1972). The effects of contingent and noncontingent rewards and controls on intrinsic motivation. *Organizational Behavior and Human Performance, 8*, 217–229. DOI: 10.1016/0030-5073(72)90047-5.

Department for Business, I. & S. (2013a). Construction 2025: Strategy, GOV.UK. Available at: https://www.gov.uk/government/publications/construction-2025-strategy (accessed on 29 April 2022).

Dubin, R. (1976). Theory building in applied areas. In M. D. Dunnette (Ed.), *Handbook of Industrial and Organizational Psychology* (pp. 17–39). Chicago: Rand McNally.

Durant, R. F., Fiorino, D. J., & O'Leary, R. (Eds.). (2017). *Environmental Governance Reconsidered: Challenges, Choices, and Opportunities.* Cambridge, MA: MIT Press.

Elster, J. (2009). Interpretation and rational choice. *Rationality and Society, 21*(1), 5–33.

Ferreira, J., Pinheiro, M. D., & de Brito, J. (2013). Refurbishment decision support tools review — Energy and life cycle as key aspects to sustainable refurbishment projects. *Energy Policy, 62*, 1453–1460.

Goh, C. S. & Rowlinson, S. (2016). Key roles in driving sustainability practice into the built environment. In *Paper Presented at 5th International Conference on Human-Environment System 2016*, Nagoya, Japan, 29/10/16 - 2/11/16.

Gorp, A. V. & Poel, I. V. D. (2008). Deciding on ethical issues in engineering design. In P. E. Vermaas, P. Kroes, A. Light, & S. A. Moore (Eds.), *Philosophy and Design: From Engineering to Architecture* (pp. 77–89). Dordrecht: Springer.

Grey, S. J. (2004). Changing frames: The discursive influence of the women's movements of New Zealand and Australia. PhD, Political Science Program, Research School of Social Sciences, Australian National University, ANU Digital Theses.

Hackett, S. & Dissanayake, S. T. (2014). *Environmental and Natural Resources Economics: Theory, Policy, and the Sustainable Society.* New York, USA: Routledge.

Harpine, E. C. (2015). Is intrinsic motivation better than extrinsic motivation? In E. Clanton Harpine (Ed.), *Group-Centered Prevention in Mental Health: Theory, Training, and Practice.* Springer International Publishing, Cham, pp. 87–107.

Hwang, B.-G., Zhu, L., & Tan, J. S. (2017a). Green business park project management: Barriers and solutions for sustainable development. *Journal of Cleaner Production, 153*, 209–219.

Hwang, B. G., Zhu, L., & Ming, J. T. T. (2017b). Factors affecting productivity in green building construction projects: The case of Singapore. *Journal of Management in Engineering, 33*(3), 04016052.

Hyde, K. F. (2000). Recognising deductive processes in qualitative research. *Qualitative Market Research: An International Journal, 3*(2), 82–90.

Jenkins, J. C. (1983). Resource mobilization theory and the study of social movements. *Annual Review of Sociology, 9*(1), 527–553.

Joachim, O. I., Kamarudin, N., Aliagha, G. U., Ufere, K. J. (2015). Theoretical explanations of environmental motivations and expectations of clients on green building demand and investment. In *Proceedings of the 2nd International Conference on Geological, Geographical, Aerospace and Earth Sciences*, Bali, Indonesia, 11–12 October 2014.

Jones, T. M. (1991). Ethical decision making by individuals in organizations: An issue-contingent model. *Academy of Management Review, 16*(2), 366–395.

Kaplan, A. (2017). *The Conduct of Inquiry: Methodology for Behavioural Science.* New York, USA: Routledge.

Kibert, C. (2012). *Sustainable Construction: Green Building Design and Delivery* (3rd edn.). Hoboken, New Jersey: John Wiley & Sons.

Knight, B. & Paterson, F. (2018). Behavioural competencies of sustainability leaders: An empirical investigation. *Journal of Organizational Change Management, 31*(3), 557–580.

Li, K. K. (2017). How does language affect decision-making in social interactions and decision biases? *Journal of Economic Psychology, 61*, 15–28.

Lynham, S. A. (2002). The general method of theory-building research in applied disciplines. *Advances in Developing Human Resources, 4*(3), 221–241. DOI: 10.1177/1523422302043002.

Marsick, V. J. (1990). Altering the paradigm for theory building and research in human resource development. *Human Resource Development Quarterly, 1*(1), 5–24.

McLaughlin, P. (2011). Climate change, adaptation, and vulnerability: Reconceptualizing societal–environment interaction within a socially constructed adaptive landscape. *Organization & Environment, 24*(3), 269–291.

Mok, K. Y., Shen, Qiping, G., & Yang, R. (2018). Stakeholder complexity in large scale green building projects. *Engineering, Construction, and Architectural Management, 25*(11), 1454–1474.

Mooi, A. (2014). What will the architect be doing next? How is the profession of the architect evolving as the focus of society shifts from sustainability to resilience or reactivist-driven design demands? *FOOTPRINT*, 119–128. DOI: 10.7480/footprint.8.1.806.

Newton, P. & Newman, P. (2015). Critical connections: The role of the built environment sector in delivering green cities and a green economy. *Sustainability, 7*(7), 9417–9443.

Opoku, A., Cruickshank, H., & Ahmed, V. (2015). Organizational leadership role in the delivery of sustainable construction projects in UK. *Built Environment Project and Asset Management, 5*(2), 154–169. https://doi.org/10.1108/BEPAM-12-2013-0074.

Pan, N. F., Dzeng, R. J., & Yang, M. D. (2011). Decision making behaviors in planning green buildings. In *International Conference on Computer Distributed Control and Intelligent Environmental Monitoring* (pp. 1710–1713). IEEE. Changsha, China, DOI: 10.1109/CDCIEM.2011.543. 19-20 February 2011.

Qian, Q. K., Chan, E. H., Visscher, H., & Lehmann, S. (2015). Modeling the green building (GB) investment decisions of developers and end-users with transaction costs (TCs) considerations. *Journal of Cleaner Production, 109*, 315–325.

Reynolds, P. D. (1971). *A primer in Theory Construction*. New York: Macmillan.

Rosenström, U. & Kyllönen, S. (2007). Impacts of a participatory approach to developing national level sustainable development indicators in Finland. *Journal of Environmental Management, 84*(3), 282–298.

Sandanayake, M., Lokuge, W., Zhang, G., Setunge, S., & Thushar, Q. (2018). Greenhouse gas emissions during timber and concrete building construction — A scenario based comparative case study. *Sustainable Cities and Society, 38*, 91–97.

Scott, J. (2000). Rational choice theory. *Understanding Contemporary Society: Theories of the Present, 129*, 671–85.

Sev, A. (2009). How can the construction industry contribute to sustainable development? A conceptual framework. *Sustainable Development, 17*(3), 161–173.

Shi, Q., Yu, T., Zuo, J., & Lai, X. (2017). Reprint of: Challenges of developing sustainable neighborhoods in China. *Journal of Cleaner Production, 163*, S42–S53.

Son, H., Kim, C., Chong, W. K., & Chou, J. S. (2011). Implementing sustainable development in the construction industry: Constructors' perspectives in the US and Korea. *Sustainable Development, 19*(5), 337–347.

Stern, C. P., Thomas, D., Abel, T., Guagnano, A. G., & Kalof, L. (1999). A value-belief-norm theory of support for social movements: The case of environmentalism. *Human Ecology Review, 6*, 81–97.

Svenson, O. (1996). Decision making and the search for fundamental psychological regularities: What can be learned from a process perspective? *Organizational Behavior and Human Decision Processes, 65*(3), 252–267.

Unit, E. P. (2021). *Twelfth Malaysia Plan 2021–2025: A Prosperous, Inclusive, Sustainable Malaysia.* Kuala Lumpur: Percetakan Nasional Berhad.

Verdugo, V. C. (2012). The positive psychology of sustainability. *Environment, Development and Sustainability, 14*(5), 651–666.

Wang, P., Liu, Q., & Qi, Y. (2014). Factors influencing sustainable consumption behaviors: A survey of the rural residents in China. *Journal of Cleaner Production, 63*, 152–165.

Zhang, J., Li, H., Olanipekun, A. O., & Bai, L. (2019). A successful delivery process of green buildings: The project owners' view, motivation and commitment. *Renewable Energy, 138*, 651–658.

Zhang, X. L., Shen, L. Y., & Wu, Y. Z. (2011). Green strategy for gaining competitive advantage in housing development: A China study. *Journal of Cleaner Production, 19*, 157–167.

Zhao, X., Tan, Y., Shen, L., Zhang, G., & Wang, J. (2019). Case-based reasoning approach for supporting building green retrofit decisions. *Building and Environment, 160*, 106210.

https://doi.org/10.1142/9789811251429_0010

Chapter 10

Green Construction Project Risk Management

Xianbo Zhao[*], Bon-Gang Hwang[†], and Ming Shan[‡]

[*]*Central Queensland University,*
Norman Gardens, QLD, Australia

[†]*National University of Singapore,*
Singapore

[‡]*Central South University,*
Changsha, Hunan, China

The past decades have witnessed an increasing number of green con-struction projects that have been developed worldwide in response to the global sustainable development goals, the active promotion from the authorities, and the increasing interest from customers. However, similar to non-green construction projects, green construction projects are inevi-tably plagued with a wide variety of risks. These risks encompass the general risks that tend to occur in all types of construction projects and the risks that are closely associated with the unique characteristics of green construction projects. Effective management of these risks is critical to the successful delivery of green construction projects. This chapter aims to identify the risks that are closely associated with green construction and present methods to analyze these risks. The risk analysis methods include fuzzy synthetic evaluation, risk path modeling, and social network analysis. A series of risk response measures are proposed to deal with the critical risks.

10.1. Introduction to green construction project risk management

The building and construction sector, including the relevant policies and standards, has significant economic, social, and environmental impacts on the society (Zuo & Zhao, 2014; Zhao *et al.*, 2019; Li *et al.*, 2020; Chang *et al.*, 2016). This sector has been widely recognized as a major consumer of natural resources and energy, and generates great quantities of construction and demolition waste (Zhao, 2021; Zhao *et al.*, 2021), and over 30% of the global construction and demolition waste is still directly sent to landfill sites without treatment (Menegaki & Damigos, 2018). Also, commercial and residential buildings globally contribute over 20% to energy consumption (Pérez-Lombard *et al.*, 2008) and are responsible for one-third of greenhouse gas (GHG) emissions in the world (WorldGBC, 2013), thereby increasing global concerns about climate change mediated by GHG emissions (Wu *et al.*, 2014; Shanmugam *et al.*, 2018; Zhu *et al.*, 2013).

Green or sustainable construction practices have a great potential for reducing worldwide energy consumption, waste generation, and GHG emissions, and have attracted increasing attention from both academics and industry practitioners (Darko & Chan, 2016). The terms "construction of green buildings," "green construction," and "sustainable construction" are sometimes used interchangeably. The fact that the construction of green buildings is part of sustainable construction merits attention. Sustainable construction practices also contribute to construction firms' competitiveness (Chang *et al.*, 2017). For existing non-green buildings, green retrofit can be performed to upgrade these existing buildings to green buildings, yielding a wide range of benefits, including operational cost savings, quality assurance, better indoor air and environmental quality, and improved employee productivity (Deloitte, 2008; McGraw-Hill Construction, 2013).

Construction projects, including green construction projects, are inevitably plagued with complex and diverse risks. Risk management has been a permanent and classic topic in construction engineering and management research, and should be integrated into green construction project management (PM) practice to assure the success of such projects. Project risk management allows decision makers to confront risks in a more realistic manner and thus improves decision-making (Mok *et al.*, 1997; Zhao *et al.*, 2014b). According to the Project Management Institute (PMI) (2017), a typical project risk management process includes planning risk management, identifying risks, performing risk analysis, planning risk response, implementing risk responses, and monitoring risks. The most significant difference in risk management between green and non-green construction projects lies in the risks identified for further analysis, response, and monitoring. This is because they are usually unique to green construction projects, closely related to the usage of new materials, technologies, and design approaches (Odom *et al.*, 2008), sustainable construction practices, and achievement of third-party green certification (Greenwald, 2012). In non-green construction projects, such risks tend to be insignificant and are thus ignored by green construction practitioners.

There have been a wide variety of risk analysis techniques available for these unique risks of green construction projects. Although these risks are unique, they should not be separated from the common risks occurring in both green and non-green construction projects. This is due to the fact that risks are dynamic and highly interdependent (Chapman, 2006; Lam, 2003), and usually interact with one another, forming a network of risk paths (Zhao *et al.*, 2017, 2018). It is oversimplified to overlook the interaction between risks. Simply ranking risks ignores the effects of top-ranked risks on other risks. Thus, the risks unique to green construction projects may cause a general risk in non-green construction practices. For example, to meet the requirements set by the green building rating schemes, contractors need to purchase special sustainable construction materials. However, the unavailability of such materials (unique risk) caused by global supply chain problems (general risk) may incur delays in construction, low productivity, and rework (general risks). In addition, risk management requires the participation of different stakeholders in a construction project. However, different stakeholders may hold different perceptions of risks given their own interests. Hence, risks should be analyzed from the perspective of different stakeholders.

Adopting various risk analysis techniques, the most significant risks can be targeted and risk responses to deal with these risks can be developed and implemented. As the green construction project progresses, there may be emerging risks that need to be monitored. In addition, to assure the success of a green construction project, the risks in the operation and maintenance phase should also be identified, analyzed, and handled. Otherwise, the GHG emission and resource consumption during the project life cycle will not meet the requirements set by the green building rating schemes.

This chapter aims to identify the risks that are closely associated with green construction and to present methods to analyze these risks. The risk analysis methods include fuzzy synthetic evaluation (FSE), risk path modeling, and social network analysis (SNA). A series of risk response measures are proposed to deal with the critical risks.

10.2. Previous research on green construction project risk management

Researchers have investigated risks occurring in green construction projects with various focus points. Some studies have been focused on occupational health and safety risks in green construction projects. For example, Dewlaney *et al.* (2012) quantified the safety risks of green construction and found that design elements and means and construction methods to achieve the credits of Leadership in Energy and Environmental Design (LEED) increased injuries: 36% increase in lacerations, strains, and sprains from recycling construction materials and a 24% increase in falls during roof work for installing solar panels. Karakhan and Gambatese (2017) evaluated the potential positive or negative impact of green design elements and construction practices related to LEED credits on the occupational health and safety of construction and maintenance workers and found that sustainable construction represented by LEED projects tended to increase base-level safety risks. Similarly, Hwang *et al.* (2018) indicated that the accident rate in green construction projects in Singapore was higher than that in non-green projects and that green and non-green projects shared the same top 10 critical safety issues. Zhang and Mohandes (2020) developed a holistic Z-numbers-based risk management framework, to deal with the safety risks faced by workers in green construction projects, based on a Hong Kong case study.

Some exploratory studies have attempted to hold a holistic view of the risk profile in green construction projects. For instance, Hwang *et al.* (2015) identified risks of green retrofit projects in Singapore and recognized "post-retrofit tenants' cooperation risk" as the top risk. Hwang *et al.* (2017a) also investigated the risks in green commercial building projects in Singapore and recognized the top five risks: "inflation," "currency and interest rate volatility worsened by the import of green materials," "durability of green materials," "damages caused by human error," and "shortage of green materials." In addition, Hwang *et al.* (2017b) assessed the risks in green residential building construction projects, compared their risk criticalities with those in non-green projects, and indicated that "complex procedures to obtain approvals," "overlooked high initial cost," and "unclear requirements of owners" were the top three critical risks in green residential projects. Ismael and Shealy (2018) investigated the critical risks in the Kuwaiti construction industry and found that a lack of public awareness and designers' and contractors' inexperience with sustainable construction were the most significant risks. El-Sayegh *et al.* (2021) assessed the risks in sustainable construction projects in the United Arab Emirates and indicated that shortage of clients' funding, insufficient or incorrect sustainable design information, design changes, unreasonably tight schedules for sustainable construction, and poor scope definition in sustainable construction were the top risks. Qazi *et al.* (2021) relied on the Monte Carlo simulation to develop a new process for prioritizing sustainability-related project risks using risk matrix data.

Some studies focused on the adoption of novel risk analysis techniques in green construction projects. For example, Yang and Zou (2014) relied on SNA to develop a stakeholder-associated risk analysis method and adopted this method to evaluate the risks and their interactions in complex green building projects, while Yang *et al.* (2016) collected risk data in China and Australia for SNA and found that reputation risk was important in both countries. In addition, Zhao *et al.* (2016a) developed the FSE approach to assess both general and unique risks in green construction projects in Singapore. Liu *et al.* (2021) adopted a meta-network modeling approach to analyze and evaluate the impact of each risk and its relationship with the project objectives of sustainable project performance.

10.3. Identifying risks of green construction projects

Risk identification is a critical phase in a project risk management process. A simple but valid method is to develop a risk checklist (Fang *et al.*, 2004). There have been a wide variety of previous studies attempting to identify the risks of green construction projects. Usually, these risks cover both unique and general risks. This is reasonable because unique risks and general risks can be interrelated while the interaction may further lead to other risks. A comprehensive literature review was performed and a list of risks reported in previous studies were identified. Table 10.1 presents a total of 50 risks, including unique risks for green projects and general risks for green and non-green projects.

10.4. Analyzing risks of green construction projects

After risk identification, the next step entails risk analysis. There have been various risk analysis techniques available to researchers and practitioners, which can be used for analyzing the risks of green construction projects. Some researchers adopted the likelihood of occurrence (LO) and magnitude of impact (MI) to rank green construction risks in terms of their criticalities (Hwang *et al.*, 2015), while some other risk analysis techniques can deal with the interrelationships among risks. The potential of three risk analysis techniques is discussed in the following sections.

10.4.1. *Fuzzy synthetic evaluation*

As risk analysis is complex and ambiguous, qualitative linguistic terms are unavoidable (Wang *et al.*, 2004). In addition, the perceptions on the likelihood and impact of risk factors by respondents are usually subjective and uncertain (Shan *et al.*, 2015b). The fuzzy set theory can deal with

Table 10.1.   Risks associated with green construction projects.

Risk category	Code	Risk factor	G/U	References
Material risk	R01	Material suitability	U	Hwang *et al.* (2017a)
	R02	Availability of green materials	U	Hwang *et al.* (2017a)
	R03	Durability of green materials	U	Hwang *et al.* (2017a)
Contractual risk	R04	Difficulty in understanding green specifications in contract details	U	Hwang *et al.* (2017a)
	R05	Breach of contract (i.e., claims and disputes)	G	Wibowo and Mohamed (2010), Zou and Li (2010), Chan *et al.* (2011a), El-Sayegh and Mansour (2015)
	R06	Intellectual property dispute (e.g., special design/construction method)	U	Jha and Devaya (2008), Al-Sabah *et al.* (2014)
Design risk	R07	Alteration and variation with the design during construction	G	Andi (2006), Zou *et al.* (2007), Marques and Berg (2011), Rebeiz (2012), Al-Sabah *et al.* (2014)
	R08	Insufficient or incorrect design information	G	Andi (2006), Tang *et al.* (2007), Roumboutsos and Anagnostopoulos (2008), Ke *et al.* (2011), Marques and Berg (2011), Al-Sabah *et al.* (2014), El-Sayegh and Mansour (2015)
Safety risk	R09	Injuries and accidents	G	Andi (2006), El-Sayegh and Mansour (2015), Hwang *et al.* (2014), Zou and Li (2010), Aritua *et al.* (2011), Chuing Loo *et al.* (2013), Hwang *et al.* (2018)
	R10	Damage caused by human error	G	Wibowo and Mohamed (2010)

(Continued)

Table 10.1.   (*Continued*)

Risk category	Code	Risk factor	G/U	References
Experience and knowledge	R11	Shortage of skills or techniques	G	Tang *et al.* (2007), Zou *et al.* (2007), Jha and Devaya (2008), Roumboutsos and Anagnostopoulos (2008), Zou and Li (2010), Aritua *et al.* (2011), Chan *et al.* (2011b)
	R12	Lack of training relating to green construction	U	Hwang *et al.* (2017b)
	R13	Lack of motivation to change their traditional practices	U	Hwang *et al.* (2017a)
	R14	Project manager's experience with green construction	U	Zhao *et al.* (2016a), Jiang (2010)
Financial and cost risk	R15	Inflation (labor and material cost increase)	G	El-Sayegh (2008), Lu and Yan (2013), Panthi *et al.* (2009), Zou *et al.* (2007), Kartam and Kartam (2001)
	R16	Currency exchange rate fluctuation	G	Hlaing *et al.* (2008), Eybpoosh *et al.* (2011)
	R17	Interest rate fluctuation	G	Hwang *et al.* (2017a)
	R18	Return on investment risk	G	Durmus-Pedini and Ashuri (2010), Lockwood (2009), Hwang *et al.* (2015)
	R19	Additional costs due to green material and equipment	U	Hwang *et al.* (2017a)
	R20	Difficulties in project budgeting due to unfamiliarity with green projects	U	Hwang *et al.* (2017a)

Table 10.1.   (*Continued*)

Risk category	Code	Risk factor	G/U	References
	R21	Inaccurate prediction of market demand	G	Tang *et al.* (2007), Jha and Devaya (2008), Roumboutsos and Anagnostopoulos (2008), Aritua *et al.* (2011), Chan *et al.* (2011a), Chan *et al.* (2011b), Ke *et al.* (2011)
	R22	Financial strength of project stakeholders	G	Hwang *et al.* (2013), Zhao *et al.* (2013b), Hwang *et al.* (2015), Wang *et al.* (2015)
Environmental risk	R23	Changes in weather	G	Chan *et al.* (2011a), Chan *et al.* (2011b), Ke *et al.* (2011)
	R24	Unforeseen adverse site conditions and geographical conditions	G	Chan *et al.* (2011a), Chan *et al.* (2011b), Ke *et al.* (2011)
	R25	Pollution restrictions	G	Yang *et al.* (2016), Yang and Zou (2014)
Performance risk	R26	Energy saving uncertainty	U	Lockwood (2009), Winston (2009), Yudelson (2010)
	R27	High expectation on green building rating	U	Shan and Hwang (2018)
Management risk	R28	Improper quality control and defective work	G	El-Sayegh and Mansour (2015), Hwang *et al.* (2015)
	R29	Claims of unverifiable benefits of green construction	U	Tollin (2011)
	R30	Inadequate insurance	G	Ling and Hoi (2006), Gruneberg *et al.* (2007), Hwang *et al.* (2017a)

(*Continued*)

Table 10.1.   (*Continued*)

Risk category	Code	Risk factor	G/U	References
	R31	Improper project feasibility and planning	G	Tang *et al.* (2007), Zou *et al.* (2007), Jha and Devaya (2008), Al-Sabah *et al.* (2014), El-Sayegh and Mansour (2015)
	R32	Delay or more time required for approval	G	Hwang *et al.* (2017a), Zou *et al.* (2007), Jha and Devaya (2008), Roumboutsos and Anagnostopoulos (2008)
	R33	Delay caused by the frequent meetings with green specialists	U	Hwang *et al.* (2017a)
	R34	Poor definition of scope and change in scope	G	Gruneberg *et al.* (2007), Tang *et al.* (2007), Zou *et al.* (2007), Jha and Devaya (2008)
Regulatory risk	R35	Import and export restrictions	G	Hwang and Leong (2013)
	R36	Change in local regulations	G	Zou and Li (2010), Aritua *et al.* (2011), Chan *et al.* (2011a), Chan *et al.* (2011b), Ke *et al.* (2011), Marques and Berg (2011)
	R37	Change in governmental policies	U	Chien *et al.* (2014), Yang and Zou (2014), El-Sayegh and Mansour (2015), Hwang *et al.* (2015)
Technological risk	R38	Selection of construction technique and sequence	G	Ke *et al.* (2011), Marques and Berg (2011), Rebeiz (2012)
	R39	Reliability and maturity of green technologies	U	Zhao *et al.* (2016a)
	R40	Technological complexity	U	Zhao *et al.* (2016a)
	R41	Lack of specifications for new green technologies	U	Tollin (2011), Zou and Couani (2012), Yang and Zou (2014)
Stakeholder risk	R42	Occupants' cooperation for retrofit	U	Hwang *et al.* (2015)
	R43	Different concerns of stakeholders	G	Hwang *et al.* (2015)

Table 10.1.   (*Continued*)

Risk category	Code	Risk factor	G/U	References
	R44	Accreditation of energy service companies (ESCOs)	U	Hwang *et al.* (2015), UNEP (2009)
	R45	Occupants' behavior in the operation phase	U	Hwang *et al.* (2015)
	R46	Occupants' environmental awareness	U	Hwang *et al.* (2015)
	R47	Special request from client about specified green technologies to be used	U	Hwang *et al.* (2017a)
	R48	Poor communications among stakeholders	G	Yang and Zou (2014), El-Sayegh and Mansour (2015), Hwang *et al.* (2015)
	R49	Resistance from client to adopt green concepts	G	Hwang *et al.* (2017a)
	R50	Limited availability and reliability of green suppliers	U	Hwang *et al.* (2017a)

Note: U = Unique risks for green construction projects; G = general risks for both green and non-green construction projects.

problems relating to ambiguous, subjective, and imprecise judgments (Zhao *et al.*, 2013a; Pedrycz *et al.*, 2011). The fuzzy set theory also allows applying mathematical operators to the fuzzy domain (Xia *et al.*, 2011; Ma and Kremer, 2015) and can quantify the linguistic facet of data and preferences for individual or group decision-making (Zimmermann, 2001; Zhao *et al.*, 2014a). Thus, the fuzzy set theory is considered as appropriate for risk assessment.

As an application of the fuzzy set theory, FSE aims to provide a synthetic evaluation of an object relative to an objective in a fuzzy decision environment with multiple criteria. The advantage of FSE lies in dealing with complicated evaluations with multiple attributes and levels. Assume there are three levels of risks: risk factors (level 1), risk groups (level 2), and the overall risk (level 3). As a multi-criteria evaluation model, the FSE model requires three basic elements: a set of basic criteria/factors, a set of alternatives, and an evaluation matrix that shows the degree to which each alternative satisfies each criterion. The FSE model involves three steps, as detailed in the following sections.

10.4.1.1. *Step 1: Calculate LO, MI, and RC of risks (level 1)*

The LO and MI of each risk can be collected in a questionnaire survey using a five-point scale. Thus, in the set of alternatives E, for both LO and MI, e_1 = very low; e_2 = low; e_3 = medium; e_4 = high; and e_5 = very high. In the evaluation matrix, r_{ij} is the degree to which the alternative e_j satisfies risk i. For example, if the results on the MI of risk "interest rate fluctuation" (R01) indicate that 20% of the respondents opined the MI as very low, 28% as low, 36% as medium, 15% as high, and 1% as very high, the membership function of the MI is given as follows:

$$\frac{0.20}{\text{very low}} + \frac{0.28}{\text{low}} + \frac{0.36}{\text{medium}} + \frac{0.15}{\text{high}} + \frac{0.01}{\text{very high}}$$

$$= \frac{0.20}{1} + \frac{0.28}{2} + \frac{0.36}{3} + \frac{0.15}{4} + \frac{0.01}{5} \tag{1}$$

It can also be written as a matrix as follows:

$$\left(R_i^{MI}\right)_{1\times5} = \left(r_{i1}^{MI}, r_{i2}^{MI}, r_{i3}^{MI}, r_{i4}^{MI}, r_{i5}^{MI}\right) \tag{2}$$

The LO and MI of risk i can be calculated using Eqs. (3) and (4), respectively:

$$\text{LO}_i = \sum_{j=1}^{5}\left(s_j \times r_{ij}^{LO}\right) \tag{3}$$

$$\text{MI}_i = \sum_{j=1}^{5}\left(s_j \times r_{ij}^{MI}\right) \tag{4}$$

where s_j denotes the score of risk i, namely s_j = 1, 2, 3, 4, 5. In previous risk management studies, risk criticality (RC) is usually used to measure how critical a risk factor is and considered as the product of LO and MI. Here, to make RC have a scale consistent with LO and MI, RC is the square root of the product of LO and MI, as shown in the following:

$$RC_i = \sqrt{LO_i \times MI_i} \qquad (5)$$

10.4.1.2. *Step 2: Calculate LO, MI, and RC of risk groups (level 2)*

The LO and MI of each risk can be aggregated to each risk group (level 2). The weight of individual risks (level 1) within a risk group, $W = \{w_1, w_2, ..., w_k\}$, needs to be determined. Here, k is the number of the risks within a risk group. The weights of the LO and MI of risk i can be calculated using Eqs. (6) and (7), respectively:

$$w_i^{LO} = LO_i \bigg/ \sum_{i=1}^{k} LO_i \qquad (6)$$

$$w_i^{MI} = MI_i \bigg/ \sum_{i=1}^{k} MI_i \qquad (7)$$

The fuzzy composition of the weight vector W and the evaluation matrix R, namely $D = W \times R$, can be used to calculate the evaluation results. Thus, the LO and MI membership functions of risk group t can be calculated using Eqs. (9)–(11), respectively:

$$d_{tj}^{LO} = \sum_{i=1}^{k} w_i^{LO} \times r_{ij}^{LO} \qquad (8)$$

$$\left(D_t^{LO}\right)_{1\times5} = \left(W_i^{LO}\right)_{1\times k} \times \left(R_i^{LO}\right)_{k\times5} = \left(d_{t1}^{LO}, d_{t2}^{LO}, d_{t3}^{LO}, d_{t4}^{LO}, d_{t5}^{LO}\right) \qquad (9)$$

$$d_{tj}^{MI} = \sum_{i=1}^{k} w_i^{MI} \times r_{ij}^{MI} \qquad (10)$$

$$\left(D_t^{MI}\right)_{1\times5} = \left(W_i^{MI}\right)_{1\times k} \times \left(R_i^{MI}\right)_{k\times5} = \left(d_{t1}^{MI}, d_{t2}^{MI}, d_{t3}^{MI}, d_{t4}^{MI}, d_{t5}^{MI}\right) \qquad (11)$$

Thus, the LO, MI, and RC of risk group t can be calculated using Eqs. (12)–(14), respectively:

$$LO_{Gt} = \sum_{j=1}^{5} \left(s_j \times d_{tj}^{LO}\right) \qquad (12)$$

$$\text{MI}_{Gt} = \sum_{j=1}^{5} \left(s_j \times r_{tj}^{MI} \right) \tag{13}$$

$$\text{RC}_{Gt} = \sqrt{LO_{Gt} \times MI_{Gt}} \tag{14}$$

where s_j = 1, 2, 3, 4, 5.

10.4.1.3. *Step 3: Calculate overall LO, MI, and RC (level 3)*

The weight of each risk group (level 2), $W_G = \{w_{G1}, w_{G2}, ..., w_{Gq}\}$, needs to be determined, which enables the aggregation of risk group results to the overall LO, MI, and RC (level 3). Here, q is the number of risk groups. The weights of the LO and MI of risk group t can be calculated using Eqs. (15) and (16), respectively:

$$w_{Gt}^{LO} = \left(\sum_{i=1}^{k} LO_i \right)_t \bigg/ \sum_{t=1}^{q} \left(\sum_{i=1}^{k} LO_i \right)_t \tag{15}$$

$$w_{Gt}^{MI} = \left(\sum_{i=1}^{k} MI_i \right)_t \bigg/ \sum_{t=1}^{q} \left(\sum_{i=1}^{k} MI_i \right)_t \tag{16}$$

where $(\sum_{i=1}^{k} LO_i)_t$ is the sum of LO of k risks under group t and $(\sum_{i=1}^{k} MI_i)_t$ is the sum of MI of k risks under group t. The LO and MI membership functions of the overall risk can be calculated using the Eqs. (17)–(20), respectively:

$$d_{Allj}^{LO} = \sum_{t=1}^{q} w_{Gt}^{LO} \times d_{tj}^{LO} \tag{17}$$

$$\left(D_{All}^{LO} \right)_{1\times5} = \left(W_G^{LO} \right)_{1\times q} \times \left(D_G^{LO} \right)_{q\times5} = \left(d_{All1}^{LO}, d_{All2}^{LO}, d_{All3}^{LO}, d_{All4}^{LO}, d_{All5}^{LO} \right) \tag{18}$$

$$d_{Allj}^{MI} = \sum_{t=1}^{q} w_{Gt}^{MI} \times d_{tj}^{MI} \tag{19}$$

$$\left(D_{All}^{MI} \right)_{1\times5} = \left(W_G^{MI} \right)_{1\times q} \times \left(D_G^{MI} \right)_{q\times5} = \left(d_{All1}^{MI}, d_{All2}^{MI}, d_{All3}^{MI}, d_{All4}^{MI}, d_{All5}^{MI} \right) \tag{20}$$

where $(D_G^{LO})_{q\times5}$ and $(D_G^{MI})_{q\times5}$ are $q\times5$ matrices that contain q matrices of $(D_t^{LO})_{1\times5}$ and $(D_t^{MI})_{1\times5}$, respectively. With the overall LO and MI membership functions, the overall LO, MI, and RC can be calculated using Eqs. (19)–(21), respectively:

$$LO_{All} = \sum_{j=1}^{5} \left(s_j \times d_{Allj}^{LO} \right) \tag{21}$$

$$MI_{All} = \sum_{j=1}^{5} \left(s_j \times d_{Allj}^{MI} \right) \tag{22}$$

$$RC_{All} = \sqrt{LO_{All} \times MI_{All}} \tag{23}$$

where s_j = 1, 2, 3, 4, 5.

Using FSE for risk analysis, it merits attention that risk grouping may impact the results because the groups influence the level-2 calculation. Also, this technique still produces a ranking of individual risks but overlooks interactions between risk groupings.

10.4.2. *Risk path modeling*

Most risks have interrelationships, which can be a one-way relationship (cause-and-effect relationship) or two-way relationship (correlation). In most cases, highly correlated risks can be merged into one; thus, a one-way relationship is a focus of risk analysis. Zhao *et al.* (2017) and Liu *et al.* (2016) defined the cause-and-effect relationship between two risks as a risk path. Several risk paths can be connected to form chains of risk paths, which show the primary and secondary risks in the chains and finally form a network of risk paths. However, if the number of risks is large, there tends to be a massive number of paths in the network. Hence, it is better to reduce the dimension of risks by categorizing risks into groups and analyzing the paths among these risk groups.

Structural equation modeling (SEM) can be used to analyze the risk grouping and paths. SEM can evaluate the measurement of latent constructs and test the relationships between latent constructs (Schreiber *et al.*, 2006). Contrary to the first-generation regression models, SEM can simultaneously model relationships among multiple independent and dependent variables (Le *et al.*, 2014; Shan *et al.*, 2015a). SEM consists of the measurement and structural models, which are also known as outer and inner models, respectively (Hair *et al.*, 2014). There are two types of SEM: covariance-based SEM (CB-SEM) and partial least squares SEM (PLS-SEM). Both approaches have strengths and weaknesses (Sarstedt *et al.*, 2011), and the weaknesses of one approach are typically the strengths of the other approach (Hair *et al.*, 2012). Hazen *et al.* (2015) provided a summary of the strengths and weaknesses of both approaches. Hair *et al.* (2014) asserted that the top reasons for using PLS-SEM include non-normal data, small sample size, and formative indicators, which have been recognized as significant advantages over CB-SEM. In contrast, CB-SEM involves constraints regarding data distribution, number of observations, and small sample sizes (Doloi, 2014).

The data on LO and MI of risks can be collected from surveys or interviews. Then, a preliminary analysis can help calculate the RC of risks. As for the sample size of surveys or interviews, there have been no hard and fast rules for the minimal sample size in PLS-SEM (Hazen *et al.*, 2015). As PLS-SEM does not require normal data distribution, it is appropriate for analyzing the data collected from a relatively small sample. PLS-SEM starts with model specification, which connects variables and constructs based on theory and logic (Hair *et al.*, 2014). Risks can be categorized according to their meanings and relevant literature review, and the preliminary relationships among risk categories are set up based on the findings from previous studies. Whether to use single-item or multi-item scales for construction measurement should be determined during model specification. Diamantopoulos *et al.* (2012) found that multi-item scales outperform single-item scales in terms of predictive validity under most circumstances, but single-item scales can perform as well as multi-item scales under some specific conditions. Additionally, previous construction management studies (e.g., Ning, 2014; Lim *et al.*, 2012) also employed both single- and multi-item scales for construct measurement. Thus, it is acceptable to adopt both single- and multi-item scales in the measurement models.

Evaluating measurement models involves checking their reliability and validity. Specifically, loadings of risks on categories should be at least 0.7, for indicator reliability; the composite reliability (CR) score should be at least 0.7 for internal consistency reliability (Hair *et al.*, 1998); the average variance extracted (AVE) value should be at least 0.5 for convergent validity (Fornell & Larcker, 1981); Cronbach's alpha coefficient should be at least 0.7 for internal consistency (Nunnally, 1978); and the square root of the AVE of each risk category should exceed the inter-category correlation and each risk should have the highest loading on the respective category for discriminant validity (Fornell & Larcker, 1981). In addition, the bootstrapping technique (Efron, 1987; Davison and Hinkley, 1997) can evaluate structural models and calculate the significance of path coefficients.

If the measurement models are reliable and valid, the structural model evaluation can be performed to model risk paths. In path modeling, the number of bootstrap samples is usually set to 5,000, as recommended by Hair *et al.* (2011), and the number of cases is the sample size. The critical *t*-values for a two-tailed test are 1.65 (significance level = 10%), 1.96 (significance level = 5%), and 2.58 (significance level = 1%). Then, researchers can check the statistical significance of risk paths and identify the primary and secondary root risks or risk groups that have chain effects on other risks or risk groups.

10.4.3. *Social network analysis*

Each stakeholder in a green construction project should assess their risks. Also, each risk can be mapped to at least one relevant stakeholder. Yang and Zou (2014) relied on SNA and developed a stakeholder-associated risk analysis method to evaluate the risks and their interactions in green construction projects. This method is appropriate for complex projects with a large number of stakeholders. The social network theory recognizes a green construction project as a system environment, which is joined by various relationships. The purpose of network analysis is to examine how relationship structures impact on behavior, and this theory is concerned with the "structure and patterning" of these relationships and seeks to identify both their causes and effects (Scott & Carrington, 2011).

The general steps of SNA include the following: (1) identifying the boundary of the network; (2) assessing meaningful and actionable relationships; (3) visualizing the network; (4) analyzing the network data; and (5) presenting the analysis results (Scott & Carrington, 2011;

Wasserman & Faust, 1994). SNA can be applied to green construction project risk analysis through the four steps detailed in the following sections.

10.4.3.1. *Step 1: Identifying stakeholders and their risks*

Every network consists of two major components: nodes and links. This step is to identify the nodes. Yang and Zou (2014) recommended the use of two methods: the classical experience-based method and the snowball rolling method. As for the classical experience-based method, core stakeholders, who include the project team and some of the key stakeholders, are engaged to perform the identification process. Core stakeholders usually identify stakeholders and risks according to pre-defined categories. As for the snowball sampling method, it engages almost all stakeholders rather than just the core stakeholders. The outcome of snowball sampling is a complete list of stakeholders, but this method is very time-consuming and may face practical and ethical challenges during the data collection process. The outcomes from this step include a comprehensive list of stakeholders and the risks associated with these stakeholders. All the risks should be coded S#R# to indicate the number of the associated stakeholder and the risk number related to this stakeholder. For example, S2R4 is the second risk associated with the fourth stakeholder.

10.4.3.2. *Step 2: Determining risk interactions*

This step involves the definition of the links in the risk network, which represent the impact between two nodes. According to Fang *et al.* (2012), the design structure matrix method is used to complete this step. This method represents relations and dependencies among risks identified in Step 1. The relationships between two risks may be independent, dependent, or interdependent. Specifically, independent risks are not related to one another; dependent relationships represent a direct impact between two risks; and interdependent relationships represent a mutually dependent relationship between two risks directly or within a bigger loop (Thompson *et al.*, 2017). This method focuses on the relationship between risks but not individual risks. The relationship is defined by the effect of one risk on the other and the likelihood of the interaction between the risks.

10.4.3.3. *Step 3: Visualizing risk network*

Once the nodes and links are identified, a risk network for green construction projects can be developed and visualized. The network can be represented by a graph $G(N,K)$, in which the risks are mapped into N nodes connected by K-weighted links. Various software packages can be used to visualize and analyze the relationship networks, such as NetMiner, UCINET, and Pajek. In most cases, in a visualized network, each link from node $SiRj$ to node $SkRt$ represents the direct effect from $SiRj$ to $SkRt$. The thickness of links shows the degrees of influence (effect × likelihood) of the relationships.

10.4.3.4. *Step 4: Deciphering risk network*

Several indicators can be calculated and used to decipher the risk network. These indicators may include but are not limited to the following: network density, network cohesion, degree of nodes, betweenness centrality, status centrality, brokerage, immediate interface, and global interface (Yang *et al.*, 2016). Specifically, density is the ratio of existing links in a network to the maximum number of links possible if every node in the group is connected with everyone else (Wasserman & Faust, 1994); cohesion indicates the distance, or the number of links, to reach nodes in a network and is based on the shortest path (Parise, 2007); degree of nodes indicates the immediate connectivity characteristic of a node and include in-degree that refers to incoming relations and out-degree that refers to outcoming relations; betweenness centrality indicates the incidence with which a given node/link falls between two other nodes/links (Pryke, 2012); status centrality shows the relative influence of a node within a network by measuring the number of the immediate neighbors (first degree nodes) and all other nodes in the network that link to the node under consideration through these immediate neighbors (Katz, 1953); brokerage describes the role and capability of a particular node in bridging different subgroups within a network under a selected partition vector; immediate interface measures the number of direct links between every pair of stakeholder/risk groups; and global interface counts the number of both direct and indirect links between every pair of stakeholder/risk groups (Yang *et al.*, 2016; Fang *et al.*, 2012).

The degree of nodes helps to identify the risks with higher immediate effects on others. Betweenness centrality helps to identify the risks and interrelationships with control over higher effects passing through it. Status centrality helps to identify the risks with higher overall effects in the entire network. Brokerage identifies the risks with critical roles between different stakeholder/risk categories. The risks with higher degree, higher betweenness centrality, higher status centrality, and higher brokerage values should be mitigated with higher priority (Yang & Zou, 2014).

10.5. Risk responses of green construction projects

The critical risks should be assigned with risk response measures. According to PMI (2017), there are five typical response strategies to deal with the risks with negative impacts: escalation, mitigation, transfer, avoidance, and acceptance. Previous studies have provided a series of response strategies to deal with the risks unique to green construction projects (Hwang *et al.*, 2017a, 2017b).

Here, some response strategies are proposed to deal with the unique risks of green construction projects. It is better to proactively plan response strategies for critical risks. For example, as a response to "accreditation of energy service companies (ESCOs)," the PM team need to check ESCOs' credibility with reference to the list of ESCOs provided by the government and seek background information on the type of past projects handled by the ESCOs. As a response to "occupants' cooperation for retrofit" in commercial buildings, retrofit work may be performed outside standard working hours; the occupants may be relocated for work; the rationale behind retrofitting the building to a green building and the potential benefits should be explained to the occupants or tenants; and financial incentives or rental rebates may be provided for tenants. As for the "high expectations on green building rating," the client should clearly understand the process to achieve a green building rating and the relevant costs to avoid any misunderstanding of the green building rating schemes. As for the "lack of specifications for new green technologies," experts and professional bodies should jointly develop specifications for green technologies and assure the quality and standard of such technologies to convince practitioners that they can help achieve the green construction objectives. As a response to "project manager's experience with green construction," more attention should be paid to the selection of project managers in terms of their experience. Sometimes, project managers' leadership styles also impact the implementation of green construction projects and the achievement of performance objectives (Zhao *et al.*, 2016b).

The steps of risk identification, analysis, and response constitute the core steps of a formal risk management process in green construction projects. Indeed, green construction project risk management does not stand alone, but is integrated with other functional PM processes, such as project schedule management, project cost management, and project stakeholder management.

10.6. Summary

This chapter explains the critical steps of risk identification, analysis, and response involved in the risk management of green construction projects. Previous studies on green construction project risk management are reviewed. Then, a list of 50 risks were identified from a literature review that included both unique risks for green projects and general risks occurring in both green and non-green projects. Three risk analysis techniques, including FSE, risk path modeling, and SNA, are discussed. Response strategies are proposed to deal with the unique risks of green construction projects.

Future research would develop a smart risk management system to help identify emerging risks, analyze stakeholder-associated risks, and propose response strategies taking account of the specific project characteristics and phases of a green construction project's life cycle.

References

Al-Sabah, R., Menassa, C. C., & Hanna, A. (2014). Evaluating impact of construction risks in the Arabian Gulf Region from perspective of multinational architecture, engineering and construction firms. *Construction Management and Economics*, *32*, 382–402.

Andi. (2006). The importance and allocation of risks in Indonesian construction projects. *Construction Management and Economics*, *24*, 69–80.

Aritua, B., Smith, N. J., & Bower, D. (2011). What risks are common to or amplified in programmes: Evidence from UK public sector infrastructure schemes. *International Journal of Project Management, 29*, 303–312.

Chan, A. P. C., Yeung, J. F. Y., Yu, C. C. P., Wang, S. Q., & Ke, Y. (2011a). Empirical study of risk assessment and allocation of public-private partnership projects in China. *Journal of Management in Engineering, 27*, 136–148.

Chan, D. W. M., Chan, A. P. C., Lam, P. T. I., Yeung, J. F. Y., & Chan, J. H. L. (2011b). Risk ranking and analysis in target cost contracts: Empirical evidence from the construction industry. *International Journal of Project Management, 29*, 751–763.

Chang, R. D., Soebarto, V., Zhao, Z. Y., & Zillante, G. (2016). Facilitating the transition to sustainable construction: China's policies. *Journal of Cleaner Production, 131*, 534–544.

Chang, R. D., Zuo, J., Soebarto, V., Zhao, Z. Y., & Zillante, G. (2017). Dynamic interactions between sustainability and competitiveness in construction firms: A transition perspective. *Engineering, Construction and Architectural Management, 24*, 842–859.

Chapman, R. (2006). *Simple Tools and Techniques for Enterprise Risk Management.* Chichester, England: John Wiley & Sons.

Chien, K. F., Wu, Z. H., & Huang, S. C. (2014). Identifying and assessing critical risk factors for BIM projects: Empirical study. *Automation in Construction, 45*, 1–15.

Chuing Loo, S., Abdul-Rahman, H. and Wang, C. (2013). Managing external risks for international architectural, engineering, and construction (AEC) firms operating in gulf cooperation council (GCC) states. *Project Management Journal, 44*, 70–88.

Darko, A. & Chan, A. P. C. (2016). Critical analysis of green building research trend in construction journals. *Habitat International, 57*, 53–63.

Davison, A. C. & Hinkley, D. V. (1997). *Bootstrap Methods and Their Application.* Cambridge: Cambridge University Press.

Deloitte. (2008). *The Dollars and Sense of Green Retrofits.* New York: Deloitte Development LLC.

Dewlaney, K. S., Hallowell, M. R., & Fortunato Iii, B. R. (2012). Safety risk quantification for high performance sustainable building construction. *Journal of Construction Engineering and Management, 138*, 964–971.

Diamantopoulos, A., Sarstedt, M., Fuchs, C., Wilczynski, P., & Kaiser, S. (2012). Guidelines for choosing between multi-item and single-item scales for construct measurement: A predictive validity perspective. *Journal of the Academy of Marketing Science, 40,* 434–449.

Doloi, H. (2014). Rationalizing the implementation of web-based project management systems in construction projects using PLS-SEM. *Journal of Construction Engineering and Management, 140,* 04014026.

Durmus-Pedini, A. & Ashuri, B. (2010). An overview of the benefits and risk factors of going green in existing buildings. *International Journal of Facility Management, 1,* 1–15.

Efron, B. (1987). Better bootstrap confidence intervals. *Journal of the American Statistical Association, 82,* 171–185.

El-Sayegh, S. M. (2008). Risk assessment and allocation in the UAE construction industry. *International Journal of Project Management, 26,* 431–438.

El-Sayegh, S. M. & Mansour, M. H. (2015). Risk assessment and allocation in highway construction projects in the UAE. *Journal of Management in Engineering, 31,* 04015004.

El-Sayegh, S. M., Manjikian, S., Ibrahim, A., Abouelyousr, A., & Jabbour, R. (2021). Risk identification and assessment in sustainable construction projects in the UAE. *International Journal of Construction Management, 21,* 327–336.

Eybpoosh, M., Dikmen, I., & Birgonul, M. T. (2011). Identification of risk paths in international construction projects using structural equation modeling. *Journal of Construction Engineering and Management, 137,* 1164–1175.

Fang, C., Marle, F., Zio, E., & Bocquet, J.-C. (2012). Network theory-based analysis of risk interactions in large engineering projects. *Reliability Engineering & System Safety, 106,* 1–10.

Fang, D., Li, M., Fong, P., & Shen, L. (2004). Risks in Chinese construction market-Contractors' perspective. *Journal of Construction Engineering and Management, 130,* 853–861.

Fornell, C. & Larcker, D. F. (1981). Evaluating structural equation models with unobservable variables and measurement error. *Journal of Marketing Research, 18,* 39–50.

Greenwald, J. (2012). Green buildings pose myriad risks. *Business Insurance, 46,* 3.

Gruneberg, S., Hughes, W., & Ancell, D. (2007). Risk under performance-based contracting in the UK construction sector. *Construction Management and Economics, 25,* 691–699.

Hair, J. F., Anderson, R. E., Tatham, R. L., & Black, W. C. (1998). *Multivariate Data Analysis with Readings.* Englewood Cliffs, NJ: Prentice Hall.

Hair, J. F., Ringle, C. M., & Sarstedt, M. (2011). PLS-SEM: Indeed a silver bullet. *Journal of Marketing Theory and Practice, 19,* 139–152.

Hair, J. F., Ringle, C. M., & Sarstedt, M. (2012). Partial least squares: The better approach to structural equation modeling? *Long Range Planning, 45,* 312–319.

Hair, J. F., Sarstedt, M., Hopkins, L., & G. Kuppelwieser, V. (2014). Partial least squares structural equation modeling (PLS-SEM): An emerging tool in business research. *European Business Review, 26,* 106–121.

Hazen, B. T., Overstreet, R. E., & Boone, C. A. (2015). Suggested reporting guidelines for structural equation modeling in supply chain management research. *International Journal of Logistics Management, 26,* 627–641.

Hlaing, N. N., Singh, D., Tiong, R. L. K., & Ehrlich, M. (2008). Perceptions of Singapore construction contractors on construction risk identification. *Journal of Financial Management of Property and Construction, 13,* 85–95.

Hwang, B.-G., Shan, M., & Phuah, S. L. (2018). Safety in green building construction projects in Singapore: Performance, critical issues, and improvement solutions. *KSCE Journal of Civil Engineering, 22,* 447–458.

Hwang, B.-G., Shan, M., & Supa'at, N. N. B. (2017a). Green commercial building projects in Singapore: Critical risk factors and mitigation measures. *Sustainable cities and Society, 30,* 237–247.

Hwang, B., Zhao, X., & Gay, M. J. S. (2013). Public private partnership projects in Singapore: Factors, critical risks and preferred risk allocation from the perspective of contractors. *International Journal of Project Management, 31,* 424–433.

Hwang, B. G. & Leong, L. P. (2013). Comparison of schedule delay and causal factors between traditional and green construction projects. *Technological and Economic Development of Economy, 19,* 310–330.

Hwang, B. G., Shan, M., Phua, H., & Chi, S. (2017b). An exploratory analysis of risks in green residential building construction projects: The case of Singapore. *Sustainability (Switzerland), 9.*

Hwang, B. G., Zhao, X., See, Y. L., & Zhong, Y. (2015). Addressing risks in green retrofit projects: The case of Singapore. *Project Management Journal, 46,* 76–89.

Ismael, D. and Shealy, T. (2018). Sustainable construction risk perceptions in the Kuwaiti construction industry. *Sustainability (Switzerland), 10,* 1854.

Jha, K. N. & Devaya, M. N. (2008). Modelling the risks faced by Indian construction companies assessing international projects. *Construction Management and Economics, 26,* 337–348.

Jiang, Y. (2010). Understanding the cost of green buildings: Evidence from Singapore. Master, National University of Singapore.

Karakhan, A. A. & Gambatese, J. A. (2017). Identification, quantification, and classification of potential safety risk for sustainable construction in the United States. *Journal of Construction Engineering and Management, 143,* 04017018.

Kartam, N. A. & Kartam, S. A. (2001). Risk and its management in the Kuwaiti construction industry: A contractors' perspective. *International Journal of Project Management, 19,* 325–335.

Katz, L. (1953). A new status index derived from sociometric analysis. *Psychometrika, 18,* 39–43.

Ke, Y., Wang, S., Chan, A. P. C., & Cheung, E. (2011). Understanding the risks in China's PPP projects: Ranking of their probability and consequence. *Engineering, Construction and Architectural Management, 18,* 481–496.

Lam, J. (2003). *Enterprise Risk Management: From Incentives to Controls.* Hoboken, NJ: John Wiley & Sons.

Le, Y., Shan, M., Chan, A. P. C., & Hu, Y. (2014). Investigating the causal relationships between causes of and vulnerabilities to corruption in the Chinese public construction sector. *Journal of Construction Engineering and Management, 140,* 05014007.

Li, S., Lu, Y., Kua, H. W., & Chang, R. (2020). The economics of green buildings: A life cycle cost analysis of non-residential buildings in tropic climates. *Journal of Cleaner Production, 252,* 19771.

Lim, B. T. H., Ling, F. Y. Y., Ibbs, C. W., Raphael, B., & Ofori, G. (2012). Mathematical models for predicting organizational flexibility of construction firms in Singapore. *Journal of Construction Engineering and Management, 138,* 361–375.

Ling, F. Y. Y. & Hoi, L. (2006). Risks faced by Singapore firms when undertaking construction projects in India. *International Journal of Project Management, 24,* 261–270.

Liu, J., Zhao, X., & Yan, P. (2016). Risk paths in international construction projects: Case study from Chinese contractors. *Journal of Construction Engineering and Management, 142,* 05016002.

Liu, M., Chong, H. Y., Liao, P. C., & Ganbat, T. (2021). Risk-based metanetwork modeling for sustainable project performance in international construction. *Journal of Infrastructure Systems, 27,* 04021020.

Lockwood, C. (2009). Building retrofits. *Urban Land, 6,* 46–57.

Lu, S. & Yan, H. (2013). A comparative study of the measurements of perceived risk among contractors in China. *International Journal of Project Management, 31,* 307–312.

Ma, J. & Kremer, G. E. O. (2015). A fuzzy logic-based approach to determine product component end-of-life option from the views of sustainability and designer's perception. *Journal of Cleaner Production, 108*, 289–300.

Marques, R. C. & Berg, S. (2011). Risks, contracts, and private-sector participation in infrastructure. *Journal of Construction Engineering and Management, 137*, 925–932.

McGraw-Hill Construction. (2013). *World Green Building Trends: Business Benefits Driving New and Retrofit Market Opportunities in Over 60 Countries*. Bedford, MA: McGraw-Hill Construction.

Menegaki, M. & Damigos, D. (2018). A review on current situation and challenges of construction and demolition waste management. *Current Opinion in Green and Sustainable Chemistry, 13*, 8–15.

Mok, C. K., Tummala, V. M. R., & Leung, H. M. (1997). Practices, barriers and benefits of risk management process in building services cost estimation. *Construction Management and Economics, 15*, 161–175.

Ning, Y. (2014). Quantitative effects of drivers and barriers on networking strategies in public construction projects. *International Journal of Project Management, 32*, 286–297.

Nunnally, J. C. (1978). *Psychometric Theory*. New York, NY: McGraw-Hill

Odom, J. D., Scott, R., & Dubose, G. H. (2008). The hidden risks of green buildings: Why moisture and mold problems are likely. *Florida Engineering Society Journal, 10*, 12–13.

Panthi, K., Ahmed, S. M., & Ogunlana, S. O. (2009). Contingency estimation for construction projects through risk analysis. *International Journal of Construction Education and Research, 5*, 79–94.

Parise, S. (2007). Knowledge management and human resource development: An application in social network analysis methods. *Advances in Developing Human Resources, 9*, 359–383.

Pedrycz, W., Ekel, P., & Parreiras, R. (2011). *Fuzzy Multicriteria Decision-Making: Models, Methods and Applications*. Chichester, England: John Wiley & Sons.

Pérez-Lombard, L., Ortiz, J., & Pout, C. (2008). A review on buildings energy consumption information. *Energy and buildings, 40*, 394–398.

PMI (2017). *A Guide to the Project Management Body of Knowledge*. Newtown Square, PA: Project Management Institute.

Pryke, S. (2012). *Social Network Analysis in Construction*. Chichester, UK: John Wiley & Sons.

Qazi, A., Shamayleh, A., El-Sayegh, S., & Formaneck, S. (2021). Prioritizing risks in sustainable construction projects using a risk matrix-based Monte Carlo Simulation approach. *Sustainable Cities and Society, 65*, 102576.

Rebeiz, K. S. (2012). Public-private partnership risk factors in emerging countries: BOOT illustrative case study. *Journal of Management in Engineering*, *28*, 421–428.

Roumboutsos, A. & Anagnostopoulos, K. P. (2008). Public private partnership projects in Greece: Risk ranking and preferred risk allocation. *Construction Management and Economics*, *26*, 751–763.

Sarstedt, M., Henseler, J., & Ringle, C. M. (2011). Multigroup analysis in partial least squares (PLS) path modeling: Alternative methods and empirical results. *Advances in International Marketing*, *22*, 195–218.

Schreiber, J. B., Nora, A., Stage, F. K., Barlow, E. A., & King, J. (2006). Reporting structural equation modeling and confirmatory factor analysis results: A review. *Journal of Educational Research*, *99*, 323–338.

Scott, J. and Carrington, P. J. (2011). *The SAGE Handbook of Social Network Analysis*. London: SAGE Publications.

Shan, M., Chan, A. P. C., Le, Y., & Hu, Y. (2015a). Investigating the effectiveness of response strategies for vulnerabilities to corruption in the Chinese public construction sector. *Science and Engineering Ethics*, *21*, 683–705.

Shan, M., Chan, A. P. C., Le, Y., Xia, B., & Hu, Y. (2015b). Measuring corruption in public construction projects in China. *Journal of Professional Issues in Engineering Education and Practice*, *141*, 05015001.

Shan, M. & Hwang, B.-G. (2018). Green building rating systems: Global reviews of practices and research efforts. *Sustainable Cities and Society*, *39*, 172–180.

Shanmugam, S., Sun, C., Zeng, X., & Wu, Y.-R. (2018). High-efficient production of biobutanol by a novel Clostridium sp. strain WST with uncontrolled pH strategy. *Bioresource Technology*, *256*, 543–547.

Tang, W., Qiang, M., Duffield, C. F., Young, D. M., & Lu, Y. (2007). Risk management in the Chinese construction industry. *Journal of Construction Engineering and Management*, *133*, 944–956.

Thompson, J. D., Zald, M. N., & Scott, W. R. (2017). *Organizations in Action: Social Science Bases of Administrative Theory*. New York, NY: Routledge.

Tollin, H. M. (2011). Green building risks: It's not easy being green. *Environmental Claims Journal*, *23*, 199–213.

UNEP. (2009). *Building and Climate Change: Summary for Decision-Makers*. Paris, France: United Nations Environment Programme.

Wang, S. Q., Dulaimi, M. F., & Aguria, M. Y. (2004). Risk management framework for construction projects in developing countries. *Construction Management and Economics*, *22*, 237–252.

Wang, T., Wang, S., Zhang, L., Huang, Z., & Li, Y. (2015). A major infrastructure risk-assessment framework: Application to a cross-sea route project in China. *International Journal of Project Management, 34*, 1403–1415.

Wasserman, S. & Faust, K. (1994). *Social Network Analysis: Methods and Applications.* Cambridge, UK: Cambridge University Press.

Wibowo, A. & Mohamed, S. (2010). Risk criticality and allocation in privatised water supply projects in Indonesia. *International Journal of Project Management, 28*, 504–513.

Winston, A. S. (2009). *Green Recovery.* Boston, MA: Harvard Business Press.

WorldGBC (2013). *The Business Case for Green Building: A Review of the Costs and Benefits for Developers, Investors and Occupants.* London: World Green Building Council.

Wu, P., Xia, B., & Zhao, X. (2014). The importance of use and end-of-life phases to the life cycle greenhouse gas (GHG) emissions of concrete — A review. *Renewable and Sustainable Energy Reviews, 37*, 360–369.

Xia, B., Chan, A. P. C., & Yeung, J. F. Y. (2011). Developing a fuzzy multicriteria decision-making model for selecting design-build operational variations. *Journal of Construction Engineering and Management, 137*, 1176–1184.

Yang, R. J. & Zou, P. X. W. (2014). Stakeholder-associated risks and their interactions in complex green building projects: A social network model. *Building and Environment, 73*, 208–222.

Yang, R. J., Zou, P. X. W., & Wang, J. (2016). Modelling stakeholder-associated risk networks in green building projects. *International Journal of Project Management, 34*, 66–81.

Yudelson, J. (2010). *Greening Existing Buildings.* New York, NY: McGraw-Hill.

Zhang, X. & Mohandes, S. R. (2020). Occupational Health and Safety in green building construction projects: A holistic Z-numbers-based risk management framework. *Journal of Cleaner Production, 275*, 122788.

Zhao, X. (2021). Stakeholder-associated factors influencing construction and demolition waste management: A systematic review. *Buildings, 11*, 149.

Zhao, X., Feng, Y., Pienaar, J., & O'brien, D. (2017). Modelling paths of risks associated with BIM implementation in architectural, engineering and construction projects. *Architectural Science Review, 60*, 472–482.

Zhao, X., Hwang, B. G., & Gao, Y. (2016a). A fuzzy synthetic evaluation approach for risk assessment: A case of Singapore's green projects. *Journal of Cleaner Production, 115*, 203–213.

Zhao, X., Hwang, B. G., & Lee, H. N. (2016b). Identifying critical leadership styles of project managers for green building projects. *International Journal of Construction Management, 16*, 150–160.

Zhao, X., Hwang, B. G., & Low, S. P. (2013a). Developing fuzzy enterprise risk management maturity model for construction firms. *Journal of Construction Engineering and Management, 139,* 1179–1189.

Zhao, X., Hwang, B. G., & Low, S. P. (2014a). Investigating enterprise risk management maturity in construction firms. *Journal of Construction Engineering and Management, 140,* 05014006.

Zhao, X., Hwang, B. G., & Phng, W. (2014b). Construction project risk management in Singapore: Resources, effectiveness, impact, and understanding. *KSCE Journal of Civil Engineering, 18,* 27–36.

Zhao, X., Hwang, B. G., & Yu, G. S. (2013b). Identifying the critical risks in underground rail international construction joint ventures: Case study of Singapore. *International Journal of Project Management, 31,* 554–566.

Zhao, X., Webber, R., Kalutara, P., Browne, W., & Pienaar, J. (2021). Construction and demolition waste management in Australia: A mini-review. *Waste Management and Research, 40,* 34–46.

Zhao, X., Wu, P., & Wang, X. (2018). Risk paths in BIM adoption: Empirical study of China. *Engineering, Construction and Architectural Management, 25,* 1170–1187.

Zhao, X., Zuo, J., Wu, G., & Huang, C. (2019). A bibliometric review of green building research 2000–2016. *Architectural Science Review, 62,* 74–88.

Zhu, J., Chew, D. A., Lv, S., & Wu, W. (2013). Optimization method for building envelope design to minimize carbon emissions of building operational energy consumption using orthogonal experimental design (OED). *Habitat International, 37,* 148–154.

Zimmermann, H. J. (2001). *Fuzzy Set Theory and its Applications.* Boston, MA: Kluwer Academic Publishers.

Zou, P. X. W. & Couani, P. (2012). Managing risks in green building supply chain. *Architectural Engineering and Design Management, 8,* 143–158.

Zou, P. X. W. & Li, J. (2010). Risk identification and assessment in subway projects: Case study of Nanjing Subway Line 2. *Construction Management and Economics, 28,* 1219–1238.

Zou, P. X. W., Zhang, G., & Wang, J. (2007). Understanding the key risks in construction projects in China. *International Journal of Project Management, 25,* 601–614.

Zuo, J. & Zhao, Z. Y. (2014). Green building research–current status and future agenda: A review. *Renewable and Sustainable Energy Reviews, 30,* 271–281.

Chapter 11

Green Construction Project Procurement Management

Sitsofe Kwame Yevu[*], **Emmanuel Kingsford Owusu**[†],
and Albert P. C. Chan[†]

[*]*Loughborough University, Loughborough, UK*

[†]*The Hong Kong Polytechnic University Hung Hom, Hong Kong*

There is overwhelming evidence that construction projects are partly responsible for the depletion of resources threatening global ecosystems. In that regard, achieving sustainable outcomes and minimizing the environmental impact of projects are essential in procurement management. Procurement forms a vital artery in the delivery of construction projects as it specifies and selects various resources expended in the project. Although green construction practices and procurement may not have gained the needed attention within project procurement, they offer a critical rethink on how construction projects can be procured via a "greener path." This chapter presents a thorough discussion on the use of green criteria in procurement management to promote green construction for projects. Subsequently, critical synthesis of research literature and industry reports was conducted to explore the application of green criteria at various phases of project procurement. Furthermore, insights on how key procurement activities such as project/product specifications, tender evaluation criteria, progress monitoring criteria, and project audits facilitate low-carbon approaches, resource preservation, and circular economy strategies were provided using practical case applications. This chapter enlightens procurement managers and researchers on effective paths to establish and evaluate the application of green procurement in construction project life cycle.

11.1. Introduction

Globally, there is demand for building and infrastructure projects in order to satisfy population increase and sustain development (Ayoub *et al.*, 2022). Such demands cannot be satisfied without considering the impact of these projects on the environment. To start and finish any construction project, the activities of procurement provide the pathway for projects to be constructed (Yevu *et al.*, 2021a). On this basis, making procurement "green" is vital if environmental conservation or green construction practices are to be implemented in construction projects. More importantly, key decisions occurring at the early stages of project development, which are usually enveloped in procurement activities, have the most direct impact on a project's environmental outcomes (Bohari *et al.*, 2020). Therefore, green procurement considers the life cycle environmental implications of decisions taken throughout the project, especially in the early stages.

Departing from the conventional way of procurement which typically focuses on cost, green procurement creates a fine balance in achieving economic and environmental goals on projects (Taghavi *et al.*, 2021). By focusing on green procurement, a demand for green materials, products, and construction practices is created at every stage in the project life cycle when building or infrastructure projects are being constructed (Wong *et al.*, 2016). Green procurement has two main advantages. On one hand, green procurement considers the environmental life cycle impact of construction products and services and checks for green compliance throughout the stages of the project on the other hand.

This chapter introduces green procurement within project procurement processes and provides use cases of green procurement at the main stages of projects. The chapter provides an overview of green procurement and its requirements in construction projects. Further, how green procurement in construction is conducted is presented and monitoring approaches for green procurement are explored. Subsequently, the applications of green requirements at various phases in project procurement are demonstrated using practical use cases in this book chapter.

11.2. Planning procurement management

The idea of procurement from construction project management (PM) perspective is the use of processes to acquire products and services for projects (Yevu *et al.*, 2022). Procurement, with its associated activities, is developed to manage contracts and agreements, purchase orders, and payments in the project cycle (PMBOK, 2021). In practice, the project manager/team coordinates with procurement experts to administer procurement activities, such as product specifications, request for proposals, statement of work/scope of work, contract documents, bidding/tendering, and selection of suppliers/construction service providers. The procurement expert(s) may come from the project team or organization and must be involved in project discussions at the early stages. This early involvement allows procurement in construction to develop a "greener path" for the achievement of environmental goals on projects.

Green procurement in construction PM is relatively an emerging concept/method/practice that promotes environmental initiatives (Sandra Marcelline *et al.*, 2022). By integrating green procurement into projects, both public and private organizations improve their environmental performance and influence their partners (e.g., constructors or suppliers) to ensure environmentally friendly products and production processes (Bohari *et al.*, 2017). Other concepts used interchangeably with green procurement in construction are sustainable procurement and green construction supply chain (Yu *et al.*, 2020). While the construction industry is increasingly being criticized for its high consumption of natural resources and materials, the application of green procurement which promises a sustainable solution to these adverse effects of construction is rather low, scarce, and fraught with uncertainties. Notwithstanding the efforts made by institutions such as the European Union (EU) to provide guidelines and codes for selecting products/services that protect or conserve the environment, concerns over how and where these measures have been applied in the processes of construction procurement remain limited for knowledge sharing in construction research.

11.2.1. *Green procurement in construction projects*

Green procurement in construction comprises of initiatives, systems, and practices that minimize environmental footprint of construction-related products and activities (Bohari *et al.*, 2020). In this regard, environmental footprint refers to the overall impact of energy consumption, greenhouse gas (GHG) emissions, and natural resource degradation pertaining to construction-related products and services. In contrast to the traditional requirement of environmental management, which focuses on only chemical hazards in construction, the criteria of green procurement extend this requirement to ensure low/zero carbon and clean production approaches. Integrating these green criteria into procurement decisions for construction products or services selection requires a step-by-step consideration (Yevu *et al.*, 2021b). The priority of green criteria in this stepwise consideration is to select products or services that use practices/technologies having low environmental impacts. To do this, green criteria in construction procurement engage one or more of these approaches, if applicable — low/zero carbon approaches, resource preservation and renewable energy use, and circular economy strategies.

11.2.1.1. *Low/zero carbon approaches*

Low-carbon approaches are practices that significantly reduce emissions (GHG) in the life cycle of construction products (Ismailos & Touchie, 2017). In procuring construction services, low-carbon approaches ensure that activities employed in these services emit less carbon into the atmosphere. More importantly, reducing the energy demand in the production of construction products is an efficient way to lower carbon emissions (Tavares *et al.*, 2021). An advanced form of low-carbon approach, with a more idealistic target, is near-zero or zero carbon emission approaches. This is, either no carbon emissions are produced or carbon emissions produced are minimal and insignificant during production and delivery of construction products and services. Identifying practices/technological solutions that embrace low-carbon approaches is a dynamic and complex process in procurement management. However, few studies have outlined some strategies and procedures designed to promote green procurement by minimizing environmental impact of construction projects during their life cycle (Bohari *et al.*, 2017). Such strategies include life cycle carbon emissions of products, ecolabelling of products, green supplier directory, and energy-efficient processes and services.

11.2.1.2. *Resource preservation and renewable energy use*

Concerning green procurement, practices or technical solutions that conserve resources expended in creating construction products and delivering services are the attributes desired. Hence, within construction supply chain, processes that exploit and destroy natural resources such as water, soil base, biodiversity, minerals, and landscapes are not selected when green procurement is to be applied in projects (Braulio-Gonzalo & Bovea, 2020). Though there has been great awareness on the environmental impacts of construction projects among stakeholders (Uttam *et al.*, 2012), green procurement offers a careful evaluation of the stages in products or services for best options. For instance, source verification of construction materials (e.g., sand and concrete), i.e., whether they are from sustainable sources or suppliers. For labor resources, health, safety, and well-being are increasingly being integrated into green procurement to advance sustainability in the planning stages of projects (Walker & Brammer, 2012). Another green criterion for construction procurement is to focus on products or services that employ renewable energy in their activities. Through this, project procurement mainly targets technological processes that incorporate renewable energy as the main source of energy for machinery in construction.

11.2.1.3. *Circular economy strategies*

Although the concept of circularity is not new in PM, it has evolved by amalgamating various strategies that oppose a linear economy (i.e., produce-use-waste landfill) (Guerra & Leite, 2021). In this regard, circular economy is increasingly becoming a key component in project performance (Charef & Emmitt, 2021), hence, green procurement has sought to include strategies of circular economy in the evaluation criteria. These strategies include reuse, refurbish, remanufacture, recycle, and recover. With these strategies, green procurement seeks to select construction products and services based on their circularity potential, that is, their ability to adapt to any circular economy strategy. Furthermore, green procurement can also use the end-of-life potential of construction materials to prioritize material selection for projects.

In construction PM, each project has its unique characteristics. Hence, green criteria applied in each project procurement may vary based on the type, goals, client demands, location, and nature of the project. Furthermore, the various requirements and practices that encapsulate green criteria are mostly presented as initiatives with broad applications and often lack detailed specifics. One possible explanation is that as projects have their differences, project and procurement managers have to adapt these green criteria to suit individual project needs for optimal outputs. These green criteria are designed to be flexible to ensure their applicability, which would in turn harness innovative solutions that are sustainable on a case-by-case basis. For instance, procurement managers can define acceptable thresholds of carbon footprints based on the context of the project, and this would stimulate innovative solutions from contractors/service providers participating in the project. Table 11.1 presents some examples of green practices and requirements adopted in project procurement.

Table 11.1.   Some green practices/requirements preferred in project procurement.

No.	Green practices/requirements preferred in project procurement	Selected references
1	Green incentives to make sustainable tenderers eligible	Bohari *et al.* (2017)
2	Applying eco-labelling schemes in the selection of products	Kuttinen and le Roux (2017), Bohari *et al.* (2017)
3	Low carbon footprint of construction products and services	Kuittinen and le Roux (2017), Sanchez *et al.* (2014)
4	Design buildings based on green specifications	Uttam *et al.* (2017), Bohari *et al.* (2017)
5	Adopting innovations with less impact on the environment	Yu *et al.* (2020), Uttam *et al.* (2017)

Table 11.1.   (*Continued*)

No.	Green practices/requirements preferred in project procurement	Selected references
6	Encouraging the use of products/ equipment that consumes less energy	Kuttinen and le Roux (2017), Sanchez *et al.* (2014)
7	Using e-procurement or web-based systems in procurement management	Yu *et al.* (2020)
8	Sustainable waste management plan for the project	Varnäs *et al.* (2009), Bohari *et al.* (2017)
9	Prioritizing products/practices with high circularity potential for reuse, recycle, recover and refurbish	Kuttinen and le Roux (2017)
10	Proof of strategies/technological solutions that eliminate waste generation	Sterner (2002), Yu *et al.* (2020)
11	Avoid purchasing hazardous materials in product compositions	Sterner (2002), Uttam *et al.* (2017)
12	Prioritizing contractors/service providers with long term strategies that promote circular economy	Varnäs *et al.* (2009), Zhang (2019)
13	Conducting life cycle assessments (LCA) of products for selection	Sterner (2002), Varnäs *et al.* (2009)
14	Green performance reporting and monitoring	Kuttinen and le Roux (2017)
15	Selecting practices that encourage the use of renewable resources	Sterner (2002), Yu *et al.* (2020)
16	Selecting locally produced materials for the project	Bohari *et al.* (2017)
17	Select construction service providers based on knowledge and experience of green construction	Bohari *et al.* (2017), Zhang (2019)
18	Reduced carbon footprint of transportation plan for the project	Sanchez *et al.* (2014)
19	Selecting construction technologies or practices that decrease materials used	Yu *et al.* (2020), Wong *et al.* (2016)
20	Adopting proven green specification model clauses in contracts	Wong *et al.* (2016), Zhang (2019)
21	Apply green technology in construction projects	Kuttinen and le Roux (2017), Wong *et al.* (2016)

Though the green practices in the table are not exhaustive, they provide a fertile foundation for developing specific green procurement practices when planning and executing construction projects.

To further appreciate the extent of research areas explored regarding green procurement, a brief contemporary literature search was conducted in Scopus on April 8, 2022. The keywords string used for the search are "Green criteria" OR "Green procurement" OR "Sustainable procurement" AND "Procurement" OR "Supply chain" OR "Purchasing" AND "Construction project" OR "Construction industry." Initial results from the search were filtered for English and journal articles. The final search results were visualized in VOSviewer (Van Eck & Waltman, 2010; Yevu *et al.*, 2021b), as shown in Figures 11.1 and 11.2. In Figure 11.1, the general overview of research discussions on green procurement is provided. Topics such as green procurement, construction industry, sustainable development, and environmental impact have dominated scholarly debates on green criteria in project procurement.

For more details on specific areas attracting green criteria applications, Figure 11.2 captures the current topics explored with green criteria

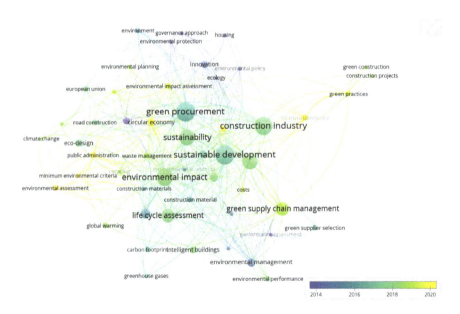

Figure 11.1.   General overview of green procurement in construction PM literature.

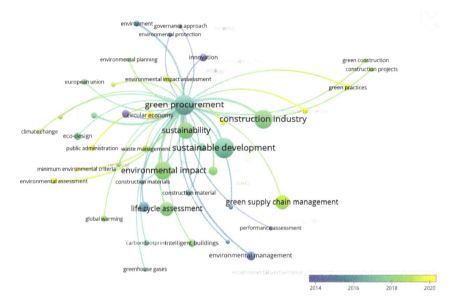

Figure 11.2.   Current trends in green procurement applications for project procurement.

in construction project procurement. Topics that have connections with green procurement and are currently trending are circular economy, minimum environmental criteria, life cycle approach, green practices, carbon footprint, ecodesign, public procurement, green supply chain management, green construction, recycling, and climate change. Put differently, these topics show research areas where green procurement is being applied in PM. While the current trends broadly reiterate priorities in green criteria (i.e., low/zero carbon approaches, resource preservation and renewable energy use, and circular economy strategies) as mentioned earlier, they further reveal avenues that have to be explored when implementing green procurement in construction projects in the future.

11.3. Conducting green procurement

Usually, project procurement is conducted with a chain of activities that starts from the project planning stage and spans throughout the life cycle of the project. This chain of activities comprises of subactivities and involves multiple stakeholders connected in a transitional manner along

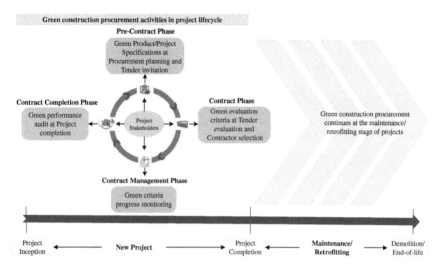

Figure 11.3.   Green procurement activities at various phases of construction projects.
Source: Adapted from Yevu (2022).

the project stages (Yevu *et al.*, 2022). Activities of the procurement cycle in tandem with the project life cycle can be divided into four phases: pre-contract, contracting, contract management, and contract completion, as shown in Figure 11.3.

The pre-contract phase focuses on assessing the need for the project and preparing for it. Subactivities employed at this stage include needs assessment, procurement planning, and tender/bid invitation. While needs assessment defines the importance and impact of the project, procurement planning covers processes on cost estimation, project/product specifications, and contract documents. Tender invitation looks at using the contract documents from procurement planning to solicit and receive proposals from tenderers/bidders regarding the project (Ruparathna & Hewage, 2013). For the contracting phase, the subactivities consist of tender evaluation and award of contract to contractor/service provider. Tender evaluation is the process that examines each bid received based on predefined evaluation criteria. Different projects may have different evaluation criteria. However, the bid or solution that provides the best value per the criteria is the one selected and subsequently awarded the contract. The contract award agreement forms the legal binding document to ensure that the project is performed as planned. In the contract management phase, procurement activities focus on progress monitoring and payments at the construction stage of the project. Project milestones are measured in correspondence to the desired outputs stipulated in the contract documents. At the contract completion phase, procurement activities are used to finalize and close out the project. Activities such as project audits, final project payments, and project file documentation are used to close out the project for the use stage (operational stage) to commence.

With numerous activities surrounding the procurement cycle for projects, there are some key activities that present critical opportunities for green procurement to influence construction practices in the project life cycle. These procurement activities are project/product specifications, tender evaluation criteria, progress monitoring criteria, and project audits (Bohari *et al.*, 2017; Sterner, 2002; Varnäs *et al.*, 2009). From these activities, green procurement practices related to low-carbon approaches, resource preservation, and circularity can be promoted at each phase of procurement as well as at the project stages. For instance, project/product specifications could be developed to describe the use of low-carbon approaches or include circularity features in construction materials and components adopted in the project. Furthermore, the tender evaluation criteria can be skewed to prioritize construction processes and methods that conserve resources or emit low GHG into the environment from method statements submitted for the project. It can also be used to check construction service providers for suitability based on their network of operations for activities/technologies that promote clean environments. To achieve these improvements that propel construction procurement toward a more sustainable outcome, conventional requirements usually demanded by project stakeholders must adapt to the changes that green procurement brings both at the product and the project level.

11.4. Monitoring green procurement processes

One major aspect of procurement that ensures the translation of plans or proposals into reality is the monitoring process (UNEP, 2016). In that regard, monitoring the procurement process at each stage forms a crucial part in implementing green procurement. Necessary controls must be set in place to ensure that the various criteria for green procurement are carried out from project planning to project completion. As mentioned earlier, key procurement activities that facilitate green procurement implementation should be the focus when monitoring construction procurement. In this process, project and procurement managers can monitor contract performance by checking green requirements compliance. Where necessary, amendments, changes, and corrections can be introduced during the monitoring process to (re)direct procurement phases toward more sustainable outputs. For example, project and procurement managers can compare and contrast method statements and work plans proposed by the contractor at the tender evaluation phase to the actual construction methods used at the progress monitoring phase in procurement. This is to ensure that the project's performance meets the requirements for green procurement as indicated. In monitoring the procurement process, modern technologies aid in gathering and assessing information for tracking and compliance purposes.

11.5. Practical case applications and discussions

As indicated by Flyvbjerg (2006), case studies demonstrate exemplars in a discipline, and without exemplars, the discipline would be ineffective in advancing knowledge and practice. In line with this, use case examples are valuable, especially in situations where there exists limited knowledge on the subject matter (Fellows & Liu, 2015). Therefore, use cases are adopted in this chapter to identify practical applications of green procurement at various phases of procurement in construction projects. Studies and industry reports that demonstrated green procurement requirements in construction were used for selecting representative examples. The criteria for selecting representative examples are studies that focused on practical application of low-carbon approaches in key procurement activities, use cases of applying green criteria to preserve resources via procurement, and use cases of applying circular economy in construction procurement. Scopus and industry reports were adopted in the search for articles/reports on the subject matter (Yevu *et al.*, 2021b). Using Scopus, keywords such as green criteria, low carbon, resource preservation, and construction procurement were used for the article search. Only English articles were considered and articles that did not present applications of green criteria in construction procurement were excluded. International reports on sustainable and green procurement in the construction industry were explored for more information on green procurement's applicability. Subsequently, contents of the representative articles/reports were examined, and their use case applications were presented based on the procurement phases identified.

11.5.1. *Precontract phase: Specifications (technical or functions' requirements)*

Technical and functional requirements are essential at the precontract phase for green procurement. In Finland, Kuittinen and le Roux (2017) report on guiding Finnish construction actors to improve their environmental competence for procurements in EU markets and emphasize that at least 10% of the materials specified in procurements should be renewable or recyclable. This mandates service consultants to include specifications of energy materials when designing buildings and describing technical requirements of materials for contracts.

According to Arts *et al.* (2006), the Dutch government formulated a framework that merges procedures for environmental criteria assessments and pre-contracting periodically at preliminary stages of projects. Using this framework, the terms of reference (TOR), which is used to invite proposed solutions from construction market actors, formulates an information outline for the proposed solution. Subsequently, this information is incorporated into the notification of intent, which is then subjected to a public review as part of the environmental criteria assessment process. The outcomes from this consultative process ensure that the TOR is more aligned toward the environmental criteria and the market actors' consent to these requirements. Therefore, the alternatives prepared as solutions by the market actors integrate these environmental requirements in their preliminary bids for the project. This approach ensures that building designers/consultants provide optimal environmental solutions to infrastructure problems. By doing this, the impact of processes proposed in the alternatives by consultants is systematically mapped out for easy evaluation.

From the study of Bohari *et al.* (2017), construction practitioners in Malaysia indicated that irrespective of the procurement setting (i.e., design and build, conventional, or partnering), technical specifications form the basis in describing products and services desired in building contracts. In response, the relevant stakeholders use these specifications to formulate minimum requirements needed on projects. This creates a performance-based environment in the pre-contract process. Therefore, details on material selection, chemical content, and functional characteristics should be integrated into contractual requirements when green procurement is applied. Subsequently, an effective avenue is presented for contract stakeholders to conform to green specifications when planning for projects. Taking material selection and chemical contents, for instance, specifications can be used to demand specified levels of carbon emissions when creating products and services to be used in projects.

In recent times, carbon labeling and ecolabeling of construction products have gained attention for onward application in technical specifications for contracts. Both schemes, carbon labeling and ecolabeling, generally calibrate the impact of the product on the environment and inform practical decision-making. In Hong Kong, a carbon labeling scheme was developed on carbon emission-intensive construction materials to guide practitioners in selecting low-carbon materials for construction (Ng *et al.*, 2018). The scheme provides the carbon footprint of key construction materials at the product level for design team and procurement practitioners to choose from when prescribing specifications and functional requirements on projects. This promotes green construction practices at the pre-contract stage since construction products are selected based on their impact on the environment. Similarly, the Carbon Reduction Label by Carbon Trust in the United Kingdom guides practitioners in formulating green specifications for project. Other schemes, such as Carbon Label in the United States and the CO2Star Carbon Labelling Project in Europe, provide the information database to determine which construction product is more friendly to the environment due to their inert processes and embodied emissions. These schemes incentivize practitioners to adopt them in contracts since the overall emissions in the supply chain of construction materials and products are captured. Key construction materials such as cement, reinforcing bar, structural steel, aluminum, glass, ceramic tiles, ready-mixed concrete, precast concrete, stainless steel, galvanized mild-steel, cast iron, brick, construction aggregate, asphalt pavement, sawn timber and plywood, and gypsum board alongside their estimated carbon footprints have been presented in these labeling schemes. Procurement practitioners can use these schemes for green procurement specifications in two ways. First, by describing sources or parameters with low/near-zero emissions in the specifications and, second, by specifying emission levels required to achieve an overall process that is low-carbon in nature. For practitioners in other countries/regions that do not have carbon labeling schemes, since the production of construction products is often similar across boundaries, these schemes could guide the development of technical and functional requirements for products and services that reflect the given situation/context.

Using information from the labeling schemes, construction actors such as suppliers, service providers, and contractors can be assessed based on their compliance to energy saving and low-carbon approaches adopted when producing construction products and services. For example, Creative Carbon Scotland created a suppliers database to identify suppliers that are committed to promoting environmentally friendly services and products for buildings. Though more effort would be needed to validate these promises, it serves as a starting point for procurement practitioners to find suppliers/contractors when applying green procurement principles. Project managers and procurement managers are encouraged to generate a database of suppliers based on how well they perform in carbon footprint assessments.

11.5.2. *Contract phase: Tender/bid evaluation*

Tender or bid evaluation is a central link in choosing the best option among several products and services for green construction. In green construction tendering systems, successful winners do not only focus on meeting conventional requirements such as cost, but they must also satisfy green practices outlined in the specifications of contract documents. The key task is to convert sustainable practices that are best managed in the specifications into criteria for the suppliers/contractors to compete against in their proposals.

In this regard, the New Zealand government adopted a tender evaluation model that integrates sustainable procurement requirements into tender evaluation processes for its agencies (UNEP, 2016). Based on a study by the UNEP (2016), the tender evaluation model applies non-cost criteria (green procurement) to the evaluation process. Using this model, the green areas assessed in the bid are a function of the sustainability risks identified in the project contract. Examples of these risks include high carbon emissions due to poor energy efficiency/travel management, poor sustainability practices of suppliers, and unsustainable materials in construction products. Procurement managers are encouraged to categorize the sustainability criteria for bid evaluation into three levels — mandatory, preferred, and leading, for suppliers/contractors (UNEP, 2016). Subsequently, the tender evaluation model establishes the appropriate ratio of green procurement to cost to be employed for submitted bids. It is worth noting that the upper limit of these ratios or weights may vary since each project is unique and may have different goals. Table 11.2 presents an illustration of green procurement to cost ratios/weightings in contracts from UNEP.

The list of issues described in the criteria for green procurement is assigned individual weights to achieve a total score. Some items in the list may include the following:

- organizational carbon footprint levels per project,
- sustainable energy for equipment,
- sustainable practices in methodology for planning managing contract (e.g., method statement),
- supplier's staff experience in sustainability issues for the project,
- previous performance on environmental impact assessments.

Table 11.2.   Green procurement to cost ratios/weightings.

Contract type	Green procurement weighting in evaluation
Project contract A	Between 50–70%. It may go up to 85% in exceptional circumstances and justifications must be provided
Project contract B	Up to 50%, justifications must be provided

Priority is given to sustainability issues that are deemed more important than others based on the project's nature and characteristics. Hence, a higher weighting is given to prioritized issues. In addition, minimum marks must be set within the green criteria in order to score the suppliers/contractors. Proposals that did not meet the minimum marks are deemed non-compliant.

The scoring method is based on the specifics in the green criteria and points are awarded accordingly. Subsequently, appropriate weights are applied and the total score for each supplier/contractor is determined. For instance, if suppliers A, B, and C had sustainability points of 170, 250, and 210, respectively, then their scores are as follows:

Supplier B	250 (Highest score) = 100 points
Supplier C	$(210 \times 100)/250 = 84$ points
Supplier A	$(170 \times 100)/250 = 68$ points

In terms of cost, considering that the lowest bid was submitted by "Supplier A," followed by "Supplier B" and "Supplier C," and their scores were represented by 100, 80, and 76, respectively, the best bid can be determined from the evaluation process using the green criteria to cost ratio (e.g., 55/45) in Table 11.3.

From the tender evaluation model in Table 11.2, Supplier B is therefore selected as the best bid since it had the highest score when green criteria and cost were combined. It is important to note that minimum thresholds for green criteria should be required in the evaluation process. Minimum green criteria thresholds serve as a caution to ensure suppliers/contractors that are capable are selected for the project.

Unlike selecting the lowest bid price as a contract method for awarding projects, the most economically advantageous tender (MEAT)

Table 11.3.   Evaluation of suppliers/contractors.

Supplier/ Contractor	Initial green criteria score	55% Weighted green criteria score	Initial cost score	45% Weighted cost score	Total score
Supplier A	68	37.4	100	45.0	82.4
Supplier B	100	55.0	80	36.0	91.0
Supplier C	84	46.2	76	34.2	80.4

contract method offers an effective way of evaluating tenders/bids regarding green criteria. In MEAT, procurement managers and project managers can establish green requirements as part of the tender evaluation process for suppliers and construction service providers. In the study of Parikka-Alhola and Nissinen (2012), the environmental award criteria were determined in a case study involving transportation service providers in Sweden. MEAT formed the basis for the procurer's evaluation equation with modifications considering life cycle assessment and environmental cost calculations. First, the life cycle inventory data for CO_2 emissions, pollutants, and energy consumption rates from trucks in three tenderers (A, B, and C) were obtained and their environmental impacts were assessed. Second, these environmental impacts were monetized based on a method that computes cost using lifetime cost of energy consumption, pollutant emissions, and CO_2 emissions during the truck's operation. Points were awarded to each tenderer based on their performance in the environmental impact assessment and the environmental cost calculation, respectively. Subsequently, a tender ranking system was developed using price-quality weightings. Though a weight of 30% was assigned for environmental award points, it did not lead to the most environmentally sound case (Tenderer B) being chosen. This could be due to dependence on irrelevant options in the price-quality ranking system and may open the evaluation process to submission of non-optimal tenders. Hence, Lundberg and Bergman (2011) emphasized that if bids/tenders are to be evaluated according to a price-quality combination system, procurement managers should put monetary value on quality which would be subtracted or added to the actual bids, instead of transforming bid prices into scores that can be added to quality score. From a green procurement perspective, this system of ranking may be appropriate if the cost of quality (i.e., green criteria) could be estimated. This would then make the lowest value the preferable award criteria.

11.5.3. *Contract management phase: Progress monitoring*

In contract management, numerous green requirements stated in the project specifications and assessed at tender evaluation are monitored for compliance during the execution of the project. Output indicators with respect to these green requirements must be clearly defined for services, machinery, products, processes, and materials in the monitoring process. The UNEP (2016) advocates the use of electronic systems in monitoring and tracking green requirements. However, where applicable, manual checks and verifications can be used to supplement data inputs for these electronic systems. Technologies such as blockchain, web-based systems, and the Internet of Things (IoT)-based technologies (e.g., radio frequency identification (RFID), tracking sensors, and global positioning system (GPS)) have potential capabilities to monitor and track green requirement performance during project execution.

Blockchain holds lots of potential for green procurement in construction due to its traceability and transparency capabilities. As such, Li *et al.* (2021) demonstrated blockchain's applicability for sustainability in prefabricated construction. With the blockchain-based platform, project participants such as clients, procurements managers, manufacturers, haulers, and contractors log into the platform to distribute information and data that cannot be altered among nodes. Since information shared is immutable, the real-time status and sources of construction materials from suppliers can be traced and checked if they are from sustainable sources. This ensures transparency in the construction supply chain, hence, project specifications that require sustainable sources of materials for projects can be verified and monitored by the procurement manager during the construction stage before interim payments are made to the contractor or supplier.

In the study of Liu *et al.* (2020), an IoT computerized platform was created to monitor real-time carbon emissions in prefabricated construction. Prefabrication stages involved in the monitoring were the production stage, transportation sage, and site construction stage. At the production stage, RFID was used to obtain data on embodied emissions of raw materials and a proximity switch was adopted to monitor the working times of machinery. The transportation stage used GPS to mainly generate the carbon emissions from freight vehicles. Different types of sensors for acceleration and pressure were employed for data acquisition and monitoring at the onsite stage. Subsequently, the computerized platform gathers data from these sensors to perform real-time monitoring of carbon emissions in the industrial chain of prefabricated construction.

This monitoring platform affords procurement managers the opportunity to realize carbon emitted in the supply chain of contractors/suppliers for compliance with green specifications on projects.

Wong *et al.* (2013) developed a virtual prototype system that estimates carbon emissions and visually demonstrates the estimated emissions of each construction activity on a project. The study focused on fuel-intensive equipment and plants onsite, such as cranes, bulldozers, excavators, and concrete pumps. The general project and equipment data were collected, and the site operational activities of these equipment were established. Subsequently, specifications on the emission levels required from the equipment/project are produced. Details on project requirements were converted into building information modeling (BIM) and mixed reality (MR) archVtypes for real-life simulation and visualization, respectively. Therefore, operational data on equipment and plants used by the contractor in a housing project were recorded and imported into the virtual prototype emission model. By doing this, the contrast between actual emissions from construction site activities and emissions levels stated in the specifications and tender evaluation can be identified. Further, the simulation tool allows remedial actions to be implemented if the actual emissions are above the levels required. In circumstances where a contractor exceeds the emission target, the procurement manager can penalize the contractor for non-compliance with requirements in the contract documents.

Furthermore, Chen and Nguyen (2019) applied a BIM-based web map service for sourcing sustainable construction materials. Locations for extracting materials/products that conform to some green construction standards are outlined and procurement managers can track the various locations that suppliers/contractors use for construction materials extraction.

11.5.4. *Contract completion: Project audits*

In project procurement management, conducting audits when closing out a project is a vital activity to check the project's performance against the requirements stated in the contract documents. Typically, green requirements are included in sustainability performance when evaluating the overall project performance. Technologies and web-based systems used for progress monitoring of green requirements during project execution can be extended to the contract completion stage when evaluating the project's performance. In line with this, multiple case studies from UNEP (2016) demonstrated the usefulness of applying web-based systems to consolidate green products and services employed in projects. In these case studies, each client organization from a country compared their green criteria for projects to what was actually performed. Countries such as Canada, Japan, Switzerland, the United States, and Australia were involved in the case studies. Sustainability performance was checked for percentage of green product procured on projects on web-based systems (e.g., e-procurement) and performance scorecards were used to rate the organization (i.e., success, mixed results, and unsatisfactory).

11.6. Summary

The purpose of this chapter was to explore the greener path in project procurement when applying green criteria for projects. At the outset, several ways of applying green criteria in project procurement were outlined in three main approaches (i.e., low/zero carbon approaches, resource preservation and renewable energy use, and circular economy strategies). Different life cycle phases in conducting project procurement were examined and key procurement activities that facilitate the application of green criteria for each phase were identified. These key procurement activities are project/product specifications, tender evaluation criteria, progress monitoring criteria, and project audits. Details on how green criteria have been applied in the key procurement activities for each procurement phase are presented in this chapter with exemplary cases from literature and industry reports. Key insights include the following:

- Among the key procurement activities, project/product specifications and tender evaluation criteria offer more green avenues to establish benchmarks and select the optimal solution in achieving green construction projects.

- The progress monitoring activity also provides opportunities for remedial actions concerning green criteria targets on projects.
- The project audit for green performance is useful in generating data-backed assessments of suppliers and contractors in achieving environmental goals on construction projects.

This chapter is essential for practitioners in the construction industry as it charts the path to ensure green criteria are applied in construction on project life cycle basis and not a piecemeal approach. Furthermore, both construction practitioners and researchers are provided with systemic guides to evaluate areas which are suitable when applying green criteria in procurement for construction projects.

Acknowledgments

This chapter is developed from a research project that is funded by the Postdoc Matching Fund Scheme at The Hong Kong Polytechnic University (Project ID: P0038801).

References

Arts, J., Nijsten, R., & Sandee, P. (2006). Very early contracting in EIA: Dutch experience with parallel procedures for procurement and EIA. In *26th Annual Meeting of the International Association for Impact Assessment.* (pp. 22–26). 23–26 May 2006, Stavanger, Norway.

Ayoub, H., Sweis, G., Abu-Khader, W., & Sweis, R. (2022). A framework to evaluate sustainable construction principles in government building projects: The case of Jordan. *Engineering, Construction and Architectural Management.* DOI: 10.1108/ECAM-01-2022-0040.

Bohari, A. A. M., Skitmore, M., Xia, B., & Teo, M. (2017). Green oriented procurement for building projects: Preliminary findings from Malaysia. *Journal of Cleaner Production, 148*, 690–700.

Bohari, A. A. M., Skitmore, M., Xia, B., Teo, M., & Khalil, N. (2020). Key stakeholder values in encouraging green orientation of construction procurement. *Journal of Cleaner Production, 270*, 122246.

Braulio-Gonzalo, M. & Bovea, M. D. (2020). Relationship between green public procurement criteria and sustainability assessment tools applied to office buildings. *Environmental Impact Assessment Review*, *81*, 106310.

Charef, R. & Emmitt, S. (2021). Uses of building information modelling for overcoming barriers to a circular economy. *Journal of Cleaner Production*, *285*, 124854.

Chen, P. H. & Nguyen, T. C. (2019). A BIM-WMS integrated decision support tool for supply chain management in construction. *Automation in Construction*, *98*, 289–301.

Fellows, R. F. & Liu, A. M. (2015). *Research Methods for Construction*. West Sussex, United Kingdom: John Wiley & Sons.

Flyvbjerg, B. (2006). Five misunderstandings about case-study research. *Qualitative Inquiry*, *12*(2), 219–245.

Guerra, B. C. & Leite, F. (2021). Circular economy in the construction industry: An overview of United States stakeholders' awareness, major challenges, and enablers. *Resources, Conservation and Recycling*, *170*, 105617.

Ismailos, C. & Touchie, M. F. (2017). Achieving a low carbon housing stock: An analysis of low-rise residential carbon reduction measures for new construction in Ontario. *Building and Environment*, *126*, 176–183.

Kuittinen, M. & le Roux, S. (2017). Procurement criteria for low-carbon building. Available at: https://julkaisut.valtioneuvosto.fi/bitstream/handle/10024/160737/EG_2017_Producement%20criteria.pdf?sequence=1.

Li, C. Z., Chen, Z., Xue, F., Kong, X. T., Xiao, B., Lai, X., & Zhao, Y. (2021). A blockchain-and IoT-based smart product-service system for the sustainability of prefabricated housing construction. *Journal of Cleaner Production*, *286*, 125391.

Liu, G., Chen, R., Xu, P., Fu, Y., Mao, C., & Hong, J. (2020). Real-time carbon emission monitoring in prefabricated construction. *Automation in Construction*, *110*, 102945.

Lundberg, S. & Bergman, M. (2011). Tender evaluation and award methodologies in public procurement. Available at SSRN 1831143. https://dx.doi.org/10.2139/ssrn.1831143.

Ng, T., Lo, I. M. C., & Cheng, J. C. P. (2018). A comprehensive Hong Kong based carbon labelling scheme covering emission intensive construction materials. Construction Industry Council Hong Kong, CIC Research Report No. CICRS_023.

Parikka-Alhola, K. & Nissinen, A. (2012). Environmental impacts and the most economically advantageous tender in public procurement. *Journal of Public Procurement*, *12*(1), 43–80.

PMBOK. (2021). *A Guide to the Project Management Body of Knowledge (PMBOK® Guide) and the Standard for Project Management* (7th edn.). USA: Project Management Institute.

Ruparathna, R. & Hewage, K. (2013). Review of contemporary construction procurement practices. *Journal of Management in Engineering*, *31*(3), 04014038.

Sanchez, A. X., Lehtiranta, L., Hampson, K. D., & Kenley, R. (2014). Evaluation framework for green procurement in road construction. *Smart and Sustainable Built Environment*, *3*(2), 153–169.

Sandra Marcelline, T. R., Chengang, Y., Ralison Ny Avotra, A. A., Hussain, Z., Zonia, J. E., & Nawaz, A. (2022). Impact of green construction procurement on achieving sustainable economic growth influencing green logistic services management and innovation practices. *Frontiers in Environmental Science*, *9*, 815928.

Sterner, E. (2002). 'Green procurement' of buildings: A study of Swedish clients' considerations. *Construction Management and Economics*, *20*(1), 21–30.

Taghavi, E., Fallahpour, A., Wong, K. Y., & Hoseini, S. A. (2021). Identifying and prioritizing the effective factors in the implementation of green supply chain management in the construction industry. *Sustainable Operations and Computers*, *2*, 97–106.

Tavares, V., Gregory, J., Kirchain, R., & Freire, F. (2021). What is the potential for prefabricated buildings to decrease costs and contribute to meeting EU environmental targets? *Building and Environment*, *206*, 108382.

UNEP. (2016). *Monitoring Sustainable Public Procurement Implementation: Recommendations and Case Studies*. Paris: United Nations Environmental Programme.

Uttam, K., Faith-Ell, C., & Balfors, B. (2012). EIA and green procurement: Opportunities for strengthening their coordination. *Environmental Impact Assessment Review*, *33*(1), 73–79.

Van Eck, N. & Waltman, L. (2010). Software survey: VOSviewer, a computer program for bibliometric mapping. *Scientometrics*, *84*(2), 523–538.

Varnäs, A., Balfors, B., & Faith-Ell, C. (2009). Environmental consideration in procurement of construction contracts: Current practice, problems and opportunities in green procurement in the Swedish construction industry. *Journal of Cleaner Production*, *17*(13), 1214–1222.

Walker, H. & Brammer, S. (2012). The relationship between sustainable procurement and e-procurement in the public sector. *International Journal of Production Economics, 140*(1), 256–268.

Wong, J. K. W., San Chan, J. K., & Wadu, M. J. (2016). Facilitating effective green procurement in construction projects: An empirical study of the enablers. *Journal of Cleaner Production, 135*, 859–871.

Wong, J. K., Li, H., Wang, H., Huang, T., Luo, E., & Li, V. (2013). Toward low-carbon construction processes: The visualisation of predicted emission via virtual prototyping technology. *Automation in Construction, 33*, 72–78.

Yevu, S. K. (2022). Electronic procurement adoption for construction projects in Ghana: Model development for the influential issues. PhD Thesis, The Hong Kong Polytechnic University, Hong Kong.

Yevu, S. K., Ann, T. W., & Darko, A. (2021a). Digitalization of construction supply chain and procurement in the built environment: Emerging technologies and opportunities for sustainable processes. *Journal of Cleaner Production, 322*, 129093.

Yevu, S. K., Yu, A. T. W., Darko, A., & Addy, M. N. (2021b). Evaluation model for influences of driving forces for electronic procurement systems application in Ghanaian construction projects. *Journal of Construction Engineering and Management, 147*(8), 04021076.

Yevu, S. K., Yu, A. T. W., Nani, G., Darko, A., & Tetteh, M. O. (2022). Electronic procurement systems adoption in construction procurement: A global survey on the barriers and strategies from the developed and developing economies. *Journal of Construction Engineering and Management, 148*(1), 04021186.

Yu, A. T. W., Yevu, S. K., & Nani, G. (2020). Towards an integration framework for promoting electronic procurement and sustainable procurement in the construction industry: A systematic literature review. *Journal of Cleaner Production, 250*, 119493.

Zhang, Y. (2020). Construction of bid evaluation index system in Government Public Project Green procurement in China based on DS evidence theory. *Sustainability, 12*(2), 651.

https://doi.org/10.1142/9789811251429_0012

Chapter 12

Green Construction Project Stakeholder Management

Chathuri Gunarathna, Nilmini Weerasinghe, Rebecca Yang, and Sajani Jayasuriya

RMIT University, Melbourne, Australia

This chapter includes eight sections to deliberate the effective stakeholder management processes and practices in green construction projects. Section 12.1 provides an introduction and the common terminology of stakeholder management. Section 12.2 identifies all stakeholders along the green construction supply chain. Section 12.3 discusses the tools and techniques for analyzing the stakeholder involvement and influences across the value chain. Section 12.4 discusses the current processes and practices of stakeholder engagement in green construction projects. A detailed comparison is conducted between the stakeholder management practices of traditional construction and green construction to identify new approaches and future directions. The challenges for stakeholder engagement in construction projects are also discussed. Section 12.5 discusses the impact of effective stakeholder management on decision-making and project success. It further provides decision-making strategies for effective stakeholder management in green projects. In Section 12.6, a demonstration case is presented to discuss real-life stakeholder management in green construction projects. The selected demonstration case is conducted to develop a solar building envelope (also known as building-integrated photovoltaics — BIPV) design and management tool. The content of this chapter is useful for project managers, project developers, and stakeholder group leaders as it provides a guide for effective stakeholder management in green construction projects. Further, the chapter contributes to the body of knowledge by specifically discussing the stakeholder management process of green construction projects, acknowledging sustainability and green concepts.

12.1. Introduction

The highest threat of construction is upon the environment; therefore, transitioning to a sustainable green construction process is prominent more than ever. With this change, the stakeholders in the built environment will face new challenges and come across new responsibilities that have not previously been a part of their professional roles. Multidisciplinary stakeholders with diverse interests interacting with one another in the different stages of the project process would make the whole process more complex and time-consuming. The stakeholder management is an effective tool for keeping such a diverse set of professionals in line to successfully deliver the project on the scheduled time and within the budget.

According to the Association for Project Management (APM) (2019), stakeholder management can be defined as "the process of identifying, analyzing, planning, and implementing the actions influencing the stakeholders." The process assists the project team to understand the stakeholder interests, assess how they impact or are impacted by the project, and establish strategies to involve stakeholders in decision-making, planning, and execution of project activities (PMI, 2017). A broader perception is given to the stakeholder management in the public and non-profit sector literature whereas the business management literature defines it in a relatively narrower perspective (Best *et al.*, 2019; Byrson & Edwards, 2017; Vitálišová *et al.*, 2021). Despite these viewpoints, the traditional stakeholder management should be reassessed and reconfigured with necessary modifications for it to work effectively under the green concept. This chapter discusses the stakeholder management process in green

Figure 12.1.   Stakeholder management process (developed based on the APM Body of Knowledge (APM, 2019) and PMI PMBOK Guide (PMI, 2017)).

construction projects under the five stages of stakeholder identification, stakeholder analysis, plan stakeholder engagement, manage stakeholder engagement, and review and improve. The five-stage stakeholder management process is shown in Figure 12.1.

12.2. Research methodology

Figure 12.2 demonstrates the research design. This chapter is developed by conducting a comprehensive literature review under five main sections: (1) stakeholder management theory and principles, (2) stakeholder management in traditional construction projects, (3) stakeholder management in green construction projects, (4) decision-making in traditional construction projects, and (5) decision-making in green construction projects. The literature review is conducted by referring to around 100 publications including books, journal papers, and conference papers. The purpose of the comprehensive literature review is to identify the stakeholder management principles, processes, its applications in the green

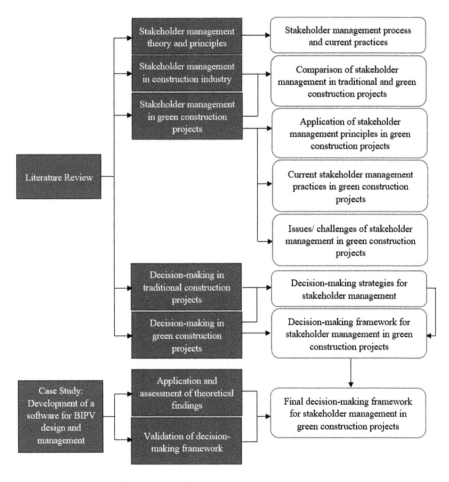

Figure 12.2.   Research design of the chapter.

construction projects, and the issues and challenges come across by the project managers. The literature findings are used to develop a decision-making framework for stakeholder management in green construction projects. A case study is selected to apply the principles and validate the developed framework. The selected case study is a software development project for building integrated photovoltaics (BIPV) design and management. The stakeholder management in this project is analyzed and the developed framework is applied to confirm its effectiveness in the project-based decision-making.

12.3. Identifying stakeholders

A large number of individuals and entities with diversified roles and responsibilities participate in different stages of the construction projects. Unlike other sectors, stakeholder participation in the construction projects is different due to its nature such as stakeholders come together to form a temporary unit, and their roles and responsibilities of them are sometimes different because of the projects and their fragmented nature. The participants show heterogeneous interests in the project objectives and maintain various relationships to play diversified roles. Identifying stakeholders and their influences is therefore critical.

12.3.1. *Who are the stakeholders?*

Stakeholder as a concept was first defined by Freeman (1984). The author defined stakeholders as "any group or individual who can affect or is affected by the achievement of the firm's objectives." The author identified stakeholder categories in an organization as clients, customers, employees, suppliers, etc. According to the Project Management Institute (PMI, 2017), stakeholders are "people, groups, or organizations that could impact or be impacted by the project." PMI (2017) provided a broader definition of stakeholders considering who may be affected or impacted by the projects. The stakeholders have been identified by active and influencing relationships between projects and the participants. They may influence project functioning, goals, development, and benefits when they support achieving the goals without opposing them (Li *et al.*, 2018b). It is noted that stakeholders can positively and negatively affect the projects as their position may vary from being supportive to adversary to the project. Also, they can be individuals, entities/organizations, or groups of individuals.

The above identification applies to green construction projects, as there are participants from multiple industries throughout the entire project life cycle performing various tasks individually and collaboratively. Here the involvement of most stakeholders is more positive in green projects and play an active role in persuading a wide range of aspects, such as economic, social, environmental, and technical, as projects are driven by sustainability targets. The numerous stakeholders have been mapped by utilizing various tools and techniques.

12.3.2. *Tools and techniques for identifying stakeholders*

Identification of all stakeholders in the entire life cycle of the project is critical, as the first step of stakeholder management. Particularly, green construction projects can be complex and comprise many processes and participants. Some of them are known stakeholders, such as clients and architects who directly contribute to the project, while some are unknown due to hidden associates, such as subcontractors, the public, or others. Nevertheless, identifying all the stakeholders is necessary for a project's success. Stakeholder identification begins with the creation of a list of stakeholders involved in the project. Also, stakeholders' attributes, roles, and responsibilities are determined (PMI, 2017). One of the common ways of identifying stakeholders is to tell who they are by the main stakeholders. In addition, the project managers may conduct brainstorming sessions, surveys, expert judgment, and interviews with primary stakeholders to identify them. Further, project documents such as project charters, business documents, and project management (PM) plans (i.e., communication plan and stakeholder registry developed at the initial stage) assist in determining the stakeholders. With the modern procurement methods, such as alliances and public–private partnerships, most stakeholders can be identified at the beginning of the projects.

The stakeholders have been categorized into various classes for identifying them straightforwardly. Srinivasan and Dhivya (2020) proposed essentially two categories by reviewing existing definitions of stakeholders as "internal" and "external" stakeholders. The "internal" stakeholders are those who are actively involved in project execution and "external" stakeholders are those who are affected and impacted by the project. This comprises both the influencers (as internal) and the claimants (as external). Berardi (2013) divided stakeholders based on the different sides of the project, client, design, construction, and public sides. Various participants are identified for each side. Zwikael and Smyrk (2019) identified two types of stakeholders, spontaneous and commissioned. Spontaneous stakeholders are those who are interested in the project regardless of any role. They are funders, beneficiaries, positive and negative impactees, customers, and influencers. The second type is commissioned stakeholders, those who play a formal role in projects, i.e., champions, project owners, steering committee members, project managers, members of the project teams, and suppliers. Further, stakeholders were classified by other researchers as internal strategic stakeholders (i.e., owner and investors), both internal and external stakeholders (i.e., public), and external and normative stakeholders (i.e., research and media), considering the life cycle of the building projects (Chan & Oppong, 2017; Srinivasan & Dhivya, 2020). A few studies identified stakeholders based on upstream (i.e., customers and investors) and downstream (i.e., suppliers) seeing the entire value chain. Identifying stakeholders through value chain could capture the whole life cycle of the projects. As a holistic approach, it is appropriate to consider the life cycle of the projects to identify and map the stakeholders.

As green construction projects continually maintain the concept of sustainability throughout the life cycle, it is important to determine the stakeholders and their attributes for the entire life cycle. Importantly, every stakeholder has different influences and viewpoints on the project objectives that will positively and negatively affect the project's success. Due to the fragmented and unique nature of green construction projects, identifying stakeholders and their roles throughout the entire project life cycle is essential. The stakeholders can be varied over time; therefore, stakeholder identification is a periodic process in green construction projects. It is also important to determine the attributes such as roles, responsibilities, and their influence in such projects over time. At this stage, stakeholder mapping is a good practice that has been used to visualize all the stakeholders in the projects. The next step is to analyze the identified stakeholders based on their attributes.

12.3.3. *Application of tools and techniques for stakeholder identification in green construction projects*

Despite the technologies used, construction projects often use stakeholder mapping to effectively identify the stakeholders (Yuan *et al.*, 2018). As an example, this section demonstrates how stakeholder mapping is used to

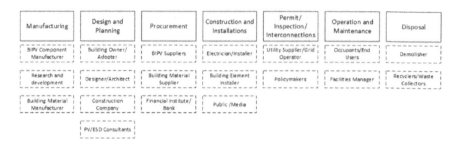

Figure 12.3.   Stakeholder mapping in BIPV.

Source: Adopted from Weerasinghe *et al.* (2020).

clearly identify the stakeholders in a BIPV project. SUPSI (2020) designed the stakeholder map of BIPV projects classifying them based on the level of influence (primary and secondary) and based on their associated industry. BIPV is a green construction technology and many industries, such as the building and construction sector, solar industry, and utility sector, make a significant contribution to project completion. Weerasinghe *et al.* (2020) identified stakeholders of BIPV projects by different life cycle stages of the projects. Figure 12.3 shows stakeholder map identified for the seven stages of the green projects. The authors highlighted that the same stakeholders may appear in multiple stages of the projects while their power and priorities can be changed. Also, the stakeholders are identified by classifying by different industries to capture the entire group.

12.4. Assessing stakeholders

Green construction projects are attracted by numerous numbers of stakeholders with a wide range of power, interests, and influences. They hold many attributes that knowingly affect the project outcome positively and negatively. The primary importance is to balance stakeholders with respect to their involvement and interest so that the project can function smoothly. Further, the expectations and interests of the stakeholders must be honored. The key benefit of this process is that it provides opportunities to engage stakeholders based on their needs and priorities. Further, this provides direction to manage stakeholders. The stakeholders' commitment, interest, and power should be fully assessed to tackle the key problems in the stakeholder management process. However, with the diversified tasks, understanding stakeholders' interests and their power has now become a challenging task.

The stakeholders hold various power and interests in the projects affecting the project goals. In building and construction projects, "client" or "building owner" vests high power in decision-making of the project while other stakeholders, such as "builders," "architects/designers," and "engineers," may significantly influence the decision-making on the project. More importantly, they maintain various relationships, such as contractual or formal, informal, and communication channels to communicate and share information. However, when stakeholders attached to the different industries form temporary units, their interests and influences are diverse, leading to conflict with project objectives (Mok *et al.*, 2018). When projects are moving toward the concept of being "green," the scenario is somewhat changed. It is said that more stakeholders are engaged in green projects than in traditional construction projects. In this regard, the participants are responsible for meeting sustainable criteria individually and as a team. The role of stakeholders and their inputs are important in achieving successful green construction projects. That is, it is not only the architect's role to make the building green; rather, the contribution of the building owner along with the other suppliers is important. According to Mok *et al.* (2018), stakeholder interests are economic, environmental, social, and functionality in green construction projects. They may apply many approaches and responsibilities toward the "green" or "sustainability" bringing narrative scope and dynamics to the projects. The following section describes tools and techniques that are used to assess the stakeholders.

12.4.1. *Tools and techniques for analyzing stakeholders*

Stakeholder analysis involves defining the nature of the stakeholders and their implications. Generally, the analysis looks at a list of stakeholders and their relevant attributes, such as interest, ownerships, knowledge, and contribution. It is a technique of systematically gathering and analyzing both quantitative and qualitative data. Various tools and techniques have evolved over the decades in analyzing stakeholders. Most of the analyses are based on stakeholder attributes, such as interest, power, and influence. The most common approach is the power/interest matrix proposed by Mendelow (1991). The author examined stakeholders based on the decision-making power of stakeholders and their interest in the projects and grouped them into four categories. These categories were actions for stakeholder groups, such as minimal effort, keep informed, keep satisfied, and key players. The matrix is modified by using alternative attributes such as power/influence grid or impact/influence grid depending on the circumstance. This matrix is a useful tool for judging the potential influence of identified project stakeholders. The salience model proposed by Mitchell *et al.* (1997) is another popular tool used in the studies of stakeholder analysis. The stakeholders have been analyzed based on their power, legitimacy, and urgency. Power represents the ability to control resources, create dependencies, and support the interests of some organization members or groups over others. Urgency expresses the degree to which a stakeholder's claims calls for immediate attention. Legitimacy describes the right of stakeholders in claiming the projects. The stakeholder impact index is another approach to determine the nature and impact of stakeholder influence, the probability of stakeholders exercising their influence, and each stakeholder's position in relation to the project. This index analyzes the relative importance of different stakeholders and the nature of their potential impact (Li *et al.*, 2018a). The importance of stakeholders will depend on the needs of the organization and the extent to which the organization is dependent on those stakeholders, relative to other stakeholders, in meeting its needs. PMI (2017) suggested common stakeholders' mapping data presentation tools, such as power/interest, power/influence or impact/influence grid, stakeholder cube, salience mode, and direction approach.

Analyzing stakeholders' relationships is a modern approach to stakeholder assessments. The use of social network analysis (SNA) for prioritizing stakeholders has been identified in many recent studies (Mok & Shen, 2016, Weerasinghe *et al.*, 2020). SNA is a suitable tool for analyzing stakeholders in complex and large projects. It is a systematic approach to examine stakeholders' interactions and interdependencies. Also, the analysis is based on the statistical background. Several studies have employed SNA to assess not only stakeholders but also their relationships with other attributes, such as critical success factors and key drivers (Liang *et al.*, 2015; Weerasinghe *et al.*, 2020). SNA provides meaningful analysis for stakeholder relationships.

12.4.2. *Application of tools and techniques for stakeholder analysis in green construction projects*

SNA and the influence/interest matrices are often used in green construction projects to analyze the stakeholder relationships and classify stakeholders based on their level of influence and interest (Yuan *et al.*, 2018). Li *et al.* (2018b) identified all stakeholders in a Net Zero energy building considering the three main stages of its life cycle, preconstruction stage, construction stage, and occupancy stage, and analyzed their involvement and contribution using SNA and the influence/interest matrices. SNA revealed that the project manager or coordinator is the most influential stakeholder in information management and the main controller of information. The study recommended that the project manager or coordinator is the best person to disseminate the knowledge on Net Zero energy buildings among the other stakeholders. Providing the project managers with necessary knowledge and training to disseminate the information can achieve better results. Also, the findings revealed that building occupants have limited understanding of the Net Zero energy applications, which creates a negative impact on the energy performance of the building during the occupancy stage. From the influence/interest matrices, it was identified that different stakeholders have different levels of influence and interest in different stages of the project. For example, in the preconstruction stage, the client and the design team have the highest influence and interest rates, whereas in the construction stage, the site supervisor and the project manager receive the highest rate.

12.4.3. *Issues and challenges of stakeholder analysis*

Traditional stakeholder analysis methods assess stakeholders on individual attributes, attitudes, and roles. It is noted that stakeholders have different levels of influence over the project processes and decisions are made at various stages by different stakeholders. These approaches create tensions and influence the project process. The stakeholder power and interest change over time. Therefore, the stakeholder assessment is not a one-time process. It should be conducted periodically throughout the life cycle stages of the project as it is always dynamic. It is also highlighted that these methods are suitable for projects that are of small size and not complex (Mok & Shen, 2016).

Stakeholder analysis methods such as SNA are recommended for large and complex projects (Mok & Shen, 2016). Understanding relationships of stakeholders helps in prioritizing the project participants. However, stakeholder relationships are dynamic throughout the project, while SNA is a snapshot of a time: static relationship. It is important to implement this method in a timely manner.

These tools attempt to identify stakeholders and visualize them based on their attributes. The cause and effect, consequence, and impact can be defined based on selected methods. The project manager should be able to balance the interest and conflicts of the stakeholders in order to accommodate them properly (Yu *et al.*, 2019).

12.5. Stakeholder engagement approaches

Stakeholder engagement is the process of involving the stakeholders in the project's decision-making by listening to, collaborating with, and informing them about the project's affairs (Bahadorestani *et al.*, 2020). It plays a vital role in ensuring the successful implementation and completion of a project. There are several definitions for stakeholder engagement put forward by different schools of thought or philosophies. According to the AA1000 Stakeholder Engagement Standard (SES, 2015) 2015, "stakeholder engagement is the process used by an organization to engage relevant stakeholders for a purpose to achieve agreed outcomes" (Accountability, 2015). APM (2019) defines stakeholder engagement as *the systematic process of identifying, analyzing, planning, and implementing the actions designed to influence the stakeholders*. Similarly, there are many definitions for stakeholder management focusing on key areas, such as business, organizational performance, change, and sustainability.

There are two main approaches to stakeholder engagement: (1) salience-based engagement and (2) demand-based engagement. In salience-based engagement, the stakeholders' salience is considered to prioritize their involvement in project's matters (Best *et al.*, 2019; Mok *et al.*, 2015). The main drawback of this approach is that the salience of stakeholders is decided based on the manager's interpretation of how much power a stakeholder holds, how legitimate his/her say about some matter is, and how urgent it is to act upon his/her claim (Bahadorestani *et al.*, 2020). Therefore, some effective stakeholder viewpoints may not be considered in the decision-making process. In the demand-based engagement, the involvement of stakeholders is prioritized based on the resource requirement (Bahadorestani *et al.*, 2020). This is in line with Pfeffer and Salancik's (1978) resource dependence theory, which suggests that the stakeholders who control the resources have more power and claim in the project. However, this approach may overlook the stakeholders with significant impact. Therefore, it is recommended to integrate both approaches in decision-making. This is highly applicable in green construction projects, as it is very much dependent on the stakeholder skills, knowledge/experience-based opinions, and availability of resources.

A well-planned stakeholder engagement not only enhances the stakeholders' comfort level and quality of working together. It also delivers technically, economically, socially, and environmentally sustainable working environment to the project. Engagement of the right stakeholders for decision-making can provide a technically feasible and flawless design, which can be easily developed into an actual building. If the project activities are planned with proper stakeholder engagement, there will be limited delays, rework, or variations. This will save money and time. If the project managers take individual stakeholder interests into consideration and execute project activities accordingly, the stakeholders will feel valued and well achieved, encouraging them to contribute more effectively to the project. A well-planned and coordinated project saves building materials and other resources and treats the environment properly. Therefore, stakeholder engagement can be considered as one of the core elements of sustainable construction. Stakeholders can be properly engaged in different ways, and they are discussed in the following section.

12.5.1. Current processes and practices of stakeholder engagement

Most of the definitions and explanations introduce stakeholder engagement as a process consisting of several stages. Each stage has several tasks to complete before moving on to the next stage. Also, there are diverse practices adopted to achieve effective stakeholder engagement. This section explains how these processes and practices are set in green construction projects and their effectiveness in achieving project success.

12.5.1.1. Stakeholder engagement process

Stakeholder engagement process typically includes identifying the stakeholder roles, analyzing the priorities, and developing a suitable engagement plan. Different institutes have slightly different processes, yet the core of the process is almost similar. For example, the AA1000 SES 2015's process of stakeholder engagement includes proper planning, preparation, implementation of the engagement plan, review, and improve (Accountability, 2015). According to the PMI's Project Management Body of Knowledge (PMBOK) Guide, stakeholder engagement process includes planning, managing, and monitoring the engagement to achieve stakeholder expectations and project success (PMI, 2017). This chapter discusses the stakeholder engagement process of green construction projects. Figure 12.4 demonstrates the steps of stakeholder engagement.

12.5.1.2. Planning engagement

The first stage of stakeholder engagement is planning. The planning process starts with determining the levels of engagement and the methods to be used in the project for stakeholder engagement. Levels of engagement decide in what way the project managers and stakeholders engage with each other, whether it is a (1) high-level engagement, such as involvement, collaboration, and empowering the other party, (2) medium-level engagement, such as consulting, negotiation, transacting, and informing the other party, or (3) low-level engagement, such as monitoring, advocating, or remaining passive with no active communication (Accountability, 2015).

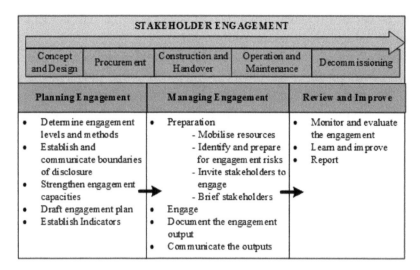

Figure 12.4. Stakeholder engagement process of green construction projects (developed based on the AA1000 SES 2015 (Accountability, 2015) and PMBOK Guide (PMI, 2017)).

For example, the project manager collaborates with the architect during the construction to make sure the design is properly developed onsite. The architect consults on the issues arising from the design whenever necessary and monitors the construction progress to make sure there is no rework or failures. There are diverse methods of engagement, such as regular meetings, online platforms, such as building information modeling (BIM), communication via email, telephone, letters, workshops, surveys, reports, and many more (Erkul *et al.*, 2019).

Stakeholder engagement always requires some boundaries for disclosure of information. It specifies what information should be shared among the stakeholders and the level of confidentiality (APM, 2019). Deciding the boundaries of information disclosure prior to stakeholder engagement is beneficial for all parties to secure their information and design copyright. For example, the drawings and other design information should be communicated to the builder, client, and other stakeholders; however, they should not be shared with the personnel outside the project. The cost information of product suppliers is confidential due to the competition they have with each other and, therefore, should be communicated with limited internal stakeholders (Zhang *et al.*, 2020). There are two main disclosure options, such as full disclosure and limited disclosure, which will be decided by either the project managers or the stakeholders who own the information (Accountability, 2015).

One of the most important steps of stakeholder engagement planning is strengthening the engagement capacities. The initial step of strengthening the engagement capacities is identifying the strengths, gaps, and weaknesses of the project team (Yuan *et al.*, 2018). Typically, every stakeholder has his/her own targets, interests, and priorities related to the project which sometimes create conflicting situations (Bal *et al.*, 2013). Therefore, it is important to identify these interests and targets and match them with the project scope to strengthen the engagement capacities. It is also important to strengthen the capacity to respond to an issue/challenge. Some stakeholders can identify an issue at an early stage and eliminate it, whereas some can deal with the issue effectively despite its severity. A project manager should identify such skillset of stakeholders and strengthen the areas they lack.

Developing an engagement plan is the next step. The plan should basically address how stakeholders can be effectively involved in the project based on their interests, needs, and expectations (PMI, 2017). Also, their skillset is highly valued in such projects. The project managers require input information and tools and techniques to develop a realistic engagement plan. A good engagement plan which pinpoints stakeholder information requirements should be developed in the early stage of the project, preferably in the inception and design stage. This plan is updated along the project life cycle considering the project changes, stakeholder additions, or leave.

The final step of planning is establishing indicators which measure and evaluate the quality of stakeholder engagement (Accountability, 2015). These indicators can be measured qualitatively or quantitatively via scale-based evaluation, survey, or general feedback. Periodical surveys can be carried out to test whether the stakeholder engagement is effectively achieved, moderately achieved, or ineffective.

12.5.1.3. *Application of planning engagement principles in green construction projects*

- Green construction projects value the specific skills, such as information communication and technology (ICT) knowledge (BIM,

AutoCAD, SketchUP, etc.), expertise knowledge on green construction applications (solar PV applications, green construction materials, energy efficiency management, etc.), prefabricated building element manufacturing, and the general skills, such as communication, negotiation, and management skills. These internal skills can be utilized and improved via workshops, seminars, and manuals.

- Aligning the personnel targets with the project scope can motivate the stakeholders to actively engage in green construction projects. For example, the architect has the knowledge and skills to use an advanced design platform and he/she wishes to use it in the projects that he/she is engaged in. Environmentally Sustainable Design (ESD) consultants can optimize building energy performance using novel tools and techniques while achieving their personal target of promoting themself as the experts in the area (Wijeratne *et al.*, 2022).

- The engagement plan of a green construction project should assign stakeholders for certain tasks considering their skills and personal expectations. For example, ESD consultants are involved in a green construction project to deliver an energy-efficient building. Their interests can be diverse such as sustainable building materials, Net Zero energy buildings, and integration of bespoke distributed renewable technologies into buildings (Lin & Chen, 2022; Martin-Chivelet, 2022). If the specific green construction project that they are involved in is a BIPV project, it matches with the ESD consultants' interests, needs, and expectations.

12.5.1.4. *Managing engagement*

After developing a proper stakeholder engagement plan, the project managers should prepare to execute it. The first step of preparation is mobilizing the required resources (Accountability, 2015). These resources include technical tools (hardware, software, and other technical equipment), human resources, financial resources, and basic infrastructure, such as office, stationary items, and other facilities.

The second step is to identify and prepare for engagement risks (Xia *et al.*, 2018). The most common risks include stakeholders' unwillingness to engage, conflicts between the stakeholders, insufficient and unequal communication of information to stakeholders, lack of balance between the strong and weak stakeholders, unrealistic expectations of stakeholders, loss of control, conflict of interests, and non-compliance with project's legal framework (Accountability, 2015).

It is important to invite stakeholders to engage and brief them about the engagement plan (APM, 2019). The stakeholders should have a clear idea about how they can engage in the project and in what ways they can contribute. Therefore, information such as scope of engagement, timeline, expected contribution from each stakeholder, resources and facilities they are provided with, related regulatory framework, expected risks and issues and how they can be managed, expected outcome, and benefits to the stakeholders should be well communicated to the stakeholders (Accountability, 2015).

The next step is the engagement. The engagement process includes maintaining proper communication and working together to meet the stakeholder needs, interests, targets, and expectations (PMI, 2017). The process must encourage the stakeholders to be actively involved in the relevant activities. Diverse communication methods, such as meetings, online discussions, emails, online design platforms, and brainstorming sessions, are conducted to finalize the design in which each stakeholder must provide their knowledge and skill-based contribution. Stakeholders should work together to develop economically viable, energy-efficient, and aesthetically valued designs. The builder should collaborate with the subcontractors and tradesmen to finalize construction without any delays. The project manager of the builder must manage all stakeholders, arrange the assignments, confirm the on-time progress, and facilitate the construction with the required resources. In both stages, addressing the risks and resolving issues are eminent.

The final step of preparation and engagement is documenting the engagement output (APM, 2019). This should capture the methods used to engage, participation level (who actively participated and who did not), timeline, a summary of stakeholder perceptions, concerns, and expectations, and a summary of interventions, recommendations, and decisions. It is important to document the outputs in such a way that it assists the later evaluation of the stakeholder engagement process (considering the previously developed indicators). Also, the outputs should be properly communicated to all stakeholders along with feedback about their personal contribution (Accountability, 2015). This reporting back can be done via a report, one-to-one meetings, an online platform, or in a stakeholder event.

12.5.1.5. *Application of managing engagement principles in green construction projects*

- Mobilizing the required resources in green construction projects should be done carefully. For example, stakeholder engagement in a green construction project requires human resources (i.e., project manager and his/her team) who have at least a basic understanding of the selected green technology.
- Green construction projects involve multidisciplinary stakeholders from different sectors such as building, prefabricated building element manufacturing, and renewable energy who have limited understanding of each other's sectors; therefore, many of the above risks can take place during stakeholder engagement. Therefore, it is crucial to identify how to deal with these risks prior to actual engagement. Encouraging and facilitating cross-sector collaboration, providing motivation to engage, and proper information management are some techniques to deal with such risks.
- Stakeholders should have a better understanding of how they should contribute to the green construction project. Considering a modular construction project as an example, the involvement of a prefabricated module manufacturer in the early design stage to understand the building requirements and design implications is important. In such situations, all parties (architect, design team, and prefabricated module manufacturer) should be well informed about their scope of engagement, level of engagement, and the expectations.
- Effective communication is essential in green construction projects due to the multiparty involvement. For example, the architect is leading the design stage and, therefore, should collaborate with ESD consultants, prefabricated building element manufacturers, and suppliers to develop a feasible green design.

12.5.1.6. *Review and improve*

Effective stakeholder engagement does not end with the execution of an engagement plan and documenting the outcome. It is a circular process which requires reviewing the engagement strategies for future improvements and modifications (PMI, 2017). The review process starts with monitoring and evaluating the engagement process (Zwikael & Smyrk, 2019). The PM should methodically monitor the commitment, participation, engagement process, and outcomes of engagement and evaluate the quality, effectiveness, and suitability of the project. It is important to assess the relationship between the effective stakeholder engagement vs achieving the objectives of the project.

The second step is learning via experience and improving stakeholder engagement based on the lessons learned (Zwikael & Smyrk, 2019). Learning and improving is important to strengthen and optimize stakeholder engagement in future projects. Since every construction project is a temporary organization built to complete one building or infrastructure, the learning is more about how to improve stakeholder engagement in similar types of future projects.

As the final step, it is important to report all learnings to use them whenever necessary. Learnings and recommended improvements should be communicated to all stakeholders, as they can help personal improvements and motivate stakeholders for future stakeholder engagement (Accountability, 2015).

12.5.1.7. *Application of review and improve principles in green construction projects*

• The involvement of different sectors such as building consultants, renewable energy consultants, sustainable design consultants, and prefabricated building element manufacturers in the design process should be evaluated considering their active participation, decision-making, innovative thinking, problem-solving, conflict management, and technology application (Shaukat *et al.*, 2022). This evaluation should also consider the project's success in terms of (1) how feasible the design is, (2) how limited the rework, variations, and defects are, and (3) how energy-efficient the building is against the simulated building performance (Bal *et al.*, 2013).

- The project managers of a green construction project can learn how to effectively engage multiparty stakeholders who have limited understanding of each other's role and use the lessons learned from this project to plan the engagement of the next project (Armenia *et al.*, 2019).
- It is preferable that the recommended improvements on stakeholder engagement be published to disseminate the knowledge among the stakeholders of the green construction industry.

12.5.1.8. *Stakeholder engagement practices in green construction projects*

Stakeholder engagement has evolved over time, introducing different trends and practices from time to time. These trends and practices improve the effectiveness of engagement and provide better results (Zwikael & Smyrk, 2019). Different organizations adopt different practices which are better suited for their organizational culture and stakeholder characteristics. Several effective stakeholder management practices can be identified in green construction projects. They are listed as follows:

- Continuous and flawless communication. Communication is the most important aspect of stakeholder management, especially when there is multidisciplinary involvement (Bohari *et al.*, 2020). Currently, green construction projects use communication methods such as emails and letters, regular face-to-face meetings, online meeting platforms, and reports. New trends include using shared platforms, such as blockchain-based information communication systems, to ensure no information gaps (Das *et al.*, 2022).
- Cross-sector collaboration from early design stage. Stakeholders from different sectors such as building, manufacturing, and renewable energy industries collaborate with one another to finalize a feasible design (Yang *et al.*, 2019). These sectors contribute to developing an optimal design by offering their expert knowledge.

- Identifying all stakeholders along the green project life cycle and assessing their skills and interests to optimize the engagement process (PMI, 2017).
- Using software and tools to facilitate the engagement process. These software and tools can be used to develop the engagement plan, allocate resources, profile the stakeholders, keep records, monitor progress, analyze outputs, and identify and assess risks (Accountability, 2015).
- Ensure all stakeholders are involved in stakeholder management activities by conducting periodic reviews (Zwikael & Smyrk, 2019).
- Consult with the stakeholders who are highly engaged or mostly affected by a specific work area (RICS, 2014). For example, involving prefabricated building envelope manufacturers in the early design stage to develop a feasible design and increase the accuracy of prefabricated products (Yang *et al.*, 2019).
- Evaluate both positive and negative impacts of stakeholder engagement to improve positive impacts and eliminate negative impacts in future green construction projects (Yang *et al.*, 2019).
- Rewards and motivation. Offering rewards or motivation to increase the active involvement of stakeholders.
- Development of stakeholder skills via workshops, seminars, and training programs (Accountability, 2015). A highly encouraged way of skills development in the green construction industry is learning from one another.
- Identify the potential risks prior to executing the engagement plan and trace the risks and issues throughout the engagement process (APM, 2019). One example of potential risks is conflicting opinions among the design team.
- Introducing stakeholder engagement principles which include being respectful to one another, purposeful related to the project, transparent and honest in actions, punctuality, and identification of the right stakeholder for the right engagement tasks (Department of Health, 2018).

12.5.2. *Comparison: Stakeholder engagement of a conventional project and a green project*

In general, green construction projects are more complex, time-consuming, and expensive than conventional building and construction projects (Weerasinghe *et al.*, 2017). Conventional project stakeholders basically consist of architects, engineers, quantity surveyors, builders, subcontractors, facilities managers, and material suppliers who are from the building industry (Abbasi *et al.*, 2021). Other parties involved in conventional projects include finance, local councils, and the client. Green construction projects have some additional stakeholders, such as ESD consultants, green material suppliers, green building designers, renewable energy technology providers, manufacturers and installers, and additional authorities to maintain the required standards. Hence, stakeholder management is complex in green construction projects (Bal *et al.*, 2013). Table 12.1 demonstrates some major differences in stakeholder engagement between the conventional and green construction projects.

Table 12.1. Stakeholder engagement in conventional vs. green construction projects.

	Green project	Conventional project
Stakeholder engagement process	• Stakeholder engagement process is complex and time-consuming • More internal and external stakeholders to consider when prioritizing, planning, and managing • Comparatively high cross-sector involvement • More effective stakeholder relationships are expected	• Stakeholder engagement process is comparatively easier • Lesser internal and external stakeholders • Lesser cross-sector involvement • Basic stakeholder relationships can be seen
Risks	• Comparatively higher risks due to stakeholder involvement from different sectors who have limited understanding of one another's line of work	• Comparatively lower risks since majority of stakeholders are from the building sector and have more experience and collaboration between one another

(Continued)

Table 12.1.   (*Continued*)

	Green project	Conventional project
Skills	• Diverse additional skills are required such as knowledge of renewable energy technologies and applications and green construction design • More communication, negotiation, and management skills are required for better engagement • Comparatively high preference on ICT skills	• Required skills are limited in comparison to green projects
Level of engagement	• Medium- and high-level of engagement can be seen • Collaboration, negotiation, consultation, and empowerment are the most preferred levels of engagement	• All levels of engagement (low, medium, and high) can be seen • Monitoring is highly preferred • Lack of empowering stakeholders
Communication	• More continuous and integrated communication and information sharing mechanism is required due to the high cross-sector involvement • Boundaries of disclosure should be comparatively high as each sector has confidential information and copyright concerns	• Communication is general and adequate • Boundaries of disclosure is comparatively low but exist
Conflicts	• More conflicts between stakeholders due to the high cross-sector involvement	• Comparatively lesser conflicts

Source: Bahadorestani *et al.* (2020), Mok *et al.* (2018), Osseweijer *et al.* (2018), Qiang *et al.* (2021), Silvius and Schipper (2019), Yang *et al.* (2019).

12.5.3. *Issues and challenges of stakeholder engagement in green construction projects*

Stakeholder engagement facilitates avoiding or resolving the issues and challenges in green construction projects (PMI, 2017). The main benefits of stakeholder engagement include but are not limited to (1) developing economically and technologically feasible design with limited variations, discrepancies, and unrealistic expectations, (2) effectively matching individual stakeholder interests, needs, and expectations with the project objectives, (3) allowing personal skills development of stakeholders, (4) integrating stakeholders from different sectors such as building and energy industries, (5) reducing conflicts and disputes, (6) creating a respectful environment for all stakeholders, (7) facilitating information sharing along the project life cycle, and (8) providing constructive criticisms and motivation for stakeholders (Bahadorestani *et al.*, 2020; Mok *et al.*, 2018; Osseweijer *et al.*, 2018). However, the stakeholder engagement process is complex and requires lots of careful planning (APM, 2019). Especially, in green construction projects, the project managers must make additional efforts to assign the right stakeholders to the right engagement activities due to the multidisciplinary and cross-sector involvement. There are several specific issues and challenges faced by the project managers when executing stakeholder management in green projects. They are explained as follows:

- Multiple stakeholders from different sectors are involved in green construction projects; however, they have limited understanding of one another's roles (Yang *et al.*, 2019). This issue creates several subissues, such as conflicts between stakeholders, miscommunication and information gaps, design errors, delays in construction, rework, and variations.
- Green construction projects require much collaboration, coordination, and negotiation (Osseweijer *et al.*, 2018). However, stakeholder involvement is discrete in green projects due to the involvement of different sectors and long project life cycle. Therefore, information communication is not continuous. Especially, the stakeholders in the later stages of the project life cycle hardly communicate with the stakeholders in the early stages. In some projects, the communication between the stakeholders in the same stage (i.e., design stage) or immediate stages is not satisfactory. The main reason for such behavior is lack of a common communication platform where all stakeholders can share their information and communicate with one another whenever necessary.

- The required skills and knowledge are sometimes not available in green construction projects. Green design requires 2D/3D designing, simulation, calculation, and optimization tools, and adequate ICT skills to use these tools (Wijeratne *et al.*, 2019). Also, qualified installers and consultants are required when using green technologies, such as BIPV, Net Zero energy buildings, and modular construction. Stakeholders with the above skills are limited in the industry and difficulties may occur in engaging them in the construction project.

- Some common issues and challenges include (1) stakeholders not willing to engage due to the lack of motivation and belief in stakeholder engagement, (2) frustration due to the high workload and lack of empowerment, (3) lack of balance between personal expectations and project objectives, (4) insufficient planning, managing, and evaluation of stakeholder engagement, and (5) inefficient documentation of stakeholder engagement (Accountability, 2015).

12.6. Decision-making strategies for stakeholder management

Stakeholder management is highly focused on involving project stakeholders in most effective ways (PMI, 2017). It is crucial for the project managers to correctly identify the most suitable stakeholders for a specific engagement to successfully complete the project. Having a predefined set of decision-making strategies is essential to achieve the above purpose (Accountability, 2015). This section discusses the decision-making strategies used in stakeholder management and develops a decision-making framework for effective stakeholder management in green construction projects.

12.6.1. *Impact of stakeholder management on decision-making and project success*

Stakeholders work together to achieve project success by contributing to the project within their chosen specialty (Buertey *et al.*, 2016). They share information, collaborate, and solve issues to execute the project while fulfilling their personal targets and expanding their knowledge, skills, and experience. Stakeholder management provides a systematic process to identify stakeholders, plan their engagement in the best suited way, manage the engagement, and evaluate outcomes for future projects (APM, 2019). This systematic process determines who is involved in the decision-making and from what level. A green construction project commences when the client introduces his/her concept to the architect. Gradually, other stakeholders join the project in all stages of the building's life cycle based on their specialty. Numerous decisions must be taken as the project develops, especially by the client, architect, builder, and building manager. They require expert opinions, knowledge, and skills to make more accurate decisions, therefore, involving other project stakeholders (Buertey *et al.*, 2016). Stakeholder management facilitates this process by delivering the best candidates for the job.

An effective stakeholder management process supports accurate and easy decision-making, while a lack of stakeholder management fuels more complications and wrong decisions. The impact of stakeholder management on decision-making therefore can be both positive and negative (PMI, 2017). The positive impacts include (1) developing a technically and economically realistic design, (2) fulfilling the green energy targets, (3) limited or no variations and rework during construction, (4) limited or no project delays, labor idling, and resource wastage, (5) creating positive stakeholder relationships, and (6) delivering a real value for money. The negative impacts include (1) developing an unrealistic design with many design inconsistencies, (2) not achieving expected sustainable outcomes, (3) many variations, rework, and repairs during the building life cycle, (4) stakeholder disputes and unwillingness to work with one another, (5) project delays and wastage, (6) difficulties in maintaining the building and low-energy performance, (7) damage to reputation, (8) stakeholder frustration and not achieving expected personal interests, and (9) worst case scenario of project termination (Buertey *et al.*, 2016; Jayasuriya *et al.*, 2020).

Given the above impacts, the project's success highly depends on achieving more positive impacts via effective stakeholder management (APM, 2019). It enables smooth design process, easy procurement stage, quick construction stage, and consistent maintenance stage until the end of the building life cycle. Proper stakeholder management can effectively capture, create, and add value to the project (Bahadorestani *et al.*, 2020). On the other hand, completing a green construction project improves the learning curve of stakeholders irrespective of their level of engagement.

12.6.2. *Decision-making strategies for stakeholder management in green projects*

Stakeholder management process requires continuous and effective decision-making to determine the optimal ways of integrating project objectives with stakeholder needs, expectations, and interests (Bahadorestani *et al.*, 2020). Dealing with multiple stakeholders is difficult and engaging them in project activities must be carefully designed (Bal *et al.*, 2013). Lack of participation in stakeholder engagement often becomes one of the key reasons for project failure (Jayasuriya *et al.*, 2020). Stakeholder participation and their level of engagement are decided by the management. Hence, it is important to have a systematic approach to decision-making to make sure that the decisions are correctly made according to a predefined guideline. Decision-making strategies are diverse and develop based on the organizational culture (Cascetta *et al.*, 2015). The following strategies are identified as suitable for green construction projects.

12.6.2.1. *Identification of decision-making context*

The PM team must initially identify the situation for which the decision-making is required. The situations may include prioritizing and ranking the stakeholders in each stage of the green construction project life cycle, who are the strong stakeholders and weak stakeholders in each project stage, whether the stakeholders should collaborate, negotiate, or consult, and what methods of engagements can be used (Accountability, 2015).

12.6.2.2. *Comprehensive analysis of the context*

The next strategy is to analyze the context carefully and in detail considering all aspects (Cascetta *et al.*, 2015). If the context is designing a prefabricated building, the stakeholders who are engaged in the designing process, what technologies and skills are required, how the stakeholders collaborate, what is their method of communication, and time frame for different design scenarios should be clearly identified and analyzed (Yang *et al.*, 2019).

12.6.2.3. *Identification and assessment of different options for the specific context*

Typically, there is an accepted process of stakeholder engagement steps for every stage of green construction projects. However, it is important to identify and assess whether there are alternatives for such engagement which provide better results than the standard process (PMI, 2017). For example, there are diverse ways of carrying out zero energy construction, such as using ecofriendly building materials, renewable energy applications, modular construction to reduce material wastage, cost management, and efficiency management, among others. Considering all these ways is essential (Wilberforce *et al.*, 2021).

12.6.2.4. *Explore the risks and constraints of all options*

Stakeholder management has both positive and negative impacts. Therefore, it is important to identify the potential options which provide a positive impact on the project's success and stakeholder's achievement (Accountability, 2015). Exploring the risks and constraints of each option can help decide whether it is worth adopting or otherwise. Considering the designing of a BIPV building, some stakeholder engagement options may be expensive and require more ICT resources or advanced drafting skills. There can be more economic options compared to these options.

12.6.2.5. *Comparison of all options to identify the most suitable option*

A proper comparison can help determine the most effective stakeholder engagement process which delivers better outcomes for the project as well as the involved stakeholders (Cascetta *et al.*, 2015). It is important to check whether these options align with the project objectives and stakeholder needs and expectations.

12.6.2.6. *Decide the adopting option and implement*

After following the above strategies, the most suitable stakeholder management option can be selected and implemented accordingly.

12.6.2.7. *Monitor and evaluate the impact of decision-making*

Monitor the impact of the decision and its contribution to project success and stakeholder achievements. If the evaluation shows negative impacts, change the approach appropriately. For example, if the decided prefabricated building designing process does not involve prefabricated module manufacturer and installer; as a result, the manufactured modules can be different from the intended design and there can be complications when installing the prefabricated modules on site (Wasim *et al.*, 2020). The lesson learned from this process is to engage the prefabricated module manufacturer and installer in the early design stage. Accordingly, the decision-making approach can be changed in the next project.

12.6.3. *A decision-making framework for stakeholder management in green construction projects*

Figure 12.5 demonstrates the proposed decision-making framework for stakeholder management in green construction projects. The framework consists of two basic layers contributing to the stakeholder management process and the decision-making process. Stakeholder management is conducted throughout the life cycle of the green construction project. Therefore, the framework demonstrates all stages of the green project life cycle along with the stakeholder management process. In each stage of stakeholder management, certain decisions should be made. In such situations, the proposed decision-making framework can be used to receive better outcomes. The following paragraph provides one example.

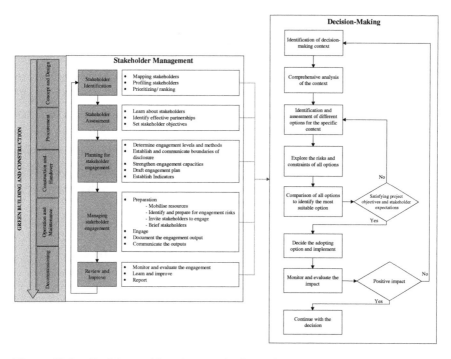

Figure 12.5. Decision-making framework for stakeholder management in green construction projects.

Assume that the project manager of the builder is planning the PV-integrated building facade installation process. Stakeholder identification and assessment are completed and the project manager is now determining the engagement levels and methods. He/she must make a decision on the levels and methods of engagement for all stakeholders involved in the installation process. Given above is the decision-making context. The project manager then analyzes the available information about the PV-integrated building façade process considering the roles of stakeholders, allocated time frame, technology requirement, and resource allocation. From the above analysis, the project manager identifies different combinations of levels and methods the stakeholders can engage in the process. These identified combinations are then analyzed for their potential risks, such as conflicts among the architect and the installer, delays in material supply, and disturbances to the other concurrent work.

The project manager also identifies the constraints, such as time and date availabilities of the installer, public holidays, and technology limitations. Once, the above step is completed, a thorough comparison is conducted between all engagement level and method combinations. If any combination is not in line with project objectives such as on-time completion, limited wastage, and achieving value for money, then these combinations should be avoided. The best option for stakeholder engagement levels and methods is selected based on the above comparison and implemented. It is important to monitor the impact of the selected option on project success and stakeholder satisfaction to make sure that there is no need for change.

12.7. Case study: Stakeholder management in green construction projects

12.7.1. *Case introduction*

The selected case is the development of a software for BIPV design and management. BIPV, which is also known as solar building envelope, is a technology that has been given attention recently, due to its functionality toward Net Zero buildings. BIPV can be applied to various parts of the building envelope, such as walls, roofs, windows, and balustrades, and provides untapped opportunities to produce green energy to meet even the total building energy demand. The growth of the BIPV among both PV and building industries is still limited due to various reasons, particularly the technical complexities. One of the reasons for ignoring BIPV by various building professionals is insufficient design capabilities and tools and resources. Unlike PV applications, BIPV has no sophisticated software, particularly in Australia. Therefore, the design and execution of BIPV software is one of the timely requirements to deploy this green technology across the world. Here, we discuss the project of design and implementation of a BIPV software as a gree construction project. The project is led by an Australian university partnering with diverse stakeholders such as building and PV industry stakeholders and funding institutions. The project duration is 2 years.

12.7.2. *Stakeholder ecosystem of BIPV tool development*

This project is performed in four sequence phases. The phases are as follows:

(a) *Planning*: The initial concept is executed in this phase and the funding has been secured. Prior to the initial screening, the project team is identified based on the resource requirements. In this stage, the primary task is a preliminary investigation that is conducted for identifying current practices, drawbacks, and future requirements of such software. This enables us to position the software in the market and deliver a product that is accepted by the end-users. Therefore, core members of the project conducted interviews with stakeholders in the entire value chain of BIPV to streamline the product's scope. The findings revealed the features and functions of the software.

(b) *Designing and prototyping*: This phase involves designing the workflow and detailed plan, identifying resources, and collecting BIPV product details. Data inputs of the software were BIPV products available in the market. Therefore, the main objective of this phase is to collect BIPV products that are suitable for Australia through local and international suppliers, manufacturers, and distributors. Also, a design workflow is developed to implement the software program.

(c) *Software development*: This phase is allocated for designing the software in the platform. An expertise in software development is largely involved in this phase to complete the task.

(d) *Testing and execution*: This phase is allocated to test the software with the assistance of end users. Afterward, the software will be ready for use in real practice. Workshops are conducted to promote the software.

In these four phases, many stakeholders from various backgrounds come together to perform a variety of tasks. The stakeholders appear in different phases of the projects and their contributions were different by phase. All stakeholders were identified and presented in the ecosystem of BIPV software design and implementation in Figure 12.6.

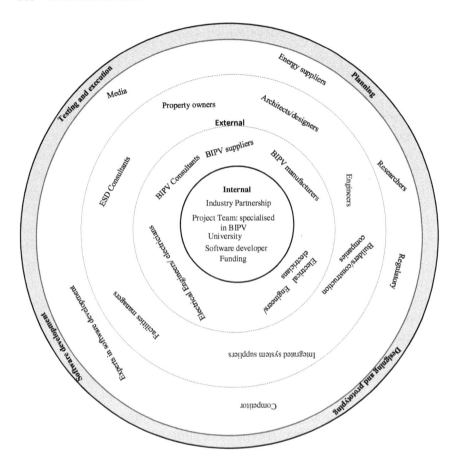

Figure 12.6.   Stakeholder ecosystem of BIPV software design and implementation.

All the stakeholders involved in the project are included by categorizing them into external and internal based on the four phases. We identified participants based on their roles. Project team consisted of researchers who specialize in BIPV. They possess skills in social, economic, and technical aspects of BIPV, while some are savvy in programming. The team leader together with six team members were directly involved in the project. The funding organizations and industry partners who contribute by providing knowledge and resources are counted as internal stakeholders. They play an important role in executing the project. The team interviewed many stakeholders in the planning phase to demarcate the project scope. These stakeholders are named as external and are in various industries, such as PV sector, building and construction sector, utility sector, and regulatory bodies. Within the four phases, stakeholders arrive and leave the project. For example, a software developer was recruited to the project as an internal stakeholder in the second phase of the project. We noticed that stakeholder involvement is dynamic and needs to identify the roles of the stakeholders and other attributes periodically.

12.7.3. *Assessing stakeholders*

The stakeholders hold a variety of interests power, roles, responsibilities, and influence on the projects. Thereby, stakeholder assessment is performed employing interest/power matrix for the planning phase of the project. This approach is suitable as this project consisted of a small set of stakeholders. The interest defines stakeholder's intention toward the project outcomes. The power defines the stakeholder's power in the execution of the project. Figure 12.7 describes the interest/power matrix of the project.

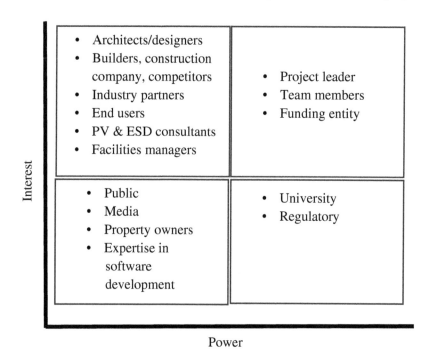

Figure 12.7.   Interest/power matrix.

The matrix distributes power and interest among the stakeholders. We realized that high power and high interest hold "project leader," "team members," and "funding entities." Their positive contribution leads to the project's success. Several stakeholders, particularly the "end users" such as architects, PV consultants, and BIPV suppliers, were identified as having a high interest, as they are interested in the outcome of the project. However, their power in the execution of the project is low. The impact of these stakeholders is very small as they provide various information to achieve the objectives. Stakeholders such as media, public, and expertise in software development were known as low interest and low power because of their involvement. University and regulatory bodies were highlighted as high-power and low-interest stakeholders. They possess high power as they have the capability of terminating the project. Accordingly, the stakeholders' power and interests are diverse with respect to their inherent roles and responsibilities. The project managers used various techniques to engage these stakeholders based on the analysis.

12.7.4. *Stakeholder engagement approaches*

The selected case has four project stages and multidisciplinary involvement. As the leading party, the university deals with the entire stakeholder management process. Project leader: the Associate Professor holds the project manager position with the assistance of her team. The stakeholder engagement process of each project stage is summarized in Table 12.2.

12.7.5. *Decision-making strategies*

Stakeholder management is mostly done within the university project team. From stakeholder identification to the review and reporting, decisions are taken focusing on the project's success and team member's satisfaction. The project leader prefers making most decisions as a team and expects contributions from all team members. Since the team members are postgraduate students, there are situations where they cannot contribute to decision-making, such as identifying industry stakeholders, legal paperwork, and handling funding. In such situations, the project leader makes the decisions considering the available information. Decision-making always

Table 12.2. Stakeholder engagement process of the case study.

Project stage	Stakeholders	Stakeholder engagement
Planning		
• Conducting interviews with the building and PV stakeholders to identify stakeholder issues and expectations on BIPV designing and management • Identifying potential partnerships and invite them • Prepare the project proposal based on interview findings • Accepting the proposal	• University project team • Funding organization • Building and PV stakeholders	• It was decided to use university project team members as interviewers due to their recently improved skills on conducting interviews (these skills are improved via a workshop). Interviews are conducted both face-to-face and via phone calls as a friendly discussion • Potential partners are identified via personal contacts. Several meetings and phone conversations are conducted in professional capacity. Agreements are signed to comply with the legal framework of all stakeholder organizations • Project proposal is developed by the university project team and submitted to the funding institute • The proposal is accepted by the funding institute and assigned a representative for them
Designing and prototyping		
• BIPV tool detail design • Resource allocation for prototyping • Collection of data inputs of the BIPV tool such as product information, terrain information and weather information • Conducting meetings with the industry partners to test the prototype	• University project team (Team members acquire the required skills) • Funding organization • BIPV manufacturers and suppliers, electrical engineers, builders, and regulatory bodies (supply input data)	• Each member of the university project team is assigned several tasks based on their personal skills and knowledge. All members collaborate with one another using online meeting platform to finalize the detailed design of the tool. Necessary resources such as computers and software are provided to the members • Regular online group meetings are conducted to discuss the progress. Project teams mainly collaborated with one another; however, the project leader on some occasions uses other measures such as consulting, informing, monitoring, and empowering the team members

(Continued)

Table 12.2.   (*Continued*)

Project stage	Stakeholders	Stakeholder engagement
		• The members who collect input data collaborate with diverse industry stakeholders to collect data. Necessary data are received as product brochures or via phone conversations and emails. • Prototype testing is conducted via online meetings with industry stakeholders

Software development

• Development of the software using the available information	• University project team • Software developer • Funding organization • Experts in software development	• The university project team has several members with software development skills; therefore, they are responsible for the actual development of the software. They collaborate with other team members whenever necessary. Several software development experts are consulted whenever necessary • Regular online group meetings are conducted to discuss the progress

Testing and execution

• Internal testing of the developed BIPV tool • Conducting workshops to introduce the software • Updating based on feedback	• University project team • Software developer • Funding organization • End users	• The initial testing is conducted within the university project team via an internal workshop and identify the errors. One of the tool designers explains how to use the tool to other members. Comments from each team member are collected and based on the comments, some updates are made • Three workshops in three different cities are conducted to introduce the software to the end-users. Workshop planning is done by the project team via face-to-face meetings. Workload is distributed among the team members. In the workshop, the participants are given the opportunity to use the tool and give feedback. Feedback is recorded • Based on the feedback, the tool is improved by the software developer

follows several strategies. If the team can contribute, the first step is to arrange a meeting online or face-to-face. An email is sent to every member with the date, time, venue, and purpose of the meeting. During the meeting, the context for the decision-making is explained to the project team. The team is asked to analyze the context and provide different options. These options are then evaluated using brainstorming and the potential risks and constraints are discussed. A verbal comparison is conducted by members pointing out the strengths and weaknesses of each option. The project leader always reminds the team of the project objectives to make sure that the proposed options satisfy them. Finally, one option is selected and based on that the decision is made. When the decided task is completed, the project leader gives feedback on its success or failure and encourages team members to learn from the experience. One example of the decision-making process is demonstrated in Figure 12.8.

12.7.6. *Validating the decision-making framework for stakeholder management in green construction projects*

The proposed decision-making framework in Section 12.6 is applied in the selected case study to validate and confirm its effectiveness in stakeholder management decision-making. On many occasions, the decision-making is much more effective and facilitates successful project progress. Due to several unforeseeable situations, the decision-making related to time allocation is not very well achieved. For example, the lockdowns and travel restrictions due to the COVID-19 pandemic in Australia delayed conducting workshops and conflicting work schedules and busy lifestyles of external parties such as information providers delayed the data collection. Nevertheless, the proposed decision-making framework is highly effective on many occasions such as identifying stakeholders, stakeholder assessment, identifying the level of engagement, and resource allocation. Based on the findings of the selected case, the framework's effectiveness can be confirmed as it facilitates the successful completion of the design tool and provides many learning and career opportunities for the project team.

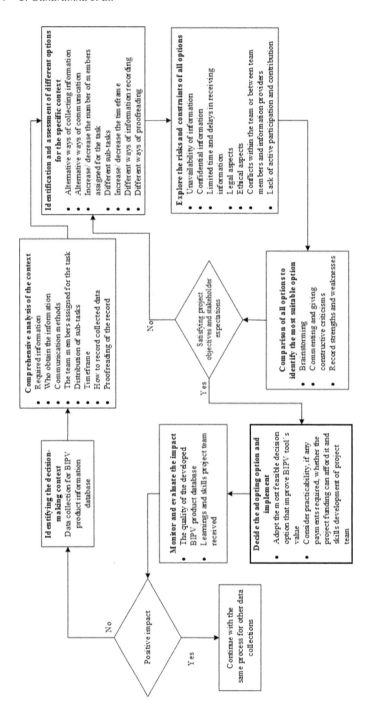

Figure 12.8.   Example of the decision-making process in the BIPV design tool development project.

12.8. Discussion and conclusion

Green construction projects are comparatively complex due to the multi-sector and multidisciplinary involvement, novel technologies, and high risk (Yang *et al.*, 2016). Unlike conventional construction, it has extra measures to take in terms of protecting the environment, reducing resource consumption and wastage, avoiding hazardous materials, installing renewable energy generating technologies, using recyclable and ecofriendly building materials, installing energy-efficient appliances, focusing on the building quality, and managing life cycle cost (Prameswari *et al.*, 2021). Green concept is not just considered in the construction stage (Farida *et al.*, 2019). It is applied throughout the whole life cycle of a green construction project, from the design stage to the end of the building's life. Therefore, stakeholders in all stages of the green construction project should have a clear understanding of the project, the technologies and applications used, and their contribution to the project (Accountability, 2015). Further, different stakeholders have different interests and targets related to the green concept. For example, property developers invest in green construction projects with diverse intentions, such as helping to protect the environment, government incentives, economic benefits, customer attraction, promotion of technologies, and many more. The application of green concept differs based on the property developer's intention: for example, if it is all about helping to protect the environment, then the property developers would prefer Net Zero energy construction and/or Net Zero energy buildings. If the intention is to gain some economic benefits, then he/she would prefer rooftop solar installation. If the intention is to develop an iconic building to attract customers and promote technologies, then he/she would prefer BIPV or modular construction. Based on the property developer's intention, the other stakeholders are engaged in the green construction project to deliver their services (Mok *et al.*, 2018). While they work to complete the project as per the property developer's requirements, they fulfill their personal goals and interests (PMI, 2017). Stakeholder management is essential to match these personal goals and interests with the project scope. Communication throughout the green construction life cycle is eminent in this context. For example, the building occupants and building managers cannot maintain the energy performance of the building without having the design information. Current research has focused on improving stakeholder communication and collaboration via online platforms such as blockchain and BIM to assist in flawless communication and effective stakeholder management (Das *et al.*, 2022; Taha *et al.*, 2020). These platforms facilitate the identification of stakeholder interests and targets, teamwork, effective engagement in work tasks, and maintaining green energy targets.

The public trust and acceptance of green construction methods are not as solid as the conventional construction methods due to a lack of awareness and high cost. Cost and trustworthy procurement are common issues when developing green construction projects. Conventional construction projects often use public–private partnership (PPP) as a common procurement method for infrastructure development and mega construction (Yang *et al.*, 2018). While it is an effective procurement method for sustainable urban development projects, such as renewable energy farms, Net Zero energy building construction, and ecofriendly material-based infrastructure development, PPP arrangement can also increase accountability and transparency among the stakeholders in green construction projects. For example, the government can support research and development for green construction in the initial stage through either financial or non-financial assistance, bringing forward technology breakthrough and reducing the risks of private sector investment (as private investors are always finding the right opportunities to build green or convert to green). A similar approach can be seen in current green energy industry called "energy performance contracts" which mitigates the financial risks of energy-efficient investments. It is a contractual arrangement between the building owner who requires an energy efficiency improvement to his/her building and the service provider (energy service company — ESCO) (Töppel & Tränkler, 2019). The service provider delivers the energy efficiency improvements with continuous monitoring and management throughout the contract period which are paid by the building owner using the financial savings or any other contractually agreed method, such as achieving energy targets or fulfilling agreed energy performance criteria. Unlike PPP, energy performance contracts can be used for both private and public projects (Hufen & Bruijn, 2016). It is quite a popular method to encourage adopting environmentally friendly products and services. In this approach, stakeholders in both parties have personal interests and a common goal to increase the building's energy efficiency. Also, it increases multidisciplinary involvement and creates new stakeholder relationships and, therefore, requires proper stakeholder management.

The above aspects are highlighted when discussing stakeholder management in green construction projects. This chapter explains how stakeholder management principles can be effectively applied to diverse green construction projects and procurement methods. Each stage of stakeholder management is discussed in the chapter along with examples from green construction projects. The issues and challenges of stakeholder management in green construction projects are explored, especially in terms of aligning the stakeholder interests and personal targets with the project scope. Seven strategies have been identified which can be effectively used in stakeholder management decision-making. A decision-making framework is proposed for stakeholder management in green construction projects and validated using a case study.

References

Abbasi, A. G., Abbasi, M., Memon, S., Mustafa, W., & Leghari, M. A. (2021). Assessment of stakeholder engagement in construction project: An empirical study of Keenjhar Lake Project. *Scopia International Journal for Science, Commerce & Arts*, *1*(2), 1–10.

Accountability. (2015). AA 1000 Stakeholder Engagement Standard 2015. Available at: https://www.accountability.org/standards/aa1000-stakeholder-engagement-standard/ (accessed on 14 April 2022).

Armenia, S., Dangelico, R. M., Nonino, F., & Pompei, A. (2019). Sustainable project management: A conceptualization-oriented review and a framework proposal for future studies. *Sustainability*, *11*(9), 2664.

Association for Project Management. (2019). *APM Body of Knowledge* (7th edn.). Buckinghamshire: Association for Project Management.

Bahadorestani, A., Naderpajouh, N., & Sadiq, R. (2020). Planning for sustainable stakeholder engagement based on the assessment of conflicting interests in projects. *Journal of Cleaner Production*, *242*, 118402.

Bal, M., Bryde, D., Fearon, D., & Ochieng, E. (2013). Stakeholder engagement: Achieving sustainability in the construction sector. *Sustainability*, *5*(2), 695–710.

Berardi, U. (2013). Stakeholders' influence on the adoption of energy-saving technologies in Italian homes. *Energy Policy, 60,* 520–530.

Best, B., Moffett, S., & McAdam, R. (2019). Stakeholder salience in public sector value co-creation. *Public Management Review, 21*(11), 1707–1732.

Bohari, A. A. M., Skitmore, M., Xia, B., Teo, M., & Khalil, N. (2020). Key stakeholder values in encouraging green orientation of construction procurement. *Journal of Cleaner Production, 270,* 122246.

Buertey, J. I. T., Amofa, D., & Atsrim, F. (2016). Stakeholder management on construction projects: A key indicator for project success. *American Journal of Civil Engineering, 4*(4), 117–126.

Cascetta, E., Carteni, A., Pagliara, F., & Montanino, M. (2015). A new look at planning and designing transportation systems: A decision-making model based on cognitive rationality, stakeholder engagement and quantitative methods. *Transport Policy, 38,* 27–39.

Chan, A. P. & Oppong, G. D. (2017). Managing the expectations of external stakeholders in construction projects. *Engineering, Construction and Architectural Management.*

Corti, P., Bonomo, P., Frontini, F., Macé, P., & Bosch, E. (2020). *Building Integrated Photovoltaics: A Practical Handbook for Solar Buildings' Stakeholders: Status Report.* Switzerland: University of Applied Sciences and Arts of Southern Switzerland (SUPSI), 1–107. Available at: https://repository.supsi.ch/12186/1/201022_BIPV_web_V01.pdf (accessed on 12 February 2024).

Das, M., Tao, X., Liu, Y., & Cheng, J. C. (2022). A blockchain-based integrated document management framework for construction applications. *Automation in Construction, 133,* 104001.

Department of Health. (2018). Stakeholder engagement framework. Available at: https://www.health.gov.au/resources/publications/stakeholder-engagement-framework (accessed on 14 April 2022).

Erkul, M., Yitmen, I., & Celik, T. (2019). Dynamics of stakeholder engagement in mega transport infrastructure projects. *International Journal of Managing Projects in Business, 13*(7), 1465–1495.

Farida, N., Handayani, N. U., & Wibowo, M. A. (2019). August. Developing indicators of green construction of Green Supply Chain Management in construction industry: A literature review. In *IOP Conference Series: Materials Science and Engineering* (Vol. 598, No. 1, p. 012021). IOP Publishing.

Freeman, R. E. (1984). Managing in turbulent times. In R. E. Freeman (Ed.), *Strategic Management: A Stakeholder Approach.* (pp. 3–28). Cambridge: Cambridge University Press.

Hufen, H. & De Bruijn, H. (2016). Getting the incentives right. Energy performance contracts as a tool for property management by local government. *Journal of Cleaner Production, 112*, 2717–2729.

Jayasuriya, S., Zhang, G., & Yang, R. J. (2020). Exploring the impact of stakeholder management strategies on managing issues in PPP projects. *International Journal of Construction Management, 20*(6), 666–678.

Li, H. X., Patel, D., Al-Hussein, M., Yu, H., & Gul, M. (2018b). Stakeholder studies and the social networks of NetZero energy homes (NZEHs). *Sustainable Cities and Society, 38*, 9–17.

Li, H., Ng, S. T., & Skitmore, M. (2018a). Stakeholder impact analysis during post-occupancy evaluation of green buildings — A Chinese context. *Building and Environment, 128*, 89–95.

Liang, X., Shen, G. Q., & Guo, L. (2015). Improving management of green retrofits from a stakeholder perspective: A case study in China. *International Journal of Environmental Research and Public Health, 12*, 13823–13842.

Lin, B. & Chen, Z. (2022). Net zero energy building evaluation, validation and reflection — A successful project application. *Energy and Buildings, 261*, 111946.

Martin-Chivelet, N., Kapsis, K., Wilson, H. R., Delisle, V., Yang, R., Olivier, L., Polo, J., Eisenlohr, J., Roy, B., Maturi, L., & Otnes, G. (2022). Building-integrated photovoltaic (BIPV) products and systems: A review of energy-related behavior. *Energy and Buildings, 262*(111998).

Mitchell, R. K., Agle, B. R., and Wood, D. J. (1997). Toward a theory of stakeholder identification and salience: Defining the principle of who and what really counts. *Academy of Management Review, 22*(4), 853–886.

Mok, K. Y. & Shen, G. Q. (2016). A network-theory based model for stakeholder analysis in major construction projects. *Procedia Engineering, 164*, 292–298.

Mok, K. Y., Shen, G. Q., & Yang, J. (2015). Stakeholder management studies in mega construction projects: A review and future directions. *International Journal of Project Management, 33*(2), 446–457.

Mok, K. Y., Shen, G. Q., & Yang, R. (2018). Stakeholder complexity in large scale green building projects. *Engineering, Construction and Architectural Management, 25*, 1454–1474.

Osseweijer, F. J., Van Den Hurk, L. B., Teunissen, E. J., & Van Sark, W. G. (2018). A comparative review of building integrated photovoltaics ecosystems in selected European countries. *Renewable and Sustainable Energy Reviews, 90*, 1027–1040.

Prameswari, F. R., Rachamawati, F., Wiguna, I. P. A., & Rohman, M. A. (2021). Importance and performance ratings analysis for implementation of green construction on building project. In *IOP Conference Series. Earth and Environmental Science, 799*(1), 12015. https://doi.org/10.1088/1755-1315/799/1/012015.

Project Management Institute. (2017). *A guide to the project management body of knowledge (PMBOK guide)*. Newtown Square, PA, Project Management Institute.

Qiang, G., Cao, D., Wu, G., Zhao, X., & Zuo, J. (2021). Dynamics of collaborative networks for green building projects: Case study of Shanghai. *Journal of Management in Engineering, 37*(3), 05021001.

Royal Institution of Chatered Surveyors (RICS). (2014). *Stakeholder Engagement*. London: RICS.

Shaukat, M. B., Latif, K. F., Sajjad, A., & Eweje, G. (2022). Revisiting the relationship between sustainable project management and project success: The moderating role of stakeholder engagement and team building. *Sustainable Development, 30*(1), 58–75.

Silvius, G. & Schipper, R. (2019). Planning project stakeholder engagement from a sustainable development perspective. *Administrative Sciences, 9*(2), 46.

Srinivasan, N. P. & Dhivya, S. (2020). An empirical study on stakeholder management in construction projects. *Materials Today: Proceedings, 21,* 60–62.

Taha, F. F., Hatem, W. A., and Jasim, N. A. (2020). Effectivity of BIM technology in using green energy strategies for construction projects. *Asian Journal of Civil Engineering, 21*(6), 995–1003.

Töppel, J. & Tränkler, T. (2019). Modeling energy efficiency insurances and energy performance contracts for a quantitative comparison of risk mitigation potential. *Energy Economics, 80,* 842–859.

Wasim, M., Vaz Serra, P., & Ngo, T. D. (2020). Design for manufacturing and assembly for sustainable, quick and cost-effective prefabricated construction — A review. *International Journal of Construction Management, 22*(15), 3014–3022.

Weerasinghe, A. S., Ramachandra, T., & Thurairajah, N. (2017, September 4–6). Life cycle cost analysis: Green vs conventional buildings in Sri Lanka. In P. W. Chan & C. J. Neilson (Eds.), *Proceeding of the 33rd Annual ARCOM Conference* (pp. 309–318). Cambridge, UK: Association of Researchers in Construction Management (4–6 September 2017).

Weerasinghe, N., Yang, R. J., Too, E., & Le, T. (2020). Renewable energy adoption in the built environment: A sociotechnical network approach. *Intelligent Buildings International, 13*(1) 33–50.

Wijeratne, W. P. U., Samarasinghalage, T. I., Yang, R. J., & Wakefield, R. (2022). Multi-objective optimisation for building integrated photovoltaics (BIPV) roof projects in early design phase. *Applied Energy, 309,* 118476.

Wijeratne, W. P. U., Yang, R. J., Too, E., & Wakefield, R. (2019). Design and development of distributed solar PV systems: Do the current tools work? *Sustainable Cities and Society, 45,* 553–578.

Wilberforce, T., Olabi, A. G., Sayed, E. T., Elsaid, K., Magharabie, H. M., & Abdelkareem, M. A. (2021). A review on zero energy buildings — Pros and cons. *Energy and Built Environment, 4*(1), 25–38.

Xia, N., Zou, P. X., Griffin, M. A., Wang, X., & Zhong, R. (2018). Towards integrating construction risk management and stakeholder management: A systematic literature review and future research agendas. *International Journal of Project Management, 36*(5), 701–715.

Yang, J., Wakefield, R., Gunarathna, C., & Weerasinghe, N. (2019). *Prefabricated Building Integrated Photovoltaics: Cost and Deployment.* London: RICS. Available at: https://www.rics.org/globalassets/rics-website/media/knowledge/research/research-reports/cost-of-prefabricated-building-integrated-photovoltaics-rics.pdf (accessed on 21 August 2020).

Yang, R. J., Zou, P. X., & Wang, J. (2016). Modelling stakeholder-associated risk networks in green building projects. *International Journal of Project Management, 34*(1), 66–81.

Yang, R. J., Jayasuriya, S., Gunarathna, C., Arashpour, M., Xue, X., & Zhang, G. (2018). The evolution of stakeholder management practices in Australian mega construction projects. *Engineering, Construction and Architectural Management, 25*(6), 690–706.

Yu, T., Liang, X., Shen, G. Q., Shi, Q., & Wang, G. (2019). An optimization model for managing stakeholder conflicts in urban redevelopment projects in China. *Journal of Cleaner Production, 212,* 537–547.

Yuan, J., Chen, K., Li, W., Ji, C., Wang, Z., & Skibniewski, M. J. (2018). Social network analysis for social risks of construction projects in high-density urban areas in China. *Journal of Cleaner Production, 198,* 940–961.

Zhang, L., Yuan, J., Xia, N., Bouferguene, A., & Al-Hussein, M. (2020). Improving information sharing in major construction projects through OC and POC: RDT perspective. *Journal of Construction Engineering and Management, 146*(7), 04020068.

Zwikael, O. & Smyrk, J. R. (2019). *Project Management.* Switzerland: Springer Nature Customer Service Center LLC.

Chapter 13

Green Construction Project Health and Safety Management

Emel Sadikoglu and Sevilay Demirkesen

Gebze Technical University, Gebze, Turkey

Safety is of utmost importance in terms of eliminating work-related injuries, accidents, and fatalities in construction projects. Occupational health and safety are an essential part of the social dimension of sustainability. A green construction project needs to focus on the health and safety of workers to become truly sustainable. Even though green construction inherently aims to improve health and safety, green design and construction practices may have both positive and negative effects on occupational health and safety. Hence, the safety risks that occur due to green construction practices should be identified and mitigated appropriately. This chapter compares health and safety in green and conventional projects. Green rating systems are inspected regarding their effect on health and safety. Common safety risks are compared in green and conventional construction projects. The chapter reviews safety management elements in green and conventional projects. The chapter further discusses a set of factors affecting health and safety performance in green and conventional construction projects. The chapter provides practical examples and case studies existing in the literature. The chapter concludes that there is no strict evidence confirming that the health and safety performance is higher or lower in green construction projects.

In different aspects, green design and construction practices may affect health and safety both positively and negatively, and several factors, such as country, contractor type, project type, and worker skills, may play an important role. Even though the existing literature discusses the health and safety risks in green construction projects, a holistic framework should be developed. Further, a comparison of health and safety performance in green and conventional projects is missing. Hence, further research is required in this area. Researchers and policymakers might benefit from the implications of this chapter to revise and revisit their studies on health and safety in green construction.

13.1. Health and safety management in construction

Health and safety are a long-visited research topic in the construction industry. The alarming rates of accidents in the industry require careful consideration of health and safety practices. According to 2019 statistics from the Occupational Safety and Health Administration (OSHA), a total of 5,333 fatalities occurred and 1,061 (20%) were in construction (OSHA, 2019). Moreover, Aksorn and Hadikusumo (2008) noted that the probability of occurrence of a fatal accident is five times more likely in the construction industry than in other industries. This proves the criticality of safety in the industry. Even though there are efforts toward improving the safety management programs implemented in construction companies, there are still challenges faced by those processes. The effectiveness of safety programs depends on many factors, such as company size, workplace conditions, project size, and worker training. Hence, safety policies and implementation standards should be set in accordance with these variables. Being the main motivation of this chapter, the health and safety performance in green construction projects is even more tricky due to several reasons, such as the reliability of green construction practices, methods, and materials used in the projects, and environmental considerations (Onubi *et al.*, 2020). Therefore, this chapter aims to contribute to the body of knowledge by first listing the main differences in health and safety in green and conventional construction. Then, the chapter provides information regarding the elements of safety management and factors affecting safety performance in green and conventional construction projects. In the final section, the chapter proposes a comparative analysis of green and conventional construction by means of practical case studies and examples in the health and safety context.

13.2. Health and safety in green and conventional construction

The US Environmental Protection Agency (USEPA) defines green building as "the practice of creating structures and using processes that are environmentally responsible and resource-efficient throughout a building's life cycle from siting to design, construction, operation, maintenance, renovation, and deconstruction. This practice expands and complements the classical building design concerns of economy, utility, durability, and comfort. Green building is also known as a sustainable or high-performance building" (NIOSH, 2010). Green design and building practices aim to improve the health and safety of the end users or building occupants and affect the environment positively (Silins, 2009; EU-OSHA, 2013). The aim of green practices is to achieve sustainability (Gambatese *et al.*, 2007). Sustainability consists of three main dimensions or pillars, which are environmental, economic, and social aspects and impacts that are considered in a balanced approach throughout the life cycle of the project (Jones *et al.*, 2010; Karakhan, 2016; Karakhan & Gambatese, 2017a).

In order for a project to be sustainable, these dimensions should be involved and equally applied in practices and processes (Karakhan, 2016; Karakhan & Gambatese, 2017a). Many engineering and construction companies in the US approach sustainability dimensions unevenly, according to the study of Jones *et al.* (2010). For instance, industrial construction companies were found to emphasize the environmental dimension, while focusing little attention on the social dimension. On the other hand, commercial construction companies were found to emphasize social pillars particularly.

Occupational health and safety are an essential part of the social dimension of sustainability (Gilding *et al.*, 2002; Gambatese *et al.*, 2007;

Chen, 2010; NIOSH, 2010, 2011; Gambatese & Tymvios, 2012; Bakhiy *et al.*, 2014; Nawaz *et al.*, 2019; Onubi *et al.*, 2020). Karakhan and Gambatese (2017a) stated that "social sustainability in construction is a life-enhancing process to accomplish social equality among all construction stakeholders in terms of health, education, economic welfare, and other human rights." Health and safety play an important role in ensuring sustainable socio-economic development of the construction industry (Rajendran & Gambatese, 2009; NIOSH, 2010). Sustainability and safety have similarities in many aspects, such as being people-centered and creating a stakeholder value (Gilding *et al.*, 2002). Both disciplines focus on protecting and developing social, economic, and environmental aspects (Nawaz *et al.*, 2019). Within the context of sustainability, adequate consideration should be given to the health, safety, and well-being of the construction workers (Hinze *et al.*, 2013).

Green construction offers promising opportunities for sustainable development (Darko & Chan, 2016). Green design and construction mostly focus on the health and safety of end users (Gambatese *et al.*, 2007; Rajendran *et al.*, 2009). On the other hand, the inclusion of concepts into the construction process is in question, in other words, green is not always equal to safety for construction workers, making it difficult to be a truly sustainable process (Gambatese *et al.*, 2007; Rajendran *et al.*, 2009; Schulte *et al.*, 2010). However, construction workers can be considered the earliest occupants and they continue to work throughout the life cycle of the green project (NIOSH, 2011). For a building to be sustainable, social and economic aspects should also be incorporated rather than just considering the environmental aspect (Rajendran *et al.*, 2009). This is because if the environmental dimension is the paramount concern, the risks may be conveyed to construction workers (Schulte *et al.*, 2010). To label a project as sustainable, the whole life cycle of the project including design, construction, operation, and decommissioning phases should incorporate sustainability, and all resources together with human resources should be sustained (Rajendran & Gambatese, 2009; Rajendran *et al.*, 2009; NIOSH, 2010). Safety can lay the foundation to achieve sustainability (Gilding *et al.*, 2002). A project with occupational health and safety issues cannot be considered a sustainable project (Gilding *et al.*, 2002; Gambatese *et al.*, 2007; Rajendran & Gambatese, 2009;

Hinze *et al.*, 2013; Karakhan & Gambatese, 2017a). According to Rajendran and Gambatese (2009, p. 1067), "the sustainable safety and health concept aims to sustain a construction worker's safety and health: from start to finish of a single project; for each future project a worker is involved in, and during the worker's remaining lifetime after retirement."

In the "Making Green Jobs Safe" Workshop in 2009, which was hosted by The National Institute for Occupational Safety and Health (NIOSH), participants agreed that there is a potential for green and sustainable practices to improve construction health and safety (NIOSH, 2010). They viewed sustainability as incomplete without the integration of health and safety concepts (NIOSH, 2010). Similarly, the Building and Construction Trades Department (BCTD), which is a department of the American Federation of Labor-Congress of International Industrial Organizations (AFL-CIO), passed the "Safe Green and Sustainable Construction" resolution and stated that true sustainability should involve construction workers' health and safety (NIOSH, 2010).

Green construction is mostly perceived as being safer than conventional construction by construction practitioners (Gambatese *et al.*, 2007). However, there is no apparent evidence for that (NIOSH, 2011). According to previous studies, green design and construction practices may affect construction health and safety both positively and negatively (Gambatese *et al.*, 2007). New technologies used in green projects can minimize some health and safety risks, especially harmful exposures. However, the installation, construction, and maintenance of these technologies may create some risks similar to conventional projects (Omar *et al.*, 2013). Green construction practices may or may not promote construction health and safety (Gambatese *et al.*, 2007). Green practices do not always favor the health and safety of construction workers during installation, construction, and maintenance (Schulte *et al.*, 2010; EU-OSHA, 2013). In several projects, the possibility of green construction practices to create health and safety hazards was revealed (Gambatese *et al.*, 2007). For instance, the CityCenter project in Las Vegas, US, was a large commercial project and obtained six Gold Leadership in Energy and Environmental Design (LEED) green certifications in 2009 (Chen, 2010; NIOSH, 2010). However, several safety issues and fatalities were observed in the project (Silins, 2009; Gambatese & Tymvios, 2012; Karakhan & Gambatese, 2017a; Nawaz *et al.*, 2019). This example indicated that green construction projects do not necessarily have good occupational health and safety records (Chen, 2010; NIOSH, 2010). Rajendran *et al.* (2009) investigated the impact of green construction on health and safety, based on data collected from 86 projects in the US, 38 of which are green and 48 of which are conventional projects. They revealed that green construction projects had a higher recordable incident rate (RIR) (mean: 6.12, median: 6.86) than conventional projects (mean: 5.63, median: 4.63). They provided suggestive but inconclusive statistical evidence. Hwang *et al.* (2018) compared "overall accident rate," which represents the number of accidents per project. They analyzed 111 green projects and 239 conventional projects. The accident rate of green construction projects (0.37) was higher than that of conventional projects (0.31). On the other hand, Karakhan *et al.* (2022) hypothesized that green construction positively affects occupational health and safety. They analyzed data from 28 projects in the US, including 20 green and 8 conventional projects. They found that green construction projects had a lower RIR (mean: 2.79, median: 1.88) than conventional projects (mean: 3.01, median: 2.31). However, there was no statistical evidence to support the hypothesis. Orogun and Issa (2021) investigated some health and safety performance metrics in seven green and seven conventional construction projects. They found that there is no statistical difference between green (RIR mean: 8.66, RIR median: 7.53) and conventional (RIR mean: 7.56, RIR median: 8.38) projects.

Despite the importance of the topic, the previous literature has not been focused heavily on health and safety management in green construction projects (Fortunato *et al.*, 2012; Karakhan & Gambatese, 2017a; Hwang, Shan and Phuah, 2018). On the other hand, the existing studies could not reach a consensus on whether green construction practices have a positive or negative effect on occupational health and safety. Hence, the potential impacts of green construction on health and safety should be evaluated further (NIOSH, 2010; Fortunato *et al.*, 2012; Omar *et al.*, 2013).

13.2.1. *Health and safety in green rating systems*

Different rating systems have been developed to evaluate sustainability based on the level of meeting certain standards. The first rating system was the Building Research Establishment Environmental Assessment Method (BREEAM), originated by the Building Research Establishment in the UK and launched in 1993. LEED was introduced in the US by the US Green Building Council (USGBC) in 1998. Comprehensive Assessment System for Building Environmental Efficiency (CASBEE) was developed in Japan in 2001 and Green Star was developed in Australia in 2003 (Marchi *et al.*, 2021). The World Green Building Council lists more than 50 green building rating tools administered by Green Building Councils worldwide (WGBC, 2022). There are commonly used systems in several countries, to name a few of them, the German Sustainable Building Council (DGNB) system in Germany, Green Globes in the US and Canada, HQE in France, and GBTool in South Africa.

When the certification systems are reviewed, safety is taken into account in terms of end users (Mattoni *et al.*, 2018; Marchi *et al.*, 2021), while there is a prevalent absence of consideration for occupational health and safety (Rajendran *et al.*, 2009; Chen, 2010; Gillen and Gittleman, 2010; Zhang & Mohandes, 2020). Even though opponents of this approach may argue that health and safety laws and regulations have already been established and used, hazards, injuries, and fatalities continue to occur in green construction projects since these are minimal standards (Chen, 2010; Hinze *et al.*, 2013). Hence, green and sustainable construction rating systems should incorporate the health, safety, and well-being of construction workers (Hinze *et al.*, 2013).

LEED is one of the most widely accepted, recognized, and used green rating systems (Silins, 2009; Karakhan & Gambatese, 2017a). There are some reasons for the motivation behind obtaining LEED certification. It helps improve the public image of owners, reduce operation and maintenance costs, and improve the health of the end users (EU-OSHA, 2013). Many studies evaluated the LEED rating system to examine health and safety in green construction projects since it is one of the most commonly utilized certification systems with a large market share and standardized categories make the analysis process clearer (Chen, 2010; Dewlaney *et al.*, 2012).

LEED rating system evaluates categories of Location and Transportation (LT), Sustainable Sites (SS), Water Efficiency (WE), Energy and Atmosphere (EA), Materials and Resources (MR), Indoor Environmental Quality (IEQ), Integrative Process, Innovation (IN), and Regional Priority. Certification is awarded at four levels: certified, silver, gold, and platinum based on achieved credits (U.S. Green Building Council, 2016). LEED rating system enables the implementation of different design alternatives, methods, or practices to obtain LEED credits (Gambatese & Tymvios, 2012). Hence, health and safety risks may change according to the design alternative or method selected (Gambatese and Tymvios, 2012).

Several researchers bring into question whether the LEED rating system is satisfactory to address the issues related to the health and safety of construction workers (NIOSH, 2010). LEED credits mainly aim to enhance occupant health, safety, and well-being (NIOSH, 2011). Even though some credits were found to support construction worker's health and safety, they are limited and there is a lack of integration of occupational health and safety into LEED credits (Gambatese & Tymvios, 2012). LEED does not explicitly state the safety of workers during construction, operation, or maintenance (Gillen & Gittleman, 2010; NIOSH, 2010; Hinze *et al.*, 2013; Karakhan & Gambatese, 2017a). Further, the requirement section of LEED credits does not include any safety standards or guidance (NIOSH, 2011). Many studies claim that the LEED certification system focuses on the environmental dimension of sustainability rather than taking a comprehensive approach to sustainability (Rajendran & Gambatese, 2009; Rajendran *et al.*, 2009; Karakhan, 2016).

In a major part of the studies, LEED credits were examined and both positive and negative potential impacts on occupational health and safety were presented (Gambatese & Tymvios, 2012). On the other hand, most credits were found to involve no additional risks since they require similar materials or tasks to non-LEED projects. Based on the literature, LEED credits that may have an impact on occupational health and safety are summarized in Table 13.1. Credits of LEED 2009 for New Construction and Major Renovations, which was updated in 2016, are presented since

Table 13.1. Impact of LEED credits on occupational health and safety.

LEED main categories and related credits	Common practices to achieve LEED credits	Falls	Electrocution	Struck-by or -against	Musculoskeletal disorders and overexertion	Inhalation and exposure to harmful substances
Sustainable Sites (SS)						
SS Prerequisite 1: Construction activity pollution prevention						dec. risk
SS 3: Brownfield redevelopment						inc. risk
SS 6.2: Stormwater design — Quality control	Increased detention system capacity, Bioswales, Detention ponds, Rainwater recycling, Vegetated filters	inc. risk		inc. risk		
SS 7.2: Heat Island effect — Roof	Green roof using membrane roofing, Thermoplastic polyolefin (TPO) roof or clay tiles	inc. risk			inc. risk	
	Vegetated roofs	inc. risk				
Water Efficiency (WE) — WE 1: Water efficient landscaping	Storm water harvesting system	inc. risk		inc. risk	inc. risk	

(*Continued*)

Table 13.1.   (Continued)

LEED main categories and related credits	Common practices to achieve LEED credits	Falls	Electrocution	Struck-by or -against	Musculoskeletal disorders and overexertion	Inhalation and exposure to harmful substances
WE 2: Innovative wastewater technologies	Dual wastewater system, Use of non-potable water	inc. risk			inc. risk	inc. risk
EA 1: Optimize energy performance	Installation of insulation and evaporative cooling chillers	inc. risk			inc. risk	
	Geothermal well	inc. risk		inc. risk		inc. risk
	Energy recovery wheel			inc. risk	inc. risk	
EA 2: On-site renewable energy	Solar energy sources, Photovoltaic (PV) panel installation	inc. risk	inc. risk	inc. risk	inc. risk	
	Wind energy sources	inc. risk	inc. risk			
EA 3: Enhanced commissioning	Additional testing and inspection	inc. risk				
MR 1.1; MR 1.2: Building reuse — Maintain existing walls, floors, and roofs; interior nonstructural elements		inc. risk				inc. risk

Energy and Atmosphere (EA)

Materials and Resources (MR)

Credit	Action				
MR 2: Construction waste management	Separating waste into different dumpsters, Redirecting recyclable and reusable materials to nearby centers	dec. risk	inc. risk	inc. risk	inc. risk
MR 3: Materials reuse				inc. risk	inc. risk
IEQ 1: Outdoor air delivery monitoring	Installation of ventilation, monitoring, and alarm system	inc. risk		inc. risk	inc. risk
IEQ 2: Increased ventilation					dec. risk
IEQ 3.1: Construction IAQ management plan- During construction	Use of cleaning products that do not include acetone, Ventilation of indoor generators	dec. risk			dec. risk
	Installation of covers over open ducts of ventilation system	inc. risk		inc. risk	
IEQ 4.1: Low-emitting materials — Adhesives and sealants	Using low-emitting materials	inc. risk			both inc. and dec. risk

(Continued)

Table 13.1.   (*Continued*)

LEED main categories and related credits	Common practices to achieve LEED credits	Falls	Electrocution	Struck-by or -against	Musculoskeletal disorders and overexertion	Inhalation and exposure to harmful substances
Indoor Environmental Quality (IEQ)						
IEQ 4.2; IEQ 4.3; IEQ 4.4: Low-emitting materials — Paints and coatings; Flooring systems; Composite wood and agrifiber products	Using low-emitting materials					dec. risk
IEQ 5: Indoor chemical and pollutant source control	Separate ventilation systems for spaces that may include harmful chemicals				inc. risk	dec. risk
IEQ 6.1: Controllability of systems — Lighting	Occupancy sensors in the facility	inc. risk				
IEQ 8.1: Daylight and views — Daylight	Natural light percolating systems, such as skylights, large windows, and building façades	inc. risk			inc. risk	

Note: inc. risk: increased risk; dec. risk: decreased risk.

Source: Fortunato *et al.* (2012), Dewlaney *et al.* (2012), Omar *et al.* (2013), Karakhan and Gambatese (2017a), NIOSH (2011), Zhang and Mohandes (2020), EU-OSHA (2013), Gambatese and Tymvios (2012), Chen (2010), Bakhiyi *et al.* (2014), Gambatese *et al.* (2007), Onubi *et al.* (2020), Silins (2009).

a major part of the literature inspected this version of LEED. Practices and methods to achieve LEED credits are given and their impact on occupational health and safety are presented as an increase or decrease in risk. The categories identifying hazard types are given based on the most mentioned hazard types in the existing studies.

One option to incorporate occupational health and safety into green construction projects is modifying the LEED rating system (Gambatese *et al.*, 2007; Chen, 2010). Health and safety should have been a prerequisite for LEED certification according to Hinze *et al.* (2013). The LEED rating system may be modified by adding credits considering health and safety, by recommending credits under the innovation in design category, or by making changes to some credits that pose health and safety risks (Chen, 2010). A Green Construction Coordinating Committee formed by NIOSH suggested the addition of worker health and safety statements to some LEED credits that are considered to have the highest potential to enhance worker safety (NIOSH, 2011). Gambatese and Tymvios (2012) recommended some modifications to the LEED rating system by specifying requirements and taking necessary precautions to eliminate risks and increase the health and safety of workers. They further proposed a pilot credit which is an enhanced construction safety plan.

The challenge of modifying LEED is the requirement of formal approval from USGBC (Chen, 2010). However, the LEED certification system provides the opportunity to offer revisions and new credits through the pilot credit system (NIOSH, 2011). After recognition of this issue, USGBC published new pilot credits that incorporate the social dimension of sustainability (Karakhan, 2016; Karakhan & Gambatese, 2017a).

Another option can be the adoption of occupational health and safety credits by other green rating systems and paving the way (Chen, 2010). Green Globes rating system by Green Building Initiative (GBI) introduces an optional credit for a plan to reduce emergencies related to construction site safety (Hinze *et al.*, 2013).

In addition to these approaches, a new health and safety system can be developed (Chen, 2010). Participants of the "Making Green Jobs Safe" Workshop specified "develop, validate, and disseminate a LEED-like safety and health rating system" as one of the priorities (NIOSH, 2011). The Sustainable Construction Safety and Health (SCSH) rating system, which was developed by researchers (Rajendran & Gambatese, 2009) at Oregon State University in the US, is the most comprehensive rating system assessing construction worker health and safety (Chen, 2010). It explicitly integrates social sustainability by considering the construction site safety (Karakhan, 2016).

SCSH rating system was established based on a literature review and Delphi survey with health and safety experts. It consists of 50 health and safety elements under 13 categories and includes the perspectives of primary parties, i.e., owners, designers, general contractors, and subcontractors. SCSH evaluates a project according to the importance and implementation level of health and safety elements (Omar *et al.*, 2013). All parties should have an individual role in enhancing collaborative occupational health and safety efforts. Rajendran and Gambatese (2009) also validated the SCSH rating system based on information collected from 25 construction projects. They found a significant negative correlation between OSHA recordable injury rate and SCSH credits when controlled for project size, facility type, and labor unionization. In other words, as the obtained SCSH credits increase, OSHA recordable injury rate decreases controlling for some parameters. However, it should be noted that developing and generalizing a new system is challenging since it requires efforts for infrastructure, administration, certification assessment team and program, and marketing (Chen, 2010).

Another approach can be establishing a criteria list rather than a formal rating system to evaluate safety performance (Chen, 2010). A scorecard system to assess contractor safety performance from the perspective of the owner was developed by Huang and Hinze (2006). Using a scorecard is user-friendly and may be strengthened further by including terms regarding worker safety in the contract (Chen, 2010).

13.2.2.   *Comparison of health and safety risks in green and conventional construction projects*

A green job should sustain and improve the environment, support workers economically, advance worker health and safety, and comply with the health and safety of communities and society (Chen, 2010). There can be both green and non-green jobs in green construction projects

(Chen, 2010). Green construction includes the construction of new buildings and the retrofitting of existing buildings. Green construction jobs can be considered in three groups according to the National Center for O*NET Development (Dierdorff *et al.*, 2009; Chen, 2010). "Green increased demand occupations" are traditional occupations without significant change where boiler technicians, insulation workers, carpenters, electricians, welders, and iron and steel workers are some examples. "Green enhanced skills occupations" include traditional occupations with some changes in tasks, skills, and knowledge, to name a few, heating and air conditioning mechanics and installers, plumbers, hazardous material handlers, and roofers. "Green new and emerging occupations" refer to new occupations required for green tasks, such as solar photovoltaic installers, weatherization installers, and technicians.

There is a range of jobs that are conducted in green construction from traditional methods to new technologies (Schulte *et al.*, 2010). The level of health and safety risks can change according to the familiarity with tasks, recognition of hazards, and work environment (Schulte *et al.*, 2010). In traditional jobs, generally, tasks are known, and hazards are recognized where established precautions can be taken. Even though some green construction practices are very similar to conventional practices, they may increase the exposure duration or frequency (NIOSH, 2010). On the other hand, in the utilization of new technologies, work may be conducted in a new environment, tasks can be unfamiliar to workers, and hazards may be unrecognized (Schulte *et al.*, 2010).

Many green construction jobs are similar to traditional jobs and create similar health and safety risks that workers in traditional jobs would be exposed to as well (Chen, 2010). Some practices in green construction are likely to have more complex elements and also may require additional work (Gambatese *et al.*, 2007; Schulte *et al.*, 2010; EU-OSHA, 2013). Increased exposure to hazards may increase the current risks or create additional risks (Gambatese & Tymvios, 2012). Even though the risks and hazards can be similar and known for some green jobs, the context is new in green construction (Chen, 2010). Green construction brings different settings which are unaccustomed to conventional construction by introducing new materials and alternative methods and creating a different work environment (Gambatese & Tymvios, 2012). The use of new technologies may create a risk of unknown hazards (Chen, 2010). As a result, these create some problems regarding health and safety management in projects (Fortunato *et al.*, 2012; Hwang *et al.*, 2018).

Safety risks, including hazards and accidents, are categorized in Table 13.1 based on the literature (Dewlaney *et al.*, 2012; Fortunato *et al.*, 2012; Omar *et al.*, 2013; Hwang *et al.*, 2018; Durdyev *et al.*, 2022) and discussed as follows.

13.2.2.1. *Falls*

Falls are one of the main causes of injuries and fatalities on construction sites (NIOSH, 2010; CPWR, 2018). Falling from roofs, ladders, and scaffolds is a major source of falls, where mostly construction laborers and roofers are affected (CPWR, 2018). According to Dewlaney *et al.* (2012), trips, slips, falling to the same level, and falling to a lower level constitute a significant portion of injuries on green construction projects. Previous studies revealed that many activities specific to green construction projects may increase exposure to falling by increasing the time that workers are required to work at height.

In green construction projects, stormwater detention systems are designed to increase capacity and detention ponds are built to achieve credit from sustainable sites part in LEED. This may increase the exposure to fall hazards (Dewlaney *et al.*, 2012; Fortunato *et al.*, 2012). In addition, in green construction projects, solar reflectivity index is aimed to be reduced and heat island effect is tried to be minimized according to sustainable sites category in LEED. In that respect, different roof covering membranes, such as thermoplastic polyolefin (TPO) roofs, are used in green construction projects that are heavier, brighter in direct sunlight, and more slippery when they are wet compared to traditional roof coverings (Fortunato *et al.*, 2012). Installation of these coverings may increase the likelihood of slips, trips, and falls (Dewlaney *et al.*, 2012; Fortunato *et al.*, 2012; Omar *et al.*, 2013; Zhang & Mohandes, 2020). Another option to reduce heat island effect is green or vegetated roofs (NIOSH, 2011; Karakhan & Gambatese, 2017a). Vegetation requires irrigation, mowing, and maintenance, where workers are exposed to work at height for longer periods of time compared to traditional roofing (EU-OSHA, 2013; Karakhan & Gambatese, 2017a; Zhang & Mohandes, 2020).

In order to earn LEED credit from optimized energy performance under the energy and atmosphere category, techniques such as installation of insulation and evaporative cooling chillers are utilized in green construction projects. However, these techniques require working at a height which results in a great chance of falling, as noted by Fortunato *et al.* (2012). Another method is the geothermal well, which is also found by Omar *et al.* (2013) to have greater risk of slipping, tripping, and falling.

To produce onsite renewable energy, photovoltaic (PV) panels use solar resources and generate clean energy (Bakhiyi *et al.*, 2014). However, PV installation poses risk of falling due to increased working time at height, using scaffolds and ladders (Fortunato *et al.*, 2012). Use of solar panels increases the traffic on rooftops during construction and maintenance (Chen, 2010). Some factors, such as extreme weather conditions, high slope angles (Bakhiyi *et al.*, 2014), and inclusion of occupational groups who are unfamiliar to work at height such as electricians (Fortunato *et al.*, 2012), can aggravate the risk. As a result, PV panel installation can cause increased exposure to falling risk and increased frequency of falls (Dewlaney *et al.*, 2012). Another way of producing renewable energy is utilizing wind power. Construction and maintenance work of wind turbines and windmills require working at height which increases the risk of falls (NIOSH, 2011).

Further, green construction projects require extra monitoring and tests which involve visitors who may not be familiar with construction site conditions (Dewlaney *et al.*, 2012). Commissioning requires ascending and descending ladders and as a result, increases exposure to fall hazards (Fortunato *et al.*, 2012). In materials and resources category of LEED, reuse of building elements may cause cave-ins and collapses which may pose a fall hazard risk, according to NIOSH (2011). To obtain envelope durability credit from the materials aspect category in the Hong Kong Building Environment Assessment Method (HKBEAM) rating system, construction workers are required to work at height for cladding of the building envelope and weatherproofing the roof, which increases the risk of falls, as indicated by Zhang and Mohandes (2020). In the water use category of HKBEAM, rainwater harvesting system can be installed to achieve recycling water credit, which requires working at height (Zhang & Mohandes, 2020).

Green construction projects utilize several systems to get credit for indoor environmental quality in LEED. Some practices, such as installation of outdoor air monitoring systems and lighting control systems, and covering ducts, increase the exposure to fall hazards due to frequent use of ladders (NIOSH, 2011; Fortunato *et al.*, 2012). Atrium design provides natural light and helps reduce energy use. However, it may pose a risk in terms of falling accidents because of exposed edges, heavy material to carry and install, complex scaffolding established on top of the atrium, and installation of fall protection systems (Gambatese *et al.*, 2007; Fortunato *et al.*, 2012; EU-OSHA, 2013). Skylights also help increase natural light; however, they create a risk of falls since they are not designed to carry heavy loads and do not include guards (Chen, 2010). Other natural light permeating systems, such as façades with glazed areas and increased open wall area, also create a risk for slips, trips, and falls (Gambatese & Tymvios, 2012; Omar *et al.*, 2013). Cleaning of these systems also exposes maintenance workers to fall hazards (NIOSH, 2011).

In addition to the increased safety risks indicated in most studies, it was also claimed that recycling programs help create and maintain cleaner construction sites, helping reduce accidents, such as slips and falls (Gambatese *et al.*, 2007; EU-OSHA, 2013).

13.2.2.2. Electrocution

Electrocution injury is most frequently caused by electric parts and mostly affects electricians and power line installers. PV panels which are widely used in green construction projects require electrical installations, increasing the probability of electrocution (Bakhiyi *et al.*, 2014). The load can be isolated from the power source in traditional systems; on the other hand, workers are required to operate on the power source itself in a solar panel system (Chen, 2010). PV installation increases the risk of electrical shock and burns due to electrical work on alternative current (AC) and direct current (DC) circuits. The electrical work of PV installation may even increase the risk of fire, as claimed by Bakhiyi *et al.* (2014). Workers may also be exposed to electrocution from nearby power lines while working on rooftops (Chen, 2010). On the other hand, solar panels become very hot due to direct sunlight and may cause burns as well. Further, tasks related to wind turbines may expose installation and maintenance workers to electrical hazards (Chen, 2010; NIOSH, 2011). Chen (2010) indicated that energy efficiency retrofitting and weatherization activities in old buildings may expose workers to electrical risks during insulation installation due to outdated wiring systems.

13.2.2.3. *Struck-by or -against*

Struck-by or -against accidents or fatalities include being struck by an object, equipment, or vehicle (CPWR, 2018). Hwang *et al.* (2018) found being struck against manually operated tools and moving or handling heavy loads to be more critical issues for conventional projects. Construction workers are more likely to be involved in these types of accidents in conventional construction projects, considering more frequent use of manually operated tools and manually moving heavy loads.

On the other hand, they found that being struck by falling objects occurs more in green construction projects (Hwang *et al.*, 2018). This was explained with the use of more prefabricated components which necessitates lifting and carrying of components that increase the likelihood of falling objects (Fortunato *et al.*, 2012). Modular and prefabricated construction increases the probability of being struck by falling objects and being struck against moving objects, as Zhang and Mohandes (2020) claim. Installation of PV panels is also considered to increase struck-by hazards due to requirement of crane operations to move materials onto roof (Fortunato *et al.*, 2012; Zhang & Mohandes, 2020). Preventive maintenance work of geothermal wells, stormwater harvesting systems, and energy recovery wheels are also found to have risk of workers getting struck-by objects (Omar *et al.*, 2013). Moreover, rainwater harvesting system installation necessitates more excavation work to embed the system underneath the building. This may cause workers to be struck by falling objects due to the trench collapsing (Zhang & Mohandes, 2020).

Waste management in green construction projects requires separating materials into different dumpsters which increases the time and effort needed (Gambatese & Tymvios, 2012). It aims to achieve construction waste management credit in the LEED category of materials and resources. The higher number of dumpsters for different types of waste occupies a place which may create bottlenecks on the construction site. They require disposal and processes required to handle waste. This also creates congestion on the construction site involving construction workers and trucks. As a result, this increases the likelihood of being struck by or struck against vehicles (Gambatese *et al.*, 2007; Chen, 2010; Fortunato *et al.*, 2012; EU-OSHA, 2013; Onubi *et al.*, 2020; Zhang & Mohandes, 2020). In addition, stormwater quality control system construction increases the time that construction workers are exposed to trenching, excavation, and heavy machines (NIOSH, 2011; Fortunato *et al.*, 2012). Considering this exposure, struck-by or -against heavy machinery hazards are more likely to occur (Fortunato *et al.*, 2012).

13.2.2.4. *Musculoskeletal disorders and overexertion*

Work-related musculoskeletal disorders are injuries of muscles, tendons, joints, and nerves caused or increased by work positions and movements, such as repetitive motions, forceful exertions, and working in confined spaces for a long time (CPWR, 2018). Construction workers suffer from a high rate of musculoskeletal disorders (NIOSH, 2010).

In green construction projects, waste management includes separation of waste to recycle. Handling of waste materials requires more time to separate and move materials which may create risk of accidents, such as lacerations, strains, sprains, and punctures (Gambatese *et al.*, 2007; Chen, 2010; NIOSH, 2011; EU-OSHA, 2013; Zhang & Mohandes, 2020). Further, wrong separation of waste requires construction workers to enter the dumpsters and categorize materials. This increases the frequency of abrasions, lacerations, and musculoskeletal injuries (Dewlaney, Hallowell & Fortunato, 2012; Fortunato *et al.*, 2012; Onubi *et al.*, 2020).

Several methods used in green construction projects are carried out in confined spaces which lead to musculoskeletal disorders. Preventive maintenance work of geothermal well systems is conducted in a confined space because of the layout of the mechanical equipment (Omar *et al.*, 2013). Preventive maintenance work of a stormwater harvesting system requires tasks in underground tanks which are confined areas. Due to layout, tasks also require working in awkward positions Omar *et al.*, 2013). Preventive maintenance work of energy recovery wheels is also conducted in a confined space Omar *et al.*, 2013).

Overexertion is one of the major causes of musculoskeletal disorders (CPWR, 2018). Lifting and carrying heavy roof-covering membranes that are used to reduce heat island effect increase exposure to overexertion (Dewlaney *et al.*, 2012; Fortunato *et al.*, 2012) and back injury (Zhang & Mohandes, 2020). Some natural light permeating systems such as atriums are designed to include large glass panes which can be heavy, causing ergonomic risks to workers (Chen, 2010). Similarly, solar panel installation requires lifting and carrying heavy panels and involves ergonomic risks due to awkward body postures and repetitive movements (Chen, 2010; Bakhiyi *et al.*, 2014). It may also cause musculoskeletal disorders such as carpal tunnel syndrome (Zhang & Mohandes, 2020). Further, in construction of modular systems, workers are required to carry and assemble the prefabricated elements. This includes heavy physical workload and may cause musculoskeletal disorders, such as carpal tunnel syndrome (EU-OSHA, 2013; Zhang & Mohandes, 2020). Besides, retrofitting existing buildings to install energy-efficient systems requires heavy workload, such as manual handling of material and equipment (EU-OSHA, 2013).

Green construction projects that aim to get credit from water efficiency part in LEED include dual wastewater systems requiring much more piping work which increases repetitive movements and overexertion (Dewlaney *et al.*, 2012; Fortunato *et al.*, 2012). Similarly, indoor chemical and pollutant source control LEED credit in indoor environmental quality category may cause overexertion. It requires separate ventilation systems for each space that may include harmful chemicals, as a result, increases the amount of drywall work, installation of additional fans, and ductwork overhead which are repetitive (Dewlaney *et al.*, 2012; Fortunato *et al.*, 2012).

Lighter construction materials are also used in green construction projects. For instance, the use of materials such as thinner bricks, which are lighter, or permeable paving stones, which provide water permeability and weigh lighter than conventional ones, may help reduce the physical workload of construction workers (EU-OSHA, 2013).

13.2.2.5. *Inhalational exposure and exposure to harmful substances*

Construction workers are exposed to several substances, such as paints, adhesives, silica, asbestos, lead, and fumes (NIOSH, 2011). Inhalational exposure to some contaminants, such as gases, vapors, dust (silica, lead, etc.), fumes, and pollutants, increases the risk of respiratory diseases (CPWR, 2018). Several construction works require tasks such as drilling, grinding, and cutting that create airborne contaminants (Gillen & Gittleman, 2010).

The inhalation issue was found to be more problematic in conventional construction projects in the study of Hwang *et al.* (2018). It was implied that the use of more environmentally friendly materials in green construction projects may reduce the likelihood of inhaling toxic gases by construction workers (Hwang *et al.*, 2018). Green construction projects provide cleaner air and reduce health hazards by minimizing volatile organic compound (VOC) materials (Gambatese *et al.*, 2007; Fortunato *et al.*, 2012). Low-VOC emitting materials for adhesives, paints, coatings, carpets, composite wood, and Agrifiber products are mostly used in green construction projects. The use of low-VOC materials reduces the adverse health effects that VOC materials cause to construction workers, such as headaches, and irritation of the eye, nose, and throat, during installation and construction (Fortunato *et al.*, 2012). Besides that, the construction indoor air quality (IAQ) management plan during construction can create a positive effect on construction workers since it helps improve IAQ (NIOSH, 2011; Karakhan & Gambatese, 2017a). Construction activity pollution prevention, which is a prerequisite in LEED sustainable sites category, is considered to have a positive effect on construction workers (Silins, 2009; NIOSH, 2011). Further, increased ventilation and indoor chemical and pollutant source control credits in indoor environmental quality category are considered to have positive benefits for maintenance workers in terms of exposure to airborne chemicals, while providing a neutral effect for construction workers (NIOSH, 2011).

On the contrary, it was reported that there is a quality issue regarding low-VOC emitting adhesives and sealants that require more rework such as additional surface preparation. The requirement of grinding and sanding produces silica dust, wood dust, etc., which cause negative health effects (Dewlaney *et al.*, 2012; Fortunato *et al.*, 2012). In waste management, construction workers may be exposed to airborne gypsum during separation of waste, which leads to respiratory problems (Fortunato *et al.*, 2012; Zhang & Mohandes, 2020). Moreover, the dust from some renewable materials used in green construction projects, such as wood and wool, may cause skin and eye irritation and respiratory diseases (EU-OSHA, 2013; Zhang & Mohandes, 2020). Some recycled materials may also pose health and safety risks. For instance, coal ash, involving fly ash, is a coal combustion byproduct that is used to strengthen concrete (Chen, 2010). Even though pouring concrete with recycled materials may not create serious risks, workers may be exposed to heavy metals and carcinogenic materials during drilling, grinding, and sawing (Chen, 2010; NIOSH, 2010).

Another consideration can be the use of nanomaterials. There are different types of engineered nanomaterials used in several construction products such as concrete, paintings, and coatings to enhance their performance. The effects of nanomaterials on human health are unknown, however, they are likely to create health and safety risks because of being similar to pollutants in terms of size (CPWR, 2018). Hence, more research investigating the nature and both short- and long-term health effects of nanomaterials are needed (Gillen & Gittleman, 2010).

Exposure may occur through inhalation of gases, smoke, and dust but may also occur through intake or contact with skin, eye, etc. (Bakhiyi *et al.*, 2014). Green construction projects that try to achieve credit from sustainable sites in LEED through brownfield redevelopment need to perform excavation, disposal, and treatment of hazardous and contaminated materials which increase exposure to harmful substances (Dewlaney *et al.*, 2012). Installation of innovative wastewater technologies increases exposure to harmful substances (Dewlaney *et al.*, 2012). Preventive maintenance work of geothermal wells includes sample collection and testing, during which workers can be exposed to chemicals leading to adverse health effects (Omar *et al.*, 2013). In preventive maintenance of stormwater harvesting systems, bleach chamber and chemical dye chamber also create risk of exposure to chemicals (Omar *et al.*, 2013). Further, reuse of building elements may create exposure to toxic materials, such as asbestos and lead (NIOSH, 2011). Reinsulation work of existing buildings exposes workers to insulation materials that include chemicals such as isocyanates and silica. These chemicals may cause dermatitis, eye and skin irritation, and respiratory diseases (Chen, 2010; EU-OSHA, 2013). On the other hand, modular construction increases assembly on the construction site while decreasing production on site. Prefabricated elements may help reduce exposure to harmful substances, such as fresh concrete mortar (EU-OSHA, 2013).

13.3. The elements of a safety management system

A good safety management system comprises a good safety plan, procedures and plans, safety training, monitoring, and reporting. Such a system might be set in the existence of good supervisors and managers having the potential to impact safety performance in construction projects (Hinze *et al.*, 1998). What is essential in safety management is to correctly identify hazards and risks. These can be identified through the root cause analysis of work-related hazards. Heberle (1998) lists the factors of an effective safety model as safety training, personal protective equipment, scheduled inspections, behavioral observations, job safety procedures, review of safety performance data, goal setting, corrective action in planning, and employee involvement and support. Tam *et al.* (2002). further mentioned the main elements of a safety management system as safety audits, safety training, safety supervision, management involvement in safety, safety promotion, the establishment of safety policies, and eradication of hazards. With such factors, safety becomes manageable and effectively organized. Figure 13.1 presents a group of five main elements that are effective in a safety management system. These main elements are listed as safety policy and procedures, audit and review, performance

Figure 13.1.   Elements of safety management.

measurement, management support for safety, and safety training and inspection.

The construction industry is among the riskiest industries with high injury rates, work-related fatalities, and worker compensation payments (McDonald *et al.*, 2009). The dynamic nature of the industry makes things even more difficult in terms of defining hazardous conditions for workers due to worksite locations and continuously changing work conditions (Hinze *et al.*, 1998). Tam *et al.* (2004) identified a set of factors affecting safety performance, such as poor safety awareness among top management and project managers, lack of training, unwillingness to input resources for safety, and reckless operations. It is the employers' and owners' responsibility to provide a safer place for workers as implied by OSHA in the US (OSHA, 2021).

Safety management systems are mainly developed to improve safety performance. Safety performance should be measured to identify the current state, observe the progress, take necessary actions, and improve the situation. Safety performance is mainly measured with two types of indicators, which are lagging and leading indicators, as indicated by Jazayeri and Dadi (2017). Lagging indicators measure data after accidents occurred and show the level of lack of safety rather than the existence of safety. For example, OSHA total recordable incident rate (TRIR) measures the number of incidents per 100 employees per year (200,000 man-hours). Lost time case incident rate (LTCR) measures the number of incidents that cause the employee to be unable to work per 100 employees per year (200,000 man-hours). Leading indicators are prospective measures that show the developing or changing status. For instance, near-miss reporting and working observation are some leading indicators (Jazayeri and Dadi, 2017). Several indicators are used in conventional and green construction projects to measure safety performance. Rajendran *et al.* (2009) used TRIR and LTCR to compare safety performance in green and conventional construction projects by considering project type, project complexity, location, funding, and contractor firm. Safety management is a need for every organization, and it is driven by proper safety training. Safety culture must be developed within the organization and conveyed to employees by clearly highlighting their roles and responsibilities in such a culture. The training should not be a short-term one rather it needs to be periodically organized and refreshed every year (Heberle, 1998). A well-organized safety model enhances workers' motivation and trust in the safety program. In this respect, safety training is an essential way of improving the ability to perform, shape behavior, and act with a sense of purpose (Demirkesen & Arditi, 2015). After safety training, workers can develop work safe behavior and learn to keep themselves from hazardous cases. On the other hand, safety training is a progressive process, which needs to be implemented in steps since it might not be very effective at the beginning. Previous studies have already revealed that workers who got safety training perform better than the ones who have not got any training yet in terms of job effectiveness (Hinze & Wilson, 2000; Reese & Eidson, 2006). Along with well-studied effect of safety training on conventional construction, studies in green construction also show its importance. Adequate health and safety training should be provided to all workers (Hwang *et al.*, 2018). Existing training programs should be assessed and enhanced to include specific hazards that can be encountered in green jobs (Chen, 2010). Governmental and regional resources are significant to qualify construction workers for green jobs. Further, unions, community, and technical colleges can play an important role in integrating health and safety into their green job training programs (Chen, 2010). Not only construction workers but also designers (architects and engineers) and contractors should be trained about safety in green construction projects. Owners should facilitate the training and bring these parties together at the earlier stages of the project, as advocated by Chen (2010).

An effective safety model might be set up with the proper equipment use. Especially, personal protective equipment (PPE) is designed in such a way that they intend to possibly prevent workers from being injured. Using PPE is also considered as an effective way to reduce accident rate in green construction projects (Hwang *et al.*, 2018). However, there is considerable resistance to using PPE in the construction industry (Feeney, 1986; Boatman *et al.*, 2015). Wong *et al.* (2020). have identified a set of factors such as accident experience, risk perception, attitude toward PPE use, safety incentives, and safety supervision in terms of promoting PPE use. They indicate that the main reason for PPE use among construction workers is associated with the safety management system of their organization which comprises a safety-offence points system, safety supervision, safety training, and safety rules and incentives.

Designing the work, systems, and processes by considering health and safety is one of the most effective prevention strategies (Chen, 2010; NIOSH, 2010; EU-OSHA, 2013). Prevention through design (PtD) aims to prevent occupational health and safety issues through architectural and/ or engineering design before the start of the project, at their source (Chen, 2010; Karakhan, 2016). NIOSH (2010, p. 8) asserted that "PtD examines hazard potential throughout the life cycle of work premises, tools, equipment, machinery, substances, and worker processes, including their construction, manufacture, use, maintenance, and ultimate disposal or reuse." To achieve PtD, designers, architects, engineers, and manufacturers should be involved in the design process (EU-OSHA, 2013). Early involvement in consideration for health and safety is significant. For example, design-build organizations, where design and construction are conducted by the same entity, were found by Chen (2010) to have better safety performance than traditional construction organizations. Further, different disciplines such as occupational health and safety and environmental protection professionals should work together. In that way, the shift of risks from the environment to the construction workers, and vice versa, can be eliminated, in the view of NIOSH (2010). PtD cannot impede all health and safety risks alone, however, it helps establish a safe workplace (Chen, 2010). Considering the hierarchy of controls, PtD is a better way to reduce hazards compared to enforcing safe work practices (Chen, 2010). Safety through design protects the construction workers more and provides a more cost-effective solution (Silins, 2009).

The essence of safety management further lies in controlling and monitoring safety policies and practices within an organization (Flin *et al.* 2000). The controlling and monitoring are sometimes used to limit liabilities and costs in terms of promoting the organization for its competitiveness in the industry. However, monitoring and controlling must be implemented to conduct an efficient safety program first. On the other hand, it is likely that there might be a set of obstacles during safety program implementation. Some workers might oppose the implementation of safety programs and act against the safety procedures and policies (Wilson & Koehn, 2000). At this point, it is of organizations' responsibility to convince workers to act safely and develop work safe behavior to avoid unsafe conditions. Indeed, an organization's willingness in developing strong safety policies would help enhance its reputation in the market. Well-set safety programs and supported safety management with all actors such as owners, designers, contractors, and subcontractors enhance company performance as well as contribute to its profitability (Demirkesen, 2011). Support and commitment from the top management is crucial to develop safety culture and to ensure workers' understanding (Hwang *et al.*, 2018).

13.3.1. *Conducting safety audit*

A safety audit is a safety assessment method to get contractors to stay in tune with the current practices, develop best practices, and sustain continuous risk reduction for the safety management system. Safety audits consist of collecting, assessing, and verifying the information for the reliability of the safety management system (Yiu *et al.*, 2018). Safety audits can be conducted for the whole project management (PM) system or for some individual areas, such as construction management system, design management system, or commissioning management system. Audits further evaluate compliance with legislative safety and environmental requirements (PMI, 2016).

The safety audit is an essential tool for the top management to observe the status of safety to improve safety performance and successfully implement safety programs in construction companies. There are internal and external audits, which are assessed to verify the system's ability in terms of predefined safety objectives and determine if any gap exists in the current safety management system (Sailendra & Shah, 2013). Teo and Ling (2006) implied that the lack of safety improvement might stem from the lack of safety auditing. They further mention that there are no standard protocols (i.e., guidelines or checklists) for safety auditing, leading to the ambiguity of the effectiveness of the auditing process.

This objective is important because the industry can adopt a standard auditing methodology and develop a benchmark for safety audit purposes. Safety auditing helps measure the success of a safety management system by bringing an active monitoring system before accidents take place (Ahmad & Gibb, 2003). Teo and Ling (2006) implied that proper safety auditing is one of the most important elements promoting safe work practices resulting from reliable and continuous feedback through observed safety levels. Hence, a safety audit is the main facilitator of determining the strengths and weaknesses of the current safety programs in organizations, where potential problems that could lead to failure of the safety program are detected (Lee, 1995). On the other hand, safety auditing is somewhat regarded as a challenging process by various organizations due to a lack of standardized guidelines or procedures. This leads to poor safety performance and in turn poor PM performance.

There might also be differences in the safety performance of construction projects regarding project type, construction methods and materials, project budget, and project requirements. The research study conducted by Hwang *et al.* (2018). revealed that worse safety performance is observed in green construction projects than in conventional construction projects. This is explained through the increasing number of green construction projects in Singapore. The study proposed a set of measures to improve the safety performance in green construction projects. For example, increasing the frequency of safety audits was proposed as a remedy for improving the safety performance in green construction projects. This can help reduce the likelihood of safety-related accidents in green construction projects. Therefore, safety audits shall be conducted more sensitively in green construction projects than in conventional construction projects.

13.3.2. *Conducting safety review*

Conducting a safety review is somewhat similar to safety audits but it is more defined as a general process, where the whole safety management system is assessed than its components. Fung *et al.* (2005) point out the role of management in terms of reviewing the safety and health system indicating that it is critical that management receives timely feedback to better assess the performance of the safety management system. In the study of Choudhry (2014), it was implied that participative goal setting and the training checklist are two important items of safety performance measures. As part of the goal-setting session, a complete safety review was conducted to put safety in order and to observe the impacts of behavior-based safety in terms of accident prevention. Gambatese *et al.* (2008) implied a strong link between designers' decisions and safe performance. In this context, they highlighted the role of safety review before mistakes turn into accidents.

According to Toole *et al.* (2006), safety reviews might be conducted as internal and external reviews. In the internal review, mostly quality assurance and quality control procedures are followed along with the cross-discipline review. In the external review, a focused safety review is conducted along with the owner review.

13.4. Factors affecting the health and safety performance of green construction projects

The construction industry is risky due to poor occupational conditions and vulnerability to hazardous situations (Pinto *et al.*, 2011). This requires the implementation of effective safety programs. It is of utmost importance to assess safety performance to establish work safe practices and reduce the likelihood of accidents. Therefore, the factors affecting health and safety performance must be considered carefully to devise better strategies.

One of the main purposes of green construction is to address occupational health and safety on construction sites. There are different opinions regarding the effectiveness of green construction practices to handle health and safety challenges in construction projects (Onubi *et al.*, 2020). For instance, Karakhan and Gambatese (2017b) reported that green construction usually has adverse effects on the site safety personnel in construction projects despite the sustainability goal of green practices. Similarly, Hwang *et al.* (2018) implied that green construction projects impose greater safety risks for workers than conventional construction. This contradicts the main purpose of green construction, which is to meet environmental, social, and economic goals. On the other hand, there are some other studies advocating green construction in terms of improving health and safety performance. For example, Ghasemi *et al.* (2015) revealed that there are various improvements in safety issues because of green construction. Jamil and Fathi (2016) ascertained that green practices contribute to the improvement of health and safety environment. Given this background, it is important to investigate factors affecting health and safety performance in green construction projects apart from conventional construction. There are different factors affecting the health and safety performance in construction projects.

Good safety performance can be achieved with the help of safety processes and implementation of best practices (Hinze *et al.*, 2013). Health and safety management system plays a crucial role in maintaining and improving safety performance (Hwang *et al.*, 2018). To achieve better safety performance, health and safety objectives should be developed, and required resources should be allocated accordingly (Mahmoudi *et al.*, 2014). A safety plan should be established to implement the safety practices (Hinze *et al.*, 2013; Orogun & Issa, 2021). Safety planning needs to be considered along with project planning at the early phases of the project (Khalid *et al.*, 2021). Accordingly, safety policy should be developed and implemented (Jazayeri & Dadi, 2017). Safety regulations are helpful in managing safety (Khalid *et al.*, 2021). Safety risk management, which is the identification and control of risks, is one of the significant factors (Khalid *et al.*, 2021). Hazards should be identified, monitored, and analyzed. Mahmoudi *et al.* (2014). concluded that risk assessment and management is the most important factor affecting health and safety at the project level. Orogun and Issa (2021) proposed that risk and hazard management is one of the crucial factors in assessing health and safety performance of green construction projects.

Leadership and commitment of top management are important factors that impact occupational health and safety (Hinze *et al.*, 2013; Mahmoudi *et al.*, 2014; Orogun & Issa, 2021). Chandra (2015) showed that project organization, leadership, and company support are potential motivators influencing sustainable construction health and safety. Leadership and management commitment was proposed as one of the factors that measure safety performance in green construction projects in the study of Orogun and Issa (2021). Mohammadi *et al.* (2018) listed a set of factors affecting the safety performance of construction projects. Some of the factors listed were management systems, culture and climate, attitude and behavior, motivation, and work condition and work pressure. Sawacha *et al.* (1999) claimed that management talk on safety affects safety performance. The top management should ensure that safety culture is internalized by all employees in the organization (Hwang *et al.*, 2018). Hwang *et al.* (2018) indicated that health and safety performance in green construction projects can be enhanced by promoting safety culture through educating and recognizing safety efforts.

Safety professionals are required at construction sites to control the implementation of safety systems (Sawacha *et al.*, 1999; Hinze *et al.*, 2013; Abas *et al.*, 2020; Orogun & Issa, 2021). Sawacha *et al.* (1999) implied that appointment of a trained safety representative on site is one of the most dominant factors affecting safety performance in the UK construction industry. Safety communication, being one of the most mentioned factors that impact safety, is significant for safety at construction sites (Orogun & Issa, 2021; Rivera *et al.*, 2021). Orogun and Issa (2021) proposed that safety communication is one of the factors in assessing the health and safety performance of green construction projects. Safety meetings should be held frequently, and participation should be increased (Orogun & Issa, 2021). According to Orogun and Issa (2021), statistical analyses showed that as the workers attend safety meetings, their unsafe behavior decreases in both green and conventional projects.

Safe working environment contributes to the reduction of accident occurrences (Abas *et al.*, 2020). Durdyev *et al.* (2022) revealed that a hazardous environment is one of the main safety risks in green construction projects. Sawacha *et al.* (1999) showed that well-designed layout and tidiness of the workplace have a positive effect on safety performance. Along with safe workplace, PPE should be provided to workers and ensured to be worn (Abas *et al.*, 2020). Using the correct type of protective equipment is a prerequisite of enhanced safety performance (Sawacha *et al.*, 1999). The use of PPE helps reduce accidents (Hwang *et al.*, 2018). In the study of Hwang *et al.* (2018), use of PPE ranked second among suggested solutions to enhance green construction projects' safety performance.

Safety training is one of the most commonly mentioned factors in improving safety performance (Sawacha *et al.*, 1999; Hinze *et al.*, 2013; Demirkesen & Arditi, 2015; Hwang *et al.*, 2018; Abas *et al.*, 2020). Durdyev *et al.* (2022) researched the safety risks in green construction projects and implied that lack of required training and the unfamiliarity of workers with the LEED requirements and methods are among the main risks. Training helps decrease the number of accidents and improve safety knowledge, awareness, behavior, and, as a result, safety performance (Hwang *et al.*, 2018; Abas *et al.*, 2020). In the study of Hwang *et al.* (2018), training ranked first among recommended solutions to enhance safety performance in green construction projects.

Safety inspection is significant to monitor tasks, risks, safety practices, people, and workplace (Abas *et al.*, 2020; Khalid *et al.*, 2021). Regular safety auditing and reviewing helps investigate the implementation of safety standards, policies, and procedures (Hwang *et al.*, 2018). Conducting safety audits and evaluations was considered as one of the significant solutions to improve safety performance of green projects as per the study of Hwang *et al.* (2018). Orogun and Issa (2021) suggested that safety control, inspection, and audit are among the factors measuring health and safety performance of green construction projects.

The factors affecting safety performance exist not only during the construction phase but also throughout the whole life cycle of the project. PtD or design for safety (DfS) helps prevent safety risks before the construction phase. Hence, it can help improve safety performance

(Hwang *et al.*, 2018). Karakhan and Gambatese (2017b) implied that several green construction rating tools, such as LEED, comprise credits for the prevention of safety issues through design. In the study of Hwang *et al.* (2018), DfS was listed as the third among selected solutions to improve safety performance in green construction projects. Hwang *et al.* (2018) recommended implementing DfS as a core syllabus in pre-employment professional courses. Orogun and Issa (2021) considered DfS as one of the factors that measure safety performance of green projects.

Health and safety contracts are also considered as a critical health and safety factor (Khoza & Haupt, 2021). The responsibilities of parties should be addressed in contracts (Sawacha *et al.*, 1999). According to the model developed by Khoza and Haupt (2021), contractual health and safety arrangement was found to have a positive and direct impact on health and safety performance. Health and safety in contracts was proposed as one of the factors that assess safety performance in green construction projects in the study of Orogun and Issa (2021).

Considering the characteristics of employees, workers' age and experience were found to impact safety performance in Sawacha *et al.*'s (1999) study. Older workers tend to have more job experience; however, they are more vulnerable to musculoskeletal disorders and overexertion, according to Gillen and Gittleman (2010). Considering the requirements of some green construction jobs, older workers may be affected negatively. On the other hand, Sawacha *et al.* (1999). indicated that older workers are more likely to be aware of safety requirements. Hence, different worker groups may influence safety performance based on their characteristics. Specialization in job functions has been further reported in the literature to be another important factor affecting health and safety performance in green construction projects (Onubi *et al.*, 2022). Moreover, workers' involvement and safety behavior management have been proposed as factors measuring green construction projects' safety performance (Orogun & Issa, 2021).

Further, other factors such as contractor type and ownership of the project by public or private entities also affect safety performance as well (Rajendran *et al.*, 2009). Lin and Mills (2001) revealed that company size and management and employee commitment to occupational health and safety are the major factors affecting safety performance in Australia.

Green construction projects need to be further investigated in terms of factors that affect health and safety performance. For example, Onubi *et al.* (2020) revealed that energy management (i.e., energy savings, using renewable resources, and using electricity control systems) has a significant and positive impact on health and safety in green construction projects. Given this background, it is implied that green construction and conventional construction differ at some point, where safety risks can be differentiated. Moreover, some factors of health and safety differently affect green construction and conventional construction projects requiring the implementation of different health and safety programs or practices.

13.5. Practical case studies and discussion

The field of health and safety research in green construction does not have a long history, which can be attributed to the fact that the introduction of green is relatively new as well (Rajendran *et al.*, 2009). Even though the field is not broad, there are several studies investigating occupational health and safety in green construction projects. Some significant studies in the area are further discussed as follows.

Gambatese *et al.* (2007). conducted one of the very first studies that considered and investigated health and safety in green construction projects. They examined a pilot study which was an LEED project by conducting focus group interviews and inspecting project documentation. They revealed both positive and negative aspects of green practices on health and safety. According to the findings of this study, all respondents considered green construction projects to be the same or safer than conventional projects.

Soon after this study, Rajendran *et al.* (2009) also examined health and safety performance in green and conventional construction projects by collecting data through questionnaire surveys and interviews. They identified green projects based on LEED certification and specified TRIR and LTCR to measure safety performance. They also considered confounding variables that may affect the safety performance of the project, such as project type, project complexity, and contractor firm. They conducted statistical tests to find out the relationship. In privately funded projects, green projects were found to have a higher median TRIR than conventional projects. In general, a comparison of TRIR values revealed that green construction projects show a higher median TRIR than conventional projects. The findings were suggestive, but however were inconclusive. Most interviews presented that there is no significant difference in the safety performance of green and conventional construction projects.

Even though these studies had some limitations in terms of sample size and generalizability, they paved the way for further research. They also emphasized the difference between green and sustainable and raised the issue of health and safety in green construction projects. Building upon these studies, most of the literature investigated the effect of practices to obtain green building rating system credits, especially LEED, on health and safety of construction workers. Safety risks in green construction projects were considered as hazards and accidents that occurred due to green practices (Dewlaney *et al.*, 2012; Zhang & Mohandes, 2020).

Gambatese and Tymvios (2012) inspected four case studies in the US and green practices were found to have no significant or additional occupational health and safety risks. However, they mentioned some potential health and safety benefits and risks of the LEED rating system and further provided recommendations to incorporate occupational health and safety into LEED certification.

Fortunato *et al.* (2012) studied the effect of additional tasks to achieve LEED certification on the safety risks of construction workers. They conducted six case studies and two validation case studies in the US. They revealed that most of the tasks are risky, such as installing green roofs and photovoltaic solar panels. It was found that 24% of LEED credits inspected pose a higher safety risk. Workers on green construction projects were found to spend longer time working at tall heights, with electrical currents, near heavy equipment, and near unstable soil compared to those working on conventional projects. The main danger was expressed as the unfamiliarity of workers with the environment and emerging new risks due to green construction practices. 25% of case studies showed that some construction occupations such as electricians and landscapers worked in unfamiliar environments such as subsurface, atria, and roof. Further, workers were required to conduct work such as additional piping, roofing, and ductwork which include repetitive movements, heavy lifting, etc. and caused overexertion injuries. Overexertion injuries are significant, considering aging construction workers and their vulnerability (Gillen & Gittleman, 2010; Fortunato *et al.*, 2012; CPWR, 2018). The study also showed that the use of low-VOC emitting materials regarding IAQ LEED credits reduces the exposure to VOC and related hazards faced by workers. Even though several negative and positive effects of green construction projects conducted according to LEED requirements on construction workers' health and safety were specified, it was found that 40% of the LEED credits inspected did not cause any change in injuries or hazards.

Dewlaney *et al.* (2012) assessed safety risks regarding LEED credits by considering frequency, severity, and exposure. They conducted interviews to collect data from LEED projects. Findings showed that the green practices put in place to achieve 12 out of 49 inspected LEED credits increase the frequency or exposure of risks to safety. In addition to previous studies, Dewlaney *et al.* (2012) found that brownfield development and daylighting credits also increase the safety risks. The most significant impacts were revealed to be lacerations, strains, and sprains due to waste management; falls due to the installation of renewable energy, e.g., solar panels; eye strain during installation of roof membranes; and harmful substance exposure during installation of innovative wastewater technologies. The study further emphasized that the most impacted safety risk category was falls.

Omar *et al.* (2013) investigated preventive maintenance work in green construction projects. Being different from other studies, the study inspected not only the construction but also the maintenance phase. A job hazard analysis, where the risk is calculated as the multiplication of hazard probability and hazard severity, was conducted. It was specified that below-grade or rooftop work is increasing in green building projects to achieve LEED credits. The most problematic health and safety issues were slips, trips, and falls due to green roof and skylight installation, hazards because of working in confined spaces such as energy recovery wheels and stormwater harvesting systems, and exposure to chemicals.

On the contrary to other studies, Bakhiyi *et al.* (2014) studied a system mostly involved in green construction practices rather than focusing on green rating systems. They examined solar panel photovoltaic systems and their effect on the environment and occupational health and safety. They assessed PV systems throughout their complete life cycle of production, operation, and end-of-life phases. Even though they are regarded as clean methods, they may produce greenhouse gases and toxic chemicals during production, and electronic waste after their useful life. Installation of PV systems may include some safety risks, such as falling from heights, falling objects, electrical shocks, burns or fires, and ergonomic risks.

Karakhan and Gambatese (2017a) quantified occupational health and safety risk by calculating as multiplication of severity and frequency. Severity was considered as the product of potential and impact. The potential of LEED credits on health and safety being positive or negative was determined by researchers. The impact of credits on health and safety was classified as low, medium, and high according to previous studies in the literature. The frequency of LEED credits obtained was determined based on the LEED scorecard review of a representative sample from the USGBC LEED project directory. It was found that 12 LEED credits have a negative impact, 4 credits have a positive impact, and 4 credits have a mixed impact on the safety performance in the construction industry. Risk plane analysis was utilized to group risks under different zones. The highest positive effect on health and safety was observed in LEED credits construction activity pollution prevention, low-emitting materials: adhesives and sealants and paints and coatings. The most negative effect on health and safety was detected in LEED credits heat island effect: roof and construction waste management. As opposed to previous studies, it was stated that the effect of onsite renewable energy on health and safety is negligible since it is obtained in only 15% of green projects in the US. The study implied that sustainable construction may create additional occupational health and safety risks "impacting the overall safety performance of the US construction industry negatively" (Karakhan & Gambatese, 2017).

Hwang et al. (2018) compared green and conventional projects and investigated their safety issues based on data collected from 30 construction companies in Singapore. In green construction projects, the most frequently occurring safety risks were found as falls, electrocution, and being struck by falling objects. Critical safety issues for both green and conventional projects were "exposure to hazardous substances," "inhalation," "moving/handling heavy loads," "respiratory failure," "being struck against manually operated tools," and "being struck by falling objects." They compared conventional and green construction projects and revealed that the safety performance of green construction projects is lower than that of conventional projects. The findings indicated that commercial projects constitute the highest accident rate in terms of project type for both conventional and green construction projects. They also showed that as the project size increases in terms of budget, the accident rate mostly increases as well. The study further provided solutions to enhance safety performance in green projects, such as training, PPE, DfS, top management commitment, and safety audits.

Previous studies mostly considered the safety risks and their comparison in green and conventional construction projects. A major part of the studies investigated the LEED rating system in the US. However, there was a dearth of studies developing a safety management framework. Zhang and Mohandes (2020) aimed to fill this gap by developing a comprehensive framework that identifies, analyzes, assesses, and controls the occupational safety risks in green construction projects. They identified practices to achieve HKBEAM credits, safety risks related to credits, and their criticality level based on the Delphi method using Z-numbers. 51 potential safety risks were identified based on data provided by experts in Hong Kong. In an analysis of safety risks, they utilized the Z-numbers-based Best Worst Method (ZBWM) and the Z-numbers-based Technique for Order of Preference by Similarity to Ideal Solution (ZTOPSIS). They evaluated safety risks based on the probability, severity, and frequency. Afterward, the risks were categorized, and evaluation strategies were recommended based on the magnitude of risks ranging from negligible to critical risks. Based on the evaluation strategy, negligible risks can be accepted, and minor risks can be transferred to third parties to control the risks. Medium risks should be mitigated with control measures, such as checking PPE and using administrative controls. Major risks should be mitigated by enhancing engineering controls, isolation, and substitution. Critical or intolerable risks should be eliminated completely. Falls due to the installation of green roofs, TPO, solar panels, atrium, rainwater harvesting system, cladding, and weatherproofing were found as critical risks. Struck-by falling objects during installation of modular elements, cladding, and weatherproofing; back injury because of installing TPO, solar panels, and heat reclaim chillers; and punctures due to waste management were reported as critical risks along with others.

Another study by Onubi *et al.* (2020) studied the effect of some green construction practices, which are energy management, waste management, and stormwater management, on construction health and safety performance. The study utilized the partial least squares structural equation modeling method on data collected through a questionnaire survey in Nigeria. The findings indicated that energy management practices have a positive effect on health and safety as opposed to previous studies. This contradiction was explained by the sample of large construction projects conducted by quality contractors. Besides, with the help of renewable energy solutions, the use of generators due to energy shortages that cause noise was eliminated. This was considered another factor explaining the positive relation. The effect of stormwater management was found to be insignificant. This was explained by the familiarity of contractors with stormwater management practices. Like previous studies, waste management practices were found to have a negative effect. Separating and recycling wastes were considered to increase risks, such as lacerations, strains, and sprains, and overexertion and struck-by hazards.

Mohandes and Zhang (2021) developed a comprehensive risk assessment model for occupational health and safety. They identified a comprehensive list of risk parameters which are severity, probability, exposure, detectability, and sensitivity to the failure of safety barriers, to the poor safety climate, to poor site safety, and to adverse environmental conditions. According to the literature review, they specified safety risks. As research methodology, they utilized Logarithmic Fuzzy-based Analytical Network Process and Interval-Valued Pythagorean Fuzzy Extended Technique for Order of Preference by Similarity to Ideal Solution. They conducted a case study in a sustainable construction project to test the model. The developed model was further compared with other assessment methods. Electrocution, crushed by falling crane-related objects, and struck-by falling loads were found critical, and recommendations regarding all identified risks were provided.

More recently, Durdyev *et al.* (2022) investigated safety risks arising from green construction practices. They proposed a fuzzy-based risk matrix by integrating the fuzzy Delphi method and fuzzy best worst method based on data collected from Kazakhstan. The related risks were identified based on literature review and expert review and then, the critical ones were determined using questionnaire survey data. The risks were analyzed based on their aggregated weights and ranked. In the evaluation stage, the safety risks were mapped in the risk matrix and an appropriate strategy (acceptance, mitigation, or elimination) was suggested. They concluded that green construction and design practices influence occupational health and safety negatively. Falling from height and back injury were assessed as severe hazards. Even though the findings reveal that workers are exposed to many risks in green construction projects, they do not necessarily indicate a cause-and-effect relationship. These risks may occur due to many other underlying reasons, such as lack of resources or lack of training.

Kim *et al.* (2022) also developed a predictive model using deep learning. They used 1,766 actual accident cases collected from Korea. Their model used some factors, such as construction scale, number of employees, and occupational classification, to predict medical day. Deep learning provided a more objective, accurate, and reliable model predicting safety accident risks which can help minimize and eliminate risks. This study differs from other studies in terms of research methodology since it utilizes deep learning rather than using linear methods.

Investigating the previous studies, green practices may have a positive, neutral, or negative impact on health and safety based on the applied methods, the familiarity of workers with the tasks, and the environment. Accident and hazard risks may be prevalent on any construction site, not only on green construction projects (Gambatese *et al.*, 2007). Negative effects of green practices may not be applicable to all companies, changing based on the nature of the project and skills of workers (Onubi *et al.*, 2020). However, the criticality of risks should be evaluated appropriately. The context should be carefully evaluated, including the country, applied practices, and rating system requirements. For example, even though several countries or jurisdictions, such as Singapore (Hwang *et al.*, 2018), Hong Kong (Zhang & Mohandes, 2020), Korea (Kim *et al.*, 2022), Nigeria (Onubi *et al.*, 2020), and Kazakhstan (Durdyev *et al.*, 2022), were inspected, the studies mostly utilize data from the US, which dominates the literature.

13.5.1. *Limitations and recommendations for future research*

Health and safety management in construction projects is a well-researched field. However, health and safety management in green construction projects has not been investigated deeply since green construction concept is a relatively new area. The existing body of knowledge compared green and conventional construction projects mostly focusing on green rating systems. Specifically, the LEED rating system has been investigated in terms of construction worker health and safety. It should be noted that most of the existing studies examined outdated versions of LEED, however, recent versions of LEED should also be investigated and analyzed (Karakhan *et al.*, 2022). Further, there is a high number of certification systems; they can also be studied and compared in the context of health and safety. Even though sustainable construction encompasses occupational health and safety, green rating systems were found to have limitations in that respect. Hence, existing rating systems should be modified, or new rating systems should be developed to incorporate occupational health and safety (Chen, 2010). The modified or newly developed rating systems are also recommended to cover not only buildings but also other types of structures such as bridges and roads (Gillen & Gittleman, 2010).

Most of the studies collected data from the US (Gambatese *et al.*, 2007; Rajendran *et al.*, 2009; Dewlaney *et al.*, 2012; Fortunato *et al.*, 2012; Omar *et al.*, 2013; Karakhan & Gambatese, 2017a). That may create a bias. Studies conducted in the US, which are also mostly related to LEED certification, seem to dominate the literature. Future studies should analyze other countries as well rather than only focusing on the US. For example, according to the study of Zhang and Mohandes (2020), in Hong Kong, some findings were found to differ from the US due to weather conditions. Considering different characteristics of developing and developed countries, more research is needed to generalize the findings and create a general framework. Another limitation of the previous studies is the lack of statistically significant and conclusive results, mainly due to small sample sizes (Orogun & Issa, 2021; Karakhan *et al.*, 2022). Future studies are recommended to be conducted using comprehensive, large-sized, and unbiased samples.

Other than the existing research stream, researchers should investigate and identify potential health and safety risks of green construction practices (Schulte *et al.*, 2010). The researchers are further recommended to conduct a life cycle safety risk analysis (Dewlaney *et al.*, 2012). All project phases should be considered. Most of the studies focus on the construction phase and there is an increasing attention to the design phase. However, the predesign, operation, maintenance, and demolition phases should also be examined.

In the existing literature, the factors affecting safety performance are not clearly categorized, and the studies that reveal the differences between green and conventional projects in terms of these factors are very limited. Moreover, a holistic framework for green construction project's health and safety management is required to lead the industry practitioners.

13.5.2. *Implications*

The results of this chapter might foster research studies to be conducted in the health and safety management of green construction projects since the background of the topic and relevant studies are available. Moreover, industry practitioners might benefit from the key outcomes of this chapter to enhance the safety performance either in conventional or green construction. Construction practitioners are recommended to identify, analyze, and mitigate the health and safety risks in green construction projects. Increased and decreased risks due to green practices should be considered. The chapter expresses safety risks which can be valuable to construction practitioners since they can be aware of these risks and take necessary precautions. Some construction management strategies, such as subcontracting or outsourcing jobs that require specific experience to specialty firms, prefabrication, and DfS, can be selected to mitigate safety risks. Being aware of safety risks arising from green construction practices can also help take into account vulnerable groups, such as older workers and immigrant workers (Chen, 2010).

The broader community might further benefit from the key findings to revisit and reshape their strategies in construction safety. Government bodies and institutions regarding green construction and occupational health and safety are recommended to exchange information (NIOSH, 2010).

Raising public awareness toward green and sustainable jobs that incorporate worker health and safety is significant to shape practices (Chen, 2010). There are different types of organizations that have impact on green construction jobs, i.e., government, policymakers, unions, standard-setting institutions, green building organizations, training organizations, and research institutions (Chen, 2010). These organizations can revise the policies and regulations according to issues raised and increase public awareness. The studies also emphasize the importance of training and education. Integration of occupational health and safety into curricula, textbooks, and examinations is significant to eliminate hazards (Chen, 2010; Schulte *et al.*, 2010). Hence, this should be considered while designing curricula and training programs.

13.6. Summary

This chapter investigates the health and safety management in green construction projects. In this respect, the chapter first presents the general safety management implementation in the construction industry including the factors affecting safety performance, and safety audits and reviews. Then, the chapter presents a comparison of safety performance in conventional and green construction projects. The distinguishing elements are discussed through practical case studies. The chapter concludes that there are different views in terms of green construction projects to evaluate them as either safer or more unsafe compared to conventional construction projects. The safety performance might differ with respect to the country of implementation, practices, and performance rating systems.

References

Abas, N. H., Yusuf, N., Suhaini, N. A., Kariya, N., Mohammad, H., & Hasmori, M. F. (2020). Factors affecting safety performance of construction projects: A literature review. *IOP Conference Series: Materials Science and Engineering*, *713*(1). DOI: 10.1088/1757-899X/713/1/012036.

Ahmad, R. K. & Gibb, A. G. (2003) Measuring safety culture with SPMT — Field-data. *Journal of Construction Research*, *4*(1), 29–44.

Aksorn, T. & Hadikusumo, B. H. W. (2008). Critical success factors influencing safety program performance in thai construction projects. *Safety Science, 46,* 709–727.

Bakhiyi, B., Labrèche, F., & Zayed, J. (2014). The photovoltaic industry on the path to a sustainable future — Environmental and occupational health issues. *Environment International, 73,* 224–234. DOI: 10.1016/j.envint.2014.07.023.

Boatman, L., *et al.* (2015). Creating a climate for ergonomic changes in the construction industry. *American Journal of Industrial Medicine, 58,* 858–869.

Chandra, H. P. (2015). Initial investigation for potential motivators to achieve sustainable construction safety and health. *Procedia Engineering, 125,* 103–108. DOI: 10.1016/j.proeng.2015.11.016.

Chen, H. (2010). Green and Healthy Jobs. A report prepared by the Labor Occupational Health Program, University of California at Berkeley. CPWR – Center for Construction Research and Training. Available at: https://lohp. berkeley.edu/materials/green-and-healthy-jobs/.

Choudhry, R. M. (2014). Behavior-based safety on construction sites: A case study. *Accident Analysis and Prevention, 70,* 14–23. DOI: 10.1016/j. aap.2014.03.007.

Darko, A. & Chan, A. P. C. (2016). Critical analysis of green building research trend in construction journals. *Habitat International, 57,* 53–63. DOI: 10.1016/j.habitatint.2016.07.001.

Demirkesen, S. (2011). *Safety Training in Construction.* Chicago, IL: Illinois Institute of Technology.

Demirkesen, S. & Arditi, D. (2015). Construction safety personnel's perceptions of safety training practices. *International Journal of Project Management,* 33(5), 1160–1169. DOI: 10.1016/j.ijproman.2015.01.007.

Dewlaney, K. S., Hallowell, M. R., & Fortunato, B. R. (2012). Safety risk quantification for high performance sustainable building construction. *Journal of Construction Engineering and Management, 138*(8), 964–971. DOI: 10.1061/ (asce)co.1943-7862.0000504.

Dierdorff, E. C., Norton, J. J., Drewes, D. W., Kroustalis, C. M., Rivkin, D., & Lewis, P. (2009). Greening of the world of work: Implications for O*NET-SOC and new and emerging occupations. Report for U.S. Department of Labor Employment and Training Administration, Washington, DC.

Durdyev, S., Mohandes, S. R., Tokbolat, S., Sadeghi, H., & Zayed, T. (2022). Examining the OHS of green building construction projects: A hybrid fuzzy-based approach. *Journal of Cleaner Production, 338*(September 2021), 130590. DOI: 10.1016/j.jclepro.2022.130590.

EU-OSHA. (2013). Occupational safety and health issues associated with green building. Available at: https://osha.europa.eu/en/publications/e-fact-70-occupational-safety-and-health-issues-associated-green-building.

Feeney, R. J. (1986). Why is there resistance to wearing protective equipment at work? Possible strategies for overcoming this. *Journal of Occupational Accidents*, *8*(3), 207–213.

Flin, R., Mearns, K., O'Connor, P., & Bryden, R. (2000). Measuring safety climate: Identifying the common features. *Safety Science*, *34*(1–3), 177–192. DOI: 10.1016/S0925-7535(00)00012-6.

Fortunato III, B. R., Hallowell, M. R., Behm, M., & Dewlaney, K. (2012). Identification of safety risks for high-performance sustainable construction projects. *Journal of Construction Engineering and Management*, *138*(4), 499–508. DOI: 10.1061/(asce)co.1943-7862.0000446.

Fung, I. W., Tam, C. M., Tung, K. C., & Man, A. S. (2005). Safety cultural divergences among management, supervisory and worker groups in Hong Kong construction industry. *International Journal of Project Management*, *23*(7), 504–512. DOI: 10.1016/j.ijproman.2005.03.009.

Gambatese, J. A. & Tymvios, N. (2012). LEED Credits: How they affect construction worker safety. *Professional Safety*, (October), 42–52.

Gambatese, J. A., Behm, M. G., & Rajendran, S. (2008). Design's role in construction accident causality and prevention: Perspectives from an expert panel. *Safety Science*, *46*(4), 675–691. DOI: 10.1016/j.ssci.2007.06.010.

Gambatese, J. A., Rajendran, S., & Behm, M. G. (2007). Understanding the effects on construction worker safety and health. *Professional Safety*, (January), *52*, 28–35.

Ghasemi, F., Mohammadfam, I., Soltanian, A. R., Mahmoudi, S., & Zarei, E. (2015). Surprising incentive: An instrument for promoting safety performance of construction employees. *Safety and Health at Work*, *6*(3), 227–232. DOI: 10.1016/j.shaw.2015.02.006.

Gilding, P., Hogarth, M., & Humphries, R. (2002). Safe companies: An alternative approach to operationalizing sustainability. *Corporate Environmental Strategy*, *9*(4), 390–397.

Gillen, M. & Gittleman, J. L. (2010). Path forward: Emerging issues and challenges. *Journal of Safety Research*, *41*(3), 301–306. DOI: 10.1016/j.jsr.2010.04.005.

Heberle, D. (1998). *Construction Safety Manual*. New York, NY, USA: McGraw-Hill.

Hinze, J. & Wilson, G. (2000). Moving toward a zero injury objective. *Journal of Construction Engineering and Management*, *126*(5), 399–403.

Hinze, J., Godfrey, R., & Sullivan, J. (2013). Integration of construction worker safety and health in assessment of sustainable construction. *Journal of Construction Engineering and Management, 139*(6), 594–600. DOI: 10.1061/(ASCE)CO.1943-7862.0000651.

Hinze, J., Pedersen, C., & Fredley, J. (1998). Identifying root causes of construction accidents. *Journal of Construction Engineering and Management, 124*(1), 67–71. DOI: 10.1061/(asce)0733-9364(2000)126:1(52).

Huang, X. & Hinze, J. (2006). Owner's role in construction safety: Guidance model. *Journal of Construction Engineering and Management, 132*(2), 174–181. DOI: 10.1061/(asce)0733-9364(2006)132:2(174).

Hwang, B. G., Shan, M., & Phuah, S. L. (2018). Safety in green building construction projects in Singapore: Performance, critical issues, and improvement solutions. *KSCE Journal of Civil Engineering, 22*(2), 447–458. DOI: 10.1007/s12205-017-1961-3.

Jamil, A. H. A. & Fathi, M. S. (2016). The integration of lean construction and sustainable construction: A stakeholder perspective in analyzing sustainable lean construction strategies in Malaysia. *Procedia Computer Science, 100*, 634–643. DOI: 10.1016/j.procs.2016.09.205.

Jazayeri, E. & Dadi, G. B. (2017). Construction safety management systems and methods of safety performance measurement: A review. *Journal of Safety Engineering, 6*(2), 15–28. DOI: 10.5923/j.safety.20170602.01.

Jones, T., Shan, Y., & Goodrum, P. M. (2010). An investigation of corporate approaches to sustainability in the US engineering and construction industry. *Construction Management and Economics, 28*(9), 971–983. DOI: 10.1080/01446191003789465.

Karakhan, A. A. (2016). LEED-certified projects: Green or sustainable? *Journal of Management in Engineering, 32*(5), 02516001. DOI: 10.1061/(asce)me.1943-5479.0000451.

Karakhan, A. A. & Gambatese, J. A. (2017a). Identification, quantification, and classification of potential safety risk for sustainable construction in the United States. *Journal of Construction Engineering and Management, 143*(7), 04017018. DOI: 10.1061/(asce)co.1943-7862.0001302.

Karakhan, A. A. & Gambatese, J. A. (2017b). Integrating worker health and safety into sustainable design and construction: Designer and constructor perspectives. *Journal of Construction Engineering and Management, 143*(9), 04017069. DOI: 10.1061/(asce)co.1943-7862.0001379.

Karakhan, A. A., Al-Bayati, A. J., Moud, H. I., & Al-Saffar, O. T. (2022). Impact of green construction on safety performance in the built environment. In *Construction Research Congress 2022.* (pp. 403–411). Arlington Virginia, United States. 2022-3-9 to 2022-3-12.

Khalid, U., Sagoo, A., & Benachir, M. (2021). Safety management system (SMS) framework development — Mitigating the critical safety factors affecting Health and Safety performance in construction projects. *Safety Science, 143*(November 2020). DOI: 10.1016/j.ssci.2021.105402.

Khoza, J. D. & Haupt, T. C. (2021). Measuring health and safety performance of construction projects in South Africa. *IOP Conference Series: Earth and Environmental Science, 654*(1). DOI: 10.1088/1755-1315/654/1/012031.

Kim, J. M., Lim, K. K., Yum, S. G., & Son, S. (2022). A deep learning model development to predict safety accidents for sustainable construction: A case study of fall accidents in South Korea. *Sustainability (Switzerland), 14*(3). DOI: 10.3390/su14031583.

Lee, H. (1995). *Environmental, Health and Safety Auditing Handbook* (2nd edn.) New York: McGraw-Hill.

Lin, J. & Mills, A. (2001). Measuring the occupational health and safety performance of construction companies in Australia. *Facilities, 19*(August), 131–139. DOI: 10.1108/02632770110381676.

Mahmoudi, S., Ghasemi, F., Mohammadfam, I., & Soleimani, E. (2014). Framework for continuous assessment and improvement of occupational health and safety issues in construction companies. *Safety and Health at Work, 5*(3), 125–130. DOI: 10.1016/j.shaw.2014.05.005.

Marchi, L., Antonini, E., & Politi, S. (2021). Green building rating systems (GBRSs). *Encyclopedia, 1*, 998–1009.

Mattoni, B., Guattari, C., Evangelisti, L., Bisegna, F., Gori, P., & Asdrubali, F. (2018). Critical review and methodological approach to evaluate the differences among international green building rating tools. *Renewable and Sustainable Energy Reviews, 82*(April 2017), 950–960. DOI: 10.1016/j. rser.2017.09.105.

McDonald, M. A., Lipscomb, H. J., Bondy, J., & Glazner, J. (2009). Safety is everyone's job: The key to safety on a large university construction site. *Journal of Safety Research, 40*(1), 53–61.

Mohammadi, A., Tavakolan, M., & Khosravi, Y. (2018). Factors influencing safety performance on construction projects: A review. *Safety Science, 109*(June), 382–397. DOI: 10.1016/j.ssci.2018.06.017.

Mohandes, S. R. & Zhang, X. (2021). Developing a holistic occupational health and safety risk assessment model: An application to a case of sustainable construction project. *Journal of Cleaner Production, 291*, 125934. DOI: 10.1016/j.jclepro.2021.125934.

Nawaz, W., Linke, P., & Koç, M. (2019). Safety and sustainability nexus: A review and appraisal. *Journal of Cleaner Production, 216*, 74–87. DOI: 10.1016/j.jclepro.2019.01.167.

Nationational Institute of Occupational Safety and Health (NIOSH) (2010). NIOSH Perspectives on Sustainable Buildings: Green and Safe. White Paper. pp. 1–16. Available at: https://www.cdc.gov/niosh/topics/greenconstruction/pdfs/nioshperspectiveonsustainablebuildings.pdf.

Nationational Institute of Occupational Safety and Health (NIOSH) (2011). Integrating Occupational Safety and Health into the U. S. Green Building Council LEED New Construction Credits: A Preliminary Report. Available at: https://www.cdc.gov/niosh/topics/greenconstruction/pdfs/integrating oshintousgbc_leed_newconstructioncredits_june2011.pdf.

Omar, M. S., Quinn, M. M., Buchholz, B., & Geiser, K. (2013). Are green building features safe for preventive maintenance workers? Examining the evidence. *American Journal of Industrial Medicine*, *56*(4), 410–423. DOI: 10.1002/ajim.22166.

Onubi, H. O., Yusof, N. A., & Hassan, A. S. (2022). Green construction practices: Ensuring client satisfaction through health and safety performance. *Environmental Science and Pollution Research*, *29*(4), 5431–5444. DOI: 10.1007/s11356-021-15705-5.

Onubi, H. O., Yusof, N., & Hassan, A. S. (2020). Adopting green construction practices: Health and safety implications. *Journal of Engineering, Design and Technology*, *18*(3), 635–652. DOI: 10.1108/JEDT-08-2019-0203.

Orogun, B. & Issa, M. H. (2021). Developing, validating and implementing performance metrics to evaluate the health and safety performance of sustainable building projects. *International Journal of Occupational Safety and Ergonomics*. DOI: 10.1080/10803548.2021.1960701.

OSHA. (2019). Commonly used statistics. Available at: https://www.osha.gov/data/commonstats.

OSHA. (2021). Workers' rights, the occupational safety and health administration. Available at: https://www.osha.gov/sites/default/files/publications/osha3021.pdf.

Pinto, A., Nunes, I. L., & Ribeiro, R. A. (2011). Occupational risk assessment in construction industry — Overview and reflection. *Safety Science*, *49*(5), 616–624. DOI: 10.1016/j.ssci.2011.01.003.

Project Management Institute (PMI). (2016). *Construction Extension to the PMBoK Guide*. Newtown Square, Pennsylvania. Project Management Institute.

Rajendran, S. & Gambatese, J. A. (2009). Development and initial validation of sustainable construction safety and health rating system. *Journal of Construction Engineering and Management*, *135*(10), 1067–1075. DOI: 10.1061/(ASCE)0733-9364(2009)135.

Rajendran, S., Gambatese, J. A., & Behm, M. G. (2009). Impact of green building design and construction on worker safety and health. *Journal of Construction Engineering and Management, 135*(10), 1058–1066. DOI: 10.1061/(asce) 0733-9364(2009)135:10(1058).

Reese, C. & Eidson, J. (2006). *Handbook of OSHA Construction Safety and Health* (2nd edn.). USA: Taylor & Francis Group.

Rivera, F. M. La, Mora-Serrano, J., & Oñate, E. (2021). Factors influencing safety on construction projects (FSCPS): Types and categories. *International Journal of Environmental Research and Public Health, 18*(20). DOI: 10.3390/ijerph182010884.

Sailendra, D. & Shah, A. (2013). Study of internal and external safety audit by gap analysis approach in indian construction organizations. *International Journal of Engineering Trends and Applications (IJETA), 2*(3), 6–12. Available at: www.ijetajournal.org.

Sawacha, E., Naoum, S., & Fong, D. (1999). Factors affecting safety performance on construction sites. *International Journal of Project Management, 17*(5), 309–315. DOI: 10.1016/S0263-7863(98)00042-8.

Schulte, P. A., Heidel, D., Okun, A., & Branche, C. (2010). Making green jobs safe. *Industrial Health, 48*, 377–379.

Silins, N. (2009). LEED & the safety profession: Green has come of age. *Professional Safety, 54*(3), 46–49. Available at: https://search.ebscohost. com/login.aspx?direct=true&db=bth&AN=37194281&site=ehost-live.

Tam, C. M., Zeng, S. X., & Deng, Z. M. (2004). Identifying elements of poor construction safety management in China. *Safety Science, 42*(7), 569–586. DOI: 10.1016/j.ssci.2003.09.001.

Tam, C. M., Tong, T. K., Chiu, G. C., & Fung, I. W. (2002). Non-structural fuzzy decision support system for evaluation of construction safety management system. *International Journal of Project Management, 20*(4), 303–313. DOI: 10.1016/S0263-7863(00)00055-7.

Teo, E. A. L. & Ling, F. Y. Y. (2006). Developing a model to measure the effectiveness of safety management systems of construction sites. *Building and Environment, 41*(11), 1584–1592. DOI: 10.1016/j.buildenv.2005.06.005.

The Construction Chart Book: The U.S. Construction Industry and Its Workers, Sixth Edition, CPWR: Silver Spring, MD. Available at https://www.cpwr. com/wp-content/uploads/publications/The_6th_Edition_Construction_ eChart_Book.pdf.

Toole, T. M., Hervol, N., & Hallowell, M. (2006). Designing for construction safety. *Modern Steel Construction, 46*(6), 55.

U.S. Green Building Council. (2016). LEED 2009 for new construction and major renovations rating system. Available at: www.usgbc.org.

WGBC. (2022). World green building council rating tools. Available at: https://www.worldgbc.org/rating-tools (accessed on 1 April 2022).

Wilson, J. M. & Koehn, E. E. (2000). Safety Management: Problems encountered and recommended solutions. *Journal of Construction Engineering and Management, 126*(1), 77–79.

Wong, T. K. M., Man, S. S., & Chan, A. H. S. (2020). Critical factors for the use or non-use of personal protective equipment amongst construction workers. *Safety Science, 126*, 104663.

Yiu, N. S., Sze, N. N., & Chan, D. W. (2018). Implementation of safety management systems in Hong Kong construction industry — A safety practitioner's perspective. *Journal of Safety Research, 64*, 1–9.

Zhang, X. & Mohandes, S. R. (2020). Occupational health and safety in green building construction projects: A holistic Z-numbers-based risk management framework. *Journal of Cleaner Production, 275*, 122788. DOI: 10.1016/j.jclepro.2020.122788.

https://doi.org/10.1142/9789811251429_0014

Chapter 14

Green Construction Project Success

Tayyab Ahmad* and **Tarek Zayed†**

*Department of Civil and Environmental Engineering,
Qatar University, Doha, Qatar*

†*Department of Building and Real Estate, The Hong Kong Polytechnic
University, Hung Hom, Hong Kong*

This chapter entails the concepts as well as a detailed understanding of "success" for green construction projects. The chapter starts with a definition of project success and the key concepts of project success, i.e., success factors and success criteria. Success criteria are the standards on which performance of a project is determined. Success factors, however, are the sociotechnical conditions to ensure that the project is developed as aspired. Differences in the development of green construction projects compared to traditional construction projects are explained to emphasize the unique nature of green construction project success. With a detailed review of research on the subject matter, this chapter provides an in-depth account of the success factors and success criteria. While providing a detailed account of green construction success criteria, the role of green certification in determining project success is explained. Success factors are explained in detail by classifying them with respect to key project stakeholders. The chapter concludes with some key takeaway messages for readers and also provides an account of the limitations in the use of presented findings. In essence, this chapter gives both the academics and practitioners of built environment a thorough understanding of how the success of green construction projects is typically determined and how the likelihood of success in such projects can be improved.

14.1. Introduction: Defining project success

Project success, which is about articulating achievements and outcomes in a project, is typically operationalized using two basic concepts, i.e., success criteria and success factors. The standards, principles, or measures of judgment to gauge the performance of a project are termed as success criteria. In the literature, these are also termed as "performance criteria," "performance metrics," and "performance indicators." An example of success criteria in the case of green construction projects can be the level of performance in environmental rating systems. For instance, the success of a green construction project is often judged based on its performance on green certification systems, such as Leadership in Energy and Environmental Design (LEED), Building Research Establishment Environmental Assessment Method (BREEAM), and Green Star. A green construction project with a Platinum level on LEED certification or a 6-star level on Green Star certification system is typically considered successful at least in environmental terms. However, success in projects is typically not defined using a single criterion, an important takeaway for readers, explained in this chapter.

The other key concept in project success encompasses "success factors," which are the enabling conditions in a project to achieve desired performance on different success criteria. Some common terms used for success factors in the literature are "critical success factors" and "success conditions." An example of success factors in green construction projects is "early involvement of environmentally sustainable design consultants in the planning stage of a project." Early involvement of these professionals in the project ensures that the sustainability measures are better incorporated into the project and "greenwashing" can be avoided.

When success factors and success criteria are considered together in the literature, success factors are considered as independent variables and success criteria are regarded as dependent variables. A number of research

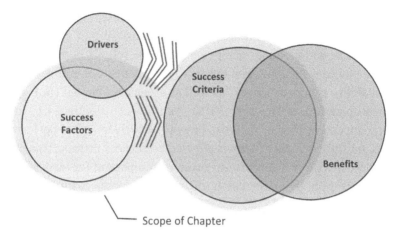

Figure 14.1.   Association of project success with project drivers and benefits.

studies have inquired about the associations among success factors and success criteria. Typically, the performance of a project in a success criterion is associated with a number of success factors, a topic discussed in detail in this chapter.

Prior to a detailed discussion on green construction success factors and success criteria, it is important to explain the association of project success with other allied concepts[1] (see Figure 14.1).

Typically, drivers are the factors setting the direction for a project. In the case of green construction projects, the term "driver" is typically used for factors setting the direction of sustainable outcomes for the project. Project drivers are typically the advantages or gains delivered from a project. The term "benefits" is often used in green construction project development literature to refer to the socioeconomic and environmental advantages delivered/expected from the incorporation of sustainability in a project. Many factors take the roles of both "success criteria" and "benefits" in the case of green construction projects. For instance, "higher energy efficiency" is both a success criterion as well as a benefit in green construction projects (Korkmaz, 2007; Ahn *et al.*, 2013). Success criteria

---

[1]A simplified association of key concepts is provided in this chapter. A more detailed understanding of the association of project success with project drivers and benefits is provided in the following study: Ahmad *et al.* (2019a).

such as "achieving green certification" are significantly influenced by project drivers such as "corporate social responsibility of client's organization." Meanwhile, some factors can have the role of both "drivers" as well as "success factors." For instance, the client's commitment toward sustainability is both a "driver" as well as a "success factor" (Bakar *et al.*, 2010; Ruparathna & Hewage, 2015). As shown in Figure 14.1, success criteria are determined or motivated by project drivers. Also, performance across multiple success criteria is affected by success factors. This chapter only addresses project success; however, it is important for readers to keep in consideration the association of project success with drivers and benefits.

14.1.1. *Scope of this chapter*

Green construction projects are construction projects developed with a diligent consideration toward sustainability. These can be building projects as well as infrastructure projects. One of the popular examples of such projects is green building projects. Among the larger domains of green construction projects, the development of green building projects has received the most attention in research. In this chapter, project success is discussed from the viewpoint of green building projects, unless otherwise mentioned. Owing to the complex nature and multistakeholder dependence of green building projects, the success factors and success criteria of these projects are generally applicable to all kinds of green construction projects.

The life cycle of construction projects can be divided into two phases: development and operation. It is a well-recognized fact in the building industry that the decisions taken during the early stages of project development have a large impact on how a project is developed and how it is operated. From a standpoint of sustainable outcomes, the development and operation phases are strongly interlinked. Provision of sustainable features and approaches during the development phase not only results in sustainable procurement of a project but also results in sustainable operations. For instance, development of a building according to green certification standards can be a success criterion in a project. This is achievable during project development; however, its benefits will be realized not only during project development but also mostly during project operation. Considering

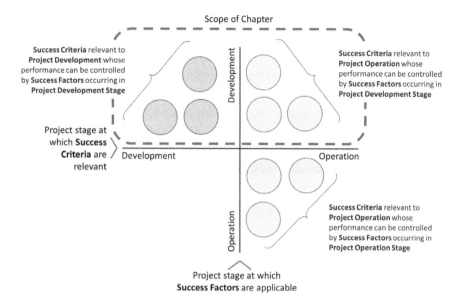

Figure 14.2.   Occurrence of success factors and success criteria across project life cycle.

the life cycle viewpoint, the scope of this chapter is limited to success criteria relevant to project development and operation but affected by success factors only occurring in project development (see Figure 14.2). Success factors occurring in project operation and success criteria affected by only these factors are beyond the scope of this chapter.

14.1.2. *Difference in project success: Green building projects and typical construction projects*

For readers, a key question at this stage can be as follows: "Why do we need special attention toward green building project success?" or "Why the lessons learned regarding project success in traditional construction projects cannot be used for green building projects?" The answer to this is that the development of green building projects differs from traditional construction projects, hence, demanding special attention toward green building project success.

Success factors for traditional construction projects have limited application when it comes to green building projects. This is because the aspirations or definition of success for green building projects is so different from their traditional counterparts that green building projects require some foundational overhauling of project development approaches. For instance, while investigating "passive houses," Rohracher (2001) claims that many approaches to traditional building development are rendered obsolete for a passive house project (a highly efficient type of green building project). The traditional planning procedures, the approaches for component certifications, as well as the quality control practices need to be revisited and revised before being applied to green building projects.

Some previous studies on green building project success have discussed differences between green and non-green building projects. Some key observations from previous studies are as follows:

- *Project objectives*: In terms of project objectives, green building projects must accomplish additional goals in comparison to traditional building projects, namely energy, land, water, and material savings, as well as environmental friendliness (Hwang *et al.*, 2017b).
- *Material supply and availability*: Material supply and availability are more critical in green building construction projects compared to traditional building construction projects (Hwang & Leong, 2013; Hwang *et al.*, 2017a).
- *Project complexity*: Compared to traditional building projects, green building projects encounter more complex problems during the construction process, and project managers are faced with greater challenges (Sang *et al.*, 2018).
- *Integration and collaboration*: The application of sustainability principles in building construction projects adds to the complexity of these projects and thus a greater integration and collaboration among project team members is required as compared to traditional projects (Riley *et al.*, 2004). According to Rohracher (2001), unlike traditional building projects, the successful development of highly efficient green building projects considerably depends on a closer interaction of users, professionals, and suppliers. This is because compared to traditional building projects, in green building projects, the variety of building components has much more complex and stronger mutual dependencies in functional terms. This consequently makes the green buildings act like machines in certain ways.

As green buildings compared to non-green building projects are more complex, have additional project objectives (such as environmental sustainability), and have increased integration and collaboration demands during their development, the success factors for traditional construction projects have limited application for green building projects. Hence, for the identification of success criteria in green building projects, an exclusive focus over these projects is warranted, a topic discussed in detail in the following section.

14.2. Success criteria in green building projects

When it comes to project success, success criteria take precedence over success conditions. This is because success criteria are the "ends" which define the "means," i.e., success factors. Recognizing the importance of success criteria in these terms, Wateridge (1998) stated that "only when the success criteria have been defined can project managers consider the appropriate factors to deliver those criteria." For instance, a project only focused toward performing well in cost and schedule criteria may adopt a different development approach as compared to a project striving to perform well in environment-related criteria. Once a consensus is developed in a project regarding the success criteria to use, it is possible to conduct intermediate or postcompletion audits to identify the reasons for project success or failure. Based on the acquired knowledge, remedial actions can be taken for a project, or the learned lessons can be applied to future projects (De Wit, 1988). Hence, by defining outcomes (i.e., success criteria) in a project, an opportunity is created to see what works (i.e., success factors) and what doesn't.

When considering success from the typical viewpoint of project management (PM), success criteria are mainly about what successful delivery of the project would look like or how the project performance will be at its handover or closeout stage. While this viewpoint can ensure success during project development, it overlooks the operation stage of projects, which is a critical stage in the case of green building projects. Accordingly, project success in this chapter is introduced from a life cycle viewpoint instead of a project development viewpoint. However, considering the theme of this book, the success criteria introduced are those which are controllable during project development phase and exclude the criteria strictly controllable during project operation.

Owing to the level of complexity, sustainability focus, special development context, and stakeholder expectations, green building projects have a dedicated list of success criteria (see Table 14.1) as identified from research studies. Even though research on green building projects is active, research on the subtopic of green building project success criteria is lacking. The list of success criteria provided in Table 14.1 is therefore not exhaustive of all the relevant criteria. Readers are urged to use this success criteria list as a reference in real projects but keep an eye out for criteria missing from this list. Except for the studies by Ahmad *et al.* (2021) and Chan and Adabre (2019), previous green building-related studies shown in Table 14.1 have used the terms "performance criteria," "performance metrics," "performance indicators," and "dependent variables," instead of using the term "success criteria." All these terms indicate a measure of project performance on some judgment criteria. It can be postulated that the use of "success criteria" term has certain connotations associated with it and this may lead to reluctance in the use of this term by the research community. In this chapter, the terms "performance criteria" and "success criteria" have been interchangeably used and imply the same meaning.

As indicated in Table 14.1, some of the success criteria are relevant during the project development stage, such as cost, schedule, and quality performance. Typically, projects are judged for their performance in these criteria until their operational benefits are not realized. Once projects are operational, the criteria relevant to operation stage (as indicated in Table 14.1) become significant. For instance, the Sydney Opera House project clearly underperformed in schedule and cost performance during its development. However, in its operational life, this project is generally regarded as a successful case based on its cultural value and its identity as a national icon.

Similar to traditional construction projects, schedule, cost, quality, and safety performance remain important for green building project success, even though during the project development stage only. "Meeting project aspirations and client's requirements" has been indicated as an important success criterion. This criterion is strongly pegged with

Table 14.1.   Success criteria of green building projects.

	Performance criteria	Project Stage	Yu et al. (2018)	Venkataraman and Cheng, (2018a)	Ahmad et al. (2019b)	Bilec (2008)	El Asmar et al. (2013)	Korkmaz (2007)	Carpenter (2005)	Molenaar et al. (2009)	Enache-Pommer and Horman (2009)	Hanks (2015)	Gultekin et al. (2013b)	Olanipekun et al. (2018)	Sang et al. (2018)	Ahmad et al. (2021)	Chan and Adabre (2019)	Sum
PM performance	Schedule performance	D	×	×			×	×			×	×	×	×				8
	Cost performance	D	×	×			×	×			×	×	×	×				8
	Quality performance	D			×		×	×				×	×		×			6
	Safety performance	D					×	×										2
	Meeting project aspirations and client's requirements	D														×		1
Environmental sustainability	Environmental sustainability	B	×	×	×	×											×	5
	— Consumption of resources and materials	B													×			1
	— Water consumption	O								×					×			2
	— Energy consumption/ energy efficiency	O								×					×	×	×	4
	— Reducing environmental impact and improving environment	B														×		1

(Continued)

Table 14.1.   (*Continued*)

Performance criteria	Project Stage	Yu et al. (2018)	Venkataraman and Cheng, (2018a)	Ahmad et al. (2019b)	Bilec (2008)	El Asmar et al. (2013)	Korkmaz (2007)	Carpenter (2005)	Molenaar et al. (2009)	Enache-Pommer and Horman (2009)	Hanks (2015)	Gultekin et al. (2013b)	Olanipekun et al. (2018)	Sang et al. (2018)	Ahmad et al. (2021)	Chan and Adabre (2019)	Sum
Economic sustainability																	
— Realizing sustainable and efficient building operations	O														×		1
Economic sustainability	B	×		×													2
— Achieving tangible benefits of sustainability	B														×		1
— Reduced lifecycle cost of project	B															×	1
— Business performance	B					×											1
Social sustainability																	
Social sustainability	B			×													1
— Building acting as a human-oriented and occupant-centric development	O														×		1
— Owner and end-users' satisfaction	O	×				×											2

Table 14.1.   (*Continued*)

Performance criteria	Project Stage	Yu et al. (2018)	Venkataraman and Cheng, (2018a)	Ahmad et al. (2019b)	Bilec (2008)	El Asmar et al. (2013)	Korkmaz (2007)	Carpenter (2005)	Molenaar et al. (2009)	Enache-Pommer and Horman (2009)	Hanks (2015)	Gultekin et al. (2013b)	Olanipekun et al. (2018)	Sang et al. (2018)	Ahmad et al. (2021)	Chan and Adabre (2019)	Sum
— Occupant turnover rate	O					×											1
— Absenteeism	O					×											1
— Indoor Environmental Quality	O					×											1
— Acoustic quality	O					×							×				2
— Ventilation	O					×							×				2
— Controllability	O					×											1
— Lighting	O					×							×				2
— Thermal comfort	O					×							×				2
Achieved green building certification	B					×	×		×				×		×		5
— Achieved certification points compared to total points	B											×					1
— Intended vs. achieved certification or score	B					×			×	×							3

Certification as a sustainability measure (row group label)

(*Continued*)

Table 14.1.   (*Continued*)

Performance criteria		Project Stage	Yu et al. (2018)	Venkataraman and Cheng, (2018a)	Ahmad et al. (2019b)	Bilec (2008)	El Asmar et al. (2013)	Korkmaz (2007)	Carpenter (2005)	Molenaar et al. (2009)	Enache-Pommer and Horman (2009)	Hanks (2015)	Gultekin et al. (2013b)	Olanipekun et al. (2018)	Sang et al. (2018)	Ahmad et al. (2021)	Chan and Adabre (2019)	Sum
Design qualities	Project acting as a source of learning	B														×		1
	Achieving good results in a reliable and consistent way	O														×		1
	Building responding to the variations in use	O														×		1
	Building responding to its surroundings	O														×		1
	Balanced design	D														×		1
	Smart character in building	D														×		1
	Organizational relationships	D	×															1
	Public recognition/ Project to act as a benchmark	B	×													×		2

Notes: D = Use/Relevance of a success criterion during project development stage; O = Use/Relevance of a success criterion during project operation stage; B = Use/Relevance of a success criterion during both project development and operation stage.
Source: Adapted from Ahmad *et al.* (2021).

quality performance. For instance, a project which meets predefined aspirations and client's requirements would also perform well in its quality criterion if the client's requirements were well articulated in the project scope. Similarly, both these criteria will be pegged with sustainability performance-related criteria in case sustainability is part of the project scope. This therefore highlights the importance of scope definition in project development. Chapter 8 covers "Green Construction Project Scope Management."

As shown in Table 14.1, for green building projects, alongside the iron triangle of schedule, cost, and quality performance, the three sustainability dimensions (i.e., social, economic, and environmental sustainability) have also been regarded as success criteria. Some studies have considered these three dimensions as performance criteria, while other studies have considered the attributes of these dimensions as performance criteria. For instance, water and energy consumption are considered as performance criteria by some studies. These are attributes of "consumption of resources and materials," a success criterion for green building projects. "Consumption of resources and materials" and "reducing environmental impact and improving environment" are two performance criteria, which are, by definition, part of "environmental sustainability." Some studies have also considered project performance in green certifications as a success criterion. Typically, green certifications such as LEED, Green Star, and BREEAM are based on sustainable development principles even though they pay more attention to environmental sustainability than the other two dimensions. This indicates that the success criteria in Table 14.1 are not mutually exclusive. Hence, a green building project opting for a certification may perform well across a number of success criteria, such as environmental sustainability. This highlights the importance of scope definition in the development of green building projects. Project goals defined well during the planning stage can help ensure synergies in project development where better project performance in some criteria also results in better performance in other criteria.

The success criteria related to PM performance (i.e., schedule, cost, and quality) and sustainability performance criteria (i.e., social, economic, and environmental sustainability) are strongly interlinked in the case of green building projects (Ahmad *et al.*, 2019b). Good or bad project performance in one of these criteria has a reinforcing or a diminishing effect on performance in other criteria. What is important to note here is that the associations among success criteria are controlled by some factors, known as "underlying conditions" (Ahmad *et al.*, 2019b). Among the myriad factors controlling the associations among performance criteria, some factors important to mention here are the use of "life cycle approach in project development," "client's vision and motivation," "integrated design approach," "project delivery method," and "project planning and management approach." Most of these factors are in the control of the project team during project development. This implies that if planned and managed adequately, the development process of a green building project can simultaneously result in good project performance across multiple outcomes (i.e., success criteria). For a thorough understanding of the associations among success criteria and underlying conditions affecting those associations, readers are referred to the detailed study conducted by Ahmad *et al.* (2019b).

Regarding local building codes, many developed regions have postulated such stringent regulatory frameworks that in terms of sustainability performance, buildings developed on regulatory codes are at par with buildings getting green certifications.[2] Even though no success criterion found from previous studies strictly mention "regulations" or "building codes," a criterion titled as "meeting project aspirations and client's requirements" addresses this issue. This is because an implicit aspiration for a project is to have it as a legal project and meeting regulatory requirements simply implies meeting legal status and therefore meeting implicit project aspirations.

Studies have indicated that for green building projects to be considered successful, they need to have balanced design (i.e., balanced attention toward different sustainability values) and have a smart character in their design. Success in such projects is not merely about the use of innovative technology; it is also about getting good operational performance

---

[2] Many local governments in Australia have embraced Green Star certification system and require building projects to have the level of sustainability performance that is at par with different levels of Green Star rating. Details regarding this are accessible using the following link: https://new.gbca.org.au/policy/local-government/.

reliably and consistently. Innovation is typically not time-tested and therefore having innovative design and achieving reliable performance results during building operations are two outcomes hard to achieve together. To be successful, green building projects need to respond to their surroundings (i.e., local ecology and urban context) and must be adaptable to future changes.

For a project to be considered successful, it may need to be publicly recognized and considered a benchmark in a local or global context. To be considered successful, projects need to act as learning grounds for future developments. This is particularly true for innovative high-performing green building projects, as these projects can inform forthcoming developments on whether a particular design approach, management approach, or a sustainable technology works or not. Projects not only need to act as learning sources based on their development approach, but they can also act as learning grounds during their operations by acting as "living labs," a concept gaining popularity during the last decade. Both the success as well as failure of performance in projects can be learned from. Currently, projects lack this transparency of their performance for the general public, however, projects developed to act as learning grounds will have transparency at their cores.

In a discussion of success criteria, an important caveat is related to the success criteria occurring during the operational stage of green building projects. Even though these criteria (such as energy efficiency and indoor environmental quality) are typically relevant in the operational stage of a project to determine its performance, the decisions made, and steps taken during project development stage affect project performance on these criteria. For instance, a disregard toward energy-saving design techniques during project development stage would result in underperformance in energy efficiency criterion during the operational life of a project. Hence, the project performance in almost all the success criteria, whether relevant to project development stage or project operation stage, can be traced back to the decisions and steps taken during project development.

Alongside the success criteria indicated in Table 14.1, the credit categories of green certification systems can also play the role of success criteria, a topic discussed in detail in the following section.

14.2.1. *Certification as a success criterion in green building projects*

In reality, credit categories of certification systems have significantly shaped the success definition of certified green building projects. To put it simpler, credit categories have the role of performance criteria within the frameworks of green certification systems. Some common examples of these credits in LEED certification system include "water efficiency" and "indoor environmental quality." To achieve the desired certification level, a project must perform well across a number of credit categories. Hence, the success of a certified green building project can be defined by its overall level of certification (as indicated in Table 14.1) or by its performance on constituent credit categories (listed in Table 14.2).

When considering green building certification systems as holistic success criteria for sustainability performance, it is important to acknowledge the limitations of these certification systems. While generally it is easy to associate project success with overall performance in green building certification systems (such as Gold or Platinum level in LEED), the use of certification as the only sustainability performance criterion is not risk-free. The following are some key issues which must be considered when using project performance in a certification system as a success criterion:

- Social and environmental sustainability attributes are generally in the purview of popular green building certification systems (see Table 14.2). When it comes to project-specific economic indicators, such as capital cost and life cycle cost performance, there is a general disregard toward economic sustainability among these certification systems (see Figure 14.3). A project only focused on social and environmental aspects may come with a significant economic burden and may not fulfill the basic needs of being successful. Hence, alongside the use of green building certification system as a success criterion, a project should also consider economic sustainability as a success criterion.
- The use of certifications as the only success measure for sustainability performance of a building faces the risk of greenwashing. Even though certification systems are gradually improving and closing the

loopholes, they are still imperfect in their scope, structure, and application. The fundamental sustainability principles overlooked in the frameworks of certification systems may not be addressed in building projects opting for certifications in case certification systems are not used as "means" to "ends" but instead as "ends." The scope of many green building certification systems is typically limited to design and as-built. In most cases, separate certification systems are required to rate the operational performance of green building projects once they enter their service lives. For instance, in Australia, Green Star (design and as-built) is the green building certification system used to rank/certify the performance of a building based on its design and as-built status. Once that building enters its service life, it can opt for NABERS certification, which ranks the operational performance of the building. As the certification oversight is typical until the delivery of a building project, a building may start to underperform in its environmental objectives. For instance, Kurnaz (2021) made a comparison of energy savings of several LEED-certified buildings. The expected energy performance of those buildings as obtained from simulations was compared with their actual energy data in the postconstruction phase. A significant discrepancy between the speculated energy performance (on which LEED certification is awarded) from real energy performance was observed with many buildings underperforming in energy criterion than previously modeled. Due to the scope limitations of green building certification systems, it is possible for a building to get a certification yet provide little benefit for the environment.

- Many building projects rigorously follow sustainability principles in their development and operation. They are by definition green and sustainable buildings but lack in terms of certifications. Hence, using certifications as a success criterion may work only for certified buildings. The performance of non-certified sustainable projects can mostly be determined using the criteria provided in Table 14.1.

14.2.2. *Story of success*

To explain the role of success criteria for a green building project, a hypothetical case can be developed. A developer organization (i.e., project client) is interested in developing a mixed-use commercial building

Table 14.2.   Credit categories of green building certification systems addressing sustainability attributes.

Sustainability attribute	BREEAM (New construction)	Green star (Design and as built)	LEED (V.4. for BD+C)	Living building challenge (3.1)
Innovative practices	Innovation	Innovation	Innovation	
Water efficiency	Water	Water	Water efficiency	Water
Sustainable materials	Materials	Materials	Materials and resources	Materials
Energy performance	Energy	Energy	Energy and atmosphere	Energy
Sustainable transport	Transport	Transport	Location and transportation	Place
Sustainable land use	Land use and ecology	Land use and ecology	Sustainable sites	
Geographically specific needs			Regional priority	
Indoor environment quality	Health and wellbeing	Indoor environment quality	Indoor environmental quality	Health + Happiness
Operational management practices to ensure sustainable outcomes	Management	Management		
Equitable and fair project development				Equity
Aesthetics, inspiration, and education				Beauty
Pollution and waste	Pollution Waste	Emissions		

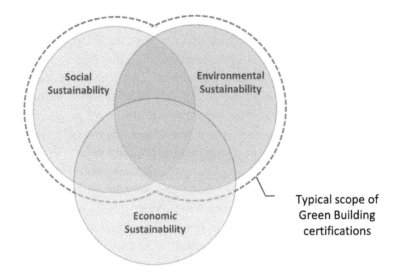

Figure 14.3.   Typical scope of green building certification systems.

entertaining retail, hospitality, and commercial office space. Driven[3] by organizational goals, corporate social responsibility, local regulatory requirements, and an overview of market demand, the developer has decided to build and operate the project as a green building. As the developer team shares these aspirations with the PM consultant and architectural consultant, ideas are generated regarding project aspirations. These ideas result in the development of project charter which includes a detailed understanding of the success criteria.

In project charter, project characteristics reflecting the current and future aspirations of the client (developer organization) are decided. The project development is planned for Victoria, an Australian state. It is decided that Green Star, a rating tool from the Green Building Council of Australia, is a reasonable certification choice in the Australian context. Striving for this certification would mean an occupant-centric and eco-friendly project development. Some local and international cases have

---

[3]Drivers of green building development are beyond the scope of this chapter; however, they have a significant influence in the use of success criteria. For a detailed understanding of the drivers involved in green building development, readers are referred to the following studies: Darko *et al.* (2017), Oyedokun (2017), Labartino (2018), Ahn *et al.* (2013), Ahmad *et al.* (2020).

been brought to the client's attention indicating that a green building may have lower operational costs. Motivated by this, the client has decided a balanced attention toward all three sustainability dimensions, i.e., human-centric, ecofriendly, and reduced operational costs. The client also realizes that they would like the project to act as a benchmark of sustainability performance, an example which can be used by future projects to learn from. To address future risks of obsolescence, they would like to see adaptability in the project implying that the building in its operational life can respond to changing market, business, environmental, and social conditions. Such adaptability of the building also adds to its sustainability outcomes as such a building can endure a longer service life, hence reducing the need for reconstruction. To make the building settle well in urban fabric, make it likable to the public, make it accessible, and make it more environmentally friendly, the client would like to see the building responding to its surroundings. The client would also like the project to have a smart character so that the building would be able to learn, inform, and execute better operational performance through smart technologies, such as the Internet of Things. They realize that in its operational life, the project needs to have consistently good performance. The project aspires to perform well not only in its operational life but also during its development. The client aims to have the building developed within the target time and cost while meeting aspired quality standards and without any accidents occurring on site. All these aspirations form the success criteria for the project in consideration and the performance on these criteria is monitored as the project moves from its inception stage to planning stage and then to construction stage.

While this section provided a detailed understanding of green building project success criteria, the following section addresses the necessary factors for achieving desired project outcomes.

14.3. Success factors in green building projects

Success factors are the enabling conditions contributing to project performance in one or multiple success criteria. When it comes to green building projects, success factors contribute to not only short-term objectives/success criteria such as cost, schedule, and quality performance but also long-term objectives, such as sustainability performance. Some studies have considered success factors as variables with multiple states. For instance, quality of workmanship has been considered a success factor by some studies (Korkmaz *et al.*, 2010b, 2011a; Swarup *et al.*, 2011). By definition, this factor is a variable with multiple states, such as "good" or "bad" workmanship. Some other studies have considered the states of variables as success factors. For instance, the "use of energy and lighting simulations" has been considered a success factor for green building projects (Enache-Pommer & Horman, 2009; Korkmaz *et al.*, 2011a; Gultekin *et al.*, 2013). This factor by definition can be considered the state of a variable, such as the project design approach. In this chapter, the green building-related success factors are presented as originally found from research studies whether as variables or as variable states. Success factors relevant to the attributes of project stakeholders are presented in Table 14.3 and success factors relevant to different aspects/attributes of

Table 14.3.   Success factors related to project stakeholders (adapted from Ahmad *et al.*, 2019a).

Stakeholder	Variable/ state	Relevance to sustainable outcomes	Success factors
Client/ Developer	V	H	Client's commitment/ involvement
	V	H	Commitment of the client's organization to provide finances for green building projects
	S	H	Client as the party proposing 'green' in the project
	V	M	The primary reason for pursuing 'green'
	V		Client type
	V		Client's ability to define the scope and make decisions
	V		Client's capability
	V		Client's ability for team procurement

(Continued)

Table 14.3.   (*Continued*)

Stakeholder	Variable/ state	Relevance to sustainable outcomes	Success factors
	S	M	Client awareness of potential savings from green building project; Clients' knowledge of green building projects
	S	M	Educating the client about the features and requirements of a green building project
	V		The relation between client and project team
Project team	V	H	Team commitment to sustainable development
	V	H	The commitment of Mechanical and Electrical engineers to implement green energy
	S	H	Support from senior management and decision-makers
	V	M	Alignment of team goals with project goals
	V		Project team integration: composition and cohesiveness, team chemistry, team's prior experience as a unit, good working relationships among team members, trust among stakeholders, a well-integrated project team
	V	M	Project team motivation
	V	M	Project ownership
	V	M	Team expertise and experience in green building development
	V		Team communication
	V		Cooperation between architects and engineers
	V		Project team composition and cohesiveness
	S		Adequate enterprise capability

Table 14.3.   (*Continued*)

Stakeholder	Variable/ state	Relevance to sustainable outcomes	Success factors
Design team	V	M	Competence of design consultant: mix-experienced design team, design team's experience in the construction industry, design team's experience in similar type and size of project, design team's decision-making effectiveness, design team's effectiveness in controlling and monitoring of economic design, design team's communication effectiveness, design team's effectiveness of managing conflicts, design team's knowledge relevant to green design, design team's knowledge of green design assessment tools, design team's skills of using design programs, design team's ability to interpret client's needs into efficient green design, design team's speed in producing green design drawings, design team's ability in overcoming green design difficulties
	V		Design team's leadership effectiveness
	V	M	Design consultant's experience and knowledge in green building projects
	V	M	Motivations of design consultants; Commitment level of the architect to produce green design
Contractor	V	M	Subcontractor's 'green' education
	S	M	Providing sustainable education to on-site construction personnel
	S		Training workers to ensure that they operate equipment fully and efficiently
	V		Competence of contractor

(*Continued*)

Table 14.3.   (*Continued*)

Stakeholder	Variable/ state	Relevance to sustainable outcomes	Success factors
Sustainability consultant	V	M	Competence of green building consultant; Experience and awareness of sustainability consultant regarding green building development; Effectiveness of consultant in terms of documentation
Project manager	V	M	Competence and skillfulness of the Project Manager; Experience and awareness of Project Manager regarding green building development
	V		Authority of the Project Manager/Leader
	V		Efforts of the Project Manager to achieve project outcomes
Local market	S	M	Supportive market environment; Market demand for green building projects and high market recognition
Public and neighboring community	S	M	Public awareness and acceptance for green building; Supportive public cognition

Notes: (1) (variable/state): V = Occurrence of a success factor as a variable; S = Occurrence of a success factor as a state of a variable.

(2) *(Relevance to Sustainable Outcomes)*: H = High degree of relevance to sustainable outcomes/criteria; M = Medium degree of relevance to sustainable outcomes/criteria.

Source: Zhou and Smith (2013), Zhang *et al.* (2017), Xia *et al.* (2014), Wang *et al.* (2013), Wai *et al.* (2012), Venkataraman and Cheng (2018b), Tang *et al.* (2019), Swarup *et al.* (2011), Shen *et al.* (2017), Robichaud and Anantmula (2010), Riley *et al.* (2005), Rasekh and McCarthy (2016), Pheng Low *et al.* (2014), Oyebanji *et al.* (2017), Olanipekun *et al.* (2018), Murtagh *et al.* (2016), Molenaar *et al.* (2009), Li *et al.* (2011, 2014), Lei (2005), Lam *et al.* (2010), Korkmaz *et al.* (2011a, 2011b), Kiani *et al.* (2018), Ihuah *et al.* (2014), Hwang *et al.* (2015, 2016, 2017c), Hwang and Ng (2013), Hanks (2015), Gultekin *et al.* (2013a), Gard (2004), Enache-Pommer and Horman (2009a), Elforgani *et al.* (2014), El Asmar *et al.* (2013), Doskočil and Lacko (2018), Dahl *et al.* (2005), Carpenter (2005), Bond (2010), Bilec *et al.* (2009), Bilec (2008), Banihashemi *et al.* (2017), Bakar *et al.* (2010), Aktas *et al.* (2012), Aktas and Ozorhon (2015).

project development are presented in Table 14.4. In terms of project stake-holders, most conditions are related to the project team, design team, and project client. This implies that project success is significantly affected by the attributes of the project team and client.

Client attributes contributing to project success: Project client/developer has a critical role in green building project development and therefore, the success factors associated with project client must be given due consideration. As indicated in Table 14.3, there are a number of client attributes which impact project success and one of the outstanding attributes can be the "type of client." In case a client is merely playing the role of a developer to develop and subsequently sell the building, the incentives and therefore motivation for sustainability outcomes may not be so high, especially when sustainability initiatives cost more and take longer to implement. On the contrary, a client who is not only a developer but also a subsequent owner of a building may have more motivation for sustainability outcomes, especially if they are related to user satisfaction and reduced life cycle costs. Another critically important client attribute is their reason for pursuing "green" in a building project. This attribute establishes the motivation to pursue sustainable outcomes in the project. For instance, in the event the reason for sustainable outcomes is mere fulfillment of local building regulations, the client may only be interested in sustainable outcomes which barely meet the regulations, nothing more. On the contrary, a client driven toward "green" because of their corporate social responsibility can be highly motivated to have better sustainable outcomes in their project. In the same context, an important question is as follows: Where did the idea of green for the project originate? In the event the idea originated from the client's side instead of the project team members, there will be higher likelihood that the client will pursue sustainable outcomes. Another related factor is "how knowledgeable the client is regarding sustainability, green building projects, and potential savings from green building projects." Higher awareness in these aspects paves the path to project success. If the client's organization lacks awareness in this regard, there must be arrangements to educate them. Typically, this role is played by architectural consultants, although sustainability consultants are better equipped with this information but may only have limited role in educating clients because of their late engagement in project development. All these attributes contribute toward the commitment of client toward sustainability, which is itself a success factor. The client's commitment needs to be strong enough to result in financial support for sustainability initiatives. While client's motivation and commitment toward sustainability outcomes matter, their capabilities also contribute toward project success. The project benefits from client's capacity to articulate the project scope well, make appropriate decisions, and bring the project team on board. Lastly, the relationship between the client and the project team also contributes to project success by affecting the flow of ideas between the two parties.

Design consultant attributes contributing to project success: For green building projects, the design consultant is often the lead consultant brought on board. The competence of these stakeholders in green building development, their leadership, and their commitment to sustainable outcomes may decide if and how a project achieves its sustainability outcomes. The competence of the design team contributing to project success can comprise many attributes (see Table 14.3), which most noticeably include their knowledge and experience of green design, knowledge of sustainability assessment, and ability to overcome green design difficulties. The leadership of the design consultant and their commitment to producing a green design affect the successful delivery of sustainable outcomes directly and indirectly.

Project manager attributes contributing to project success: The project manager also has a significant role to play in the success of a green building project. In this regard, an important attribute is the authority of the project manager in the project as a leader. If the project manager can practice such leadership, it is possible to align the efforts of the entire project team toward project goals. As a leading authority, the efforts of the project manager to achieve project outcomes significantly contribute to project success. The competence and skillfulness of the project manager in green building development is particularly important as their awareness and previous experience in such projects can enable them to address the particular challenges of green building projects.

Sustainability consultant attributes contributing to project success: Owing to the critically important role of the sustainability consultant in green building development, the attributes of this stakeholder have much contribution toward project success. Sustainability consultants need to be well experienced and aware of green building development. Also, they need to be well aware of the documentation required for green building certification.

Contractor attributes contributing to project success: The contractor is the party executing the project design on the construction site, which implies that the competence of the contractor in terms of the experience and awareness related to green building development can contribute to the successful delivery of sustainable outcomes. The contractor may need to train their workers for efficient use of construction equipment. They may also need to provide sustainable education to onsite construction personnel. Since the contractor is responsible for the jobs performed by subcontractors, they are also responsible for the "green" education of subcontractors.

Project team attributes contributing to project success: The project team as a whole needs to have some attributes to realize the successful development of a green building project. The team should have expertise and experience in green building development. The team needs to be committed to sustainable development and should have its goals aligned with project goals. Particularly, mechanical and electrical engineers should be committed to implement energy saving in design. The project team should exhibit enterprise capabilities and should take ownership of the project. The team should be so well integrated that it works as a unit, and particularly architects and engineers should have good cooperation among them. Different parties in the project team should be able to openly communicate which leads to a collaborative project environment.

In terms of the project development aspects, a large number of success factors (see Table 14.4) are related to team formation, procurement, and contractual aspects; project planning; project design; and project monitoring, risk management, and quality assurance. Some of the highly studied success factors (see Tables 14.3 and 14.4) include client's commitment, project team integration, team expertise and experience, team

Table 14.4.   Success factors related to project attributes.

Theme	Variable/ State	Relevance to sustainable outcomes	Success factors
Budgetary and financial issues	V	H	Cost premium of green building projects; Cost of sustainable materials, products and technology
	S		Strong financial capability of client; Adequate funding and resources for project development
	S		Innovative financing methods
Innovation and diffusion	S		Innovative management approaches
	S	M	Use of innovative technological approaches
	S		Advanced machinery and equipment
	V	M	Use of technology
	S		Adopting tried and tested technologies; Using appropriate construction technology
	S	M	Use of advanced technology and automation for construction work by the contractor
	S	H	Incorporating innovation in design
	S		Effective and efficient software development and application
Knowledge, awareness and perceptions	S	H	Understanding of project and project objectives
	V	H	Knowledge management
	S	H	Reliability and quality of the specification, guide and benchmarking systems
Policy	S	M	Adequate policy system
	S	H	Effective environmental compliance and auditing programs
	S		Adequate policy execution

Table 14.4.   (*Continued*)

Theme	Variable/ State	Relevance to sustainable outcomes	Success factors
Project constraints	V	M	Project site condition
	V		Project type
	V		Project size; Scope of work
	V		Land issues
	V	H	Geography and climatic conditions
	V		Economic environment
	V		Socio-political environment
	V	H	Availability of sustainable building materials
	V	M	Good accessibility and provision of adequate alternative transport modes
Project focus, goals and ambitions	S	H	Defining project goals: the selection of green features that naturally align with the other project goals; aligning sustainability with the business case and corporate strategy
	S	H	Clear and realistic goals and objectives; Clear priorities of stakeholders
	S	H	Ensuring that the preliminary budget is aligned with project goals
	V	H	Importance of 'green' for the project
	S	H	Ensuring cost-effectiveness of work; Finalizing economic and ecological goals based on cost/ benefit analysis

(*Continued*)

Table 14.4.   (*Continued*)

Theme	Variable/ State	Relevance to sustainable outcomes	Success factors
Integration	V	H	Timing of introducing 'green'
	S		Transparent delivery process
	S		Adequate information/communication channels
	S		Level of design integration; Integrated design approaches
Project monitoring, risk management and quality assurance	V		Performance monitoring, feedback and control
	V		Schedule control
	S		Regular health and safety reports during construction and operational stages
	S		Incorporating effective risk management
	S		Implementing troubleshooting
	S		Strong/detailed plan effort in design and construction
	V		The completion level of construction documents
	S		Use of commissioning process
	S		Use of envelope mock-ups
	V		Quality of workmanship
	S		Quality control inspections
Project design	S	H	Client maintaining active participation in the green design process
	S	M	Use of quantitative metrics
	S	M	Use of energy and lighting simulations
	S	H	Strong/detailed effort in design
	S	M	Regular inspection of design specification and building code to prevent discrepancy

Table 14.4.   (*Continued*)

Theme	Variable/ State	Relevance to sustainable outcomes	Success factors
	S	M	Economic design and efficient use of resources
	S	M	Appropriate land use and development plan
	S		Check for errors and discrepancies in design documents before submitting for approval to avoid deviations or corrections
	S		Performing sufficient studies and analysis on project requirements and complexity before work commences
	S	M	Adding flexibility in design to allow future expansion
	S		Simplicity/low level of complexity in building design
	S		Design of building to fulfill constructability
	S	H	Design focus on energy-efficiency
	S		Ensuring that the interior fit-out matches the base building
	S	H	Design team's attention to green design and construction details
Expert engagement	S		Timing of contractor's involvement; Contractor's involvement in design stages
	S		Designer's involvement in construction stages
	S		Timing of key participants' involvement; Early involvement of key project participants

(*Continued*)

Table 14.4.   (*Continued*)

Theme	Variable/ State	Relevance to sustainable outcomes	Success factors
	S		Involvement of the Facility Management team in the design stage
	S	H	Involvement of a green consultant; Involvement of a green professional throughout the project development; Dedicated department for sustainability
	S		Involvement of commissioning professional from the project onset
Project planning	S		Selection of prime location for the project
	S		Site selection based on community input
	S	H	Designing building as per standards; Following LEED checklist and documenting system at the feasibility stage
	S	M	Efficient compilation and submission of documentation for certification
	S		Avoiding setback in review and approval of documents
	S	H	Early evaluation and adoption of environmental considerations
	S		Minimal scope changes; Minimizing change orders during construction; Avoiding design changes
	S		Effective change management
	S		Realistic schedule estimate
	S		Realistic cost estimate
	S		Adequate project planning

Table 14.4.   (*Continued*)

Theme	Variable/ State	Relevance to sustainable outcomes	Success factors
	S	M	Using whole life costing approach; Whole life PM
	S		Adequate allocation of resources
	S	M	Community engagement; Active stakeholder involvement; Consulting meetings with tenants/end-users
Team formation, procurement and contractual aspects	S		Clearly articulated responsibilities; Creating accountabilities, expectations, roles and responsibilities
	V		Design team's effectiveness in controlling and monitoring design development
	V		Project delivery method
	V		Contractual terms used
	S	M	Contracts having incentives for implementing sustainable practices and exceeding sustainability goals; Contract incentives/penalties
	S		Completeness and adequacy of project design and specifications
	S	H	'Green' requirements in the contract
	V		Contractual relations for consultants
	V		Contractual relations for core team members
	S		Procurement method costs
	V		The primary process for team selection/ procurement
	S		Selection of companies relative to the project size
	S	H	Importance of sustainability-related criteria in the request for proposal

Table 14.4.   (*Continued*)

Theme	Variable/ State	Relevance to sustainable outcomes	Success factors
	S		Contractor's procurement: Emphasis on high-quality workmanship; Comprehensive contractors' portfolio investigation in terms of their level of awareness of the sustainability concept and their previous records of sustainable project implementation; Checking contractors' resources and capabilities before awarding the contract; Using the open-book subcontracting process which allows the client to have access to the estimates and pricing submitted by subcontractors

Notes: (1) (regarding variable/state): V = Occurrence of a success factor as a variable; S = Occurrence of a success factor as a state of a variable.

(2) *(regarding relevance to sustainable outcomes)*: H = High degree of relevance to Sustainable outcomes/criteria; M = Medium degree of relevance to Sustainable outcomes/criteria.

Source: Adapted from Ahmad *et al.* (2019a), Zhou and Smith (2013), Zhang *et al.* (2017), Xia *et al.* (2014), Wang *et al.* (2013), Wai *et al.* (2012), Venkataraman and Cheng (2018b), Tang *et al.* (2019), Swarup *et al.* (2011), Shen *et al.* (2017), Robichaud and Anantatmula (2010), Riley *et al.* (2005), Rasekh and McCarthy (2016), Pheng Low *et al.* (2014), Oyebanji *et al.* (2017), Olanipekun *et al.* (2018), Murtagh *et al.* (2016), Molenaar *et al.* (2009), Li *et al.* (2011, 2014), Lei (2005), Lam *et al.* (2010), Korkmaz *et al.* (2011a, 2011b), Kiani *et al.* (2018), Ihuah *et al.* (2014), Hwang *et al.* (2015, 2016, 2017c), Hwang and Ng (2013), Hanks (2015), Gultekin *et al.* (2013a), Gard (2004), Enache-Pommer and Horman (2009a), Elforgani *et al.* (2014), El Asmar *et al.* (2013), Doskočil and Lacko (2018), Dahl *et al.* (2005), Carpenter (2005), Bond (2010), Bilec *et al.* (2009), Bilec (2008), Banihashemi *et al.* (2017), Bakar *et al.* (2010), Aktas *et al.* (2012), Aktas and Ozorhon (2015).

communication, competence of design consultant, competence of project manager, support from senior management, adequate funding of project, defining project goals, design integration, performance monitoring and control, risk management, completion level of construction documents, involvement of sustainability consultant, stakeholder engagement, project delivery method, contractual terms, and team procurement process. Some highly studied success conditions are related to the timeliness of project activities. For instance, the timing of contractors' involvement, the timing of key participants' involvement, and the early adoption of environmental considerations.

While all of the reported factors contribute to project success, some of the success factors have a direct relation to the achievement of sustainable project objectives compared to other factors (see column 3 of Tables 14.3 and 14.4). For instance, "cost of sustainable materials" is a success factor highly relevant to the achievement of sustainable objectives/outcomes/criteria in a project. In case sustainable materials are too expensive to be used on a project, their lack of affordability is counterproductive in achieving project sustainability. On the contrary, the "authority of project manager" is a success factor which results in project success across multiple criteria instead of only sustainability criteria/outcomes.

14.4. Conclusion

This chapter started with an overview of the key concepts in project success, i.e., success factors and success criteria. First, the associations of project success with project drivers and benefits were explained. Subsequently, the distinction of green building projects (as a type of green construction projects) from traditional construction projects was explained which supports the need for a focused study on green building project success. This was followed by a detailed discussion regarding the success criteria of green building projects. Some associations among success criteria were also explained. Lastly, a detailed account of success factors involved in green building projects was provided. Success factors were arranged in terms of the characteristics of project stakeholders and the attributes of project development. The success factors directly related to the achievement of sustainability outcomes/criteria include the following:

- *Project client*: Client's commitment/involvement in project sustainability, commitment to provide finances for sustainable elements, active participation in green design process, and awareness of green building projects and potential savings from them; process of educating the client about green building features and requirements; client as the key party (driver) proposing "green" in a project; and the primary reason why the client is pursuing "green" (for example, for better marketing or higher Return on Investment (ROI).

- *Project team*: Project team's motivation and commitment to sustainable development, and expertise and experience in green building development; team aligning its goals toward project goals; high degree of team integration (details in Table 14.3); and team taking project ownership.

- *Design consultant*: Design consultant's competence (details in Table 14.3), motivation and commitment toward green design, attention to green design and construction details, and experience and knowledge in green building projects.

- *Contractor and subcontractor*: Subcontractor's "green" education; process of providing sustainable education to onsite construction personnel; and contractor's use of advanced technology and automation for construction work.

- *Sustainability consultant*: Sustainability consultant's competence, experience and awareness in green building development, and effectiveness/professionalism in matters of documentation.

- *Engineering consultant*: Mechanical and electrical engineers' commitment toward the use of green energy.

- *Project manager*: Project manager's competence, skillfulness, experience, and awareness of green building development.

- *Market and public recognition*: Market demand for green building projects; and public awareness and acceptance for green building projects.

- *Budgetary and financial issues*: Affordability of sustainable materials, products, and technology.

- *Expert engagement*: Involvement of a green consultant throughout the project development and having a dedicated department for sustainability during project development.

- *Innovation and diffusion*: Innovation in design and using innovative technological approaches.

- *Timeliness*: Early introduction of "green" concept in project.

- *Knowledge, awareness, and perceptions*: Project team's understanding of project and project objectives; and reliability and quality of the specifications and benchmarking systems.
- *Policy*: Project following environmental compliance and auditing programs.
- *Project constraints*: Availability of sustainable building materials; and good project accessibility and provision of adequate alternative transport modes.
- *Project design*: Strong/detailed effort in design; design focus on energy efficiency; use of quantitative metrics; use of energy and lighting simulations; regular inspection of design specifications and building codes to prevent discrepancy; economic design and efficient use of resources; appropriate land use and development plan; and flexibility in design for future expansion.
- *Project focus, goals, and ambitions*: Defining clear and realistic sustainability goals and objectives; clear priorities of stakeholders; ensuring that the preliminary budget is aligned with project goals; importance of "green" for the project; ensuring cost-effectiveness of work; and finalizing economic and ecological goals based on cost/benefit analysis.
- *Project planning*: Designing building as per standards; following LEED checklist and documenting system at the feasibility stage; early evaluation and adoption of environmental considerations; efficient compilation and submission of documentation for certification; using the whole life costing approach; whole life Project Management (PM); community engagement; active stakeholder involvement; and consulting meetings with tenants/end-users.
- *Team formation, procurement, and contractual aspects*: "Green" requirements in the contract; importance of sustainability-related criteria in the request for proposal; contracts having incentives for implementing sustainable practices and exceeding sustainability goals; and contract incentives/penalties.

The purpose of this chapter was to provide a comprehensive account of the concept and content related to green building project success. The following are some recommendations for readers when using the findings provided in this chapter:

- This chapter has provided a detailed account of success factors and success criteria of green building projects. While green building projects are a large segment of sustainable construction projects, they do not entirely represent sustainable construction projects. Alongside green building projects, green infrastructure projects also constitute sustainable construction projects. While the key concepts and many individual factors discussed in this chapter may also apply to the larger domain of sustainable construction projects, readers are suggested to look for specialized studies on green infrastructure projects elsewhere.

- This chapter provided a detailed account of green building project success in terms of their success factors and success criteria. It must be noted that there is no equal emphasis of research studies on all the success factors and criteria reported in this chapter. This implies that success factors and criteria do not have equal importance. It is logical to state that some criteria are more representative of green building project success than other criteria. Also, some success factors contribute more toward project success than other factors.

- Success criteria and factors do not occur in isolation, instead they occur in factor networks where change in one factor introduces changes in other factors. This therefore implies that there is more value in studying these factors (both success factors and success criteria) together instead of individually. The interrelationships among success factors and interrelationships among success criteria have not received much attention in research studies. Future research can develop this area of inquiry.

- In real green building projects, one may not find a complete representation of the success criteria provided in this chapter. A real-life project may have used some criteria listed in this chapter and missed the rest. The logic of this lies in the fact that every project is developed in a unique context where different aspirations lead to different criteria for success/performance judgment. Similarly, a real green building project may have been successfully developed but may have only partially relied on the success factors provided in this chapter.

- Even though in this chapter authors have attempted to provide a comprehensive account of success factors and success criteria related to green building projects, the lists of factors are by no means complete. Researchers and industry experts should be on the lookout for factors missing in the lists provided. Sustainability in buildings is an evolving topic. In a temporal context, such projects may keep on evolving and therefore future inquiries should keep looking for factors missed by previous studies.

References

Ahmad, T., Aibinu, A. A., & Stephan, A. (2019a). Managing green building development — A review of current state of research and future directions. *Building and Environment, 155*, 83–104.

Ahmad, T., Aibinu, A. A., & Stephan, A. (2020). Green buildings in Australia: Explaining the difference of drivers in commercial and residential sector. In R. Roggema & A. Roggema (Eds.), *Smart and Sustainable Cities and Buildings* (pp 535–547). Cham: Springer International Publishing.

Ahmad, T., Aibinu, A. A., & Stephan, A. (2021). Green building success criteria: Interpretive qualitative approach. *Journal of Architectural Engineering, 27*, 04020045.

Ahmad, T., Aibinu, A. A., Stephan, A., & Chan, A. P. (2019b). Investigating associations among performance criteria in Green Building projects. *Journal of Cleaner Production, 232*, 1348–1370.

Ahn, Y. H., Pearce, A. R., Wang, Y., & Wang, G. (2013). Drivers and barriers of sustainable design and construction: The perception of green building experience. *International Journal of Sustainable Building Technology and Urban Development, 4*, 35–45.

Aktas, B. & Ozorhon, B. (2015). Green building certification process of existing buildings in developing countries: Cases from Turkey. *Journal of Management in Engineering, 31*.

Aktas, C. B., Ryan, K. C., Sweriduk, M. E., & Bilec, M. M. (2012). Critical success factors to limit constructability issues on a net-zero energy home. *Journal of Green Building, 7*, 100–115.

Bakar, A. H. A., Abd Razak, A., Abdullah, S., Awang, A., & Perumal, V. (2010). Critical success factors for sustainable housing: A framework from the project management view. *Asian Journal of Management Research, 1*, 66–80.

Banihashemi, S., Hosseini, M. R., Golizadeh, H., & Sankaran, S. (2017). Critical success factors (CSFs) for integration of sustainability into construction project management practices in developing countries. *International Journal of Project Management*, *35*, 1103–1119.

Bilec, M. M. (2008). *Investigation of the Relationship Between Green Design and Project Delivery Methods*. Lawrence Berkeley National Laboratory.

Bilec, M. M., Ries, R. J., Needy, K. L., Gokhan, M., Phelps, A. F., Enache-Pommer, E., Horman, M. J., Little, S. E., Powers, T. L., & McGregor, E. (2009). Analysis of the design process of green children's hospitals: Focus on process modeling and lessons learned. *Journal of Green Building*, *4*, 121–134.

Bond, S. (2010). Lessons from the leaders of green designed commercial buildings in Australia. *Pacific Rim Property Research Journal*, *16*, 314–338.

Carpenter, D. S. (2005). Effects of contract delivery method on the LEED (trademark) score of US Navy Military Construction Projects (Fiscal years 2004–2006). Master Dessertation, Oregon State University.

Chan, A. P. C. & Adabre, M. A. (2019). Bridging the gap between sustainable housing and affordable housing: The required critical success criteria (CSC). *Building and Environment*, *151*, 112–125.

Dahl, P., Horman, M., Pohlman, T., & Pulaski, M. (2005, April 5-7, 2005). *Evaluating Design-Build-Operate-Maintain Delivery as a Tool for Sustainability*. Paper presented at the Construction Research Congress 2005: Broadening Perspectives — Proceedings of the Congress, San Diego, California.

Darko, A., Zhang, C., & Chan, A. P. (2017). Drivers for green building: A review of empirical studies. *Habitat International*, *60*, 34–49.

De Wit, A. (1988). Measurement of project success. *International Journal of Project Management*, *6*, 164–170.

Doskocil, R. & Lacko, B. (2018). Risk management and knowledge management as critical success factors of sustainability projects. *Sustainability*, *10*, 1438.

El Asmar, M., Hanna, A. S., & Loh, W.-Y. (2013). Quantifying performance for the integrated project delivery system as compared to established delivery systems. *Journal of Construction Engineering and Management*, *139*, 04013012.

Elforgani, M. S. A., Alnawawi, A., & Rahmat, I. B. (2014). The association between client qualities and design team attributes of green building projects. *ARPN Journal of Engineering and Applied Sciences*, *9*, 160–172.

Enache-Pommer, E., & Horman, M. (2009, April 5-7, 2009). *Key Processes in the Building Delivery of Green Hospitals*. Paper presented at the Construction Research Congress, Seattle, Washington, USA.

Gard, P. T. (2004). Fast and innovative delivery of high performance building: Design-build delivers with less owner liability. *Strategic Planning for Energy and the Environment, 23*, 7–22.

Gultekin, P., Korkmaz, S., Riley, D. R., & Leicht, R. M. (2013). Process indicators to track effectiveness of high-performance green building projects. *Journal of Construction Engineering and Management, 139*, A4013005.

Hanks, N. M. (2015). Investigation into the effects of project delivery methods on LEED targets. MSc Thesis, University of San Francisco.

Hwang, B. G. & Leong, L. P. (2013). Comparison of schedule delay and causal factors between traditional and green construction projects. *Technological and Economic Development of Economy, 19*, 310–330.

Hwang, B. G. & Ng, W. J. (2013). Project management knowledge and skills for green construction: Overcoming challenges. *International Journal of Project Management, 31*, 272–284.

Hwang, B. G., Shan, M., & Supa'at, N. N. B. (2017b). Green commercial building projects in Singapore: Critical risk factors and mitigation measures. *Sustainable Cities and Society, 30*, 237–247.

Hwang, B. G., Zhao, X., & Tan, L. L. G. (2015). Green building projects: Schedule performance, influential factors and solutions. *Engineering, Construction and Architectural Management, 22*, 327–346.

Hwang, B. G., Zhu, L., & Ming, J. T. T. (2016). Factors affecting productivity in green building construction projects: The case of Singapore. *Journal of Management in Engineering, 33*, 04016052.

Hwang, B. G., Zhu, L., & Tan, J. S. H. (2017c). Identifying critical success factors for green business parks: Case Study of Singapore. *Journal of Management in Engineering, 33*, 04017023-1--04017023-13.

Hwang, B. G., Shan, M., Phua, H., & Chi, S. (2017a). An exploratory analysis of risks in green residential building construction projects: The case of Singapore. *Sustainability, 9*, 1116.

Ihuah, P. W., Kakulu, I. I., & Eaton, D. (2014). A review of Critical Project Management Success Factors (CPMSF) for sustainable social housing in Nigeria. *International Journal of Sustainable Built Environment, 3*, 62–71.

Kiani Mavi, R. & Standing, C. (2018). Identifying critical success factors for green business parks: Case Study of Singapore. *Journal of Cleaner Production, 194*, 751–765.

Korkmaz, S. (2007). Piloting evaluation metrics for high performance green building project delivery. Doctoral dissertation, The Pennsylvania State University.

Korkmaz, S., Riley, D., & Horman, M. (2010). Piloting evaluation metrics for sustainable high-performance building project delivery. *Journal of Construction Engineering and Management, 136*, 877–885.

Korkmaz, S., Riley, D., & Horman, M. (2011a). Assessing project delivery for sustainable, high-performance buildings through mixed methods. *Architectural Engineering and Design Management, 7*, 266–274.

Korkmaz, S., Swarup, L., & Riley, D. (2011b). Delivering sustainable, high-performance buildings: Influence of project delivery methods on integration and project outcomes. *Journal of Management in Engineering, 29*, 71–78.

Kurnaz, A. (2021). Green building certificate systems as a greenwashing strategy in architecture. *Bartın University International Journal of Natural and Applied Sciences, 4*, 72–88.

Labartino, I. (2018). Building certification as a driver in green building design: The holistic appoarch of WELL. Doctoral dissertation, Politecnico di Torino.

Lam, P. T., Chan, E. H., Poon, C. S., Chau, C. K., & Chun, K. P. (2010). Factors affecting the implementation of green specifications in construction. *Journal of Environmental Management, 91*, 654–661.

Lei, Z. (2005). Is private finance initiative a good mechanism to deliver sustainable construction? In *The 2005 World Sustainable Building Conference*, September 27–29, 2005. (pp. 4035–4042). Tokyo.

Li, Y. Y., Chen, P.-H., Chew, D. A. S., & Teo, C. C. (2014). Exploration of critical resources and capabilities of design firms for delivering green building projects: Empirical studies in Singapore. *Habitat International, 41*, 229–235.

Li, Y. Y., Chen, P.-H., Chew, D. A. S., Teo, C. C., & Ding, R. G. (2011). Critical project management factors of AEC firms for delivering green building projects in Singapore. *Journal of Construction Engineering and Management, 137*, 1153–1163.

Molenaar, K., Sobin, N., Gransberg, D., McCuen, T., Korkmaz, S., & Horman, M. (2009). Sustainable, high performance projects and project delivery methods: A state-of-practice report. *White Paper for the Design-Build Institute of America and the Charles Pankow Foundation.*

Murtagh, N., Roberts, A., & Hind, R. (2016). The relationship between motivations of architectural designers and environmentally sustainable construction design. *Construction Management and Economics, 34*, 61–75.

Olanipekun, A. O., Xia, B., Hon, C., & Darko, A. (2018). Effect of motivation and owner commitment on the delivery performance of green building projects. *Journal of Management in Engineering, 34*, 04017039-1--04017039-14.

Oyebanji, A. O., Liyanage, C., & Akintoye, A. (2017). Critical Success Factors (CSFs) for achieving sustainable social housing (SSH). *International Journal of Sustainable Built Environment, 6*, 216–227.

Oyedokun, T. B. (2017). Green premium as a driver of green-labelled commercial buildings in the developing countries: Lessons from the UK and US. *International Journal of Sustainable Built Environment, 6*, 723–733.

Pheng Low, S., Gao, S., & Lin Tay, W. (2014). Comparative study of project management and critical success factors of greening new and existing buildings in Singapore. *Structural Survey, 32*, 413–433.

Rasekh, H. & Mccarthy, T. J. (2016). Delivering sustainable building projects–challenges, reality and success. *Journal of Green Building, 11*, 143–161.

Riley, D., Sanvido, V., Horman, M., Mclaughlin, M., & Kerr, D. (2005). Lean and green: The role of design-build mechanical competencies in the design and construction of green buildings. In *Construction Research Congress*, (pp. 1–8).

Riley, D. R., Magent, C. S., & Horman, M. J. (2004). Sustainable metrics: A design process model for high performance buildings. In *CIB World Building Congress*, (pp. 1–9). May 2–7, Toronto, CIB, The Netherlands.

Robichaud, L. B. & Anantatmula, V. S. (2010). Greening project management practices for sustainable construction. *Journal of Management in Engineering, 27*, 48–57.

Rohracher, H. (2001). Managing the technological transition to sustainable construction of buildings: A socio-technical perspective. *Technology Analysis & Strategic Management, 13*, 137–150.

Ruparathna, R. & Hewage, K. (2015). Sustainable procurement in the Canadian construction industry: Current practices, drivers and opportunities. *Journal of Cleaner Production, 109*, 305–314.

Sang, P., Liu, J., Zhang, L., Zheng, L., Yao, H., & Wang, Y. (2018). Effects of project manager competency on green construction performance: The Chinese context. *Sustainability, 10*, 3406.

Shen, W., Tang, W., Siripanan, A., Lei, Z., Duffield, C. F., Wilson, D., Hui, F. K. P., & Wei, Y. (2017). Critical success factors in Thailand's green building industry. *Journal of Asian Architecture and Building Engineering, 16*, 317–324.

Swarup, L., Korkmaz, S., & Riley, D. (2011). Project delivery metrics for sustainable, high-performance buildings. *Journal of Construction Engineering and Management, 137*, 1043–1051.

Tang, Z. W., Ng, S. T., & Skitmore, M. (2019). Influence of procurement systems to the success of sustainable buildings. *Journal of Cleaner Production, 218,* 1007–1030.

Venkataraman, V. & Cheng, J. C. (2018). Critical success and failure factors for managing green building projects. *Journal of Architectural Engineering, 24,* 04018025.

Wai, S., Yusof, A. M., Ismail, S., & Tey, K. (2012). Critical success factors for sustainable building in Malaysia. In *International Proceedings of Economics Development and Research.* (pp. 123–127). IACSIT Press.

Wang, N., Wei, K., & Sun, H. (2013). Whole life project management approach to sustainability. *Journal of Management in Engineering, 30,* 246–255.

Wateridge, J. (1998). How can IS/IT projects be measured for success? *International Journal of Project Management, 16,* 59–63.

Xia, B., Skitmore, M., Wu, P., & Chen, Q. (2014). How public owners communicate the sustainability requirements of green design-build projects. *Journal of Construction Engineering and Management, 140,* 04014036-1--04014036-6.

Yu, T., Shi, Q., Zuo, J., & Chen, R. (2018). Critical factors for implementing sustainable construction practice in HOPSCA projects: A case study in China. *Sustainable Cities and Society, 37,* 93–103.

Zhang, L., Li, Q., & Zhou, J. (2017). Critical factors of low-carbon building development in China's urban area. *Journal of Cleaner Production, 142,* 3075–3082.

Zhou, L. & Smith, A. J. (2013). Sustainability best practice in PPP: Case study of a hospital project in the UK. In *International Conference on PPP Body of Knowledge.* Preston, UK.

Chapter 15

Embodied Energy Assessment of Onsite Construction Processes of Concreting Work: Models and Validation

L. Pinky Devi[*] and Sivakumar Palaniappan[†]

[*]*Department of Civil Engineering, Nagarjuna College of Engineering and Technology, Bangalore, India*
[†]*Department of Civil Engineering, Indian Institute of Technology Madras, Chennai, India*

The built environment life cycle consists of manufacturing of materials, onsite construction, operation, periodical maintenance, repair, and the end-of-service life phases. Among these phases, the onsite construction-related impacts are often ignored or underestimated due to challenges in gathering reliable field data from construction sites or poor documentation of site data. Given the fact that many developing countries are expected to witness major construction and infrastructure development initiatives in the coming decades, the assessment of sustainability metrics such as the embodied energy and embodied carbon of onsite construction processes assumes significance. Further, the onsite construction phase-related impacts are expected to be significant at the aggregate (national) level considering all development projects in a given time period. When the energy efficiency of the operational phase reaches a threshold limit as in the case of low-energy or low-carbon buildings, the next focus of improvement is the construction phase consisting of materials and onsite construction processes. This chapter presents a framework for assessing the energy use of onsite construction processes along with the identification of several technological and operational parameters. A set of regression models are presented to assess the electricity and fuel use for concreting construction processes using field data gathered from four major high-rise building construction projects in India. The application and validation of the proposed models are demonstrated using data gathered from two additional case studies in the Indian context. The methodology and the models presented in this chapter are useful for construction planners to assess the sustainability metrics along with the project performance metrics, thereby facilitating the integration of sustainability metrics in project planning.

15.1. Introduction

The construction industry that contributes to infrastructure and industrial development is one of the major consumers of natural resources and uses about 40% of the total energy consumed in the entire world (Economy Watch, 2010). The industry is a significant contributor to global greenhouse gas emissions (UNEP, 2001; Sandanayake *et al.*, 2018; Ge & Friedrich, 2020). Globally, there is a significant increase in greenhouse gas emissions due to the use of fossil fuels (Olivier & Peters, 2020). More than 50% of the global greenhouse gas emissions are caused by China, the US, European Union, India, Japan, and Russia. Several developed countries aim to achieve the Net Zero energy goal by 2050. The Government of India aims to reach the Net Zero energy target by 2070 and reduce the carbon intensity of the nation's economy by 45% by 2030. Sustainability-related goals are being considered in the international and national building standards.

The life cycle of a building consists of four major phases, namely mining of raw materials and manufacturing/production, onsite construction (site installation), use stage or operation, and the demolition stage or end of service life. The building life cycle energy is the sum of the initial embodied energy used for manufacturing materials and initial construction, recurring embodied energy, operating energy, and demolition energy. Construction energy refers to the energy used for materials and onsite construction processes. According to Cole and Kernan (1996), the relative significance of the construction energy with respect to the life cycle energy increases when the energy efficiency of the operational phase reaches a threshold (as in the case of low-energy or Net Zero energy buildings) or due to reduced building service life. Further, in our research,[1] construction energy is found to be a significant component of the life cycle energy for residential buildings with natural ventilation or partial air-conditioning. This highlights the need for accurate assessment of energy use and emissions of onsite construction processes pertaining to the built environment.

The current procedures used for quantification of energy use for onsite construction processes are based on technological parameters. Parameters related to operational and site-based aspects are not considered in detail. The models that exist in the literature to quantify the embodied energy and emissions mainly focus on building materials (Chang *et al.*, 2010; Shukla *et al.*, 2009). There are several studies available in the existing literature related to energy use and emissions of onsite construction processes. These include the following: (i) Construction Environmental Decision Support Tool (CEDST) developed using hybrid life cycle assessment (LCA) to estimate the energy use, emissions and waste generation of the construction phase, by Guggemos and Horvath (2005); (ii) Global Environmental Model/Management-21P (GEM-21P) to assess CO_2 emissions of production of materials and construction, by Baek *et al.* (2013); (iii) energy use and emissions of earthmoving activities, by several researchers (Ahn *et al.*, 2009; Lewis & Hajji, 2012; Devi & Palaniappan, 2014, 2017); (iv) emissions of heavy duty construction equipment, by Fitriani and Lewis (2014); and (v) embodied energy and emissions of buildings construction processes, by several researchers (Li *et al.*, 2010; Abanda *et al.*, 2013; Li *et al.*, 2014; Hong *et al.*, 2014; Kim *et al.*, 2015; Dong & Thomas, 2015; Ding *et al.*, 2020; Cang *et al.*, 2020).

Several existing studies in the literature quantify energy use and emissions based on the technological parameters (equipment parameters, such

---

[1]Devi & Palaniappan (2014), (2019).

as engine power) and emission factors available in the literature/standards. Only a few studies are based on the actual fuel use records or energy meter readings. This chapter presents a set of models to determine the energy use of onsite construction considering operational-, project-, and site-related parameters in addition to technological parameters. The proposed models are based on the as-built (actual) data gathered from four major building construction projects in India, thus representing construction practices in emerging/developing nations.

Given the scale of development that is expected to happen in many developing countries including India, this is expected to be significant at the aggregate (national) level. This chapter proposes a framework for the assessment of energy use for onsite construction processes. A set of empirical models are presented to assess the energy use for typical onsite construction processes based on field data gathered from Indian construction projects. The scope of this chapter is limited to concreting work, as this is one of the work packages that involve energy-intensive construction activities. The models are validated using two real case studies considered in the Indian context.

15.2. Conceptual framework for assessment of construction energy use

Figure 15.1 shows a conceptual framework for assessing the energy use for construction projects considering materials and onsite construction. The energy use for construction consists of two components, namely manufacturing of materials and onsite construction. The embodied energy associated with building materials depends on material type/technical specifications, the quantity of materials used, and the energy intensity of materials. Technical specifications of materials greatly influence energy intensity of materials, for example, virgin steel versus recycled steel or stainless steel versus normal steel. The energy intensity of materials depends on several aspects, such as the mining of raw materials, source of raw materials, quality of raw materials, processing of raw materials, technical specifications of materials, choice of technology used during manufacturing, fuel type, and packaging.

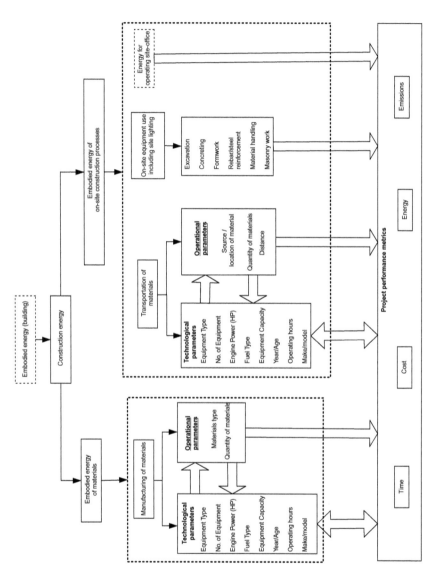

Figure 15.1. Framework for assessing the energy use in the onsite construction phase.

The embodied energy of onsite construction processes refers to the energy used for transportation of resources, onsite equipment uses, temporary structures, such as scaffolding and formwork, and site-related infrastructure and facilities, such as site office, inventory storage, material handling (tower crane/material hoist), and site lighting. Transportation refers to the movement of materials, equipment, and human workforce to the site as well as from the site. The energy use for transportation depends on several factors, such as the location of manufacturing plants, location of the construction site, location of equipment vendors, location of construction worker's housing, and the choice of vehicles, trucks used for transport, and fuel type. A variety of construction equipment is used during onsite construction for site clearance, excavation, concreting, formwork, rebar bending and cutting, material handling, masonry work, mechanical, electrical, and plumbing (MEP) work, and related specialized services and interior and finishing work. In general, the energy used for equipment (both the manufacturing and onsite construction) depends on numerous factors, such as the equipment type (model), number of equipment units used, engine power, equipment capacity, age (model year), type of contract, operating hours per day, fuel type, and fuel mileage.

The framework presented in Figure 15.1 was developed based on the field data gathered from four major high-rise building projects completed by leading construction contractors in India. In general, numerous factors influence the energy used for manufacturing materials and onsite construction processes, and these factors are broadly classified into two groups, namely technological factors and operational factors. Further, the project-related and the site-related factors also influence the construction energy use. Additional inputs on factors influencing the construction energy use are provided by Cole and Rousseau (1992), Kofoworola and Gheewala (2009), Kara *et al.* (2010), Dixit *et al.* (2010), Santero *et al.* (2011), and Monahan and Powell (2011).

Figure 15.2 presents a framework for assessing the energy use for concreting work and the influence of technological and operational parameters. The concreting work package during building construction involves production, transportation, pumping, compaction, and curing, as illustrated in Figure 15.2. Concrete is produced either through

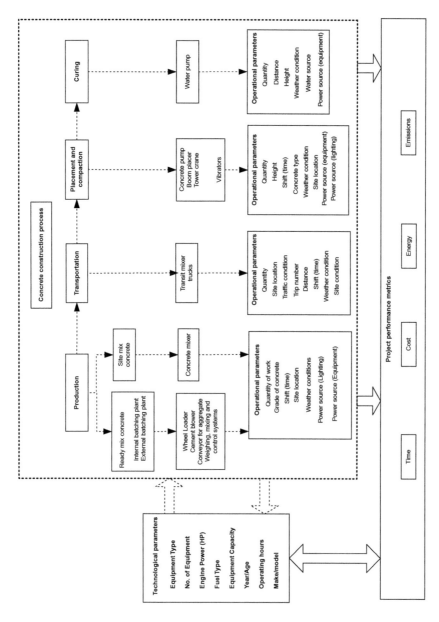

Figure 15.2. Framework for assessing the energy use for concreting work.

ready-mixed concrete plants or at the construction site through concrete mixers. The production of ready-mixed concrete involves the use of control systems for weighing/batching and mixing, cement blower, conveyor, and wheel loader. Site-mixed concrete is prepared using a concrete mixer powered by electricity or diesel. A large construction project site typically has an internal batching plant to cater to high demand. To meet excessive demand or handle temporary interruption in production, concrete is also procured from an external batching plant. For small-scale projects, concrete is sourced from an external ready-mixed batching plant or produced at the site using a concrete mixer.

Transit-mixer trucks are used to transport the concrete from the batching plant to the site. There are several options available to move concrete within the site, for example, concrete pump, tower crane, or boom placer. Compaction of concrete requires concrete vibrators. Curing concrete requires either a water pump or spraying machine, depending upon the type of curing method chosen. Additional details on the influence of technological and operational parameters on the energy use for onsite construction processes are provided by Devi and Palaniappan (2017) and Devi (2017).

15.3. Predictive models for onsite construction energy use

A set of predictive models are presented to determine the energy use for onsite construction processes with reference to concreting work. These models are based on the field data gathered from four major construction projects completed by leading contractors in India. These four building construction projects are located in Chennai (southern India). Among these four projects, one project is based on conventional RCC structural frames, and the other three projects are based on monolithic concrete structures (shear wall frame structure). The number of floors in these projects ranges from 10 to 20. The total volume of concreting work completed per project in these case studies ranges from 30,000 to 80,000 cubic meters. The total built-up area per project in these case studies ranges from 65,000 to 173,000 square meters. This chapter considers the following items related to concreting work: (1) batching plant, (2) wheel loader, (3) transit mixer trucks, (4) pumping of concrete, (5) curing, (6) material handling using tower crane (formwork and steel), (7) rebar bending and cutting, and (8) site lighting and site office.

15.3.1. *Batching plant*

The capacity of the batching plant is decided based on the volume of concreting work. When the demand for concrete is less than 5,000 cu.m. per month and the project duration is at least 12 months, an internal batching plant with a production capacity of 30 cu.m./hour is chosen. Moreover, when the demand exceeds 5,000 cu.m. per month with the project duration exceeding 24 months, a batching plant of 56 cu.m./hour or two batching plants of 30 cu.m./hour are deployed. The total operating hours of the batching plant and the grade of the concrete produced influence the energy use per unit amount of concrete produced.

Table 15.1 presents the data gathered for an internal ready-mixed concrete batching plant with 30 cu.m./hour production capacity. The concrete quantity produced per day, electricity meter readings, and operating hours are noted for each sample and the average values are reported for each production range considering all samples. Electricity use for

Table 15.1. Electricity use for batching plant with 30 cu.m./hour capacity.

| Number of samples | Concrete production | | Electricity meter (kWh) | Operating hours | Productivity (cu.m/hour) | Energy use (kWh per cu.m.) |
	Range (cu.m./day)	Average (cu.m./day)				
115	0–50	26	71	2.02	12.9	3.00
96	51–100	71	156	4.06	18.2	2.21
74	101–150	122	242	6.35	19.6	1.98
78	151–200	175	296	8.92	20.1	1.70
45	201–250	221	347	11.09	20.3	1.57
25	251–300	268	413	13.40	20.2	1.54
7	301–350	334	465	15.29	22.0	1.39
Total 440	0–350	118	215	6.3	17.8	2.12

Table 15.2.   Electricity use for batching plant with 56 cu.m./hour capacity.

| Number of samples | Concrete production | | Electricity meter (kWh) | Operating hours | Productivity (cu.m./hour) | Electricity use (kWh/cu.m.) |
	Range (cu.m/day)	Average (cu.m/day)				
14	0–50	22	167	1.4	17.27	11.7
14	51–100	76	482	2.8	28.02	6.4
9	101–150	124	682	4.5	28.04	5.4
19	151–200	172	641	6.7	28.24	3.7
46	201–250	225	785	7.7	30.23	3.5
50	251–300	277	812	9.5	30.12	2.9
53	301–350	326	929	11.0	30.54	2.8
35	351–400	371	961	11.8	32.29	2.6
20	401–450	417	976	12.6	33.43	2.3
6	451–500	468	1,082	14.0	33.78	2.3
266	0–500	268	799	8.9	29.82	3.1

concrete production was analyzed using 440 samples gathered on a daily basis. Table 15.2 presents the concrete quantity produced, electricity meter data, and operating hours for a 56 cu.m./hour batching plant. Average values are derived considering all data samples in each production range. It is observed that the increase in the daily concrete production results in increased productivity (cu.m./hour) and decreased electricity use (kWh/cu.m.). However, the electricity use for concrete production becomes constant when the production exceeds 400 cu.m./day. Table 15.3 presents the predictive regression models developed for both types of batching plants. The scope of the model, the validity of the input parameters, the number of samples used, and the coefficient of determination (R^2) are summarized for each model.

15.3.2. *Wheel loader*

Wheel loader equipment is used for moving aggregates and other materials on site. The model for assessing the fuel use (diesel) of wheel loaders is presented in the following using 16 samples:

$$y = 0.2619x - 90.332 \qquad (15.1)$$

Table 15.3. Predictive models: electricity use for batching plant and related items.

Internal batching plant capacity	Scope	Regression model	Validity of the model, number of samples and R^2
30 cu.m./hour	Monthly	$y = 2.1622x - 137.68$ y — Electricity use (kWh/month) x — Concrete produced (cu.m./month)	$1326 < x < 5239$ 16 months data from two projects $R^2 = 0.88$
30 cu.m./hour	Per cu.m. of concrete	$y = 0.00002x^2 - 0.012x + 3.1524$ y — Electricity use (kWh/cu.m) x — Concrete produced (cu.m./day)	$0 < x \leq 350$ 440 samples $R^2 = 0.95$
56 cu.m./hour	Monthly	$y = 0.0008x^2 - 10.119x + 50712$ y — Electricity use (kWh/month) x — Concrete produced (cu.m/month)	$5501 < x < 9529$ 9 months $R^2 = 0.80$
56 cu.m./hour	Per cu.m. of concrete	$y = 3E\text{-}05x^2 - 0.0283x + 8.1629$ y — Electricity use (kWh/cu.m) x — Concrete produced (cu.m/day)	$0 < x \leq 500$ 266 samples $R^2 = 0.98$

where "y" is the diesel fuel used for wheel loaders (liters/month), "x" is the concrete quantity produced (cu.m./month), and the applicable range of input parameter is $1,328 < x < 5,901$.

15.3.3. *Transit mixer trucks*

Transit mixer trucks are used to transport concrete from the batching plant to the site. Each data sample refers to the concrete quantity transported and the fuel used for one transit truck per month. A total of 178 data samples were gathered from four case studies. All the four case studies considered have an internal batching plant. Several factors influence the fuel used by transit mixer trucks, for example, transportation distance, truck model, make, capacity, traffic conditions, site location, site conditions, and the working shift (day or night). The traffic conditions and the shift are insignificant in this study since all four case studies refer to the internal batching plant located within the site and the site location and site conditions are the same. It is observed that transporting concrete at night results in shorter travel time and waiting time which in turn reduces the fuel use.

Multiple regression models were developed taking into account the concrete quantity transported, travel distance, age (model year), make, and truck capacity. A vital observation is that the make is not a significant variable influencing the fuel use. The model for determining the fuel use for transit mixer trucks is presented in the following:

$$TF = 0.4954 * Q + 49.05 * A + 0.18692 * D - 148.92 \quad (15.2)$$

where TF is the total diesel fuel used by one transit mixer truck (liters/month), Q is the concrete quantity transported per transit mixer truck (cu.m./month) ($53 < Q < 2{,}130$), A is the age of the transit mixer truck with reference to base year 2,014 ($1 < A < 15$), and D is the total distance traveled by one transit mixer truck (km/month) ($31 < D < 948$).

The R^2 value is found to be 0.87 which indicates the fitness of the model. The concrete quantity transported, the age of the truck, and the travel distance are the three significant variables influencing the fuel use.

15.3.4. *Pumping of concrete*

The fuel use for pumping concrete depends on the building height and type of concrete. For example, pumping of self-compacting concrete (SCC) takes less time than normal concrete resulting in lesser fuel use. A total of 78 data samples were gathered for concrete pumping documenting the model year, make, pump capacity, height of placing concrete, type of concrete, type of pump, and quantity of concrete pumped.

15.3.4.1. *Normal concrete*

The model built for determining the fuel use for pumping normal concrete is based upon data corresponding to 17 concrete pump months. Age of the equipment is not identified as a significant variable. The model for determining the fuel use for pumping normal concrete is presented in the following:

$$CPF_{Normal} = 0.6468 * Q + 16.43\ 21 * H - 161.705 \qquad (15.3)$$

where CPF_{Normal} is the total diesel fuel use for pumping normal concrete using concrete pump (liters/month), Q is the quantity of concrete pumped per concrete pump (cu.m./month) ($505 < Q < 2,562$), and H is the height of placing concrete (m) ($0 < H < 30$).

The R^2 value is found to be 0.94 for the above model. The concrete quantity and height of pumping are identified as the two significant parameters that influence the fuel use.

15.3.4.2. *Self-compacting concrete*

The total number of "concrete pump months" used for developing the model is 61. The quantity of concrete pumped and the height of placing are identified as significant parameters. The equipment age and the capacity are identified as not significant. The model for determining the fuel use for pumping SCC is presented in the following equation. The R^2 is found to be 0.90 for the model:

$$CPF_{SCC} = 0.5344 * Q + 18.7906 * H - 500.839 \qquad (15.4)$$

where CPF_{SCC} is the total fuel use for concrete pump (liters/month), Q is the quantity of concrete pumped (cu.m./month) ($280 < Q < 4,416$), and H is the height of placing concrete (m) ($0 < H < 48$).

The equipment age is not a significant parameter for both the normal concrete and SCC, as the data relate to concrete pumps which are relatively newer (2 and 4 years old).

15.3.5. *Curing of concrete using water pump*

The electricity used for curing depends on the building height, the source of water, and the transport distance to the site. For curing of concrete using a water pump, this study uses an average electricity consumption (kWh/cu.m.), as presented in Table 15.4. The data samples gathered were grouped based on the concrete quantity cured, model year (age), make,

Table 15.4.   Curing of concrete using water pump.

No. of samples	Concrete quantity (cu.m./month)	Electricity meter (kWh)	Electricity use (kWh/cu.m.)	Model year	Make	Capacity
10	3,312	2,412	0.86	2008	WP1	10 hp
6	4,724	4,225	0.90	2012	WP2	10 hp
21	5,115	9,143	1.91	2012	WP1	15 hp

and capacity. Other operational factors, such as the height of pumping, are not considered due to lack of data.

15.3.6. *Material handling using tower crane: Formwork and steel*

The two types of formworks applied in the multi-storeyed building construction are the conventional formwork (using wooden runners, plywood, mild steel plates with mild steel props, and cup locks staging) and the monolithic ("mivan") formwork. This phase involves four activities, namely making/preparation, transportation, lifting, and placing. The embodied energy of formwork for a given project depends on the number of repetitions of use and the assembly of the formwork through site lighting and equipment.

It is noted that the carpentry work done during daytime reduces the electricity use for site lighting. The average number of repetitions of use for wooden formwork (plywood) and monolithic aluminum formwork are 8 and 75, respectively. The use of aluminum formwork results in less cycle time and minimum masonry and carpentry work. The aluminum formwork is mostly imported from Korea and as a result, the transport cost and the embodied energy associated with materials and transport are more compared to wooden formwork. Additionally, the energy used for transportation, lifting, and placing is influenced by the building height, shift (time), and the source of electricity.

15.3.6.1. *Electricity use for tower crane operations based on number of lift cycles*

Field data related to 43 "tower crane months" are used to develop the model for determining the electricity use. Data gathered consists of number of lift cycles, equipment age, capacity, number of buildings served by a tower crane, height of the working space, and the experience of the equipment operator. The height of the working space (30 m), operator's experience, and the capacity of the tower crane are not considered in model development. The model for determining the electricity use of tower crane lifting operations based on lift cycle is presented as follows:

$$ETC_{lift\ cycle} = 0.3212 * N + 251.8516 * S - 26.5155 \qquad (15.5)$$

where $ETC_{lift\ cycle}$ is the electricity use for lifting of materials (kWh/month), N is the number of lift cycles per month ($526 < N < 2{,}862$), and S is the number of buildings served by a tower crane ($1 < S < 4$).

The R^2 of the above model is 0.6015, implying that there are other variables that affect electricity use which are not present in the model. It is inferred that age is not a significant parameter, but the height of working space and the type and quantity of material lifted may be influential parameters. Due to lack of data, both of these parameters are not included in the model development. The experience of the tower crane operators is found to be 6–8 years. From the contractor's feedback, the operator experience is considered as one of the important factors that influence productivity as well as electricity use. This model is applicable for sites where a tower crane serves multiple buildings, for example, 2–4.

15.3.6.2. *Electricity use for tower crane operations based on the material quantity lifted*

Data related to 58 "tower crane months" are considered in developing the model based on the material quantity lifted. Several parameters influence the electricity use by tower crane, namely the quantity of materials lifted (MT), equipment age, lifting capacity, number of buildings served concurrently by a tower crane, height of the working space, and the operator's experience. The MT per month, equipment age, and the height of working space are the three significant variables that affect electricity use. The model for determining the electricity use by tower crane for materials lifting is presented as follows:

$$ETC_{MT} = 1.811 * Q + 73.91 * A + 44.55 * H - 590 \qquad (15.6)$$

where ETC$_{MT}$ is the electricity use for lifting of materials (kWh per month), Q is the quantity of material lifted (MT/month) ($79 < Q < 1,809$), A is the age of the tower crane with reference to base year 2014 ($1 < A > 11$), and H is the height of the working space (m) ($29 < H > 49$).

15.3.7. *Rebar bending and cutting*

The steel rebar is cut and bent according to the shop drawings and specifications. The process of cutting and bending the rebar based on site requirements is done either at the construction site or at a centralized rebar fabrication facility. The major processes are bending and shearing, transportation, lifting, and placing, which are done either manually or using machinery. It is also noted that most of the bar bending and cutting work is done during the daytime. The electricity use (and the energy use) for rebar bending and cutting depends on many operational factors, such as the quantity of work, transportation distance, building height, shift (time), and the source of electricity. Data gathered over a period of 16 months were used for building the model. The model for determining the electricity use for rebar bending and cutting is presented as follows ($R^2 = 0.88$):

$$y = 1.9659 * x + 9.817 \tag{15.7}$$

where y is the electricity use for rebar bending and cutting (kWh /month) and x is the quantity of rebar cut and bent per month (MT) ($165 < x < 621$).

15.3.8. *Site lighting and site office*

The model for predicting the electricity used for the site lighting is presented in the following equation based on 16 samples ($R^2 = 0.88$):

$$y = -0.0004x^2 + 7.0886x - 2,347.8 \tag{15.8}$$

where y is the electricity use for the site lighting (kWh/month) and x is the total concrete quantity used (cu.m./month) ($1,327 \leq x \leq 5,901$).

The electricity use for the site office varies from 1 to 4 kWh per cu.m. of concrete depending upon the use of air conditioning and the scale of concrete produced and used.

15.4. Validation of the proposed models

Data gathered from two case studies (Case study "A" and Case study "B") are used to validate the results generated by the predictive models. Both case studies are based on the conventional RCC-framed structure. These case studies "A" and "B" are 35 m and 45 m tall buildings, respectively. These case studies are G+7 and G+10, respectively. Data corresponding to 6 months of construction duration were used for validation of models. The amount of concreting work done during the data collection period in these case studies are 17,150 and 23,164 cu.m., respectively. Figure 15.3 shows

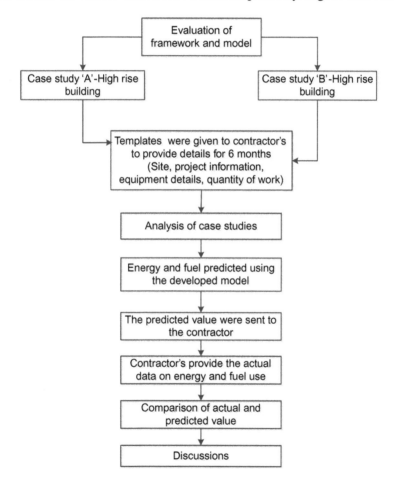

Figure 15.3. Flowchart for evaluation of predictive models.

the methodology used to evaluate the proposed models. The models were used to predict the electricity and fuel used by construction equipment for onsite construction processes. The list of construction equipment and processes considered are batching plant and its components (batching plant, cement blower, conveyor, and wheel loader), transit mixer trucks, concrete pump, tower crane (material handling), water pump for curing of concrete and dewatering, rebar bending and cutting, site office (lights, air conditioning, computer, printer, and photocopying machines), and site lighting for safety and night timework. First, the models were used to predict the electricity and the fuel use for case studies "A" and "B." Second, the actual data were gathered for case studies "A" and "B" from the contractor. The predicted values were compared with the actual data and the differences in the results are noted. Figure 15.4 shows the differences between the predicted values by the models and the actual data gathered from the two case studies.

The difference in the results of the models and the actual data observed at the site is less than 10% for transit mixer trucks, concrete pumps, and site lighting. In the case of batching plant, wheel loader, water pump, and rebar bending and cutting, the difference between the results of

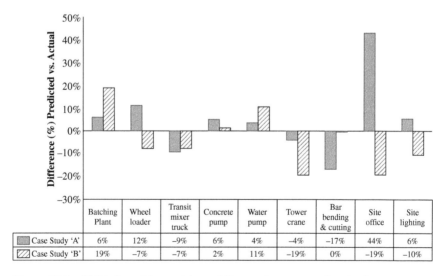

	Batching Plant	Wheel loader	Transit mixer truck	Concrete pump	Water pump	Tower crane	Bar bending & cutting	Site office	Site lighting
Case Study 'A'	6%	12%	–9%	6%	4%	–4%	–17%	44%	6%
Case Study 'B'	19%	–7%	–7%	2%	11%	–19%	0%	–19%	–10%

Figure 15.4.   Validation of the models — difference between predicted values and actual data based on two case studies.

the models and the actual data exceeds 10%, but it is less than 20%. In the case of rebar bending and cutting for Case "B," the model results are exactly the same as the actual data and hence there is no error in the prediction. In the case of the concrete pump for Case "B," the difference in the results is only 2%. In the case of the site office for Case "A," the difference in the results is significant, which indicates that the model did not include relevant site-related parameters, such as area of the site, amount of work done, number of electrical fittings at the site as well as site office, area of the site office, and type and the number of equipment used at the site office.

15.5. Summary and conclusion

This chapter presents a framework to assess the energy use of onsite construction processes based on data gathered from four construction projects in India. Majority of the studies reported in the literature use technological factors, such as engine horsepower, load factor, and operating hours of the equipment to determine the energy use for onsite construction processes. Actual as-built field data gathered from four Indian case studies are used to develop a set of predictive models to assess the fuel and electricity use for concreting work. Detailed methodology is presented to assess the energy use for concreting construction processes of high-rise buildings. It is observed that numerous factors related to operation, technology, construction site, and the scale of the project influence the energy use for construction processes. Several factors, such as the type of concrete, floor level, number of buildings served by the tower crane at a time, capacity of the construction equipment used, transportation distance, equipment model, and the age of the equipment, are found to influence the energy use for concreting work. Further, the work demand, the rate at which the work is performed, and the utilization rate of the equipment also influence energy use.

The methodology and the models presented in this study are useful for construction planners to evaluate the sustainability metrics in addition to the project management performance metrics and perform trade-off analysis considering alternate construction scenarios. The limitation of this study is that the models are based upon the data gathered from four high-rise building case studies and the sample size is limited in certain activities.

Acknowledgments

The first author acknowledges the research scholarship provided by the Ministry of Education, Government of India during the period of the study reported in this chapter. The authors express their sincere thanks to the contractors and project engineers who participated in the reported study and supported data collection during site visits. Further, the authors thank the general assistance provided by the staff members of the Department of Civil Engineering, Indian Institute of Technology Madras during the study.

References

Abanda, F. H., Tah, J. H. M., & Cheung, F. K. T. (2013). Mathematical modelling of embodied energy, greenhouse gases, waste, time–cost parameters of building projects: A review. *Building and Environment*, *59*, 23–37.

Ahn, C., Rekapalli, P., V., Martinez, J. C., & Pena-Mora, F. (2009). Sustainability analysis of earthmoving operations. In *Proceedings of the 2009 Winter Simulation Conference* (pp. 2605–2611).

Baek, C., Park, S.-H., Suzuki, M., & Lee, S. H. (2013). Life cycle carbon dioxide assessment tool for buildings in the schematic design phase. *Energy and Buildings*, *61*, 275–287.

Cang, Y, Yang, L., Luo, Z., & Zhang, N. (2020). Prediction of embodied carbon emissions from residential buildings with different structural forms. *Sustainable Cities and Society*, *54*, 101946.

Chang, Y., Ries, R. J., & Wang, Y. (2010). The embodied energy and environmental emissions of construction projects in China: An economic input — output LCA model. *Energy Policy*, *38*, 6597–6603.

Cole, R. J. & Kernan, P. C. (1996). Life-cycle energy use in office buildings. *Building and Environment*, *31*(4), 307–317.

Cole, R. J. & Rousseau, D. (1992). Environmental auditing for building construction: Energy and air pollution indices for building materials. *Building and Environment*, *27*(1), 23–30.

Devi, L. P. (2017). Studies on energy use for high-rise building construction processes. Doctoral dissertation, Building Technology and Construction Management, Department of Civil Engineering, Indian Institute of Technology Madras, Chennai, India.

Devi, L. P. & Palaniappan, S. (2014). A case study on life cycle energy use of residential building in Southern India. *Energy and Buildings*, *20*, 247–259.

Devi, L. P. & Palaniappan, S. (2016). A framework for the assessment of energy use of high-rise building construction processes. Construction Research Congress 2016, ASCE. https://doi.org/10.1061/9780784479827.102.

Devi, L. P. & Palaniappan, S. (2017). A study on energy use for excavation and transport of soil during building construction. *Journal of Cleaner Production*, *164*, 543–556.

Devi, L. P. & Palaniappan, S. (2019). Life cycle energy analysis of a low-cost house in India. *International Journal of Construction Education and Research*, *15*(4), 256–275. https://doi.org/10.1080/15578771.2018.147 6935.

Ding, Z, Liu, S., Luo, L., & Liao, L. (2020). A building information modeling-based carbon emission measurement system for prefabricated residential buildings during the materialization phase. *Journal of Cleaner Production*, *264*, 121728.

Dixit, M. K., Fernández-Solís, J. L., Lavy, S., & Culp, C. H. (2010). Identification of parameters for embodied energy measurement: A literature review. *Energy and Buildings*, *42*(8), 1238–1247.

Dong, Y. H. & Thomas, S. Ng. (2015). A life cycle assessment model for evaluating the environmental impacts of building construction in Hong Kong. *Building and Environment*, *89*, 183–191.

Economy Watch. (2010 June 29). A report on "Construction Industry Trends. Available at: http://www.economywatch.com/world-industries/construction/trends.html.

Fitriani, H. & Lewis, P. (2014). Comparison of predictive modeling methodologies for estimating fuel use and emission rates for wheel loaders. Construction Research Congress 2014: Construction in a Global Network. Available at: https://ascelibrary.org/doi/10.1061/9780784413517.063.

Ge, M. & Friedrich, J. (2020). 4 charts explain greenhouse gas emissions by countries and sectors. World Resource Institute. Available at: https://www.wri.org/blog/ 2020/02/greenhouse-gas-emissions-by-country-sector.

Guggemos, A. A. & Horvath, A. (2005). Comparison of environmental effects of steel- and concrete-framed buildings. *Journal of Infrastructure Systems*, *11*(2), 93–101.

Hong, T., Ji, C., Jang, M., & Park, H. (2014). Assessment model for energy consumption and greenhouse gas emissions during building construction. *Journal of Management in Engineering*, *30*(2), 226–235.

Kara, S., Manmek, S., & Herrmann, C. (2010). Global manufacturing and the embodied energy of products. *CIRP Annals — Manufacturing Technology, 59*, 29–32.

Kim, J., Koo, C., Kim, C.-J., Hong, T., & Park, H. S. (2015). Integrated CO_2, cost, and schedule management system for building construction projects using the earned value management theory. *Journal of Cleaner Production, 105*, 275–285.

Kofoworola, O. F. & Gheewala, S. H. (2009). Life cycle energy assessment of a typical office building in Thailand. *Energy and Buildings, 41*(10), 1076–1083.

Lewis, P. & Hajji, A. (2012). Estimating the economic, energy, and environmental impact of earthwork activities. Construction Research Congress 2012 ©ASCE, 1770–1779.

Li, X., Yang, F., Zhu, Y., & Gao, Y. (2014). An assessment framework for analyzing the embodied carbon impacts of residential buildings in China. *Energy and Buildings, 85*, 400–409.

Li, X., Zhu, Y., & Zhang, Z. (2010). An LCA-based environmental impact assessment model for construction processes. *Building and Environment, 45*(3), 766–775.

Monahan, J. & Powell, J. C. (2011). An embodied carbon and energy analysis of modern methods of construction in housing: A case study using a lifecycle assessment framework. *Energy and Buildings, 43*(1), 179–188.

Oliver, J. G. J. & Peters J. A. H. W. (2020). Trends in global CO_2 and total greenhouse gas emissions. A report by PBL Netherlands Environmental Assessment agency, The Hague, 2020, PBL publication number: 4331.

Sandanayake, M., Lokuge, W., Zhang, G., Setunge, S., & Thusharc, Q. (2018). Greenhouse gas emissions during timber and concrete building construction — A scenario based comparative case study. *Sustainable Cities and Society, 38*, 91–97.

Santero, N. J., Masanet, E., & Horvath, A. (2011). Life-cycle assessment of pavements. Part I Critical review. *Resources, Conservation and Recycling, 55*, 801–809.

Shukla, A., Tiwari, G. N., & Sodha, M. S. (2009). Embodied energy analysis of adobe house. *Renewable Energy, 34*(3), 755–761.

UNEP — Energy and Cities: Sustainable Building and Construction, Sustainable Buildings and Climate Initiative, Summary of main Issues, for Decision-Makers, ETC Side Event at UNEP Governing Council, 2001 — Nairobi, Kenya. Available at: http://www.unep.or.jp/ietc/focus/EnergyCities1.asp (assessed on 23 September, 2016).

Chapter 16

Postconstruction Management of Green Projects

Adeleye Ayoade Adeniran[*]**, Emma Ayesu-Koranteng**[*]**,
Lukuman Musibau**[†]**, Winston Shakantu**[*]**,
and Sijekula Mbanga**[*]

Nelson Mandela University, Port Elizabeth (Gqeberha), South Africa
[†]*Federal Polytechnic Ede, Osun State, Nigeria*

The focus for most projects is the design and construction stages, which cover a brief span, while the postconstruction phase, which covers a longer span, is rarely brought to the fore. It should be considered that meeting "sustainability goals" does not end after the building design is completed but continues further. The postconstruction stage is the time to start the occupation and maintenance of the completed project. At this phase in a project life cycle, many projects have been characterized by poor performance, not only because of design or construction failure but also because of postconstruction management issues. When conceptualized, these issues are rarely on the front burner of projects, hence the continuous dilapidation/failure of projects before they run their projected life cycle. This chapter seeks to bring to the fore the need for postconstruction management of green projects by adopting management techniques to ensure sustainability (being enjoyed by the present and future users alike). The chapter is proposed to present the green project life cycle, which will help underscore the aim and scope of its postconstruction management as well as the management principles that will be required. The chapter further identifies the factors that could influence the use and postconstruction management of green projects and the effect of such factors that gravitate projects toward depreciation and obsolescence. The chapter closes by discussing postconstruction management strategies for green projects as a baseline for decision-makers, developers, and stakeholders who promote green construction culture and enforce green regulations to drive sustainability.

16.1. Introduction

Whether local or international, businesses and organizations have recently understood that "green" is important and mostly use it to market and sell their products and services. This is because the ecosystem is currently at a critical point, while human activities continue to deplete the ecosystem functions irreversibly.

While there have been several discussions about green businesses, green projects, their management, and their managers, not a lot has been on the table about its postconstruction management, and this is thought-provoking because a project's life cycle is the basis of a business. Projects are the engine room for conceptualizing business ideas and their implementation. Projects, by definition, use resources; hence should the project, its management, and postproject management (PM), therefore, not be a key area of focus?

Green building, as defined by the US Environmental Protection Agency (1987), is a structure and the application of resource-efficient and environmentally responsible processes throughout the building life cycle: "from planning to design, construction, operation, maintenance, renovation, and demolition." This definition is in tandem with the definition of sustainable development by the World Commission on Environment and Development (1987) as the "ability to make development sustainable — to ensure that it meets the needs of the present without compromising the ability of future generations to meet their own needs." According to the World Green Building Council (2016), "a 'green' building is one that, through its architecture, construction, or operation, reduces or eliminates negative effects on our climate and natural environment while also having the potential to create positive influences." Ding *et al.* (2018) indicated that in China, green building is defined as a structure that, to the greatest degree, conserves resources of land, water, energy, and materials; protects the environment; and reduces emissions during its life cycle in order to offer humans a suitable, healthy, and innovative use environment that is also in accord with nature.

Green building projects protect valuable natural resources while also improving our quality of life, and their features include "efficiency in energy, water and other resources use; renewable energy use; reduction measures of pollution and waste while enabling of recycling and reuse; excellent indoor ambient air quality; non-toxic, ethical, and sustainable materials usage; consideration of the environment in design, construction, and operation; consideration of the quality of life of occupants in design, construction, and operation; and a design that enables adaptation to a changing environment."

These features speak to sustainability and toward meeting the sustainability standards. As stated by Tang and Lee (2016), it involves a series of activities that require close cooperation at all stages by various stakeholders, including but not limited to the client, contractor, architects, and engineers. The green building practice essentially expands and reinforces the traditional building design concerns of utility, comfort, durability, and economy (Robichaud & Anantatmula, 2011). The three pillars of sustainability must be recognized throughout the production process and after the construction is completed by consistent maintenance management.

The value of maintenance management is based on the need for organizations to continue improving their capacity to create value for consumers while also improving the cost efficiency of their operational processes (Gann & Salter, 2000). Hence, maintenance management has a vital support function in physical assets investment. Maintenance management cost in the UK manufacturing industry, for instance, is between 12 and 23% of its total operating costs, according to Srivastava *et al.* (2020), and largely in the mining industry to about 40–50%, as documented by Kumar *et al.* (2013). While these costs are high in the short to medium term, maintenance management helps organizations optimize their competitive advantage in the long run by procuring the right mix of real assets and greatly using those already in place to achieve business requirements.

Maintenance management has been identified in the traditional construction sector as a larger service for postconstruction activity and processes (Ismail, 2020). However, while green building construction projects grow in complexity and scale, the need to monitor the green building elements for maintenance management action will come to the fore. Mohamed *et al.* (2019) highlighted the need for this in their investigation of the post-Grenfell fire of 2017, which was adduced to maintenance management issues.

This event points to the fact that issues which are not considered holistically during construction activity can pose a challenge for society due to improper and poor maintenance management performance.

With this scenario, beyond the construction phase of green building, this chapter in the following sections presents a case for the postconstruction management of green projects by considering its life cycle, the aim and scope of green project postconstruction management, the principles of green project postconstruction management, factors influencing the use and postconstruction management of green projects, and effects of depreciation and obsolescence on green projects and makes a case for management strategies for green projects.

16.2. Green project life cycle

Ding *et al.*'s (2018) definition of green building underscores the focus of the green concept in the span of life of a building because of the additional requirements for implementing green building projects. This additional requirement underpins the life cycle of a green project, causing it to deviate from the traditional project life cycle of conceptualization, implementation, and feedback. Figure 16.1 depicts the life cycle of a green project adapted from Romano *et al.* (2014).

The consciousness of the detrimental consequences of traditional building influences paved for new ways of conceiving structures that need to change while focusing on people's well-being, planet protection, and economic profit and not jeopardizing safety and reliability throughout its

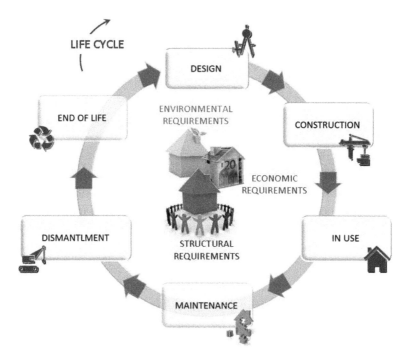

Figure 16.1. Green project life cycle.

entire life cycle. Therefore, the life cycle of a green building is balanced among the three dimensions of sustainable development: environmental, economic, and structural/physical requirements. The design phase is where sustainable structures are conceived, considering all the sustainability dimensions.

Environmental performance is assessed during the design phase using the life cycle assessment (LCA), which permits environmental impacts to be assessed from raw material mining (including the supply chain) to the product's end of life (Ingrao *et al.*, 2018) (see Chapter 17).

The use of LCA in the construction industry has become a critical concern for green building design, allowing architects and engineers to assess the environmental impacts produced by a building over its entire life cycle (Dossche *et al.*, 2017). In addition, the LCA influences material and technology selection, promoting specific design criteria and recycling. As noted by Raouf and Al-Ghamdi, the design team's primary responsibilities are to describe the aim of each green construction activity, the prerequisites to accomplish the green construction, the documentation needs, and the managing and verifying specifications for a contractor (Raouf & Al-Ghamdi, 2019).

While a holistic decision is made during the design phase, Olubunmi et al. (2016) alleged that it is equally important to create a cooperative environment during the construction period to stimulate collaboration among all stakeholders.

The in-use phase is the phase specified in the construction agreement that follows the construction stage and sometimes is referred to as the guarantee/warranty phase (Sechrest & Price, 1985). Alexander (2013) argues that the client provisions for the occupation could move the project from managing a worksite to an involved working facility with minimal disruption and cost. Therefore, it is essential to plan for work as soon as possible to address any issues during the planning and development phases. Other than being the longest phase in terms of time, the occupation phase is considered one of the most critical stages because most natural impacts occur. Once a green building is completed and adapted to its use, it tends to suffer a fair rate of wear and tear once occupied, and maintenance management sets it immediately. The maintenance management problems normally associated with a new building are usually small, but as the complexity of new equipment increases, the associated challenges of its operation will tend to grow, resulting in depreciation and probably obsolescence (Shafique et al., 2018). Bearing this in mind, post-occupancy assessment must be performed as a fundamental instrument to illustrate whether the venture goals have been accomplished or not (Abisuga, 2020). The evaluation helps guarantee that the project conveys its objectives and helps distinguish the lessons learned, especially with the obtainment preparation, so that future projects will note them for productivity (Salem, 2018). The performance assessment will emphasize where modifications and restructurings are required for the building and its expansion contexts to distinguish cost in utilization. The findings will aid in enhancing good practice and also affect future strategic plans.

When the green building reaches its obsolescence stage in its cycle, it is dismantled. The dismantling method would have been identified from the design stage, making it possible for building components and material reuse. The reuse of the components will reduce the consumption of new resources and energy, waste generation, and protect the environment because, at the very end of life, limited components, which are classified as non-reusable and nonrecyclable, will be disposed of as waste.

16.3. Obsolescence and depreciation: End of life of green projects

As defined by Pourebrahimi *et al.* (2020), obsolescence is a loss of performance, utility, value, or suitability caused by physical decay, technical improvements, political changes, social and economic changes, and modifications in consumer and stakeholder requirements. Depreciation is defined by Albu and Albu as "any loss of utility caused by physical damage to the asset or its components due to its age and regular wear and tear, which is embodied in a loss of value" (Albu & Albu, 2021). From these two definitions, it is clear that a structure or its component may be degraded by a variety of variables other than physical deterioration, implying that the action of these other variables in reducing the utility of buildings cannot be overemphasized (Pinder & Wilkinson, 2000).

With this in mind, it is safe to align with Grover and Grover (2015), who opined that the concept of obsolescence is difficult to describe due to the overlapping of the multiple reasons that cause it, hence making it difficult to find common causes among distinct types of obsolescence. Bortolini and Forcada (2018) also indicated that while physical degradation can be predictable and quantifiable for intervention, legal and social elements are more complex, if not impossible, to predict over time.

The social and legal service life of a component or building, according to the International Organization for Standardization (2016), includes the time after completion until human desires or regulatory obligations force their change for considerations apart from economic considerations. Farahani *et al.* (2019) opined that the prerequisites for determining the end of service life of a building can, and most likely would, change during the building's service life, implying that the building may become obsolete in response to fluctuations in performance requirements before its technical service life expires.

Based on these arguments and viewpoints, it is acceptable to conclude that the concept of social and legal service life, whether in traditional or green building projects, might be subjective; hence a conceptual explanation of how aesthetic, legal, and social issues can influence a building's end of service life is offered in this direction.

16.3.1. *Aesthetic obsolescence*

The study of beauty and its polar opposite, ugliness, is generally referred to as aesthetics, as Huron (2016) puts it. Since beauty or ugliness is subjective, aesthetic obsolescence is possibly the most difficult topic to define and almost impossible to simulate. To define aesthetic obsolescence, different authors have used different terms.

For example, Wilkinson *et al.* (2014) see it as concepts that relate to an outdated or old-fashioned appearance of a building or its components, while Johnston (2016) connects it with the changes in style, fashion, image, or stylistic attributes of a building, which could be as a result of architectural styles.

Human needs and wants are insatiable; hence the continuous changes in style, fashion, and aesthetic values stipulate new requirements regarding the buildings' appearance or material choices (Pourebrahimi *et al.*, 2020).

In a larger sense, aesthetic obsolescence happens when a structure becomes outdated despite keeping proper functionality and serviceability because users believe it no longer fits current fashion or its style is antiquated (Wilkinson *et al.*, 2014).

With green building projects currently in demand by tenants, financiers, and governments, traditional buildings that do not refurbish or upgrade with green building characteristics will deteriorate and become obsolete.

16.3.2. *Social obsolescence*

A few authors, such as Rodi *et al.* (2015), described social obsolescence as the decline of the building components' serviceability or usefulness due to societal change in the sense of taste.

The implication of this is that a new building or its component can still be disposed of before the end of its useful life or acceptable degradation levels for the reason that more advanced and seemingly better solutions are accessible (Pinder & Wilkinson, 2000). Changes may influence such obsolescence in the expectancy levels because of personal needs and experience (Silva *et al.*, 2022); hence cultural obsolescence is another dimension of social obsolescence and can be influenced by cultural values, and local traditions, the users' working conditions and lifestyle (Krivý, 2013). As a result, obsolescence varies at the global, regional, and local levels because what is acceptable varies from place to place. In general, social obsolescence is founded on cultural shifts, which typically occur as a result of changes in lifestyle, tastes, and demands; preconceived notions; corporate culture; and collective and individual preferences, among others (Thomsen & Straub, 2021).

The continuous clamor for green building will see users inclining to characterize the need for intervention based on subjective criteria and individual perceptions.

16.3.3. *Legal obsolescence*

Liu *et al.* (2020) identified this type of obsolescence to be one arising from changes in legislation and standards. For example, new building regulations can make buildings legally obsolete, requiring intervention, maintenance, or replacement of their components to fulfill current standards (Alonso *et al.*, 2020). Muminović *et al.* (2020) opined that legal obsolescence might arise as a building design and rehabilitation control mechanism. Another aspect of legal obsolescence is "political obsolescence," which arises as to the common good and the community interests change (Wilkinson *et al.*, 2014). According to Pourebrahimi *et al.* (2020), "political obsolescence" overlaps the concept of social obsolescence, but instead of dealing with interpretive concepts, political obsolescence is transformed into regulations, and thus it is commonly referred to as legal obsolescence. Buitelaar *et al.* (2021) termed it "statutory obsolescence," but it is still described when the building becomes obsolete due to an inability to meet minimum standards.

16.3.4. *End of life*

The physical deterioration or functional loss of performance of a green building or its components does not restrict its end of life. On the contrary, the life span can be indefinitely extended as long as the facility remains beneficial, taking into account social and cultural criteria, as well as emotional attachment. However, whenever a supposedly suitable replacement is discovered, the end of service life can also occur prematurely, for the same reasons or due to regulatory frameworks.

According to Preiser and Vischer (2006), the motives for users to engage in maintenance and rehabilitation pursuits are, in increasing order of importance, as follows: aesthetics, social issues, psychological issues, functionality, safety in use, and health. However, even though users recognize the importance of preventing physical deterioration, they have a low sensitivity to the issue, and it is not easy to define what reasonable acceptance criteria are.

A given element is often replaced for aesthetic reasons, regardless of its technical performance. Even if the end of the service life is caused by physical deterioration of the building structures, the time it occurs is frequently influenced by architectural and aesthetic considerations. According to Alaimo and Accurso (2008), there is a significant relationship between performing maintenance actions and the social and urban environment of the building, particularly those predicated on its aesthetic appeal. The constituents and service life of a building can be influenced by legal considerations, which are frequently associated with cultural and economic factors. National building codes and owner expectations can characterize the performance standards that should be reached during the building's life span. The requirements imposed by standards are typically related to safety issues, whereas the owners' demands are more subjective and usually related to economic or aesthetic motivations (Silva & de Brito, 2019).

New regulations, as well as new urban development plans and policies, can also motivate buildings to reach the end of their useful life (Ahn *et al.*, 2013).

16.4. The scope and aim of green project postconstruction management

Any investment or project, traditional or green, aims to secure optimum returns, which may be financial, prestigious, religious, or other satisfaction forms. Therefore, to achieve the aim of a green building project, there is a need for the following:

- the collection of all as-built drawings and warranty and maintenance manuals,
- certification of all vendor bills after collecting all documents and attending snags,
- preparation of detailed statements of vendors' key contacts, in case of any defects,
- preparation of completion certificate based on all documents and drawings,
- assisting in appointing a suitable Green Facility Manager (GFM),
- handing over all documents and delivering basic guidelines to the GFM.

At this phase, the onus lies on the GFM to ensure seamless "occupation" and "maintenance," which will underscore the scope of postconstruction management. They are discussed from the facility management point of view, and divided into two broad categories: operations and management (Kamaruzzaman *et al.*, 2018).

Operational scope refers to the staff's everyday routine support roles, including operating and maintaining all physical elements to guarantee functionality, enhance the physical assets' value, and provide a healthy and safe environment (Jensen & van der Voordt, 2020). These tasks are comparatively short term in nature and involve cleaning, repairing, and redecorating, among others. More importantly, good postconstruction management practice is founded on these routines and services (Chinemenma *et al.*, 2021).

Gehani (1995) identified that management roles are distinguished at strategic and tactical levels. Non-routine planning and consultation at the strategic level aim to make the best use of the organization's facilities and physical resources over the long term (Newell *et al.*, 2003). According to Badke-Schaub *et al.* (2011), management strategy deals with the complexities of ambiguous, non-routine situations that can affect the overall direction and future of the organization. Bowen *et al.* (2018) documented that there is consultation and non-routine planning at the strategic level to make the best, long-term use of the organization's physical resources and overall facilities. In agreement, Musyoka (2018) stated that management strategy deals with the intricacies of non-routine ambiguous activities that can impact the objectives and future of the whole system. Hence, strategic decisions require an integrated approach, reactive or proactive, whereby the organization has one vision.

On the other hand, the tactical level depends on the policy direction of strategic planners tasked with sophisticated and complex processes because they involve specific, routine, and short-term managerial preventive operations (Tien, 2019) and activities on this level support accountable workplace behavior as well as the continuity of working environments (Suzuki, 2017).

16.5. Principles of green project postconstruction management

Management research has a long history, and many authors have approached it from various perspectives, with different rationalists emphasizing different beliefs. For example, the Taylor school of thought highlighted the engineering aspect and emphasized human interaction, Brech and Terry focused on decision-making, Davis accentuated leadership, and others, such as Richman, underscored coordination and integration (Riaz & ur Rehman, 2017).

Koontz (2010) gave a broad description of management as the practice of designing and maintaining an atmosphere where people working as a team competently achieve a selected number of goals. Primarily, this definition implies that managers carry out the managerial functions of planning, organizing, leading, staffing, and controlling to achieve a set of productivity.

However, because of the components and objectives of green building, its postconstruction management principles go beyond the traditional management principles and include specifics discussed as follows.

16.5.1. *Sustainable management*

Green building's effective, sustainable management is important to creating and fostering a healthy living environment that facilitates security and safety for its inhabitants within the purview of the sustainable development targets. A modern and sustainable asset management process that supports well-planned and managed infrastructure such as water supply, sewage systems, and communications networks is a significant contributing factor to achieving this goal (Yang *et al.*, 2021).

Qin *et al.* (2016) posited that the development, management, and maintenance of a green building must be supported by holistic asset management systems and other mechanisms, such as risk management, engineering PM, and a life cycle approach to asset management. Furthermore, Federman (2017) reiterated that advanced approaches such as automated data collection, geographic information systems, building information modeling, and improved asset planning and design help support the systems of green building.

16.5.2. *Resilience*

The design and facilities of green building are intended to ensure that they have an extended life cycle by guaranteeing that the space is environmentally friendly, durable, and adaptable to maximize alternatives for future use (De Neufville & Scholtes, 2011). Furthermore, regarding greenhouse gas emissions, conservation of energy, and toxicity, the choice of materials has a considerable impact on the environmental performance of buildings; hence, materials with high recycling capability, resilience, and long life are desirable material characteristics for green building.

As a result, Howe (2011) noted that green building materials are chosen based on the criteria, such as reused and recycled content, zero or low off-gassing of harmful air emissions, zero or low toxicity, sustainably and quickly ecofriendly harvested components, high recyclability, ruggedness, longevity, and local production.

16.5.3. *Water efficiency*

As a result of its relative "abundance," water is the most critical resource exploited because all human activities rely on it, and it has no alternative (Gleick, 1996). Unfortunately, Barbier (2019) reported that the perceived abundance has encouraged water wastage and led to water stress in most parts of the world. Water efficiency reduces water usage and minimizes wastage through improved technology and practices (Pereira *et al.*, 2012). Green buildings are sustainable buildings that demand water conservation while preventing pollution, encouraging the reuse of greywater and recycled treated water, and ensuring potable water is used for potable activities alone (Sheth, 2017).

16.5.4. *Energy efficiency*

Buildings consume around 40% of the world's energy (Harputlugil & de Wilde, 2021), releasing about a third of the total global carbon (Du *et al.*, 2019). The resultant effect of carbon emissions is the energy crisis, global warming, and climate change, which have become one of humanity's major challenges (Erickson, 2017).

Significant attempts have been made to reduce energy consumption and improve its efficiency, and the concept is associated with the energy supply required to achieve desired environmental conditions that reduce energy consumption (Paramati *et al.*, 2022). The elements that contribute to energy consumption in buildings include lighting, heating, cooling, and air conditioning (Alizadeh *et al.*, 2020), and green building endeavors to reduce energy costs in buildings via its design and optimization of variables (Peña *et al.*, 2022). Furthermore, for ease of postconstruction management, green building projects integrate the mechanisms of the variables from the beginning of the construction phase, thereby ensuring the reduction of the implementation costs and adding values that benefit the user (Pacheco *et al.*, 2012). Hence, green building projects go beyond conventional codes, having higher sustainability goals in energy saving, carbon emission reduction, and indoor air quality (IAQ) improvement.

16.5.5. *Waste efficiency*

The construction sector involves numerous resource-intensive activities that generate a significant volume of waste (Wu *et al.*, 2015), which has been said to contribute to the depletion of the ecosystem (Zhang *et al.*, 2019). Illankoon and Lu (2020) observed that minimizing production waste is a critical sustainability target in green building rating systems. Abandoned and surplus materials resulting from building processes, such as construction, renovation, and demolition, are construction waste (Saidu & Shakantu, 2016). Green building standards, on the other hand, have credits for evaluating waste efficiency, reducing virgin resource usage and landfilling; and incentivizing the reuse and recycling of original building parts and components, the use of green materials, the implementation of minimal-waste design and construction technologies, and the development of better waste management strategies (Ghisellini *et al.*, 2018).

16.5.6. *Indoor air quality*

The quality of air around and within structures and buildings is referred to as IAQ, and it is well known that it impacts occupants' comfort, health, and well-being (Steinemann *et al.*, 2017). Green building incorporates methods to reduce indoor air pollutant sources and increase energy efficiency in buildings (McGill *et al.*, 2016). However, although encasing can save energy and reduce the infiltration of outdoor pollutants, an unintended consequence can be a significant rise in toxic elements from indoor air contaminants (Sharpe *et al.*, 2020).

The World Health Organization's "Guidelines for Air Quality" reported that the main health implications of indoor air pollution include respiratory infection, irritation, and sick building syndrome, among others (World Health Organization, 2000). As a result, maintaining high IAQ is critical to ensuring the health of building occupants and, hence, one of green building postconstruction management's vital principles.

16.5.7. *Conservation*

While there is no single definition of conservation, it is possible to gain perspective by assuming that it is a set of activities that preserve or restore ecosystem health and prevent or recover species from extinction (Sutton, 2004). Early efforts to conserve materials and energy in buildings necessitated a comprehensive approach to addressing numerous dimensions of sustainability (Bibri & Krogstie, 2017). A green building will only accomplish its goals within the confines of conservation of resources, such as water, energy, and materials, as well as improved IAQ in the built environment (Ahn *et al.*, 2013).

16.5.8. *Sustainable maintenance*

Green building pushes the utilization of all earth-friendly materials, the execution of practices to reduce waste, and the improvement of IAQ (Nasier, 2021). This use indicates ecological, monetary, financial, and social advantages, and the accomplishments of a green building will rely upon the quality and viability of green frameworks, which have a goal of sustainable development (Sarkar *et al.*, 2020). Furthermore, achieving sustainable maintenance will help achieve health and safety performance, improved environment, adoption of lean manufacturing and other sustainable engineering techniques, and improved working conditions (Cherrafi *et al.*, 2017). Meanwhile, best practices in manufacturing and maintenance processes are needed to reduce waste.

Every aspect of a legal protocol must be met in the design and maintenance of green building within the ambit of green and sustainable principles (Franco *et al.*, 2021). This means that incorporating recyclable and recycled materials into all phases for energy efficiency and long-term maintenance is vital.

16.6. Factors that will influence the use and postconstruction management of green buildings

The United Nations has underscored the vital role of management in creating a sustainable living environment. While green building projects have been expanding rapidly to solve the construction industry's sustainability challenges in the recent past, this rapid expansion calls for identifying the overarching factors influencing their use and postconstruction management. The factors are politics/policy, socioeconomic, human resource and organizational, physical and environmental, technological, ethical/moral, and legal, as adapted from Adeniran *et al.* (2021) (see Figure 16.2).

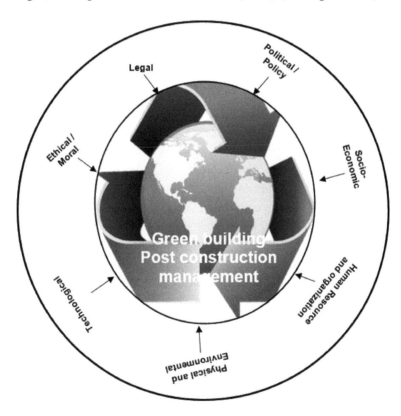

Figure 16.2. Factors that will influence the use and postconstruction management of green building.

16.6.1. *Political and policy factors*

Politics/policy factors are ideologies and legislations that influence decision-making, social systems and participation, security and stability, service delivery, and access. Whatever impacts the other factors may have on management, politics and policy may threaten them because they influence people's rights. As a result, political and policy factors may present challenges to green building postconstruction management, and their interaction may influence its success.

Chan *et al.* (2018) showed that the most dominant factor influencing green building technologies was government-related factors, highlighting the government's role in promoting its adoption. Political factors include the support and promotion given by the government. As identified by Love *et al.* (2012), the lack of government incentives is one of the factors influencing the development of green construction; thus, their role is vital. Various governments and organizations advocate promoting sustainable construction, but Han (2019) indicated that a lack of promotion causes the slow spread of green practices.

Also, a critical influencer, highlighted by Oke and Aigbavboa (2017), includes governments' necessary and appropriate guidelines and regulations. In the same vein, Mashwama *et al.* (2020) identified that the government needs to play a huge role in implementing green construction as there was limited government involvement and the complexity of codes and regulations on green building in emerging economies was an issue.

Gurgun *et al.* (2018) also stated that politics and economic crises influence importation and green materials prices. This means that whether materials are needed for construction or postconstruction management, their availability will be influenced by the government that makes policies.

16.6.2. *Socioeconomic factors*

Marker *et al.* (2014) stated that social influence provides the most significant contribution to the adoption of green building technology, and this influence can reduce transaction costs. The social influences of green building postconstruction management are premised on quality of life, health, and well-being in the buildings, the community, and the societal environment. At a building level, the social influences are centered on health, comfort, and satisfaction (Chen *et al.*, 2020). A subfactor of social idiosyncrasies are cultural elements that significantly impact green building adoption and processes as acceptance of innovation at its early phase is encouraged where cliques are expressive (Chuah, 2018). The issue of uncertainty is a major cultural dimension that influences the adoption of green building technology, and it is inherent in the level of risk tolerance (Muthukrishna & Schaller, 2020). A greater degree of uncertainty creates rigid rules in societal structure and is expected to slow the approval and implementation of new technologies (Kapoor & Klueter, 2021).

The economic factor influences environmental sustainability by ensuring minimum-cost processes that encourage optimal allocation of resources and discourage waste (Singh & El-Kassar, 2019). For example, Thacker *et al.* (2019) argued that a building has direct (associated with the life cycle costs and benefits of land, materials, and labor, among others) and indirect (including environmental costs associated with infrastructure, loss of biodiversity, etc., and social benefits, such as job creation) economic impacts through its development, use, and disposal. The socioeconomic benefits of a green building that influence its postconstruction management are greater tenant demand, building value insurance, lower occupancy cost, higher rents or sales prices, and human capital savings (Appleby, 2013).

16.6.3. *Technological factors*

Even though green building technologies have been encouraged in the construction industry to deal with sustainability issues, their adoption is still influenced by a series of impediments. Ahmed *et al.* (2021) defined green building technologies as technologies incorporated into building design and construction to make the final product sustainable. Green building technology influences a wide range of significant sustainability benefits that are not likely to be derived from adopting traditional building technologies; as documented by the United Nations Environment Programme (2009) that with the adoption of appropriate green building technologies, a 30–80% cut in building energy consumption is attainable.

In addition, several researchers (Simpeh & Smallwood, 2015; Luthra *et al.*, 2015) have indicated that green building technology adoption influences several other environmental, economic, and social benefits, such as improved indoor environmental quality, improved productivity, water efficiency, enhanced human health and well-being, and higher property value. Some of the key influencers with respect to technological factors are knowledge systems and data capturing, benchmarking and assessment, technologies of the future changing the construction process, and technologies to mitigate the impact (Kerin & Pham, 2020).

The technology factors associated with green building projects are broad, comprising land, water resources, energy, materials, construction and building technology, and indoor environment, among others; thus, every piece of technological development is critical to green building development.

16.6.4. *Organizational and human resource factors*

Kraus *et al.* (2020) have asserted that policymakers and researchers have come to a compromise that increased pollution, resource depletion, and biodiversity loss, which are the causative factors of environmental degradation, are deeply rooted in organizational and human behavior.

Chew (2004) classified human resource management factors as organizational (company culture and policies, leadership, consultation, communication, working relationships, effective integration, and satisfying work environment) and human resource (effective selection, training and career development, motivation, equity, and challenging opportunities and assignments). The introduction of green buildings has necessitated the change concepts, Kaizen, lean management, business reengineering, or Total Quality Management (TQM), which devolve greater emphasis on personnel (Taplin & Winterton, 2019; Buckley *et al.*, 2017). According to Solaimani *et al.* (Solaimani *et al.*, 2019), these concepts imply active engagement in the change initiative, leading to a more process-oriented and holistic work design.

Hence, human interactions with the system and natural environment are complex and diverse and thus influence the use and postconstruction management of green building.

16.6.5. *Physical and environmental factors*

The adoption of green building technology seeks to guarantee sustainable construction against conventional technologies' physical and environmental challenges (Zhang *et al.*, 2019). One of the contextual or external factors that influence the adoption of an innovation such as green building was identified by Sanderford *et al.* (2015) as the attributes of the built environment, which are physical and environmental. Physical and environmental attributes that will influence the use and postconstruction management of green buildings are the topography (Vyas *et al.*, 2019b), climate (Mohanta & Das, 2022), size (Ikudayisi *et al.*, 2022; Brueckner and Colwell, 1983), access (Vyas *et al.*, 2019), location (Hashim *et al.*, 2012), density (Mansour *et al.*, 2022), land use mix (Fruth *et al.*, 2019), landscape (Luo *et al.*, 2020), and infrastructure (Olawumi & Chan, 2020; Liberalesso *et al.*, 2020), among others.

16.6.6. *Legal factors*

Certain legally enforceable rights, which reflect the extent and effectiveness of control, are considered legal factors, and the basis of green building management will depend on the form of rights, privileges, and obligations that subsist in it (Adeniran *et al.*, 2021). These highlight specific laws and regulations that may impact an industry's business environment, and such legal analysis may consider employment, health and safety, consumer, advertising, and antitrust legislation (Ulubeyli & Kazanci, 2018).

Therefore, the legal factors must be clearly understood if they are to be used to maximum advantage against the challenges they might bring. Examples of legal factors that can influence the postconstruction management of green building include government legislation (Ulubeyli &

Kazanci, 2018), right to rely, risk averseness, the standard of care and compensation (Raouf & Al-Ghamdi, 2019), spatial planning regulations (Biernacka & Kronenberg, 2018), and institutional framework (Darko & Chan, 2018), to mention a few.

16.6.7. *Moral and ethical factors*

Morality and ethics are mental phenomena inseparable from human intentionality; thus, their considerations in the prescriptions for management practice cannot be wished away (Pertiwi, 2018). Some of the moral and ethical issues that can influence green building postconstruction management include misappropriation of funds allocated for maintenance management (Mbaiwa, 2015), sharp practice (Assaad & El-Adaway, 2020), money laundering and tax invasion (Berghoff & Spiekermann, 2018), and bribery (Chang *et al.*, 2018; Chan *et al.*, 2017), among others.

16.7. Postconstruction management strategies for green projects

Green development is fast becoming a popular concept to accommodate growth while minimizing impacts on natural resources. Each phase of green development — design, construction, and postconstruction — is all-important. Postconstruction, which is the longest in the life cycle, refers to people moving into and managing their properties and the neighborhoods in which they are situated. Figure 16.3 presents a framework for the postconstruction management of green building. The inner circle represents the green building postconstruction management, while the second layer represents the strategies that will ensure that the influences in the outer layer have a positive influence on the green building environment.

The outer layer contains the factors that influence green building postconstruction management. They could be exogenous or endogenous, as discussed in the previous section.

The middle layer shows the five management types vital to postconstruction management: strategic management, performance management, maintenance management, estate management, and sustainable waste management; they all work within reactive and preventive maintenance.

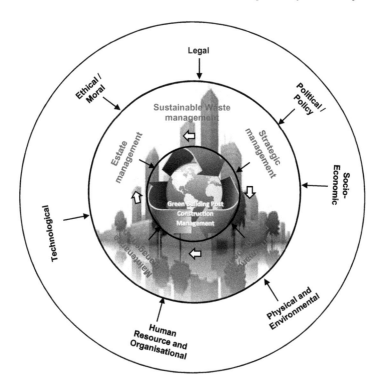

Figure 16.3.   Framework for postconstruction management of green building.

Strategic management is defined by McGee and Sammut-Bonnici as "the process of evaluation, planning, and implementation designed to maintain or improve competitive advantage" (McGee & Sammut-Bonnici, 2015). Corporate vision, business models, global strategy, competitive techniques, global strategy, collaborative action, and mergers are all part of the planning process (Bindra *et al.*, 2019).

Leadership is required during the implementation phase to control strategic processes, build the applicable organizational structure, steer the organization through corporate governance, and develop management culture (Samimi *et al.*, 2020). Sandradewi *et al.* (2022) contended that every other management activity is deficient for resource deployment and implementation when strategic management is lacking.

According to Baron and Armstrong (2007), "performance management is a strategic and integrated approach to enhancing the effectiveness of organizations by improving the performance of the people who work in them and developing the capabilities of teams and individual contributors." Performance management also ensures the success of set goals by linking performances and targets to the core objective and goals of the organization (Aguinis *et al.*, 2012). Hence, performance management will aid in increasing efficiency by establishing links between corporate strategy, budgeting, and service monitoring and evaluation for the success of postconstruction management of green building.

Maintenance management involves all activities of management that determine the maintenance objectives, priorities, strategies, and responsibilities (Márquez, 2007). Therefore, maintenance management is a significant support function in building performance because it will guarantee the sustenance of functional, structural, economic, and aesthetic conditions (Waziri & Vanduhe, 2013) throughout the life cycle of a green building project. Furthermore, maintenance itself is defined according to BS 3811 as "a combination of any actions carried out to retain an item in or restore it to an acceptable condition" (Chanter & Swallow, 2007).

Olajide (2017) defined estate management as "the direction and the supervision of interest(s) in the land and landed property to secure optimum return which may not always be financial, but it can be a social benefit, status, prestige, political power or some other goal or group of goals." Green buildings are landed properties built for a goal, and therefore the estate management function is vital for the postconstruction management of green building.

The traditional waste management approach is to plan waste generation, collection, and disposal systems as separate operations, but they are intimately connected, and each can influence the other. Moreover, the planning required for these operations necessitates a delicate balance between manufacturing subsystems, transportation systems, land use patterns, urban growth and development, and public health considerations (Li *et al.*, 2018). Therefore, various improvement methods which will ensure prevention, minimization, reuse, recycling, recovery, and disposal should be harnessed to ensure the benefits of a chosen approach to excellent management toward sustainability in waste management.

From the preceding, it can be seen that all the five management types are vital postconstruction management of green building.

16.7.1. *Maintenance approach*

The postconstruction management personnel will be primarily responsible for the selection of the approach to be used, and this decision must be consistent with established policies in order to achieve the initial goal and reap the benefits of the green building project. While it is essential to note that no single format can fit all maintenance circumstances, rather, any format used should be tailored to a green building project's explicit requirements and program. As illustrated in Figure 16.4, from BS3811 (1993), there are various approaches to maintenance that can be divided into planned and unplanned maintenance (Idris *et al.*, 2022).

Planned maintenance is defined by Au-Yong *et al.* (2018) as work performed at a prespecified time to prevent or reduce the possibility of a facility failing, with appropriate tasks assigned based on cost-effectiveness and safety (Basri *et al.*, 2017). Such work is scheduled and implemented in expectation of a failure, and the activities include regular inspection, cleaning, testing, and routine checks to prevent component breakdown (Saxena, 2022), as well as condition or time-based maintenance that results from prior knowledge of a component's condition as a result of periodic inspection (Blokus-Dziula & Soszynska-Budny, 2022). The benefits of planned maintenance include ensuring that assets live through their predetermined lifespan while long-term repair costs are significantly kept low and enhancing safety, due to a reduction in the likelihood of catastrophic failure (Alileche, 2018). This maintenance approach is best suited for green building as the target is to ensure sustainability and avoid breakdowns.

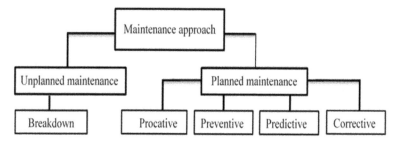

Figure 16.4.   Maintenance approach adapted from BS 3811, 1993.

16.8. The benefits of effective postconstruction management of green projects

The benefits of effective postconstruction management of green projects may not be measurable in the short term, and the maintenance costs are likely to be high until the benefits begin to have an impact. One of the benefits is that it will ensure that the green building is compliant and safe for use by everyone who has access to it (Atlam & Wills, 2020). In addition, postconstruction management of green building will guarantee the overall functionality of every space in the green building (Amato *et al.*, 2020). Also, functional and clean facilities are valuable and lead to comfortable and long-term residents because fewer incidences of breakdown occur when assets, such as HVAC units, elevators, and boilers, operate as efficiently as possible (Eini *et al.*, 2021). A further benefit is that postconstruction management of green buildings will reduce the number of onsite potential accidents or incidents, thus helping be free of litigations and liabilities (Jeong *et al.* 2022). Finally, a well-maintained property retains its market value, and it is thus expected that a green building project with adequate postconstruction management will continue to maintain its value over time (Zalejska-Jonsson, 2020).

16.9. Conclusion

This chapter attempted to make a case for the importance of postconstruction management of green projects and concludes that the postconstruction phase in the life cycle of a green building project is the longest and as such that phase must be well taken care of to avoid or eliminate obsolescence. The chapter concludes that while green building culture is being promoted, planned maintenance must be projected for postconstruction management of green building and stakeholders must be intimated of the process to make green building projects more efficient during the longest term of its cycle and enhance knowledge in adapting sustainability in the green construction industry.

References

Abisuga, O. (2020). Integrated collaborative facilities management framework for post-occupancy evaluation of higher education facilities. Doctoral dissertation, University of New South Wales, Sydney, Australia.

Adeniran, A. A., Mbanga, S., & Botha, B. (2021). A framework for the management of human settlements: Nigeria and South Africa as cases. *Town and Regional Planning, 78*, 1–15.

Aguinis, H., Gottfredson, R. K., & Joo, H. (2012). Using performance management to win the talent war. *Business Horizons, 55*(6), 609–616.

Ahmed, A. M., Sayed, W., Asran, A., & Nosier, I. (2023). Identifying barriers to the implementation and development of sustainable construction. *International Journal of Construction Management, 23*(8), 1277–1288.

Ahn, Y. H., Pearce, A. R., Wang, Y., & Wang, G. (2013). Drivers and barriers of sustainable design and construction: The perception of green building experience. *International Journal of Sustainable Building Technology and Urban Development, 4*(1), 35–45.

Alaimo, G. & Accurso, F. (2008). The assessment of durability of discontinuous roofing: An experiment on sandwich panels. In *11th International Conference on Durability of Building Materials and Components*. (Vol. 3, pp. 1029–1036). Istanbul Technical University, Istanbul, Turkey. 11 May 2008–14 May 2008.

Albu, S. & Albu, I. (2021). Depreciation of the economic value of historic properties. *Open Journal of Applied Sciences, 11*(11), 1256–1267.

Alexander, K. (2013). *Facilities Management: Theory and Practice*. Routledge.

Alileche, L. (2018). Use of BIM for the optimal management of existing buildings. Doctoral dissertation, Université de Lille, France.

Alizadeh, R., Soltanisehat, L., Lund, P. D., & Zamanisabzi, H. (2020). Improving renewable energy policy planning and decision-making through a hybrid MCDM method. *Energy Policy, 137*, 111174.

Alonso, A., Patricio, J., Suarez, R., & Escandon, R. (2020). Acoustical retrofit of existing residential buildings: Requirements and recommendations for sound insulation between dwellings in Europe and other countries worldwide. *Building and Environment, 174*, 106771.

Amato, A., Andreoli, M., & Rovai, M. (2021). Adaptive reuse of a historic building by introducing new functions: A scenario evaluation based on participatory MCA applied to a former carthusian monastery in Tuscany, Italy. *Sustainability*, *13*(4), 2335.

Appleby, P. (2013). *Sustainable Retrofit and Facilities Management*. Routledge, Oxford.

Assaad, R. & El-Adaway, I. H. (2020). Enhancing the knowledge of construction business failure: A social network analysis approach. *Journal of Construction Engineering and Management*, *146*(6), 04020052.

Atlam, H. F. & Wills, G. B. (2020). IoT security, privacy, safety and ethics. In *Digital Twin Technologies and Smart Cities* (pp. 123–149). Cham: Springer.

Au-Yong, C. P., Ali, A. S., & Chua, S. J. L. (2018). A literature review of routine maintenance in high-rise residential buildings: A theoretical framework and directions for future research. *Journal of Facilities Management*. *17*(1), 2–17. https://doi.org/10.1108/JFM-10-2017-0051.

Badke-Schaub, P., Daalhuizen, J., & Roozenburg, N. (2011). Towards a designer-centred methodology: Descriptive considerations and prescriptive reflections. In *The Future of Design Methodology* (pp. 181–197). London: Springer.

Barbier, E. (2019). The water paradox. In *The Water Paradox*. (pp. 1–269). Yale University Press, London.

Baron, A. & Armstrong, M. (2007). *Human Capital Management: Achieving Added Value Through People*. Kogan Page Publishers, London.

Basri, E. I., Razak, I. H. A., Ab-Samat, H., & Kamaruddin, S. (2017). Preventive maintenance (PM) planning: A review. *Journal of Quality in Maintenance Engineering*, *23*(2), 114–143. https://doi.org/10.1108/JQME-04-2016-0014.

Berghoff, H. & Spiekermann, U. (2018). Shady business: On the history of white-collar crime. *Business History*, *60*(3), 289–304.

Bibri, S. E. & Krogstie, J. (2017). Smart sustainable cities of the future: An extensive interdisciplinary literature review. *Sustainable Cities and Society*, *31*, 183–212.

Biernacka, M. & Kronenberg, J. (2018). Classification of institutional barriers affecting the availability, accessibility and attractiveness of urban green spaces. *Urban Forestry & Urban Greening*, *36*, 22–33.

Bindra, S., Parameswar, N., & Dhir, S. (2019). Strategic management: The evolution of the field. *Strategic Change*, *28*(6), 469–478.

Blokus-Dziula, A. & Soszynska-Budny, J. (2022). Condition-based maintenance and availability analysis of wind farm infrastructure. *Journal of Infrastructure Systems*, *28*(2), 05022001.

Bortolini, R. & Forcada, N. (2018). Building inspection system for evaluating the technical performance of existing buildings. *Journal of Performance of Constructed Facilities*, *32*(5), 04018073.

Bowen, A., Kuralbayeva, K., & Tipoe, E. L. (2018). Characterising green employment: The impacts of 'greening' on workforce composition. *Energy Economics*, *72*, 263–275.

Brueckner, J. K. & Colwell, P. F. (1983). A spatial model of housing attributes: Theory and evidence. *Land Economics*, *59*(1), 58–69.

Buckley, P., Found, P., Griffiths, G., & Harrison, G. (2017). *Staying Lean: Thriving, Not Just Surviving*. CRC Press, Cardiff.

Buitelaar, E., Moroni, S., & De Franco, A. (2021). Building obsolescence in the evolving city. Reframing property vacancy and abandonment in the light of urban dynamics and complexity. *Cities*, *108*, 102964.

Chan, A. P. C., Darko, A., Olanipekun, A. O., & Ameyaw, E. E. (2018). Critical barriers to green building technologies adoption in developing countries: The case of Ghana. *Journal of Cleaner Production*, *172*, 1067–1079.

Chan, A. P., Darko, A., Ameyaw, E. E., & Owusu-Manu, D. G. (2017). Barriers affecting the adoption of green building technologies. *Journal of Management in Engineering*, *33*(3), 04016057.

Chang, R. D., Zuo, J., Zhao, Z. Y., Soebarto, V., Lu, Y., Zillante, G., & Gan, X. L. (2018). Sustainability attitude and performance of construction enterprises: A China study. *Journal of Cleaner Production*, *172*, 1440–1451.

Chanter, P. & Swallow, B. (2007). *Building Maintenance Management* (2nd edn.). Oxford: Blackwell Publishing Ltd.

Chen, C. F., Yilmaz, S., Pisello, A. L., De Simone, M., Kim, A., Hong, T., Bandurski, K., Bavaresco, M. V., Liu, P. L., & Zhu, Y. (2020). The impacts of building characteristics, social psychological and cultural factors on indoor environment quality productivity belief. *Building and Environment*, *185*, 107189.

Cherrafi, A., Elfezazi, S., Govindan, K., Garza-Reyes, J. A., Benhida, K., & Mokhlis, A. (2017). A framework for the integration of green and lean six sigma for superior sustainability performance. *International Journal of Production Research*, *55*(15), 4481–4515.

Chew, J. C. L. (2004). The influence of human resource management practices on the retention of core employees of Australian organisations: An empirical study. Doctoral dissertation, Murdoch University.

Chinemenma, O. A., Chisom, N. C., & Uzoamaka, O. E. (2021). The impact of facility management on office buildings performance in Nigerian Universities. *Indiana Journal of Humanities and Social Sciences*, *2*(7), 19–28.

Chuah, S. H. W. (2018 December). Why and who will adopt extended reality technology? Literature review, synthesis, and future research agenda. *Literature Review, Synthesis, and Future Research Agenda*. Universiti Sains Malaysia, Malaysia, pp. 1–56. http://dx.doi.org/10.2139/ssrn.3300469.

Darko, A. & Chan, A. P. C. (2018). Strategies to promote green building technologies adoption in developing countries: The case of Ghana. *Building and Environment, 130*, 74–84.

De Neufville, R. & Scholtes, S. (2011). *Flexibility in Engineering Design*. MIT Press, Massachusetts.

Dossche, C., Boel, V., & De Corte, W. (2017). Use of life cycle assessments in the construction sector: Critical review. *Procedia Engineering, 171*, 302–311.

Du, Q., Li, Z., Li, Y., Bai, L., Li, J., & Han, X. (2019). Rebound effect of energy efficiency in China's construction industry: A general equilibrium analysis. *Environmental Science and Pollution Research, 26*(12), 12217–12226.

Eini, R., Linkous, L., Zohrabi, N., & Abdelwahed, S. (2021). Smart building management system: Performance specifications and design requirements. *Journal of Building Engineering, 39*, 102222.

Erickson, L. E. (2017). Reducing greenhouse gas emissions and improving air quality: Two global challenges. *Environmental Progress & Sustainable Energy, 36*(4), 982–988.

Farahani, A., Wallbaum, H., & Dalenbäck, J. O. (2019). Optimised maintenance and renovation scheduling in multifamily buildings — A systematic approach based on condition state and life cycle cost of building components. *Construction Management and Economics, 37*(3), 139–155.

Federman, A. (2017). Documentation for the conservation of built heritage: Analysis of recording methodologies. Doctoral dissertation, Carleton University.

Franco, M. A. J. Q., Pawar, P., & Wu, X. (2021). Green building policies in cities: A comparative assessment and analysis. *Energy and Buildings, 231*, 110561.

Fruth, E., Kvistad, M., Marshall, J., Pfeifer, L., Rau, L., Sagebiel, J., Soto, D., Tarpey, J., Weir, J., & Winiarski, B. (2019). Economic valuation of street-level urban greening: A case study from an evolving mixed-use area in Berlin. *Land Use Policy, 89*, 104237.

Gann, D. M. & Salter, A. J. (2000). Innovation in project-based, service-enhanced firms: The construction of complex products and systems. *Research Policy, 29*(7–8), 955–972.

Gehani, R. R. (1995). Time-based management of technology: A taxonomic integration of tactical and strategic roles. *International Journal of Operations & Production Management, 15*(2), 19–35.

Ghisellini, P., Ji, X., Liu, G., & Ulgiati, S. (2018). Evaluating the transition towards cleaner production in the construction and demolition sector of China: A review. *Journal of Cleaner Production, 195*, 418–434.

Gleick, P. H. (1996). Basic water requirements for human activities: Meeting basic needs. *Water International, 21*(2), 83–92.

Grover, R. & Grover, C. (2015). Obsolescence — A cause for concern? *Journal of Property Investment & Finance, 33*(3), 299–314. https://doi.org/10.1108/JPIF-02-2015-0016.

Gurgun, A. P., Bayhan, H. G., Polat, G., & Turkoglu, H. (2018). Schedule risk assessment in green building projects. In *Euro-Med-Sec-2. The Second European and Mediterranean Structural Engineering and Construction Conference: Responsible Design and Delivery of the Constructed Project* 23–28 July 2018, Beirut, Lebanon 379 (Vol. 1) 1–6.

Han, H. (2019). Governance for green urbanisation: Lessons from Singapore's green building certification scheme. *Environment and Planning C: Politics and Space, 37*(1), 137–156.

Harputlugil, T. & de Wilde, P. (2021). The interaction between humans and buildings for energy efficiency: A critical review. *Energy Research & Social Science, 71*, 101828.

Hashim, A. E., Samikon, S. A., Nasir, N. M., & Ismail, N. (2012). Assessing factors influencing performance of Malaysian low-cost public housing in sustainable environment. *Procedia-Social and Behavioral Sciences, 50*, 920–927.

Howe, J. C. (2011). Overview of green buildings. *Environmental Law Reporter News & Analysis, 41*, 10043.

Huron, D. (2016). Aesthetics. In S. Hallam, I. Cross, & M. Thaut (Eds.), *The Oxford Handbook of Music Psychology* (pp. 233–245). Oxford University Press, Oxford.

Idris, M. F. M., Saad, N. H., Yahaya, M. I., Mohamed, W. M. W., Shuib, A., & Amin, A. N. M. (2022). Strategy practiced by rolling stock maintenance: A case study within the urban rail. *Pertanika J. Sci. Technol, 30*(2), 1019–1032.

Ikudayisi, A. E., Chan, A. P., Darko, A., & Adegun, O. B. (2022). Integrated design process of green building projects: A review towards assessment metrics and conceptual framework. *Journal of Building Engineering, 50*, 104180.

Illankoon, I. C. S. & Lu, W. (2020). Cost implications of obtaining construction waste management-related credits in green building. *Waste Management, 102*, 722–731.

Ingrao, C., Messineo, A., Beltramo, R., Yigitcanlar, T., & Ioppolo, G. (2018). How can life cycle thinking support sustainability of buildings? Investigating life cycle assessment applications for energy efficiency and environmental performance. *Journal of Cleaner Production, 201*, 556–569.

Ismail, Z. A. (2020). Maintenance management practices for green building projects: Towards hybrid BIM system. *Smart and Sustainable Built Environment*, 10(4), 616–630. https://doi.org/10.1108/SASBE-03-2019-0029.

Jensen, P. A. & van der Voordt, T. J. (2020). Typology of value adding FM and CREM interventions. *Journal of Corporate Real Estate*, 22(3), 197–214. https://doi.org/10.1108/JCRE-09-2019-0042.

Jeong, G., Kim, H., Lee, H. S., Park, M., & Hyun, H. (2022). Analysis of safety risk factors of modular construction to identify accident trends. *Journal of Asian Architecture and Building Engineering*, 21(3), 1040–1052.

Johnston, K. M. (2016). Obsolescence and renewal: Transformation of post war concrete buildings. Doctoral dissertation, University of Maryland, USA.

Kamaruzzaman, S. N., Myeda, N. E., Zawawi, E. M. A., & Ramli, R. M. (2018). Developing facilities management (FM) competencies for Malaysia: Reference from international practice. *Journal of Facilities Management*, 16(2), 157–174. https://doi.org/10.1108/JFM-08-2017-0036.

Kapoor, R. & Klueter, T. (2021). Unbundling and managing uncertainty surrounding emerging technologies. *Strategy Science*, 6(1), 62–74.

Kerin, M. & Pham, D. T. (2020). Smart remanufacturing: A review and research framework. *Journal of Manufacturing Technology Management*, 31(6), 1205–1235. https://doi.org/10.1108/JMTM-06-2019-0205.

Koontz, H. (2010). *Essentials of Management*. Tata McGraw-Hill Education, New Delhi.

Kraus, S., Rehman, S. U., & García, F. J. S. (2020). Corporate social responsibility and environmental performance: The mediating role of environmental strategy and green innovation. *Technological Forecasting and Social Change, 160,* 120262.

Krivý, M. (2013). Don't plan! The use of the notion of 'culture' in transforming obsolete industrial space. *International Journal of Urban and Regional Research*, 37(5), 1724–1746.

Kumar, U., Galar, D., Parida, A., Stenström, C., & Berges, L. (2013). Maintenance performance metrics: A state-of-the-art review. *Journal of Quality in Maintenance Engineering, 19*(3), 233–277. https://doi.org/10.1108/JQME-05-2013-0029.

Li, J., Zuo, J., Cai, H., & Zillante, G. (2018). Construction waste reduction behavior of contractor employees: An extended theory of planned behaviour model approach. *Journal of Cleaner Production, 172,* 1399–1408.

Liberalesso, T., Cruz, C. O., Silva, C. M., & Manso, M. (2020). Green infrastructure and public policies: An international review of green roofs and green walls incentives. *Land Use Policy, 96,* 104693.

Liu, H. Y., Maas, M., Danaher, J., Scarcella, L., Lexer, M., & Van Rompaey, L. (2020). Artificial intelligence and legal disruption: A new model for analysis. *Law, Innovation and Technology, 12*(2), 205–258.

Love, P. E., Niedzweicki, M., Bullen, P. A., & Edwards, D. J. (2012). Achieving the green building council of Australia's world leadership rating in an office building in Perth. *Journal of Construction Engineering and Management, 138*(5), 652–660.

Luo, L., Fang, W., Wang, X., & Quan, R. (2020 March). Application of green building in landscape planning of characteristic towns. In *IOP Conference Series: Materials Science and Engineering* (Vol. 782, No. 5, p. 052026). 3rd International Conference on Energy Material, Chemical Engineering and Mining Engineering (EMCEME 2019), 28–29 December 2019, Qingdao, China. IOP Publishing.

Luthra, S., Kumar, S., Garg, D., & Haleem, A. (2015). Barriers to renewable/sustainable energy technologies adoption: Indian perspective. *Renewable and Sustainable Energy Reviews, 41*, 762–776.

Mansour, S., Al Nasiri, N., Abulibdeh, A., & Ramadan, E. (2022). Spatial disparity patterns of green spaces and buildings in arid urban areas. *Building and Environment, 208*, 108588.

Marker, A. W., Mason, S. G., & Morrow, P. (2014). Change factors influencing the diffusion and adoption of green building practices. *Performance Improvement Quarterly, 26*(4), 5–24.

Márquez, A. C. (2007). *The Maintenance Management Framework: Models and Methods for Complex Systems Maintenance*. Springer Science & Business Media, London.

Mashwama, N., Thwala, D., & Aigbavboa, C. (2020). Obstacles of sustainable construction project management in South Africa construction industry. In M. Mashwama, D. Thwala, C. & Aigbavboa (Eds.) *Sustainable Ecological Engineering Design*, (pp. 305–314). Cham: Springer.

Mbaiwa, J. E. (2015). Community-based natural resource management in Botswana. In *Institutional Arrangements for Conservation, Development and Tourism in Eastern and Southern Africa* (pp. 59–80). Dordrecht: Springer.

McGee, J. & Sammut-Bonnici, T. (2015). *Wiley Encyclopedia of Management, Volume 12: Strategic Management*. John Wiley & Sons.

McGill, G., Oyedele, L. O., McAllister, K., & Qin, M. (2016). Effective indoor air quality for energy-efficient homes: A comparison of UK rating systems. *Architectural Science Review, 59*(2), 159–173.

Mohamed, I. F., Edwards, D. J., Mateo-Garcia, M., Costin, G., & Thwala, W. D. D. (2019). An investigation into the construction industry's view on fire prevention in high-rise buildings post Grenfell. *International Journal of Building Pathology and Adaptation, 38*(3), 451–471. https://doi.org/10.1108/IJBPA-05-2019-0048.

Mohanta, A. & Das, S. (2022). Maintainability performance prediction of green building envelope in warm-humid climate. *Journal of Performance of Constructed Facilities, 36*(3), 04022013.

Muminović, E., Radosavljević, U., & Beganović, D. (2020). Strategic planning and management model for the regeneration of historic urban landscapes: The case of historic center of Novi Pazar in Serbia. *Sustainability, 12*(4), 1323.

Musyoka, G. W. (2018). Stakeholder involvement and service delivery: Provision of affordable housing by national housing corporation in Kenya. Doctoral dissertation, University of Nairobi.

Muthukrishna, M. & Schaller, M. (2020). Are collectivistic cultures more prone to rapid transformation? Computational models of cross-cultural differences, social network structure, dynamic social influence, and cultural change. *Personality and Social Psychology Review, 24*(2), 103–120.

Nasier, S. (2021). Sustainable green materials for new construction. *Materials Today: Proceedings, 37*, 3505–3508.

Newell, S., Huang, J. C., Galliers, R. D., & Pan, S. L. (2003). Implementing enterprise resource planning and knowledge management systems in tandem: Fostering efficiency and innovation complementarity. *Information and Organization, 13*(1), 25–52.

Oke, A. E. & Aigbavboa, C. O. (2017). Drivers of sustainable value management. In A.E. Oke & C. O. Aigbavboa (Eds.) *Sustainable Value Management for Construction Projects*, (pp. 179–182). Cham: Springer, Johannesburg, South Africa.

Olajide, S. E. (2017). *Elements of Estate Management.* Mauritius: Lap Lambert.

Olawumi, T. O. & Chan, D. W. (2020). Application of generalised Choquet fuzzy integral method in the sustainability rating of green buildings based on the BSAM scheme. *Sustainable Cities and Society, 61*, 102147.

Olubunmi, O. A., Xia, P. B., & Skitmore, M. (2016). Green building incentives: A review. *Renewable and Sustainable Energy Reviews, 59*, 1611–1621.

Pacheco, R., Ordóñez, J., & Martínez, G. (2012). Energy efficient design of building: A review. *Renewable and Sustainable Energy Reviews, 16*(6), 3559–3573.

Paramati, S. R., Shahzad, U., & Doğan, B. (2022). The role of environmental technology for energy demand and energy efficiency: Evidence from OECD countries. *Renewable and Sustainable Energy Reviews, 153*, 111735.

Peña, M., Biscarri, F., Personal, E., & León, C. (2022). Decision support system to classify and optimise the energy efficiency in smart buildings: A data analytics approach. *Sensors, 22*(4), 1380.

Pereira, L. S., Cordery, I., & Iacovides, I. (2012). Improved indicators of water use performance and productivity for sustainable water conservation and saving. *Agricultural Water Management, 108*, 39–51.

Pertiwi, K. (2018). Contextualising corruption: A cross-disciplinary approach to studying corruption in organisations. *Administrative Sciences, 8*(2), 12.

Pinder, J. & Wilkinson, S. J. (2000). The obsolescence of office property: A new research agenda. In *16th Annual ARCOM Conference. Glasgow Caledonian University.: Association of Researchers in Construction Management*, (pp. 375–384). 6–8 September 2000, Glasgow, UK.

Pourebrahimi, M., Eghbali, S. R., & Roders, A. P. (2020). Identifying building obsolescence: Towards increasing buildings' service life. *International Journal of Building Pathology and Adaptation, 38*(5), 635–652. https://doi.org/10.1108/IJBPA-08-2019-0068.

Preiser, W. & Vischer, J. (Eds.). (2006). *Assessing Building Performance.* Routledge, London.

Qin, X., Mo, Y., & Jing, L. (2016). Risk perceptions of the life-cycle of green buildings in China. *Journal of Cleaner Production, 126*, 148–158.

Raouf, A. M. & Al-Ghamdi, S. G. (2019). Building information modelling and green buildings: Challenges and opportunities. *Architectural Engineering and Design Management, 15*(1), 1–28.

Riaz, M. & ur Rehman, M. H. (2017). The effectiveness of school management in improvement of schools. *Educational Research International, 6*(2), 161–169.

Robichaud, L. B. & Anantatmula, V. S. (2011). Greening project management practices for sustainable construction. *Journal of Management in Engineering, 27*(1), 48–57.

Rodi, W. N. W., Hwa, T. K., Said, A. S., Mahamood, N. M., Abdullah, M. I., & Abd Rasam, A. R. (2015). Obsolescence of green office buildings: A literature review. *Procedia Economics and Finance, 31*, 651–660.

Romano, E., Negro, P., & Taucer, F. (2014). Seismic performance assessment addressing sustainability and energy efficiency. *JRC Scientific and Policy Reports.* Available at: https://data.europa.eu/doi/10.2788/5391.

Saidu, I. & Shakantu, W. (2016). The contributions of construction material waste to project cost overruns in Abuja, Nigeria. *Acta Structilia: Journal for the Physical and Development Sciences, 23*(1), 99–113.

Salem, D., Bakr, A., & El Sayad, Z. (2018). Post-construction stages cost management: Sustainable design approach. *Alexandria Engineering Journal, 57*(4), 3429–3435.

Samimi, M., Cortes, A. F., Anderson, M. H., & Herrmann, P. (2020). What is strategic leadership? Developing a framework for future research. *The Leadership Quarterly, 33*(3), 1–22.

Sanderford, A. R., Keefe, M. J., Koebel, C. T., & McCoy, A. P. (2015). Factors influencing US homebuilders' adoption of green homebuilding products. *Journal of Sustainable Real Estate, 7*(1), 60–82.

Sandradewi, K., Kusumaningrum, A., & Pradana, A. I. (2022). Research and development barriers in management and business area: Strategic management overview. *International Journal of Economics, Business and Accounting Research (IJEBAR), 6*(1), 405–415.

Sarkar, A., Qian, L., & Peau, A. K. (2020). Overview of green business practices within the Bangladeshi RMG industry: Competitiveness and sustainable development perspective. *Environmental Science and Pollution Research, 27*(18), 22888–22901.

Saxena, M. M. (2022). Total Productive Maintenance (TPM); as a vital function in manufacturing systems. *Journal of Applied Research in Technology & Engineering, 3*(1), 19–27.

Sechrest, D. K. & Price, S. J. (1985). *Correctional Facility Design and Construction Management*. National Institute of Justice, Washington DC.

Shafique, M., Kim, R., & Rafiq, M. (2018). Green roof benefits, opportunities and challenges–A review. *Renewable and Sustainable Energy Reviews, 90*, 757–773.

Sharpe, R., Osborne, N., Paterson, C., Taylor, T., Fleming, L., & Morris, G. (2020). Housing, indoor air pollution, and health in high-income countries. In *Oxford Research Encyclopedia of Environmental Science*. https://doi.org/10.1093/acrefore/9780199389414.013.34.

Sheth, D. (2017). Water efficient technologies for green buildings. *International Journal of Engineering Innovation and Scientific Research, 1*, 5–10.

Silva, A. & de Brito, J. (2019). Do we need a buildings' inspection, diagnosis and service life prediction software? *Journal of Building Engineering, 22*, 335–348.

Silva, A., de Brito, J., Thomsen, A., Straub, A., Prieto, A. J., & Lacasse, M. A. (2022). Causal effects between criteria that establish the end of service life of buildings and components. *Buildings, 12*(2), 88.

Simpeh, E. K. & Smallwood, J. J. (2015). Factors influencing the growth of green building in the South African construction industry. In *Smart and Sustainable Built Environment (SASBE) Conference 2015* (pp. 311–320). 9–11 December 2015, University of Pretoria, Pretoria, South Africa.

Singh, S. K. & El-Kassar, A. N. (2019). Role of big data analytics in developing sustainable capabilities. *Journal of Cleaner Production, 213*, 1264–1273.

Solaimani, S., van der Veen, J., Sobek II, D. K., Gulyaz, E., & Venugopal, V. (2019). On the application of Lean principles and practices to innovation management: A systematic review. *The TQM Journal, 31*(6), 1064–1092.

Srivastava, A. K., Kumar, G., & Gupta, P. (2020). Estimating maintenance budget using Monte Carlo simulation. *Life Cycle Reliability and Safety Engineering, 9*(1), 77–89.

Steinemann, A., Wargocki, P., & Rismanchi, B. (2017). Ten questions concerning green buildings and indoor air quality. *Building and Environment, 112*, 351–358.

Sutton, P. (2004). A perspective on environmental sustainability. *Paper on the Victorian Commissioner for Environmental Sustainability*, 1–32.

Suzuki, T. (2017). *TPM in Process Industries*. Routledge, New York.

Tang, H. T. & Lee, Y. M. (2016). The making of sustainable urban development: A synthesis framework. *Sustainability, 8*(5), 492.

Taplin, I. M. & Winterton, J. (Eds.). (2019). *Rethinking Global Production*. Routledge, London.

Thacker, S., Adshead, D., Fay, M., Hallegatte, S., Harvey, M., Meller, H., O'Regan, N., Rozenberg, J., Watkins, G., & Hall, J. W. (2019). Infrastructure for sustainable development. *Nature Sustainability, 2*(4), 324–331.

Thomsen, A. & Straub, A. (2021). Service life and the cause-effect processes underlying ageing and decay: A discussion. *CIB W080*, 48–54.

Tien, N. H. (2019). *International Economics, Business and Management Strategy*. Dehli: Academic Publications, Rohini, Delhi.

Ulubeyli, S. & Kazanci, O. (2018). Holistic sustainability assessment of green building industry in Turkey. *Journal of Cleaner Production, 202*, 197–212.

United Nations Environment Programme (UNEP) (2009). *Buildings and Climate Change: Summary for Decision Makers available online at* https://wedocs. unep.org/20.500.11822/32152 (accessed on 7 February 2022).

USEPA. (2019). Green building. Available at: https://archive.epa.gov/green building/web/html/ (accessed on 20 May 2022).

Vyas, G. S., Jha, K. N., & Patel, D. A. (2019a). Development of green building rating system using AHP and fuzzy integrals: A case of India. *Journal of Architectural Engineering, 25*(2), 04019004.

Vyas, G. S., Jha, K. N., & Rajhans, N. R. (2019b). Identifying and evaluating green building attributes by environment, social, and economic pillars of sustainability. *Civil Engineering and Environmental Systems, 36*(2–4), 133–148.

Waziri, B. S. & Vanduhe, B. A. (2013). Evaluation of factors affecting residential building maintenance in Nigeria: Users' perspective. *Civil and Environmental Research, 3*(8), 19–24.

WCED. (1987). World commission on environment and development. *Our Common Future, 17*(1), 1–91.

Wilkinson, S. J., Remøy, H., & Langston, C. (2014). *Sustainable Building Adaptation: Innovations in Decision-making.* John Wiley & Sons, West Sussex.

World Green Building Council. (2016). What is green building? | World Green Building Council. [online] *Worldgbc.org.* Available at: https://www.worldgbc.org/what-green-building (accessed on 20 May 2022).

World Health Organization. (2000). *Guidelines for Air Quality* (No. WHO/SDE/OEH/00.02). Geneva: World Health Organization. Available at: http://apps.who.int/iris/handle/10665/66537 (retrieved 15 May 2022).

Wu, Z., Fan, H., & Liu, G. (2015). Forecasting construction and demolition waste using gene expression programming. *Journal of Computing in Civil Engineering, 29*(5), 04014059.

Yang, F., Wen, X., Aziz, A., & Luhach, A. K. (2021). The need for local adaptation of smart infrastructure for sustainable economic management. *Environmental Impact Assessment Review, 88*, 106565.

Zalejska-Jonsson, A. (2020). Does facility management affect perception of building quality? A study of cooperative residential buildings in Sweden. *Facilities, 38*(7/8), 559–576.

Zhang, L. W., Sojobi, A. O., Kodur, V. K. R., & Liew, K. M. (2019). Effective utilisation and recycling of mixed recycled aggregates for a greener environment. *Journal of Cleaner Production, 236*, 117600.

Zhang, Y., Wang, H., Gao, W., Wang, F., Zhou, N., Kammen, D. M., & Ying, X. (2019). A survey of the status and challenges of green building development in various countries. *Sustainability, 11*(19), 5385.

Chapter 17

Green Construction Project Life Cycle Management

Cheng Siew Goh

Northumbria University, Newcastle upon Tyne, UK

Life cycle management (LCM) is an integrated system approach for managing the total life cycle of goods and services toward sustainable production and consumption. It helps decision-makers to make informed decisions by examining activities associated with the entire project life cycle. LCM is of particular interest in green construction in which an optimum use of resources and circularity are often emphasized for minimal environmental impacts. This chapter reveals how LCM contributes to green construction by offering a more systematic and holistic view in examining the costs and benefits of green construction projects throughout their entire life cycle. Various life cycle stages of green construction projects are reviewed to understand the impacts of different inputs and outputs for consideration along the life cycle stages, hence pinpointing potential hotspots for improving the value chain. Tools and methodologies of LCM, such as life cycle assessment (LCA), life cycle costing (LCC), and social life cycle assessment (SLCA), are also discussed to demonstrate the potential of leveraging LCM tools in offering more credible and robust results for managing green construction projects. LCM helps facilitate more innovative and critical thinking for the development of green construction projects, thereby promoting the delivery of sustainable development goals within the built environment.

17.1. Introduction

The construction industry is a project-oriented sector and project management (PM) plays a significant role in promising the success of construction projects. Projects in the construction environment cannot be treated as static undertakings (Jaafari, 2000). Emphasis should be placed on the added complexity of construction PM by issues engendered by a range of construction stakeholders with different levels of uncertainties and uncontrollable risks. As a result, PM in construction shall be able to give optimum flexibility while offering an effective approach for managing value chains throughout the life cycle.

There has been an increasing awareness of environmental issues in the past few decades. Climate change and environmental concerns have called for a paradigm shift toward adopting more sustainable and greener approach in creating built assets, infrastructure, and facilities. The green movement has diffused into the construction industry gradually, with rising demands for green construction in the market to reduce the environmental footprints. Finite resources are required to be managed in a more environmentally responsible manner while reducing carbon emissions and waste production. Green construction necessitates the implementation of more holistic and integrated PM strategies to incorporate green design and green materials in construction projects in the very early project stage. An integrated management approach is pivotal to guarantee the success of green construction for providing greater environmental, social, and economic benefits to all stakeholders.

In view of the pressing need for a more thorough PM methodology, life cycle management (LCM) could offer an impetus to embrace the new management philosophy for green construction in the field of construction PM, by offering a holistic and interconnected management perspective on sustainability performance and environmental impacts of a project over the life cycle. LCM helps facilitate the transition from the traditional linear economy to the circular economy by unlocking a thoroughly managed value chain for green construction.

The objective of this chapter is to present the potential of adopting LCM for managing green construction projects and the contributions of LCM in facilitating more innovative and critical thinking for the development of green construction projects. Life cycle thinking (LCT) is not a totally new concept in the field of green construction. Life cycle assessment (LCA) has been extensively used as a tool to evaluate the environmental impacts of green construction projects (Russell-Smith & Lepech, 2015; Sartori *et al.*, 2021). Life cycle costing (LCC) is also widely adopted to examine the cost impacts of green construction projects. The application of life cycle principles in LCA and LCC gives a specific emphasis on either environmental or economic impacts. They might not give a full spectrum to examine the whole supply chain of managing green construction projects. There is little research to explore the use of LCT as a management approach for managing green construction projects. The necessity for life cycle PM in capital projects was highlighted by Jaafari (2000), but to date, a link between LCM and green construction projects has not yet been found. This chapter therefore aims to bridge the gap by demonstrating the urgent need to incorporate LCM into the management approach of green construction projects.

17.2. Life cycle management

LCM is a management concept to embrace LCT in understanding the impacts of a product or service over the entire life span, from the extraction of raw materials to production, in-use, and disposal. The primary goal of LCT is to minimize resource consumption and reduce environmental impacts while improving socioeconomic performance during the life cycle (Remmen *et al.*, 2007). LCT evaluates the impacts of all kinds of activities associated with a product or service from the upstream to the downstream of a supply chain. According to Remmen *et al.* (2007), LCT expands the established concept of cleaner production from a facility-based environmental management system to an integrated management system that is beyond the organization's boundaries by examining interactions with internal and external stakeholders (Remmen *et al.*, 2007). As advocated by Mazzi (2020), LCT offers the totality of the system with an evaluation of the product life cycle using a long-term time horizon and multidimensional views. It looks beyond the short-term business success and targets long-term achievements and value creation (Sonnemann *et al.*, 2015).

The concept of LCT emerged in the 1980s (Baitz, 2015). Various similar terms, such as product LCM, information LCM, application LCM for software, and data LCM, have evolved as different ways of embracing LCT in management methodologies. LCT gained attention when product LCM emerged in manufacturing and aerospace industries in the 1980s (Aram & Eastman, 2013; Li *et al.*, 2021). The concepts of LCT and LCM received wider acknowledgment when LCA was developed and became popularized in 1997 as part of an international ISO standard.

In LCT, there are six RE-philosophies, namely rethink, repair, replace, reduce, recycle, and reuse. Table 17.1 summarizes RE-philosophies and their principles in applications.

The definition of LCM is however not definitive where diverse definitions of LCM can be found in the literature. The UNEP's definition is seen to be a more widely accepted definition: "a product management system focusing on the minimization of environmental and socioeconomic burdens associated with a product or product portfolio throughout its entire life cycle and value chain" (Remmen *et al.*, 2005). In short, LCM is an integrated approach for managing the total life cycle of goods and services toward sustainable production and consumption. It helps decision-makers to make informed decisions by giving a complete picture from the raw material extraction and assembly to in-use and end of life of a product or service. LCM should be integrated at all levels of an enterprise for

Table 17.1.   The 6 RE-philosophies in LCT.

RE-Philosophy	Principles
Rethink	Rethink the purposes and functions of a product for optimum efficiency
Repair	Repair the product easily
Replace	Replace hazardous substances or materials with safer solutions
Reuse	Design for disassembly for reuse
Reduce	Reduce resource consumptions and reduce socioeconomic impacts
Recycle	Adopt recyclable materials or products

improving operations and products/services to ensure information and decisions are made based on a full system or a life cycle perspective (Hunkler *et al.*, 2003).

In practice, LCM is regarded mainly as a business management approach that collects, structures, and disseminates information from different programs and tools evaluating the environmental, social, and economic performance of a product or service during its life cycle. It facilitates transparent communication internally and externally (Hunkler *et al.*, 2003; Rebitzer & Buxmann, 2005) and offers a full understanding of interdependency of business to support decisions and actions for improved sustainability. It is considered as a product stewardship framework to offer a comprehensive portfolio to pinpoint potential hotspots with critical ecological and environmental consequences.

LCM can assist to make more informed decisions by describing and examining all activities associated with a product or service throughout the supply chain, hence effectively managing and evaluating the potential impacts of the product. The literature has identified numerous purposes for adopting LCM in practice, as presented in Table 17.2.

17.2.1. *Life cycle management and project management*

The prevalent PM frameworks adopt an enterprise-specific and staged approach for all projects under all circumstances, with the specification of major activities and deliverables for each project phase for management control (Labuschagne & Brent, 2005). However, these PM frameworks have limited considerations for managing environmental impacts and there is a clear need to revise them to incorporate sustainability and environment into the decision-making processes of a project (Labuschagne & Brent, 2005). The functionality of LCM has been augmented from merely creating, storing, sharing, and managing product data to improving project and enterprise performance with informed decision-making through efficient resource use and agile problem-solving (Aram & Eastman, 2013).

Although LCM is mainly adopted in the product- or organization-based system, its application can be of great value in managing projects. The Project Management Institute defined projects as "a temporary endeavor undertaken to create a unique product or service." A project is

Table 17.2.   Different purposes of adopting LCM in the literature.

LCM functions and purposes	Aram and Eastman (2013)	Guo et al. (2010)	Hunkeler et al. (2003)	Li et al. (2021)	Nilsson-Lindén et al. (2021)	Rebitzer and Buxmann (2005)	Remmen et al. (2007)
Evaluate environmental, social, and economic impacts of a product over its entire life cycle			x		x	x	x
Support the business assimilation of integrated product policy, ecolabeling, design for environment, green procurement, and other related business or government initiatives in relation to a product/market	x		x			x	
Connect environmental improvement with economic efficiency						x	
Facilitate transparent internal and external communication			x			x	
Improve decision-making by integrating technological, economic, environmental, and social aspects of an organization and the goods and services			x	x			
Facilitate the transition from linear economy to circular economy					x		
Create the explicit link between organizations and their natural resource use and pollutant emissions				x	x		
Assess the total environmental impacts of products				x	x		
Assess the entire product portfolio of an enterprise rather than a product	x			x			
Integrate each phase of PM from planning to closeout		x					
Capture and provide access to product and process information and provide integrity of information throughout the life cycle of a product	x						

seen as a vehicle to deliver a product or service that could have environmental, social, and economic consequences. Aligning PM methodologies with the sustainability goals shall be considered during the project life cycle. The capabilities of LCM include workflow and program management modules as well as project control applications for standardizing, automating, and making management operations intelligent (Li *et al.*, 2021). This makes LCM a compelling approach to address the limitations of existing PM methodologies in the green movement.

17.3. Life cycle management in the construction context

Although LCM is traditionally rooted in the manufacturing industry, the demand for it has now gradually expanded to a broad range of industries, including the architectural, engineering, and construction industry (Aram & Eastman, 2013). The potential application of LCM has been examined in the construction sector over the past decades. Jaafari (2000) proposed the use of life cycle PM model as a proactive approach to project implementation in construction. Goh (2018) examined the potential of embracing the principles of LCT and LCM in developing a more integrated sustainability approach for assessing sustainable practice in the built environment. Guo *et al.* (2021) employed a virtual prototyping-based communication and collaboration platform for the implementation of LCM in construction projects. Patel and Ruparathna (2023) integrated building information modeling (BIM) with LCT for road infrastructure planning to provide decision support resources to local governing bodies and construction teams. Li *et al.* (2021) also integrated the functionalities of BIM with product LCM by developing a BIM-enabled building LCM for construction projects. This shows that LCM has gained the attention of global researchers for potential applications and knowledge transfer from the manufacturing and software industries to the construction industry.

The construction industry is highly fragmented considering the involvement of vast amounts of stakeholders with different interests and objectives during the development of built assets. Fragmentation in the construction sector requires different specialists for contribution but it is essential to have good communication and coordination through the construction supply chain to effectively organize and manage project resources. In addition, PM in construction is required to be carried out throughout several discrete yet continuous project stages. The maintenance and operation stage of built assets is found to be the most disconnected phase from the other project stages (Li *et al.*, 2021). Optimizing performance at one stage of project processes may not be beneficial or succeed if the quality of work and performance in other stages falls short. Lack of communication and collaboration between stakeholders in different project phases is acknowledged as a key issue of effective PM and LCM can help solve the issue by integrating each phase of PM, from planning to closeout, with better information sharing and stakeholder coordination (Guo *et al.*, 2010).

17.3.1. *Life cycle phases in construction projects*

Defining explicit project life cycle phases is essential to warrant proper implementation of LCM to understand the material inflow and outflow in the upstream to downstream activities. If activities are not clearly defined and documented by each department or entity independently, this may pose challenges in integrating the elements of people, processes, business systems, and product management information for continuous improvement. It would result in piecemeal management as these elements are managed in disconnected manners at different times across the life cycle with unstandardized approaches by different people (Li *et al.*, 2021). As a result, LCM would be of importance to the construction industry to give a more systematic approach to manage resources for better efficiency and effectiveness.

Various project life cycle phases exist in the literature as well as in construction practice, owing to different interests and goals of a broad range of stakeholders involved in construction projects. The number and the names of phases adopted in each approach vary from one another (Labuschagne & Brent, 2005). The complexity and diversity of projects, organizations, and industries exacerbate the difficulties in reaching an agreement about the life cycle phases of a project. Despite the classification variants of defining life cycle phases, a construction project can generally be divided into five generic phases: initiation/planning, design,

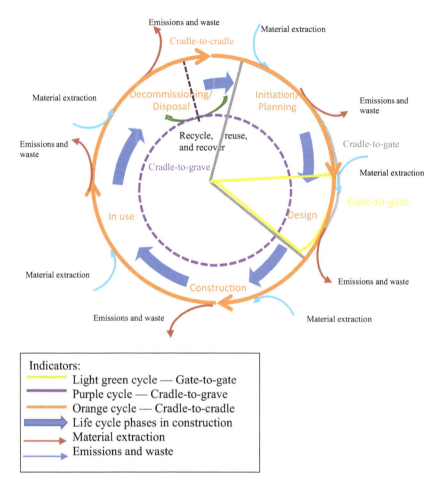

Figure 17.1.   Life cycle phases and system boundaries in LCM.

construction, in-use, and decommissioning/disposal, as displayed in Figure 17.1.

It is important to note that LCM shall be practiced in conjunction with proper considerations of system boundaries in the life cycle. LCM evaluates all activities associated with each phase of the project life cycle, including their inputs, processes, and outputs. It is necessary to understand the three main phases of a life cycle: cradle, gate, and grave. Cradle is the starting point in which impacts of elements are inputs to the process (e.g., resource extraction). A gate is the activity point where a milestone is achieved, with a finished output completed to move to the next phase in a life cycle. A grave is the endpoint with the ultimate disposal of the outputs. As presented in Figure 17.1, there are different types of system boundaries defined in the LCM implementation:

- *Cradle-to-gate*: from raw material extraction to gate. This is mostly applicable to upstream value chains.
- *Gate-to-gate*: from one defined point along the life cycle to the subsequent defined point along the life cycle.
- *Cradle-to-grave*: from raw material extraction through product use and disposal, i.e., end of life.
- *Cradle-to-cradle*: a closed cycle from raw material extraction through product use and disposal, whereas the end product is subsequently recycled, recovered, and reused at end of life.

17.4. Life cycle management and green construction

The building and construction industry accounts for about 41% of primary energy use and 40% of greenhouse gas emissions and the trend is expected to continue growing in the upcoming years (Russell-Smith & Lepech, 2015). According to Russell-Smith and Lepech (2015), the cradle-to-site effects of buildings (i.e., from material extraction, manufacturing, transportation, and onsite construction) are often overlooked as compared to the entire operational impacts. It is vital to employ a management approach in the building and infrastructure production process to manage construction projects with more environmentally friendly methods.

LCM is developed based on the concept of LCT that goes beyond the traditional focus on the production site and construction process, and it takes into account the environmental, social, and economic impacts of a product from cradle to grave (Remmen *et al.*, 2007). The contribution of LCM toward the transformation of green construction is evident. LCM gives a prominent means to diffuse environmental performance more directly into the organizational and project performance. As the main goals of LCM are to reduce environmental impacts (e.g., natural resources consumption and carbon emissions), LCM can be viewed as one of the best toolboxes of environmental management to estimate the direct environmental and economic costs of construction projects over the life cycle. Life cycle considerations in terms of resource use, transportation, material reuse or recycling, and disposal are taken into account to assess the whole system impacts of a construction project across the life span. LCM offers a great opportunity to facilitate links between three key aspects of sustainability, i.e., environment, society, and economy, throughout the entire value chain.

Green construction focuses on sustainability and LCM is of value to enhance the shortcomings of existing sustainability management strategies, such as limiting the environmental impacts from a single point of view. According to Mazzi (2020), various environmental management tools are found to have limits of decreasing environmental impacts of a process by allocating them at other times, upstream or downstream of the supply chain and this leads to problem shifting — unintentionally creating other environmental problems elsewhere. It is therefore important to consider decisions taken with a system perspective to balance trade-offs in economic, social, and environmental implications.

17.5. How life cycle management facilitates green construction

Improving the environmental performance is one of the main objectives of LCM. The implementation of LCM implies the understanding of the entire production process in construction projects, from natural material extraction, material/product conversion, product integration, product assembly into a finished building system, shipping, product use, and product disposal along the value chain. Both positive and negative impacts generated by the projects are evaluated in detail. LCM allows the project team to identify environmental hotspot areas in green construction projects for improvement.

In green construction, projects are designed and developed in a way to eliminate negative impacts on the climate and natural environment, while preserving the natural resources and enhancing the living quality of people. The principles of green construction are in line with the objectives of LCM, and there is a complementary relationship between them in contributing to the project deliverables and outcomes. LCM adopts a holistic, transdisciplinary, and multidimensional approach to assess the extending internal consequences and externalities of green construction projects.

In addition, LCM promotes green design principles, such as design for environment, design for disassembly, and design for recycling. It also refers to policies and frameworks, such as circular economy, sustainable consumption and production, resource efficiency, ecoefficiency, dematerialization, and industrial ecology for implementation (UNEP/SETAC Life Cycle Initiative, 2012).

In Zuo *et al.*'s (2017) work, the need of adopting LCM in the construction industry is identified and tools such as LCA and LCC are widely acknowledged as important decision tools for green buildings. The relationships and trade-offs between environmental, economic, and social impacts can be revealed with the application of an integrated LCM approach. The following section introduces tools and methodologies of LCM for green construction in the environmental, economic, and social aspects.

17.6. Tools and methodologies of life cycle management for green construction

17.6.1. *Environment: Life cycle assessment*

LCA is used as a formalized environmental management approach of assessing ecological impacts throughout the life cycle of a product, service, or system, from raw material acquisition, production, transportation, use, maintenance, and end of life. Environmental issues in construction are highly complex, interrelated, and multifaceted. A sophisticated quantitative tool such as LCA offers a great solution to understand the environmental impacts of raw materials, intermediate products, and final products by considering all inputs, outputs, and flows within a process, product, or system.

As defined by ISO 14040 (2006), four key stages are prescribed in conducting LCA practice: (1) goal and scope definition, (2) inventory analysis, (3) life cycle impact assessment, and (4) life cycle interpretation.

The scope of LCA is subject to the intended use and subjects of the study; here the depth and breadth of an LCA study can vary significantly. In Stage (1) — Goal and Scope Definition — it is important to determine the purposes of conducting LCA study, the product functions, the use of LCA results, and the intended audiences. System boundaries in the project life cycle (e.g., cradle-to-gate and cradle-to-grave) should be set to establish the scope of the study. Once the purposes and system boundaries are established, Stage (2) — Inventory Analysis — is carried out to collect and aggregate input and output data to measure the material use, energy use, waste, and discharges in each life cycle phase. Detailed life cycle impact assessment is performed in Stage (3) to evaluate the magnitude and severity of environmental consequences. Input–output analysis is involved to give accurate quantification of impacts to understand activities in their temporal orders. The results are subsequently interpreted in Stage (4) to draw conclusions and recommendations by identifying the environmental burdens, impacts, and areas for improvement.

The ISO 14040 (2006) standard provides established standards to facilitate the implementation of LCA studies of a given product or service by defining terms and consistent system boundaries of applications. There are two types of studies: LCA studies and life cycle inventory (LCI) studies. The difference between LCA and LCI is that LCI performs only an inventory analysis and an interpretation, with an exclusion of life cycle impact assessment.

Environmental performance measurement is found to lack a common measure, hence resulting in a proliferation of a variety of metrics and indicators (Hunkler *et al.*, 2001). In LCA, natural resource use and pollutant emissions across the life cycle are often studied. According to the International Council of Chemical Associations (2016), the common environmental metrics adopted in LCA include the following:

- Cumulative energy demand (CED)
- Cumulative fossil energy demand (CFED)
- Cumulative renewable energy demand (CRED)
- Global warming potential (GWP)
- Ozone depletion potential (ODP)
- Acidification potential (AP)

- Eutrophication potential (EP)
- Photochemical ozone creation potential (POCP)
- Consumptive water footprint and water emissions
- Eco and human toxicity assessment
- Direct and indirect land use change
- Respiratory effects
- Nuisance
- Ionizing radiation
- Indoor environmental quality

CED refers to the total energy consumed over the entire life cycle in delivering the functional unit where CRED and CFED are subsets of CED that consider fossil fuels and non-fossil fuel-based energy. GWP is commonly known as carbon footprints that reflect greenhouse gas emissions. Water emissions are also measured in LCA by using consumptive water footprint and water emissions to capture the total life cycle requirements of water to deliver the functional unit. Specific chemical emissions and their impacts on human health and ecosystems are assessed using eco and human toxicity assessment.

The value of LCA to green construction projects is evident. LCA develops a more systematic approach to quantify the environmental aspects and the impacts of green construction. It gives transparency to the design process and allows decision-makers to understand the impacts of their decisions on the environmental contexts (Sartori *et al.*, 2021). Various green building rating systems have also incorporated LCA into their credit systems to increase awareness of ecological impacts of green construction projects. The incorporation of LCA increases quantitative measures in green building rating systems, hence improving the scientific values behind the credits with numerical evidence in comparing alternative design choices (Sartori *et al.*, 2021). LCA can also stimulate practitioners to search for more authentic and innovative green solutions for construction projects to unlock the barriers. Nevertheless, LCA focuses on environmental damage on a wider scale, where specific local ecology and community contexts are often ignored, as noted by Sartori *et al.* (2021). It does not inform practitioners regarding the impacts on social and economic pillars of sustainability either.

17.6.2. *Economic: Life cycle costing*

LCC is used to calculate all costs and economic impacts associated with a product or system across its life cycle. LCC requires a thorough understanding of the budgetary movements within the life cycle of a project by considering not only initial cost but also operation, maintenance, administration, recurrent, and end-of-life costs. All terms in LCC practice shall be expressed on monetary values that are tangible. Intangible impacts, such as comfort and environmental load, are ignored in LCC calculations.

Having an origin from financial cost accounting, LCC was first employed in 1933 by the United States of America General Accounting Office to assess the life cycle costs of tractors. The adoption of LCC in construction gained prominence when there was increasing consciousness on the building operational and maintenance costs as well as the trend of value for money (Gundes, 2006). LCC is also used to consider economic and financial forecasts of a product or service throughout its life cycle by taking into account time value of money. It compares alternative design options in construction projects by considering both revenues and expenditures to be incurred from a construction project. Maximizing cost-effectiveness and efficiency is the primary goal of conducting LCC in order to assist decision-makers in making a more informed decision for a better return on investment.

Despite focusing on investment returns, there have been efforts to employ LCC in environmental decision-making, particularly in the building sector (Gundes, 2006). LCC helps demonstrate the total cost of ownership of green buildings by assessing a range of green strategies with different initial costs and implications for subsequent operational costs employed in buildings. Recent changes to green finance, green leases, and public–private partnerships procurement have also increased the importance of LCC in the transition to green buildings.

The total cost consumed by resources in LCC can, to an extent, reflects the environmental and social burdens of green building systems, but there are challenges associated with the inability of LCC to include all kinds of environmental costs in the calculations (Gundes, 2006). To address this, some efforts integrating LCC and LCA in sustainability assessment are made by extending existing LCC programs to include LCA or vice versa (Zuo *et al.*, 2017). For instance, environmental LCC has been established as an effort to apply LCC in parallel with LCA. Environmental LCC attempts to give a framework to evaluate decisions with consistent but flexible system boundaries. An integration of LCA and LCC can avoid double counting the environmental impacts in both financial and physical terms. The financial costs of life cycle environmental aspects and their associated impacts shall be accounted for by internalizing the costs, such as applying the polluter pays principle to reflect the real monetary flows covered by the respective actors (Swarr *et al.*, 2011).

LCC has been recognized as a valuable approach to the development of green construction. Various studies show that the initial costs of green buildings are substantially higher than conventional buildings and LCC is a great tool to demonstrate how the economic benefits of green construction can outweigh the cost premium (Li *et al.*, 2020). The adoption of LCC also gives a comprehensive view to examine the effectiveness of green construction to achieve optimal economic returns by considering cost and benefits. However, LCC also has some pitfalls in examining externalities and social impacts of green construction projects.

17.6.3. *Social: Social life cycle assessment*

Social life cycle assessment (SLCA) is a tool to evaluate social and socio-economic effects of a product or project on stakeholders throughout the life cycle. It has roots in social impact assessment (SIA), which was used to assess the social impacts of activities. Despite having some commonalities, SIA may cover a glance at some phases of a project life cycle while SLCA provides a stronger basis for assessing the social and socioeconomic aspects of projects and the potential positive and negative impacts along the entire life cycle phases (Andrews, 2009).

The UNEP's Guidelines for SLCA of Products defined social impacts as consequences of positive or negative pressures on social endpoints (i.e., well-being of stakeholders) and they encompass three main dimensions: (1) behaviors, (2) socioeconomic processes, and (3) capitals (Andrews,

2009). Due to the dynamic and complex relationships between the three social dimensions, stakeholder categories and socioeconomic subcategories need to be classified to assist with the operationalization of SLCA (Andrews, 2009).

Stakeholder identification and classification are of great interest in SLCA, and stakeholder involvement is crucial to review the inclusion of an extensive array of social issues in SLCA that could be crucial to determining the social impacts and hotspots in the projects. Diverse social sustainability indicators are required to quantify socioeconomic impacts of green construction projects. The identification and assessment of social impacts in life cycle calculation are said to be extremely challenging in view of the diverse nature, the variety of stakeholder groups, and the tendency of a change in time (Gundes, 2016). There is neither a standardized set of social sustainability indicators nor a consistent method of evaluating social impacts. Unlike environmental and economic assessments that are rooted in technical and mathematically quantifiable metrics, the nature of assessment in SLCA is found to be qualitative and highly subjective. In addition, a lack of data also leads to difficulties in developing widely accepted social indicators and assessment techniques in SLCA.

As a result, SLCA is often neglected by the scientific community and it is still in the infancy stage of development, as compared to the other two life cycle methodologies. Nevertheless, social parameters shall not be removed from the assessment of green construction projects, as there is a mutual interdependency of social, environmental, and economic aspects for the whole life performance of green construction projects. Leading green building rating systems such as the US Leadership in Energy and Environmental Design (LEED) and the Japan Comprehensive Assessment System for Built Environment Efficiency (CASBEE) have given more emphasis on social impacts in their evaluation (Sartori *et al.*, 2021). It can be deduced that social impact assessment is now receiving more attention in the prevalent evaluation of green construction performance.

17.7. Conclusion

This chapter reveals how crucial LCM is in the transition to green construction by offering a more systematic and holistic PM methodology.

LCM allows construction stakeholders to understand the environmental impacts associated with all activities, including their inputs, processes, and outputs, along the life cycle stages. This would assist construction stakeholders to pinpoint potential hotspots for improving environmental performance along the value chains of their green construction projects. The application of LCM also examines the whole life costs and benefits of green construction projects. Leveraging LCM tools such as LCA, LCC, and SLCA can give decision-makers more credible and robust results to support their decision-making for developing and managing green construction projects. Since LCM offers the totality of the project system using a long-term time horizon and multidimensional views, it looks beyond the short-term success and emphasizes long-term achievements and value creation of green construction projects. This could reassure construction stakeholders over the potential value of pursuing green by offering a full lens of environment and economic footprints. In short, LCM facilitates more innovative and critical thinking for the development of green construction projects, thereby promoting the delivery of sustainable development goals within the built environment.

References

Andrews, E. S. (2009). Guidelines for social life cycle assessment of products: Social and socio-economic LCA guidelines complementing environmental LCA and Life Cycle Costing, contributing to the full assessment of goods and services within the context of sustainable development. UNEP/Earthprint.

Aram, S. & Eastman, C. (2013). Integration of PLM solutions and BIM systems for the AEC industry. In *ISARC*. In *Proceedings of the International Symposium on Automation and Robotics in Construction* (Vol. 30, p. 1). IAARC Publications. 11th to 15th August 2013. Montreal, Quebec, Canada.

Baitz, M. (2015). From projects to processes to implement life cycle management in business. In: G. Sonnemann & M. Margni, (Eds.), *Life Cycle Management* (pp. 93–104). Dordrecht: Springer.

Goh, C. S. (2018). Towards an integrated approach for assessing triple bottom line in the built environment. In R. Amoêda & C. Pinheiro (Eds.), *Proceedings of 2017 International Conference on Advances on Sustainable Cities and*

Buildings Development. 15–17 November 2017, Green Lines Institute, Portugal.

Gundes, S. (2016). The use of life cycle techniques in the assessment of sustainability. *Procedia-Social and Behavioral Sciences, 216*, 916–922.

Guo, H. L., Li, H., & Skitmore, M. (2010). Life-cycle management of construction projects based on virtual prototyping technology. *Journal of Management in Engineering, 26*(1), 41–47.

Hunkeler, D., Saur, K., Stranddorf, H., Rebitzer, G., Schmidt, W. P., Jensen, A. A., & Christiansen, K. (2003). *Life Cycle Management*. SETAC, Brussels.

International Council of Chemical Associations. (2016). *An Executive Guide: How to Know If and When It's Time to Commission a Life Cycle Assessment*. Brussels, Belgium: International Council of Chemical Associations.

ISO 14040 (2006). Environmental management — Life cycle assessment — Principles and Framework (ISO 14040:2006). Geneva: ISO.

Jaafari, A. (2000). Life-cycle project management: A proposed theoretical model for development and implementation of capital projects. *Project Management Journal, 31*(1), 44–52.

Labuschagne, C. & Brent, A. C. (2005). Sustainable project life cycle management: The need to integrate life cycles in the manufacturing sector. *International Journal of Project Management, 23*(2), 159–168.

Li, L., Yuan J., Tang M., Xu Z., Xu, W., & Cheng, Y. (2021). Developing a BIM-enabled building lifecycle management system for owners: Architecture and case scenario. *Automation in Construction, 129*, 103814.

Li, S., Lu, Y., Kua, H. W., & Chang, R. (2020). The economics of green buildings: A life cycle cost analysis of non-residential buildings in tropic climates. *Journal of Cleaner Production, 252*, 119771.

Mazzi, A. (2020). Introduction life cycle thinking. In Jingzheng Ren & Sara Toniolo (Eds.), *Life Cycle Sustainability Assessment for Decision-making* (pp. 1–19). Elsevier.

Patel, K. & Ruparathna, R. (2021). Life cycle sustainability assessment of road infrastructure: A building information modeling (BIM) based approach. *International Journal of Construction Management, 23*(11), 1837–1846.

Rebitzer, G. & Buxmann, K. (2005). The role and implementation of LCA within life cycle management at Alcan. *Journal of Cleaner Production, 13*(13–14), 1327–1335.

Remmen, A., Jensen, A. A., & Frydendal, J. (2007). *Life Cycle Management: A Business Guide to Sustainability*. Nairobi, Kenya: UNEP/SETAC.

Russell-Smith, S. V. & Lepech M. D, (2015). Cradle-to-gate sustainable target value design: Integrating life cycle assessment and construction management for buildings. *Journal of Cleaner Production, 100,* 107–115.

Sartori, T., Drogemuller, R., Omrani, S., & Lamari, F. (2021). A schematic framework for life cycle assessment (LCA) and green building rating system (GBRS). *Journal of Building Engineering, 38,* 102180.

Sonnemann, G., Gemechu, E. D., Remmen, A, Frydendal, J., & Jensen, A. A. (2015). In Sonnemann, G., Margni, M. (Eds.), *Life Cycle Management: Implementing Sustainability in Business Practice.* (pp. 7–21). Dordrecht: Springer.

Swarr, T. E., Hunkeler, D., Klöpffer, W., Pesonen, H. L., Ciroth, A., Brent, A. C., & Pagan, R. (2011). Environmental life-cycle costing: A code of practice. *The International Journal of Life Cycle Assessment, 16*(5), 389–391.

UNEP/SETAC Life Cycle Initiative. (2012). *Greening the Economy Through Life Cycle Thinking.* Ten years of the UNEP/SETAC Life Cycle Initiative. Paris, France.

Zuo, J., Pullen, S., Rameezdeen, R., Bennetts, H., Wang, Y., Mao, G., Zhou, Z., Du, H., & Duan, H. (2017). Green building evaluation from a life-cycle perspective in Australia: A critical review. *Renewable and Sustainable Energy Reviews, 70,* 358–368.

https://doi.org/10.1142/9789811251429_0018

Chapter 18

Digital Green Construction Project Management

Mohammad Sakikhales[*]**, Stephen Au Ling Ming**[†]**, and Amos Darko**[‡]

[*]*University of Greenwich, Greenwich, UK*

[†]*MTECH Engineering Co., Ltd., Hong Kong, China*

[‡]*University of Washington, Seattle, WA, USA*

The concern about the sustainability impact of construction has increased rapidly over the past few years and green construction has become a focal point of discussion and an important player to achieve sustainability goals. While green construction is not a new topic, it has been emphasized in the light of new digital technologies and modern software packages. Digital technologies and software, such as building information modeling (BIM), the Internet of Things (IoT), digital twins, and artificial intelligence and machine learning, make many promises to improve the project management (PM) of green construction projects. This chapter explores the benefits of digital technologies and software for designing for sustainability, and for schedule, cost, quality, resource, communications, stakeholder, risk, health and safety, and construction site management for green construction projects to transform the way buildings are designed and constructed by reducing their environmental footprint, improving efficiency, and better use of resources.

Practical cases are introduced. The chapter emphasizes the need to fully integrate integrated digital delivery and digital twins into green construction PM. Despite the many benefits that digital green construction PM can offer, this practice is not free from challenges. Some significant challenges and solutions for digital green construction PM are discussed. The insights from this chapter will help practitioners to unlock the full value of digital in the management of their green construction projects. Researchers and students will benefit through an understanding of the past, present, and future developments of the field.

18.1. Introduction

Digital green construction project management (PM) is defined as the use and application of digital technologies and software to improve the process of managing and delivering a green construction project. This is a relatively new trend in the construction industry, and it is expected to continue to be a trend in the future. Digital green construction PM involves applying digital tools across various PM functions (e.g., schedule, cost, and quality management) in green construction projects. It is a highly data-driven approach that leads to both greener and smarter construction, with various benefits in improved collaboration, communication, coordination, data and information management, transparency and accountability, productivity, risk mitigation, profits, decision-making, delivery times, sustainability, efficiency, accuracy, costs, quality, and health, safety, well-being, and compliance (Loring, 2023; Stewart, 2022; ConstructionPlacements Admin, 2022).

Digital green construction PM practices can be used to manage and optimize construction projects with a focus on sustainability and environmental friendliness. They can streamline project planning and scheduling, coordination, and execution by integrating cutting-edge digital solutions, such as building information modeling (BIM), the Internet of Things (IoT), blockchain, digital twins, artificial intelligence and machine learning (AI/ML), reality modeling, and cloud computing. Throughout the project's lifetime, green construction PM seeks to improve the schedule, lower costs, minimize waste, improve health and safety, and mitigate environmental effects. It seeks to allow project stakeholders, such as clients, architects, engineers, contractors, subcontractors, consultants, and suppliers, to communicate in real time, make data-driven decisions, and improve the quality of the project and project outcomes. Digital technologies have the innate potential to help achieve the goals of green construction PM.

This chapter examines the benefits of digital technologies and software for designing for sustainability, and for schedule, cost, quality, resource, communications, stakeholder, risk, health and safety, and construction site management for green construction projects, with practical cases introduced. The chapter emphasizes the need to fully integrate integrated digital delivery and digital twins into green construction PM. Finally, the chapter discusses pressing challenges of digital green construction PM and offers solutions to them to promote digital green construction PM.

As Autodesk (2023) indicates, BIM is the foundation of digital transformation in the construction industry. As such, most of the digital green construction PM applications discussed in this chapter are BIM-based, although a case for digital twin-based applications is made at the end of this chapter. Autodesk (2022) further stated that digital twins are "still pretty new to the construction industry." Thus, not many applications are seen in the green construction PM space yet. We believe that digital twin provides a better solution for digital/smart green construction PM, but the best way to get to digital twin is to start with BIM. This chapter explains why.

18.2. Using digital technology and software to design for sustainability

Green construction project designers must design for sustainability (DfS). For instance, designing the project with circularity in mind will principally mean that no project asset at the end of its life cycle will become waste but will instead remain incorporated in the supply chain. The project must be designed, constructed, operated, and deconstructed in a way that copies the closed-loop systems that exist in nature. In addition, optimizing the performance and sustainability of the project demands a different approach which must start in early conceptual planning. The conventional design process needs to be changed through the following actions:

- integrating new contracting documents that eliminate silos in the design processes,
- focusing on the larger portfolio approaches rather than project perspective — need for scalability,
- providing access to a single energy/carbon model shared with all relevant stakeholders,
- full team commitment to collaborative and integrated processes early in the design process,
- deploying building energy modeling before design development and validated as design modifications are introduced,
- integrating decision-making using data and information management processes,
- providing value engineering options with data demonstrating impacts to building performance, first costs, and long-term operating costs.

BIM offers powerful digital technology and software to achieve these goals. The technology provides a methodology to consolidate all project information in a single working environment for all project stakeholders. This allows the stakeholders to perform simulation analysis for making the right decisions at the first time to optimize the project performance for customer wisdom and creating impact to better and sustainable living environments for human beings. BIM can be applied for various purposes throughout the entire life cycle of the project (life cycle BIM), as summarized in Figure 18.1 that was presented in the World Economic Forum's (2016) report "Shaping the Future of Construction: A Breakthrough in Mindset and Technology."

Moreover, Figure 18.2 shows the digital construction portfolio that must be addressed from design and construction to facility management. This digital construction portfolio is prepared by the second author's company, MTECH Engineering Co., Ltd. Green construction projects must implement the "green BIM," i.e., using BIM tools to achieve sustainability (in design) and/or improved building performance objectives on the project (McGraw-Hill Construction, 2010). In addition to the traditional BIM

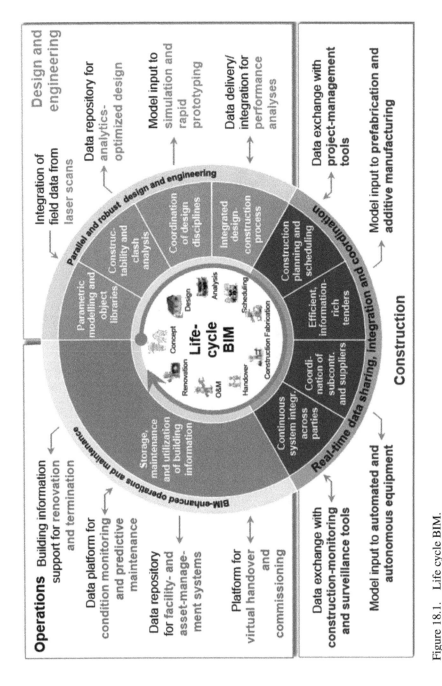

Figure 18.1. Life cycle BIM.

Source: The Boston Consulting Group cited in World Economic Forum (2016).

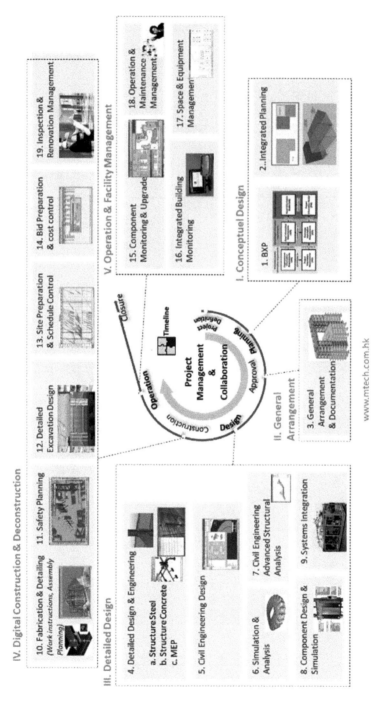

Figure 18.2.   Digital construction portfolio by MTECH Engineering Co., Ltd.
Source: www.mtech.com.hk.

scope of work, green BIM tools should also include the 3Rs concept of *reduce*, *reuse*, and *recycle* in their sustainability analysis of the project design (Pelsmakers, 2013). The system should offer better integration with facility operation maintenance manuals for more effective low-carbon management. The use of cloud-based BIM technology to enable the management of building sustainability using "big data" is also required. Green BIM has been found by many researchers to be effective for integrating and accomplishing project sustainability goals.

Due to the accumulation of life cycle information of the building, BIM can be effectively used for designing the building by considering circularity ("circular BIM"). Thus, using BIM at the early design stage can help recognize the materials flow (Akanbi *et al.*, 2018), where life cycle assessment (LCA) can be adopted by considering the materials' flow of the building in all phases based upon the cradle-to-cradle system boundary (Herczeg *et al.*, 2018; Russell-Smith & Lepech, 2015). In order to estimate the salvage performance of building elements right from the early design stage in the circular economy, Akanbi *et al.* (2018) developed a whole life performance estimator based on BIM. Sanchez *et al.* (2019) proposed a semi-automated deconstruction programming method for buildings using BIM to enhance the deconstruction planning and design for reusing the materials in a circular economy. Such tools help improve the green construction project performance by (1) process automation, (2) resolving circularity issues before site works start, (3) supporting quantitative analysis, (4) low-cost exploration of alternatives, (5) managing project tasks in compliance with circularity and sustainability, (6) managing circularity across the whole project life cycle, and (7) an iterative design process for meeting project constraints.

LCA is critical to DfS. To quantify the building's environmental impacts, LCA requires data on all the components' materials. The BIM model contains technical building information, and these required data could be extracted from the model. Therefore, the environmental impacts of the building may be quantified by integrating BIM and LCA software and models, such as One Click LCA and SimaPro. This practice has been reviewed and demonstrated by Teng *et al.* (2022). There is a need to document all the reasonable assembly and material options for the building elements in order to quantify the impact and corresponding uncertainty related to not knowing exactly what the type of material is. A functional database must therefore be created to compile all the different options for each assembly and all the corresponding life cycle inventories.

In the following, we provide an example of how the integration of BIM and LCA works + the project life cycle in practice:

1. For starting mechanical, electrical, and plumbing (MEP) design, for example, requirements for indoor quality are needed:

   a. As required by the customer, maximum temperatures, etc. must be defined.
   b. The result is a target value for each space, which the MEP designer must fulfill (e.g., max. 26° C > simulation > target value 1.2 kW cooling).

2. Spaces with requirements are linked to service area charts (e.g., air handling unit service areas):

   a. Linking is made using ifcSpaces (ifcZones are created with external software to IFC file).
   b. Analysis is performed using Solibri or other software.

3. Dynamic simulation of energy and comfort is performed according to the requirements, building BIM model (LOD100), and service area charts, as demonstrated in Figure 18.3:

   a. Every space is simulated.
   b. Alternative simulations and comparison for different envelopes, windows, etc.: beginning of life cycle costing calculations, as shown in Figure 18.4.
   c. Material specification with carbon emission information is created and input into the BIM models.

4. As-design BIM model (LOD350) for detailed design:

   a. Modeling and coordination to validate the design (Figure 18.5).
   b. Update the sustainability requirements.

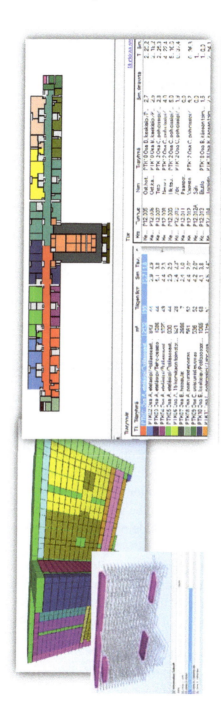

Figure 18.3. Results of dynamic simulation of energy and comfort based on the LOD100 BIM model.

Figure 18.4.   Life cycle costing calculations for different simulations.

Figure 18.5.   Coordination of BIM modeling process for detailed design.

There is a need for collaboration for the green design — BIM-based materials' passport management. Under the BIM task execution system Plannerly, the BIM modeling task card is created to specify that materials' passport information must be input into the BIM model elements (e.g., the door) and be verified before releasing the model to be used. Figures 18.6–18.8 demonstrate the verification of the BIM model using Plannerly.

Another way to check what building elements are in compliance with environmental requirements (or have the material passport) is through the filtering of the database via the BIM viewer Dalux, as shown in Figure 18.9. All the panels with pink color in the figure can be recycled.

c.   All the as-design material passports are exported via 5D BIM for costing purposes (see Section 18.4 and Figure 18.10).

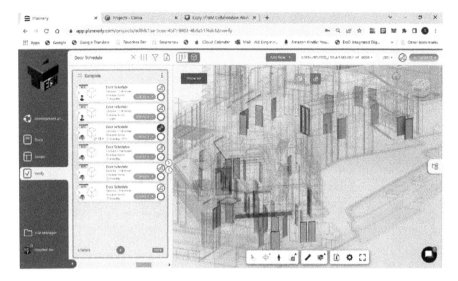

Figure 18.6.   Screen capture of the display of verified BIM models in Plannerly.

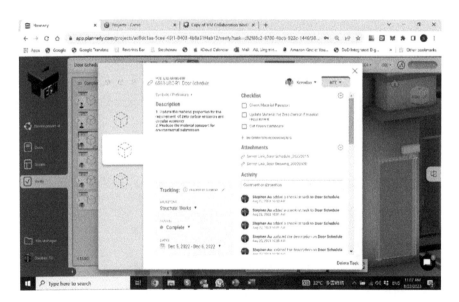

Figure 18.7.   Screen capture of the display of the task card for the verified BIM models in Plannerly.

Figure 18.8.   Sorting of the doors according to different material compliance via Plannerly verify function.

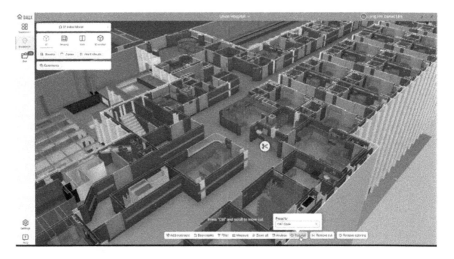

Figure 18.9.   Color display of green material compliance building elements via the filtering function of Dalux BIM Viewer.

ID	Type of Door	Width (m)	Depth (m)	Total Length (m)	Steel (kg/m^3)	Steel Percentage in volume (%)	Life expectancy (yr)	Wastage (%)	Plywood thickness (m)
B1	C45	0.2	0.8	12	400	2	50	4	0.018
B2	C45	0.3	0.5	520	400	2	50	4	0.018
B3	C45	0.3	0.8	269	400	2	50	4	0.018
B4	C45	0.3	0.9	65	400	2	50	4	0.018
B5	C45	0.4	0.6	72	400	2	50	4	0.018
B6	C45	0.4	0.8	109	400	2	50	4	0.018
B7	C45	0.4	0.9	28	400	2	50	4	0.018
B8	C45	0.5	0.8	289	400	2	50	4	0.018
B9	C45	0.5	0.9	252	400	2	50	4	0.018
B10	C45	0.5	1	4	400	2	50	4	0.018
B11	C45	0.5	1.1	9	400	2	50	4	0.018
B12	C45	0.55	0.8	132	400	2	50	4	0.018
B13	C45	0.55	0.9	39	400	2	50	4	0.018
B14	C45	0.55	1.1	26	400	2	50	4	0.018
B15	C45	0.55	1.2	6	400	2	50	4	0.018

Figure 18.10.   Exporting the LCA information from the BIM model.

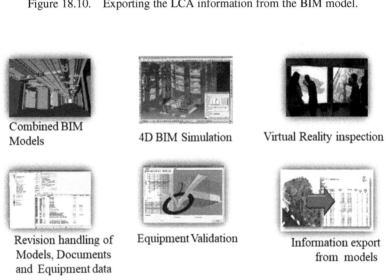

Combined BIM Models

4D BIM Simulation

Virtual Reality inspection

Revision handling of Models, Documents and Equipment data

Equipment Validation

Information export from models

Figure 18.11.   As-construction BIM models for different BIM uses.

5. As-construction BIM models (LOD350 or LOD400) for construction (Figure 18.11).

6. As-built BIM Models (LOD500) for facility management (Figure 18.12).

BIM can also be integrated with digital technologies such as IoT and blockchain technology to better track emissions during the planning and

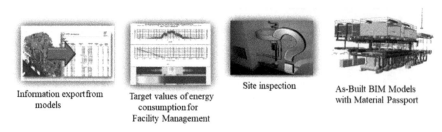

Information export from models

Target values of energy consumption for Facility Management

Site inspection

As-Built BIM Models with Material Passport

Figure 18.12.   Different as-built BIM models for operation and maintenance.

design stages and throughout the green construction project. Xu *et al.* (2023) have recently developed an integrated IoT-BIM-based monitoring system for tracking and visualizing embodied carbon emissions of buildings. Improved tracking and visualization of emissions can create motivations for reducing them.

Connecting the BIM model to a decision-making tool and to sustainability metrics (such as those found in green building rating tools) helps enable useful decisions in the early project design stage. It allows detailed sustainability trade-off analysis to be performed by referring to real project data. This process provides a means for modeling the impacts of decisions concerning design, operations, maintenance, and occupant behavior modification, thereby promoting a sustainable built environment through the use of multidimensional visualization technology. Ansah *et al.* (2019) have reviewed the practice of connecting BIM to green building rating tools, while Farzad Jalaei is among the researchers who have contributed significantly to advancing this practice for designing sustainable projects. Jalaei has developed several integrated BIM-based tools to automate green design assessment frameworks at the conceptual design stage of building projects (Jalaei *et al.*, 2020; Jalaei & Jrade, 2015; Jalaei & Jrade, 2014).

It is crucial that green construction project clients, designers, managers, and contractors embrace digital technology and software to DfS, achieving sustainability goals, such as climate mitigation, better health and well-being, circularity, waste reduction, and natural resources conservation by design. Take waste reduction for example. Improper design and unexpected changes in design have been identified by researchers as major causes of construction waste generation. Innes

(2004) indicated that inappropriate project design decision-making and unexpected design changes may lead to an increase of up to 33% in the volume of construction waste. Therefore, it is important to incorporate digital technology and software to improve green construction project design decision-making, a subject tackled in Chapter 9.

18.3. Digital technologies and software for schedule management

Construction scheduling software has been around for a long time. The concept of scheduling changed with the development of the Gantt chart around a century ago and then evolved during the space war between the former Soviet Union and the United States. Methods such as the Critical Path Method (CPM) and Program Evaluation and Review Technique (PERT) were developed at that time, and for a couple of decades, these approaches have been the main methods for construction scheduling. Microsoft Project and Primavera were the two main players for years, although there have been other software packages on the market. However, in recent times, new digital technologies have transformed the way scheduling is conducted.

The technological improvement in tools has offered a significant opportunity for programmers to plan, monitor, and optimize project schedules and make them more accurate and efficient. The main advancement is probably BIM-based scheduling tools, popularly known as 4D modeling. Although 4D does not limit itself to construction scheduling and can be referred to by other simulations or analyses that involve time, as shown in Figure 18.13, it is widely understood that 4D is construction scheduling. The concept behind BIM-based construction scheduling is to link the timeline to the elements in the model, as illustrated in Figure 18.14. Consequently, an animation or video will be created. It is also possible to overlay the animation with other data, such as the cost breakdown.

These tools can improve field efficiency by visualizing the planned construction schedule and reducing schedule delays due to missing information on the green construction project (Viscuso *et al.*, 2020). According

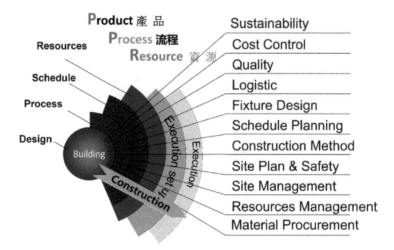

Figure 18.13.   Problems addressed through 4D BIM simulation.

to Zhang *et al.* (2016), a 3D representation of the schedule can improve PM at each stage by minimizing interference between different activities in the same area. In addition to the most tangible benefits, a visualized schedule provides a platform for people to discuss and resolve potential challenges and reduce any rework. Consequently, an optimized schedule will help reduce the carbon footprint of the whole green construction project. Software packages such as Synchro and Navisworks were pioneers in these fields. However, there is also a need to improve collaboration in scheduling and the communication of the schedule. Therefore, new tools are moving from standalone software to more cloud-based ones. A tool such as cmBuilder is a typical example of this generation.

The next step is to bring the schedule into reality by integrating it with virtual reality (VR) and augmented reality (AR) technologies. Some BIM software packages offer the integration of VR and AR (for example, Bentley). The last invention in software and scheduling is the application of AI/ML for scheduling. There have been many academic attempts in the past couple of years to bring AI/ML to construction project scheduling (Abioye *et al.*, 2021; Darko *et al.*, 2020b; Debrah *et al.*, 2022). ALICE is one of the commercially available AI-powered construction simulation and optimization platforms.

In the specific domain of green construction PM, very limited attempts have been made to benefit from the power of AI/ML in

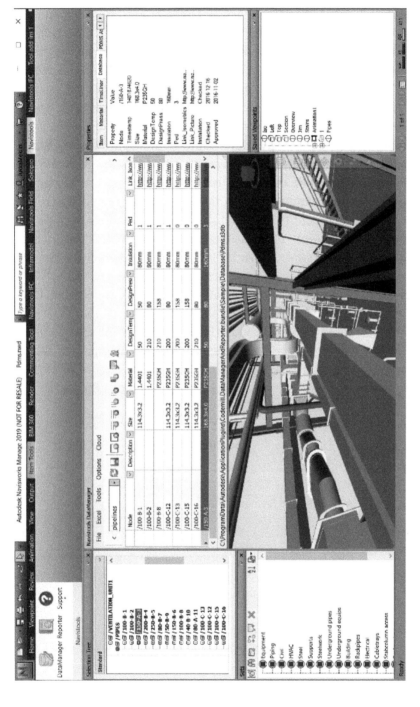

Figure 18.14.   BIM-based construction scheduling.

scheduling, as recently pointed out by Darko *et al.* (2023). Existing AI/ML-based construction project scheduling tools may face challenges when being applied in green construction projects, especially if they do not cater for scheduling for green or sustainable features and requirements. How do you schedule green features and requirements using AI/ML? Following the same logic behind Lisa Matthiessen and her colleagues' "budgeting methodology" for green construction projects presented in Chapter 4, "the only effective way to schedule for green features and requirements in construction projects is to identify the goals and build an appropriate schedule model for them. If they are seen as upgrades or additions, the time required to meet those requirements will also be seen as an addition. It is possible to establish goals and durations from the very beginning of the project. Other methods are ineffective and unnecessary" (Matthiessen and Morris, 2004). Building such AI/ML models has been advocated to improve green construction project PM and delivery. The "Green Building Project Cost & Duration Predictor" developed by Darko *et al.* (2023) is a typical example, as shown in Figure 18.15.

The ML-based web application (Figure 18.15) is the first developed for automated or digital, fast, and accurate green building project cost and

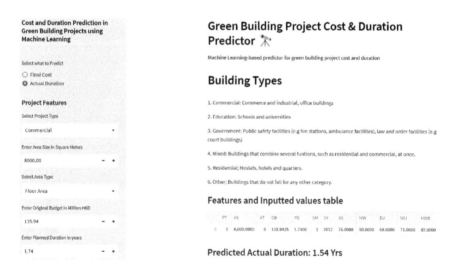

Figure 18.15.   Green building project cost & duration predictor (Darko *et al.*, 2023).
Source: https://ml-based-green-predictor.streamlit.app/.

duration prediction. It identifies the green building rating goals and other goals of the project and estimates the project duration based on them. The benefits of such tools are seen in accurate project estimates, avoidance of overruns, and improved project sustainability and delivery performance.

18.4. Digital technologies and software for cost management

The story of digital technologies for cost planning in green construction projects is similar to scheduling. The concept of cost planning has also been around for years. It has relied mainly on measuring 2D drawings and using spreadsheets, which is a tedious and laborious task. One of the main challenges is that any change in design would result in a long process of updating the cost. However, with the new digital tools, cost planning can rely on software packages to provide a faster and more accurate cost estimation in green construction projects. With the advance in BIM-based cost planning, or 5D BIM, tools such as CostX are leveraging the parametric nature of the BIM authoring tools to run the quantity takeoff faster and more accurately, which will result in more accurate material use. This will not only reduce the embodied energy of the green construction project but also potentially reduce the wastage of materials (Abioye *et al.*, 2021). In addition, it will reduce the carbon footprint related to transport and inventory and the green design process.

Studies have shown the advantages of implementing BIM early in the green construction process to increase the efficiency of the cost-estimating processes (Valentini *et al.*, 2017). For instance, a construction management company might estimate costs using the building data that the green designer has provided. This estimate may be carried out by the construction manager during the phases of conceptual design, design development, and construction documents. In addition, BIM can assist cost estimation operations in the other project phases by ensuring consistency between the green design configuration and quantity estimation, providing accurate quantity analysis, or both. However, the total number derived from models must be coupled with other information because the information contained in building information models may be insufficient to generate a cost estimate (Wu *et al.*, 2014). The AI-powered tools on the market, such as Kreo, are promising faster material lists, cost estimations, and quotes. For green construction projects specifically, the "Green Building Project Cost & Duration Predictor" (Figure 18.15) offers a typical example of using AI/ML in cost estimation (Darko *et al.*, 2023). If BIM provides project information and if AI/ML uses such information for cost and time estimating, then a piece good advice for the green construction project manager is to look at leveraging integrated BIM-AI/ML tools to improve the estimating process. Zhang *et al.* (2022) have reviewed the literature on BIM-AI integration in the construction industry.

18.5. Digital technologies and software for quality management

The green construction project's various phases are all impacted by the quality control process. Early identification and rectification of errors through proper quality control and coordination processes can help minimize costs, rework, time delay, and material wastage due to delayed correction activities. Procedures must be established and put into action in order to guarantee information and model quality at every stage and before information exchanges. From the initial planning and design phases to the actual construction and final delivery, the digital approach enables better quality management to be implemented. Each party involved in the BIM model has a designated individual who is in charge of coordinating the model and taking part in all significant BIM activities (Viscuso *et al.*, 2020). The BIM procedure throughout the life cycle of the green project must be planned in advance by taking into account the model's content, amount of detail, format, and party in charge of updates, as well as the distribution of the model and data to other parties. This will create a golden thread of information that can improve the quality of the information delivered.

In addition, through simulation and monitoring, potential quality issues (e.g., clashes or conflicts between different elements) can be identified and addressed in advance, reducing rework and costs and wastes associated later in construction. BIM provides a visual representation of

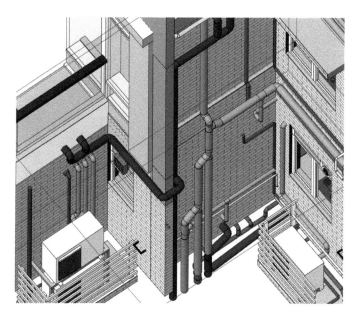

Figure 18.16. Display of part of a typical BIM model of a residential building project depicting the spatial relationships between various elements.

various elements, including building services, fixtures, equipment, and builder's work modifications (Figure 18.16). By depicting these elements in a single drawing, it allows different trades to understand their spatial relationships and identify and resolve potential clashes or conflicts.

The BIM model helps coordinate the installation and routing of building services, such as electrical, plumbing, heating, ventilation, and air conditioning (HVAC), and fire protection systems (Figure 18.17). It ensures that the necessary openings, recesses, chases, or modifications are incorporated into the building structure to accommodate these services without conflicts.

The clash detection function of the model needs to be highlighted with regard to its benefits to quality management. By combining different elements in a single drawing, the BIM model facilitates clash detection. It allows stakeholders, including architects, engineers, contractors, and sub-contractors, to review the drawing and identify and resolve potential clashes or conflicts between different elements, such as building services, structural components, or equipment installations.

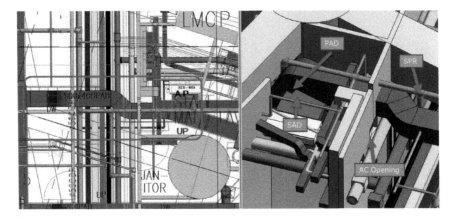

Figure 18.17.   Display of 3D MEP BIM model with 2D drawing for coordination.

The key benefit of all these BIM functions is "early identification of problems." Identifying clashes or conflicts early in the project is crucial to avoid costly rework or delays. The 3D enables stakeholders to identify potential clashes and conflicts before construction begins or during the design development stage. This allows for timely resolution through design modifications or coordination meetings.

It's important to note that the actual cost of changing design faults can vary significantly based on project-specific factors. It is advisable to consult with a construction professional, such as a contractor or estimator, to assess the specific circumstances and estimate the potential cost implications accurately.

Digital technologies, such as Laser Detection And Ranging (LADAR), have provided the opportunity to scan the sites at various stages to be checked against the design. The model can then be used to compare the elements of the production to the planned ones in a design/planning vs as-built process. This is illustrated in Figure 18.18 where the actual construction site progress of a Class A high-rise commercial building project in Hong Kong is being compared with the virtual planning in BIM. The construction site can be scanned at various stages through handheld devices, using robotics such as Boston Dynamics robots or drones, to compare outcomes and potentially find issues to address quickly. This will help reduce the amount of rework and improve the quality of the final green construction project.

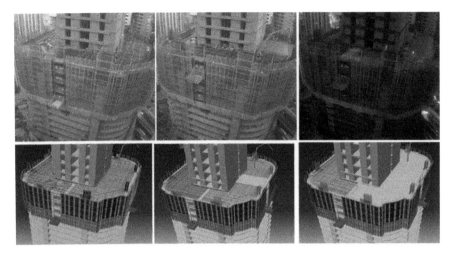

Figure 18.18.   The capture of day 4 construction site progress vs the virtual planning in BIM of a Class A high-rise commercial building project in Hong Kong.

In Hong Kong, the Digital Works Supervision System (DWSS) is another technology that provides smart quality inspection solutions to green construction projects. It is a web-based centralized platform for collecting information and managing the workflows of construction site activities to improve efficiency, safety, and quality performance (Development Bureau, 2020). DWSS also hosts all different smart site applications deployed on site. DWSS is used for onsite quality inspection to ensure compliance with the approved drawings or the as-construction BIM models. An inspection mobile solution is able to access, record, and distribute the project information, including installation, commissioning, or corrective tasks through notes and annotations, drawings, photos, plans, and sketches from mobile devices on the field. It then sends the report in real time through a well-defined workflow to the operator, subcontractor, back office, and client instantly. So, construction quality inspection tasks can be performed digitally. Also, scheduled or *ad hoc* site health and safety inspection can be performed at anytime, anywhere.

Comprehensive inspection reports (Figure 18.19) can be automatically generated from mobile devices and desktop and laptop computers. As the project proceeds, these data as well as the updated BIM model are

Total Quality Management

🖨 Print

No.	Subject	Method	Extent	Time	Acceptance criteria	Documentation	Finished
QC							
廚房安裝檢查							
QC-001	廚房安裝檢查	Check according to BIM mdoel		Once every week	Compliance with BIM model	QC Inspection Report	
浴室安裝檢查							
QC-002	浴室安裝檢查	Check according to BIM mdoel		Once every week	Compliance with BIM model	QC Inspection Report	6
門安裝檢查							
QC-003	門安裝檢查	Check according to BIM mdoel		Once every week	Compliance with BIM model	QC Inspection Report	7

Figure 18.19.   Report generated by Dalux Build.

handed over to the operational phase. Dashboard on key performance indicators is updated in real time for quality performance analysis. Finally, task monitoring or support can be done both onsite and from the back office at any time.

18.6. Digital technologies and software for resource management

A shortage of labor and materials has been reported in various regions. According to a 2019 research conducted in the US by the Associated General Contractors of America and Autodesk, 80% of contractors struggle to recruit skilled labor (AGC, 2019). In the UK, this issue has been accelerated after Brexit, and companies continue to struggle with workforce challenges. While headline inflation is decreasing, according to a study by construction cost consultancy Currie & Brown, the skills shortage is expected to result in an 8.3% increase in labor costs by 2023. The study highlights that this might increase lead times by as much as 50% and compel contractors to rescope projects (Currie & Brown, 2023). While this is not the final answer to the root causes of this challenge, finding smarter ways to assign resources can reduce the negative impact. New software packages such as Vico can monitor not just the schedule but also the workforce, equipment, and materials of a green construction project.

These software packages can easily allocate or relocate resources. For instance, tasks or equipment can be assigned to various team members. After gathering data through the process, these tools can also be used to optimize resource usage. Without a good understanding of time and cost, the project might overallocate resources (time, people, and materials) to the project. BIM-based tools for scheduling and cost planning (see Sections 18.3 and 18.4) can depict a clear image of the green construction project to prevent double work, material waste, and delays. In addition to better planning, as these tools can track the resources, they can provide better visibility for the green project team members.

18.7. Digital technologies and software for communications management

The construction industry has long suffered from a lack of transparency and inefficiency. The efficiency rate in the construction industry is around 30%, and the rework rate is normally between 15% and 75% (Changali *et al.*, 2015). The ability to have real-time communication between various parties involved in the green construction project can significantly increase the efficiency of the whole project. This is especially important because as highlighted in Chapter 1, communication and coordination across a multidisciplinary and interdisciplinary team is the most significant challenge to delivering a successful green construction project. Currently, communication between project stakeholders is largely by emails, faxes, phone calls, mobile communication apps, face-to-face meetings, and written reports. But all of them are idle and spread in different individual or workgroup working platforms.

The enhanced communication offered by digital tools and platforms can lead to better decision-making. A basic premise of BIM, for instance, is coordination, communication, and collaboration by different stakeholders at different stages of the project life cycle to insert, extract, update, or modify information in the model to support and reflect the roles of that stakeholder, as proclaimed by the US National Institute of Building Sciences (2023). In addition, the flow of information will have the potential to prevent delays and guarantee access to the most up-to-date information. Being transparent about who has done what is when the construction industry can provide higher accountability for green construction projects.

Traditional information-sharing techniques can have a negative impact on PM, supply chain control, and participant trust. The actual digital shift in this context affects and develops the ways that green project contractors communicate with one another. An enhanced BIM strategy ensures the flow of digital information and provides a single database comprising all the information generated and shared by the operators during all stages of the green construction project process (Hsiao, 2017).

In this context, the idea of a common data environment (CDE) becomes particularly significant. The BIM Wiki (2023) says the following:

> The CDE is the single source of information used to collect, manage, and disseminate documentation, the graphical model and non-graphical data for the whole project team (i.e., all project information whether created in a BIM environment or in a conventional data format). Creating this single source of information facilitates collaboration between project team members and helps avoid duplication and mistakes.

Figure 18.20 shows an example of a CDE setup for the second author's company's BIM project execution. The upper layer, Plannerly, is an online BIM task execution platform which is used to define and to monitor the scope of works, schedules, and resources and deliverables based on the agreed BIM execution plan. The purpose of the bottom layer, Dalux Box Pro, is to capture, share, review, and manipulate all data and information throughout the project life cycle from design and construction to operation and maintenance. Structural data, consisting of formalization and centralization, is an organized way of distributing work with administrative control mechanisms.

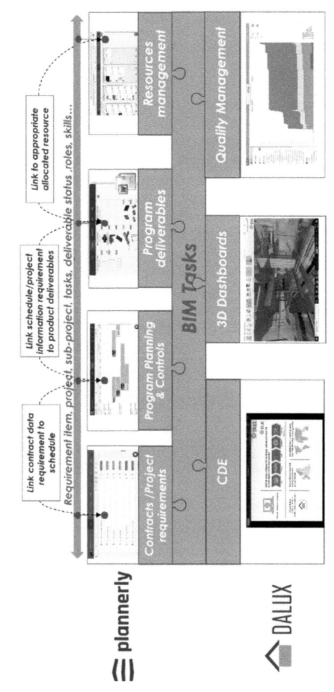

Figure 18.20.   The architecture of CDE for MTECH BIM project execution.

18.7.1. *Digital information delivery process*

The BIM modeling and coordination work on a complex project is a significant task. Plannerly hosts all the modeling and BIM delivery activities and provides a portal to the project team to manage all BIM scope, uses, deliverables, schedules, resources, and quality.

Through Dalux, all information, activities, and people are connected for online real-time project coordination, communication, and collaboration. We are able to run in-depth, interactive engagement sessions and design reviews under any media through the cloud anywhere at anytime. All communications are captured and act as a single version of truth in one unified platform for the project moving forward.

The link up of Plannerly and Dalux Box Pro puts the BXP on life. The ISO19650 standard is embedded into the daily project tasks (Figure 18.21). This enables seamless real-time data application and exchange between project stakeholders in a way that everyone can benefit from the project's success. For example, the BIM modeler can easily understand the detailed requirements of the modeling tasks through the Plannerly task card, as shown in Figure 18.22.

ISO19650 CDE Workflow

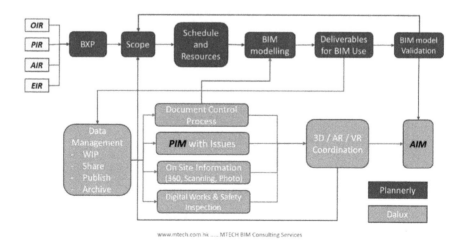

Figure 18.21.   The ISO19650-compliant CDE workflow introduced by MTECH.

Figure 18.22.   The BIM modeling task card created by Plannerly.

The CDE also provides automatic AI-driven verification of BIM model quality according to the requirements, checklist, and completeness (Figure 18.23). Based on the set rule, the model can automatically check if requirements, such as carbon emission data and LCA compliance, are met before it is being released for use. For any noncompliance, feedback route is created for correction.

After the model is released and shared, engineers are able to conduct in-depth studies on the design or construction issues through multiple sources of data, including 2D drawings, the 3D BIM model, laser scanning point clouds, and 360 photos (Figure 18.24). They are also able to conduct interactive engagement sessions and design reviews through the cloud by desktop and mobile without having to get everyone in the same physical space. This approach has proved incredibly successful, capturing more viewpoints (e.g., BIM models for the building and 3D laser scanning point cloud data for the landscaping and site formation) for knowledge sharing than ever before while reducing travelling, costs, and carbon footprints.

In addition, the CDE allows online 2D and 3D BIM issues tracking for real-time access, commenting, and updating (Figure 18.25). The result is

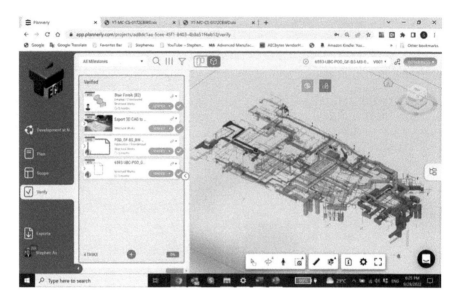

Figure 18.23.   Automatic BIM model quality verification by assigning AI rules in Plannerly.

Figure 18.24.   Display of laser scanning point cloud together with BIM model in the single environment via Dalux BIM Viewer.

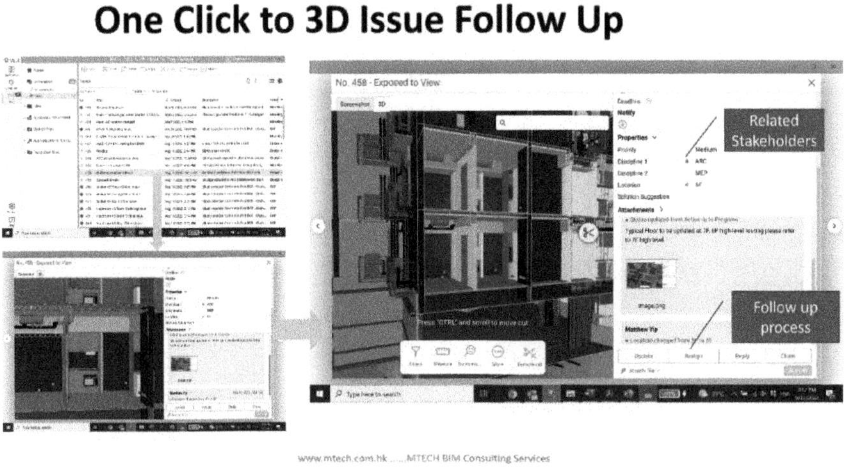

One Click to 3D Issue Follow Up

Figure 18.25.   Display of design issues tracking under the Dalux CDE.

not only for problem-solving but also for design optimization and innovation.

Furthermore, an AR of the BIM model through a mobile device can be used for onsite construction task verification and follow-up (Figure 18.26). All comments are updated in the CDE so that everyone can react instantly.

Collaboration is essential to the success of a green construction project. However, effective collaboration can only be achieved through effective coordination and communication. BIM and CDE are crucial for improving coordination, communication, and collaboration between the numerous experts and stakeholders involved in a green construction project.

18.8.   Digital technologies and software for stakeholder management

The Association for Project Management (2021) states that the process of identifying, assessing, planning, and carrying out measures to influence stakeholders — individuals or organizations that have an interest in the project, play a part in it, or are influenced by it — is known as stakeholder management. Any project that aims to fulfill sustainability objectives in

Figure 18.26. AR display through Dalux BIM Viewer for site installation verification comparing with BIM model.

the built environment, such as green construction projects, must manage its stakeholders effectively if it is to succeed, a subject tackled in Chapter 12. The interactions between several stakeholders involved in green construction projects are dynamic, complicated, and oftentimes fraught with conflicts (Abdelkhalik & Azmy, 2022). In order to ensure agreement, cooperation, communication, and satisfaction among all parties involved in green construction projects, good stakeholder management is crucial. Digital technologies and methods for managing green construction projects are proven to be effective enablers for enhancing stakeholder management (Wen & Qiang, 2022). Bal *et al.* (2013) suggested six steps to achieve this: (1) identification, (2) relating stakeholders to different sustainability-related targets, (3) prioritization, (4) managing,

(5) measuring performance, and (6) putting targets into action. Various tools are available for the green construction project manager to collect, analyze, and track data for environmental, social, and governance (ESG) reports and maximize the value of the data. These tools can identify and prioritize stakeholders based on their challenges. Construction firms should develop a unified communication system that combines desktop, tablet, mobile, and landline access on one platform, enabling onsite staff, project managers, and those in the office to stay connected on any device.

Stakeholders can establish and develop their life cycle BIM database over time, which would be a valuable source of information for all the stakeholders involved in the process. Additionally, it looks to be of added value for customers, stakeholders, and design companies, enabling a continual development of knowledge for both the current project's BIM database and those of the next projects. According to UNI 11337 (2018), the innovative potential of BIM enables stakeholders to take advantage of various project levels. For example, by fusing 3D geometric models and schedule data, a 4D aspect can be created that can offer several practical benefits to simplify site planning and management for green construction projects (Gazzaniga *et al.*, 2020).

18.9. Digital technologies and software for risk management

Risk has been defined as a situation or event that can have positive or negative impacts on the green construction project. There are many risks associated with green construction projects, including running over time, moving costs, and a lack of quality. (Chapter 10 provides a comprehensive account of these risks.) If the benefits of using digital tools, which were discussed in the previous sections, can be used to mitigate the risk of running over time and cost and even find a solution that can help finish the project earlier and with a lower budget, then this in turn can be calculated as a saving in the total footprint of the green construction project. Many other risks can be mitigated through enhanced coordination, communication, and collaboration between stakeholders. For this section, we can focus on environmental risk. As discussed earlier in Section 18.2, a more enhanced BIM-based LCA can be performed using BIM-based tools such as One Click LCA to evaluate the impact of the materials. By evaluating the embodied energy of different materials, BIM and BIM-based building performance simulation can help the practitioner select a material with a smaller ecological footprint. In addition, various BIM-based automated environmental impact assessments of infrastructure projects can use the information in the model to integrate them with the U.S. Energy Information Administration (EIA) databases. BIM and BIM-related technologies as risk management tools have been discussed by several researchers, including Darko *et al.* (2020a) and Zou *et al.* (2017).

18.10. Digital technologies and software for health and safety management

Health and safety have been major challenges for the construction industry. Construction is still a sector with a high incidence of accidents, and digital tools can mitigate the situation. Many health and safety issues that can be neglected based on 2D drawings and spreadsheets can be easily identified by viewing a 3D model and also using an immersive environment. These technologies can give the technician the ability to visualize the green construction project from design to construction and propose the best measures to reduce risks (Pinto *et al.*, 2018).

BIM allows the implementation of health and safety management throughout the whole life cycle of a green project to improve safety. Tools such as CerTus HSBIm by ACCA Software or 3DRepo (Figure 18.27) can simulate how the site looks, how it would evolve, and how practitioners can use it to avoid risks. There are also a lot of platforms that can simulate health and safety issues for training purposes, such as site induction. This training can also be provided through VR, AR, digital twins, and computer vision to immerse the trainee in the environment. The real-time and dynamic visualizations and analyses of the project site provided by digital twins are particularly significant to improving health and safety on green construction projects.

A key factor in improving health and safety procedures in green construction management is technology and software. Construction organizations may greatly enhance safety procedures and reduce dangers on job sites by putting innovative instruments and software systems to use. The possibility of accidents and mistakes is decreased because of the exact

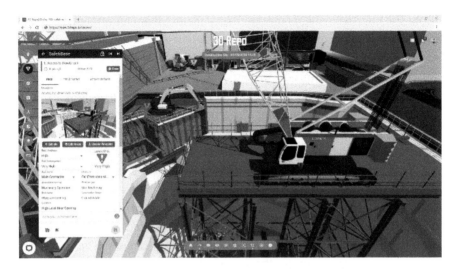

Figure 18.27.   BIM-based health and safety analysis.

project planning, clash detection, and risk assessment capabilities of BIM software. In addition, wearable technology with sensors can track employees' vital signs, spot potential dangers, and instantly notify both staff members and managers. There is some research suggesting incorporating wearables to control the safety of workers including slips and trips, sensing environmental concerns, collision avoidance, falling from a high level, and electrocution (Ibrahim *et al.*, 2023). However, significant obstacles to the adoption of wearable devices by organizations relate to cost, technology, and human factors. Furthermore, AR and VR technologies provide immersive training experiences that let employees practice difficult skills in a secure virtual setting. These technological developments not only raise the bar for health and safety but also encourage an industry-wide culture of proactive risk management in green construction projects.

18.11. Intelligent construction site management

It is vital to maximize efficiency on green construction projects. However, before inefficiencies can be improved, we must first have the ability to identify where those inefficiencies lie.

The inherent complexity of construction projects makes it challenging to pinpoint which areas of a project are running optimally and which have room for improvement. There are many factors that can affect a project's progress, so to accurately address inefficiencies, we need the ability to wade through all that information and identify where to focus our efforts. By analyzing internal processes and onsite performance, it becomes possible to sort through the noise and begin to see where optimizing efficiency is possible. Maximizing the efficiency of resources, systems, and workflows ensures that performance reaches its full potential and that green construction projects are delivered on time and on budget.

To better assess project performance, managers should track projects on a granular level. Monitoring individual tasks enables accurate measurement and identification of inefficiencies and areas for improvement. But data that are focused on the progress and performance of individual tasks are often limited to manually compiled firsthand reports. The quality of these data is dependent on the knowledge and experience of the team compiling it. This leaves room for misinterpretation due to gaps in information, delays in accessing the relevant data, the subjectivity of the person analyzing it, and the quality of the data being presented.

Buildots provides companies with accurate and objective datasets that represent what is happening on their construction project sites week-by-week. Site engineers use wearable 360° cameras to capture the site conditions by walkthroughs. Using its advanced AI capabilities, Buildots compares these data to the BIM model used for construction and flags any discrepancies (Figure 18.28). With this information, a green

Figure 18.28.   Site construction performance analysis by Buildots.

construction project manager can accurately track real-time progress compared to the project's critical path and make scheduling adjustments as required. The AI platform is able to collect, analyze, and report on large volumes of data to the most minute detail. In this way, we can track all activities on any element through the course of its life on the construction site.

18.12. The case for digital twins and integrated digital delivery

Green construction projects and their performance can be very *dynamic* in nature, requiring dynamic approaches for their better management. During a green construction project, many decisions often must be made based on incomplete information, assumptions, and the personal experiences of the construction professionals. Currently, project changes or adjustments are a fact of life at all stages of design and construction and even throughout the entire project life cycle. Motawa *et al.* (2007) indicated that changes in construction projects are very common and likely to occur from different sources, by various causes (e.g., the changing economic environment and climate in which projects operate), at any project stage, and may have considerable negative impacts on project performance. These changes can impact and create uncertainties in decisions made earlier on the project, ultimately changing the desired performance of the project over time. For example, changes in prices due to fluctuations may affect project cost performance. Changes in weather can affect energy, sustainability, and time performance. What if the digital green construction PM tools and approaches are able to capture these dynamics, changes, and uncertainties in real time for better decision-making and project performance?

Most of the BIM-based approaches discussed earlier have an important limitation in this aspect. They are concerned only with *static* building information models taking no account of varying nature of the difficulties on a green construction project. In addition, the static nature of those BIM-based approaches does not allow for continuous performance monitoring, assessment, understanding, and improvement.

Richard Ferris is Head of Engineering at Lendlease, a multinational construction and real estate company. John Turner is VP of Innovative Solutions at Gafcon. In their article "From BIM to Twin!," it is stated that "BIM is limited by the input provided to it by all the stakeholders." In addition to being static, BIM does not also offer real-time data and information, monitoring, assessment, understanding, and improvement of project performance.

According to Ferris and Turner (2020), "the evolution of BIM is the digital twin." Digital twins provide a dynamic virtual platform that rapidly and accurately captures data for performance evaluation purposes, generating a range of insights, scenarios, and representations enabling more soundly based decision-making than is likely with any other platform (Smart Cities Council Australia New Zealand, 2020). In simple terms, a digital twin is defined by Darko *et al.* (2022) as "a realistic dynamic virtual model of a physical object, system, environment, or process (physical twin)." It responds and behaves like its physical twin. The Digital Twin Consortium (2023) states the following:

- digital twin systems transform business by accelerating holistic understanding, optimal decision-making, and effective action,
- digital twins use real-time and historical data to represent the past and present and simulate predicted futures,
- digital twins are motivated by outcomes, tailored to use cases, powered by integration, built on data, guided by domain knowledge, and implemented in information technology (IT)/operational technology (OT) systems.

The use of digital twins will help green construction project stakeholders and managers in automatically obtaining highly accurate and fast real-time data by live data flows and a connection between the real physical project and a unified dynamic virtual model of the project. This dynamic model is constantly updated using real-time data supplied by IT/OT systems, smart IoT sensors, and other sources, such as environmental, social, and economic datasets. When this is done in a cost-effective way, stakeholders can unlock considerable value over the life cycle of their projects and solve key project and business issues and challenges more dynamically (Smart Cities Council Australia New Zealand, 2020).

All these lead to better green construction PM. The digital twin-based approaches will integrate the capabilities of BIM and many other digital tools — smart IoT sensors, AI/ML, blockchain, quantum computing, VR, AR, LADAR, etc. — for better green construction PM. Such integration enables real-time information response, improved simulation modeling, and optimized green construction project life cycle management, a subject tackled in Chapter 17.

The above case for using digital twins to improve green construction PM does not mean to say that the existing BIM-based approaches are not useful. They are. Why? Autodesk (2022) stated that "digital twins can be created without BIM but bringing them to their full potential starts with the integrated workflows and information sharing that already power the BIM process — starting with BIM is a much more efficient way to get there." Therefore, it is just a matter of converting the already existing BIM-based approaches into digital twin-based ones by equipping them with dynamic, real-time, and bidirectional data and information management capabilities. This requires a good knowledge and understanding of IT/OT applications. Darko *et al.* (2022) explain how the BIM-based green building assessment approaches discussed in Section 18.2, for instance, can be transformed into digital twin-based ones, while the concept of a digital twin for data-centric management of production in construction projects has been discussed by Sacks *et al.* (2020).

Despite the benefits, the potential of digital twins in green construction PM has not been sufficiently explored. With the global digital twins market expected to expand in the coming years, the potential of the technology in green construction PM should be further explored by researchers and practitioners.

Integration of the various green construction project life cycle stages, from design and manufacturing to construction and asset delivery and management, is crucial to achieving efficiency, quality, and sustainability in the built environment. Through the use of digital technologies, including digital twins, IDD, as defined by the Singapore Building and Construction Authority (2021), "integrates work processes and connects stakeholders working on the same project throughout the construction and building life cycle. This includes design, fabrication, and assembly onsite, as well as the operations and maintenance of buildings."

Just like digital twins, IDD builds upon the use and application of BIM and virtual design and construction (VDC). According to the Building and Construction Authority (2021), IDD covers four areas:

- *Digital design*: Engaging stakeholders to achieve design objectives through collaborative and coordinated design, to meet client's, regulatory, and downstream requirements.
- *Digital fabrication*: Translating design to standardized components for automating offsite production.
- *Digital construction*: Just-in-time delivery, installation, and monitoring of onsite activities to maximize productivity and minimize rework.
- *Digital asset delivery and management*: Real-time monitoring for operations and maintenance to enhance asset values.

These features show that IDD and digital twins are closely related in that the latter facilitates the former and that both IDD and digital twins have the potential to improve green construction PM ensuring that client's requirements are met throughout the project life cycle. There is therefore a need to fully integrate IDD and digital twins into green construction PM.

18.13. Challenges and solutions for digital green construction project management

Adopting and implementing digital technologies and software to improve the way green construction projects are managed and delivered is not free from challenges. Despite the many benefits discussed in this chapter, some significant challenges must be addressed. In the following, we discuss some of these pressing challenges and offer solutions to them.

18.13.1. *Deployment costs*

Implementing digital technologies can require spending countless sums on training programs, and new software, hardware, processes, workflows, and staff. This can create challenges for green project managers who already are under pressure to balance costs with the need to achieve sustainability. To solve this challenge, priority must be given to digital technologies and tools that deliver the most value to the project. Some digital technologies can help to reduce even the original project cost. It may be easier to justify investments in these technologies. As mentioned earlier in Section 18.9, if the digital tools can help to mitigate the risk of running over cost, which is typical of construction projects, and even find a solution that can help to finish the project with a lower budget, then this in turn can be calculated as a saving in the total cost footprint of the green construction project, justifying the investment in the digital tools.

18.13.2. *Lack of digital skills and infrastructure*

Construction professionals may lack the IT/OT skills necessary to deploy technologies, such as IoT. Likewise, many construction project sites do not have the required digital infrastructure, e.g., reliable hardware and internet connectivity, as indicated by Gyan Consulting (2023). Collaboration with capable IT/OT experts or having them on the project team is critical to addressing this challenge. Relevant education and training can also be provided to the project team. In addition, the project organization must upgrade its digital infrastructure by, for example, implementing reliable hardware and internet connectivity.

18.13.3. *Security and privacy risks*

If digital technologies are implemented without cybersecurity planning or awareness specific to those technologies, they may form a weak link in the project network and impose significant threats to the project organization. Sufficient security and privacy protection must be put in place by, for instance, using technologies, such as blockchain.

18.13.4. *Sustainability risks*

Green projects aim to reduce energy consumption and carbon emissions. However, the use of digital technologies may run contrary to this goal, as the technologies also use energy and emit carbon. It is essential to deploy energy- and carbon-efficient technologies that contribute to achieving the green goals of the project.

18.13.5. *Human–machine interaction during decision-making*

Can project managers trust the recommendations or decisions of a digital tool such as AI? It can be difficult, especially if they lack an understanding of how the AI came up with the recommendations or decisions (the "black box syndrome"). It can also be difficult because of "Techlash," defined by Linkov *et al.* (2020) as "a distrust that the technologies have users' best interests at heart, given some questionable behavior on the part of the organizations that build and/or promote them." The answer to this problem is to use technologies that include clear quantifications and visualizations of user confidence in their decisions, such as actionable and interpretable AI proposed by Linkov *et al.* (2020).

18.13.6. *Interoperability issues*

Many digital tools and methods designed by researchers and organizations are proprietary and designed for specific applications, leading to issues of interoperability in heterogeneous digital systems related to data exchange, security, storage, scalability, and communication. It is recommended to use technologies that support open standards to promote interoperability.

18.13.7. *Tight schedules*

With time running out to meet global sustainability goals, green projects frequently have tight schedules because of the need to deliver the projects "as soon as possible." Hence, the time required to properly plan, manage, and implement digital strategies can be a challenge. Project managers must ensure that the project schedule allows for the proper planning, management, and implementation of both digital and green strategies. Synchronizing the green project schedule and digital delivery schedule is a key indicator for successful digital green construction PM. In addition, the solutions offered to overcome the "deployment costs" challenge earlier are applicable to this "tight schedules" challenge as well, and vice versa.

18.13.8. *Other considerations for digital success*

Digital transformation is fundamentally about enabling people to manage information effectively, improve processes, and apply technology wisely. Technology alone is not the solution to the challenges we face, but technology applied wisely is a key enabler. We need purpose-led technology, not technology-led change. Effective information management requires the right people to have the right information at the right time to make better decisions. And better decisions lead to better outcomes.

18.13.9. *Added value with digital as default*

By defining a "digital as default approach" and a core digital process that starts with the end result in mind, we build an operation system to facilitate the green project.

The key to a digital as default approach is to ensure that the base requirements are captured at the start of the project. This means that the project team can develop the digital information in a standardized format that can be utilized by the best technology available at the time, leading to many benefits, such as the following:

- More time to do the right thing. Through the CDE, everyone gets good quality data that enables them to optimize quality and innovation through cooperation.
- Less pressure on error detection and correction, making people happier and healthier, and building trust and harmony.
- Smart people — doing "less" and earning "more," with effectiveness and efficiency achieved.
- Overall, it is about the achievement of sustainability, digitalization, as well as smartness.

18.14. Summary

The use and application of digital technologies and software in the management and delivery of green construction projects has several benefits in improved collaboration, communication, coordination, data and information management, transparency and accountability, productivity, risk mitigation, profits, decision-making, delivery times, sustainability, efficiency, accuracy, costs, quality, and health, safety, well-being, and compliance of the green construction projects.

This chapter explored the benefits of digital technologies and software for designing for sustainability, and for schedule, cost, quality, resource, communications, stakeholder, risk, health and safety, and construction site management for green construction projects, with practical cases introduced. The chapter emphasized the need to fully integrate integrated digital delivery and digital twins into green construction PM. Finally, the chapter discussed pressing challenges of digital green construction PM and offered solutions to them to promote digital green construction PM. To ensure digital success, it is recommended to define a "digital as default approach" and a core digital process that starts with the end result in mind. The technologies should be applied wisely, where the process changes that will improve project performance are first identified before identifying and implementing the digital technologies and solutions that will enable those process changes and unlock the associated benefits. For example, the need to pursue digital must be driven by process changes defined, for example, as "increase design productivity by 30% by streamlining the design process through BIM collaboration and communication." Rather than defining a process change, for example, as "make BIM software available to all project team members." This can increase the likelihood that digital technologies and tools will add real value to the project and deliver better project outcomes (McKinsey & Company, 2019).

The insights from this chapter will help practitioners unlock the full value of digital in the management of their green construction projects. Researchers and students will benefit through an understanding of the past, present, and future developments of the field.

References

Abdelkhalik, H. F. & Azmy H. H. (2022). The role of project management in the success of green building projects: Egypt as a Case Study. *Journal of Engineering and Applied Science*, *69*, 61. https://doi.org/10.1186/s44147-022-00112-5.

Abioye, S. O. *et al.* (2021). Artificial Intelligence in the construction industry: A review of present status, opportunities and future challenges. *Journal of Building Engineering*, *44*, 103299. DOI: 10.1016/j.jobe.2021.103299.

AGC. (2019). Eighty percent of contractors report difficulty finding qualified craft workers to hire as firms give low marks to quality of new worker pipeline. Available at: https://www.agc.org/news/2019/08/27/eighty-percent-contractors-report-difficulty-finding-qualified-craft-workers-hire-0 (accessed on 15 July 2023).

Akanbi, L. A., Oyedele, L. O., Akinade, O. O., Ajayi, A. O., Delgado, M. D., Bilal, M., & Bello, S. A. (2018). Salvaging building materials in a circular economy: A BIM-based whole-life performance estimator. *Resources, Conservation and Recycling*, *129*, 175–186.

Ansah, M. K., Chen, X., Yang, H., Lu, L., & Lam, P. T. (2019). A review and outlook for integrated BIM application in green building assessment. *Sustainable Cities and Society*, *48*, 101576.

Autodesk. (2022). What is a digital twin? How intelligent data models can shape the built world. Available at: https://www.autodesk.com/design-make/articles/what-is-a-digital-twin.

Autodesk. (2023). Building information modeling. Available at: https://www.autodesk.com/solutions/aec/bim.

Bal, M., *et al.* (2013). Stakeholder engagement: Achieving sustainability in the construction sector. *Sustainability*, *5*(2), 695–710. DOI: 10.3390/su5020695.

BIM Wiki. (2023). Common data environment CDE. Available at: https://www.designingbuildings.co.uk/wiki/Common_data_environment_CDE.

Building and Construction Authority (BCA). (2021). Integrated Digital Delivery (IDD). Available at: https://www1.bca.gov.sg/buildsg/digitalisation/integrated-digital-delivery-idd (accessed on 10 July 2023).

Changali, S., Mohammad, A., & van Nieuwland, M. (2015). The construction productivity imperative. McKinsey & Company. Available at: https://www.mckinsey.com/business-functions/operations/our-insights/the-construction-productivity-imperative (accessed on 19 July 2023).

ConstructionPlacements Admin. (2022). Digital construction: What is digital construction management? Available at: https://www.construction placements.com/digital-construction/#Books_On_Digital_Construction_ Management.

Currie & Brown. (2023). UK construction market outlook. Available at: https:// www.curriebrown.com/media/2650/uk-mor-report_final.pdf (accessed on 19 July 2023).

Darko, A., Chan, A. P. C, Yang, Y., & Tetteh, M. O. (2020a). Building information modeling (BIM)-based modular integrated construction risk management– Critical survey and future needs. *Computers in Industry, 123*, 103327.

Darko, A., Chan, A. P. C., Adabre, M. A., Edwards, D. J., Hosseini, M. R., & Ameyaw, E. E. (2020b). Artificial intelligence in the AEC industry: Scientometric analysis and visualization of research activities. *Automation in Construction, 112*, 103081.

Darko, A., Glushakova, I., Boateng, E. B., & Chan, A. P. C. (2023). Using machine learning to improve cost and duration prediction accuracy in green building projects. *Journal of Construction Engineering and Management, 149*(8), 04023061.

Darko, A., Jayasanka, T. A. D. K., Chan, A. P. C., Jalaei, F., Ansah, M. K., & Opoku, D. J. (2024). Digital twin-based automated green building assessment framework. In S. Skatulla & H. Beushausen (Eds.), *Advances in Information Technology in Civil and Building Engineering. ICCCBE 2022*. Lecture Notes in Civil Engineering, Vol. 357. Springer, Cham. https://doi. org/10.1007/978-3-031-35399-4_43.

Debrah, C., Chan, A. P. C., & Darko, A. (2022). Artificial intelligence in green building. *Automation in Construction, 137*, 104192.

Development Bureau. (2020). Digital works supervision system. Available at: chrome-extension://efaidnbmnnnibpcajpcglclefindmkaj/https://www.devb. gov.hk/filemanager/technicalcirculars/en/upload/374/1/C-2020-03-01.pdf (accessed on 15 June 2022).

Digital Twin Consortium. (2023). What is a digital twin? Available at: https:// www.digitaltwinconsortium.org/initiatives/the-definition-of-a-digital-twin/.

Ferris, R. & Turner, J. (2020). From BIM to twin! Available at: https://www. brighttalk.com/webcast/18347/447781.

Gazzaniga, G., Coppola, L., Daniotti, B., Mirachi, C., Pavan, A., & Savoia, V. (2020). Decision-making BIM platform for chemical building products. In B. Daniotti, M. Gianinetto, & S. Della Torre (Eds.), *Digital Transformation of the Design, Construction and Management Processes of the Built*

Environment. Research for Development. Cham: Springer. https://doi. org/10.1007/978-3-030-33570-0_6.

Gyan Consulting. (2023). Digital transformation construction challenges and solutions. Available at: https://www.linkedin.com/pulse/digital-transformation-construction-challenges-solutions/.

Herczeg, G., Akkerman, R., & Hauschild, M. Z. (2018). Supply chain collaboration in industrial symbiosis networks. *Journal of Cleaner Production, 171,* 1058–1067.

Hsiao, J. I.-H. (2017). "smart" contract on the blockchain-paradigm shift for contract law?. *US-China Law Review, 14*(10). DOI: 10.17265/1548-6605/2017.10.002.

Ibrahim, K., Simpeh, F., & Adebowale, O. J. (2023). Benefits and challenges of wearable safety devices in the construction sector. *Smart and Sustainable Built Environment.* https://doi.org/10.1108/SASBE-12-2022-0266.

Innes, S. (2004). Developing tools for designing out waste pre-site and on-site. In *Proceedings of Minimising Construction Waste Conference: Developing Resource Efficiency and Waste Minimisation in Design and Construction.* London, UK: New Civil Engineer. October 2004.

Jalaei, F. & Jrade, A. (2014). Integrating BIM with green building certification system, energy analysis, and cost estimating tools to conceptually design sustainable buildings. In *Construction Research Congress 2014: Construction in a Global Network* (pp. 140–149). Atlanta, Georgia.

Jalaei, F. & Jrade, A. (2015). Integrating building information modeling (BIM) and LEED system at the conceptual design stage of sustainable buildings. *Sustainable Cities and Society, 18,* 95–107.

Jalaei, F., Jalaei, F., & Mohammadi, S. (2020). An integrated BIM-LEED application to automate sustainable design assessment framework at the conceptual stage of building projects. *Sustainable Cities and Society, 53,* 101979.

Linkov, I., Galaitsi, S., Trump, B. D., Keisler, J. M., & Kott, A. (2020). Cybertrust: From explainable to actionable and interpretable artificial intelligence. *Computer, 53*(9), 91–96.

Loring, J. (2023). What is digital construction? 7 best practices. Available at: https://global.hitachi-solutions.com/blog/digital-construction/.

Matthiessen, L. F. & Morris, P. (2004). *Costing Green: A Comprehensive Cost Database and Budgeting Methodology.* Davis Langdon.

McGraw-Hill Construction. (2010). *Green BIM: How Building Information Modelling is Contributing to Green Design and Construction: Smart Market Report.* McGraw-Hill Construction. Bedford, MA.

McKinsey & Company. (2019). Decoding digital transformation in construction. Available at: https://www.mckinsey.com/capabilities/operations/our-insights/decoding-digital-transformation-in-construction.

Motawa, I. A., Anumba, C. J., Lee, S., & Peña-Mora, F. (2007). An integrated system for change management in construction. *Automation in Construction*, *16*(3), 368–377.

Pelsmakers, S. (2013). BIM and its potential to support sustainable building. *National Building Specification*. Available at: https://www.thenbs.com/knowledge/bim-and-its-potential-to-support-sustainable-building#:~:text=Yet%20the%20inherent%20power%20of%20BIM%20is%20its,carbon%20or%20for%20better%20use%20of%20fewer%20materials. Accessed March 12, 2024.

Pinto, D., Rodrigues, F., & Baptista, J. S. (2018). The contribution of digital technologies to construction safety. *Occupational Safety and Hygiene, VI*, 115–119. DOI: 10.1201/9781351008884-20.

Russell-Smith, S. V. & Lepech, M. D. (2015). Cradle-to-gate sustainable target value design: Integrating life cycle assessment and construction management for buildings. *Journal of Cleaner Production*, *100*, 107–115.

Sacks, R., Brilakis, I., Pikas, E., Xie, H. S., & Girolami, M. (2020). Construction with digital twin information systems. *Data-Centric Engineering*, *1*, e14.

Sanchez, B., Rausch, C., & Haas, C. (2019). Deconstruction programming for adaptive reuse of buildings. *Automation in Construction*, *107*, 102921.

Smart Cities Council Australia New Zealand. (2020). Data leadership guidance note: Digital twin. Available at: https://bit.ly/3S5pnib.

Stewart, O. (2022). Digital construction — Everything you need to know. Available at: https://www.sablono.com/en/blog/digital-construction#:~:text=Digital%20construction%20is%20using%20digital,and%20efficient%20ways%20of%20working.

Teng, Y., Xu, J., Pan, W., & Zhang, Y. (2022). A systematic review of the integration of building information modeling into life cycle assessment. *Building and Environment*, *221*, 109260.

US National Institute of Building Sciences. (2023). What is a BIM? Available at: https://www.nationalbimstandard.org/faqs#faq1.

Valentini, V., Mirarchi, C., & Pavan, A. (2017). Comparison between traditional and digital preliminary cost-estimating approaches. *Innovative Infrastructure Solutions*, *2*(1), 1–8. https://doi.org/10.1007/s41062-017-0066-7.

Viscuso, S., Talamo, C., Zanelli, A., & Arlati, E. (2020). BIM management guidelines of the construction process for general contractors. In B. Daniotti, M. Gianinetto, & S. Della Torre (Eds.), *Digital Transformation of the Design, Construction and Management Processes of the Built Environment. Research for Development.* Cham: Springer. https://doi.org/10.1007/978-3-030-33570-0_17.

Wen, S. & Qiang, G. (2022). Managing stakeholder concerns in green building projects with a view towards achieving social sustainability: A Bayesian-network model. *Frontiers in Environmental Science, 10.* DOI: 10.3389/fenvs.2022.874367.

World Economic Forum. (2016). Shaping the future of construction: A breakthrough in mindset and technology. PDF report. https://www.weforum.org/publications/shaping-the-future-of-construction-a-breakthrough-in-mindset-and-technology/ (accessed 12 March 2024).

Wu, S., Wood, G., Ginige, K., & Jong, S. W. (2014). A technical review of BIM based cost estimating in UK quantity surveying practice, standards and tools. *ITcon, 19,* 534–562. https://www.itcon.org/2014/31.

Xu, J., Zhang, Q., Teng, Y., & Pan, W. (2023). Integrating IoT and BIM for tracking and visualising embodied carbon of prefabricated buildings. *Building and Environment,* 110492.

Zhang, C., Zayed, T., Hijazi, W., & Alkass, S. (2016). Quantitative assessment of building constructability using BIM and 4D simulation. *Open Journal of Civil Engineering, 6,* 442–461. DOI: 10.4236/ojce.2016.63037.

Zhang, F., Chan, A. P., Darko, A., Chen, Z., & Li, D. (2022). Integrated applications of building information modeling and artificial intelligence techniques in the AEC/FM industry. *Automation in Construction, 139,* 104289.

Zou, Y., Kiviniemi, A., & Jones, S. W. (2017). A review of risk management through BIM and BIM-related technologies. *Safety Science, 97,* 88–98.